THE NEW CORPORATE ACC

This book is about Corporate Social Responsibility (CSR) and the law, a pairing which at first sight might seem a contradiction in terms. The adoption by companies of CSR policies is, after all, routinely characterised as voluntary – a matter of business going the extra mile beyond what the law requires. If CSR is self-governance by business, however, it is self-governance that has received a firm push from external social and market forces, from forces of social accountability.

At the same time law is playing a much more significant role than the image of CSR suggests, and this legal accountability – the focus of the book – is set to increase. Legal intervention should not, however, be seen as making social accountability redundant. Wider ethical standards and social and market forces are also necessary even to make legal regulation effective.

How law is being used, and by whom is also significant. Little of the new law is conventional state regulation. Law is being brought into play in subtle and indirect ways, private law is being used in innovative ways, and the initiative lies as much with private organisations as with the state. At the same time governments are using social and market forces to foster CSR. What is demonstrated in the context of corporate social responsibility is the emergence of a new, multi-faceted, corporate accountability.

DOREEN McBARNET is Professor of Socio-Legal Studies at the Centre for Socio-Legal Studies, University of Oxford.

AURORA VOICULESCU is Lecturer in Law at the Centre for Law, Open University.

TOM CAMPBELL is Professorial Fellow at the Centre for Applied Philosophy and Public Ethics (CAPPE), Charles Sturt University.

THE NEW CORPORATE ACCOUNTABILITY

Corporate Social Responsibility and the Law

Edited by

DOREEN McBARNET, AURORA VOICULESCU,
TOM CAMPBELL

CAMBRIDGE
UNIVERSITY PRESS

CAMBRIDGE UNIVERSITY PRESS
Cambridge, New York, Melbourne, Madrid, Cape Town,
Singapore, São Paulo, Delhi, Tokyo, Mexico City

Cambridge University Press
The Edinburgh Building, Cambridge CB2 8RU, UK

Published in the United States of America by
Cambridge University Press, New York

www.cambridge.org
Information on this title: www.cambridge.org/9780521142090

© Cambridge University Press 2007

First published 2007
First paperback edition 2009

A catalogue record for this publication is available from the British Library

ISBN 978-0-521-86818-1 Hardback
ISBN 978-0-521-14209-0 Paperback

CONTENTS

v

Contributors

BRUNO AMANN is Professor in Management Sciences at the University of Toulouse. His research interests are in the areas of family business, corporate governance and property rights. He is the author and editor of several books and has published extensively in French research reviews.

STEPHEN BOTTOMLEY is Professor of Commercial Law at the Australian National University and Director of its Centre for Commercial Law. He is the author, with Roman Tomasic and Rob McQueen, of *Corporations Law in Australia* and, with Simon Bronitt, of *Law in Context* (Federation Press, 2005). He is editor, with David Kinley, of *Human Rights and Commercial Law* (Ashgate, 2002) and, with Suzanne Corcoran, of *Interpreting Statutes* (Federation Press, 2005).

JÉRÔME CABY is Professor of Corporate Finances, Graduate Business School (IAE), Université Panthéon-Sorbonne, France. He has been a faculty member there for five years and is currently Dean. He is conducting research in corporate finance mainly on corporate governance, shareholder value analysis and family business management. He has published many papers in French specialist research reviews and five books as author or editor. He is also a Managerial Editor at Pearson Education. He is monitoring research in corporate finance, and teaches postgraduate classes at Paris University, and also in international programmes codeveloped by IAE and foreign universities such as the Georgia State University, University Ain Shams (Cairo), University Galatasaray (Istanbul), UIBE (Beijing).

KEVIN CAMPBELL is a Lecturer in the Department of Accounting, Finance and Law, University of Stirling. His most recent work has been in the area of financial regulation in offshore finance centres, the attitude towards the impact of the Research Assessment Exercise among academic lawyers in the United Kingdom, the behaviour of the UK stock market, and corporate finance in the transitional economies of Central and

Eastern Europe. He has published numerous articles, among others in the *Journal for Law and Society*, the *Company Financial and Insolvency Law Review*, the *Business Law Review*, *Applied Financial Economics*, and the *International Journal of Business Studies*.

TOM CAMPBELL is a Professorial Fellow in the Centre for Applied Philosophy and Public Ethics, Charles Sturt University, Canberra, where he manages the Business and Professional Ethics Program, and Visiting Professor in the School of Law, King's College, London. He was formerly Professor of Law at the Australian National University. He is the author of *The Theory of Ethical Positivism* (Dartmouth, 1996), *Justice* (Macmillan, 2001), *Rights: A Critical Introduction* (Routledge, 2005) and co-editor of *Human Rights and the Moral Responsibilities of Public and Private Sector Organisations* (Kluwer, 2004).

ANTHONY FORSYTH has a PhD from the University of Melbourne, and is a Senior Lecturer and Coordinator of the Corporate Law and Accountability Research Group in the Department of Business Law and Taxation, Faculty of Business and Economics, at Monash University, Melbourne.

CAROLA GLINSKI is a research fellow at the Centre for European Environmental Law at the University of Bremen, Germany. She obtained her law degree from the Free University of Berlin in 1993, and passed her second state examination in law in 1996. After two years' practice as a solicitor, she obtained a Masters Degree in Development Policy from the University of Bremen in 2000. Her research focuses on the field of European and international environmental law and on global governance, on which she has published *Environmental Justice and the South African Legal System* (Herzogenrath: Shaker Verlag GmbH, 2003) and a number of articles and book contributions.

NEIL GUNNINGHAM is an interdisciplinary social scientist and lawyer who specialises in safety, health and environmental regulation. He currently holds Professorial Research appointments in the Regulatory Institutions Network, Research School of Social Sciences, and in the School of Resources, Environment and Society, at the Australian National University. His books include (with Sinclair) *Leaders and Laggards: Next Generation Environment Regulation* (Greenleaf, 2002), with Kagan and Thornton, *Shades of Green: Business, Regulation and Environment* (Stanford University Press, 2003), with Grabosky, *Smart Regulation: Designing Environmental* Policy (Oxford University Press, 1998), and, with Johnstone, *Regulating Workplace Safety* (Oxford University Press, 1999).

NICOLA JÄGERS is a senior researcher and lecturer at Tilburg University in the Netherlands. She holds a master's degree in history and law. She obtained her PhD at the Netherlands Institute of Human Rights (SIM) in 2002. The dissertation was published as a book entitled *Corporate Human Rights Obligations: In Search of Accountability* (Intersentia, 2002). Moreover, she has published several articles and book contributions on the issue of corporate social responsibility. Her present research focuses on the role of non-governmental organisations in international economic institutions in the context of mainstreaming human rights.

JACQUES JAUSSAUD is Professor of Management Sciences at University of Pau (Université de Pau et des Pays de l'Adour), France. His research interests are in the area of international management, including organisation and control of multinational companies, with a particular focus on Japan, China and other Asian countries. He has published widely in these areas in various academic journals including, in 2006, the *Journal of International Management* and *International Management*. He has co-edited several books, such as *Perspectives on Economic Integration and Business Strategy in the Asia–Pacific Region* (Macmillan 1997), *China and India, Economic Performance and Business Strategies of Firms in the Mid 90s* (Macmillan, 1998), *Changing Economic Environment in Asia and Business Strategies* (Palgrave, 2001) and *Economic Dynamism and Business Strategy of Firms in Asia: Some Recent Developments* (China Economic Publishing House, 2006).

DAVID KINLEY holds the Chair in Human Rights Law at Sydney University Law School. He is author of numerous texts and articles in the field of human rights generally, and specifically in the area of the interaction of human rights with the global economy. He has also advised and worked with many different governments, corporations, non-governmental organisations and international organisations on a variety of international human right law matters.

MARINA KURKCHIYAN is a Research Fellow in Socio-Legal Studies at the University of Oxford, and a Fellow of Wolfson College. Previously she has held appointments at the London School of Economics, the University of Michigan at Ann Arbor, and Yerevan State University in Armenia. She is an empirical sociologist who specialises in legal culture and regulation, and she has conducted empirical research in many countries including the Ukraine and Russia. As a consultant to the World Bank, the Department for International Development, the Open Society Institute and the United

Nations Development Programme, she has completed a number of official reports. Her academic papers dealt with various aspects of development, law and social structure such as education, poverty relief, the informal economy and health care. Her recent work is reported in *Economic Crime in Russia* (edited with Alena Ledeneva), (Kluwer Law International, 2000), *Law and Informal Practices* (edited with Denis Galligan), (Oxford University Press, 2003), and *The Armenians: Past and Present in the Making of National Identity* (edited with Edmund Herzig), (Routledge Curzon, 2004).

DOREEN McBARNET is Professor of Socio-Legal Studies at Oxford University, and a Fellow of Wolfson College. She joined the Centre for Socio-Legal Studies after some years as a Lecturer in Sociology at Glasgow University where she graduated in History and Sociology. Her research has addressed various areas of law, beginning with doctoral work on the criminal justice process. However, her main interest for many years now has been business and the law, particularly in the context of corporate finance, tax avoidance, creative accounting and corporate responsibility, and she taught the core course on Corporate Responsibility for the MBA at Oxford's Said Business School. Her publications include the books *Conviction* (Macmillan, 1981, 1983), *Creative Accounting and the Cross-Eyed Javelin Thrower* (Wiley 1999) with C. Whelan, and *Crime, Compliance and Control* (Ashgate, 2004). Her work for the current book is based on research funded by an ESRC professorial fellowship, and she has been awarded the CBE for services to social science.

CHRISTOPHER McCRUDDEN is Professor of Human Rights Law and Fellow and Tutor in Law, Lincoln College, at Oxford University, and Overseas Affiliated Professor of Law, University of Michigan Law School. He is a Member, in the Office of the First Minister and Deputy First Minister, Panel of Experts on the Single Equality Bill (2003–) and a Member of the Procurement Board of Northern Ireland (2003–) and of the European Commission's Expert Network on the Application of the Equality Directives (1986–2003). He is member on the Editorial Board of several journals, including the *Oxford Journal of Legal Studies*, the *Law in Context* Series (Cambridge University Press), the *International Journal of Discrimination and the Law*, the *Journal of International Economic Law*, and *European Public Law*. He has published numerous journal articles, is the author (with Sandra Fredman and Mark Freedland) of *An EU Charter of Fundamental Rights* (Sweet & Maxwell, 2000) and has edited *Anti-discrimination Law* (Ashgate/Dartmouth, 2004).

LAWRENCE E. MITCHELL is John Theodore Fey Research Professor of Law at The George Washington University Law School and the Director of the Sloan Program for the Study of Business in Society. He is author of *Corporate Irresponsibility: America's Newest Export* (Yale University Press, 2001), which became the subject of much attention in the United States and Europe. For six years he practised corporate law in New York City. He is the editor of *Progressive Corporate Law* (1995). Professor Mitchell has done substantial work in using economic sociology to address corporate law issues.

PETER T. MUCHLINSKI is the Professor of Law and International Business at Kent Law School, University of Kent. Prior to rejoining KLS he was the Drapers' Professor of Law in the Law Department of Queen Mary and Westfield College, University of London, from 1998 to 2001. He specialises in international and European business law, competition law, law and development and commercial regulation. His more recent work concentrates on the social dimension of the regulation of international business, with emphasis on human rights and multinational enterprises and upon the impact of globalisation upon legal research methodology. He is the author of *Multinational Enterprises and the Law* (Blackwell Publishers, 1995, revised paperback edition 1999) and (with Julia Black and Paul Walker) editor of *Commercial Regulation and Judicial Review* (Hart Publishing, 1998). In 1990 he qualified as a barrister in the field of commercial and European law and is a door tenant at Brick Court Chambers, London. He acts as a principal adviser to the United Nations Conference on Trade and Development (UNCTAD) on investment issues. During the period of June–October 2003 he worked at UNCTAD in Geneva as a Senior Legal Expert in the Division on Investment Technology and Enterprise Development.

JUSTINE NOLAN lectures in international human rights law at the University of New South Wales, Sydney, and is the Deputy Director of the Australian Human Rights Centre. She specialises in examining the relationship between human rights and business. Prior to joining UNSW, she was the Director of the Business and Human Rights programme at the Lawyers Committee for Human Rights in the United States (now Human Rights First), where she worked closely with a number of multinational corporations and the United Nations in developing and implementing mechanisms for protecting human rights in business operations.

CHRISTINE PARKER is Senior Lecturer in the School of Law at the University of Melbourne, Australia. She is author of *The Open Corporation:*

Effective Self-Regulation and Democracy (Oxford University Press, 2002) and *Just Lawyers: Regulating Access to Justice* (Oxford University Press, 2003). She is co-editor of *Regulating Law* (Oxford University Press, 2004).

JUAN PIÑEIRO is Professor of Corporate Finance at the University of Santiago de Compostela, Spain. He has published extensively in Spanish, English and French and is the co-author of several books including, most recently, *Corporate Social Responsibility* (Palgrave, 2006), *Sustainability Accounting and Reporting* (Springer, 200), *Analisis y calculo de las Operaciones Financieras* (Torculo, 2003). He is also coordinator of the journal, *Revista Galega de Economia*, and co-editor of *Revista de Gestao Portuaria, Ambiental e de Negocios do Brasil.*

PATRICK SCHMIDT teaches political science at Macalester College in St Paul, Minnesota. He has previously held appointments at Southern Methodist University, Dallas, Texas, and at the Centre for Socio-Legal Studies, Oxford. He is the author of numerous articles on American courts and of the book *Lawyers and Regulations: The Politics of the Administrative Process* (Cambridge University Press, 2005). He is also co-author, with Simon Halliday, of *Human Rights Brought Home: Socio-Legal Studies of Human Rights in the National Context* (Hart Publishing, 2004).

AMY SINDEN is an Associate Professor at Temple University Beasley School of Law and a member scholar of the Center for Progressive Reform. Her recent academic writings have criticised the misuse of economic theory in environmental law, arguing against the use of cost-benefit analysis in environmental standard setting and countering claims that private property rights can solve environmental problems in the absence of government regulation. She has also written about the application of classical human rights norms to environmental conflicts. Her articles have appeared in a number of books and academic journals, including the *Iowa Law Review*, the *University of Colorado Law Review*, and the *Harvard Environmental Law Review.*

DOUGLAS VICK died in a tragic accident before this book reached publication. He was a Lecturer in Business Law in the Department of Accounting, Finance and Law, Stirling University, and also a Visiting Fellow with the Stirling Media Research Institute. Prior to that, he held the post of Honourable Abraham L. Freedman Teaching Fellow and Lecturer in Law at Temple University School of Law in Philadelphia, Pennsylvania. He was also an Associate Attorney in the Litigation Department of Pepper, Hamilton and Scheetz, a large Philadelphia law firm, and he was a Law

Clerk for the Honourable Howard G. Munson, Chief Judge of the United States District Court for the Northern District of New York, Syracuse, New York (1986–1988). He was awarded a Juris Doctor degree by the Albany Law School of Union University in 1986. He was admitted to the bars of New York and Pennsylvania. He published numerous articles in the *Modern Law Review*, the *Journal of Law and Society*, the *Federal Communications Law Journal*, the *Virginia Journal of International Law*, the *Buffalo Law Review* and the *Journal of Media Law and Practice.*

AURORA VOICULESCU is Lecturer in Law at the Open University and an Associate Research Fellow at the Centre for Socio-Legal Studies, Oxford University. Between 1999 and 2003 she was a British Academy Post-doctoral Fellow in Law at Lincoln College, Oxford University. Her teaching, research work and publications are in the area of human rights, in particular in connection with collective and corporate agency and responsibility. In this context, her research focuses on the interplay between human rights discourse and global market agencies such as transnational corporations and intergovernmental economic and financial institutions. She is on the Editorial Board of the *Journal for Commonwealth Law and Legal Education.* She is the author of *Human Rights and Political Justice in Post-Communist Eastern Europe: Prosecuting History* (Edwin Mellen Publisher, 2000).

NATALIE ZERIAL has a law degree from the University of Sydney where she worked as a research assistant for Professor David Kinley, and also spent one semester on academic exchange at the University of Cornell, where she worked as a research assistant for Associate Professor of Law, and Director of the Cornell Death Penalty Project, John Blume. She also did clinical work with lawyers from the Centre for Constitutional Rights on Guantanamo Bay litigation. In 2007 she is the tipstaff for Mr Justice Windeyer of the New South Wales Supreme Court.

Introduction

DOREEN McBARNET

This book is about the relationship between corporate social responsibility (CSR) and the law, and it is a book addressed to the many people in business, non-governmental organisations (NGOs), governments, academe and society more generally who are currently concerned with what corporate social responsibility involves and with its potential impact on both business and society. The objective is to inform and to stimulate the growing debate both on corporate social responsibility itself and on its potential role in the area of business regulation, law and ethics.

At first sight, the pairing of CSR and the law might seem a contradiction in terms. The adoption by companies of CSR policies is, after all, routinely characterised as voluntary – a matter of business going the extra mile beyond what the law requires. Describing CSR as voluntary is however a little misleading. The adoption of CSR policies by business has taken place in a very specific context. If CSR is self-governance by business, it is nonetheless self-governance that has received a very firm push from external social and market forces. From the start, 'voluntary' CSR has been socially and economically driven. What is more, the reality – as this book demonstrates at length – is that law is playing a much more significant role than the image of voluntary or NGO and market-driven CSR suggests, a role that could increase still further.

This book explores how this is happening and how it could develop in the future. It also demonstrates the operation, in the arena of CSR, of a complex interaction between government, business and civil society, private law, state regulation and self-regulation, at national and international levels, with social, legal, ethical and market pressures all being brought to bear in ways that cut across traditional pigeonholes, and interrelate with and foster each other. Indeed, as Chapter 1 argues, the multiple sources and interweaving forms of corporate governance – legal and extra-legal – coalescing under the banner of CSR might be seen as a new, multi-faceted corporate accountability.

1

Analysing CSR and the law takes us into a broad spectrum of areas of law and policy, and of business and social practice. The contributions to this book are multidisciplinary and interdisciplinary – drawing on law, sociology, political science, economics, business management, accounting and philosophy. They are international and multinational, in terms of the contributors themselves, the issues addressed and the jurisdictions covered, often comparatively. The areas of law and legal process covered are wide-ranging. Company law, securities, tort, contract, criminal, international, human rights, trade law, tax, accounting and environment law all come under discussion, though that discussion is consciously written not for lawyers or business executives alone but to interest and inform the layman. Different perspectives and methods are brought to bear. Some chapters analyse law and policy, some look at the politics behind legal developments, some at the social and economic forces at work. Several chapters are based on empirical research, while others speculate on future developments or take a moral or normative perspective, considering not what is but what should be and why. Some contributors are critical, others hopeful of CSR, some neutral observers, others advocates. Despite the range of disciplines, areas and perspectives covered, however, there is a single, clear focus throughout on exploring the relationship between CSR and the law.

The book is presented in five parts. Part One, on *Corporate Social Responsibility and the Law*, comprises a single long chapter by McBarnet setting out the development, context and critique of CSR, as background for the rest of the book, and exploring the interface between CSR and the law, which is analysed as CSR *beyond* law, *through* law and *for* law. CSR *beyond* law addresses the familiar concept of CSR as an extra-legal movement, CSR *through* law demonstrates the increasing intervention of law in what can really no longer be seen as 'voluntary' CSR. CSR *for* law reminds us that law itself has its limits and argues that CSR has a role to play in complementing law, by providing wider ethical standards and forces of social accountability, and by not only making demands on business beyond those of formal law, but making formal law itself more effective. The chapter also conceptualises the developing interaction between voluntary, or market-driven, CSR and the law, as a new corporate accountability.

This new corporate accountability is addressed in a range of ways in the chapters that follow. With the more familiar territory of CSR *beyond* the law set out in Part One, Parts Two to Four of the book focus in particular and in depth on the new corporate accountability as demonstrated by

CSR *through* law, while the wider ethical issues also raised in Part One are returned to in greater depth in Part Five.

Part Two, *Bringing Law into Corporate Social Responsibility*, looks in detail at some of the innovative legal mechanisms being used to make inroads on 'voluntary' CSR, exploring the often subtle and indirect ways in which law is being used to enforce voluntary CSR standards and to legally back social accountability. This also demonstrates how private law is increasingly being used to regulate business, often by private organisations such as NGOs.

Chapter 2, by McBarnet and Kurkchiyan, explores the operation of 'contractual control', showing how business is increasingly being 'regulated' by business through private contractual arrangements – for example in the CSR standards required in supply contracts – and assesses the impact and potential of the practice. In Chapter 3 McCrudden shows how governments, as purchasers of goods and services, can also exercise such control through their procurement policies, focusing particularly on the European Union. Chapter 4, by Glinski, reassesses the legal status of voluntary codes of conduct adopted by businesses, asking: are they really voluntary? It shows how law is being used, and could be used more extensively, to hold corporations legally accountable to their own voluntary corporate codes.

Chapter 5, by McBarnet and Schmidt, analyses the creative use of the all but moribund US Alien Tort Claims Act, originally enacted in the eighteenth century to deal with piracy, but used in the late twentieth and early twenty-first centuries to hold multinational corporations liable for human rights abuses overseas. This analysis demonstrates, specifically, the creative use of domestic private law, by private organisations, to enforce rights established in public international law. More generally, it demonstrates the dynamic potential of law and the fact that corporate practices can prove in practice to be less immune from legal sanction than is often assumed. Jägers, in Chapter 6, examines the emergent development of the status of NGOs, within the particularly testing context of the World Trade Organisation, from social catalyst to a legally recognised role. Chapter 7, by Parker, straddles the themes of Parts Two and Three, demonstrating the interlinking of state regulation and voluntary action. It looks at government control through 'meta-regulation', showing the less direct legal tools governments can bring into play both to foster CSR policies and to facilitate private enforcement.

Parts Three and Four, *Expanding Legal Accountabilities*, review a range of areas of law, showing how the accountability of corporations in substantive law is being stretched through new legislation or challenged through new interpretation – or suggesting how it should be. Governments are also shown to be using new approaches to legal regulation.

Part Three focuses particularly on company law. Chapter 8, by Campbell and Vick, analyses the expansion of CSR accountability fostered by the United Kingdom's new legal disclosure strategy which is based on a three-way interplay of law, voluntary CSR and the financial market. It reviews developments in the law, analyses the politics and economic models behind them, and assesses the practical impact of socially responsible investment. In Chapter 9, Mitchell looks from current law and practice to potential routes to enhanced corporate responsibility through the role of the Board. Chapter 10, by Bottomley and Forsyth, reviews recent developments in corporate law, drawing particularly on experience in Australia, and focusing on its impact on the interests of employees. In Chapter 11, Amann, Caby, Jaussaud and Piñero analyse policy and practice in the United States, Japan, France and Spain on the exercise of shareholder rights for CSR goals. Chapter 12, by Voiculescu, examines law and policy in the European Union in relation to CSR, showing how CSR goals are being approached not only through the overt routes set out in the Green Paper, but through subtler methods such as the use of legal instruments established in relation to human rights. This chapter leads us through company law to human rights, and so to Part Four.

Part Four analyses some of the expanding legal accountabilities confronting business in the context of human rights and the environment, as well as examining the way law is widening its approach to the basic concept of holding a company, as opposed to an individual, responsible at all. In Chapter 13, Voiculescu considers the concept of corporate legal responsibility in the CSR context, drawing lessons from recent developments in a range of jurisdictions in the specific and testing arena of corporate criminal responsibility. Chapter 14, by Muchlinski, traces developments in international law, showing how the traditional idea that international law, in a context such as human rights, applies to states rather than corporations has been eroded, and the practical issues arising. Chapter 15, by Kinley, Nolan and Zerial, takes this further, analysing the politics behind the controversial UN Human Rights Norms for Corporations.

Chapter 16 takes us to the issue of CSR and the law in the context of the environment, with Gunningham examining the role of the licence to operate, in a range of senses, as a mechanism of corporate control. Sinden, in Chapter 17, approaches environmental and human rights issues from a more normative perspective, arguing that the power wielded by multinational corporations justifies the imposition of an obligation of responsibility.

Part V concludes the book with Campbell's analysis, in Chapter 18, of the concept of CSR and of its moral foundations, drawing on a number of themes raised throughout the book, and asking particularly whether human rights can provide a moral grounding for CSR, and for the social, political and legal forces sustaining the new corporate accountability.

Thanks are due to all those who have contributed chapters to this book, to Tom Campbell and Aurora Voiculescu for contributing both chapters and editorial support, and to Ewen Miller for his hard work copy-editing. Thanks are also due to the Economic and Social Research Council,[1] whose award of a professorial fellowship to Doreen McBarnet contributed significantly by funding both the specific empirical research and analysis behind Chapters 1, 2 and 5, and the more general research project on 'Regulation, responsibility and the rule of law', which inspired exploration of the new corporate accountability.

December 2006

[1] ESRC Professorial Fellowship RES-051-0031.

PART ONE

Corporate Social Responsibility and the Law

Corporate social responsibility beyond law, through law, for law: the new corporate accountability

DOREEN McBARNET

It is difficult to open a newspaper these days without coming across some reference to corporate social responsibility (CSR). As the ready resort to acronym suggests, it is a term that has entered into routine usage in debates both about business and within business. Post-Enron, and in a world in which the role of business in human rights and the environment is a matter of standard debate, the social and ethical responsibilities of business have become key issues, and CSR has become a much talked about element in corporate governance.

CSR essentially involves a shift in the focus of corporate responsibility from profit maximisation for shareholders within the obligations of law[1] to responsibility to a broader range of *stake*holders, including communal concerns such as protection of the environment, and accountability on ethical as well as legal obligations. It is a shift from 'bottom line' to 'triple bottom line',[2] as it is sometimes put, from 'profits' to 'people, planet and profits', or indeed to 'profits and principles', to cite Shell International's social reports. These broader concerns are not necessarily seen as in conflict with shareholder interests but as protecting them long term. CSR is not philanthropy, contributing gifts from profits, but involves the exercise of social responsibility in how profits are made.

I would like to thank the Economic and Social Research Council (ESRC) which is funding this research through its Professorial Fellowship Scheme (RES-051-27-0031). The work on CSR is part of a larger programme of research on 'Regulation, responsibility and the rule of law'. This chapter draws on a number of working papers including 'New sources of leverage in the regulation of global business: harnessing CSR', plenary lecture at the first Regnet conference, Canberra, December 2003.
[1] M. Friedman, 'The Social Responsibility of Business is to Increase its Profits', *New York Times Magazine*, 13 September 1970.
[2] J. Elkington, *Cannibals with Forks: The Triple Bottom Line of 21st Century Business* (Oxford: Capstone, 1997).

Typically, CSR policies involve a commitment by corporations, usually expressed in their statements of business principles or corporate-specific codes of conduct, to enhanced concern for the environment, human rights, fairness to suppliers and customers, and opposition to bribery and corruption. The range of issues involved is constantly expanding, with matters such as the promotion of 'diversity' in the workforce, ethical policies on the supply chain, responsible marketing, especially with regard to marketing to children, and even demand for a responsible approach in the food business in relation to obesity, recently added to the agenda. After Enron, CSR is also regarded as not only involving social and environmental issues but as going to the heart of core business operations such as accounting and even tax policies, and has become an issue for corporate governance in the narrower sense of the term. The language of business ethics is also frequently brought into play, with environmental and social impact seen as part of a new business ethics. The trend to a shift of language in business from CSR to simply CR, corporate responsibility, reflects this. CSR has indeed become something of a portmanteau concept which incorporates a broad sweep of ethical concerns from saving the planet to demanding honesty and fairness in business dealings.

The institutionalisation of CSR as a business issue has been demonstrated by the increasingly routine adoption of CSR policies in major companies. In 2001, 73 per cent of the United Kingdom's FTSE 100 companies had codes of conduct or statements of business principles. By 2004, this was up to 91 per cent.[3] In the United States, all of the Fortune 500 companies have introduced codes of conduct. The publication of CSR reports has increased with eighty-three of the FTSE 100 companies reporting in 2005,[4] ninety of the top hundred European companies and fifty-nine of the US top hundred producing CSR reports for 2005–06.[5]

The range of sectors adopting CSR policies has widened. The financial sector, which a decade before felt far from the frontline of social and environmental issues faced by the likes of oil and clothing companies, has acknowledged it too is affected by CSR just as much as its clients, and reporting there doubled in 2004–05. By 2005, even tobacco companies and arms manufacturers, sectors beyond the pale for many CSR advocates, were producing CSR reports. The number of 'ethics officers' in US corporations has been on the rise,[6] and company structures have increasingly

[3] UK Institute of Business ethics survey, 2005.
[4] Context, *Directions: Trends in CSR Reporting 2003–04* (2005).
[5] Context, *Reporting in Context* (2006).   [6] *Ethical Corporation*, 26 July 2005.

included dedicated CSR managers and directors expressly responsible for CSR. Indeed, making CSR a matter for board-level responsibility has become established practice among leading companies.

Companies are recruiting the services of CSR consultancies to produce CSR codes, write or verify CSR reports, train staff in CSR and market their CSR credentials. They are signing up to CSR initiatives and putting themselves up for CSR awards. In a survey in December 2005 by management consultants McKinsey, only 6 per cent of the 4,238 executives surveyed worldwide agreed with the Milton Friedman line that the sole purpose of business was to produce high returns for shareholders; 84 per cent thought high returns had to be balanced with contributions to the broader public good.[7]

This chapter examines the interface between CSR and the law. At first sight that may seem a contradiction in terms. The adoption of CSR policies is, after all, routinely characterised as voluntary – a matter of business going the extra mile beyond what the law requires. As Chris Tuppen, social and environmental programmes manager at British Telecom (BT), put it in the company's first social report: 'The key issue is really what companies are going to do beyond mere compliance with the law.'[8] Ricoh, the digital office equipment company, markets itself under the headline 'Ricoh goes beyond compliance; we're going beyond the legal framework.'[9]

The UK government's major review of company law, reporting in 2001,[10] underlined this approach by opting to retain CSR as a voluntary matter rather than making it a direct legal obligation, and the theme has been reiterated since, with Stephen Timms, Energy and Corporate Responsibility Minister, describing CSR as 'going beyond legal requirements'.[11] The Department of Trade and Industry's line is to 'see CSR as the voluntary actions that business can take, over and above compliance with legal requirements'.[12] The European Commission took the same approach in its Green Paper on CSR, defining CSR as 'a concept whereby companies integrate social and environmental concerns in their business operations and in their interaction with their stakeholders on a voluntary

---

[7] McKinsey, 'Global Survey of Business Executives: Business and Society', *McKinsey Quarterly* 2 (2006), 33–9.

[8] BT Social Report (1999); and see S. Perrin, 'Show how much you care', *Accountancy* September (1999), 44–5.

[9] See, for example, *Financial Times* special report on corporate governance, 15 December 2004.

[10] Department of Trade and Industry, *Company Law Review Report* 2001.

[11] *Ethical Corporation*, September 2004, p. 13.

[12] www.csr.gov.uk/whatiscsr.shtml

basis'.[13] The subsequent 'Communication on CSR' reported that business respondents to the Green Paper 'stressed the voluntary nature of CSR', with the Commission noting 'large consensus' that CSR is 'behaviour by businesses over and above legal requirements, voluntarily adopted'.[14] Indeed, it made 'recognition of the voluntary nature of CSR' the first principle of its framework for action.[15] The United Nations' Global Compact for business is signed up to on a voluntary basis.

The voluntary adoption of CSR by multinational corporations might seem rather paradoxical in a context where multinationals have been seen for some time as in many ways stronger than nation states, with consequent implications for the feasibility of effective governmental control over their practices. Why would business voluntarily commit itself to standards beyond the requirements of law? The reality is that describing CSR as voluntary is a little misleading. The adoption of CSR policies by business has taken place in a very specific context. If CSR is self-governance by business, it is nonetheless self-governance that has received a very firm push from external social and market forces. From the start, 'voluntary' CSR has been socially and economically driven.

Section I of this chapter sets out some familiar themes in the CSR debate, reviewing the social and market pressures that lie behind businesses' 'voluntary' adoption of CSR policies – the 'drivers' so often referred to in discussions of CSR in a business context – though it introduces some new perspectives too. It looks, in short, at the conventional concept of CSR as *beyond* the law, in the dual sense both of involving goals beyond the requirements of law, and of being driven by extra-legal forces – extra-legal forces that we might see as constituting a new corporate *social* accountability. It also examines the argument that CSR is *against* the law, contravening the legal duty of managers to owners, along with a range of wider criticisms of 'voluntary' CSR and, indeed, of social accountability.

Section II, however, moves the discussion on from the conventional understanding of CSR, by questioning just how voluntary CSR really is, or can remain, not only in social and economic terms but in legal terms. It analyses the many ways in which law is in fact being used to make business adoption of CSR policies much more of a legal obligation than the discourse of voluntarism – and indeed the current demands from many non-governmental organisations (NGOs) to supercede voluntarism with regulation – would suggest. It explores the interface between CSR and the law by analysing the growing phenomenon of CSR being brought about

[13] COM (2001) 366.   [14] COM (2002) 347.   [15] COM (2002) 347, p. 8.

through law, though often in subtle, indirect and creative ways, and not necessarily through government action.

Section III explores the interface between CSR and the law in reverse, shifting focus from the role of law in CSR to the role of CSR in law. Calls for less emphasis on voluntarism and more on legal regulation of business, as the only effective way to secure a more responsible approach by business to its impact on society, may expect more of law than law can in fact provide. For a range of reasons, well rehearsed in many years of socio-legal research, law is not always as effective as might be hoped in regulating business, partly because of compromise in the substance of law and problems in enforcement, but also because of the attitude to law and compliance taken by business itself.

Business is extremely adept at finding 'arguably legal' ways to circumvent regulatory control, using the art of 'creative compliance'[16] to simultaneously escape legal control and any threat of penalty for doing so. The pervasive nature of such an approach to law in business suggests the need for some further, extra-legal driver not only to secure a commitment in business to socially responsible policies *beyond* the law, but to secure businesses' responsible compliance *with* the law. It may be that we need to look not only to law to enhance the effectiveness of socially and economically driven CSR, but to socially and economically driven CSR to enhance the effectiveness of law. Section III explores this issue of CSR *for* law.

The chapter concludes by observing the multiple sources and interweaving forms of corporate governance – legal and extra-legal – which are coalescing under the banner of CSR, and considers their potential as the basis of a new, multi-faceted corporate accountability.

I. Corporate social responsibility beyond the law

Discussions of business adoption of CSR policies routinely present it as the product of a number of external drivers, notably the role of civil society, particularly activist NGOs focused on business activities, the facilitation of campaigns against business as a result of the new technology (notably the internet), along with trends in business itself such as outsourcing and branding making it more vulnerable to CSR critique, and the growth of a socially responsible consumer and investment market. To this we might add the impact of Enron and related scandals, the role of

---

[16] For the development of this concept, see D. McBarnet, *Crime, Compliance and Control* (Aldershot: Ashgate, 2004) (collected essays).

the CSR industry itself, the response of business to new opportunities, and the strategic use of an ideology which could meld new CSR demands and traditional business interests in the 'business case' for CSR.[17] Corporate social responsibility emerges as the product of a new level of social accountability for business which is, however, seen by many as inadequate without the development of further legal accountability too.

A. New pressures, new vulnerabilities: civil society, the new technology and trends in business

In the McKinsey survey of business executives, only 8 per cent thought companies were motivated to champion social or environmental causes out of genuine concern.[18] Certainly business was, at least in the beginning, more reactive than proactive in the development of the contemporary CSR movement.[19] Some familiar examples – Shell and Nike – can be drawn on to demonstrate this and provide background for later analysis.

One of the leaders in the adoption of explicit CSR policies, codes and reports was Shell, its 'transformation' having become a classic business school case study,[20] and it was very much responding to major public relations (PR) crises resulting from both environmental and human rights issues, particularly in Nigeria.[21] The company's operation in a state run by a military dictatorship accused of major human rights abuses, the impact of oil extraction on the Ogoni people and the Niger Delta environment, the execution of Ogoni leader Ken Saro-Wiwa and the campaigns of human rights organisations pointing the finger not just at the Nigerian

---

[17] For more detail on these arguments, see D. McBarnet, 'Human Rights and the New Accountability', in T. Campbell and S. Miller (eds.), *Human Rights and Moral Responsibilities of Corporate and Public Sector Organisations* (Dordrecht: Kluwer, 2004), pp. 63–80, on which this section draws. Also D. Vogel, *Market for Virtue: Potential and Limits of CSR* (Washington, DC: Brookings, 2005).

[18] McKinsey 2006.

[19] Though there is also a much older tradition of philanthropy or something more akin to contemporary social responsibility or business ethics among specific firms, such as the religious roots of Cadbury or Rowntree.

[20] P. Mirvis, 'Transformation at Shell', *Business and Society Review* 105, 1 (2000), 63–84.

[21] 'Shell in Nigeria' has become a classic business school case study in CSR courses. See Harvard Business School case studies *Royal Dutch/Shell in Nigeria* (Boston: Hárvard Business School Publishing 9–399–126, Rev. 20 April 2000) and *Royal Dutch/Shell in transition* (Boston: Harvard Business School Publishing 9–300–039, 4 October 1999), and management texts, for example M. McIntosh, D. Leipziger, K. Jones and G. Coleman, *Corporate Citizenship* (London: FT/Pitman, 1998). See too G. Chandler, 'Oil Companies and Human Rights', *Business Ethics: A European Review* 7, 2 (1998), 69–72.

dictatorship but at Shell amounted to a PR disaster, which was only exacerbated when Shell's plan to dump its Brent Spar oil rig at sea was met by much publicised resistance by Greenpeace.

NGOs played a major part in the publicity and pressure that prompted Shell's 'transformation', not only Greenpeace on the environmental side, but Amnesty International, Pax Christi and others on the human rights front, and the development of the CSR movement generally has to be seen in the context of the growth of a highly active and activist civil society, which has put significant pressure on business via campaigns, publicity, boycotts and pressures both for more transparency and for more socially responsible policies and practices. There is nothing new about organised protest by civil society (witness, for example, the nineteenth-century campaigns against slavery), but one of the ironies of the recent era of deregulation of business (in terms of state control) has been the simultaneous expansion of constraints imposed by civil society. Non-governmental activity on a global scale has now become a key part of the discourse of globalisation and is routinely identified – by governments, commentators and business itself, as one of the key 'drivers' of the contemporary CSR movement.[22]

The growing voice of civil society has of course been aided by another often cited 'driver', the new technology, expanding easy global communication, and making for instant worldwide publicity. There is now, it is frequently said, 'no hiding place' for corporate activity. The internet provides a ready forum for instant criticism and publicity, with websites on all kinds of issues pointing the finger at specific companies. The new technology means even one person can have a major impact, as in the case of Mike Kasky in his campaigns against Nike, of which more later.[23]

All this can be seen as resulting in a new level of social accountability that goes beyond that required by law. Take another classic case, that of Nike. Nike, like many other multinational companies, has its shoes and clothing produced in cheap labour countries by independent suppliers. Some of its Vietnamese, Indonesian and Chinese suppliers were exposed as using child labour, requiring employees to work long hours, beyond even the high legal minimum of the countries in question, at less than even the low statutory minimum wage, and in some places in conditions

---

[22] The European Union, for example, acknowledged the importance of social and market pressures, noting that civil society must be recognised as playing a significant role in this new business governance; COM (2002) 347, p. 5.

[23] See also John Braithwaite and Peter Drahos, *Global Business Regulation* (Cambridge: Cambridge University Press, 2000).

where carcinogens in the air were above the permitted level.[24] In short, both Nike's own code of conduct and, in some cases, local law, were being broken, but not by Nike. Under traditional criteria Nike was neither accountable nor responsible, as Nike's chief executive officer (CEO) was quick to point out.

But Nike was *held* responsible and held to account by civil society campaigners. Again, the Nike experience has become an icon of what can go wrong if companies stick to too narrow a notion of corporate responsibility – demonstrations, protests, 'shoe-ins' where Nike trainers were publicly thrown away, very public rejection of sponsorship, weeks of anti-Nike cartoons in the press, and a fall in profits, which Nike itself attributed to its association with child labour. The Nike case is a clear demonstration of civil society in action through social protest, and a classic naming and shaming campaign.

The Nike case demonstrates another contextual factor – trends in business practice such as outsourcing and branding. Nike was particularly vulnerable to such adverse publicity because of the importance to its business of the Nike brand. Indeed, Nike is in a sense only a brand: production is all subcontracted. In its emphasis on branding, however, it can be seen to have created its own nemesis. The very fact that the name is so well known made it an easy target for critique, in what Klein labels the 'brand boomerang'.[25] At the same time, the trend to outsourcing and subcontracting means companies have less automatic direct control over the conditions under which their products are made. Though this can be seen cynically as an advantage when no *legal* responsibility or accountability is attached, it becomes a source of risk when the new *social* accountability is brought into play. Hence the increasing corporate attention to 'ethical trading' and supply chain policy.

Brand vulnerability in general is seen to be on the increase, as the proportion of corporate value that comes not from tangible assets such as property and stock but from 'intangibles' has risen. Intangible value is essentially the difference between what the tangible property is worth and what the market will pay, and is put down to such factors as brand and reputation, intellectual property and knowledge bases. A study of FTSE 100 companies in 2005 found that 60 per cent of the companies'

---

[24] In November 1997, an employee leaked a report by the company's auditors exposing conditions in Vietnamese factories supplying it (*The Guardian*, 13 June 1998), and the story then featured repeatedly in all forms of media.

[25] N. Klein, *No Logo* (London: Flamingo, 2000), p. 345.

market value had to be categorised as intangibles,[26] with a not dissimilar figure (53 per cent) attributed in 2006 to the US Fortune 500.[27]

When the brand becomes so important, the argument goes, so does reputation. Companies cannot afford to risk their reputation coming under challenge. According to research by insurance company Aon, the top 2000 private- and public-sector organisations regard damage to reputation as their biggest risk.[28] Social, environmental and ethical issues are now seen as key sources of reputation risk, a fact reflected in the risk identification and risk management sections of corporate CSR reports, and reputation risk has become a key concept in the discourse of CSR, pushing CSR issues up the corporate agenda.

B. Market factors: consumers and investors

Market factors can also be seen as key contextual drivers. Attacking brand reputation on CSR grounds would be ineffective if consumers and investors did not care. Further drivers can therefore be identified in a growing trend to what we might think of as 'concerned consumption'.

The CSR consumer market, once seen as purely a niche market, is growing significantly. A UK survey in October 2006 found that more than a third of consumers are prepared to spend more on 'ethical' foods, compared to 25 per cent in 2002, while in the US LRN study of ethics in the market, 70 per cent of those surveyed reported they had decided not to purchase products or services from a company they thought had questionable ethics.[29] More valuable than what people say is evidence of actual spending patterns, and there is clear evidence of rising CSR-oriented consumer practice. A survey by the Co-operative Bank in November 2006 put the UK ethical consumption market at £29 billion, an 11.4 per cent rise on the previous year compared to a 1.4 per cent rise in household expenditure more generally.[30]

The sale of 'Fairtrade' products alone rose 40 per cent in 2005 and 265 per cent from 2002 to 2005, constituting in itself a £230 million market.[31] Fairtrade guarantees producers a price that at least covers the cost

---

[26] Vivien Beattie and Sarah Jane Thompson, 'Intangibles and the OFR', *Financial Management* June (2005), 29.

[27] Corporatewatch.com; *The Guardian*, 6 November 2006.

[28] Aon insurance group, 2000, reported in SustainAbility, *The Changing Landscape of Liability* (London: SustainAbility, 2004), p. 17.

[29] www.lrn.com/news/releases, 30 January 2006.   [30] *Financial Times*, 27 November 2006.

[31] Mintel survey; *The Guardian*, 14 October 2006.

of production and is usually better than market price, as well as providing a premium for social and environmental projects. The producers in turn must meet set standards on labour and the environment.[32] Marks & Spencer reported a 27 per cent rise in sales in three months when it switched all thirty-eight of its tea and coffee lines to Fairtrade sources in 2006.[33] Organic food sales doubled from 2000 to 2006, with £1.6 billion spent in 2005–06.[34] Ethical trading encompasses not just food but a wide range of materials and products such as organic cotton and sustainably produced timber, with pressure on the mining industry also increasing from the gold and diamond trade.

Socially responsible investment (SRI) is another major development, with investment funds screening companies by triple bottom line criteria rather than simply on the basis of financial performance or value. In the United Kingdom, FTSE (the Financial Times Stock Exchange Index) introduced in 2001 the FTSE4Good index using criteria based on CSR. Dow Jones in the United States has its Sustainability Index. There are 'socially responsible', ethical and 'green' investment trusts. FTSE4Good's approach is to raise the bar over time, 'engaging' companies to meet higher standards at each review and dropping companies that fail to do so. In its first three years it dropped eighty-seven companies, including household names such as Goldman Sachs and Avon, while the introduction of more demanding human rights criteria resulted in fifty-three companies developing new policies and practices to ensure continued inclusion.[35] Companies included in these indices make much of it in their CSR reports.

Socially responsible investment funds for individual investors may be relatively small beer, though growing – the LRN Survey of ethics in the US investor market found 50 per cent of individual stockholders had at some point decided not to purchase shares in a company because they believed it had questionable ethics.[36] However, SRI is increasingly a concern for the giants of the investment field too, such as pension funds. SRI investment in France rose 76 per cent in 2004, with 60 per cent of that accounted for by institutional investors.[37] The twenty-four-fold rise in SRI funds in Australia to A$7.7 billion over the period 2000 to 2005 is particularly attributable to pension fund investment.[38]

Major pension funds can wield significant influence. CalPERS, the Californian Public Employees Retirement Scheme Fund, with an international

---

[32] *The Guardian*, 28 June 2006.   [33] *ibid.*, 31 July 2006.
[34] *ibid.*, 3 November 2006.   [35] *Ethical Corporation*, October 2004, p. 30.
[36] www.lrn.com/news/releases, 30 January 2006.
[37] *Ethical Corporation*, September 2005, p. 4.   [38] *Financial Times*, 5 June 2006.

investment portfolio of \$217.6 billion,[39] announced in February 2002 that it was pulling out of investment in businesses in Thailand, Indonesia, Malaysia and the Philippines because they did not meet CalPERS' CSR criteria.[40] In June 2006, the Norwegian government pension fund, one of the largest in the world, with spending power of \$230 billion, withdrew investment from Wal-Mart and Freeport McMoRan Copper and Gold on human rights and environmental grounds.[41] In the previous year it had divested from oil company Total on the grounds of complicity in human rights violations in Myanmar, the former Burma. NGOs, it might be added, have also targeted banks and other financial institutions to demonstrate their own CSR credentials by investing only in socially responsible ways, and by ensuring their clients comply with the banks' stated social and environmental standards.[42]

The employment market is also identified by some as a driver of CSR. In the United Kingdom, a MORI poll in August 2006 found 92 per cent of employees considered it important that their employers be socially responsible and 60 per cent said they felt strongly about it.[43] It has been argued that good corporate citizenship can be used to attract, retain and motivate the best workers.[44]

C. The corporate social responsibility industry and ethical scandals

There is another factor which should be added to the usual list of 'drivers'. This is the emergence of a whole new CSR industry. As well as socially responsible investment funds and 'ethical banks',[45] there are CSR consultancies advising on policies, offering training, and writing codes of conduct or CSR reports. CSR reporting needs standards against which to report, so there are CSR standard-setting organisations and CSR reporting certification firms. There are companies publicising the publication

---

[39] Investment portfolio market value \$217.6 billion as of 30 September 2006, cited in *CalPERS' Facts At A Glance*, available at www.calpers.ca.gov/eip-docs/about/facts/investme.pdf.

[40] *Business Week Online*, 25 February 2002.   [41] www.socialfunds.com/news, 16 June 2006.

[42] For example, CR Coalition, *A Big Deal? CSR and the Finance Sector in Europe*, 1 December 2005; 'My money, clear conscience', a campaign launched by Belgian NGOs against investment in the defence industry. *Ethical Corporation*, May 2005, p. 10.

[43] *The Guardian*, 6 November 2006.

[44] Marc Benioff and Karen Southwick, *Compassionate Capitalism: How Corporations Can Make Doing Good an Integral Part of Doing Well* (Franklin Lakes, NJ: The Career Press, 2004).

[45] The Triodos Bank, for example, has advertised positions under the headline, 'Would you like to work for an ethical bank?'

of social reports – 'with up to 150 reports released each month, how can you ensure your report is read by the people who matter?'[46] The big accountancy firms now include CSR consultancy as well as green and social responsibility audits. There are CSR specialist law firms. There are companies organising CSR conferences and publishing CSR magazines and newsletters.

All of these businesses have a vested interest in selling CSR, with the result that CSR has itself become a business and a market factor. In addition, companies themselves are constructing whole bureaucracies of CSR managers who also have a vested interest in – and often a positive passion for – keeping up CSR momentum.

There have been some ironies in relation to the CSR industry, of course. Arthur Andersen worked in 1999 with the London Business School on a survey on reputation management in relation to CSR and ethics. In the process, it marketed the services of its own 'ethics and responsible business practices consulting group', arguing that, with reputation an 'increasingly valuable corporate asset', companies needed 'robust programmes for guiding employee behaviour' and expressing concern that 'adoption of programmes to manage business ethics risk is by no means evident in all large companies'.[47] Two years later, with its own collapse after its involvement with Enron, that advice must have had something of a hollow ring.

The Enron collapse itself, and other business scandals of the early 2000s based on accounting scandals – Worldcom in the United States, HIH in Australia, Parmalat in Italy – have also boosted concerns about the ethical aspects of CSR and brought CSR and ethical risk more overtly onto the corporate governance agenda.

D. *Voluntary corporate social responsibility and the business case*

The idea of 'CSR drivers' has become something of a cliché, referred to as a taken-for-granted background to CSR by all parties involved. The factors involved are real enough, but just how much impact they have, and how inevitable and sustainable that impact is, could do with more testing empirical research, and there is certainly plenty of scope for criticising dependence on these drivers as a means of securing CSR, as we shall see.

---

[46] Advertisement in *Ethical Corporation* (June 2005), p. 17 for subscriptions to ReportAlert.info.

[47] Arthur Andersen/London Business School, *Ethical Concerns and Reputation Risk Management* (1999), p. 7.

The question can also be asked as to just who is doing the driving, since CSR has also been positively embraced by significant segments of big business, seen not just as a problem to be dealt with but as an opportunity to be seized in the pursuit of competitive advantage.

Companies use their CSR credentials in marketing as they press for more market share:

> 'CSR company of the year.'
> Once could be deemed lucky, twice is just plain responsible.[48]

This was Marks & Spencer's full-page advertisement in the UK national press in the summer of 2006. CSR branding has moved from niche to mainstream. The Body Shop created an early niche market in ethical products, but the brand was taken over in 2006 by mainstream company L'Oréal wanting in on the CSR market. Likewise Nestlé, another company that features in business school case studies for various CSR crises, launched a Fairtrade coffee in 2005, despite having previously dismissed Fairtrade as merely a niche market, while Cadbury Schweppes went partially organic by taking over Green & Black's. The concept of 'bottom of the pyramid' business has attracted attention to the fact that even the purchasing power of the very poor of the world adds up in aggregate to a significant market, and new markets are being found in meeting needs in developing countries while simultaneously doing profitable business. Vodafone's provision of mobile phone services in sub-Saharan Africa – which as well as providing social contact has facilitated entrepreneurship in an area lacking adequate communications – is a good example. If CSR can be seen as a way of making money it can also be seen as a way of saving it. Energy conservation and other green measures, for example, also cut costs. BP's internalisation of CO^2 emissions reportedly saved a net $600 million.[49]

This combination of reactively responding to social and market pressures, protecting the brand from reputational risk, and proactively seizing cost-saving techniques and market opportunities is usually packaged as the 'business case' for CSR. CSR is seen essentially as in harmony with the traditional pursuit of profit rather than in conflict with it. Market opportunities and cost savings make for short-term profit, while CSR activity without direct and immediate financial reward can be seen as brand enhancement, beneficial to long-term shareholder value. Presented in this

---

[48] See, e.g., *The Guardian*, 14 July 2006, referring to its Business in the Community Awards.
[49] BiTC, Insight Investment and FTSE, *Rewarding Virtue*, November 2005.

way, CSR is perfectly rational for business, the much cited 'win-win' situation for business *and* the rest of the world. Good (ethical) business is
good (profitable) business.

E. Corporate social responsibility against the law?

The business case has been a very useful way of packaging, and indeed
marketing, CSR. In particular, it neatly sidesteps the criticism that it is
simply not legitimate for management to adopt CSR policies, putting the
interests of other stakeholders before those of shareholders, with any social
benefit coming from investment and economic development – the view
classically summed up by Milton Friedman as '[t]he social responsibility of
business is to make profits'.[50] Managers are reminded that it is the owner's
money they are spending. Particularly attacking corporate philanthropy,
critics have asked: whose company is it?

> Corporate philanthropy is charity with other people's money . . . When
> Robin Hood stole from the rich to give to the poor, he was still stealing . . .
> he was still a bandit – and less of one, arguably, than the vicariously chari-
> table CEO, who is spending money taken . . . from people who have placed
> him in a position of trust to safeguard their property.[51]

Attacking CSR by attacking corporate philanthropy could be seen as something of a mishit, both because the extent to which philanthropy detracts
from profits tends to be exaggerated – corporate philanthropy by the
United Kingdom's FTSE 100 companies, including donations, gifts in
kind, staff time and attributed management costs, in fact amounts to less
than 1 per cent per annum of pre-tax profits[52] – and because CSR is in any
case about how companies make profits rather than about how they give
them away. But similar arguments are made too in relation to core CSR
issues such as environmental issues, supply chain standards and other
'selfless sacrifice for stakeholders'.[53] Management is seen as having simply
no right to spend shareholders' money in the interests of the wider social
good.

---

[50] Friedman, 'The Social Responsibility of Business'; see also D. Henderson, *Misguided Virtue:
False Notions of Corporate Social Responsibility* (London: Institute of Economic Affairs,
2001).

[51] *The Economist*, 22 January 2005, CSR survey supplement, p. 8.

[52] *ibid.*, p. 4.   [53] *ibid.*, p. 9.

This position has indeed been framed by critics of CSR as a legal point, particularly in the context of Anglo-American company law,[54] with CSR seen as effectively constituting a breach of managerial duty. The legal role of managers is seen as one of stewardship for the owners of the company. Their legal obligation therefore is to focus on profit maximisation for shareholders, constrained only by the need to comply with any other legal regulations imposing particular duties on them.[55] CSR can be seen in this context not so much as management proudly going beyond legal obligation, but, in effect, as management going beyond its legal powers (acting 'ultra vires') or even breaching its fiduciary duty to the owners. It is CSR against the law.

This is, however, an oversimplification of the law, which is rarely quite so cut and dried as this suggests. While the rules of statutory company law, in a number of jurisdictions, might 'on their face' seem to support this view,[56] the effective meaning of law depends on how those rules are interpreted in practice, and interpretation over the years has in fact been more complex and subtle. As CSR has grown in significance and critics have overtly raised legally based objections to it, so have legal champions emerged to draw attention to this and to overtly argue the case that company law, far from preventing CSR, can be seen as permitting, and perhaps even requiring, CSR practices.

John Parkinson,[57] an influential participant in the UK Company Law Review, took a strong line on this issue, demonstrating from analysis of case law in the United Kingdom and elsewhere that while profit maximisation may be a management obligation, courts have in practice tended to leave a good deal of discretion to management in terms of how they achieve that goal, and far from insisting on short-term profit maximisation, have accepted the justification of attention to wider constituents and interests as a means of enhancing long-term shareholder value. Indeed, Parkinson argues that even the Ford Motor Company case,[58] which he describes as a 'rare example of a successful challenge' to management – though it is one that is often cited by those who see an expanded CSR as against the law – need not have been lost. Managers had reduced dividends, with

---

[54] The stakeholder approach taken in Germany, for example, raises different issues.

[55] Friedman, 'The Social Responsibility of Business'; Henderson, Misguided Virtue; and see critiques in The Economist, 22 January 2005, CSR survey supplement (see nn. 51–53).

[56] Parkinson, 'The Legal Context of Corporate Social Responsibility', Business Ethics: A European Review 3, 1 (1994).

[57] ibid. Also see Mitchell for a US perspective: L. Mitchell, 'Roles and Incentives; the Core Problems of Corporate Social Responsibility', Ethical Corporation, October 2005.

[58] Dodge v. Ford Motor Company case, 170 NW 668 (1919).

the motivation of making cars cheaper and increasing employment. The case, says Parkinson, might well have been won by management, had the same facts been presented (as they reasonably could have been) as motivated rather by long-term shareholder interests. In effect, what we have here is the 'business case' again, being argued within the context of law itself.[59]

This approach may indeed be enhanced in future cases by the growing extra-legal awareness and promotion of CSR, judicial change often being influenced by what is seen as changing public opinion. Mitchell has argued that the assumption in the 1980s and 1990s in the United States that the legal obligation of management was to maximise shareholder profit – 'in its extreme version short term shareholder profit' – can be attributed more to the market culture of the time than to legal construction, though he sees the legal establishment as having tended to go along with it: 'the trend in corporate law is to accept it as the basic norm'.[60] A different social and market culture could impact in a different way. Social accountability and legal accountability can interrelate.

The business case has been a highly useful concept in the CSR movement, employed by NGOs to persuade business to adopt CSR policies, within business to justify their adoption, and by lawyers to justify a wider rather than a narrower legal interpretation of corporate responsibility. It provides the means of adopting a new model of corporate social responsibility that is simultaneously the traditional model. CSR is in shareholders' interests. As Shell put it, in its first social report: 'Principles or profits: does there have to be a choice?'[61] CSR is presented as a matter of principles *for* profits, meeting the demands and opportunities of a new context and a new market. The implication is that the voluntary adoption of CSR, within the context of social and market drivers, is a reliable way of harnessing the market for the social good.

F. *Challenging social accountability and voluntarism*

Useful for all parties as the business case for CSR may be, there are problems with it. For some the problem is the business case itself as a source of motivation, and the belief that business should be ethical regardless of the business case. As Sir Geoffrey Chandler, founder-chair of the Amnesty

---

[59] It can be seen as particularly effective if CSR is distinguished from philanthropy, though Parkinson argued even philanthropy could be justified by the business case on reputational grounds.

[60] Mitchell, 'Roles and Incentives'.   [61] The Shell Report, 1998

International Business Group, has put it, 'ultimately you do it because it is right'.[62] There has to be a moral element involved in the way business is done. So long as the only justification for adhering to CSR is shareholder value, it cannot be assumed that in a conflict of demands CSR will win out. 'People sometimes argue that, if it makes good commercial sense to respect human rights then market forces will secure compliance. It is not self-evident however that human rights norms are always good for business.'[63] Google and Yahoo in 2006 admitted sacrificing their own principles for entry to the lucrative Chinese internet market: 'the requirements of doing business in China include self-censorship – something that runs counter to Google's most basic values and commitments as a company'.[64]

Attractive as the concept of profits and principles as a harmonious unity may be, the problem is that sometimes there does have to be a choice, and one concern of CSR advocates is that where there is a clash of interests, voluntary CSR may not be adequate to ensure that CSR goals, even if they can be seen as in the long-term or reputational interests of the company, will be selected over short-term profit or securing limited business opportunities. Oil companies, for example, cannot choose where oil reserves are to be found. If the choice is to work with a government noted for human rights abuse, or to miss out on a limited business opportunity, what will the choice be? Some companies make a point of expressly declaring their voluntary codes trump commercial considerations. BT's code of business practice, for example, requires employees to 'stick to our business principles', adding: 'This might mean that we have to reject potential new business if it looks as though it would force us to compromise.'[65] And in fact companies do report instances of choosing to lose immediate business opportunities rather than take reputational risks. But the concern for critics is whether such policies can be depended on, and can be depended on for companies in general. Would voluntary CSR survive a major market downturn?

There are other issues with voluntary CSR. How many companies adopt voluntary CSR policies? The practice may now be prevalent among big

[62] 'Does Capitalism Deserve to Survive?', keynote lecture, MBA course on corporate responsibility, Said Business School, Oxford University, 30 April 2003.

[63] International Council on Human Rights Policy, *Beyond Voluntarism: Human Rights and the Developing International Legal Obligations of Companies* (Versoix, Switzerland: ICHRP, February 2002), p. 8.

[64] Testimony to the US Congress International Relations Subcommittee, *Financial Times*, 16 February 2006.

[65] BT, *The Way We Work* (2004).

business, but what about small- and medium-sized companies? What about global variations in the take-up of voluntary CSR? The McKinsey survey found significant variations between countries in executive assessment of the social role of business. How reliable and transparent is CSR reporting? Though they acknowledge Shell to have 'a pretty reasonable reputation for corporate responsibility', NGOs producing 'The Other Shell Report' have criticised Shell for failing to report legal actions against it.[66] How real are corporate CSR policies in practice? How are they implemented, followed through, enforced? How selective are those policies? Though Wal-Mart, in a Damascean conversion, set itself new environmental goals in 2005, CSR ideas did not seem to affect its practices regarding employees.[67] Is CSR fundamentally just PR?

There are criticisms too of the efficiency of extra-legal – market and civil society – pressures as a means of fostering CSR. Does the 'market for virtue' work?[68] Good companies, it is argued, do not necessarily prosper, nor 'bad' ones lose out, and there are reports that FTSE4Good and Dow Jones Sustainability companies have underperformed by 3 per cent and 8 per cent since their inception,[69] though, of course, investors might in the long run still prefer an under-performer to a temporary over-performer such as Enron, which ends up bankrupt.

NGO pressure on big brand names has been criticised as necessarily patchy in impact. After all, when we burn our Nike shoes in a grand protest, do we go barefoot or wear trainers from another brand, and how do we know the factories where they were made are, in CSR terms, any better? Nor is brand sensitivity an issue for all business, but only for high-profile brand names.

How strong are CSR consumer markets? They may be growing but how many consumers will be willing to opt for CSR over price? How reliable are CSR certifications? Reports have been published of Fairtrade-certified coffee allegedly being produced by labourers paid less than the minimum wage, or from illegal plantings in protected rainforest.[70] How fair is fairtrade? How much of the premium price differential goes to the producers as opposed to the retailers? Marks & Spencer has promised not to increase its margins on Fairtrade products, but is this the norm?[71]

---

[66] Reported in *Ethical Corporation*, September 2004, p. 47.
[67] *The Independent*, 2 November 2005. A leaked memo noted 46 per cent of children of employees either had no health insurance or relied on emergency government programmes set up for the indigent and unemployed. Health plans had been cut to cut costs.
[68] Vogel, *Market for Virtue*.   [69] Goldman Sachs Report, *Ethical Corporation*, June 2005.
[70] *Financial Times*, 9 September 2006.   [71] *Financial Times Magazine*, 22 July 2006.

How deep does socially responsible investment go? How closely do investment funds investigate the practices of the companies they assess? Are investment policies based on 'best in class' (the least bad in a poorly performing, in CSR terms, sector), as practiced by some SRI investors, what we would expect from socially responsible investment? In 2005 FTSE4Good dropped eleven banks for failing to meet its standards at the same time as the Dow Jones Sustainability Index, taking a 'best in class' approach, added fifteen.[72]

And then there is the issue of what the socially responsible approach is, especially given the breadth of the concept, where conflicts of interest between multiple stakeholders can arise. How is support for developing countries via fair-trade purchases to be balanced against the environmental impact of the 'food miles' involved?

Concern has also been expressed over putting pressure on business through extra-legal means – NGOs and the market – on grounds of democratic deficit and the rule of law – the idea of CSR *against* the law once again, at a more abstract level. By what authority do NGOs set social standards? Is it legitimate for unelected organisations not only to set standards but to enforce them through extra-legal means, such as adverse publicity, protests and boycotts, particularly when the case they make may be contestable? Greenpeace, having protested over Shell's plans for disposing of the Brent Spar oil rig, and secured a change of policy, later agreed the original plan would have been the best solution. Indeed, it is because of pressure from business on these fronts that leading NGOs Greenpeace, Amnesty and Oxfam introduced a joint code of conduct to govern their own operations in June 2006, committing themselves to ensure 'the high standards that we demand of others are also respected in our own organisations'.[73] The same question of legitimacy can indeed be applied to business overreaching its role and making public-interest decisions, when, as the *Economist* put it in a critique of CSR, 'the proper guardians of the public interest are governments, which are accountable to all citizens'.[74]

G. The call for legal regulation

One result of such concerns has been a call to end reliance on voluntary corporate action as a route to corporate social responsibility, and to

---

[72] www.socialfunds.com, news report, 8 September 2005.
[73] *Financial Times*, 3 June 2006.   [74] *The Economist*, 22 January 2005.

introduce more regulation through law. In the European Union, Socialist and Green Members of the European Parliament (MEPs) have argued against a purely voluntary policy on CSR and urged the European Commission to impose binding rules.[75] Even at the Green Paper stage, the 'large consensus' for voluntary CSR did not include trade unions and civil society organisations who 'emphasised that voluntary initiatives are not sufficient to protect workers' and citizens' rights'.[76] Naomi Klein, despite her elaboration of the power of NGO and market pressure for CSR through the brand boomerang, nonetheless concludes that they are not enough, calling for international regulation to control corporate practice.[77] John Ruggie, UN Special Representative for Business and Human Rights, talking of supply chain issues, argued 'compliance efforts cannot fully succeed unless we bring governments back into the equation'.[78]

Sir Geoffrey Chandler has called for more legal regulation, seeing voluntary CSR as a 'curse'[79] distracting from the need for effective external control. Friends of the Earth, in its response to the European Union's Green Paper, has also noted:

> we remain very concerned that CSR may be used as a convenient excuse by companies to undermine necessary legislation and regulation that support sustainable development . . . While CSR may be valuable in terms of promoting better corporate behaviour it can never be seen as an alternative to good public policy and legislation . . . Voluntary commitments are hardly the basis for ensuring responsible corporate behaviour.[80]

There is concern, in effect, that voluntary CSR will be used *against* law to prevent new legal protections or dilute old ones. Academics too, Shamir for example, have criticised voluntary CSR as a way of staving off regulation.[81] Vogel argues there are limits to what NGOs and the market can

---

[75] www.euractiv.com, 14 July 2005.
[76] 'Communication from the Commission concerning CSR', COM (2002) 347, p. 4.
[77] Klein, *No Logo*.
[78] Remarks at the forum on CSR, Bamberg, Germany, 14 June 2006.
[79] G. Chandler, 'The Curse of "Corporate Social Responsibility"', *New Academy Review* 2, 1 (2003).
[80] Friends of the Earth, December 2001, p. 2.
[81] R. Shamir, 'Between Self-regulation and the Alien Tort Claims Act: On the Contested Concept of Corporate Social Responsibility', *Law and Society Review* 38, 4 (2004). It is not just business that has argued voluntary CSR means legal regulation is not needed. Harvard Business School academic Debora Spar has argued 'spotlight' controls of companies through brand targeted campaigns have made legal regulation redundant; D. Spar, 'The Spotlight on the Bottom Line', *Foreign Affairs*, 13 March 1998, cited in Klein, *No Logo*, p. 434.

achieve and underlines the need for effective government regulation.[82] While market-driven CSR should be valued, it 'should not be regarded as a long-term substitute for the rule of law'.[83]

The argument is that only legal regulation can provide 'systematic impact'.[84] It would apply to and be enforceable against all business, not just those companies which voluntarily choose or are pressed by brand vulnerability to adopt it. It would be fairer, making for a level playing field for business, it would have more legitimacy, based on and providing due process of law, and, most importantly, it would be more effective.

H. Responding to the critique

Two responses should be made at this stage to this critique of 'voluntary' CSR and social accountability, and to the accompanying call for more legal regulation. The first is to urge caution in being too critical of CSR 'beyond the law' and dismissing it as 'just PR'. The second is to question just how accurate it is to describe the present state of CSR as purely extra-legal. The reality on both points is more complex.

First, if it is important to keep a critical eye on new developments, and to be wary of taking them always at face value, it is also important to avoid being so critical that valuable steps forward are lost, and real commitment to improvement abandoned because whatever is accomplished it is never enough. 'The best should not be allowed to be the enemy of the better', as Vogel puts it.[85] Nor should CSR developments be viewed only through the cynical lens of vested interest. Many of the individuals in the CSR business have found in CSR a way of combining involvement in business with a genuine wish to make a social difference. Awareness is growing within business.[86] NGOs and others acknowledge that real changes of practice have been accomplished.

---

[82] Vogel, *Market for Virtue*.

[83] D. Vogel, 'The Limits of the Market for Virtue', *Ethical Corporation*, September 2005, p. 46.

[84] Ruggie, remarks at CSR forum, Bamberg Germany, 14 June 2006 (see n. 78).

[85] Vogel, 'The Limits of the Market for Virtue', p. 44.

[86] The Unilever/Oxfam research project on Unilever's operations in Indonesia was reported by both the NGO and the business participants as a significant learning experience; J. Clay, *Exploring the Links between International Business and Poverty Reduction: a Case Study of Unilever in Indonesia* (Oxford: Oxfam/The Hague: Novib/London: Unilever, 2005).

There has also been a steady escalation of demands on business, and a dynamic – and indeed competitive – response.[87] Critics, assessors for socially responsible investment or verifiers of CSR reports have moved from seeking evidence of CSR policies on paper to seeking clear evidence of their implementation – moving from 'tell me' to 'show me', as Shell has put it. It is not just socio-legal scholars who know that policies 'in the books' do not necessarily mean policies 'in action'. Pressure has moved on from seeking evidence of attention to CSR issues within multinational corporations themselves to seeking evidence of their attention to these issues in their supply chains and in the practices of their joint-venture partners.

In any case, as I have argued elsewhere,[88] even if CSR were to be seen as just PR, it may be that 'just PR' will do. Policies first adopted for PR purposes may not be allowed to remain at that level, and strategies can take on their own momentum, both internally and externally. Within the organisation, CSR staff may put pressure on boards to move beyond PR to embedded practice, noting that 'just PR' will not work even as PR. Externally PR has its own function as a means of leveraging practice. The more a company adopts what we might think of as 'halo branding', the more vulnerable it is to criticism if the halo slips. Both BP and Shell, generally presented as leaders in the CSR field, have experienced this effect in recent years, Shell when its reserve accounting was found to be misleading in 2004, BP in 2006 when it faced a barrage of CSR and ethical crises in its US operations, with accusations of oil price manipulation,[89] allegations of 'unethically trying to induce a settlement' in a personal injury lawsuit brought by victims of the 2005 fatal fire at its Texas City refinery,[90] and safety and environmental disasters in Alaska and elsewhere attributed not to misfortune but to serious systems failure and unethical practices.

NGOs are well aware of the enhanced vulnerability of companies that have adopted the strategy of halo branding and the leverage this provides. Witness Peter Frankental of Amnesty International: 'From an NGO perspective, a company that ties its flag to the mast of human rights is offering

---

[87] Marks & Spencer's commitment not to increase margins on its Fairtrade products was followed by Sainsbury's announcement that it would have no differential in price between its Fairtrade and non-Fairtrade bananas, mainstreaming Fairtrade (for bananas at least) so that customers did not have to pay a premium for 'ethical consumption'; *The Guardian*, 13 December 2006.

[88] McBarnet, 'Human Rights and the New Accountability', and 'New Sources of Leverage', Regnet plenary lecture.

[89] *The Guardian*, 7 September 2006.   [90] *Financial Times*, 6 September 2006.

a hostage to fortune. If it fails to deliver on its stated commitments, its credibility will be at stake.'[91]

While this comment was made in the context of human rights, it could be applied to any social, environmental or ethical commitment. PR can be a double-edged sword, and a source of reputational and market leverage in itself. Voluntary, or market-driven, CSR should not be too readily dismissed in the call for more law.

In any case, law is no longer quite so separate from CSR as the debate might suggest. The image of CSR as the voluntary adoption of policies beyond the obligations of law is beginning to look increasingly shaky as new legal pressures and new legal mechanisms to enforce CSR policies are brought into play – and brought into play not only by governments and intergovernmental agencies, but also, once again, by civil society.

II. Corporate social responsibility through law

Law is playing an increasing role in enforcing 'voluntary' CSR policies. Few of the commitments which companies normally sign up to in their voluntary CSR policies (addressing such issues as health and safety, discrimination and corruption) are entirely free of legal obligation anyway. Indeed, companies routinely make commitments in their codes of conduct to comply with the law, though that is obviously a legal obligation. However, even what are presented as voluntary CSR codes and policies, 'beyond mere compliance', are in fact increasingly being encroached on by law. New legal developments are directly and indirectly fostering voluntary CSR and market pressures, while new legal tools are being evolved, and old ones used creatively, to make what businesses have perceived as voluntary, or beyond the law, in fact legally enforceable.

This is not, on the whole, state regulation that we are discussing, nor indeed international law, though both come into the picture, but other facets of law, often private law being used by private parties, NGOs, business itself, and indeed governments under a different hat. This raises interesting angles on the nature of legal governance and on law's capacity to empire-build. It also shows how social and market forces increasingly interplay with law, with more complex forms of governance emerging. Legal doctrines and processes are being used by NGOs as part of their

---

[91] P. Frankental, 'Can Branding Reinforce Human Rights?' in M. McIntosh (ed.), *Visions of Ethical Business* (London: Pricewaterhouse Coopers, Financial Times and Malcolm McIntosh, 1998).

strategy, and market forces are being stimulated and facilitated by legal measures. At the same time, of course, much of the momentum for legal intervention has come from the CSR movement and from the change of culture it reflects and promotes.

How is law being brought into play? Governments are fostering CSR through indirect regulation, old legal rights are being put to new uses, and private law – tort law and contract law – are being used, tort law to extend the legal enforceability of CSR issues, contract law to give CSR standards the weight of legal obligation.

A. Government: fostering corporate social responsibility through indirect regulation

Despite the fact that governments have shown themselves reluctant to make the adoption and implementation of CSR policies a mandatory requirement of company law, governmental legislation has nonetheless played a part in fostering CSR. The United Kingdom, in its review of company law in the 1990s, opted to keep CSR a voluntary matter.[92] At the same time, however, the UK government also introduced legislation which not only encouraged, but in practical terms necessitated, the adoption of CSR policies by major companies. The route was indirect, using disclosure as the tool, and indirect in another sense too, in that it was accomplished through legislation directed at investors in business corporations rather than at the businesses themselves.

In July 2000 pension funds were required by new UK legislation[93] to state whether and how they took into account in their investment decisions social, environmental and ethical considerations. There was no legislative obligation on them to do this, the requirement was merely to disclose whether they did so or not. Nonetheless, the practical consequence was that pension funds have increasingly chosen to take into account the CSR policies of the companies they invest in. What pension fund, with its own reputation in mind, would want to declare publicly that it considers ethical, social and environmental issues irrelevant? This in turn had a knock-on effect on companies seeking investment from pension funds. Pension funds are major players in the stock market – members of the National

---

[92] It has been observed that governments encouraged the emergence of the CSR concept, arguing, at the 1992 Earth Summit, for 'responsible entrepreneurship' but through voluntary initiatives (Paul Hohnen, *Ethical Corporation*, 2 May 2005).

[93] Occupational Pension Schemes (Investment, and Assignment, Forfeiture, Bankruptcy etc.) (Amendment) Regulations 1999, SI 1999 No. 1849.

Association of Pension Funds control a sixth of the UK stock market[94] – and their demands could not easily be ignored. Similar legislation has followed in Germany, Belgium and Australia.

Reference has already been made to the role of SRI as a market pressure on companies to adopt CSR policies. This legislation could be seen as making mainstream investment of necessity 'socially responsible' to one degree or another. So underlying the social and market pressures making CSR rather less voluntary than the word might suggest, there can also be seen to be legal forces at work. These legal forces are subtle in their approach in that they are indirect and, in legal terms, non-mandatory. In practical, *socio*-legal terms, however, once the legal obligation to disclose was in place, the pressure was on to disclose a positive approach to CSR. Governmental regulation has thus quietly bolstered and, indeed, created a whole new level of market pressure, and indirectly fostered voluntary CSR. There has been another knock-on effect too, in that listed companies, through the voice of the Confederation of British Industry (CBI), have in turn criticised financial institutions for failing to themselves provide the level of disclosure they demand, increasing the pressure for further disclosure in the financial sector itself.[95]

Disclosure is also the approach taken by the European Union in its requirement for companies to produce a 'business review' as part of their statutory annual reports, describing the 'principal risks and uncertainties' they face. This expressly requires reporting on 'non-financial' performance, 'including information relating to environmental and employee matters'.[96]

The requirement has been implemented in the United Kingdom in the Company Law Act of 2006. In fact, the business review is a weaker requirement than was first proposed in the United Kingdom, where the original intention was for a more demanding 'Operating and Financial Review' (OFR). The proposed UK law had set out more detailed requirements and more overt reference to CSR issues. Companies would have been required to disclose their strategies for identifying and dealing with risk, expressly

---

[94] *The Guardian*, 22 August 2005. The same article reports the National Association of Pension Funds' (NAPF's) announcement that while it was not issuing guidelines for pension fund trustees, it was nonetheless 'urging' them 'to ask the investment managers who oversee their pension funds to consider corporate social responsibility when investing on their behalf' as 'CSR should be a "normal part of the investment process"'. The NAPF had already 'been telling company boards that "failure to take account of their wider role in society could cause serious damage to their prospects", but was now going one step further'.

[95] *Ethical Corporation*, May 2005, p. 4.

[96] European Accounts Modernisation Directive 2003/51/EC No. 2003 L178/2.

including risk from social, environmental and ethical factors – a wider express list than that of the European Union, and clearly CSR-led. They would also have had to disclose their policies on these issues. This too was set to foster the voluntary adoption of CSR policies by business, since one obvious way to demonstrate CSR risk control is to adopt express CSR policies, implementation strategies and compliance programmes. However, despite the years of consultation that lay behind it, the OFR was suddenly dropped in November 2005 as, it was said, a demonstration of the Labour government's reduction of red tape for business.

Ironically, however, the reaction from business to the dropping of the OFR was far from supportive. Investment funds wanted the disclosure, reflecting as it did the new concern with reputational risk.[97] Social and environmental responsibility, they argued, should both be put at the heart of corporate decision-making and reported accordingly, preferably in the statutory annual report.[98] What is more, many large companies had already invested heavily in introducing the policies, the staff and the mechanisms for identifying, measuring and reporting CSR risk.

The result was that, even before the new, weaker legislation was in place, or compliance required (not till 2008), companies were producing OFR-like reports. By March 2006, eighty-five of FTSE 100 companies had published non-financial reports, three had reported via a parent company or subsidiary and the remaining twelve had included some non-financial reporting in their annual report.[99] For many companies this was simply a continuation of their voluntary CSR reports with a new focus on the language of risk and performance indicators. For some it was anticipation of expected legislation, law affecting practice even before it comes into play. At the same time practice also influenced law. The introduction of the legal requirement for disclosure could be seen as itself facilitated *politically* by the fact that the practice had already begun in response to social and market pressure, while it was facilitated *practically* by the prior existence

---

[97] The London Stock Exchange's Combined Code on Corporate Governance, and the Turnbull Report (1999) before it, had already included reputation as an asset to be protected by companies, and required internal reviews and reputation risk management with, it has been suggested, directors potentially open to attack for breach of fiduciary duties if they did not pay this issues sufficient attention (Philip Goldenberg, partner in Berwin Leyton, quoted in the *Financial Times*, 9 March 2002). By 2006, as we have seen, reputation risk inevitably included CSR issues.

[98] See the Association of British Insurers position paper reported in the *Financial Times*, 30 November 2006.

[99] CorporateRegister.com; *The Guardian*, 6 November 2006.

of reporting standards produced by international NGOs. Market forces, voluntary action and legal obligation intertwined.

The United Kingdom's new disclosure requirements did not in fact stop at replacing the OFR with the business review. Legal requirements were beefed up again with two requirements: first, that the business review be audited and, second, that companies disclose information on their supply chain and other contractual relationships. With conditions in a company's supply chain and the activities of its joint-venture partners (in relation, for example, to human rights)[100] key issues in the CSR debate, this could become another significant factor for CSR by fostering more CSR-conscious supply and joint-venture policies. There is also potential for further pressure via disclosure, with the 2006 Companies Act including a reserve power to allow the government to require institutional directors to disclose how they have voted at annual meetings.[101] This was included with the express purpose of fostering voluntary disclosure. The resort to law will take place only if 'managers fail to come clean on their voting records voluntarily'.[102]

In effect, while supporting a voluntary approach to CSR, UK government strategy – with significant civil society lobbying behind it – has been to legislatively support and strengthen the market pressures on companies to pay attention to CSR issues. In effect, it has used law to boost the potential for social accountability.[103] Similar practices had already been adopted elsewhere. Even before the European Union's new requirements, France had required disclosure of social and environmental issues in companies' annual reports.[104]

Indirect fostering of CSR-related policies, particularly in more narrowly focused corporate governance – though also in relation to such issues as the environment and corruption – can be seen in the United States too, though there largely through enforcement strategies. It was noted earlier that all the US Fortune 500 companies have for some time had corporate codes of conduct or statements of principle in place. One factor in this was government action which, again though not directly mandating such codes, in practice fostered their adoption. When the Foreign Corrupt

---

[100] See the reference to Shell in Nigeria earlier and McBarnet and Schmidt, Chapter 5 in this volume. A late amendment allowed companies to veto data where it might be exploited by extremists (*Financial Times*, 1 November 2006).

[101] *Financial Times*, 4 November 2006.

[102] *Financial Times*, 6 June 2006, quoting Alastair Darling, Trade and Industry Secretary.

[103] See Friends of Earth, 2001, n. 80.

[104] Nouvelles Regulations Economiques, applicable from 2002 annual reports.

Practices Act introduced tougher penalties for corruption, the Sentencing Commission also introduced scope to mitigate them *if* a corporation could demonstrate it had a code of conduct in place and an active programme for its propagation and enforcement.[105] Not surprisingly, such programmes subsequently proliferated.

Since then the Sarbanes-Oxley Act, in reaction to Enron, has required companies to introduce codes of ethical conduct. These were narrowly defined and directly mandated only for chief executive officers and chief financial officers. However, once again, by making evidence of a corporate 'culture of integrity' a mitigating factor in any future prosecution, the Sentencing Commission has indirectly fostered a wider application of codes and code implementation, including company-wide communication and training in ethics.[106] Other agencies, such as the Environment Protection Agency, take account of internal policies in deciding on penalties. The Securities and Exchange Commission requires both codes of ethics and evidence of effective implementation procedures, as do, since 2004, the New York Stock Exchange and NASDAQ. The courts in Delaware (where some 58 per cent of the Fortune 500 companies are legally based) have also lent the weight of law to this by holding boards responsible for the implementation of compliance systems consistent with the sentencing guidelines.[107]

No wonder that for public companies operating in the United States, Paine *et al.* see codes of conduct as 'arguably a legal necessity'.[108] A similar use of enforcement policies has been mooted in the United Kingdom, using the carrot as much as the stick, in the idea of risk-based enforcement, where companies that demonstrate themselves to be 'responsible' would be treated with more trust and less regulatory inspection.[109]

CSR policies and ethical codes may then be upheld by governments as a matter for voluntary business practice, yet at the same time actively fostered by subtler or more indirect legislative or regulatory action.

---

[105] See Simon Webley, 'The Nature and Value of Internal Codes of Ethics', paper presented at the conference on *The Importance of Human Rights in International Business*, University of Exeter, 15–17 September 1998.

[106] US Sentencing Commission, *Federal Sentencing Guidelines Manual* (2004).

[107] L. Paine, R. Deshpande, J. Margolis and K. Bettcher, 'Up to Code: Does your Company's Conduct meet World Class Standards?', *Harvard Business Review* December (2005), 122–33.

[108] *ibid.*, at 122. Also see Parker on meta-regulation, Chapter 7 in this volume.

[109] See the 'Hampton Review', P. Hampton, *Reducing Administrative Burdens, Effective Implementation and Enforcement* (HM Treasury, 2004), discussed in BiTC, Insight Investment and FTSE, *Rewarding Virtue*.

In the United Kingdom's case, not all of the government's interventions have in fact been indirect. The 2006 Companies Act also sets out a duty on directors to act in the way they consider 'in good faith, would be most likely to promote the success of the company for the benefits of its members as a whole'.[110] Discharging this duty requires attention to factors such as the interests of employees, relationships with customers and suppliers, and impact on the environment, effectively codifying the wider understanding of directors' duties noted in our earlier discussion of case law. Interestingly, Margaret Hodge, the Industry Minister, also declared that the current legislation would be only a 'first step' in imposing tougher standards on directors.[111]

B. Civil society and the law: shareholder activism

It is not just governments that are using law, often indirectly, to foster CSR. NGOs, and members of civil society more generally, are increasingly moving beyond the conventional indirect route of lobbying for changes in legislation to using the mechanisms of law directly themselves in order to produce change at the level of business practice.

NGOs have, for example, used company law to gain legal status and a legal voice within companies, making themselves not just external pressures on companies but internal pressures too. They have done this through the simple expedient of buying shares, making themselves share-holders and exercising shareholder rights to bring resolutions to annual general meetings (AGMs). Such actions have provided a new means for their conventional role of awareness-raising, with significant publicity raised through reporting of their actions at AGMs.

More than publicity has resulted, with changes in corporate policy also being accomplished. In California in 2004, the Interfaith Center on Corporate Responsibility, an umbrella organisation filing for a group of shareholding NGOs, withdrew a resolution destined for Occidental's AGM only when the company agreed to adopt a human rights policy.[112] NGOs have thus used the opportunities available in law to move from the role of advocates outside the corporation to the role of legal actors within it. The shareholder resolution brought by the Ecumenical Council for Corporate Responsibility (ECCR) to Shell's 2006 AGM was introduced

---

[110] Companies Act 2006, s. 172(1), coming into force in 2008.
[111] *Financial Times*, 25 October 2006.
[112] William Baue SocialFunds.com, 19 March 2004 (*Ethical Corporation*, 20 March 2004).

as being proposed because of concerns about 'the loss of production, environmental costs and reputational risk' (all 'business case' concerns) 'faced by *our* company'.[113]

Amnesty International USA[114] has also extended the tactic into a base for more conventional campaigning by asking 'ordinary Americans to voice their concerns and priorities to institutional investors holding shares in their names, asking them to support shareholder resolutions addressing human rights'.[115] Two resolutions pressed in 2006 were first, in relation to Dow Chemicals, seeking more help for the remaining 100,000 and more victims of Bhopal, and, second, in relation to Chevron, regarding health and environmental issues in the Ecuadorian Amazon which Amnesty alleged were caused by the operations of Chevron's subsidiary Texaco.

This 'Share Power' campaign, and the general exercise of shareholder rights to promote CSR, confronts and exploits the narrow legal interpretation of corporate responsibility as primarily to further shareholders' interests by making shareholders advocates of CSR. Major shareholders are also exercising their rights in order to raise CSR issues. The UK Institutional Shareholders Committee specifically noted corporate responsibility as one of the items that should be raised with companies, on the basis, for example, of reputational risk.[116]

C. Private actors, private law: enforcing human rights

Civil society has also played a very direct role in bringing law into play, often in innovative and even surprising ways, to enforce CSR, and increasingly to make it a legal obligation. Instead of just seeking to influence state or international legislation, they have turned to the mechanisms offered in *private law*, essentially tort and contract, and used them to make direct legal inroads on 'voluntary' CSR.

One of the most creative examples is the use, in the United States, of the Alien Tort Claims Act. The Alien Tort Claims Act (ATCA), a US statute relating to 'piracy on the high seas', dates back to 1789, and was rarely used in two centuries. It is, nonetheless, currently proving the bane of multinational corporations who are being pursued, via ATCA, through

---

[113] www.eccr.org.uk; my emphasis.
[114] AIUSA has held an activism portfolio of shares in companies it might want to target since 2001 (*Ethical Corporation*, October 2005, p. 25).
[115] *Ethical Corporation*, 12 September 2005, and see October 2005.
[116] BiTC, Insight Investment and FTSE, *Rewarding Virtue*.

the US courts.[117] The goal is to have them pay out compensation – and be seen to take responsibility – for human rights abuses committed abroad by foreign governments with which they have been operating in joint venture. The use of ATCA is an example of highly creative legal enforcement by NGOs concerned with human right abuses, but with no way of enforcing claims through more conventional legal routes.

ATCA was first pressed into the service of human rights by a human and civil rights activist organisation, the Center for Constitutional Rights, in the case of *Filártiga* v. *Peña-Irala*.[118] This first case was concerned with human rights but not with business. However, ATCA has since been developed into a tool to hold multinational corporations to account on human rights issues, via the *Unocal* case, brought to court by the CCR again, along with Earthrights International and Amnesty International.[119] The *Unocal* case was settled out of court in 2005, but it has left a legacy of valuable precedents and procedures, a long list of pending cases on the same theme – involving such companies as Shell, Texaco, Chevron, Rio Tinto, Coca-Cola and Gap – and gained extensive publicity for the issues involved. It has also encouraged others to find legal means within their own jurisdictions to enforce respect for human rights on business, while the United Nations has set up a panel of experts to look into formulating an international law standard on corporate aiding and abetting liability.[120] The case also gave institutional shareholders ammunition for pressing corporations on human rights. Unocal has subsequently merged with Chevron, and, as a result of the ATCA case, pension funds such as CalPERS have put additional pressure on Chevron to publish and implement its human rights policy,[121] legal initiatives again fostering market action.

Human rights have been on the CSR agenda for some time, and it has become routine practice for multinationals to sign up to voluntary human rights commitments such as the UN's Global Compact, and to include respect for human rights in their own codes of conduct. But the use of ATCA by NGOs has made it clear to multinationals that commitment without compliance is not enough, and that, in some situations at least, there are legal means to enforce it.

---

[117] See McBarnet and Schmidt, Chapter 5 in this volume, for a detailed analysis.
[118] *Filártiga* v. *Peña-Irala*, 630 F 2d 876 (2d Cir. 1980).   [119] See Chapter 5, pp. 164–9.
[120] See, for example, www.Earthrights.org, news, July 2006.
[121] www.socialfunds.com/news, 17 August 2005.

D. Legal accountability on voluntary commitments

Law has been used innovatively by civil society in other ways. Repeated
reference has been made to the voluntary construction and publication, by
most major businesses these days, of corporate codes of conduct and CSR
reports. Corporations can, however, find themselves held to account on
these voluntary initiatives, not just socially but legally. Once in place, and
with an active civil society to press the case, such voluntary declarations
may turn out to have legal implications. Nike is once again key here. In
Kasky v. *Nike*,[122] Marc Kasky, an activist on environmental issues and
labour rights, brought a legal case against Nike on the basis that it had
made false statements in response to the criticisms in the late 1990s that
sweated labour was being used in the factories that supplied it. Nike had
stated in its CSR reports that its suppliers adhered to its code of conduct
which did not permit sweated labour, and Kasky argued this was simply
untrue. Indeed, it was false and misleading and therefore in violation of
California's legislation on unfair competition and false advertising.

Like *Unocal*, the *Kasky* case ended by being settled out of court, with
Nike paying $1.5 million[123] to the NGO, Fair Labor Association.[124] But
it has had its effect in firing a warning shot on the use of CSR as PR,
and on the adoption of policies without adequate implementation and
verification. Though it was anticipated that one result might be a cessation
of voluntary CSR communications from corporations, CSR reporting has
in fact continued. As another participant, a spokesman for one of the
several NGOs that supported Kasky via '*amicus* briefs', put it, 'Companies
will continue to tell their side of the story, as they have a real market
reason for doing so: to attract capital and new consumers. None of that
has changed as a result of this lawsuit, the companies just need to be more
careful that what they say is accurate'.[125]

Though Nike's first response was to announce that it would no longer
produce a CSR report, in fact it not only resumed its CSR reporting but

[122] *Kasky* v. *Nike, Inc.*, 45 P 3d 243 (Cal. 2002).

[123] P. Rudolph, 'Ethical Reporting and the Law', *Ethical Corporation*, 3 February 2005.

[124] An industry-sponsored non-profit organisation promoting adherence to international
labour standards and improved working conditions (*Ethical Corporation*, 23 September
2003). Nike was a founding member of the Fair Labor Association in the wake of the
criticisms of its suppliers' practices in the 1990s.

[125] Adam Kanzer, general counsel and director of shareholder advocacy for Domini Social
Investments, which filed an *amicus* brief in support of Kasky (www.socialfunds.com,
2003). Other parties in the *amicus curiae* briefs included NGOs Reclaim Democracy,
Public Citizen, Global Exchange and the Sierra Club, along with four members of Congress
(www.reclaimdemocracy.org, 9 April 2003).

made it more transparent, publishing for the first time in its report of activities in 2004 a list of more than 700 suppliers around the world, thus facilitating assessment by NGOs or others.[126] The report, published in July 2005, began: 'We've been fairly quiet for the past three years in Corporate Responsibility because of the Kasky lawsuit. So we're using this report to play a little catch-up and draw a more complete picture'. Nike has also become an advocate, putting pressure on industry more generally to follow its example. 'No one company can solve these issues that are endemic to our industry.'[127] Presenting his original response to criticisms on its supply chain as 'bumpy' and 'an error', Nike's chairman and former Chief Executive Officer (CEO) Philip Knight sets out publication of their supply chain as 'an effort to jump-start disclosure and collaboration throughout the industry'.[128]

This demonstrates the potential impact of private litigation. There can be a significant knock-on effect from even a single case in motivating the targeted company to raise the standards of its competitors rather than be left at a competitive disadvantage itself. Interestingly, Knight also stood down as CEO in favour of a new CEO, chosen 'in part on [his] track record in corporate responsibility'.[129]

There is plenty of scope in law in other jurisdictions too to transform not just voluntary CSR reports, but also voluntary codes of conduct, into standards to which companies can be held legally accountable. A 2005 European Directive specifically, if in somewhat limiting terms, includes non-compliance by a company with its code of conduct as an instance of a misleading commercial practice.[130] Carola Glinski has argued that, despite the 'long-standing opinion of the vast majority of authors, [that] such codes of conduct merely create moral obligations but have no legal effect whatsoever', there is scope within European law for such cases to be brought, on grounds not dissimilar to the *Kasky* case, leading her to ask whether private codes of conduct can really be seen as voluntary rather than legally binding.[131]

---

[126] *Nike Corporate Responsibility Report for 2004* (July 2005).
[127] Hannah Jones, Vice President of Corporate Responsibility, reported by Laureen Foster and Alexandra Harney in *Dow Jones and Reuters Factiva*, 22 April 2005.
[128] *Nike Corporate Responsibility Report for 2004*, p. 2.   [129] *ibid.*
[130] EC Unfair Commercial Practices Directive 2005/29/EC, OJ 2005 No. L149/22. This is limited to situations 'where the commitment is not aspirational but is firm and is capable of being verified, and the trader indicates in a commercial practice that he is bound by the code': Article 6(2)(b).
[131] See Chapter 4 of this volume.

As a result of *Kasky* v. *Nike*, and similar legal developments elsewhere, business organisations have been put on notice to be wary of their CSR PR, and perhaps to be conscious that their voluntary codes of conduct and CSR reports may prove less voluntary than they thought. If CSR codes and reports could once have been taken for granted as useful PR with no legal repercussions, that may no longer be the case.[132]

E. Business, governments and contractual control

Several of the examples so far have indicated the complex interplay between legal and market forces that is involved in CSR, the source of legal initiatives in both government and private actors, and the use of both regulatory and private law. That intricate interplay is very much in evidence in what we might call 'contractual control'. It is not just NGOs and private activists who have been using private law to transform voluntary commitments into legal obligations. So too has business itself. Large companies have been using private law to impose CSR policies on *other* businesses. So indeed have governments.

There is a growing trend for major companies to include CSR commitments in the terms and conditions they set out for their contracts with their own suppliers.[133] While the market power of large companies vis-à-vis suppliers is itself clearly an important factor in any influence accomplished, it is becoming regarded in business as best practice to formalise this as a legal obligation. The adoption of this controlling role by big business over its suppliers may be less surprising and less altruistic than it seems. Some of the companies whose reputations have been hardest hit by the CSR movement have found themselves pilloried for the practices of external suppliers which were not their legal responsibility, but for whose actions they were nonetheless held accountable. Nike's experience vis-à-vis the child labour practices of its south-east Asian suppliers epitomises this. It may be no wonder then that companies increasingly require their external suppliers, as well as their own companies, to adopt CSR codes of conduct, and are using the legal mechanism of contract to do so. So the pressures of market and civil society have had the knock-on effect of business exercising legal control over business. It might also be noted that the production of contracts is itself facilitated by companies'

---

[132] Likewise, Oxfam's concern that voluntary CSR meant victims had no recourse to remedies has been disproved, in some situations at least (Oxfam International, *The European Commission's Green Paper: Promoting a European Framework for CSR, a Submission by Oxfam International*, January 2002, p. 5).

[133] See McBarnet and Kurkchiyan, Chapter 2 in this volume.

ability simply to incorporate standards already set by NGOs such as the International Labour Organisation.

Nor is it just business organisations that are using contract as a means of promoting CSR. National, local and indeed supranational governments are not only using conventional regulatory law to foster CSR, but are also using their market power, and private law, by including CSR obligations in their own procurement contracts. The UK government, for example, has proposed requiring specified 'green' standards for the companies whose goods and services it purchases, covering energy efficiency, greenhouse gas emissions, the efficient use of natural resources and raw materials, transport, pollution controls and appropriate sourcing of environmentally sensitive goods such as timber.[134] Californian and Massachusetts state procurement policies are well known for their policy-driven stance, while a number of European states and the European Union have also taken CSR procurement on board.[135] Government procurement has enormous market power, with UK government procurement spending, for example, amounting to some £150 billion per annum.[136] Indeed, one CSR advocate has suggested that governments could do far more for CSR by forgetting about regulation and using their contractual power.[137] In a sense we have come full circle here, back to market forces and consumer power, but in this case the consumers are both business itself and government, and consumer power is expressed in legal form through contractual obligation.

F. Corporate social responsibility: beyond the law or through the law?

There is then increasing legal intervention in the arena of CSR, to an extent where its voluntariness must be questioned not only in terms of the social and market forces, but in terms of the legal forces driving it. There is also a significant interplay between legal, market and social forces, with each fostering and being fostered by the other. Indeed, even the general trend to increasing intervention by law feeds back into market pressures through the threat of financial and reputation risk inherent in CSR-related litigation. Insurance firms have begun to put pressure on business on the

---

[134] *Financial Times*, 9 June 2006.
[135] The European Commission's Communication on CSR included discussion of its own capacity to include CSR requirements in its procurement policies; COM (2002) 21. And see McCrudden, Chapter 3 in this volume.
[136] *Financial Times*, 9 June 2006.
[137] In a nice twist, NGOs are using the Freedom of Information Act to find out about government procurement, who they have contracts with, and exploring CSR issues. Friends of the Earth alone was reported in March 2005 as having put in 'about 100' requests for information (*Ethical Corporation*, 29 March 2005).

need to pay attention to CSR issues on the grounds of increased litigation risk and higher premiums.

This increased legal intervention emanates in part from regulatory initiatives by government that are more subtle than direct mandating of CSR. But the voluntary nature of CSR is also being brought into question by the development of strategic uses of private law, often in highly creative ways, by both government and civil society. Law is not just a tool of government, and governmental regulation is not the only way to try to control business through law. Civil society too is increasingly deploying legal mechanisms to constrain business. What is more, law is being deployed to *enforce*, rather than just to encourage, commitments by business to ethics, human rights, and social and environmental responsibility.

These initiatives are not seen by all as the best way to make CSR a legal rather than a voluntary matter. There are criticisms and concerns that these initiatives, just like voluntary CSR, might divert from the full-scale legal regulation some see as the only way to ensure real corporate accountability. Indirect fostering of CSR by governments as opposed to outright regulation can be seen as too soft, private litigation as patchy in target and impact, contractual control as too limited, and creative uses of law such as ATCA as too reliant on the quirks of specific legal systems. Sir Geoffrey Chandler, an eloquent champion of the need for corporate accountability on human rights, sees ATCA only as 'a crude weapon' being used because it is 'all that is available'.[138] Even Paul Hoffman, lead advocate in the ATCA case against Unocal, has observed: 'International legislation, will, at the end of the day, be a better means of curbing corporate behaviour than law suits.'[139] What is really required, in other words, is mandatory legal regulation.

As an ideal this is hard to refute. But, in practice, mandatory legal regulation has its limitations too. Indeed, there may be scope not only for regulation to contribute to the efficacy of CSR, but for CSR to contribute to the efficacy of regulation. Hence the concern to explore the idea of CSR *for* law.

III. Corporate social responsibility for law

For a range of reasons, well rehearsed in many years of socio-legal research, legal regulation is not always as effective as might be hoped in controlling

---

[138] 'The Slow March to Corporate Accountability', *Ethical Corporation*, May 2004, p. 23.
[139] Quoted in magazine news story 'Under the Shadow of ATCA', *Foreign Direct Investment*, 5 June 2006. See McBarnet and Schmidt, Chapter 5 in this volume.

business. Indeed, the pressure from civil society for voluntary CSR has come about partly in recognition of the failure of legal regulation. This is often presented as a failure to establish effective global regulation in an era of global business, a view which might suggest that, in time, global institutions of governance could arise, filling the legal vacuum and making way for effective legal regulation. Or it is seen as a matter of, in time, strengthening the substantive standards and enforcement of law in developing countries. The limitations of law as a means of controlling big business are, however, much more endemic than these views imply.

A. Limits in the law and the role of extra-legal corporate social responsibility

The issue of globalisation is real enough. While big business is transnational, global institutions for the governance of business remain poorly developed, particularly when it comes to enforcement, and competition between different jurisdictions allows business to play the game of regulatory arbitrage, moving away from a high regulation area to a less demanding legal environment, or achieving a more amenable legal environment where it is, through the threat of such a move.

But there are other more general limitations in law. In both international and national settings, business can influence both the substance of law and how it is enforced through lobbying and negotiation, introducing compromise and weakening control. Even in the minor examples cited in this chapter, we can see the effect of lobbying in UK government backtracking on the OFR. Nor can governments necessarily be relied on to prioritise corporate responsibility over what they see as national or commercial interests, not least in areas such as corruption.[140] While market, social and private litigation pressures on business are criticised as patchy, the same could also be said of regulatory enforcement, not just in the international context because of lack of effective institutional means, but generally, as decades of socio-legal research have demonstrated. Even in the context of state regulation, resources can be limited, penalties often weak enough to be treated as just another business cost, a licence to be paid, rather than a significant deterrent, and enforcement techniques can be inefficient, alienating those willing to comply voluntarily while failing

---

[140] See, for example, the controversy in 2006 over the UK government putting a stop to a Serious Fraud Office investigation into Saudi Arabia's dealings with UK company BAE Systems, prompting legal action by NGOs against the government. *Financial Times*, 19 December 2006.

to constrain those who do not. Business non-compliance with law is far from unusual, and enforcement far from fully effective.

Given these limits, extra-legal pressures from NGOs and the market can check or balance business influence on government and provide useful supplements to the resources of law. Business lobbying has already become a CSR issue, with calls for more transparency on the part of business. At the same time, the lobbying strength of disparate pressure groups on the environment, employees, human rights and so on has been enhanced by the very concept of CSR. Though this concept is sometimes criticised as being too open-ended, one consequence of that is its capacity to encompass a wide range of more specific interest groups making for a stronger pressure point in relation to both business and government. The UK company law debate of the early 2000s saw 130 different organisations, with interests in many different aspects of CSR, lobby in a unified campaign as the Coalition for Corporate Responsibility (CORE). This coalition effect can be seen in a range of situations. The campaign in 2005 for a more CSR-oriented approach by Europe's finance sector[141] was a coordinated project which included case studies on tax practices, climate issues, corruption, poverty and human rights – the range of coverage strengthening the critique. Even where campaigns are more disparate, the uniting label of 'CSR' provides focus for both the framing of critiques and proposals and the organisational response.

Enforcement and implementation too may be enhanced by the scrutiny of civil society and the market. Labour rights commentators on the United Kingdom's 2006 codification of 'enlightened shareholder value' duties for directors, while welcoming their potential to enhance discussion of social issues at board-level, may also have been right to observe that their impact in practice 'may well depend on the willingness of trade unions, NGOs and socially oriented shareholders to query how boards have interpreted the "enlightened" part of their mandate'.[142] Legal intervention does not necessarily render social and market pressure redundant, but may merely shift its focus from seeking the introduction of rights and duties to pressing for their effective implementation.

The idea of CSR can also raise awareness of the impact of corporate and consumer practice and enhance voluntary adoption of policies that go beyond the law, a factor which should not be overlooked. Braithwaite's model of a pyramid of legal enforcement, increasingly influential among

---

[141] CR Coalition, *A Big Deal?*   [142] *Ergon: Focus on Labour* (7 December 2006), 6.

regulators round the world, reminds us of the value of encouraging voluntary virtue before enforcing it.[143]

However, it is on yet another count that CSR may have its most significant contribution to make to the effectiveness of legal control. One of the most problematic limitations in legal control lies not in law itself but in how business responds to it. Business is extremely adept at managing law to circumvent and pre-empt legal control, through the art of 'creative compliance'.[144] Much legal regulation is frustrated by clever legal gamesmanship that creatively structures or restructures the legal form of business practices in such a way that it can be claimed they fall outside the ambit of disadvantageous law and beyond the reach of legal control. Creative compliance is normal routine practice for business and for the legal and accounting firms that serve it. It is after all readily justified as perfectly legal, not breaking the law but merely using it in creative ways.

Creative compliance can be found in any regulatory context, wherever there is the motivation to resist legal control and the resources to employ legal skills to do it through technical circumvention rather than simple breach of law. Tax avoidance and creative accounting are classic examples, but health and safety legislation, environmental regulation, and employee and consumer rights – indeed, any unwelcome legal constraints – are all potentially subject to circumvention in the same ways. Law is scrutinised for opportunities for avoidance with a range of techniques routinely employed: searching for gaps in the law – 'where does it say I can't?'; seeking out opportunities in the 'ex-files' of exemptions, exceptions and exclusions to see if transactions can be restructured to fit within them, whether they naturally do so or not; scrutinising detailed definitions and thresholds which can then be used as guidelines for structuring practices or transactions to fall outside them; constructing innovative methods the law has not yet come to address. The concept and practice of creative compliance are discussed in detail elsewhere.[145] The important

---

[143] Ayers and Braithwaite, *Responsive Regulation* (Oxford: Oxford University Press, 1992).

[144] See, for example, D. McBarnet, 'Law, Policy and Legal Avoidance', *Journal of Law and Society*, Spring (1988), 113–21; D. McBarnet, 'Whiter than White Collar Crime: Tax, Fraud Insurance and the Management of Stigma', *British Journal of Sociology*, September (1991), 323–44, McBarnet, *Crime Compliance and Control*; D. McBarnet, 'After Enron: Corporate Governance, Creative Compliance and the Uses of Corporate Social Responsibility', in J. O'Brien (ed.), *Governing the Corporation* (Chichester: John Wiley, 2005), pp. 205–22; and see D. McBarnet and C. Whelan, *Creative Accounting and the Cross-eyed Javelin Thrower* (Chichester: John Wiley, 1999).

[145] See previous footnote.

point in this context is the pertinence to all this of the idea of corporate social responsibility.

B. Creative compliance and corporate social responsibility

Of all the obstacles to effective legal control of business, creative compliance is arguably the most intractable. Enforcement in theory could be enhanced with more resources and more powers, but enforcement can only be exercised where law is broken not where it is, arguably, complied with. Changing the law can make creative compliance more difficult but it cannot eradicate it. Specific changes to specific definitions only result in adaptation, with the new rules replacing the old as guidelines for new creative structures of circumvention. Hence the adoption of regimes based on broad principles rather than specific prescriptive rules. But principle-based regulation is not a panacea in itself. It is difficult to put into practice without its application resulting in reversion to a series of rules, and it invites criticism on the basis of involving too much uncertainty and retrospectivity, and too much power for regulators. In any case, principles still have to be expressed in words, and even requirements phrased in broad conceptual terms can be subject to creative compliance.[146]

The result is that changes to the law alone cannot easily tackle creative compliance, because creative compliance is the product not just of limits in the law but of a mind-set which seeks to exploit those limits, and, crucially, which sees this exploitation as perfectly legitimate. This is a mind-set in which law is seen not as an authoritative and legitimate policy to be implemented, but as a body of decontextualised words, and as a raw material to be worked on to one's own advantage, regardless of the intentions of the legislators in making the law or the objectives they are seeking to meet. It is about the letter rather than the 'spirit' of the law. It is a mind-set which sees the application of law essentially as a game, a game in which it is legitimate to come up with creative avoidance techniques – however 'bullish', 'spurious' or 'sailing close to the wind' the legal arguments used to justify them are perceived *by those constructing them* to be.[147] It is a mind-set in which responsibility for making the law invulnerable to the search for loopholes or to creative circumvention is taken to lie wholly with those making law, not with those targeted by it.

---

[146] For detailed examples, see McBarnet and Whelan, *Creative Accounting and the Cross-eyed Javelin Thrower*, or McBarnet, 'After Enron: Corporate Governance' (see n. 144).

[147] These are all quotations from corporate lawyers in my research interviews.

It is a mind-set where what is 'arguably legal', and only that, defines what is legitimate. And that is where corporate social responsibility comes into play.

CSR is, as we have seen, presented by business as 'what companies are going to do beyond mere compliance with the law'.[148] Going 'beyond legal compliance' is key to the image of social responsibility. That view of CSR, however, assumes a base-line of compliance that is in fact problematic, not only because of the significant amount of non-compliance that takes place in business, but because of the routine practice of creative compliance. The attraction of creative compliance is precisely that it can claim to be compliant with the law, or, as it is often more circuitously put, not, on a strict literal interpretation of the law, illegal. If that claim succeeds, there is a simultaneous escape from both legal control and any adverse legal repercussions. In some contexts this would be, and has been, seen as not only legitimate but admirably astute. But in the context of a new business environment in which companies are keen to present themselves as socially responsible, the practice of creative compliance may raise some uncomfortable questions.

For companies holding themselves out as going beyond mere compliance, is compliance with a strict literal interpretation of the law enough? Is meeting the letter of the law while deliberately frustrating its spirit *responsible* compliance? Are the *consequences* of creative compliance socially responsible? Is it socially responsible to use legal creativity to escape intended controls, obviate employment rights or circumvent health and safety protections? Is aggressive tax avoidance socially responsible? Is there not a certain irony in companies taking credit in their CSR reports for contributing to community education or health at the same time as using every arguable form of legal creativity to avoid paying the tax that might have funded them from the public purse? Nor is it just social welfare that is impeded by creative compliance but the functioning of capital markets themselves, through creative compliance in such contexts as accounting, capital adequacy regulation and corporate governance, though of course failure in the market has social effects too for investors, creditors, employees and pensioners. Is it socially responsible or ethical to use, in any context, legal arguments that 'sail close to the wind' to circumvent legal control?

Such questions imply a misfit between CSR claims and compliance practices, and indicate potential for CSR to become a source of leverage

---

[148] BT Social Report (1999).

in getting companies to reassess their attitudes to law and compliance. As I have argued elsewhere, though CSR is generally presented as going beyond legal obligations, it may be that business could best 'demonstrate a new attitude to corporate social responsibility not so much by *surpassing* law's requirements, but by meeting those requirements *in spirit* at last'.[149]

C. Creative compliance on the corporate social responsibility agenda

Such questions are no longer being raised only in the abstract. The issue is beginning to appear on the CSR agenda as a result of growing interest among NGOs, consultancies and investment funds, particularly in relation to tax avoidance. Government is also addressing the issue, and employing the language of corporate responsibility and corporate ethics to do so.

New dedicated NGOs have emerged, using classic strategies of naming and shaming campaigns. The Tax Justice Network (TJN), an international NGO launched in the United Kingdom in 2003, has taken a key role in stirring up publicity and provoking responses. While its interests extend more widely to poverty in developing countries and the role in that of tax lobbying, evasion, corruption and international tax competition, TJN has also embraced the issue of tax avoidance and CSR. The Davos World Economic Forum (WEF) in January 2005 was seized by NGOs[150] with a CSR agenda as an opportunity to make 'Corporate Social *Irresponsibility* Awards', and tax avoidance joined more conventional CSR issues as one of the award categories. The two NGOs organising the ceremony described it as a reminder 'to members of the WEF and other large corporate groups that the public expects them to be responsible stewards of the environment; insists on their respect for human rights and labour rights; and does not tolerate tax avoidance'.[151] The TJN nominated the 'winner' on tax avoidance, accountancy firm KPMG, for its marketing of 'abusive' tax avoidance schemes.[152]

Not far behind NGOs have been consultancies advising a rethink of attitudes to tax in particular, and in some cases to compliance more generally.

---

[149] McBarnet, 'After Enron: Corporate Governance'.
[150] The Berne Declaration and Pro-Natura-Friends of the Earth Switzerland.
[151] www.evb.ch/en/p25003167.html
[152] Tax Justice Network, *Tax Justice Focus* 1, 1 (2005), newsletter of Tax Justice Network re US exposees.

Ironically, given its brush with infamy over 'abusive' tax avoidance, or indeed because of it, KPMG has taken a lead role here. In its 2004 paper, 'Tax in the Boardroom', it acknowledges tax strategy now carries reputational risk, due not only to changing governmental attitudes but to the role of the CSR movement. Tax planning is seen as key in this. Corporate tax planning, KPMG notes, can range from the 'social duty'-end of the spectrum to the 'shareholder duty'-end. While conventionally corporate duty was seen to fall on the shareholder duty-end of the spectrum, requiring minimisation of tax by all legal means, KPMG warn that the balance may be less clear now because of reputational damage and the risk that poses – despite the legality of the techniques involved – to long-term shareholder value: 'Boards should recognise, when overseeing the design and monitoring of tax strategies and policies, that contemporary debates about governance, corporate social responsibility and ethics mean that even legal tax-minimisation activity can generate reputational liabilities that can destroy shareholder value'.[153]

Investment organisations have entered into the debate, with Henderson Global Investors producing an influential report based on a survey of the chairmen of FTSE 350 companies. This was explicitly presented as a response to the fact that tax, including what some view as 'inappropriate tax avoidance', is coming under greater scrutiny and that commentators are suggesting that 'approaches to tax should be seen as a matter of corporate social responsibility'.[154] Conferences, workshops and internet debates on the subject are also springing up in rapid succession. In a multiplicity of ways, tax avoidance has emerged as an issue for the corporate social responsibility agenda, and as an ethical rather than just a technical legal concern.

To some managers, and many lawyers, this is entirely inappropriate, there being, in traditional legal thinking, no place for ethical judgement in tax law. But CSR also operates, as business keeps telling us, beyond law, and in the new context of social as well as legal accountability, it is in the courts of public opinion not just in the courts of law that business practice is being judged. Creative compliance in areas such as tax avoidance may pass the test of legality but fail on the test of social responsibility.

In the United Kingdom, the tax authorities have expressly brought the language of CSR into their discussions of tax avoidance, and developed

---

[153] KPMG, 'Tax in the Boardroom' (2004), p. 8.
[154] Henderson Global Investors, *Tax, Risk and Corporate Governance*, February 2005.

initiatives to get 'tax on the boardroom agenda'. The Organisation for Economic Co-operation and Development (OECD) too sees tax avoidance as firmly on the agenda of the 'corporate social responsibility' movement: 'Tax is where environment was ten years ago.'[155]

It is not surprising that tax avoidance has caught the eye of critics geared to CSR. In terms of its consequences, it is clearly a public welfare issue. It is also, of course, a challenge for business in that it goes to the heart of the issue of profit maximisation and provides a real test of whether companies adopting CSR policies embed them throughout the organisation – including the core departments of tax and accounting – seeing them as relevant to financial and legal issues as well as the more established agenda of environment, human rights and so on.

D. The spirit of the law

Though tax avoidance has particularly caught the CSR imagination, there are indications that a more general concern with creative compliance as a CSR and reputational risk could also evolve. Part of the tax debate, and of wider relevance for legal compliance more generally, is the increasing discussion of compliance with the spirit of the law. A report by BiTC, Insight Investment and FTSE looked more generally to the issue of compliance with the spirit and not just the letter of the law, as did Sustainability's report on tax.[156]

This language has begun to emerge too in statements of regulatory policy. Some of the indirect regulatory strategies mentioned earlier, US measures encouraging the adoption of corporate codes of conduct, were geared to fostering good ethical practices, a goal which could be seen as part of the CSR agenda. For the regulators, however, in the wake of Enron, those good ethical practices were much more specifically geared to fostering a corporate culture of compliance with the law. Importantly, the compliance sought was not technical or creative compliance, but compliance with the spirit of the law.

Former US Securities and Exchange Commission (SEC) chairman William Donaldson, for example, has pressed home the importance of investors being able 'to see for themselves that companies are living up to their obligations and embracing the spirit underpinning all securities

---

[155] Jeffrey Owens, OECD, quoted by Vanessa Houlder, *Financial Times*, 22 November 2004.
[156] BiTC, Insight Investment and FTSE, *Rewarding Virtue*.

laws ... beyond just conforming to the letter'.[157] Enron had demonstrated just where a disregard for the spirit of the law – and in Enron's case, the letter of the law too – could lead. Just as important, the publicity surrounding Enron had revealed just how routine creative accounting and aggressive tax avoidance – 'gaming the system', as the then-SEC chairman Harvey Pitt put it – was among businesses in general.[158] One result of Enron was clear concern to tackle creative compliance, not just fraud, and the regulatory response relates to this.[159] UK regulators too increasingly discuss compliance in terms of the spirit of the law. And regulatory and market pressures interrelate: the more the regulators raise the issue, the more the market – as Henderson Global Investors emphasise – sees risk in ignoring it.

There are indications that the idea of compliance with the spirit of the law is being taken on board by business. In their 2006 corporate codes of conduct, twenty-three of the top fifty corporations in the US Fortune 500 and twenty-six of the FTSE 100 committed themselves expressly to compliance with the spirit of the law.[160] These are small numbers and what this commitment means in practice is, like many of the issues raised in this chapter, a matter for ongoing or further research. Likewise, exactly how companies will deal with the CSR pressures on the issue of tax remains to be seen. Information on amount of tax paid and on tax planning policy has begun to appear in the CSR reports of a handful of UK companies. To date, on the issue of tax planning, companies have defended their right to legally minimise tax, as one would expect. The key will be where the line will be drawn in practice on the level of aggressive artificial and creative avoidance techniques employed in doing this. There are, however, indications that the idea that tax minimisation has to be balanced against reputation risk minimisation and the maintenance of good relations with the tax authorities has been taken on board.

The issue of legal compliance, and of what it means to comply with the law *responsibly*, does seem to be entering the CSR agenda. Bringing CSR ideas to the issue of legal compliance raises the threshold on what is required for businesses' legal behaviour to be deemed legitimate. Courts of

[157] W. H. Donaldson, 'U.S. Capital Markets in the Post-Sarbanes-Oxley World: Why Our Markets Should Matter to Foreign Issuers', lecture at London School of Economics, London, 25 January 2005.

[158] H. Pitt, remarks before the Annual Meeting of the American Bar Association's Business Law Section, Washington, 12 August 2002.

[159] For a detailed analysis of Enron and its aftermath for creative compliance, see McBarnet, 'After Enron'.

[160] This is the subject of ongoing research under the ESRC Professorial Fellowship Scheme.

law may be unwilling or find it difficult to hold companies to legal account for what is arguably technically lawful behaviour – although every now and then they do just that, with 'new approaches' which 'lift the corporate veil', look through form to substance, or reinterpret how transaction forms are read, and changing social demands might encourage this. But courts of public opinion, markets and investors can set their own standards for what they hold to be legitimate, and they may set the bar higher than what is 'arguably technically legal', viewing even legal compliance through the lens of what is ethically acceptable or socially responsible. Indeed, companies which fly the banner of CSR invite the imposition of such standards. As Shell put it, 'there is also an inseparable responsibility to ensure that our businesses are run in a way that is ethically acceptable to the rest of the world and in line with our own values'.[161]

In adopting CSR policies and holding themselves accountable to standards beyond legal compliance, companies may not have anticipated CSR reaching from calls for social responsibility on such issues as environmental concerns to calls for social responsibility in relation to legal compliance itself. But CSR has its own momentum, and the potential is there for the market to exercise judgement, and flex its muscles, in the arena of legal compliance too.

All the usual provisos, the limits of market and social forces, of course apply. Nonetheless, those who call for CSR *through* law might also consider the potential for CSR to work *for* law, putting pressure on business to review its attitude to law and compliance, shifting the threshold of social responsibility and ethical legitimacy from compliance with the letter of the law to compliance with its spirit and so, potentially, enhancing the effectiveness of legal control.

IV. Conclusion: a new corporate accountability?

The idea of CSR as voluntary self-regulation, or even as market- and NGO-driven self-regulation, has invited criticism, and it certainly has its limitations. But the view that CSR policies are voluntary or can be treated with impunity as 'just PR' is becoming less and less sustainable. Not only have there been growing market and social pressures, but there has also been increasing legal intervention, fostering and enforcing CSR, often in subtle and indirect ways, through private as well as state initiatives, and there is pressure for further regulatory intervention.

[161] Shell Report (1998).

Nonetheless, even if CSR is becoming increasingly a legal issue, a significant part of its value may lie still in its original conceptualisation as going beyond the law, as being ultimately about business ethics in its ends and social and market pressures in its means. Law may for many reasons, not least because of the value placed on democracy and the rule of law, be the preferred mechanism for corporate accountability. But given the limits of law, we also need extra-legal ethical, social and economic pressures, both to make demands beyond the range of formal law and to make formal law effective. Different eras throw up different ideas that capture the public's moral imagination. CSR happens to be the idea of the moment which might be harnessed to that end.

In short, social and legal means need not be seen as alternatives for furthering corporate responsibility, but as complementary controls in a new style of corporate accountability that involves both legal and ethical standards. Nor need the state be seen as the only viable source of corporate governance. Both legal and social accountability have a role to play. This chapter has demonstrated the multiplicity of sources of governance in operation and a multiplicity of mechanisms being employed, all far more complex than the traditional state-based 'command and control' model of legal regulation.

Law is not just a tool of government, and governmental regulation is not the only way to try to control business through law. Civil society organisations too are increasingly deploying legal mechanisms to constrain business. What is more, they are deploying law to *enforce*, rather than just to encourage, commitments by business to ethics, human rights, and social and environmental responsibility. At the same time, governments are using the market through their procurement power, and facilitating market and NGO pressures with enhanced disclosure. Business organisations are not only adopting internal CSR policies but are themselves exercising legal and market control over other businesses, as well as lobbying and organising (especially when stung by NGO attention themselves) to raise industry standards on CSR and level the playing field. International organisations, both public and private, are setting standards. NGOs and businesses are working in partnership, with NGOs advising rather than only criticising business.

What is emerging in the arena of CSR is a complex interaction between government, business and civil society, private law, state regulation and self-regulation, at national and international levels, with social, legal, ethical and market pressures all being brought to bear in ways that cut across traditional pigeon-holes, and which, as this chapter has tried to demonstrate, interrelate with and foster each other. How this will work out remains to be seen. Not all of these forces are new, though the intensity and spread may be. Many of the developments described here are in their infancy or more indicative of potential than accomplishment. Backlash is always a possibility. All of these forces have their limits. Nonetheless, under the banner of Corporate Social Responsibility, there may be emerging a new, interweaving, multi-faceted form of corporate accountability.

PART TWO

Bringing Law into Corporate Social
Responsibility

2

Corporate social responsibility through contractual control? Global supply chains and 'other-regulation'

DOREEN McBARNET AND MARINA KURKCHIYAN

Legal control of the social impact of business can be exercised through private law as well as through state regulation, and it can be exercised by business itself. Self-regulation is a familiar theme in discussions of corporate social responsibility (CSR) and the law. What has received less attention is the significance for CSR of what we might describe as 'other-regulation', the imposition of CSR standards on one business entity by another, through mechanisms such as contract.

Some of the companies whose reputation has been hardest hit by the CSR movement have found themselves pilloried for the practices of external suppliers which were not their *legal* responsibility but for whose actions they were nonetheless held accountable. Nike's experience vis-à-vis the child labour practices of its south-east Asian suppliers epitomises this.[1] It may be no wonder then that many major companies are not only disseminating their adopted CSR principles and policies throughout their own subsidiary companies worldwide, but are increasingly adopting policies that encourage their external suppliers, and indeed their joint venture partners, to adhere to them. Some companies take this even further, setting, for example, working conditions or environmental standards for their suppliers as part of the supply contract, and initiating their own enforcement mechanisms. Reputational risk is by no means exclusive to suppliers in developing countries, as British Airways' experience in 2005 with UK suppliers Gate Gourmet demonstrated. However, with developing countries increasingly the primary site of production, and issues there

Thanks to the Economic and Social Research Council (ESRC), which has funded this research through its Professorial Fellowship Scheme as part of a project on 'Regulation, responsibility and the rule of law'.
[1] See Chapter 1 in this volume.

the particular target of critical attention, the focus for CSR in supply is, in its first stages at least, very much on *global* sourcing.

Based on empirical research, this chapter examines the use of supply contracts as a mechanism of 'other-regulation'.[2] It explores how companies are exercising contractual control, and assesses the potential of this mechanism for extending CSR through private law.

The idea of business corporations using private law to raise working conditions, environmental and ethical standards in business in other business enterprises carries with it a certain irony since the standards they are setting include many that historically they themselves only adopted under pressure as a result of employee activism, or under legal obligation as a result of government intervention. The irony is all the greater in the context of developing countries, since outsourcing to developing countries was originally motivated by lower cost, which was in turn affected by lower wages and lower regulatory standards (or laxer enforcement). Indeed, multinational companies (MNCs) have been criticised for actively working to keep legal standards down, lobbying for regulatory laws and tax regimes favourable to foreign investment and playing on competition among developing countries for MNC trade and investment. Some have even been accused of using private law to, effectively, prevent improvement in government regulatory standards. Amnesty International has reported on the 'stabilisation' clauses in contractual agreements underpinning major investment projects, notably the building of the Baku-Tbilisi-Ceyhan and the Chad-Cameroon oil pipelines, which required governments to pay compensation to the oil companies involved if they introduced new environmental or social legislation which 'affected the "economic equilibrium" (read profitability) of the pipeline'.[3]

Hence the irony of the idea of MNCs seeking to raise standards, and using contract to do so, though of course the 'business case' concept of CSR makes the justification the same, with the bottom line being protected in this case not by minimising direct costs but by minimising the potential costs of reputational damage and consequent loss of market share. Outsourcing to developing countries and taking advantage of what

---

[2] The idea that private law has a regulatory capacity is not new, but that regulatory capacity had tended to be seen as incidental, either as a side effect of private contracts in correcting failures of the market system such as duress or undue influence – see M. J. Trebilcock, *The Limits of Freedom of Contract* (Cambridge, MA.: Harvard University Press, 1993) – or as a happy accident in its potential to collude with public law for the provision of public goods – see Hugh Collins, *Regulating Contracts* (Oxford: Oxford University Press, 1999). What was new in the CSR-oriented supply contracts was their tendency to stipulate requirements that reached into the realm of public law deliberately, and from the outset.

[3] CR Coalition, *A Big Deal? CSR and the Finance Sector in Europe*, 1 December 2005, p. 21.

the Organisation for Economic Co-operation and Development (OECD) calls 'weak governance' zones has become not just an opportunity but a significant source of risk.[4] There is also, of course, a host of new legal pressures on business in relation to CSR.[5]

This situation provides interesting potential for change. MNCs have been criticised, rightly, for their immense negative influence on global labour conditions, human rights and the environment, but of course, conversely the power that could be harnessed to exert positive influence is also immense, and this is recognised by governments, international organisations, non-governmental organisations (NGOs) and indeed business. Though Wal-Mart is hardly a company noted for its social responsibility, its Chief Executive Officer (CEO) and President Lee Scott announced in 2005 the 'personal discovery' which led to his adoption of a new environmental approach at Wal-Mart, noting: 'Our size and scale means that even one small environmental change in our policies or our customers' habits has exponential impacts all over the world'[6] – a potential that has been described as 'the Wal-Mart effect'.[7] It is frequently noted that multinational companies can have more economic clout and power than governments, and the OECD has talked of the capacity for multinational enterprises to use their influence to make positive contributions to economic, environmental and social progress.[8]

The use of supply contracts could provide a means of employing this corporate influence to CSR ends. Alternatively, it could be merely the latest form of CSR rhetoric, or doomed to be no more than rhetoric by the scale of the practical problems involved. So how are businesses putting CSR contracts into operation and what potential is there for such 'contractual control' to make a difference to CSR standards in practice?

The research reported here is based on analysis of the corporate codes of conduct, websites and CSR reports of thirty-five FTSE 100 multinational companies[9] and five foreign-based multinational companies, with a number of follow-up telephone interviews; on reports by NGOs, governments and international organisations; on press reports; and on interviews

---

[4] OECD, 'The OECD Risk Awareness Tool for Multinational Enterprises in Weak Governance Zones' (2006).

[5] See Chapter 1 and at various places in this volume.

[6] *Greenpeace Business* 85 (May 2006), 11, at images-na.ssl-images-amazon.com/images/G/02/00/00/00/24/28/58/24285882.pdf.

[7] C. Fishman, *The Wal-Mart Effect: How an Out-of-town Superstore Became a Superpower* (London: Allen Lane, 2006).

[8] OECD, 'Guidelines for Multinational Enterprises' (2000), at www.oecd.org/dataoecd/56/36/1922428.pdf.

[9] For the year 2004–05, published 2005.

at three NGOs. It also draws on more in-depth research at five companies, including some analysis of internal documentation.[10] This latter element is pilot work with the objective of raising issues rather than providing any definitive description of typical practice across the board. Companies selected for the pilot research were, indeed, chosen from those regarded as leaders in good practice on CSR in the supply chain, this approach being most likely to reveal fundamental issues rather than those resulting from obviously cosmetic policies.

Section I below analyses the emergent practice of fostering CSR through contractual control, section II describes what is currently taken to be 'best practice' in how it is approached, and section III offers a critical evaluation of its current status and its potential.

I. Supply chains on the corporate social responsibility agenda and the emergence of contractual control

Most large businesses are supplied, with both the goods they retail and the goods they use in their administration, by other businesses, which in turn buy from other businesses still, and so on down the supply chain. Increasingly, big business 'outsources' to contractors rather than directly manufacturing goods itself, contracting factories, usually these days in developing countries, to make the goods for them, and these factories may in turn subcontract. Supply may be agricultural too, and there are similar issues in mining, though our focus will be largely on factories. The supply chain has become a growing issue on the CSR agenda, with big business held to account by NGOs and the media for practices in the factories or farms they contract for supply. Working conditions, low pay, job insecurity, child labour, poor health and safety standards, environmental damage, have all featured in a multitude of damning reports. One report from a group of NGOs (Association for Sustainable and responsible Investment in Asia (ASrIA), Co-operative Insurance Society (CIS) and Impactt) reported employees typically working up to two hundred hours of overtime a month in China (where the legal limit is thirty-six hours' overtime a month) resulting in working time of twelve to thirteen hours a day seven days a week.[11] In similar vein, an Oxfam

---

[10] The work at this stage has not yet included interviews with suppliers.

[11] Association for Sustainable and responsible Investment in Asia, 'An SRI Perspective on The Impactt Overtime Project: Tackling Supply Chain Labour Issues Through Business Practice' (2005), p. 2, at www.asria.org/publications/lib/050921_impactt_overtime_web_combine.pdf.

study revealed that in Chile 75 per cent of women in the agricultural sector are hired on temporary contracts and put in more than sixty hours a week during a season, and yet one in three of them still earns less than the minimum wage.[12]

Companies are increasingly being held to account for activities some way down the supply chain, with McDonald's, for example, criticised by Greenpeace for buying chicken from companies which in turn buy chicken *feed* from companies which are alleged to use soya grown in conditions marked by 'illegal land grabbing', 'slave labour' and environmental destruction in the Amazon rainforest. Greenpeace consequently slates McDonald's 'claims to be rainforest friendly'.[13]

Some companies are adopting CSR strategies for the supply chain in response to direct experience of adverse media attention. Marks & Spencer, for example, was the subject of a World in Action 'expose' of one of its supply factories in Morocco in 1996 where, among other things, child labour was alleged. Marks & Spencer took a libel case to court and won, but, having prided itself on its ethical reputation, the company was stung by the experience, and the development of both its general CSR policy and its supply policy was spurred by the experience. Other companies report the adoption of CSR supply policies as a pre-emptive measure, or in response to socially responsible investment (SRI) analysts making supply a key criterion of investment. Some are coming under pressure from their own CSR auditors or verifiers. Ernst & Young, for example, recommended to BP in its verification report that it provide more information on how it seeks to influence its suppliers and contractors on CSR policies.[14]

The supply chain is becoming increasingly recognised as an area of reputational – and indeed insurance – risk, with a number of companies beginning to develop a 'risk-based approach to supplier engagement' and 'systems to identify higher risk suppliers'.[15] Much of the reporting by companies of their CSR concerns in supply is put very clearly in terms of risk management: 'a supplier CSR questionnaire . . . will enable . . . procurement professionals to determine whether a supplier represents a significant risk due to poor human rights, employment, ethical or environmental

---

[12] Oxfam, 'Trading Away Our Rights: Women working in global supply chains' (2004), p. 5, at www.oxfam.org.uk/what_we_do/issues/trade/trading_rights.htm.

[13] *Greenpeace Business* 85, 6 (May 2006).

[14] BP social report for year 2004 (2005). The 2005 verification report (2006) notes improved coverage. Available at www.bp.com/sectiongenericarticle.do?categoryId = 9008328 &contentId = 7015269.

[15] Vodafone Corporate Social Responsibility Report for 2004–2005, p. 24.

performance'.[16] Where suppliers used to feature in CSR reports in terms of the reporting company's commitment to treat suppliers fairly, it is now the suppliers' practices that are key.

AstraZeneca notes as key drivers for its focus on corporate responsibility in 'the management of external spend': the need to minimise risk of business interruption due to a supplier having a safety, health or environmental (SHE) accident; insurers becoming more interested in SHE; employee preference for such values; intensified media attention and public opinion; and 'the need to ensure, maintain and safeguard AstraZeneca's reputation as a good corporate citizen'.[17] This puts in a nutshell the business case for 'other-regulation' in the supply chain.

Business has responded to this developing situation by, as ING puts it, 'cranking up' supply strategy.[18] British Telecom (BT), for example, launched a supply chain initiative in 2001 and integrated all its CSR requirements for suppliers in a single CSR approach in 2005;[19] the Boots Group Code of Conduct on Ethical Trading was approved in June 2000 with the expectation of auditing all suppliers by April 2006;[20] IKEA launched its 'The IKEA Way on Purchasing Home Furnishing Products' in 2000;[21] and Marks & Spencer announced its 'Global Sourcing Principles' in 2001.[22] In their CSR reports, fifty-four of the UK 250 had begun by 2005 to report on supply chain issues.[23]

Our sample companies demonstrated a range of declared policies on CSR and supply, most very recent. Some simply noted 'encouraging', 'inviting' or 'expecting' suppliers to operate in a way consistent with the purchasing company's business principles. Some had adopted specific procedures such as distribution of business principles and guidance to suppliers, provision of specific codes of principles for suppliers, or the addition of CSR criteria to the questionnaires on quality,

---

[16] WPP CSR Review (2003), p. 23.
[17] AstraZeneca, 'CR Principles in Purchasing', Corporate Responsibility Guideline 1, version 1 (2005), p. 3.
[18] ING Corporate Responsibility Report (2005).
[19] See British Telecom, 'BT's Purchasing Principles', at www.selling2bt.bt.com/working/purchasing/default.asp.
[20] The Boots Group, 'Code of Conduct for Ethical Trading' (2005), at www.boots-csr.com/library/EthicalTrading.pdf.
[21] IKEA Group, 'The IKEA Way on Purchasing Home Furnishing Products', at www.ikea.com/ms/en_US/about_ikea/social_environmental/purchasing_home_furnishing_products.pdf.
[22] Marks & Spencer, 'Global Sourcing Principles' (2005), at images-na.ssl-images-amazon.com/images/G/02/00/00/00/24/28/58/24285882.pdf.
[23] Context and Salter Baker, 'Directions Report' (2005).

financial soundness and so on, issued to potential suppliers as a basis for selection.

The emergent trend, however, is for contractual control. Best practice is increasingly being treated as setting up a contractual obligation on suppliers to meet specified CSR standards. Contract coverage is extending beyond the traditional concerns with product specification, price, delivery dates, quality, financial incentives and penalties, mechanisms for dispute settlements and the like, to corporate social responsibility obligations. Companies already adopting this approach are addressing it in stages, usually adding the CSR terms on the next occasion when a contract comes up for renewal, with some committing to a timed schedule for having all suppliers on CSR-inclusive contracts, and 'global templates' for contracts which include CSR being developed.

II. Mapping contractual control

In exercising contractual control, what CSR issues are addressed, what kind of contracts are used and how are they enforced?

A. Key issues

Adhering to the buying company's own code of conduct tends to be one general requirement, and this will normally cover a sweep of issues including business ethics, environment and human rights. But specific supplier codes are increasingly being established and becoming the basis of contractual obligation. What these focus on varies to some extent by industry. Some companies have had environmental standards as a contractual obligation for some time (environment having been the vanguard issue in CSR). However, not surprisingly given the focus of recent critique, the primary concerns in supplier codes are labour issues.

Prohibition of child labour tends to be given a prominent place, being one of the most emotive of CSR issues. Other key issues are freedom from discrimination, wages set at a level that people can live on, proper provision for health and safety, acceptable working conditions, reasonably restricted working hours, a respect for human dignity, and recognition and rights for worker associations, including the right to collective bargaining. BT's 'Sourcing With Human Dignity' code, for example, addresses child labour, forced labour, cruel, harsh and inhuman treatment, discrimination, freedom of association and collective bargaining, health and safety, wages, working hours and regular employment entitlements.[24] There is also a separate code for suppliers on environmental impact. These codes do not simply state standards as bald principles but set out specific detailed requirements.

1. Private law and state law

The standards set out in supplier codes sometimes go beyond the substantive requirements of domestic law in the supplier's country, but it would often be more accurate to see contractual control as a potential enforcement mechanism for state or international law that is espoused locally in the lawbooks but not in practice.

In one way or another, most of the countries of the developing world have harmonised their legal systems to generally accepted requirements of international labour standards and relevant UN conventions. Most of them have already become members of the World Trade Organisation, or are making efforts to be admitted to it by reforming their legal framework. And in any case, they are all members of the United Nations and have therefore signed up to the relevant treaties. It is also true, however, that in some cases the obligations undertaken at international level have not been transposed into domestic law, or in other cases have been added only after the insertion of loopholes that allow various malpractices to continue. For example, the law in China limits both working hours and maximum permitted overtime. But at the same time, the law permits companies to apply to the Department of Labour for a formal extension to the legal limits, so in effect enabling business firms legally to avoid legal constraint.

Though the ethical supply codes of different companies express their requirements in a variety of ways, their labour requirements in particular tend to echo international law and norms, effectively reproducing the fundamental principles espoused by the International Labour Organisation. Contractual control can therefore be seen as a potential mechanism for implementing international norms, with multinationals' private law potentially compensating for failures in state law.

However, the real inadequacies lie not so much in the substance of local law as in its enforcement. In some instances highlighted by campaigners, law has been deliberately disregarded by the state in order to make the country more attractive, in terms of costs, to foreign investors. In other

---

[24] British Telecom, 'GS18 – Sourcing with Human Dignity Standard', at www.selling2bt.bt.com/working/humandignity/default.asp.

cases, misapplying or ignoring the law has been treated as an opportunity for personal gain by corrupt officials. Law can also be ignored by the victims for various reasons, starting with cultural unfamiliarity. People may simply be unaware of the rights law confers on them, or they may be inhibited by a social imperative telling them that resort to law is not socially acceptable. And, of course, the imbalance of power between employer and employee may be too great for any law to have effect. People can be far too desperate to earn something, however little and by whatever means, to dare to confront the management if doing so might have even the slightest impact on their employment prospects.

Some MNC managers reported the unwelcome realisation that by taking on CSR responsibilities they have acquired a greatly expanded role. In effect they are stepping into the shoes of the government in the supplier countries, by policing and enforcing the non-commercial law of the land. In our interviews with people responsible for monitoring CSR implementation in the supply chain, it became clear that the main CSR task, as they now see it, is to monitor the implementation of national law. As one interviewee put it: '99 per cent of our requirements are legal requirements; they are not set by us. They are included in our code, but 99 per cent or even 100 per cent of them are legal requirements that should be observed anyway.'

Not surprisingly, purchasing companies took considerable care to learn local law. In some cases, the policy was to invest resources in building up a complete database of all the applicable laws of each country that they operate in, and then to add an extra ongoing system to keep it up to date by monitoring legislative changes and adding them to the database as appropriate. In other cases, companies contract a local agent within the region, consulting them on local legislation and requiring them to inform the western company whenever significant changes occur. Regardless of the method adopted for achieving it, familiarity with local non-commercial law has become central to the interpretation and implementation of supply companies' CSR obligations in any particular social setting.

That said, company policies are not only concerned with enforcing compliance with local law. Some supply codes also made it clear that where domestic law falls below international standards, it is international standards that should be observed, and on some issues the standard is expressly set higher than in domestic law. Marks & Spencer, for example, in its 'Global Sourcing Principles' stipulates: 'Each supplier must, as a minimum, fully comply with all relevant local and national laws and regulations . . . Moreover, *whatever the local regulations,* workers should normally be at least 15 years old.'[25] BT also expressly requires, where local laws and corporate standards 'address the same subject, [that] the provision which affords the greater protection to the employee should be applied'.[26] Higher standards may also be required for selected suppliers. AstraZeneca notes, 'for strategic suppliers, additional criteria beyond legal compliance should be incorporated'.[27]

2. 'Soft' contracts

What about the contract itself? What kind of legal tool is being employed? In the broadest view of relations between business entities, there is a wide variety of interactions that might be described as a 'contract'. Depending on the specifics of the industry, the character of the business relationship, the duration of the business engagement and the already established conventions in the industry, the contract could range from an oral agreement through various stages of formalisation such as an e-mail exchange or a brief letter of agreement to an elaborately drafted, signed and witnessed document. For instance, in a food industry that is dominated by the characteristics of fast, seasonal, direct handling of perishable products, the agreement is of necessity often reached by telephone or e-mail exchange. By contrast, the medical and beauty product industries are highly regulated, require licensing all the way along the supply chain and routinely encourage everyone concerned to agree upon the most carefully crafted contracts. However, it should be stressed that, as Jenkinson and Mayer point out: 'Overall, formal, legal contracting appears less relevant to trades between firms than economic theory would lead us to believe... Whatever the mechanism, there is growing evidence of the significance of informal arrangements, but as yet there is insufficient evidence on precisely how they work.'[28]

Another dimension that affects the place and importance of contract in business agreements is the multilayered structure of subcontracting. In some cases companies entered into a contractual relationship with a different western-based supplier, which then subcontracted production to factories in a developing country. Although the company intending to retail the products still expects the subcontractors in such cases to comply with the requisite codes, and they do monitor both the quality of the

[25] Marks & Spencer, 'Global Sourcing Principles', p. 2 (our emphasis).
[26] BT, 'Sourcing with Human Dignity', code standard 1.
[27] AstraZeneca, 'Corporate Responsibility Principles' (2005), p. 7.
[28] T. Jenkinson and C. Mayer, 'The Assessment: Contracts and Competition', *Oxford Review of Economic Policy* 12, 4 (1996), 3.

product and the working conditions in the factory if their brand name is attached to the product, all this is done not on the basis of direct contracts, but through the intermediate partner.

Contract types can be broken down into the 'soft,' or relational contract, and the 'discrete', well-defined contract, which specifies all the relevant terms within its pages.[29] 'Soft' contracts are normal usage in many areas of business and tend to typify the legal organisation of long-term business relations, characteristic of much supply, and valued for the greater reliability and trust they build up over time, while prescriptive 'discrete' contracts are more likely in one-off deals. One company broke down the ratio in its supply contracts as two thirds long-term relationships on 'soft contracts', and one third who were 'in and out' on discrete contracts. How soft the contract is also usually depends on how far conditions are simply imposed by one party or involve a more collaborative approach, and how far the issues are open to interpretation and further negotiation, rather than imposed as strict and sharply defined obligations from the outset.[30] CSR requirements are normally set out in agreements designed at the 'softest' end of the spectrum.

A closer look at supply contracts demonstrates this. The actual contract can be quite minimal. Where a written document is needed in order to start business with a supplier in a retail industry, the common practice is to use a short letter of agreement, followed later by a commercial document describing terms and conditions of business in detail. Our research suggests that the CSR obligations set out in the letter of agreement are typically very brief and very broad, for example: 'By supplying the goods . . . the Supplier expressly warrants that they will conform to all [the purchasing company's] Policies, which are notified by [the Company] to the Supplier in connection with the supply of goods', with the terms and conditions usually also establishing the right to assess and monitor compliance: '[the purchasing company] reserves the right to carry out a Social Accountability Assessment at the Supplier's premises'.

On the substance of what is to be complied with, the key documents for determining the criteria therefore become the company's own code of conduct and related policies, and any specific supplier code. Suppliers may indeed be required to complete a questionnaire demonstrating how

[29] On relational contract, see I. R. Macneil, 'Relational Contract Theory as Sociology: A Reply to Professors Lindenberg and de Vos', *Journal of Institutional and Theoretical Economics* 143, 2 (1987), 272–90.

[30] On relational contract, see D. Campbell and P. Vincent-Jones (eds.), 'Contracts and Economic Organisation', *Socio-Legal Initiatives* (Aldershot: Dartmouth, 1996).

they meet the codes' standards, with the response taking on contractual status: 'If your response is accepted and becomes part of the contract then you will be expected to meet these commitments as you would with any other contractual clause.'[31]

Codes can, however, be quite 'soft' in the way their requirements are expressed. Supply codes demonstrate careful phrasing to leave space for adjustment: suppliers 'must meet all *the appropriate* relevant industry and country standards' or 'must work *towards* higher standards'; '*as a norm* they [employees] should be free to join a lawful union or a workers association'; 'the code of conduct should be observed *wherever it is possible*' (our emphases). This 'openness' is typical of codes of conduct in general and has been heavily criticised as making them mere 'statements of lofty intent'[32] and 'awfully slippery'.[33] They certainly allow a great deal of space for claims that they have been successfully attained. But to contracting companies they also serve important practical purposes, put in terms of flexibility and practicability on the one hand, and the need for partnership on the other.

3. Flexibility and practicability

The broad contractual obligation and general policy statement is usually followed by more informal explanation of the standards required and the conditions that are to be imposed by means of auditing. The 'soft' contract puts the matter of the social performance of the supplier clearly onto the agenda of communication between the corporation and the supplier, while also fixing in place the right of the company to conduct social auditing. At the same time it gives ample flexibility to both sides in deciding the actual level of standards that, in the words of corporate representatives, it is 'appropriate' and 'reasonable' to expect from an individual supplier in a particular country under a specific set of circumstances. Companies noted to us their internal discussions, even before embarking on a CSR supply policy, on what standards could realistically be demanded of suppliers.

Flexibility was seen as important. For example, in explaining why it is necessary to express CSR conditions initially at a high level of generality while still keeping a reference to the corporate code of conduct in the contract, we were told:

---

[31] British Telecom, 'Working with BT – the generic standards', at www.bt.com.
[32] S. P. Sethi, 'Standards for Corporate Conduct in the International Arena: Challenges and Opportunities for Multinational Corporations', *Business and Society Review* 107, 1 (2002), 20–40, at 23.
[33] Naomi Klein, *No Logo* (London: Flamingo, 2000).

Even if the audit was positive before we actually start working with the supplier, you cannot assume that the standards are going to stay the same for ever. Change of management or change of law might affect what standard is feasible. For example, you don't have to allow unions in a special economic zone in Bangladesh. The local law bans the unions there. Now, if we are using a supplier in Bangladesh special economic zone, we don't demand true freedom of association because legally they cannot do it. But next year, the law may change, so the next year we would require it. So the standard shifts, and we should have a flexible tool available to respond to all the possible changes.[34]

Obviously, there is a direct commercial rationale behind the frequent reluctance of major firms to press hard for the supplier to meet the highest of the standards set by a literal reading of the code of conduct. In any business firm governed by the imperative of making profits, the interests of buying policy will have to be set against the elaborate and costly hedging of risks involved in full scale CSR implementation. But companies also reported legal, economic and cultural factors which tend to make more rigorous demands both difficult and even counterproductive.

The legal problem arises when local law is not just less demanding than the purchasing company's code, but conflicts with it.[35] The obvious example, noted already in passing, is the almost universal CSR requirement for suppliers that workers must have freedom of association. In some countries, with China – a prominent supplier-factory country – among them, independent trade unions are formally prohibited by the government, and the prohibition is rigorously enforced. In such cases, interviewees reported, suppliers are still encouraged by the purchasing company to initiate some kind of workers' representative body that can operate with the consent of the management and consult with it about the running of the business. Western managers readily acknowledge that they are fully aware of the superficiality of this requirement. An alternative, or supplementary, strategy, as in another of our cases, is for companies to tackle this issue through political rather than contractual influence, working at the macro rather than the micro level, by engaging in a lobbying campaign through the Ethical Trade Organisation to change local law.

The economic constraint is that the resources of the local suppliers are often so limited that even a CSR-conscious management cannot afford sufficient investment to raise standards such as health care and

---

[34] Interview conducted in Nottingham, 24 January 2006.
[35] Indeed, some companies expressly require adherence to higher standards than local law requires only where they do not conflict with law; see, for example, BT, 'Sourcing with Human Dignity'.

safety provision, welfare payments, ventilation and equipment specifi-
cations to international level. Improvements could come mainly from
improved productivity and better management, but these cannot be
achieved overnight, and they may never be attainable without long-term
planning, sophisticated training and perhaps supervision – external management – as well. On these grounds purchasing companies argue that
it is enough for the supplier to acknowledge the problems, be willing to
discuss them, and demonstrate an interest in sorting them out; it is not
realistic at such an early stage to enforce maximum compliance with a
CSR code – instead of producing a reformed supplier, it would put it
out of business. Alternatively, of course, purchasing companies could pay
more to cover these costs, as the price of reputational insurance, a point
we shall return to later.

There is also a cultural dimension that purchasing companies feel constrains the demands they can make of suppliers. If they are to achieve
genuine application of the CSR code they will find themselves tackling
issues that are far beyond their competence. How are they to enforce gender equality in an enterprise that operates in a fiercely sexist society? How
are they to harmonise CSR policy on under-age labour with an accepted
local concept of childhood when there are different sets of social expectations on when childhood ends and adulthood starts? How are they to take
account of such matters as family autonomy, the central role of tradition
and the primacy of filial duty?

The matter becomes even more complicated when moral issues are
considered in local context. For example, if there is a very big gap between
the usual local standard and the standard required by a foreign company,
could that destabilise the community? What should be done if a family
desperately needs the earnings that the child brings home? How can a ban
on child labour in the relatively better-paid export industries be justified,
if the inevitable consequence of such a ban would be that the children
concerned are forced to seek employment in the much worse conditions
typical of enterprises that only supply the domestic market, or in the
classic example, if the likely alternative is prostitution? How can a child's
contribution be either quantified or morally evaluated when her or his
work is done at home? Many of the outsourcing contracts are subdivided
and the various parts handed downward, eventually finding their way
to individual families who perform a given task collectively as a private
household.[36]

---

[36] See 'Trade, Labour Standards and Development: Where Should they Meet?', *DFID
Background Briefing Note* (London: Department for International Development, 2000).

4. Partnership

Soft contracts are also explained in relational terms. 'Partnership' or 'alliance' are the concepts most frequently utilised to describe the characteristically flexible relationships set up by 'soft' contracts. Partnership especially is frequently referred to in justifying the vagueness built into relational contracts. It implies that business partners are able to work together in personal terms; that they have a mutual desire to work things out; that they are willing to share risks and rewards; that they exercise mutual understanding; that they try to help each other instead of controlling and punishing each other; and that the relationship is altogether a win-win scenario. Partnership assumes the building of trust and suggests that the parties are engaging in a constructive dialogue. There is a clear business case for the partnership approach, with 'adversarial' supply relationships being blamed for poor quality, delays and lack of supplier commitment.[37]

In contractual control it is established practice to present the MNC-supplier relationship as a partnership. CSR contractual terms are often being introduced as new obligations in established supply relationships, and purchasing companies are keen to stress their commitment 'to work with the suppliers, not to walk away', and always to help them find a solution to the demands of CSR.

Companies described their contributions in this partnership deal as 'working at both levels, with the managers and with the workers', in order, as one of the interviewees put it, 'to bring life into the code of conduct document'. At the managerial level it meant training and advice. BT, for example, set up a training programme in 2004 for all BT suppliers to help them implement environmental management systems compatible with international standards. It might also mean demonstrating to suppliers the business case advantages of CSR, offering advice on how to improve productivity, or helping to find a simple solution to problems without extra cost – 'free consultancy', as one interviewee put it. BT reports: 'We help them to understand when they are breaking the law or how to do things differently, and how to make more profit.'[38] NGOs recognise the importance of this consultancy on the 'business benefits' of CSR, seeing it as leading to more willingness on the part of suppliers to experiment, and thereby to more sustainable change.[39]

---

[37] S. Sivadasan, J. Efstathiou, A. Calinescu and L. H. Huatuco, 'Supply chain complexity', in S. New and R. Westbrook (eds.), *Understanding Supply Chains* (Oxford: Oxford University Press, 2004), p. 133.

[38] British Telecom, 'Social and Environmental Report' (2005).

[39] ASrIA, 'An SRI Perspective', p. 5.

Such advice may be quite minor and simple. One example we were given was presented as an improvement to work conditions that could be made without any financial loss to the supplier. Workers had to spend long hours on their feet with only a short break in the middle. The advice was to extend the break from thirty minutes to one hour. The interviewee reported that the outcome was that, despite the longer break, productivity had remained the same, while the suppliers were delighted to discover that they had gained a reduction in reported problems of occupational health, a fall in staff turnover and a markedly more contented workforce.[40] In another case, an investment was made by the purchasing company to set up capacity-building courses that would provide training for all the managers who were responsible for each of the various stages of their supply chain. The curriculum focused on ways to plan and manage production in such a way that human resources would be more efficiently utilised.

At shop-floor level, the purchasing company's role is seen as creating as much employee awareness as possible on what the CSR code of conduct says, and all its implications, and explaining local law and employee rights under it. Booklets and posters have been produced and distributed to workers. A few companies have attempted to take the instructional methodology a little farther. BT reports that it has set up 'mandatory awareness training' for at least some of the workers covered by its code of conduct. Marks & Spencer has sponsored the production of videos in the various local languages, explaining both the code and the relevant laws of the land in each case. The firm requires the local managers of the supplier companies to take charge of arranging for all the workers to view the completed videos.

B. Enforcing contractual control

The same kind of thinking that lies behind the adoption of soft contracts also colours the approach to enforcement.

Enforcement is an important part of supplier strategy for MNCs serious about how their CSR policies are viewed. Critics, assessors and SRI investment analysts have long since moved beyond being impressed by the adoption of policies alone, and want to see proof of implementation. Best practice therefore involves sophisticated monitoring processes, and, as we

---

[40] For other cases demonstrating how better management of code compliance can bring positive benefits to supplier firms as profitable businesses, see 'Managing Compliance with Labour Codes at the Supplier Level', *ETI Briefing Paper No. 3*, based on presentations and discussions from the ETI Biennial Conference (12–13 May 2005).

have seen, the right to monitor compliance is likely to be expressly written into the terms and conditions of the contract: '[The Company] reserves the right to carry out a Social Accountability Assessment at the Supplier's premises'. In line with the partnership model, however, the enforcement approach is not punitive but follows the 'compliance model' approach. MNC policy is more about bringing their suppliers into compliance over time than immediately resorting to penalties.

Best practice involves on-site monitoring of all suppliers at the outset, to check whether they meet the requirements, identifying and reporting shortcomings and carrying out follow-up assessments of progress towards rectifying them, usually over an agreed period of time. There will also be a 'continuous improvement' programme and continued periodic audits.

Companies particularly concerned about CSR branding tend to have in place provisions for in-house auditing. In itself, supplier auditing is not new for any big corporation. There are long-established and well-tested schemes for routine quality auditing as an essential part of purchasing policy, and as it was put to us by one respondent: 'we always looked around to ensure that as far as we were concerned, the factory that we were using was of a good standard'. CSR contracting has now added explicit criteria for measuring conditions and practices, all listed and publicly available for reference in the written code of conduct, making social auditing more systematic. Also, there was a general acknowledgment that this is a very different type of auditing, requiring new skills.

> If quality auditing used eyes, social auditing uses voices, understanding, and all the senses. You have to talk to people. Previously, working in Asia and visiting factories, I was looking at the quality of goods and at the quality of the facilities; I was looking at the process, but also at what was the health and safety condition ... But we were not good at understanding things like what wages people should be paid, above what age should people be working in this country, what are the unions like, what does discrimination mean in the Indian context. Those were things that we had never really delved into because we would never need to do it in the UK.[41]

To perform the new CSR tasks, companies have had to extend their existing auditing capacity by recruiting and training new staff, retraining existing staff who were already working as assessors so that they were equipped to operate in the new field, and developing appropriate methodology and training, including guidance on how to gain access to information by

---

[41] Interview conducted in London, 17 December 2005.

an informal approach and how to assure respondents that they could be certain of confidentiality. In some cases this staff training evolved into training the staff of the supplier companies. When that was completed, the corporation could hand over the work and grant the suppliers accreditation so that they could themselves audit compliance farther down the supply chain.

In assessing the strengths and weaknesses of in-house auditing, it should be said on the positive side, as indeed one NGO interviewee did, that if done well, the audit does expose at least some of the problems in the supplier factories, demonstrate the company's commitment to taking ethical issues seriously and send a signal to the suppliers that the monitoring process cannot be ignored.

However, in-house audit is also open to criticism on the grounds of conflict of interest. In its decision-making, management has to strive for a balance between criteria determining the quality of the product, criteria measuring the commercial aspects of the prospective contract, and criteria that indicate the degree of acceptability or otherwise of the social performance of the supplier. On at least a short-term assessment, the suspicion of critics is that business will be business: that the primary concern of any company – profit – will suggest to the decision-makers that if one of three categories has to be marginalised, it is not a good idea to choose either quality or price. It is for this reason that in the campaigning literature especially, the objectivity of in-house audit, fairly or otherwise, is often questioned.

External audit is a response to this concern, and social auditing has become a globalised business in itself. Financial and quality auditing firms such as Ernst & Young and PricewaterhouseCoopers have extended their services to include the new demand for social auditing. In addition, new social auditing organisations have also emerged, some of them commercial and others not-for-profit. The current trend is towards greater reliance on global audit firms. There is also pressure on supplier factories to secure their own certification directly, by initiating and paying for independent auditing in order to be in a position to bid for new contracts. This obviates the need for meeting different standards set by different purchasing companies in multiple audits, although some purchasing companies are already sensitive to this, permitting replacement of their own standards with 'a similar ethical trading standard as a reasonable alternative where suppliers are already working towards this alternative'.[42]

---

[42] BT, 'Sourcing with Human Dignity'.

The main criticism advanced by those who have observed and commented on the practice of external auditing is that its goal of objectivity causes it to be superficial, formal and biased in favour of quantification. The big specialist firms tend to work on the basis of a standardised, predetermined and strict methodology which cannot easily be adjusted to fit any particular case. Such rigidity requires indifference to the individual peculiarities of a society, and precludes any allowance for its distinctive culture, its attitudes towards gender, its religious proclivities and so forth. Reliance solely on third-party auditing is also sometimes seen as a company's way of deflecting criticism and protecting its image if there should be a public relations crisis, as opposed to a system that would encourage the management to face up in a responsible manner to problems that they can see for themselves. Some companies, such as IKEA and Marks & Spencer, have grasped this nettle and now practice both in-house and independent auditing at the same sites, which gives them a chance to 'calibrate' the consistency of the two sets of findings.[43]

1. Audit and detection

However, whether in-house or external, social auditing of suppliers has limits as an enforcement tool. It is merely a snapshot and while it may be good at detecting some issues, especially the immediately visible ones such as specific flaws in health and safety conditions at the workplace, there are other issues that an audit approach is unlikely to be effective in discovering. These are the systemic violations of a code of conduct such as excessive overtime, anti-union policies, discrimination in any of its many forms, or sexual harassment.[44] The methodology does not allow the auditors to do what they would need to do to uncover the subtle way in which violations of that kind can take place and then be covered up.

And cover-ups certainly occur. For example, factories routinely presented false data to auditors.[45] There are reports of sophisticated systems of deception with two sets of books, or working hour records, or convoluted plots such as setting up a fully compliant 'model factory' which then subcontracts the bulk of the job to other outlets operating away from the view of the auditors.[46] Factory managers have learned how to

---

[43] PricewaterhouseCoopers, 'Sourcing Overseas for the Retail Sector', p. 10.

[44] Alison Maitland, 'Social audits are failing to detect factory abuses', *Financial Times*, 2 November 2005, p. 8. See also *WRAP Newsletter*, January 2005.

[45] ASrIA, 'An SRI Perspective', p. 5.

[46] Clean Clothes Campaign, 'Looking for a Quick Fix: How Weak Social Auditing is Keeping Workers in Sweatshops' (The Netherlands: Clean Clothes Campaign, 2005), p. 25.

prepare their facilities for audits to convey a false impression of working conditions in plausible fashion. Employee contracts compliant with the requisite codes may be available on record, while 'shadow contracts' are set up whereby employees agree to give up not just employee protections such as limits on overtime but basic human rights, agreeing not to marry, become pregnant or be involved in a relationship.[47] Workers are coached about what to say to outsiders, and reports suggest that sometimes a climate of fear exists among workers who expect that they might have to discuss working conditions with an outside inspector.[48]

Similar practices occur in the context of environmental standards, with, for example, reports of dealers in China 'laundering' wood illegally logged in Indonesia by stamping it as though it is from a sustainable source.[49] One purchasing company noted:

> It's a nightmare trying to ensure the wood we get . . . doesn't come from such sources . . . they know what we want to hear in terms of being environmentally friendly. So you can go to the sawmill, where they reassure you that the wood comes from managed forests and they show you all the stamps – but I'm not always convinced.[50]

Indeed, the local legal culture in many developing countries provides a supportive environment for such evasive and corrupt behaviour, because law is so often associated in the public mind with an oppressive regime with little normative authority.[51] Audits, as they do even in the traditional financial context, may be dealing with only an illusion of compliance.

Despite these detection limitations, audit does throw up significant problems. Boots, for example, in 2005 reported 2,500 breaches identified through its supplier verification programme.[52] What action is taken if violations of the supplier code are detected? What sanctions underlie the enforcement of contractual control?

2. Sanctions

In the general spirit of partnership, the auditing of social performance along the supplier chain is commonly presented by a retail corporation as

---

[47] Panorama, 'Nike and Gap', BBC, 15 October 2000
[48] ASrIA, 'An SRI Perspective', p. 5.   [49] *Greenpeace Business*, 85, p. 8.
[50] 'Sisco Merchandising', reported in the *Independent on Sunday*, 13 July 2005.
[51] M. Kurkchiyan, 'The Illegitimacy of Law in Post-Soviet Societies' in D. T. Galligan and M. Kurkchiyan (eds.), *Law and Informal Practices: the Post-Communist Experience* (Oxford: Oxford University Press, 2003), pp. 25–46.
[52] www.bitc.org.uk/resources/case_studies/afe_sc_05_bootssvp.html.

being 'about learning, not about policing', and as being 'most importantly an awareness raising process'. The BT website suggests that 'the evaluation increases the supplier understanding of how to work in partnership with BT'. In short, within the framework of partnership, a negative finding from auditing does not bring about confrontation, censure, penalty or a break in the relationship. Instead, it is a part of the process of transforming business culture in the factory by consensus.

In terms of legal consequences, non-compliance with the contract is highly unlikely to ever result in a court case. Despite the insistence by one interviewee that contractual obligation is important to get the issues taken seriously, he was quick to add 'even though it is highly unlikely we would ever go to court'. As is usual in business contracts more generally, any sanction for non-compliance normally consists of economic leverage rather than legal procedure. As Collins notes, 'perhaps the most pervasive and effective non-legal sanction comprises a refusal to deal with the other party in the future'.[53] Not repeating an order or declining to place a new one are the strongest measures likely to follow from contractual non-compliance.

However, in the partnership approach taken in CSR supply contracts even this is a rarity. In noting that no legal action has been taken in ten years, Unilever 'emphasises that the key to its successful partnerships with suppliers is that it does not have adversarial relationships'.[54] Pressed to explain whether non-compliance would indeed result in such a radical response as cancelling or not renewing a contract, interviewees proceeded to give thoughtfully phrased explanations of what non-compliance really means in this context. For them it was defined not as a failure to reach the required standards of performance (even if a supplier should do so repeatedly), but rather as an attitude of mind. Non-compliance was a non-cooperative stand on the part of the supplier. Only if a supplier knowingly fails to cooperate would they pull out: 'if for example, we went there and found a major problem and they refused to do anything about it, then we would, hypothetically, walk away', though even in this case the interviewee added: 'but we have not actually done that in any case at this stage'.

BT's report on the implementation of its 'Sourcing with Human Dignity' (SWHD) Labour Standard in the three years 2003–05 notes only one instance of contract termination in the period. This involved a

[53] Collins, *Regulating Contracts*, p. 101.
[54] In its Unilever Indonesia research report with Oxfam: J. Clay, 'Exploring the Links between International Business and Poverty Reduction: a Case Study of Unilever in Indonesia' (Oxford: Oxfam and Unilever, 2005), p. 65.

subcontractor who had been found 'upon re-assessment, to persistently allow serious shortfalls of the SWHD standard, including excessive and forced overtime and intimidation of workers. The contractor falsified records to try to hide this from assessors. As a result, we stopped placing orders with that company'.[55] In another example, the supplier simply refused to cooperate with the changes required. The particular contract represented a very small part of the supplier's overall business, and to lose it would mean only a small loss. It did not therefore make commercial sense to meet the purchasing company's condition, which in this situation was to raise the wages of the workers. Unusually, the supplier decided not even to play the deception game of manufacturing an illusion of compliance, but to walk openly away from the contract. For some purchasing companies their approach depends on the issue at stake. For H&M child labour was taboo: 'If we find child labour being employed by the same supplier – or one of his subcontractors – on a second occasion, we cease our co-operation with the supplier for good. This has occurred on a few occasions'.[56]

Nonetheless, there is a difference in the enforcement policy between suppliers with which a purchasing firm has an already established business relationship, and a prospective new one. With previously contracted business partners, policy is always at the softest possible end of the soft approach. The understanding is that within the spirit of partnership, a gradual improvement will be made. We were repeatedly told that with such partners, although it is theoretically possible to break an ongoing series of contracts that are already in place, it is not likely to happen in practice.

When it comes to selection of new suppliers, however, a harder line can be taken. There is less at stake with no working relationship and existing supply channel to lose, and more emphasis on risk. It was also recognised that the publicity within a country or region that follows from a rejection has a useful demonstration effect. This is not to say, however, that CSR performance has become the decisive factor in contracting a new supplier. Even though social auditing has now become a commonplace and much-trumpeted element in corporate supply policy, it remains just one factor among others in procurement decisions, though there were minimum CSR standards, with issues such as child labour, once again, taboo. H&M, for example, insisted that though its policy is to work for improvement,

---

[55] BT, 'Social and Environmental Report', Suppliers section, p. 02.
[56] H&M website, www.HM.com.

'certain basic requirements must always be met. For example a supplier who refuses to allow trade unions or has employees who are younger than the law or our code of conduct allow, will never be accepted as a supplier, even if he is prepared to say that he intends to carry out improvements'.[57]

III. Evaluating contractual control

How are we to assess the potential contribution of contractual control as a means of fostering corporate responsibility in the supply chain? The use of contract for this purpose is in its infancy, but this exercise in mapping how contractual control is currently operating raises a number of questions. Is contractual control too 'soft' to be effective? What influences the effective spread of contractual control? Who bears the cost of contractual control and does the 'partnership' of MNC and supplier need to become more of a two-way venture? Should there be any concern about counterproductive effects in the wider social context?

A. Soft contracts, symbolic control?

The way in which contractual control is currently being exercised has raised questions about its potential impact. With 'soft' contracts the norm in contractual control and a clear reluctance to sanction, some will undoubtedly ask whether CSR can be effectively extended through contract or whether this is just an example of CSR as public relations, with MNCs protecting their own reputation but perhaps to little other practical effect. It is, however, important to put this 'soft control' in context. The soft contract/soft enforcement approach is not confined to CSR matters, but is typical of contracts in general where long-term relations are involved.[58] Nor is it simply a product of the private nature of contractual control, since it typifies many branches of state regulation too.

Limited resources and detection problems hiding the 'dark figure' of non-compliance are as common in state regulation as in private. The policy of allowing time for suppliers to remedy failings is exactly paralleled by the 'compliance' approach of Hawkins' UK water pollution inspectors, who also demonstrate the same 'law as last resort approach', with only tiny numbers of breaches resulting in prosecution. When they do opt

[57] www.HM.com, July 2006.
[58] S. Macaulay, 'Non-Contractual Relations in Business: A Preliminary Study', *American Sociological Review* 28, 1 (1963), 55–67.

for recourse to legal sanction the driving factor is, exactly as here, the attitude and lack of cooperativeness of the culprit.[59] Indeed, although some state regulatory agencies, especially in the United States, prefer to 'go by the book',[60] the favoured approach to regulation in many agencies has for some time been Braithwaite's 'enforcement pyramid' with soft approaches tried first to foster compliance and 'big sticks' only brought in as last resort, though it is deemed important that they be there as ultimate sanction.[61]

Lack of rigorous regulatory enforcement in the business context has been criticised for decades in socio-legal and criminological literature as merely 'symbolic' control,[62] but the key question is, what works? Is the goal to punish or to secure compliance by the optimal means? The answer in this context must be to secure compliance, though of course that still raises the question of effectiveness in achieving that goal, and some NGOs have questioned whether the current approach is accomplishing enough remediation.

The fact is, however, that purchasing companies are on something of a cleft stick on this issue. If they were to take a less 'soft' approach they might well find themselves subject to even more criticism. The preference for progressive improvement and reluctance to use the 'ultimate penalty of contract termination', as Unilever puts it,[63] is hardly surprising. Contract termination would in many instances lead to factory closure and job loss, and setting that sequence of events in play could be seen as extreme corporate *irresponsibility*. The impact of contractual control is, in any case, affected by more than the approach to enforcement.

B. Limits in the current reach of contractual control

Whatever the ultimate overall impact of contractual control, it is important to recognise the factors that are currently causing variation and limiting capacity across different companies according to their market position, across different sectors, across different tiers in the supply chain, and across CSR issues.

---

[59] Keith Hawkins, *Environment and Enforcement* (Oxford: Clarendon Press, 1984).

[60] E. Bardach and R. Kagan, *Going by the Book: the Problem of Regulatory Unreasonableness* (Philadelphia, PA: Temple University Press, 1982).

[61] I. Ayres and J. Braithwaite, *Responsive Regulation* (Oxford: Oxford University Press, 1992).

[62] W. G. Carson, 'Some Sociological Aspects of Strict Liability and the Enforcement of Factory Legislation', *Modern Law Review* 33, 4 (1970) 396; F. Pearce and S. Tombs, 'Ideology, Hegemony and Empiricism', *British Journal of Criminology* 30 (1990), 424.

[63] Clay, 'Exploring the links', p. 65.

1. Uneven corporate participation

This paper has approached contractual control for CSR from a 'current best practice' perspective. The practice is no more than emergent and only a limited number of companies are involved to date. These tend to be the 'premium brands' which have the commercial incentive and resources to engage at this level. In this group is the handful of companies that either sell at the top end of their sector or for whom CSR branding is particularly important. Other situations in which companies can afford to invest in CSR contractual control is where they have a special niche in their domestic market, as in the case of BT. Bigger companies are also better placed to monitor than smaller companies are.

The big question is how far CSR concerns are likely to become requirements for suppliers among 'value brands', businesses for whom competing on price is all. As John Ruggie, UN Special Representative for Business and Human Rights, put it at a recent CSR event for business, 'Is the fundamental business model of value brands, as opposed to the premium brands you represent, compatible with any concept of sustainable compliance? I do not know the answer, but we need one, because there are far more of them than there are of you'.[64]

2. Uneven participation across sectors

The use of CSR codes, on supply as more generally, varies across business sectors. Rhys Jenkins attributes this to the fact that CSR codes were adopted in response to consumer pressure, rather than from internal business management need. It is driven by the imperative of risk reduction and not by corporate desire to create social benefits. Consequently, it is concentrated in industries that specialise in consumer goods, such as garments, footwear, toys or food, all of which are particularly concerned about brand name damage.[65] In industries focused on durable goods where prices on products are relatively high, such as the car industry, discussions about codes of conduct rarely take place.[66] The pattern is even more pronounced in industries farther removed from the customer, such as raw material production.

---

[64] Remarks delivered at a forum on corporate social responsibility, Germany, 14 June 2006, at www.fairlabor.org/all/resources/NGO_Ger06/Ruggie_keynote.pdf.

[65] Though even there Clean Clothes Campaign estimates only 10 per cent of all garment production workplaces in the world are audited each year.

[66] Rhys Jenkins, 'Corporate Code of Conduct', *Technology, Business and Society Programme Paper Number 2* (New York: UN Research Institute for Social Development, 2001), p. 27.

Even within the consumer goods sector, there are variations depending on the characteristics of the industry. If the business involves a lasting relationship that can justify investment or make risk consideration a significant factor, then it is more likely that a code of conduct will be taken seriously.

3. Uneven impact along the supply chain

Even 'best practice' companies do not cover the entire supply chain with CSR and do not include in the monitoring schemes suppliers of products that do not carry the brand name – at least, it was sometimes added, 'not yet'. In those situations the risk factor for the corporation is not considered to be high. This effectively excludes a large proportion of suppliers further down the chain. As noted earlier, some companies operated double standards according to whether suppliers were 'strategic' or not, for example including in all contracts a minimum requirement of meeting local laws relating to Corporate Responsibility and Safety, Health and Environment, but noting that 'for strategic suppliers, additional criteria beyond legal compliance should be incorporated'.[67]

Likewise, if brand protection is key, procurement that is not directly retail related, such as supplies for the administration of the business, tends to be seen as a lower priority, though, that said, some companies do include their administrative supplies – BT requires specified environmental criteria for paper and stationery, for example – and one company that prided itself on its ethical supply policy nonetheless was caught out by the revelation that timber used in its shop fronts came from an environmentally unacceptable source.

Other factors include the volume of the purchasing order, and the nature of the relationship between retailer and supplier. If a supplier has contracted for a short-term or for a one-off purchase, then CSR compliance is often not even mentioned. This is how it was explained:

> In some instances we were in a factory maybe only one week, for just one order, we never went back again. For instance, this year we wanted a radio for sale at Christmas. The next year we do not want the radio, thank you, it is an MP3 player that we are interested in, not radios any more. And it is a different factory. We were going to be in that new factory maybe one week, maybe even only a few hours, you just do not know. We took the view that it is even unethical to request that factory to pay minimum wage, to make sure that unions were in place, to cut their hours to a reasonable level. And

---

[67] AstraZeneca, 'Corporate Responsibility Principles', p. 7.

all this for a small order? We are not going to work with them over time, so we are not making any contribution; we are not giving them any tools to do it, any skills to improve productivity. In cases when we are only with them for a season – as commonly happens in the gift business – the standard that we operate was that the factory should look reasonable.[68]

Another variable that affected the purchaser's policy was whether a given supplier works exclusively for it or has other clients. It is considered worthwhile to make investments in a factory from which the purchasing company can gain exclusively, but illogical to take on costs for improvements from which competitors can then freely benefit.

And, of course, there is the issue of how far down the supply chain the purchaser goes. Best practice recognises the need to go beyond 'tier 1' suppliers, the direct contractors, to their subcontractors, 'tier 2' and beyond, but at best this tends to be seen as an issue to be dealt with in stages, and a difficult one, very much dependent on the cooperation of first-tier suppliers, without which 'by definition many of these workers [in tier 2 and beyond] remain unseen and out of reach'.[69] Some purchasing companies complain that it is easier for those with short supply chains to make this commitment. For those with long, many-tiered supply chains, 'it's like signing an open cheque'. Where MNCs limit the range of their supply chain responsibility, they may in effect be simply passing risk to their tier 1 suppliers. One tier 1 supplier, concerned about the veracity of its own (tier 2) supplier's environmental certification, noted anxieties about potential repercussions vis-à-vis their MNC customer: 'now, everything they do has to be good practice. It means they could refuse stuff from me if it turned out anything was wrong. And because we have to pay upfront for everything in China with no recourse, that would be terrible for us'.[70]

4. Uneven coverage of issues

The CSR issues that are targeted by purchasing companies tend to be dictated by risk and critique, hence the focus on labour rights in developing countries rather than the wider range of CSR concerns. Nor are the labour issues focused on necessarily the ones that are deemed most important locally. Prominence is usually given to those issues that would

---

[68] Interview conducted in London, 3 March 2006.
[69] R. Casey briefing paper for J. Ruggie, *Meaningful Change: Raising the Bar in Supply Chain Workplace Standards*, at www.reports-and-materials.org/Ruggie-briefing-paper-for-Thailand-consultation-June-2006.pdf, p. 19.
[70] 'Sisco Merchandising', *Independent on Sunday*, 3 July 2005.

be most likely to provoke emotional reactions among western consumers, for instance child labour. Other issues, such as job security, get less attention. A number of reports have suggested that job security is available only to a minority of employees in supplier companies.[71] We have been given figures showing that on average 20–25 per cent of the workforce in a typical factory are lucky enough to have a stable contract. In some places the rate of turnover reaches 150 per cent. Most of the workers are employed on a temporary basis, without any benefits, receiving much less than the living wage that they need. Typically, most of those part-time or temporary workers often are not included on the checklist provided to the auditors. Among those also excluded from the official labour record are the armies of homeworkers who evidently have no prospect of benefiting from the rules of ethical trading.

In these early stages, then, CSR-oriented contractual control is limited in coverage. The question is whether the practice will expand or whether the factors driving it will remain, or be allowed to remain, limited in reach.

C. Towards real partnership?

Many scholars are sceptical about the use by business of the notion of partnership, seeing it as often more rhetoric than fact: 'It [partnership] is used as a political weapon. Partnerships are "good". So, many relationships have to be presented as "partnership", especially by the party that stands to gain most from it'.[72] 'Partnership' implies that parties cooperate on equal terms, but in the MNC–supplier relationship the symmetry of power is massively and visibly distorted. Decision-making is monopolised by the MNC, and the supplier has little bargaining power. It is not in a position to negotiate the level of standards that it can afford to take responsibility for, nor can it demand generous purchasing terms that would enable it to invest in the facilities and training that would bring about major CSR improvements or indeed greater efficiency.

Though MNCs invest in CSR management and audit, and contribute training and guidance, compliance cost is usually a matter for suppliers.[73] As the Marks & Spencer website makes clear: 'It is the supplier's

---

[71] Oxfam, 'Trading Away Our Rights', p. 19.
[72] Mary Huntington, 'Outsourcing: Perfecting Partnerships,' *Management Consultancy*, 10 January 1997, at www.managementconsultancy.co.uk/management-consultancy/features/2077255/outsourcing-perfecting-partnerships.
[73] Clean Clothes Campaign, 'Looking for a Quick Fix', p. 90.

responsibility to achieve and maintain these standards.'[74] These expenses can sometimes include substantial expenditure if the work involves projects like renovating buildings, buying new machinery or increasing wages. Some suppliers have initiated the auditing of their own premises and procedures in order to obtain the requisite certification, partly as a response to the expense of having to deal with as many different audits as they have purchasers, but then they have to pay themselves both the auditing bill and any consequential bill for repair or upgrading. Even when purchasing companies do the auditing in-house, additional expenses are commonly imposed on the supplier, as may be spelt out indeed in the terms and conditions of the contract: 'In the event of the need for independent interpreters to be used as part of this process, then the Suppliers will be required to provide funding to cover the cost of their engagement and any expenses associated with their travel and accommodation.'

It is clear that for some suppliers the expenses of facing a full-scale audit and then having to act on the recommendations are too high for their resources. A report from TraidCraft on whether CSR makes any difference suggests that in many cases when a code of conduct is applied as an additional standard, compliance with it has led to workers finding themselves in an even more insecure situation.[75]

The degree of choice that suppliers are left within such a partnership was spelled out by one of our interviewees: 'These suppliers don't have to deal with us. I mean, if they want to do business with us they know the basic requirements that they have to meet. And it is on that understanding that we enter into business with them; they don't have to reach that agreement and they don't have to work with us.' In practice, some small suppliers are being pushed out of business, while others, as we have seen, have developed sophisticated schemes of evasion. Only a very few of the bigger suppliers are able to put the required improvements into place, engage in genuinely transparent auditing and then exercise some real bargaining power with the retailer.

But even in an ideal version of a partnership, where a company is willing to harmonise its commercial interest to the capacity of the supplier and to help it to extend that capacity, and where on the other hand the

[74] Marks & Spencer, 'Global Sourcing Principles' (August 2005), p. 2, at www2. marksandspencer.com/thecompany/ourcommitmenttosociety/suppliers/supplier_global. shtml.

[75] TraidCraft, 'Corporate Social Responsibility – Does It Make Any Difference?', *Fair Trade Tool Kit* (London, October 2004), p. 2, at www.traidcraft.co.uk/template2.asp?pageID = 1510&fromID = 1503.

supplier is making sincere efforts to improve working conditions and comply with the codes, one should bear in mind that partnership requires investment in terms of both time and money, and that it works only if it is a long-term and exclusive relationship.[76] This description of the ideal model fits only a part of the *western* retail industry, which means that a partnership relationship cannot be possible in a substantial proportion of the industry's outsourcing agreements, which are short-term, one-off and seasonal. The ideal model also conflicts with the very nature of the global market. Globalised trade is in a state of constant flux, with corporations required by the system to be ready to switch not just product lines and factories but whole markets and countries, just for a small price cut.

There is growing evidence that even though companies are pressuring suppliers to bear the potential costs of CSR, they are at the same time reluctant to review their own purchasing practices – even though those practices are a major contributor to the poor labour conditions often found in the supply chains, and indeed often lead to the flouting of both codes and laws.[77] Many NGOs have pressed this home and The Ethical Trade Initiative has taken up the issue with business.[78] Indeed, business, or at least key players in business, are beginning to acknowledge this too. Nike convened a task force chaired by its CEO to look at its own role in non-compliance on the part of suppliers, and found half of the instances of serious non-compliance could be traced back to its own demands: flexible production, fast turnaround, surge orders, changed orders, and the like. For example:

> Terms of the standard supply agreement generally specify that the factory pays the air freight if the factory cannot make delivery by a certain date; when orders arrive late, factories will choose to work more hours rather than be burdened by the obligation to pay a costly air freight bill. The push to meet production goals within the time constraints directly lead to compliance issues and abuse of workforce rights.[79]

---

[76] Some authors point out a danger for collusion in any lasting relationship. See F. L. Jeffries and R. Reed, 'Trust and Adaptation in Relational Contracting', *The Academy of Management Review* 25, 4 (2000), 876–7.

[77] Insight Investment and Acona Ltd., 'Buying your Way into Trouble? The Challenge of Responsible Supply Chain Management' (2004); TraidCraft, 'Buying Matters. Consultation: Sourcing fairly from developing countries' (2006), p. 3.

[78] 'Bridging the gap between commercial and ethical trade agendas: Pioneering approach to purchasing practices', *ETI Briefing Paper No. 5*, ETI Biennial Conference (12–13 May 2005).

[79] R. Casey briefing paper for J. Ruggie, *Meaningful Change*, p. 24.

The purchase terms lead to conflict with the CSR terms of the contract. Reporting on such issues, Special UN Representative for Business and Human Rights John Ruggie concluded: 'Capacity building in the supply chain is desirable and necessary, but it won't take care of the brand-induced problems.'[80]

What all of this suggests is the need for the partnership model to become more genuinely collaborative, with MNCs recognising the need to revise their procurement policies as part of their CSR policy on supply, rather than simply expect, even with their support in other ways, a one-sided raising of standards on the part of suppliers.

A more genuinely two-way partnership could help in other ways. Suppliers are not usually invited to be part of the process of designing the objectives of the CSR policy, which therefore tend to be geared to the moral expectations of western customers rather than local needs. Research among supply factory employees frequently indicates that the priorities of the local workers are different from those outlined in CSR codes. For instance, two urgent needs from the perspective of the workers – who are predominantly women in many outsourced industries – are the provision of safe transportation home and the guarantee of getting a job back again after a break in employment forced by pregnancy. Neither issue is commonly found in the social audit list of MNCs.[81]

More input from suppliers could help smooth out the kind of moral and cultural clashes we have already noted. Research for the United Nations has suggested that 'most examples of unsuccessful remediation attempts stem from a lack of ability to create a business case using specific local circumstances. Without a business case that is culturally and socially acceptable, there may be compliance but there will not be long term sustainable change, nor will there be meaningful integration of standards and best practices'.[82]

Finally, more partnership could also help stimulate local 'ownership' of issues, allowing the possibility of CSR developing as an integrally embedded rather than an externally imposed concept.

---

[80] J. Ruggie, remarks delivered at CSR forum, Germany, at www.fairlabor.org/all/resources/NRO_Ger06/Ruggie_keynote.pdf.

[81] See R. Pearson and Gill Seyfang, 'New Hope or False Dawn?: Voluntary Codes of Conduct, Labour Regulation and Social Policy in a Globalized World', *Global Social Policy* 1, 1 (2001), 49–78; and see TraidCraft, 'Corporate Social Responsibility', p. 2.

[82] R. Casey briefing paper for J. Ruggie, *Meaningful change*, p. 38.

D. A macro perspective

This latter point may have relevance at macro level too. All engagement in social policy, whether public or private in source, has to be aware of potential impact on the wider social and economic situation, for good or ill, particularly from the perspective of developing countries, where so much of the focus of contractual control currently is, and where so much of the advantage is hoped for.

As private law, contractual control necessarily has limited targets, being relevant only to the factories that work with multinationals and are exporting goods. Other people working in local markets do not benefit from the improvements that CSR might bring. Ironically, the more effective CSR through contractual control becomes, the more likely it is to create a new dimension of inequality in societies that typically already suffer from far too much of it. Consciousness of the gap between the continuing poor and the newly better-off could be socially disruptive.

It has also been suggested that the private, foreign and corporate nature of contractual control could be seen as underlining the failure of government to raise standards and undermining its authority, or as distracting attention from, and diminishing, the role of both governments and labour movements, so actually serving as a barrier to sustainable 'home-grown' change.[83]

IV. Conclusion

CSR through private 'other-regulation' is in its early stages and it is hardly surprising to find limited coverage to date and limitations in its operation. But the strategy of implementing CSR through contractual control does have a valuable role to play.

Despite its patchy impact so far, it is generally accepted in the literature, even by NGOs well aware of its limitations, that it has achieved positive results. On the issue of labour conditions where attention has particularly focused, CSR supply policy has improved working conditions in supply factories and raised awareness among workers of their rights and entitlements, and there is some anticipation that it may help trigger more fundamental, if slow, cultural changes in the treatment of

[83] A. Cramer, P. Pruzan-Jorgensen, H. Jorgensen and M. Jungk, 'Strengthening Implementation of Corporate Social Responsibility in Global Supply Chains' (Washington, DC: World Bank Group Social Responsibility Practice, 2003).

ordinary people in the workplace.[84] Though the focus is still largely on labour conditions and some environmental issues, the establishment of the principle of contractual control opens the way to influence on a wider CSR agenda.

The conceptual focus in contractual control on CSR *in supply*, rather than just in developing countries, has opened a new avenue for calling for action too on conditions in the west, with NGOs now drawing attention to the fact that numerous code violations occur there as well – that sweatshops and homeworking also exist in MNCs' own backyards, that 'British homeworkers' are part of 'global supply chains' too: 'We tend to think that all of these horror stories happen in Asia; the reality is that right under our noses, there's some of the worst exploitation.'[85]

The uneven impact to date of contractual control, and the necessarily patchy effect of any private control mechanism, may suggest that either a more profound evolution of the business case for CSR will be necessary for this mechanism to have wide effect, or that it can be no substitute for forms of control more universal in their application (in theory at least) – business-wide standards or state regulation. Business itself recognises that 'progress will only happen once a critical mass of participation is achieved', and the learning experience of contractual control is in fact proving a jumping-off point for more collective business initiatives.[86] But it is important to remember that there are many collective initiatives in progress which seem to still leave much work to be done, and though government control might be ideal, while it is absent or simply – and inevitably – imperfect, private controls have their part to play too.

Contractual control will also evolve, as companies compete on ethical branding, and as pressure mounts. CSR through contractual control is a response to critique, and CSR critique inevitably evolves with the response to it. Many of the limits noted here will become the new agenda for further pressure and potentially for further change. Indeed, contractual control should be seen as an expression not just of private control *by* MNCs, but of private control *of* MNCs by market and social forces. Contractual control

---

[84] Jason Clay (Principal Author), *Exploring the Link Between International Business and Poverty Reduction: A Case Study of Unilever in Indonesia* (Eynsham, UK: Information Press, 2005), report commissioned by Oxfam GB, Novib Oxfam Netherlands and Unilever.

[85] Bas Norris, National Union of Knitwear, Footwear and Apparel Trades (KFAT), quoted in *Made at home*, Oxfam Briefing Paper 63 (May 2004), p. 1.

[86] R. Casey briefing paper for J. Ruggie, *Meaningful Change*, p. 28.

is voluntary use of private law by MNCs, but it is also a response to external demands that they take responsibility for improving poor working and environmental standards rather than simply, as has traditionally been the case, take advantage of them. The question is whether MNCs will prove willing to exercise that responsibility by reviewing their commercial and production demands in order to make it possible for their CSR demands to be met.

3

Corporate social responsibility and public procurement

CHRISTOPHER MCCRUDDEN

Public procurement (the purchase by public bodies of goods and services from others) has proven to be a dedicated follower of political fashion. Historically, we see consistent attempts to link public procurement with the government policy of the day, in areas as diverse as national industrial policy, reducing unemployment, improving employment conditions, support for small businesses, local development, employment of disabled workers and equal pay for men and women, to mention only a few.[1] With the increasing popularity of 'corporate social responsibility', it is hardly surprising, then, that corporate social responsibility (CSR) has become linked to the use of public procurement. This chapter considers the 'new' use of public procurement in the pursuit of CSR in the European context, but considers in particular the relationship between CSR, public procurement *and the law*.

I. Old wine in new bottles?

Is the role of public procurement in CSR something new, or simply a new label for an old phenomenon? In another context, I have sketched out the historical development of the use of public procurement for social policy purposes, tracing its origins to the nineteenth century.[2] I argued that public procurement is an extraordinarily adaptable tool, which has often been used to meet a regulatory need when other methods of regulation are not considered acceptable, available or effective. In the CSR context, a similar development appears to be happening: governments often seem to be unwilling to regulate business using traditional command and control

---

[1] A book-length study of these uses of public procurement by the author, from which this chapter draws extensively, is Christopher McCrudden, *Buying Social Justice* (Oxford: Oxford University Press, 2007).

[2] Christopher McCrudden, 'Using Public Procurement to Achieve Social Outcomes', *Natural Resources Forum* 28 (2004), 257–67.

regulation.[3] Procurement appears to be among a group of useful alternative regulatory mechanisms. The use of public procurement to deliver CSR may also be seen as simply old wine in new bottles in another respect: the content of the CSR principles that are 'enforced' by public procurement echoes the content of many of the social linkages over the past 200 years. Many issues frequently linked to CSR now have all been linked to public procurement in the past, without using the CSR banner. Not surprisingly, those interest groups that were previously identified with the use of procurement to achieve these social goals, such as trade unions, jumped on the CSR bandwagon.

However, in at least two respects, the development of CSR has markedly expanded the types of policies that are now commonly linked to public procurement: in increasing the role of public procurement in addressing environmental issues, and in increasing the role of public procurement in addressing social conditions in other countries. We now see, increasingly, issues such as fair trade, reducing the use of child labour and sustainable development featuring on the public procurement agenda. Increasingly, as CSR became more and more associated with sustainable development, so too did public procurement, leading to the development of the concept of sustainable procurement, for example. CSR did not generate these as policy issues, of course, but it provided a useful label by which these issues could be addressed. In another respect, linking CSR to procurement may be different than linkage has been in the past, in indicating that a significant shift of governance may be under way, at least in some countries.

One important driver for the introduction of CSR requirements into public procurement is the desire to narrow the gap between aspiration and practice by firms: procurement came to be seen by some governments as a method of providing (market-based) incentives to firms to adopt and fulfil CSR obligations, by linking these obligations with access to government contracts.[4] Public procurement becomes one of a range of initiatives, a 'portfolio approach',[5] in which different initiatives support

---

[3] For a discussion of the failure to pass legislation in Australia, the United States and the United Kingdom to enforce standards of good practice for multinational enterprises based in those countries in respect of their overseas operations, see Adam McBeth, 'A Look at Corporate Code of Conduct Legislation,' *Common Law World Review* 33, 3 (2004), 222–54.

[4] For example, 'Promoting Global Corporate Social Responsibility: The Kenan Institute Study Group Consensus' (September 2003) recommended the use of US government procurement policies as tools to promote global CSR; at www.iccr.org/news/press_releases/pdf%20files/recommendations_rpt.pdf.

[5] Simon Zadek, Sanjiv Lingayah and Maya Forstater, 'Social Labels: Tools for Ethical Trade: Final Report' (European Commission, 1998), pp. 10, 58, 75.

each other.[6] At the international level, this approach is usefully illustrated by the incorporation of public procurement as an element for achieving compliance with the draft Norms on the Responsibility of Transnational Corporations and Business Enterprises with Regard to Human Rights.[7]

Governments stand to gain if business adopts CSR principles.[8] Matten and Moon, for example, have argued that CSR 'encourage[s] companies to assume more responsibilities as most welfare states in Europe are increasingly facing limits to their ability to tackle social issues in the way they traditionally did'.[9] If welfare states (particularly in Europe) are in decline, then there will be pressure from governments and others on business to fill the gap of welfare provision. It is therefore in the interests of government that the CSR project is not seen to fail.

II. Public procurement as equivalent to private procurement

Although an important context, the relationship between public procurement and CSR cannot *only* be seen as a compliance gap-filling measure. The relationship between procurement and CSR is more complex than this suggests.

We need to step back a little and look at the relationship between procurement and CSR more broadly. Increasingly, the distinction between public and private in general, and public procurement and private procurement in particular, is becoming blurred. There are several aspects to these developments. First, with the advent of privatisation and contracting out, functions that would traditionally have been carried out by government are now increasingly carried out, under contract, by the private sector. This has led to an argument that when this happens, some of the 'public-sector ethos' should carry over to the private sector. This is,

---

[6] David Hess 'Corporate Social Responsibility and the Law', in José Allouche (ed.), *Corporate Social Responsibility*, vol. I (Basingstoke: Palgrave Macmillan, 2006), p. 173. Compare Olivier de Schutter, 'The Accountability of Multinationals for Human Rights Violations in European Law' in Philip Alston (ed.), *Non-state Actors and Human Rights* (Oxford: Oxford University Press, 2005), p. 227.

[7] See David Weissbrodt and Maria Kruger, 'Norms on the Responsibilities of Transnational Corporations and Business Enterprises with Regard to Human Rights', *American Journal of International Law*, 97 (2003) 901, n. 108.

[8] Moon has argued that there are three reasons for government to encourage CSR: 'it can substitute for government effort; it can complement government effort; and it can legitimise government policies'. J. Moon, 'Government as a Driver of Corporate Social Responsibility', ICCSR Research Paper Series No. 20-2004, 2004, p. 2.

[9] Dirk Matten and Jeremy Moon, '"Implicit" and "Explicit" CSR: A conceptual framework for understanding CSR in Europe', ICCSR Research Paper Series No. 29-2004, 2004, p. 24.

perhaps, most strikingly the case in the context of utilities privatisation, where the argument is that certain 'public' values should be transferred over to the private providers.[10] More generally, the 'growth of CSR activity in the 1990s occurred in response to widespread concerns about increases in corporate power through privatization and globalization'.[11] Second, with increasingly tight public-sector budgets and the increasing emphasis on efficiency and 'value for money', public bodies were urged (in some cases required) to become more like the private sector. Private-sector values, ethos and management styles were increasingly incorporated into public-sector management. This was strikingly so in several countries with regard to public procurement activities, contributing to the dramatic extent of reform in the management of public procurement in developed countries over the past twenty years.

Private-sector firms increasingly incorporate CSR principles into private procurement.[12] If private-sector firms do so, why should public-sector bodies not also? After all, shouldn't the public sector become more like the private sector? CSR suggests to the private sector that business should go beyond purely economic considerations, and go beyond strictly legal obligations, appreciating the social and environmental externalities involved in its operations, including its supply chain. Incorporation of social and environmental concerns into *public* procurement appears to involve a similar acceptance of responsibility by government. Are government service providers to be viewed as public corporations that comply with the law, including those pertaining to the environment and workplace practices, but do not normally go beyond it?[13] If so, there would be no justification for incurring additional costs to purchase goods and services that meet environmental or social criteria beyond what laws and regulations require. The assumption underlying this model is that the citizenry, or its elected representatives, have already embodied their social and environmental preferences in existing legislation. If they now expect even better performance, whether of the public sector or the private sector, they will change that legislation.

In contrast with this model, however, are government service providers to be viewed as having a broader mandate, including safeguarding the

---

[10] See Christopher McCrudden, 'Social Policy and Economic Regulators: Some Issues for the Reform of Utility Regulation', in Christopher McCrudden (ed.), *Regulation and Deregulation: Policy and Practice* (Oxford: Oxford University Press, 1998), pp. 275–94.

[11] Allouche (ed.), *Corporate Social Responsibility*, p. xxiv.

[12] McBarnet and Kurkchiyan, Chapter 2 in this volume.

[13] This paragraph draws substantially on comments by David O'Connor, Third Expert Meeting on Sustainable Public Procurement, United Nations Headquarters, New York, USA, 14–17 June 2005.

environment and the social fabric, protecting the interests of vulnerable members of society and of future generations? On this view, government is a social welfare optimiser, seeking to internalise in its policies and practices all relevant externalities. This calls for a more activist role of government with respect to its procurement decisions. The sheer size of the public procurement market, for example, might be used to encourage the development of 'green' products at an affordable price for the general market, simply by guaranteeing a sufficient number of public purchases to create viability. For example, 'Japan has successfully used green procurement of low emission cars to stimulate technological innovation in the motor industry'.[14] Efforts such as these contributed to the adoption by the OECD Council of a recommendation advocating green public procurement.[15] From this viewpoint, public bodies have CSR responsibilities themselves as purchasers, and public procurement is not just a mechanism for ensuring compliance by others with their CSR responsibilities but an important element in how the public sector can satisfy its own CSR responsibilities.[16]

III. Responsible public procurement as 'leading by example'

The more we equate public bodies with private firms, the more similarities appear. If we equate the relationship between private firms and their consumers with the relationship between public bodies and their citizens, it would be strange indeed if public bodies did not react similarly. Indeed, some see the role of government as being in part to represent the collective preferences of citizens. The inclusion of social and environmental conditions should not only be seen as about the consequences of procurement decisions and the leverage those consequences give us on policy. A common intuition, surely, runs rather this way: when the government buys purchases, it acts in the name of its citizens and ought to uphold certain standards. 'We' do not want 'our' public goods purchased from companies that discriminate or pollute because it is sordid, it would dirty our hands, and not (only) because we are hoping to use government spending to alter the social landscape.[17]

---

[14] Roger Cowe and Jonathon Porritt, *Government's Business: Enabling corporate sustainability* (London: Forum for the Future, 2002), p. 33.

[15] OECD Press Release, 23 January 2002, at www.oecd.org.

[16] This is the message, for example, of such studies as Lisa Mastny, 'Purchasing Power: Harnessing Institutional Procurement for People and the Planet', Worldwatch Paper 166 (July 2003).

[17] Don Herzog, personal communication.

Private-sector procurement, as we have seen, increasingly engages with CSR. Government increasingly encourages the private sector to ensure that its supply chains are in CSR compliance. Governments also act to facilitate such initiatives.[18] The British government, for example, supported the creation of the Ethical Trading Initiative, which brings together companies, non-governmental organizations (NGOs) and trade unions in order to help purchasers to secure goods that are produced in conditions in developing countries that meet environmental and social standards. Not surprisingly, the result of this is also to shine a spotlight on the procurement practices of those bodies that advocated that firms should use their procurement operations in this way.[19] A prominent example was the reaction of some NGOs to the UN launch of the Global Compact. Did the United Nations itself comply with the principles of the Global Compact in its procurement practices? When the answer was 'not yet', a degree of embarrassment was apparent.[20] Governments, in other words, operate both as regulators of the market and also as participants in the market. When principles they espouse in the former are not applied in the latter, the government appears to lack coordination, or appears to be simply hypocritical. An important driver, then, for the incorporation of CSR standards in public procurement is the need to be seen to be leading by example:[21] if government expected firms to ensure that their supply chains are clean, then the least government can do is to ensure that its own house is in order too.

[18] Thomas Loew, Kathrin Ankele, Sabine Braun and Jens Clausen, 'Significance of the CSR debate for sustainability and the requirements for companies: Summary', p. 8 (example of the German federal government's encouragement of codes of practice in private-sector procurement).

[19] See, for example, Cowe and Porritt, *Government's Business*, p. 46 (where the British Government is encouraged to apply the same standards in its procurement as it is commending to others.); 'EU Accused of Using Illegally Logged Timber', at www.tendersdirect.co.uk, in which Greenpeace alleged that illegal timber was being used in new EU buildings in Brussels: 'If true, the allegations would be an acute embarrassment for the EU. Last year the Commission launched its own action plan to combat illegal logging and the trade in illegal timber.'

[20] 'Role of UN Global Compact, Human Rights and Business Matters', Spring/Summer 2001, including the correspondence between Kenneth Roth, Executive Director of Human Rights Watch, and John G. Ruggie, Assistant Secretary General, at www.amnesty.org.uk/business; Peter Utting, 'The Global Compact and Civil Society: Averting a Collision Course', *UNRISD News* 25. For subsequent developments, see 'Report on the Third Expert Meeting on Sustainable Public Procurement', United Nations Headquarters, New York, USA, 15–17 July 2005.

[21] Cowe and Porritt, *Government's Business*, p. 32; Gianni Zappalà, 'Corporate Citizenship and the Role of Government: the Public Policy Case, Information and Research Services', Department of the Parliamentary Library Research Paper No. 4 (Canberra, 2003), pp. 2, 17.

IV. European Community and CSR in procurement

The development of the EC approach to the relationship between CSR and procurement illustrates several of these points. The movement for corporate social responsibility was actively pursued in several member states during the 1990s. This included, in some states, the use of public procurement in this context.[22] However, CSR was relatively slow in being recognised and incorporated into EC policy.[23] The European Community's framework for CSR began to be developed soon after the Lisbon Council appealed to companies' sense of social responsibility in March 2000. A Green Paper was published by the Commission in 2001, and a Communication followed in 2002. This established the EU Multi-Stakeholder Forum on CSR, which deliberated and published a report in 2004. In 2006 the Commission published a further Communication on CSR. In the Community context, CSR includes promoting responsible production, promoting responsible consumption, promoting the transparency and credibility of CSR practices and promoting responsible investment.

There were two linked aspects to the idea of corporate responsibility as it developed at the European level. One related to the practices of European enterprises operating outside the European Community, particularly in developing countries. A second related to the activities of enterprises operating within the European Community. In both, though to somewhat differing degrees, whether to use public procurement was an element of the debate. In 1999 the Parliament adopted a resolution on EC standards for European enterprises operating in developing countries.[24] The principal element of the wide-ranging Resolution was a request to the Commission and the Council to make proposals 'to develop the right legal basis for establishing a European multilateral framework governing

---

[22] See, e.g., Anders Rosdahl, 'The Policy to Promote Social Responsibility of Enterprises in Denmark' (September, 2001), p. 9, paper prepared for the European Commission-DG EMPL Peer Review Programme.

[23] For discussion of earlier initiatives at the EC level, see, S. MacLeod and D. Lewis 'Transnational Corporations: Power, Influence and Responsibility', *Global Social Policy*, 4, 1 (2004) 77, 85.

[24] The European Parliament had a long history of prior involvement in this issue. For example, its Resolution on the Commission's Action Programme relating to the implementation of the Community Charter of Fundamental Social Rights for Workers, A3–175/90, 13 September 1990, insisted that in the trade agreements and cooperation treaties 'social clauses should be incorporated under which the contracting parties would undertake to abide by ILO standards' (para. 10), 'international treaties and conventions on working conditions and the rights of workers' (para. 22), and that they should also take 'environmental considerations into account and that penalties should be imposed for failure to comply with contractual arrangements' (para. 23).

companies' operations worldwide'.[25] Amongst the other actions the Resolution called on the Commission 'to bring forward proposals for a system of incentives for companies complying with international standards developed in close consultation and cooperation with consumer groups and human rights and environmental NGOs – such as in procurement, fiscal incentives, access to EC financial assistance and publication in the Official Journal'.[26] A 1999 Commission publication on codes of practice considered possible methods of making social labels more effective through public policy interventions. Among the methods listed were 'using public procurement in promoting labelled products'.[27]

It was really only in 2001, however, that the debate began in earnest at the EC level, with the publication of three important Communications for the Commission to the Parliament with relevance to the issue. Two, relating to the European Community's role in promoting human rights and democratisation in countries outside the Community,[28] and relating to the promotion of core labour standards and improving social governance in the context of globalisation,[29] did not mention procurement, but a third, presented the same day as the second, the Commission's Green Paper 'Promoting a European Framework for Corporate Responsibility',[30] responded to the Parliament's recommendations regarding procurement. The Green Paper was intended to launch a debate on the promotion of corporate social responsibility within the European Community. In the context of a discussion on social and environmental labelling, the Green Paper accepted that there is 'increasingly a need for a debate regarding the value and desirability – in the context of the Internal Market and international obligations – of public actions aimed at making social and eco labels more effective'.[31] The Commission gave several examples of such action, including 'use of public procurement and fiscal incentives in promoting labelled products'.[32]

---

[25] Resolution of the 15th January 1999, Code of conduct for European enterprises operating in developing countries, OJ No. C104/180, 14 April 1999, para. 11.

[26] Para. 28.

[27] Quoted in Colleen Hanley, 'Avoiding the Issue: The Commission and Human Rights Conditionality in Public Procurement', *European Law Review* 27 (2002), 714.

[28] European Commission, 'The European Union's Role in Promoting Human Rights and Democratisation in Third Countries', 8 May 2001, COM (2001) 252 final.

[29] European Commission, 'Promoting Core Labour Standards and Improving Social Governance in the Context of Globalisation', 17 July 2001, COM (2001) 416 final.

[30] European Commission, 'Promoting a European framework for Corporate Social Responsibility', 18 July 2001, COM (2001) 366 final.

[31] *ibid.*, para. 83.   [32] *ibid.*

The responses to the Green Paper varied considerably.[33] Lewis and MacLeod have, however, described 'the remarkable homogeneity between individual corporate responses as well as the responses of industry representatives'.[34] They characterise these as involving 'a definite emphasis on self-regulation, a lack of enthusiasm for enforcement mechanisms, temporization of implementation requirements, the voluntary nature of CSR, good practice and a general abhorrence of a "one-size fits all" approach to CSR'.[35] Although welcoming the Commission's initiative, the Council fired a warning shot, asking the Commission to 'query carefully the added value of any new action proposed at European level'.[36] The Committee of the Regions, however, in its response to the Green Paper, accepted 'that local and regional authorities can give a lead in relation to promoting good CSR practices by ensuring that their purchasing and procurement strategies are CSR compliant'.[37] The Parliament, perhaps unsurprisingly, took an even stronger position. A report from the Committee on Employment and Social Affairs[38] proposed a draft Resolution to be adopted by the Parliament which urged the Council to 'take into account the Parliament's position on the principle of corporate social responsibility in the directive on public procurement',[39] and called on the Commission to bring forward proposals:

> to promote the contribution of EU companies towards transparency and good governance world-wide, including through the setting up of a blacklist to prevent the tendering for public contracts by EU companies ... for non-compliance with minimum applicable international standards (ILO core labour standards, OECD guidelines for multinational companies); and to establish a compliance panel to ensure that companies awarded contracts in the context of EC public procurement ... comply with EU human rights obligations and development policies and procedures as well as minimum standards according to the ... ILO and OECD Guidelines in the execution of those contracts; companies on the blacklist would be ineligible for EU contracts or awards for a period of three years.[40]

---

[33] For a discussion, see Lewis and MacLeod, *Transnational Corporations*, p. 85.
[34] *ibid.*, p. 86.   [35] *ibid.*
[36] Council Resolution on the follow-up to the Green Paper on corporate social responsibility, OJ No. C86/3, 10 April 2002.
[37] Opinion of the Committee of the Regions on the Green Paper on Promoting a European Framework for Corporate Social Responsibility, OJ No. C192/1, 12 August 2002.
[38] 30 April 2002, A5-0159/2002.
[39] Para. 32, draft Resolution.   [40] Para. 59, draft Resolution.

The Parliamentary Resolution reflected these recommendations closely.[41]

The European Commission produced its Communication on corporate social responsibility in July 2002.[42] The Commission's treatment of procurement needs to be seen in the context of the developments in the procurement reform package. By the time of its response, the Commission had issued its Interpretative Communications on the possibilities for integrating social and environmental considerations into public procurement. As regards the integration of social considerations into the directives, the Commission was essentially unwilling to go beyond what it had said in these Communications. In the section dealing with external relations policy, however, the Commission was more forthcoming. Where:

> public support is provided to enterprises, this implies co-responsibility of the government in those activities. These activities should therefore comply with the OECD guidelines for multinational enterprises, and, inter alia, not involve bribery, pollution of the environment or child or forced labour. Making access to subsidies for international trade promotion, investment and export credit insurance, as well as access to public procurement, conditional on adherence to and compliance with the OECD guidelines for multinational enterprises, *while respecting EC international commitments*, could be considered by EU Member States and by other States adherent to the OECD Declaration on International Investment.[43]

In addition, the Commission announced its intention to 'integrate further social and environmental priorities within its management, including its own public procurement'.[44] The Council, in its Resolution responding to the Commission, whilst welcoming the general thrust of the Commission's approach, did not discuss procurement issues explicitly, and

[41] P5-TA(2002)0278, European Parliament Resolution on the Commission Green Paper on promoting a European framework for corporate social responsibility, paras. 28 and 54.

[42] European Commission, 'Corporate Social Responsibility: A business contribution to Sustainable Development', 2 July 2002, COM (2002) 347 final.

[43] *ibid.*, para. 7.6. The reference to respecting international commitments presumably refers to the WTO Government Procurement Agreement, *inter alia*.

[44] *ibid.*, para. 7.7. As regards the formal legislative provisions governing Commission procurement, however, the Commission took the position that they should reflect the procurement directives and that any changes in the existing Regulations (Commission Regulation (EC, Euratom) No. 2342/2002 of 23 December 2002 laying down detailed rules for the implementation of Council Regulation (EC, Euratom) No. 1605/2002 on the Financial Regulation applicable to the general budget of the European Communities, OJ No. L357/1, 31 December 2002) should wait the completion of the legislative package, discussed in Chapter 4 in this volume.

restricted itself to supporting 'the intentions of the Commission, in par-ticular to focus its strategy on . . . integrating CSR into Community poli-cies', and calling on the member states 'to integrate, where appropriate, CSR principles into their own management'.[45]

V. Opposition to corporate social responsibility in European public procurement

It would be misleading to suppose that attempts to use public procure-ment for CSR purposes are unopposed. There are two, rather different, objections. The first arises more specifically in the context of CSR. The use of public procurement has led to objections that CSR should, as we shall see from the European Commission's definition, be 'voluntary'.[46] 'Voluntary' in this context does not necessarily mean 'motivated by phi-lanthropy' but rather that it should not be legally required.

The second objection is based on a general objection to the use of procurement for social policy purposes. This objection derives from a concern that the adverse effects of such linkages outweigh any good that may come of them. Common general objections are: that such linkage increases the costs of procurement; that linkage leads to a reduction in the transparency of the procurement process; that linkage leads to greater bureaucratisation of procurement; or that it increases the opportunity for corruption. In the EC context, a particular concern, given that one of the primary functions of the organisation is to reduce barriers to the creation of a vibrant internal market, is that such linkages increase the opportunity for, or have the effect of, reducing competition. To the extent that government addresses these problems, there may well come a time where there is seen to be a tension between achieving these goals, and using public procurement to achieve CSR.

One of the main features of the Commission's proposals was the estab-lishment of a European Multi-Stakeholder Forum to include social part-ners, business networks, consumers and investors to exchange best prac-tice, to establish principles for codes of conduct and to seek consensus on evaluation methods and tools such as social labels. These issues came to the fore in this Forum, hosted by the European Commission between 2002 and 2004, which provided an important context in which the various

---

[45] Council resolution of 6 February 2003 on corporate social responsibility, OJ No. C39/3, 18 February 2003.
[46] See also in Voiculescu, Chapter 12 in this volume.

interested groups (such as representatives of business, trade unions and NGOs) could discuss future European CSR policy, and help to shape the Commission's future approach.[47] As regards the use of public procurement to encourage business to adopt CSR, it quickly emerged that the representatives of business were adamantly opposed, whereas the trade unions and NGOs were in favour. The three 'Round Tables' in which discussions took place could simply report the disagreement. In the Round Table on the diversity, convergence and transparency of CSR Practices and Tools, '[i]t was suggested by NGOs and trade unions that public authorities could play a number of roles in driving CSR and related activities, through actions in the areas of procurement policies, export credit schemes, trade policies and eligibility for subsidies and taxes'. Business and employer organisations, however, 'stressed the view that linking public policy or funding sources with CSR could have damaging consequences for SMEs, could distort competition and would involve disregarding the voluntary nature of CSR'.[48] In the Round Table on fostering CSR among SMEs, participants 'had fundamentally different views on the issue'. Some supported further analysis, 'looking particularly at how SMEs might benefit from calls for tender with social and environmental criteria', whilst others 'argued that the practical problems of introducing . . . social and environmental criteria into public procurement (particularly if those are built on what is accepted as voluntary practice) are too great'.[49] The emphasis on CSR being voluntary was also stressed during the course of the third Round Table, as well as the argument that it 'would amount to discrimination against other bidders'.[50] In light of this, it was not surprising that the Final Report of the Forum merely recorded disagreement on the issue and set out the arguments for and against. Given the extent to which the Commission had committed itself to going forward with CSR initiatives on the basis of a voluntary approach, it was not surprising that mention of public procurement was entirely absent from the 2006 Commission Communication on CSR, much to the disappointment of trade unions and NGOs.[51]

---

[47] Michel Capron, 'Forum plurilatéral européen sur la RSE: la raison d'une déconvenue', available at www.lux-ias.lu/PDF/Capron.pdf.

[48] Round Table on 'The diversity, convergence and transparency of CSR Practices and Tools', Final Report (2004), para. 3.5.

[49] Round Table on 'Fostering CSR among SMEs', Final Version (3 May 2004), para. 3.1

[50] Round Table on 'Improving Knowledge about CSR and Facilitating the Exchange of Experience and Good Practice', Final Version (29 April 2004), p. 12.

[51] See European Parliament Socialist Group statement.

VI. Corporate social responsibility and procurement:
European legal issues

A third objection to the use of public procurement for CSR purposes related to the legality of such uses. In Europe, in addition to national legal provisions governing public procurement, there are two additional sets of legal requirements: those arising under EC law (in particular, but not exclusively, arising from a series of Directives on public procurement that began in the 1970s), and those arising under international law (in particular, but not exclusively, arising from the World Trade Organisation (WTO) Government Procurement Agreement). The complexity of these provisions, and the uncertainty as to whether particular linkages were permissible, acted as a constraint on risk-averse public authorities adopting procurement-linkages for CSR purposes.[52]

In practice, the most effective single intervention of the Community in advancing the use of public procurement for CSR purposes was the attempted clarification of the legal position under EC law. If there were a risk of being sued, some public authorities would prefer not to act. Indeed, for the Commission, the clarification of the legal position was identified as part of the Commission's strategy for encouraging CSR, as it meant removing an existing barrier to the further adoption of CSR policies in the member states.[53] The Community had a role to play, therefore, if only in improving legal clarity.

This strategy had two aspects. First, the Commission produced Interpretative Communications of the existing Directives. In 2001, the Commission published an Interpretative Communication that set out the Commission's view on the use of public procurement for environmental purposes. In October 2001, an equivalent Communication was published relating to the pursuit of social policy in public procurement. Second, the Community was pursuing a general legislative reform of these Directives. In the context of the use of procurement linkages for social and environmental purposes, the Commission's primary strategy was to resist incorporating any requirements to pursue social or environmental policies into

---

[52] See, e.g., finding of a survey into determinants of green public procurement, Luke Brander and Xander Olsthoorn, 'Three scenarios for Green Public Procurement', December 2002, Institute for Environmental Studies, Vrije Universiteit, The Netherlands, at p. 20ff. See also Janet Morgan and Jan Niessen, 'Immigrant and Minority Businesses: Making the Policy Case', *European Journal of Migration and Law* 4, 329 (2003) at 332, 334.

[53] 'Report on the Expert Meeting on Sustainable Public Procurement Copenhagen', Denmark, 2–3 December 2002, at www.un.org/esa/sustdev/sdissues/consumption/SPP-Report-rev.pdf, European Commission view by Herbert Aichinger.

EC procurement law, and to argue that the Commission's interpretative communications brought sufficient clarity into the interpretation of the existing Directives to justify little substantive change from these Directives in the new Directives. The Commission succeeded to some extent, fending off many amendments, supported by trade unions, NGOs and the European Parliament, that would have required member states to include environmental or social criteria in their public procurement, but accepting the inclusion of substantial numbers of 'recitals' at the beginning of the new Directives incorporating various of the clarifications originally set out in the interpretative Communications, and introducing some change into the drafting of the substantive provisions of the new Directives.[54]

The result of the process, taken as a whole, was to leave substantial amounts of discretion to the member states, and to the public authorities in the member states, to decide whether to include CSR policies in public procurement. NGO activity then shifted to the member states, since the new Directives had to be incorporated into domestic law in each member state, thus providing an ideal opportunity for public pressure to be brought to bear. The result was a blossoming of activism around the issue of social and environmental standards in national procurement practices, and the development of significant levels of activity in these areas. From the point of view of the Commission, this aspect of their CSR strategy largely worked. 'Clarifying the law' meant that the issue was put on national agendas.

Clarifying the law is a continuing issue, however, for the Commission. The very scope of the CSR agenda means that legal issues will continue to require clarification. A brief and partial list must suffice: the impact of the EC state aid rules on procurement linkages; the extent to which issues relating to employment conditions are permissible under the new Directives; the legality of attempts to promote gender and racial equality issues using public procurement; issues relating to the new directives' provisions on sheltered workshops and access to disabled users; the legality of SME-development policies; the permissibility of incorporating 'sustainable development' in public purchasing; the relationship between procuring renewable energy and the directives; the use of eco-labels and

---

[54] See, e.g., Sue Arrowsmith, 'An Assessment of the New Legislative Package on Public Procurement', *Common Market Law Review* 41 (2004), 1–49; Christopher H. Bovis, 'Public Procurement in the European Union: Lessons from the Past and Insights to the Future', *Columbia Journal of European Law* 12, 1 (2005), 53; Joël Arnould, 'Secondary Policies in Public Procurement: The Innovations of the New Directives', *Public Procurement Law Review* 4 (2004), 30.

environmental management schemes under the new directives; the extent to which CSR impacts differently on procurement in the utilities sector; the impact of the EC procurement directives on 'fair trade' issues. Partial attempts, mostly in the context of green procurement, have been made to address some of these legal issues. A Handbook on Green Public Procurement was published in August 2004 giving further explanations and best practice examples.[55]

VII. Corporate social responsibility, procurement and the 'soft power' of the Commission

The other element in the strategy of the Commission that links CSR with public procurement is the use of the Commission's ability to muster 'soft power'[56] – through the provision of information, and the attempt to guide the production of better coordinated standards, in the hope that public bodies will see the adoption of public procurement as a method of ensuring compliance in particular circumstances. This strategy has, in particular, attempted to address the problem of the more permissive regime that emerged out of the legal strategy: the proliferation of different standards and requirements that any particular firm may be subject to. Anna Diamantopoulou, when she was Commissioner responsible for Employment and Social Affairs in the European Commission, argued that the plethora of different standards applicable to CSR, not least in the public procurement context, 'carries the risk of "accidental" new barriers to trade in the EU's internal market'.[57]

Good examples of this approach in practice are to be found in the development of approaches to linking public procurement with policies for green public procurement and policies for disabled workers. As regards green procurement, there have been several interlinking elements

---

[55] SEC(2004/1050).

[56] Joseph S. Nye, Jr, *Soft Power: The Means to Success in World Politics* (New York: Public Affairs, 2004).

[57] Anna Diamantopoulou, Commissioner responsible for Employment and Social Affairs, European Commission, 'The role of public policies in promoting CSR', Address at the Presidency Conference on Corporate Social Responsibility, Venice, 2003, p. 6. See also 'Can Procurement be used to promote equality? Lessons from experiences at home and abroad', Summary note of EDF Seminar Series, 2 March 2006. See also David O'Connor's identification of 'the risk of proliferation of sustainable procurement criteria and the need for harmonization across jurisdictions', Report on the Third Expert Meeting on Sustainable Public Procurement, United Nations Headquarters, New York, USA, 15–17 July 2005.

to the strategy, in addition to clarifying the law.[58] The Commission has encouraged member states to draw up publicly available action plans for greening their public procurement.[59] The review of the Lisbon Strategy in 2004 again stressed the need for national and local authorities to set up action plans for greening public procurement by the end of 2006.[60] In January 2005, the Commission urged that such plans should establish objectives and benchmarks for enhancing green public procurement as well as guidance and tools for public procurers.[61] The Commission has also worked with other groups (such as the International Council for Local Environmental Initiatives (ICLEI) and Eurocities) to spread and clarify the message. For example, Local Environmental Management Systems and Procurement (LEAP) is a project co-funded by the European Commission and ICLEI that aims to provide a series of practical tools for assisting public authorities in implementing sustainable procurement and its integration with existing environmental management systems.[62] The Commission has also established an environmental database containing basic environmental information, referring to national and EU eco-labels where appropriate.[63]

As regards the use of procurement for meeting the needs of those who are disabled, the Commission has supported the establishment of a Pilot Project ('Build for All') to mainstream disability policies, in particular promoting accessibility to the built environment. The Commission had established an Expert Group on Full Accessibility, which delivered its conclusions at the end of 2003, the European Year of People with Disabilities. The report[64] identified a lack of awareness as one of the most important obstacles to achieving accessibility in the built environment. The report also recommended that Guidelines should be produced that would help tenderers to comply with the new provision of the Directive. In January 2005, the Commission helped launch the 'Build for All Reference Manual', as part of a public consultation. The manual gives guidance

---

[58] europa.eu.int/comm/environment/gpp. See further Catherine Day, 'Buying green: the crucial role of public authorities', *Local Environment: The International Journal of Justice and Sustainability* 10, 2 (2005), 201.
[59] Communication on Integrated Product Policy (IPP) of 18 June 2003.
[60] Report by the High Level Group headed by Mr Wim Kok (November 2004).
[61] Communication on the Report on the implementation of the Environmental Technologies Action Plan (January 2005).
[62] www.iclei-europe.org/leap.
[63] ec.europa.eu/environment/gpp/transport_and_communication_services_en.htm.
[64] '2010: A Europe Accessible for All' (October 2003), available at www.eca.lu/upload/egafin.pdf.

on the establishment of essential accessibility criteria, and a methodology for step-by-step implementation of accessibility as provided for by the EC Public Procurement Directives. According to the Manual, Corporate Social Responsibility is one of the reasons for why the issue needed to be addressed:[65]

> The concept of Corporate Social Responsibility is increasingly pressed for by political decision makers at all levels of Government and, as a result, is increasingly being highlighted as an important criterion in Public Procurement decisions. That is to say that there is a growing tendency to require that companies who are entrusted with the execution of large public Works contracts are actively engaged in pursuing Corporate Social Responsibility within their structures.

VIII. Developments in the member states

The linkages between public procurement and CSR were being developed in the member states during the 1990s. This activity substantially increased, however, during and after the process of 'clarification' discussed above. We can point to several significant legal developments in the member states. Among those 'CSR-supportive policies' in the field of public procurement listed on the Commission's CSR website, the Belgian example fits into this category. In November 2001, the Belgian government approved the introduction of a social clause for certain federal public procurement contracts favouring the inclusion of disadvantaged groups (for example, 5 per cent of the total share of the contract is to be used to hire long-term unemployed people).[66] Since March 2001, the French law on public procurement authorises the inclusion of social and environmental considerations among the clauses of public procurement contracts (article 14). A new reform, which was adopted in 2006, introduced sustainable development and high quality environment in public procurement criteria.[67] We can also point to significant developments in the practice of procurement, although changes in practice are very uneven across the Community. The 2005 European Commission survey on the state of play on green public procurement in the member states found that seven member states (Austria, Denmark, Finland, Germany,

---

[65] European Commission, 'Build for All Reference Manual' (January 2005), p. 8.

[66] ec.europa.eu/environment/gpp/pdf/Stateofplaysurvey2005_en.pdf.

[67] 'The New Code des Marchés Publics was promulgated in Decree No. 2006-975 of 1 August 2006, available at: www.legifrance.gouv.fr/texteconsolide/AMHFN.htm.

the Netherlands, Sweden and the United Kingdom) were practising a significant amount of green public procurement. In these countries, 40–70 per cent of all tenders published on Tenders Electronic Daily (TED) during the past year included environmental criteria. However, in the remaining eighteen countries, this figure was below 30 per cent.[68]

Whilst the approaches developed by the Community go some way to explain the development of responsible procurement in the past decade, it is by no means a complete explanation, whether at the level of the Community or domestically. Particularly in the latter, whilst Community law appeared to *permit* public bodies to introduce social and environmental issues, it did not require it, so we need further explanations. In particular, three developments encouraged the greater use of public procurement to achieve social and environmental objectives in member states: the growth of the environmental movement, and its gradual evolution into a movement for 'sustainable development', developing strategies for greening public procurement;[69] the alliance between 'old social movements', such

---

[68] M. Bouwer, K. de Jong, M. Jonk, T. Berman, R. Bersani, H. Lusser and P. Szuppinger, 'Green Public Procurement in Europe' (2005), at europa.eu.int/comm/environment/gpp/media.htm#state.

[69] The United Nations Conference on Environment and Development (UNCED) held in Rio de Janerio, Brazil in 1992 (the so-called 'Earth Summit') was a turning point for the development of the use of public procurement for green purchasing. The Rio Declaration on Environment and Development was adopted by more than 178 governments. Agenda 21, as it came to be called, was a plan of action to be taken globally, nationally and locally by organisations of the United Nations, governments and others in many areas in which humans impact on the environment. Agenda 21 (para. 4.23, chapter 4) called for governments to exercise leadership through government purchasing (procurement was addressed in element C of the CSD Work Programme on Changing Consumption and Production Patterns adopted at the third session of the CSD in 1995). A Commission on Sustainable Development (CSD) was created in December 1992 to ensure effective follow-up of UNCED, to monitor and to report on implementation of the agreements at the local, national, regional and international levels. The 1997 Programme for the Further Implementation of Agenda 21 further encouraged governments to take the lead in changing consumption patterns by improving their own environmental performance with action-oriented policies and goals on procurement, the management of public facilities and the further integration of environmental concerns into national policy-making. The full implementation of Agenda 21, the Programme for Further Implementation of Agenda 21 and the Commitments to the Rio principles, were reaffirmed at the World Summit on Sustainable Development (WSSD) held in Johannesburg, South Africa from 26 August to 4 September 2002. The changing of consumption and production patterns was, indeed, seen as one of the overarching objectives of and essential requirements for sustainable development, as recognised by the heads of state and governments in the Johannesburg Declaration. The Johannesburg Plan of Implementation called for the development of 'a 10-year framework of programmes in support of regional and national initiatives to accelerate the shift towards sustainable consumption and production' (chapter 3). The

as trade unions, with new social movements, such as organisations claiming rights for disabled persons, in focusing on public procurement as a strategy; and the development of new forms of governance, such as the increasing requirement that major policies that cross departmental functions, such as gender equality, should be 'mainstreamed' throughout government, including in procurement.

IX. Corporate social responsibility and procurement in the United Kingdom

A fourth explanation for the growth of social procurement at the national level derives from national approaches to CSR. Perhaps most significant, in this context, is the changing use of public procurement in the United Kingdom because this is linked more explicitly to a CSR agenda than in most other member states.[70] During the 1980s and 1990s, under successive Conservative governments, public procurement had been significantly reformed, in part by reducing the use of public procurement for social policy purposes. This was in part due to the need to cut public budgets; more efficient public procurement was thought to require a concentration on economic elements predominating in the idea of 'value for money'. Local authorities, for example, which had experimented with incorporating social issues into their procurement, were substantially stripped of their ability to do so in 1988. However, alongside this increasing emphasis on an economically driven conception of 'value for money', the other most significant development was the expansion of contracting as a method of governance. Public bodies were increasingly required to contract out several basic services. In local government, for example, a regime of

framework should strengthen international cooperation and increase exchange of information and best practices to facilitate the implementation of national and regional programmes to promote sustainable consumption and production. '[R]elevant authorities at all levels' were encouraged 'to take sustainable development considerations into account in decision-making, including on national and local development planning, investment in infrastructure, business development and public procurement' (para. 19). This would include actions to '[p]romote public procurement policies that encourage development and diffusion of environmentally sound goods and services'. For further developments, see 'Overview of progress towards sustainable development: a review of the implementation of Agenda 21', the Programme for the Further Implementation of Agenda 21 and the Johannesburg Plan of Implementation, Report of the Secretary-General, E/CN.17/2006/2, 15 February 2006, para. 46.

[70] Darren Ford, 'Public-sector Procurement and Corporate Social Responsibility', in Christopher Stephen Brown (ed.), *The Sustainable Enterprise: Profiting from Best Practice* (London: Kogan Page, 2005), p. 49.

'compulsory competitive tendering' (or CCT) required a market-driven element to be introduced into service provision that resulted in work, previously done in-house by council employees, now being done by employees of private-sector firms operating under contract to the public body. The election of a Labour government in 1997, however, led to significant changes in this approach to procurement that more and more enabled it to be incorporated into the new government's increasingly strong CSR agenda.

The Labour government's approach to CSR is increasingly seen in the academic literature as part of an approach to governance based on partnership between business and the public sector, which aimed to meet the need for better public services without the tax and spend approach that had traditionally been associated with Labour governments. This led, for example, to considerably increased use of public-private partnerships in areas as diverse as the provision of housing, the building and running of schools and the provision of social transfer payments. This increased use of the private sector resulted in 'business . . . assum[ing] a far greater profile in social life than hitherto'.[71] However, it also brought additional political risks to government, increasing the likelihood that the government would be seen as being no different to the Conservative administrations that they replaced, and be 'punished for the irresponsibility of business'.[72] Together with this partnership approach to business came increased use of the rhetoric of CSR, leading to the United Kingdom being seen as one of the leading exponents of CSR in Europe.

One of the tools that government has used in helping to ensure that CSR is being delivered in the United Kingdom is the use of public procurement. It is by way of procurement, rather than increased use of traditional command and control regulation through legislation, that CSR is not infrequently being encouraged. As a result, there has been a significant shift in approach in policy on the use of procurement to deliver social and environmental outcomes. Two significant changes have been apparent. The first is that some of the most aggressively economically driven legislation on procurement introduced by the Conservative governments has been significantly changed, most notably the shift from CCT to a 'best value' approach, and the amendment of the 1988 restrictions on the use of procurement for social purposes in local government. This has led to an increased interest in the use of social and green procurement by major local government purchasers, not least in London. We can see this as one

---

[71] Moon, 'Government as a Driver', p. 7.   [72] *ibid.*, p. 18.

of the 'initiatives [taken] to adjust the regulatory environment for CSR'.[73] The second identifiable change is the extent to which public procurement has been referred to in policy pronouncements since 2000 as a method of helping to deliver particular social or environmental goals, and the extent to which this is justified by using CSR-influenced language.[74] The third identifiable change is the extent to which there have been attempts to put CSR procurement into practice. The more high profile attempts, for example, have been the Public Sector Sustainable Food Procurement Initiative,[75] the purchasing of sustainable timber products,[76] the purchase of 'green' electricity,[77] and the incorporation of 'fair trade' into some procurement.[78] Interestingly, in contrast to the debate at the EC level over the use of public procurement as an instrument of CSR, there has been relatively little opposition by business in Britain to these developments, and in some of these cases representatives of business have been involved directly in urging the use of public procurement.[79] Indeed, delivery of social outcomes through public procurement has become increasingly seen as a business advantage in tendering for future government contracts.[80]

[73] ibid., p. 14
[74] Strategy Unit, 'Ethnic Minorities in the Labour Market' (March, 2003); CRE, 'Guidance on equality and procurement' (July 2003); National Procurement Strategy for Local Government (October 2003); Office of Government Commerce (OGC)/DEFRA, 'Joint Note On Environmental Issues' (October, 2003); National Employment Panel, 'Report to Chancellor' (March 2005); Office of Deputy Prime Minister, 'Code of Practice on Workforce Matters' (September 2005); Women and Work Commission, 'Shaping a Fairer Future' (February 2006); The Equalities Review, 'Interim Report for Consultation' (March 2006).
[75] Ford, 'Public-sector Procurement and Corporate Social Responsibility', p. 52.
[76] Office of Government Contracts, 'Information Note 9/2002, Timber Procurement by Government Departments' (December 2002); Office of Government Commerce, 'Timber Procurement by Government Departments: New Guidance and Revised Model Contract Specification Clause' (September 2003).
[77] Department for Environment, Food and Rural Affairs, 'Changing Patterns: The UK Government Framework for Sustainable Consumption and Production' (September 2003).
[78] Office of Government Commerce, 'Guidance on Fair and Ethical Trading' (2005).
[79] One example is the CBI membership of the Women and Work Commission. There may be several reasons. Moon has sought to explain why, in general, business may urge governments to be a driver of CSR: 'This could be for reasons either of wishing to increase competitors' costs or of wishing to penalise free riders which enjoy the reputational goods and propitious governance systems that CSR may generate for business in general' (Moon, 'Government as a Driver', p. 19).
[80] See, e.g., Accord, 'Corporate Social Responsibility Report' (2004) available at www.accordplc.com/xsl/downloads/CSRFINAL.pdf.

X. Use of public procurement for corporate social responsibility purposes and its relationship to law

The use of public procurement to achieve increased compliance and its relationship to *law* is complex and multi-faceted. Whilst public procurement *policy* has assiduously tracked government policy more generally, government procurement *law* has generally lagged behind changes in policy developments, leaving lawyers and policy-makers to interpret the existing law to conform to the changing policy preferences, to change the existing law to reflect these preferences, or to restrict linking public procurement with the delivery of these policy preferences. We have seen that the potential mismatch between existing public procurement law and CSR has required EC procurement law to be re-examined to see to what extent there are legal barriers to delivering CSR through public procurement.

Examining the relationship between public procurement law and CSR brings into focus aspects of public procurement that are not generally examined in this context, in particular the nature of public procurement itself, and how it differs from procurement by private firms. It also brings into focus the importance of which definition of CSR we adopt. This arises because CSR has been seen by some to be defined by the absence of legal obligation. Corporate social responsibility, according to the European Commission, is 'a concept whereby companies integrate social and environmental concerns in their business operations and in their interaction with their stakeholders *on a voluntary basis*'.[81] What does 'voluntary' imply in this context? What role, in particular, does this imply for public policy and law? Whether CSR should be undertaken only on a voluntary basis or can be complemented with a governmental regulatory framework is, of course, a central issue in the debates surrounding CSR more generally.[82] In this chapter, we examined this debate through a case study of a hitherto largely unexplored issue: the developing relationship between CSR and public procurement, concentrating particularly but not exclusively on the debate among the EC institutions surrounding the relationship between public procurement and

---

[81] European Commission, 'Promoting a European framework', COM (2001) 366 final (emphasis added).

[82] For a recent review of some of the academic literature, see Marta de la Cuesta González and Carmen Valor Martinez, 'Fostering Corporate Social Responsibility Through Public Initiative: From the EU to the Spanish Case', *Journal of Business Ethics* 55 (2004), 275–93.

CSR.[83] We can identify three differing relationships, drawing on the helpful analytical structure developed by Doreen McBarnet.[84]

One way of viewing the relationship between public procurement requirements and the law is by seeing to what extent such procurement requirements go *beyond the law*, requiring companies to take action that they would not otherwise have been required to take. This type of analysis, whatever its merits in each particular legal system, has little utility as a comparative tool. The extent to which public procurement requires corporations with which government is contracting to go beyond what is otherwise legally required, or merely to comply with the law, depends crucially on how far particular legal systems incorporate into law requirements that in other jurisdictions are left instead to the private sector to deal with on a voluntary basis. An example should make the issue clear. In the United States, the federal government has used public procurement as one of a raft of measures to ensure compliance by government contractors with extensive legal prohibitions on employment discrimination; these obligations apply to employers generally. In this case, public procurement does not go beyond the legal requirements on business; rather it reflects them. Public procurement is also used, however, to require businesses to undertake affirmative action measures that are not otherwise applicable to businesses generally. In this case, public procurement goes beyond what the law otherwise requires. Different jurisdictions draw the lines very differently between what is legally required and what is not in the social and environmental fields. Until recently, for example, most European countries did not have extensive prohibitions on racial discrimination. If we define CSR as involving businesses going *beyond the law*, then CSR procurement will differ significantly from jurisdiction to jurisdiction depending on the extent of social and environmental legislation otherwise applicable in that jurisdiction. Nor, as Fox, Ward and Howard have argued, does the rigid 'voluntary versus regulatory' divide 'make sense in the context of developing country economies where tools to encourage compliance with minimum legislation can be understood as a significant element of the CSR agenda'.[85]

Most developed countries now have extensive legal regulation of the use of government procurement. The reasons for this are complex and

---

[83] For a description of the development of CSR in the European Union, see Kristina K. Herrmann, 'Corporate Social Responsibility and Sustainable Development: The European Union Initiative as a Case Study', *Indiana Journal of Global Legal Studies* 11, 2 (2004), 205–32.

[84] McBarnet, Chapter 1 in this volume.   [85] Fox, et al., *Public Sector Roles*, p. 1.

multifaceted. Suffice it to say that there are often much more extensive limits on how governments can behave in undertaking procurement activity than will apply to private parties contracting together. This has given rise to considerable debate in most jurisdictions as to whether existing legal restrictions on public procurement restrict the use of CSR public procurement. A prominent issue, therefore, in the relationship between public procurement, CSR and the law is how far CSR procurement is *against the law*. This debate has involved considering the restrictions on public procurement that arise at the national level, at the regional (particularly at the EC) level, and under WTO agreements. One feature of the debate is the extent to which there is disagreement at each of these levels as to what the implications of the legal restrictions are for CSR public procurement. The other feature of the debate is the apparent effect of this uncertainty on the willingness of public bodies to engage in CSR public procurement.

One effect of this uncertainty is that some jurisdictions have attempted to clarify what public bodies are able to do to use public procurement for achieving social and environmental goals by law. Here the issue is how far CSR procurement has been facilitated *through the law*. There have been differing mixes of three basic approaches that have been adopted in different jurisdictions on different social and environmental issues. In some contexts, legislation explicitly requires public bodies not to give contracts under certain circumstances.[86] In other contexts, legislation requires public bodies simply to consider the use of procurement for achieving social and environmental purposes. This may be done explicitly, for example by allowing the award of contracts on a preferred basis to sheltered workshops established to provide employment for severely disabled workers. Or it may be done by implication, for example in the increasingly frequent requirement that public bodies 'mainstream' equality issues in their policies and practices.

---

[86] For example, in Northern Ireland contracts may not be awarded to employers who are systematically in breach of the fair employment legislation (Northern Ireland Fair Employment and Treatment Order, 1998). In Taiwan, the Government Procurement Act 1998 'introduced a new requirement that products bearing the "Green Mark" ecolabel . . . should be given priority in government procurement and benefit from a price advantage of 10 percent' (Fox, et al., *Public Sector Roles*, p. 13); Halina Ward, *Legal Issues in Corporate Citizenship* (IIED, February 2003), p. 1. See also www.epa.gov.tw. In South Africa, recent legislation, the Minerals and Petroleum Resources Development Act (No. 28 of 2002), introduced affirmative procurement requirements as part of a raft of measures to increase black economic empowerment. See R. Hamann, 'Mining companies' role in sustainable development: the 'why' and 'how' of corporate social responsibility from a business perspective', *Development Southern Africa* 20, 6 (2003), 237, at 250.

Law may, therefore, require the use of public procurement for some CSR purposes, permit it but not require it for other CSR purposes, and prohibit its use for a third group of CSR purposes. When a particular legal system does this at the same time (as is the case in many jurisdictions), it is likely to give at least the appearance of policy incoherence, leading to legal uncertainty. The uncertainty of the legal position regarding linkage to achieve CSR goals is a recurrent theme. Legal uncertainty has been seen as a feature of domestic, European and international law.[87] Uncertainty to this degree is one barrier to the further development of CSR. Adopting linkage in public procurement is likely, therefore, to give rise to a need to ensure policy coherence and consistency across government, ensuring that all sections of government are 'singing from the same hymn sheet'. One of the sites in which the debate about the appropriate role of CSR is played out is in the legal domain, by which I mean to encompass both legislative and interpretative contexts.

Increasingly, the need to resolve legal difficulties, and create clear rules of the game to allow CSR to flourish, may require legal intervention, but this appears to give rise to a tension with the underlying principle of voluntarism, if that is defined as the absence of legal regulation. Halina Ward has argued that the 'voluntary/regulatory' divide 'operates as a brake on discussions of new legislation or regulation as a response to contested CSR issues'.[88] The ambiguity in the public procurement context is whether we define public procurement as government regulation (in which case it appears akin to 'regulation' and thus contrary to the spirit of CSR's voluntarism) or as a market operation in which government acts as a purchaser (in which case it appears akin to the incentive-based market-mechanisms discussed earlier and fits in squarely with CSR voluntarism). The reality, of course, is that it is both, occupying an ambiguous space between the two, hence its attraction in many ways.

In the EC context, an approach to the issue appears to have developed in the form of an *enabling model of law*. This involves legal regulation enabling the relationship between CSR and public procurement to flourish, for example by explicitly setting out a common standard of what public bodies may do in the use of procurement for achieving CSR goals, but not requiring it, and in reducing legal uncertainties that might lead

---

[87] The confusion in the area of WTO law is well illustrated in Zadek, Lingayah and Forstater, 'Social Labels', p. 77. See also A. Cramer, P. Pruzan-Jorgensen, H. Jorgensen and M. Jungk, 'Strengthening Implementation of Corporate Social Responsibility in Global Supply Chains' (Washington, DC: World Bank Group Social Responsibility Practice, 2003), p. 31.

[88] Ward, *Legal Issues*, p. 1.

to unwillingness to use public procurement for CSR purposes. In this context, then, the Community fulfils one traditional function of government, which is to create the conditions for market-mechanisms to operate effectively. In the UK context, we see government taking one step further towards embracing a regulatory role for procurement in the name of CSR, but one that appears to be accepted by business as an acceptable price for an otherwise business-friendly environment.

4

Corporate codes of conduct: moral or legal obligation?

CAROLA GLINSKI

I. Introduction

Corporate social responsibility (CSR) is of particular importance in the context of transnational economic activities, especially when production takes place in countries where social and environmental protective standards are low, be it due to insufficient legislation or lack of enforcement. Many of the so-called developing countries especially do not avail themselves of appropriate regulation of industrial processes, of labour standards and of adequate control mechanisms.[1] Also, many of the smaller countries lack the power to deal adequately with big transnational corporations. Spectacular accidents like the Bhopal disaster,[2] but also continuous exploitation and pollution (of people and the environment)[3] caused by transnational economic activities, are the consequence and have brought this issue onto the international agenda.

Nevertheless, until now environmental, and also health and safety aspects of transnational economic activities, have not undergone immediate regulation in public law. International conventions have not been

---

This chapter partly builds on a paper presented at Oniati in June 2005, to be published in O. Dilling, M. Herberg and G. Winter (eds.), *Responsible Business: Self-Governance and the Law in Transnational Economic Transactions* (Oxford: Hart Publishing, 2007).

[1] See the cases studies on Brazil by J. Kleba, 'Kontrollkompensation, Rechtssynergie, greenwashing? Recht und Selbststeuerung von Multinationalen Konzernen in Brasilien', in G. Winter (ed.), *Die Umweltverantwortung multinationaler Unternehmen* (Baden-Baden: Nomos, 2005), pp. 115–45, and on Kenya by E. Chege Kamou, 'Environmental Regimes and Direct Investment in Third World Countries', in G. Winter (ed.), *ibid.*, pp. 147–85.

[2] See, e.g., U. Baxi, *Inconvenient Forum and Convenient Catastrophe: The Bhopal Case* (Bombay: Indian Law Institute, 1986).

[3] For example, for Texaco in Ecuador, see S. MacLeod, 'Maria Aguinda v. Texaco Inc: Defining the Limits of Liability for Human Rights Violations Resulting from Environmental Degradation', *Contemporary Issues in Law* (1999), 188–209. For the conduct of Thor Chemicals and Cape plc in South Africa, see H. Ward, 'Towards a New Convention on Corporate Accountability? Some Lessons from the Thor Chemicals and Cape PLC Cases', *Yearbook of International Environmental Law* (2001), 105–43.

adopted, nor do high-standard countries have any direct regulative power over the production standards in developing countries, due to the international law principle of sovereignty. Those countries where the parent companies are situated cannot regulate on the subsidiaries' behaviour in their host countries, nor have those countries where products from low-protection countries are marketed regulative power on the production patterns.[4] This is the background where corporate social responsibility in the form of 'self-regulation' comes in and has been regarded as an instrument to bridge the gap between the different national protection levels, at least to a certain extent.

As a matter of fact, there are a considerable number and variety of self-regulatory instruments. Some were initiated by national or supranational institutions,[5] some were negotiated with non-governmental organisations (NGOs) or trade unions, and others have been unilaterally adopted by individual enterprises, groups of enterprises or by business associations.

With a view to the relationship between CSR and the law, one can find two extreme positions. The long-standing opinion among business, NGOs and also many lawyers is that codes of conduct and other self-regulatory instruments create moral obligations at best but have no legal effect whatsoever. At the other end of the spectrum, some academics have developed rather generalising ideas of legal pluralism which might lead – very generally speaking – to the recognition of self-regulation of the different social sectors (e.g. the business sector) as a source of law that is as valid a source law as formal national or international law.[6] In contrast, this chapter focuses on already possible private law effects of corporate self-regulation in order to bridge, at least to a certain extent, the legal gap public law leaves. It thereby proposes to take a sector-specific approach and to assess potential legal effects of private regulation with a view to the

---

[4] On foreign direct investment, see the analysis by K. Böttger, *Die Umweltpflichtigkeit von Auslandsdirektinvestitionen im Völkerrecht* (Baden-Baden: Nomos, 2002). On the relationship between international trade and the protection of the environment, see, e.g., P. C. Mavroidis, 'Trade and Environment after the *Shrimps-Turtles* Litigation', *Journal of World Trade* 34 (2000), 73–88.

[5] See, e.g., the Global Compact initiative by Kofi Annan, unglobalcompact.org; the EC Commission's Communication on Corporate Social Responsibility, COM (2002) 347 final.

[6] See in particular the contributions in G. Teubner (ed.), *Global Law without a State* (Aldershot: Dartmouth, 1997). See also G. Teubner, 'Global Private Regimes: Neo-Spontaneous Law and Dual Constitution of Autonomous Sectors?', in K.-H. Ladeur (ed.), *Public Governance in the Age of Globalization* (Aldershot: Ashgate, 2004), pp. 71–87, and 'Societal Constitutionalism: Alternatives to State-Centred Constitutional Theory?', in C. Joerges, I.-J. Sand and G. Teubner (eds.), *Constitutionalism and Transnational Governance* (Oxford: Hart Publishing, 2004), pp. 3–28.

different purposes and effects of the various self-regulatory instruments and the requirements of the respective fields of law, while taking into consideration the particularities of the transnational sphere. Until now, case law that is directly concerned with corporate social or environmental self-regulation of transnational economic activities does not seem to be available. Therefore, this chapter is based on legal doctrine and theory as well as on case law on comparable phenomena and questions, as indicated in the respective paragraphs.[7]

In essence, two types of corporate self-regulation can be distinguished: *published* codes of conduct, guidelines or agreements on the one hand;[8] and *internal* regulation in contracts, management handbooks or simply through the internal organisation by multinational enterprises of their environmental and safety management on the other hand.[9]

Self-regulation may also have different purposes. A published set of rules may primarily aim at marketing effects but also at the improvement, harmonisation and standardisation of production methods or business conduct. The latter is even more valid for internal regulation. However, standardisation may also aim at creating legal effects, in particular at defining requirements for lawful conduct in order to exclude 'black sheep' from the market, or to establish a legally 'safe harbour' for those who comply with the private rules. Other aspects, such as avoiding legislation, may also be important for safeguarding the companies' capacity to define their own standards.

As a consequence, two prototypes of legally relevant effects will be distinguished in the first part of this chapter: a market effect which creates legitimate expectations (II), and a standardisation effect which might define the legally required conduct (III). In the second part, a model is developed under which transnational corporations can be held liable for damage caused by their subsidiaries in developing countries if they fail to organise their structures adequately by using self-regulatory instruments (IV). The chapter concludes that private self-regulation is relevant in law: on the one hand, voluntary social and environmental commitments

---

[7] One reason for the reluctance of potential claimants and courts may be that little research has been carried out on the socially binding effect of corporations' published social and environmental commitments as well as on their internal steering mechanisms. For this, see M. Herberg, *Globalisierung und private Selbstregulierung: Umweltschutz in multinationalen Unternehmen* (Frankfurt am Main: Campus, 2007).

[8] See, e.g., the websites of Bayer at www.bayer.com/about-bayer/social-responsibility; of BP at www.bp.com; of BASF at corporate.basf.com/en/sustainability; and of Shell at www.shell.com.

[9] See in particular M. Herberg, *Globalisierung und private Selbstregulierung*.

may produce a variety of binding legal effects; on the other hand private self-regulation may even be required by law in industries with high potential for causing pollution and damage.

II. Market effects

Published self-regulation usually aims at market effects. Typical examples are codes of conduct, social and environmental reports, and labels and messages transported in advertisements. They are used as marketing tools, designed to build confidence for improving a corporation's reputation and market share. This is particularly true for private regulation of social and environmental standards for production in, or trade with, developing countries.[10] Nevertheless, companies can be surprised to find that they are held to the promises they made in voluntary codes or other public statements, as happened to Nike.[11]

Relevant legal effects can be based on the legal protection of the addressees' legitimate expectations in the compliance with these self-regulatory instruments in contract law, as well as in the law of misleading advertisement that forms part of the law of unfair competition.

Two potential legal effects must be distinguished. First, public statements on one's own environmental conduct in low-standard countries, in whichever form, can of course be binding on the author of such statements. Second, widely publicised codes of conduct may be able to set a standard with an effect that goes beyond their immediate signatories. This means that they may be able to set a standard that all traders or producers of the same line of business must comply with unless they indicate otherwise. Thus, they may have an external effect on third parties that have not been involved in the regulatory process or that have not agreed to the code of conduct.

A. Defining one's own behaviour: setting individual standards[12]

There cannot be any doubt that a corporation is allowed to make binding promises concerning its own behaviour by establishing or signing a

---

[10] See also E. Kocher, 'Unternehmerische Selbstverpflichtungen zur sozialen Verantwortung – Erfahrungen mit sozialen Verhaltenskodizes in der transnationalen Produktion', *Recht der Arbeit* (2004), 27–31.

[11] See Chapter 1 in this volume.

[12] For a detailed analysis, see C. Glinski, 'Produktionsaussagen im Kauf- und Werberecht', in G. Winter (ed.), *Die Umweltverantwortung multinationaler Unternehmen*, pp. 216–28.

(corporate) code of conduct. To varying extents, all legal orders recognise the protection of confidence in promises. Where, in a business context,[13] one party attracts confidence by another party, the other party must be protected by law. The key element consists of a (self-)binding behaviour that makes the impression of being serious. Sociological research into codes of conduct and other self-regulatory instruments has revealed that they all use the language of promises. Otherwise they fail in their intention to gain, or regain, reputation.[14] The only crux, in particular with advertising messages, can lie in their vagueness. However, even from vague statements, or promises, one can extract a binding minimum content.[15] Another issue is that codes of conduct sometimes explicitly declare not to be binding, and there appears to be wide belief that promises in codes of conduct can be invalidated in such a way. However, declarations on the non-binding character of a statement are inconsistent with the expectations the statement aims to create otherwise. Thus, they can only destroy the addressee's expectations if they are as visible and as prominent as the confidence-building features.[16]

The recognition and support of self-regulatory instruments by official authorities, such as the UN Global Compact logo, increases public trust further.[17] Also, discrepancy in expertise and knowledge between the producer and the consumer makes the consumer more dependent on the producer's information, so that his/her trust in the producer's statements deserves even more protection.[18] Besides, ethical consumption is the only way in which people can take influence on production patterns in low-standard countries.[19]

---

[13] This may only be different in a social context, see R. Fehlmann, *Vertrauenshaftung – Vertrauen als alleinige Haftungsgrundlage* (St Gallen: University of St Gallen, 2002), pp. 179–80.

[14] See M. Herberg, 'Codes of Conduct und kommunikative Vernunft', *Zeitschrift für Rechtssoziologie* 22 (2001), 25.

[15] See J. Köndgen, *Selbstbindung ohne Vertrag* (Tübingen: Mohr, 1981), pp. 301–2.

[16] For example, small print is not capable of countering the overall impression of advertising, and the same is true for a declaration of the non-binding character at the very end of a long code of conduct; see Köndgen, *Selbstbindung*, p. 184. See also German case law on environmental advertising, e.g., Bundesgerichtshof (BGH), *Wettbewerb in Recht und Praxis* (1989), 163; BGH, *Wettbewerb in Recht und Praxis* (1991), 159.

[17] See Köndgen, *Selbstbindung*, p. 233.

[18] See I. Roth, *Umweltbezogene Unternehmenskommunikation im deutschen und europäischen Wettbewerbsrecht* (Frankfurt am Main: Lang, 2000), p. 2.

[19] See T. Wilhelmsson, 'Contribution to a Green Sales Law', in T. Wilhelmsson, *Twelve Essays on Consumer Law and Policy* (Helsinki: Publications of the Department of Private Law, University of Helsinki, 1996), pp. 284–5.

In fact, EC policy and legislation do make use of this confidence-building effect of codes of conduct, social and environmental reports, and labels.[20] As consumers shall thereby be given incentives for ethical purchasing, the only logical consequence would be that consumers must be afforded legal protection of their confidence in the environmental and social performance of producers.[21] In this context, it should be noted that, at EC level, environmental law and private law do not act entirely separately from each other. Instead, Article 6 of the EC Treaty contains a horizontal environmental clause according to which environmental protection requirements must be integrated into the definition and implementation of all EC policies and activities,[22] and this is recognised to be a rule for interpreting all primary and secondary EC law. Thus, it also applies to internal market law, including EC consumer contract law and law of unfair competition, where the wording of relevant provisions is open to interpretation.

1. Contracts of sale

In the first place, binding promises can be introduced into a contract. Contract law is based on the principle of party autonomy that allows the contracting parties to determine freely their mutual obligations according to their own needs. The consent of the parties is to be assessed objectively. Although the contracting parties usually pursue their own interest, this does – of course – not exclude altruistic intentions and expectations, which equally deserve the protection afforded by contract law. A typical example would be the purchase of a 'fair trade' product.

---

[20] In particular, the Sixth Community Environment Action Programme aims at improving environmentally sound production by promoting more sustainable consumption patterns within the European Community but also abroad in connection with foreign direct investment and trade, Decision No. 1600/2002/EC, OJ 2002 No. L242/1, paras. 2, 5, 13–14, and so does the Green Paper on Integrated Pollution Control, COM (2001) 68 final, p. 20. With the Regulation on eco-labelling, Regulation 1980/2000/EC, OJ No. L237/1, and Regulation 761/2001/EC, allowing voluntary participation by organisations in a Community eco-management and audit scheme (EMAS), OJ 2001 No. L114/1, these thoughts have made their way into EC secondary legislation. More recently, in its 'Communication on Corporate Social Responsibility', the European Community has turned its eye directly to the performance of multinational enterprises, COM (2002) 347 final, p. 1.

[21] See, e.g., Wilhelmsson, 'Green Sales Law', p. 278.

[22] Although the precise scope of this clause is being discussed controversially, see, e.g., N. Dhondt, *Integration of Environmental Protection into other EC Policies* (Groningen: Europa Law Publishers, 2003), pp. 143–83. See also C. Glinski and P. Rott, 'Umweltfreundliches und ethisches Konsumverhalten im harmonisierten Kaufrecht', *Europäische Zeitschrift für Wirtschaftsrecht* (2003), 654.

Nevertheless, former German sales law, and also the sales law of other countries, was fairly restrictive in recognising the binding effect of such promises, in particular where they were not made by the seller but by the producer and where they did not relate to the physical properties of goods but only to production patterns.[23]

These deficiencies can and must be overcome by interpreting the EC sales law provisions on the conformity of a good with the contract (and their national implementations) in such a way that the conformity requirement includes all the qualities that determine the value of a product. According to Article 2 (2)(d) of the Consumer Sales Directive 1999/44/EC[24] that sets the minimum standards for the member states' consumer sales laws, the concept of conformity includes conformity with public statements on the specific characteristics made about them not only by the seller, but also by the producer or his representative, particularly in advertising or on labelling. Codes of conduct and environmental reports constitute such relevant public statements as well. In fact, it is one of the very modern features of EC consumer sales law to acknowledge that the producer's statements may have a far greater effect on the purchasing decisions of consumers than the immediate contact between the seller and the consumer.[25] Besides, the concept of conformity extends not only to product-related characteristics of the goods in question, such as their toxicity, but also to the circumstances under which they were produced. Especially where the price of the ethically produced goods is higher than the price of goods produced otherwise, the specific production patterns are usually decisive for the purchase. The only reservation to be made is that public statements must relate to the 'specific characteristics' of a good. The emphasis is on the term 'specific'. This means that public statements must relate to facts that can be proven, which is usually the case with labelling or codes of conduct but not necessarily with advertising spots,[26] although a fact content can usually be extracted from any statement on social or environmental performance.[27]

---

[23] See, e.g., K.-N. Peifer, 'Die Haftung des Verkäufers für Werbeangaben', Juristische Rundschau (2001), 265–6, on German law.

[24] Directive 1999/44/EC on certain aspects of the sale of consumer goods and associated guarantees, OJ 1999 No. L171/12.

[25] See also D. Staudenmayer, 'The Directive on the Sale of Consumer Goods and Associated Guarantees – a Milestone in the European Consumer and Private Law', European Review of Private Law (2000), 551.

[26] See also Staudenmayer, 'The Directive', 552.

[27] See above, in section II A. 'Defining one's own behaviour: setting individual standards'.

Sales law, therefore, offers the consumer or the trading partner[28] the opportunity to enforce promises that are related to the circumstances of the production. This can be of particular relevance if it comes to mass protests against specific producers that have been identified to act against their public statements, as in the case of the anti-Nike movement. Furthermore, consumer associations may sue for injunctions,[29] stopping sellers from selling goods that are not in conformity with the producers' public statements without correcting these statements.

2. Law of misleading advertisement

With a view to the law of misleading advertisement, the situation is similar. The law of misleading advertisement forms part of the law of unfair competition. Nowadays, it is recognised that the law of unfair competition serves three purposes: the protection of competitors, the protection of competition as a public good and the protection of consumers.[30] This is particularly true for the law of misleading advertisement.

Insofar as the free decision of the average consumer can be influenced by a published code of conduct or a label, and so on, through which the signatories promise to apply ethical or environmentally sound production patterns, the respective legitimate expectations of consumers are protected by the law. Non-compliance is a violation of the law of misleading advertisement. In principle, there are no further requirements.

In fact, it has, for example, always been possible to derive from German law on misleading advertisement and also from EC law, namely from Directive 84/450/EEC on misleading advertising.[31] The notion of 'advertising' comprises all measures that aim at increasing one's own or another's sales. Clearly, all the above-mentioned public statements qualify as advertising, even social or environmental reports.[32] Advertising does not only relate to product properties but also to clean production and to

---

[28] These considerations may of course apply in contract law in general. Germany, for example, has extended these rules to all sales contracts.

[29] Under Directive 98/27/EC on injunctions for the protection of the consumers' interests, OJ 1998 No. L166/51, as implemented by the member states.

[30] See, e.g., the aims of the German Gesetz gegen den unlauteren Wettbewerb (Act against Unfair Competition, UWG), as laid down in § 1.

[31] Directive 84/450/EEC relating to the approximation of the laws, regulations and administrative provisions of the member states concerning misleading advertising, OJ 1984 No. L250/17.

[32] See also the US case of *Marc Kasky* v. *Nike, Inc., et al.*, 2 Cal. Daily Op. Serv. 3790.

the 'clean' image of a company.[33] Publicised codes of conduct or other self-regulatory instruments with social or environmental content usually express the specific engagement and also competence of a trader in this field that is not restricted to the production of a specific type of good but extends to all goods produced by this company. Even industry-wide codes of conduct may constitute advertising if a certain industry competes with another industry, as, for example, the oil industry competes with the natural gas industry.

German courts have already created a body of case law on environmental advertising. For example, longer texts, such as codes of conduct or environmental reports, have to be informative and true.[34] A product that is described as being environmentally sound must not be below average in this respect.[35] Negative aspects that are not mentioned must not nullify the mentioned positive aspects. The same rules apply to traders that hold themselves out as being environmentally friendly.[36] Particularly high requirements apply to traders in dirty industries, such as extraction industries.[37] The use of environmental labels necessitates a high level of transparency concerning their content, their issuer and their evaluation, since labels make the impression of being somehow official.[38] In terms of transparency, the mentioning of internal social or environmental guidelines that are not publicly accessible[39] is particularly problematic.

The new EC Directive on unfair commercial practices, Directive 2005/29/EC,[40] pays much attention to the power of codes of conduct by introducing Article 6(2)(b), under which a trader who does not comply with 'commitments that are firm and capable of being verified' is acting unfairly. However, one word of caution must be added: the Directive applies to 'any act, omission, course of conduct or representation,

---

[33] For details, see G. Federhoff-Rink, *Umweltschutz und Wettbewerbsrecht* (Heidelberg: Verlag Recht und Wirtschaft, 1994), pp. 84–90; E. B. Zabel, *Die wettbewerbsrechtliche Zulässigkeit produktunabhängiger Image-Werbung* (Konstanz: Hartung-Gorre, 1998), pp. 20–6.

[34] See Federhoff-Rink, *Umweltschutz*, p. 249.

[35] See Roth, *Umweltbezogene Unternehmenskommunikation*, p. 241. The OLG Düsseldorf, *Gewerblicher Rechtsschutz und Urheberrecht* (1988), 59, has required a significant improvement of the environmental characteristics compared to competing products.

[36] See Roth, *Umweltbezogene Unternehmenskommunikation*, pp. 242–3, 248.

[37] See Federhoff-Rink, *Umweltschutz*, p. 85.

[38] See Bundesgerichtshof, *Rechtsprechung des Bundesgerichtshofs in Zivilsachen* 105 (1989), 277.

[39] One example is the website of BASF at corporate.basf.com/de/sustainability/ grundwerte/leitlinien.htm?id = 7_dK98ndrbcp1E1.

[40] OJ 2005 No. L149/22.

commercial communication including advertising and marketing, by a
trader, directly connected with the promotion, sale or supply of a product
to consumers' (Article 2(d)), and therefore seems to exclude measures
that are merely indirectly connected with the promotion, sale or supply
of a product to consumers.[41] With this formula, advertisement with the
'clean' image of a company might be taken out of the scope of application
of the Directive, although such an interpretation would not be in line
with EC environmental policy on legislation and the policy on corporate
social responsibility. Consequently, such advertisement would remain in
the competence of the member states.

The traditional remedy in unfair competition law is the injunction
which regularly can only be invoked by consumer associations or public authorities. More recent national legislation (e.g., in Germany) also
allows consumer associations to sue for damages.[42] Only a few national
legislations grant individual consumers rights under their laws of unfair
competition.[43] Directive 2005/29/EC does not require the introduction
of individual rights but does not prohibit them either.[44]

B. Setting general standards by creating reasonable consumer expectations

There is a second route by which codes of conduct and other publicly
accessible private regulation can become legally binding: they can shape
consumer expectations in a more general way and therefore set standards
that all traders – at least in the same line of business – are bound by. It
is, for example, possible that carpets can be expected not to have been
woven by children if a majority of carpet producers adhere to a respective
code of conduct that is well-known to consumers. The relevant legal
criteria here are the 'reasonable consumer expectations'[45] towards the
'normal' product. Under Directive 1999/44/EC, consumer goods must
'show the quality and performance which are normal in goods of the
same type and which the consumer can reasonably expect'. Similarly,
Directive 2005/29/EC prohibits misleading the 'average consumer', who is

---

[41] What this means exactly is rather unclear; see H. Köhler and T. Lettl, 'Das gel-
tende europäische Lauterkeitsrecht, der Vorschlag für eine EG-Richtlinie über unlautere
Geschäftspraktiken und die UWG-Reform', *Wettbewerb in Recht und Praxis* (2003), 1034.

[42] German Unfair Competition Act of 2004, § 10. Damages have to be paid to the public
purse, and the prerequisites are very restrictive.

[43] One example is Spanish law.   [44] Recital (9).

[45] See, e.g., N. Reich and H.-W. Micklitz, *Europäisches Verbraucherrecht* (4th edn, Baden-
Baden: Nomos, 2003), p. 655.

defined as being reasonably well-informed and reasonably observant and circumspect.[46] This not only covers misleading actions but also misleading omissions (Article 7 of Directive 2005/29/EC). Both sales law and the law of misleading advertising require a trader to correct an assumption that an average consumer legitimately makes but that the product does not comply with. As a consequence, a carpet that has been woven by children would not be in conformity with a sales contract unless the parties have agreed on this fact. And it would be a misleading omission and therefore an unlawful commercial practice not to lay open that the carpet was produced by children.

Whether or not a code of conduct has such a consumer expectations shaping effect is primarily a matter of fact. Although the 'reasonable' consumer expectations include a normative element, they nevertheless depend on the expectations of real consumers. Clearly, a code of conduct will only be able to have such an effect if the most important traders or the majority of traders adhere to it. Furthermore, intensive publicising will be necessary since the consumer side will otherwise not be aware of the code.

III. Standardisation of lawful conduct

Going even further, private regulation of corporate social responsibility might even set standards of lawful behaviour that are binding not only on those producers who have agreed on the relevant private rule but also on those who have not committed themselves or even declared otherwise. In the field of commercial practices, industry-wide codes of regulation particularly might be able to produce this effect, whereas in the field of technical standards even the internal practice of some corporations may be equally relevant.

Importantly, this type of legal effect is independent from shaping expectations and from communication of the private rules beyond the concerned circles. However, in order to create such a broad binding effect, special legitimacy requirements must be met that differ from one field of law to another.

In private law, standardisation mainly plays a role where there is a general clause that needs to be concretised. Here, standardisation aims at the middle level between the general clause and the court's decision of the individual case by regulating the 'normal' case in a certain context. For

[46] See recital (18).

the following, ethical or fairness standards and technical standards shall be distinguished.

A. Setting fairness standards for commercial practices

Private regulation of fair business conduct might be a mechanism to civilise competition by prohibiting practices that are regarded as detrimental, but it might also serve to exclude competition by 'black sheep'. Instruments that may have such an effect could be codes of conduct, agreements or simply a common conviction. In legal terms, private regulation may concretise or define the general fairness requirement of unfair competition law,[47] thereby potentially elevating the previous standard to a higher level.

The criteria for concretising the general clause may differ throughout the various legal systems insofar as a more empirical or a more normative approach to fairness can be taken. With an empirical approach that emphasises the normal market practice, national and international business usages, but also guidelines, recommendations or codes of conduct established by business associations or professional bodies, could gain considerable importance. However, it is difficult to imagine that a legal system would refrain completely from exercising normative control. Normally, unfair competition laws refer to 'good faith', 'good morals' and 'good practices', expressions that refer at least partly to extra-legal 'norms' not merely usages, as the element 'good' demonstrates.[48] These extra-legal norms are in principle subject to societal (consent on) values.[49]

Private regulation concerning ethical production patterns, including social and environmental conduct in low-standard countries, might qualify for concretising a general fairness clause.

The protected interests in most unfair competition laws are the protection of competitors, of consumers and of the public good of fair competition as such. As the concretising effect of private regulation is broadly binding on all producers, including those 'outsiders' who have not agreed on the relevant private rule, the legitimacy towards these outsiders has to

---

[47] In contrast, where no general clause exists, and the example would be the law of unfair competition of the United Kingdom, private regulation cannot create rules with an effect on those who have not agreed on them.

[48] See H. Köhler, 'Zur Umsetzung der Richtlinie über unlautere Geschäftspraktiken', *Gewerblicher Rechtsschutz und Urheberrecht* (2005), 796.

[49] For a detailed analysis, see G. Teubner, *Standards und Direktiven in Generalklauseln* (Frankfurt: Athenäum, 1971).

be secured. At the same time, consumer interests may be affected, in particular, where higher fairness standards lead to increased purchase prices. Obviously, one of the main interests of the not-so altruistic consumers is directed towards cheap consumer prices. The public good of a fair and undistorted competition should normally not be negatively affected by the introduction of higher fairness standards, unless competition is reduced by the cartel-type exclusion of certain competitors that do not adhere to the higher standards.

Thus, first of all the consensus among the competing corporations is essential. Therefore, fairness standards will have to be based on a collective code of conduct or an agreement.[50] The relevant group is the one that competes in a certain market, for example the European market. If not all the members of the relevant group agree, the consensus certainly has to be broad, which means that the vast majority of traders has to adhere to the relevant rule.[51] Moreover, the consensus must reflect the group interest of the competitors, which means that it must be theoretically acceptable by all members of the group. This requires the rule to be adopted by a representative variety of the group members in order to prevent unfair exclusion. Consequently, a number of big companies cannot effectively create rules that disadvantage small and medium enterprises. And companies from industrialised countries cannot establish rules that are equally valid for companies from the developing world.

The disregard of some few corporations can be justified by the following considerations. The law itself calls for some objective standard that does not take account of each individual opinion. Furthermore, the standardisation of fairness increases legal certainty and therefore serves the public interest and also the group interest.

With a view to different social and environmental standards in industrialised and developing countries, two 'norms' might be subject to a consensus, with different groups of corporations concerned. First of all, the consensus might relate to the unfairness of deliberately taking advantage of a gross imbalance in the protection of public goods such as the environment by moving production into low-protection countries.[52] The group

---

[50] International certification systems may play an important role in indicating even a 'transnational' consensus; see E. Kocher, 'Unternehmerische Selbstverpflichtungen im Wettbewerb – Die Transformation von "soft law" in "hard law" durch das Wettbewerbsrecht', *Gewerblicher Rechtsschutz und Urheberrecht* (2005), 651.

[51] See also Kocher, 'Unternehmerische Selbstverpflichtungen', 649.

[52] See also R. Knieper and H. Fromm, 'Anmerkung', *Neue Juristische Wochenschrift* (1980), 2020.

concerned would be composed of multinational corporations, mainly but not necessarily, from industrialised countries. Thus, consensus would have to be reached between these multinational corporations.

Even more far-reaching would be a consensus to the effect that production methods that deviate so grossly from the basic requirements of good morals and public order even render the trade with such products unlawful. The group concerned here would be all producers that apply such production methods and compete, for example, on the European market, including corporations that are genuinely situated in their home countries. Thus, consensus would have to include a representative number of corporations from developing countries as well.

Finally, such a consensus must not ignore the interests of the consumer side. Here, one must not rely on the altruistic consumer but take account of the average consumer.[53] In contrast, a representative variety would not need to include the most unscrupulous consumers.

Competition lawyers might argue here that competition law is not concerned with issues that lie prior to the actual competition on the marketplace, and in particular with environmental aspects of the production process, but that these issues are subject to public law only. German case law on this issue is not entirely consistent.[54] In 1992, the Bundesgerichtshof (German Supreme Court, henceforth BGH) held that a trader acted in breach of the law of unfair competition because he gained an advantage over his competitors by paying less than the minimum wage to his employees.[55] In contrast, in 2000 the BGH adopted a narrow view in a case in which a German producer of lumber had violated German environmental law and could therefore sell lumber more cheaply than his competitors.[56] However, this opinion is generally on the decrease. In fact, even competition lawyers argue in favour of the introduction of social and environmental standards in World Trade Organisation (WTO) law in

---

[53] Obviously environmental groups and non-governmental organisations in the field of developing policy do not represent the whole spectrum of consumers but merely those concerned with the protection of the environment and of the people in developing countries. Consumer associations might be more representative, but do not necessarily have a democratic mandate either. Consumer assent could therefore best be assessed by consumer polls.

[54] See R. Sack, 'Die lückenfüllende Funktion der Generalklausel des § 3 UWG', *Wettbewerb in Recht und Praxis* (2005), 540–2.

[55] BGH, 3/12/1992, *Gewerblicher Rechtsschutz und Urheberrecht* (1993), 980. For more details on this line of cases, see Kocher, 'Unternehmerische Selbstverpflichtungen', 648–9.

[56] BGH, 11/5/2000, *Neue Juristische Wochenschrift* (2000), 3351.

order to level out gross differences in social and environmental standards. And consensus on the relevance of grossly unequal production methods for competition could overcome the reluctance of courts to include them in competition law.

In practice, the requirement of a broad consensus of producers and consumers will only relate to grossly unacceptable practices such as, for example, production that destroys the lives of indigenous peoples (like Texaco's oil production in Ecuador) or ruthless cutting down of the rain forest in contradiction to 'modern' techniques of sustainable forestry. Thus, the law of unfair competition could – at least to a certain level – fill the gap that results from the lack of harmonisation of social and environmental standards worldwide. Producers from developing countries are protected by the criterion of consensus: there will be no legal effect of private regulation to their disadvantage unless they agree.

B. Technical standardisation in tort law

Technical self-regulation may aim at harmonisation in order to facilitate economic transactions, at informing the profession, or at providing guidance to employees or subsidiaries in order to improve their performance and to prevent damages. However, it may also aim at creating legal effects by establishing a legally 'safe harbour' for those who comply with the private rules.[57] Technical self-regulation mainly comes in the form of private norms adopted by one or more corporations, the usual or actual practice of one or more corporations, or measures that are recognised as necessary by one or a number of corporations.

In legal terms, it might define the required standard of due diligence in classical fault-based tort law. In very general terms that would mean (1) if the conduct was not in line with the relevant technical norm, there would be a strong presumption of negligence and (2) vice versa, if the conduct was in line with the relevant technical norm, there would be a presumption of due diligence and therefore against negligence even though damage was caused. Such a standardisation effect has already been discussed controversially with a view to semi-private technical norms adopted by recognised standardisation organisations or institutes such as the Deutsches Institut für Normung eV (DIN), the British Standards

---

[57] See, e.g., D. Hart, 'Ärztliche Leitlinien – Definitionen, Funktionen, rechtliche Bewertungen', *Medizinrecht* (1998), 12–13, for medical guidelines.

Institution (BSI), the Comité Européen de Normalisation (CEN), and the International Organisation for Standardisation (ISO).[58] These presumptions may either form part of substantive law or merely impact on the burden of proof.[59] In contrast, it is common ground that technical norms do not have an immediate binding effect in tort law.

Clearly, the legally required standard of due diligence is a normative standard not an empirical one. Therefore, it cannot simply be related to a custom or a common practice as it might be unacceptably lax.[60] Instead, its concretisation has to lead to the correct determination of the one legally required conduct in a particular situation, taking account of the two main purposes of tort law.[61] One purpose is the compensation of the victim, which in fact means the allocation of damages, the other purpose is the prevention of damage, a purpose of ever increasing importance especially in the field of environmental liability.[62] For the prevention of damage, it is essential that the standard of due diligence is technically or substantially correct, a question that can be answered best by experts. In contrast, the decision on the allocation of damages – which means the determination of the required conduct, the compliance with which exempts from liability – is a question that has to reflect the public interest. It is a question of societal values, for example of the individual freedom to act or public interest in

---

[58] See, e.g., P. Marburger, *Die Regeln der Technk im Recht* (Cologne: Heymanns, 1979), pp. 429–91; J. Falke and H. Schepel, *Legal Aspects of Standardisation in the Member States of the EC and EFTA*, vol. 1, *Comparative Report* (European Communities, 2000), pp. 231–45; J. Falke, *Rechtliche Aspekte der Normung in den EG-Mitgliedstaaten und der EFTA*, vol. 3, *Deutschland* (European Communities, 2000), pp. 448–60; K. Finke, *Die Auswirkungen der europäischen technischen Normen und des Sicherheitsrechts auf das nationale Haftungsrecht* (Munich: Beck, 2001).

[59] See in particular Marburger, *Regeln*, pp. 445–8. For a more recent overview, see Finke, *Auswirkungen*, pp. 15–21.

[60] See generally G. Brüggemeier, *Common Principles of Tort Law* (London: BIICL, 2004), 66–7. For German law, see *Münchener Kommentar zum Bürgerlichen Recht* – H-P Mertens, § 276 no. 60. For US tort law, see, e.g., *Texas and Pacific Ry Co.* v. *Beymer*, 189 US 468, 470 (1903, per Holmes, J); *The TJ Hooper*, 60 F 2d 737 (2d Cir. 1932, per Learned Hand, CJ). For English law, see, e.g., *Edward Wong Finance Co. Ltd v. Johnson Stokes and Master* [1984] AC 296. This was different in pre-industrialisation US case law where the legal requirement of due care was held never to exceed social custom; see H. Schepel, *The Constitution of Private Governance* (Oxford and Portland, OR: Hart Publishing, 2005), pp. 340–3.

[61] See Brüggemeier, *Common Principles*, pp. 66–7. See also Falke, *Rechtliche Aspekte*, p. 452.

[62] See, e.g., W. Wurmnest, *Grundzüge eines europäischen Haftungsrechts* (Tübingen: Mohr Siebeck, 2003), pp. 94–100, for the tort law systems in the EC; Brüggemeier, *Common Principles*, pp. 3–7, for German and US tort law. For the increasing purpose of prevention in environmental law, see in particular P. Marburger, 'Grundsatzfragen des Haftungsrechts unter dem Einfluß der gesetzlichen Regelungen zur Produzenten und Umwelthaftung', *Archiv für civilistische Praxis* 192 (1992), 28–31.

economic development versus the protection of health and safety or the environment.[63]

Still, it is worth considering the tort law consequences of technical self-regulation. Below the legal effect of defining a 'safe harbour' there are two other legal effects one should be aware of: the setting of individual standards of diligence; and the setting of generally applicable minimum standards of diligence.

1. Individual standard of diligence

Corporations can be held liable if they violate their own (internal) technical norms or deviate from the usual conduct that they have recognised as necessary. This is true even if their own individual standards exceed what is legally required in general. Here the private rules or usual conduct of a corporation are used (by law) in order to establish an individually higher standard of diligence.

The reason is that tort law liability was traditionally based on individual fault. This has changed insofar as (more) objective standards of negligence have evolved.[64] This objective standard, however, merely has the purpose of introducing a minimum standard, thereby raising the diligence required from those who lack certain abilities.[65] This is in line with the increasingly important purpose of prevention. In contrast, the objective approach has not lowered the diligence requirements for those who have special knowledge and abilities.[66]

Strictly speaking, this is not an issue of standardisation at all, since here private regulation or practice does not take effect on other producers (outsiders) but is only binding on the respective corporation. Therefore, there is no reason for further legitimacy considerations. This is different with the following effects, where private regulation may have a real standardising effect that it is binding on outsiders.

---

[63] For an overview of the societal background of tort law in the course of the change from the pre-industrialisation period to industrial society, see, e.g., Brüggemeier, *Common Principles*, pp. 3–17.

[64] See generally (but with special focus on German and US tort law) Brüggemeier, *Common Principles*, pp. 65–73, 76–82. For objective standards in the different European legal orders, see, e.g., C. von Bar, *Gemeineuropäisches Deliktsrecht*, vol. II (Munich: Beck, 1999), pp. 248–53; Wurmnest, *Grundzüge*, pp. 113–24. Typical notions are the standards of the 'reasonable man' (United Kingdom, United States), or of the '*bon père de famille*' (France).

[65] See, e.g., E. Deutsch and H.-J. Ahrens, *Deliktsrecht* (4th edn, Cologne: Heymanns, 2001), pp. 62–3. Exceptions are only made where children or disabled persons are concerned.

[66] See, e.g., *Münchener Kommentar zum Bürgerlichen Recht* – H.-P. Mertens, § 267 no. 56. For example, a chief physician is held to his own skills even if they are superior to those of the average doctor.

2. Baseline or minimum standard the non-compliance of which attracts liability

Beyond this individual effect, private regulation by (a certain variety of) corporations defines the minimum standard, the breach of which constitutes liability. Private regulation here includes the common practice as well as the measures recognised as necessary – no matter whether it is based on an agreement between corporations, or simply exercised or (internally) regulated in parallel. Outsiders – that is, producers who do not adhere to the relevant practice or rule – are bound by this minimum standard defined by the practice or regulation of others as well.

This essentially stems from the tort law requirement of negligence, according to which damage must be predictable and avoidable. Here, the individual ability to recognise and avoid damage is replaced by the respective abilities within a certain line of business or category of producers. The binding effect on outsiders is a (legitimate) consequence of the legal decision in favour of objective standards. This objective approach is also reflected by the term 'duty of care'.[67]

All measures to prevent damage that are usually applied in practice or that are deemed adequate by the relevant category of producers must be regarded as measures that the members of the same profession or business can recognise and take.[68] Notably, this determination of the minimum standard does not disallow producers to take different measures as long as they achieve the same level of safety.[69] With a view to semi-private technical norms Falke and Schepel have observed a growing international consensus that 'compliance with standards is a necessary but not necessarily sufficient condition for the exemption of liability in tort'.[70] An illustrative example from English law is the case of *Ward* v. *Ritz Hotel*. The balustrade of the hotel's balcony was lower than the relevant British norm and a guest fell down and was injured. Whereas the judge in the first instance denied the relevance of a breach of an institutionalised norm

---

[67] See, e.g., Brüggemeier, *Common Principles*, pp. 109–12.

[68] This result could also be derived from (German) case law concerning institutionalised technical norms, compliance with which was not regarded as sufficiently diligent as the standard of the actual practice was already higher; see, e.g., Landgericht Berlin, 18 October 1996, *Neue Juristische Wochenschrift – Entscheidungsdienst Versicherungs- und Haftungsrecht* (1997), 94. This means that at least this standard of the actual practice has to be complied with.

[69] The burden of proof then falls on the producer; see, e.g., Marburger, *Regeln*, p. 470; Falke, *Rechtliche Aspekte*, pp. 453–4.

[70] Falke and Schepel, *Legal aspects of standardisation*, p. 233.

for establishing negligence, the majority of the Court of Appeal held that the failure to comply with the relevant technical norm constituted negligence.[71]

This legal effect of a minimum standard of due diligence has, however, some prerequisites. First of all, the private rule or practice must be established or followed by a representative variety of corporations. In contrast, a great number of adhering corporations is not necessary since the relevant criterion is not consent but the general ability within the relevant category of producers, or peer group ('*Verkehrskreis*'), to recognise and follow the rule.

The second prerequisite is the correct determination of the peer group. In the context of an industrialised country, the relevant peer group is the respective line of business that is also usually subjected to the same public law requirements. This may be different in a developing country where domestic producers at a low level of environmental and safety standards meet producers that are subsidiaries of and controlled by multinational corporations. Under such circumstances, the relevant category of producers cannot simply be identical with the line of business but has to take into consideration other criteria such as technological know-how, (environmental and safety) management abilities, access to technology and financial resources. Consequently, this approach leads to different standards within the same line of business, where sophisticated producers – in particular, subsidiaries of multinationals – have to adhere to the higher standard of their peer group.

With such a consideration of different peer groups that forms part of tort law, it is also possible to level out – at least with the legal consequences of tort law – the different protection standards globally. These different tort law requirements on different categories of producers in the same line of business should not be in breach of international law – and in particular of the principle of national treatment that is usually enshrined in investment agreements – so long as the nationality of the producer or his link with a foreign investor as such are not relevant criteria.[72]

---

[71] *Ward* v. *The Ritz Hotel (London)* [1992] PIQR 315. For examples from German case law, see, e.g., BGH, 4 April 1989, *Neue Juristische Wochenschrift – Rechtsprechungs-Report* 1989, 921; BGH, 12 November 1996, *Neue Juristische Wochenschrift* 1997, 582; BGH, 27 April 1999, *Neue Juristische Wochenschrift* 1999, 2593.

[72] For the difficult relationship of investment agreements and environmental standards, see, e.g., I. Madalena, 'Foreign Direct Investment and the Protection of the Environment: the Border between National Environmental Regulation and Expropriation', *European Environmental Law Review* (2003), 70–82.

3. 'Safe harbour'

In contrast, the final legal effect of a 'safe harbour' may be the one actually intended by corporations. By producing their own (technical) codes or norms, corporations may hope that courts refer to these self-regulatory requirements when determining the correct standard of lawful conduct, the compliance with which exempts the producer causing damage from liability. As a consequence, the victims and/or the general public (would) have to bear the costs of the damage. Ironically, corporations may find that this type of binding effect proves elusive.

This standard of a safe harbour is usually higher than or at least as high as the baseline or the minimum standard but – in principle – not necessarily the highest state of the art. Obviously, third persons (the victims) and the public interest (e.g., in environmental protection, public safety or simply in avoiding public costs of remedying the damage) are directly concerned by any regulation with regard to a safe harbour. Therefore, private regulation of a safe harbour would not only presuppose the substantive correctness of the standard derived from 'ideal expertise',[73] but also a fair and representative procedure to ensure the reflection of the public interest.[74]

As a first consequence, technical *self*-regulation by corporations *unilaterally*, although relevant for defining an individual or an objective minimum standard, lacks the legitimacy to define a safe harbour for

---

[73] This has to be ensured by the selection of the experts according to their qualifications, independence and reliability. The technical and scientific expertise must include and balance different opinions and different fields of science concerned. Furthermore, the decision procedure has to be transparent, the norms have to be published and explained, and ideally they have to be externally evaluated and their application monitored; see, e.g., W. Hoffmann-Riem, 'Öffentliches Recht und Privatrecht als wechselseitige Auffangordnungen – Systematisierung und Entwicklungsperspektiven', in W. Hoffmann-Riem and E. Schmidt-Aßmann, *Öffentliches Recht und Privatrecht als wechselseitige Auffangordnungen* (Baden-Baden: Nomos, 1996), pp. 320–2. Also, norms can be regarded as reliable if there is empirical evidence that their adherence has effectively prevented damage, for example in other countries.

[74] A representative variety of the concerned interests (including social and environmental interests) has to be considered. Also, general prerequisites of fair procedure must be met, for example, interests have to be balanced to make sure that the less powerful (social and environmental) interests have an equal opportunity to give an input as the traditionally powerful economic interests or well-informed circles. This includes the guarantee that the representatives of these other interests obtain all relevant information in due time, and that certain interests cannot be overruled. It may even be necessary to support such interests as the protection of life and health over-proportionately in order to reflect their human rights value. See, e.g., Hoffmann-Riem, 'Öffentliches Recht und Privatrecht', pp. 319–20.

producers to the disadvantage of third persons or the general public, as there are no safeguards for their substantial correctness (although they may in fact reflect the state of the art) or for the reflection of the public interest.

However, a number of tort law-specific objections must be raised against *multilateral* technical regulation as well. To start with, the existence of an 'ideal' committee that really reflects the 'ideal expertise' and the public interest is not very likely, as the oft-mentioned shortcomings of ISO, CEN and DIN demonstrate, where – despite all precautions – the producers and users of technology dominate the standardisation process, simply because of their superior knowledge and their resources.[75]

But there are further important reasons why a safe harbour cannot be established. Also, environmental liability law – that is, liability for damages caused by industrial installations – follows a (worldwide) trend towards strict liability. In principle, fault-based liability in these circumstances is a relict anyway. In order to be in line with this tendency towards strict liability, the standard of due diligence required by fault-based tort law should reasonably reflect the highest state of the art that can be answered by the 'ideal expert'. Any safe harbour below appears inadequate.

Legitimacy considerations also prevent private regulation from establishing a safe harbour in tort law. If a private committee, no matter how pluralistic, could determine a standard of due diligence below the highest state of the art, it would decide that in the case of compliance with this lower standard the victims have to bear their damage without any compensation. Thus, a private committee would be allowed to place a special burden on a group of persons (the future victims) that cannot be identified in advance and that cannot therefore be included in the decision-making process proportionately to their potential suffering. This is a problem that – for tort law – cannot be solved by requirements of fair procedure.[76] Importantly, future victims of industrial accidents usually have no choice as to whether or not they expose themselves to the risk of uncompensated damage.[77] Moreover, a private committee has no alternative compensatory mechanisms available.

---

[75] See, e.g., R. Krut and H. Gleckman, *ISO 14001 – A Missed Opportunity for Sustainable Global Industrial Development* (London: Earthscan, 1998); Falke, *Rechtliche Aspekte*, p. 452.

[76] In contrast, the contractual limitation of liability between a producer and members of a local community would seem possible but this is no matter of standardisation of due diligence.

[77] This may be different in product liability.

Therefore, the general exclusion of liability for certain conduct below the highest state of the art can only be decided by a democratically legitimated legislator,[78] and it should then be accompanied by an insurance solution.[79] Political reasons for such a decision may be the wish to attract (risk) technology, or to offer an incentive to establish some reasonable standard at all, in particular where – like in low standard countries – there is no adequate public law regulation on the subject matter.

Therefore, tort law does not really give room for the determination of a safe harbour, no matter whether it is by a corporate code of conduct, by the ideal pluralistic committee or by semi-private institutionalised norms. In principle, due diligence in environmental liability requires diligence at the highest state of the art. A general decision in favour of an exclusion of liability for conduct below the highest state of the art can only be decided upon by a democratically legitimated legislator. Apart from this, the justification for not meeting the highest state of the art in the individual case can only be decided by the civil courts. In exceptional cases it may, for example, be acceptable not to apply the highest standard of safety where the costs incurred are grossly disproportionate to the preventive effect of the measure or to the severity of the damage. This task necessitates the weighing of the respective interests of the producer and the victim in order to achieve justice in the individual case, although the decision may be influenced by societal values on the correct allocation of damages.

The same result can be found in literature and case law from other member states of the European Community (concerning semi-private institutionalised technical norms). Falke and Schepel observe that in tort law, 'non-compliance is of greater legal significance than compliance with standards', and compliance 'leads to scarcely more than a mere indication of fulfilling duties of care (at all)'.[80] For example, in the 'ice hockey case', a spectator was injured by a puck that flew over the board. Although the

---

[78] See also K. Sach, *Genehmigung als Schutzschild?* (Berlin: Duncker and Humblot, 1994), p. 236.

[79] See, e.g., Brüggemeier, *Common Principles*, pp. 3–7, for the introduction of insurance to balance shortcomings in protection by tort law during industrial development in Germany and in the United States.

[80] Falke and Schepel, *Legal aspects of standardisation*, pp. 235 and 233, with further references. Further arguments used in literature are, for example, that standardisation aims at regulating the general or typical case, whereas further or more specific safety measures may be necessary in the individual case, which is relevant in tort law. Besides, practice shall be left with the responsibility to evaluate critically their own production patterns and to improve them accordingly once they discover risks, instead of simply relying on standards. See, e.g., Falke, *Rechtliche Aspekte*, pp. 451–5.

height of the board was in compliance with the relevant German standard, the German Bundesgerichtshof regarded this norm as generally too low. The court held that 'they (the technical norms) do not always determine the ultimate care that can be expected in a particular case and do not discharge the judge from his duty to take account of the safety interests of potential victims himself'.[81]

IV. Liability of parent companies[82]

Another important issue of corporate social and environmental responsibility is the liability of parent companies for damage caused in developing countries. Although the market effects of transnational corporate self-regulation can be enforced with the mechanisms of contract law and the law of unfair competition in those countries where the products are marketed, this nevertheless is merely an indirect remedy in the transnational context. These mechanisms do not confer remedies on the people in substandard countries who suffer damage from a 'breach' of (self-regulatory) standards. Tort law, in contrast, offers an immediate sanction for a breach of standards. On the contrary, it provides for damages and is a direct remedy for these people. In terms of corporate social and environmental liability, however, this can only be seriously effective if it is not only the subsidiary in the developing country that is liable but if the corporate responsibility of the parent company can be translated into liability for damage caused, where appropriate.

The fundamental problem with a view to addressing damage claims to parent companies lies, apart from jurisdiction,[83] in the legal separation between the parent company and the subsidiary in a substandard country that has been enshrined in virtually all company laws worldwide.

This principle of legal separation makes it almost impossible to hold parent companies liable for damages their subsidiaries have caused under

---

[81] BGH, 29 November 1983, *Neue Juristische Wochenschrift* 1984, 801.

[82] For a detailed analysis, see C. Glinski, 'Haftung multinationaler Unternehmen für Umweltschäden bei Auslandsdirektinvestitionen', in G. Winter (ed.), *Die Umweltverantwortung multinationaler Unternehmen* (Baden-Baden: Nomos, 2005), pp. 231–85.

[83] See, e.g., the decision by the Victorian Supreme Court in *Dagi and others* v. *BHP*, cited by P. Prince, 'Bhopal, Bougainville and Ok Tedi: Why Australia's *Forum Non Conveniens* Approach is Better', *International and Comparative Law Quarterly* 47 (1998), 593–5. Concerning the decisions by the House of Lords in the *Cape Industries* case [2000] 4 All ER 268, see P. Muchlinski, 'Corporations in International Litigation: Problems of Jurisdiction and the United Kingdom Asbestos Cases', *International and Comparative Law Quarterly* 50 (2001), 11–12; Ward, 'Towards a New Convention', 129.

the law of corporations. Attempts to introduce direct remedies for tort victims through the law of corporations have regularly proved unsuccessful.[84] Despite this legal separation, it is remarkable that all the new initiatives on corporate social and environmental responsibility address the multinational corporation as a whole. This is true for the OECD *Guidelines for Multinational Enterprises*,[85] Kofi Annan's *Global Compact*,[86] the EC Commission's *Communication on Corporate Social Responsibility*[87] and similar national initiatives.[88] Even further go the 'Norms on the Responsibility of Transnational Corporations and other Business Enterprises with Regard to Human Rights'[89] and an NGO representatives' call for a 'Corporate Accountability Convention'[90] both of which demand the introduction of the transnational corporations' liability for damages.

In this context, tort law can play an important role, in particular since it is independent from the barriers built by the law of corporations.[91] Prominent examples for this approach are the cases of *Cape Industries*[92] and *Thor Chemicals*.[93]

[84] See, e.g., Muchlinski, 'Corporations in International Litigation', 1; G. Teubner, 'Unitas Multiplex – Das Konzernrecht in der neuen Dezentralität der Unternehmensgruppen', *Zeitschrift für das gesamte Gesellschaftsrecht* (1991), 189.

[85] On their version of 2000, see S. Tully, 'The 2000 Review of the OECD Guidelines for Multinational Enterprises', *International and Comparative Law Quarterly* 50 (2001), 394.

[86] Available at www.unglobalcompact.org. For critical comments, see, e.g., A. Zumach, 'Der "strategische Handel" des Generalsekretärs – Ernüchternde Erfahrungen mit dem Globalen Pakt von Davos', *Vereinte Nationen* 50 (2002), 1.

[87] COM (2002) 347 final.

[88] See the French Décret no. 2002–221 du 20 février 2002 pris pour l'application de l'article L. 225–102–1 du code de commerce et modifiant le décret no 67–236 du 23 mars 1967 sur les sociétés commerciales (French Decree no. 2000-221 of 20 February 2002 concerning the application of Article L. 225-102-1 of the Commercial Code and amending Decree no. 67-236 of 23 March 1967 concerning the commercial companies), O.J. (France) no. 44 of 21 February 2002, p. 3360. (O J No. 44 of 21 Feb, 3360).

[89] UN document E/CN.4/Sub.2/2003/12/Rev.2 (2003). For an account, see P. Muchlinski, 'Human Rights, Social Responsibility and the Regulation of International Business: The Development of International Standards by Intergovernmental Organisations', *Non-State Actors and International Law* 3 (2003), 135–45; K. Nowrot, 'Die UN-Norms on the Responsibility of Transnational Corporations and Other Business Enterprises with Regard to Human Rights – Gelungener Beitrag zur transnationalen Rechtsverwirklichung oder das Ende des Global Compact?', in C. Tietje, G. Kraft and R. Sethe (eds.), *Beiträge zum Transnationalen Wirtschaftsrecht* 21 (2003).

[90] For details, see Ward, 'Towards a New Convention', 107–9.

[91] For English law, see *Williams* v. *Natural Life Health Foods Ltd* [1998] 1 WLR 830, with a critical comment by R. Grantham and C. Rickett, 'Directors' "Tortious" Liability: Contract, Tort or Company Law?', *Modern Law Review* 62 (1999), 133. For German law, see P. Hommelhoff, 'Produkthaftung im Konzern', *Zeitschrift für Wirtschaftsrecht* (1990), 761.

[92] *Lubbe and Others* v. *Cape plc* [2000] 4 All ER 268.

[93] *Sithole and Others* v. *Thor Chemicals Holdings Ltd and Others* [1999] All ER (D) 102. See Muchlinski, 'Corporations in International Litigation', 3–4.

A. Detrimental influence on the production process

If the parent company influences the production process, for example, by giving instructions or by issuing environmental management handbooks, and the subsidiary causes damage while following these instructions, the parent company is liable if the procedures followed were below the required standard of a reasonable operator.[94] This result should be obvious in all legal orders. The parent company should also be liable if it unduly restricts the subsidiary's funds for environmental management.

B. Responsibility for the environmental management

In *Cape Industries* and *Thor Chemicals*, the claimants sued under the tort of negligence. In *Cape Industries* they claimed that the parent company was in breach of its duty of care towards the employees and the neighbours of the plant that was run by its South African subsidiary. They argued that the parent company acted negligently by establishing a company and a plant in South Africa and not taking care of its proper safety and environmental management afterwards. Unfortunately, the defendants settled the claims once the English courts had decided to have jurisdiction for the cases so that no case law was available.[95]

In *Amoco Cadiz*,[96] the State Court of Illinois found that the oil spill was caused negligently by the parent company that had been responsible for the safety and the maintenance of the ship.[97] Thus, the reason for the parent company's liability was the allocation of responsibility for this element of the operation of the subsidiary. The same rule should apply under German tort law.[98] Apart from actual influence on the production patterns, the appearance is of some relevance. If a parent company makes the impression of controlling production patterns, this may cause a duty of care. In this context, publicised instruments of self-regulation that imply control over the subsidiaries' safety and environmental performance can play an important role.

---

[94] See, e.g., H. P. Westermann, 'Umwelthaftung im Konzern', *Zeitschrift für das gesamte Handelsrecht* 155 (1991), 239–40.

[95] For details, see Ward, 'Towards a New Convention', 113–22.

[96] *In re Matter of Oil Spill by the Amoco Cadiz*, F 2d 1279, 1303 (7th Cir. 1992).

[97] See J. E. Antunes, 'Neue Wege im Konzernhaftungsrecht – Nochmals: Der "Amoco Cadiz"-Fall', in U. H. Schneider, P. Hommelhoff, K. Schmidt, W. Timm, B. Grunewald and T. Drygala (eds.), *Festschrift für Marcus Lutter zum 70. Geburtstag* (Köln: Otto Schmidt, 2000), p. 1007.

[98] See Hommelhoff, 'Produkthaftung', 764, on tort law rules for product liability.

This idea of liability corresponding to the responsibility for the running of a plant is even more strongly anchored in modern environmental liability laws that focus on the notion of the 'operator'. Under the US Comprehensive Environmental Response, Compensation and Liability Act (CERCLA), courts have adopted a wide interpretation of the notion of 'operator' that included companies that had the control over or participated in the actual running of the plant. Some courts even regarded those who had the opportunity to control as operators.[99] Under the German Environmental Liability Act, the operator is the one who exercises the decisive influence on the operation of the plant, that is, the one who has the legal and factual power to make the necessary decisions on the operation and the one who benefits economically from the operation.[100] Thus, the operator is the one who controls the risks that stem from the plant and who is therefore able to avoid damages.[101] This is also meant to serve as an incentive for investment into safety management.[102] Hence, determination of the subsidiary's environmental management – for example, by technical guidelines – is a strong indicator for the parent company's being the real operator.[103] The same is true for centralised environmental units that control the environmental conduct of the whole corporation.[104] Finally, the EC Environmental Liability Directive 2004/35/EC[105] defines 'operator' as any person who operates *or controls* the occupational activity or, where this is provided for in national legislation, to whom decisive

[99] For details, see U. Vettori, *Haftung für Ökoschäden im Recht der USA* (Berne: Lang, 1996), pp. 106–8; F. Ochsenfeld, *Direkthaftung von Konzernobergesellschaften in den USA: die Rechtsprechung zum Altlasten-Superfund als Modell für das deutsche Konzernhaftungsrecht?* (Berlin: Duncker and Humblot, 1998), pp. 46–73; M. Landwehr, *Die Durchgriffshaftung in konzernverbundenen Gesellschaften* (Frankfurt am Main: Lang, 2002), pp. 113–15. However, in *United States v. Bestfoods*, 118 S. Ct 1876 (1998), the US Supreme Court took a more restrictive view and held that only those who have actively caused the pollution are the 'operator'.

[100] See Verwaltungsgericht Mannheim, *Neue Zeitschrift für Verwaltungsrecht* (1988), 562.

[101] See U. H. Schneider, 'Die Überlagerung des Konzernrechts durch öffentlich-rechtliche Strukturnormen und Organisationspflichten', *Zeitschrift für das gesamte Gesellschaftsrecht* (1996), 239; A. Hucke and H. Schröder, 'Umwelthaftung von Konzernen', *Der Betrieb* (1998), 2206.

[102] See G. Teubner, 'Die "Politik des Gesetzes" im Recht der Konzernhaftung', in J. F. Baur, K. J. Hopt and K. P. Mailänder (eds.), *Festschrift für Ernst Steindorff zum 70. Geburtstag am 13. März 1990* (Berlin: de Gruyter, 1990), p. 265.

[103] See Westermann, 'Umwelthaftung', 240; Schneider, 'Überlagerung des Konzernrechts', 239–40.

[104] See K. Schmidt, 'Haftungsrisiken für Umweltschutz und technische Sicherheit im gegliederten Unternehmen – Gesellschafts- und konzernrechtliche Betrachtungen', *Umwelt- und Technikrecht* 26 (1993), 84.

[105] OJ 2004 No. L143/56.

economic power over the technical functioning of such an activity has been delegated, a definition that is understood to encompass parent companies.[106] In all these laws, self-regulatory instruments can play an important role in providing evidence of control over the subsidiary's environmental conduct.

C. Lack of corporation-wide safety and environmental management

The two approaches discussed so far have one thing in common: they do not hold liable a parent company that simply leaves the responsibility to a subsidiary which is not capable of dealing with risks appropriately, be it for lack of financial resources or for lack of technical knowledge and experience, whereas the parent company avails itself of the necessary know-how and financial means. This is the situation that regularly arises in transnational corporations which include subsidiaries in developing countries.

The next step would therefore be to recognise the parent company's duty to organise the corporation in such a way that damage can best be avoided. A parallel can be drawn to product liability law. Whilst in product liability law potentially dangerous products are put into circulation, here dangerous technologies are exported. Product liability law holds the producer liable for damages since he is the one who is responsible for the design of the product and is best suited to instruct users and to monitor the functioning of the product in practice.[107] In a transnational corporation, the parent company that designs a product which is then produced by subsidiaries worldwide will be liable for damages. Transposed to production processes, this would mean that the parent company which develops technology and makes it available to a subsidiary in a developing country has to take responsibility for its proper functioning and use. This includes the duty to instruct and educate the users – that is, the employees of the subsidiaries – on safety and environmental issues. The parent company would also have to monitor the functioning and use of the technology in practice, and to take into account the lower level of education of employees in developing countries, as well as climatic differences and so on. In case of problems, the parent company would have to take action, for example by taking over certain functions or by introducing

---

[106] See C. Leifer, 'Der Richtlinienentwurf zur Umwelthaftung: Internationaler Kontext, Entstehung und öffentlich-rechtliche Dimension', *Natur und Recht* (2003), 604.
[107] See Hommelhoff, 'Produkthaftung', 763–7.

additional safety elements. In fact, this is exactly what the German chemical industry is already doing.[108] However, such taking over would not be a voluntary legal duty under tort law. It is safe to say that some of the duties cannot be delegated at all but must be fulfilled by the skilled and experienced personnel of the parent company that has developed a certain technology.

In conclusion, this would mean that parent companies of transnational corporations are obliged to introduce a corporation-wide safety and environmental management system that allocates responsibilities where they can best be exercised. Otherwise they are liable for damage that occurs from insufficient management and control. If, however, a reasonable structure has been established, and a subsidiary still causes damage, the parent company is not liable but only the subsidiary in question. Usually, the burden of proof for such a structure would lie with the parent company.[109] Self-regulatory instruments would become an important tool for establishing a corporation-wide safety and environmental management system. Tort law would then serve as an incentive to introduce environmentally friendly corporate structures and production schemes.[110] Whether or not such adequate management systems are already in place cannot be decided at this stage. The practice of the German chemicals industry to use a worldwide system of codes of conduct, guidelines, handbooks and auditing schemes appears to be rather progressive. Certainly, the requirements of the ISO for management systems, such as ISO 9000[111] and ISO 14000,[112] do not reach an adequate standard since they merely apply to individual enterprises, not to a whole multinational corporation and, moreover, they are far too unsophisticated for the necessities of safety and environmental management.[113]

Only such a duty to organise a transnational corporation adequately does justice to demands that transnational corporations should guarantee not only their own compliance with human rights, social standards and environmental standards but also the compliance of all their subsidiaries.

[108] See Herberg, 'Codes of Conduct', 39.
[109] See G. Brüggemeier, 'Enterprise Liability for Environmental Damage: German and European Law', in G. Teubner, L. Farmer and D. Murphy (eds.), Environmental Law and Ecological Responsibility (Chichester: Wiley, 1994), pp. 90–2, for the organisation of enterprises.
[110] See Brüggemeier, 'Enterprise Liability', pp. 91–2.
[111] The ISO 9000 series is concerned with quality management.
[112] The ISO 14000 series is concerned with environmental management.
[113] See Krut and Gleckman, ISO 14001; A. Matusche-Beckmann, Das Organisationsverschulden (Tübingen: Mohr, 2001), pp. 355–74.

V. Conclusion

There is no doubt that corporate social responsibility – although usually regarded as a set of voluntary self-commitments and self-regulation – produces a variety of legal effects. Even if social responsibility deals with public-interest issues such as the protection of the environment, of health and safety, and of labour standards, it has legal effects in private law, although these effects may rarely be intended by the respective corporations. These legal effects are limited to their binding effect. First of all, self-regulation creates immediate obligations for those who adopt the rules. This is true for sales law and for advertisement law but also for tort law. Second, private corporate regulation is well capable of setting minimum standards for a whole group of corporations, including outsiders, for fair business conduct, as well as for due diligence in tort law, if the authors of the rules are sufficiently representative. And self-regulation of multinational corporations is of increasing importance in light of the parent companies' responsibility – and indeed liability – for failure to build a corporation-wide safety and environmental management system. Thus, self-regulation is able to produce a truly transnational regulative effect that goes beyond the individual obligation but sets standards for all producers of the same category, thereby bridging the gap with private law mechanisms where public law mechanisms are not available. In contrast, private corporate regulation cannot create a 'safe harbour' by limiting the legal obligations of those who adhere to it, to the disadvantage of, for example, the victims of environmental damage.

5

Corporate accountability through creative enforcement: human rights, the Alien Tort Claims Act and the limits of legal impunity

DOREEN McBARNET AND PATRICK SCHMIDT

Commitment to to human rights has become a regular feature of voluntary corporate codes of conduct and corporate social responsibility (CSR) reports. Though human rights abuse can occur anywhere, debate in the international business context tends to concentrate on developing countries. This debate has focused partly on such concerns as labour conditions, increasingly seen as part of the human rights canon, or freedom of speech, as in the case of Google and other internet-related businesses operating in China. But it has also involved claims of egregious and fundamental human rights abuses such as torture, extra-judicial killings, slave labour and genocide, being carried out, if not directly by commercial organisations themselves, by governments for or with corporate benefit.[1] Businesses can have more than just a geographical connection with these issues through the location of their operating companies in countries with poor human rights records. They may also be directly involved in their core business with the governments of those countries, as their commercial partners in joint ventures.

For international business operating in such contexts, human rights issues are increasingly recognised as a significant risk factor in relation to CSR reputational capital.[2] Non-governmental organisations (NGOs) such as Amnesty International publish the names of companies operating in areas noted for human rights abuse,[3] and publicity campaigns aimed at

Thanks are due to the ESRC for funding this research as part of the professorial fellowship awarded to McBarnet on the theme 'Regulation, responsibility and the rule of law'.

[1] For example, see EarthRights, 'Help defend ATCA', at www.earthrights.org/site_blurbs/help_defend_atca.html.

[2] Hence, for example, Shell's *Management Primer on Business and Human Rights*, at www.shell.com.

[3] www.amnesty.org.

mobilising market pressure against such companies pounce on indications of corporate involvement in, or benefit from, human rights abuses.

But can the pressure on international business regarding human rights be extended to *legal* risk and *legal* accountability? Human rights are part of international law traditionally dealing with nation states, and though there are currently many interpretations that argue human rights obligations should and do also apply to private corporations, along with bids to extend its express reach to business,[4] these remain at the level of proposal and debate. Voluntary corporate commitments, such as to the UN Global Compact – which includes respect for international human rights – involve no mechanism for enforcement.

Bringing multinational corporations (MNCs) to account for human rights abuses abroad is difficult for other reasons, too. International publicity and market campaigns can be waged against the brand name and holding company, with its headquarters in New York or London, Paris or Sydney, but legally the issue may be more complex. Multinationals typically have elaborate corporate structures. Operating companies working with abusive regimes are frequently subsidiaries or other separate legal entities, and the brand company may have no clear legal liability for the behaviour of such units. Then there is the question of jurisdiction, with any legal accountability usually a matter for the country where the offence or damage takes place, which does little practical good if the country in question is run by the dictatorship whose business arm is part of the joint venture involved in the alleged abuses. And if the abuses are not directly carried out by the multinational business itself, but by its joint venture partner, how can the business corporation be held to legal account?

Yet despite all these obstacles, NGOs have succeeded in establishing the legal accountability of MNCs, in the US domestic courts, for human rights abuses abroad. They have done so by using private law to fill the public law gap. In 1996 a lawsuit was brought in the United States against international oil company Unocal over complaints of murder, rape, slave labour, forcible eviction and other egregious human rights abuses[5] carried out by the army of Myanmar (formerly known as Burma) for Unocal's joint venture with the Myanmar government. Unocal was accused of knowingly using forced labour (forced by the army by means of these

---

[4] See Chapters 14 and 15 of this volume.
[5] Torture was also on the list but those complaints were dismissed on the basis there were insufficient facts to justify examination. Torture is one of the complaints against Shell in the *Saro-Wiwa* case, *Wiwa* v. *Royal Dutch Shell Petroleum*, 226 F 3d 88 (2d Cir. 2000).

violations) to construct its Yadana gas pipeline.[6] In June 2005, after nearly ten years of litigation, Unocal settled the case out of court for a sum which must, under the terms of the settlement, remain undisclosed, but which reportedly amounted to many millions of dollars. Further suits have been pursued or are in process involving a list of leading international companies, including oil concerns Shell, Texaco, Chevron and Talisman, as well as other companies such as Rio Tinto, Coca-Cola, WalMart and Gap.

Unocal's settlement out of court means that no company has to date actually been found legally liable, but the result of the *Unocal* case, the preceding cases on which it built, and the Supreme Court case, *Sosa*,[7] that followed, is the establishment of a legal procedure by which business corporations can be held to account for human rights abuses, even where they have been carried out in foreign jurisdictions.[8] International human rights, in the US context at least (and NGOs in other jurisdictions are looking for opportunities to follow suit), are no longer a matter of voluntary commitment, but a matter of potential legal liability.

This legal accountability was accomplished through creative legal enforcement by NGOs and their lawyers, conducted through the civil courts. The legal tool used to achieve the apparently legally impossible task was an arcane and virtually redundant statute of 1789 called the Alien Tort Claims Act (ATCA), a 'tort' being a 'wrong' over which the victim can sue in the civil courts. Originally set up in the context of such offences as piracy on the high seas,[9] it would allow foreign (hence 'alien') citizens to sue for recovery of their property or damages when pirates tried to dispose of it in US ports. The statute was little used in the 200 years that followed, until it was spotted as a potential tool for creative enforcement in the context of international human rights. Faced with legal obstacles to client goals, the skill of lawyers is to find ways to legally accomplish the apparently legally impossible. That is indeed exactly how corporate

---

[6] R. Chambers, 'The Unocal Settlement: Implications for the Developing Law in Corporate Complicity in Human Rights Abuses', at www.globalpolicy.org/intljustice/atca/2005/09unocal.pdf.

[7] *Sosa* v. *Alvarez-Machain*, 542 US 692 (2004).

[8] Even if favourable precedent from superior appellate courts does not flow from settled litigation, protracted litigation that is substantial enough to compel settlement by its nature usually has been able to create doubt about who might prevail on the merits. Sometimes in the form of opinions from sympathetic judges, these opinions help to form a roadmap to future possibilities. See, e.g., *Doe* v. *Unocal*, 395 F 3d 932 (9th Cir. 2002).

[9] Protection of ambassadorial rights and violation of safe-conducts were also seen as potential targets.

lawyers earn their fees, and our prior research in areas like corporate finance readily demonstrates the routine use of legal creativity to accomplish what financial analysts, for example, have described as 'sheer magic' in financial engineering.[10] In this case, however, legal creativity was turned *against* corporate interests by NGOs. ATCA was, as one commentator put it, 'not drafted to clobber corporations'[11] – it had to be actively worked on to achieve this outcome.

This creative accomplishment of corporate accountability was a long, slow process, and not without setbacks and the indignant protest that 'US businesses are not pirates'.[12] From the first 'Eureka!' moment when the idea of using ATCA in the context of human rights emerged – as far back as the 1970s – to the establishment of the principle of corporate accountability in the US courts for international human rights abuses, there was a long list of specific legal problems to counter, and specific principles to establish. The story is worth telling not only for the legal development it describes but also to demonstrate the process, and significance for corporate responsibility, of legal creativity itself. Drawing on both legal and empirical research,[13] including interviews with key participants, this chapter analyses how ATCA's legal magic was accomplished, its immediate consequences, and its wider implications both for the future relationship between CSR and the law, and for the new corporate accountability more generally.

I. The process of creative enforcement

For nearly two centuries, ATCA was no more than an obscure statute making a bare procedural statement on a matter of jurisdiction: 'The district courts shall have original jurisdiction of any civil action by an alien for a tort only, committed in violation of the law of nations or a treaty of the United States.'[14]

For ATCA to become a tool of corporate accountability, three key transformations were necessary. It had to be established, first, that the 1789

---

[10] D. McBarnet and C. Whelan, 'Creative Compliance and the Defeat of Legal Control: the Magic of the Orphan Subsidiary', in K. Hawkins (ed.), *The Human Face of Law* (Oxford: Oxford University Press, 1997).

[11] *Foreign Direct Investment*, 5 June 2006, at www.fdimagazine.com.

[12] P. Rozenweig, press room commentary (Heritage Foundation, 28 April 2003), at www.heritage.org.

[13] Case law, legal history, interviews with key participants, press coverage, legal, business and NGO websites.

[14] 28 USC §1350.

statute's reference to the law of nations could apply in the context of contemporary international law on human rights; second – given the focus of international law on states – that it could apply to private actors rather than just governments and state officials; and third, that it could apply to business corporations. A fourth important issue was whether it could apply where corporations were complicit in the violations without necessarily executing them themselves. Along the way, human rights activists using ATCA in suits against companies also had to overcome an array of specific defences.

To put it in terms of a staged transformation may seem to suggest a deliberate twenty-five-year strategy to catch business in the ATCA net. That would be misleading. The process was more gradual than that, with one bold step encouraging another, and ambitions developing in stages, with success in the context of state violation of human rights leading on to the recognition of new strategic possibilities in relation to business accountability – though even that was more complex than it sounds. Each case could take years to reach resolution, and steps towards a second stage might be taken without necessarily knowing the final outcome of the first.

The context also changed over the period. The process took place against a developing debate in international law in which an explicit drive for recognition of corporate responsibility in the human rights area was, by the latter part of the twenty-five-year period, clearly emerging, helping facilitate the argument in the courts that ATCA should apply to business corporations, too. This would have been more difficult to press when the use of ATCA was first mooted.

Context was important more generally. Vitally, how would judges receive the innovative arguments? In using Unocal, a California-based oil company, as their test case on business accountability, the initiating NGOs and their lawyers were able to have the arguments heard in the first instance before a reputedly liberal-minded Californian judiciary, who, it was hoped, would be sympathetic to the issues involved. Political context was relevant too, with the early steps helped by a supportive Carter administration. The combination of a shift of focus from pursuing foreign policemen in the first modern ATCA case to pursuing US businesses in Unocal, a very different government approach in the Bush administration, and the impact of 9/11 and the discourse of terrorism made for a more difficult political context later. But by that time a number of battles had already been won and there was real momentum, though there was still uncertainty about how the Supreme Court would respond in the important 2004 *Sosa* case.

The transformation began with a chance encounter, on the streets of New York in 1979, between the father of a tortured and murdered Paraguayan, and the Paraguayan police chief responsible. The result was the *Filártiga* case,[15] the resurrection of ATCA and the accomplishment of the first key step towards establishing ATCA as a contemporary legal tool for enforcing human rights.

A. *From piracy to human rights*

The significance of *Filártiga* could not have been predicted from the text of ATCA or from the facts of the case. Dr Joel Filártiga was a committed opponent of Paraguay's long-time dictator-president, Alfredo Stroessner. The penalty for his activities, in 1976, was the brutal torture and murder of his son, Joelito, by Americo Peña-Irala, the Inspector-General of Police in Asuncion. Joelito's sister Dolly was brought to Peña's home to view the body of her brother and she too was threatened. The Paraguayan justice system offered little meaningful recourse, though a formal, plodding procedure was observed. When Dr Filártiga raised a criminal action against Peña and the police, his attorney was threatened and ultimately disbarred. The substance of the criminal investigation was hijacked by a confession to Joelito's murder by the son of Peña's companion, who claimed to have found Joelito with his wife – a defence that eventually won an absolution from a Paraguayan court.[16] In 1979, coincidentally, both Dolly and Peña were living in the United States, the latter having overstayed his tourist visa to set up residence in Brooklyn.

With little evidence of any crimes committed in the United States, Peña was arrested and faced imminent deportation, or a 'voluntary departure', if no grounds could be found to hold him. Lawyers from the Centre for Constitutional Rights (CCR) became involved in an attempt to hold Peña in the United States, but they lacked optimism as they plotted a legal strategy. Given just one day to file a lawsuit, Filártiga filed a claim for wrongful death by torture, seeking compensation and punitive damages of $10 million. The key would be establishing the jurisdiction of US courts for a suit by a non-US citizen against another non-US citizen for torture conducted abroad, and Peter Weiss, a senior attorney with CCR, argued that ATCA could provide it. A temporary restraining order kept Peña in

---

[15] *Filártiga* v. *Peña-Irala*, 630 F 2d 876 (2d Cir. 1980).
[16] Richard Alan White, *Breaking Silence: The Case That Changed the Face of Human Rights* (Washington, DC: Georgetown University Press, 2004), p. 262.

the country, as Filártiga's attorneys argued to a federal district court that Congress had given courts jurisdiction to try suits by aliens for torts that rise to the level of violations of international law.

Scant historical records exist for the exact origins of ATCA, and there was little subsequent case history to give much further idea of its scope. Only twice before 1980 had ATCA been ruled sufficient grounds to establish jurisdiction. The first instance was in 1795, when a court took jurisdiction in a case brought by a French plaintiff concerning the ownership of slaves on board a Spanish prize ship, taken at sea.[17] There is some irony in the fact that a statute now being used in the cause of human rights was first used to restore slaves to their owners. The second instance, like the first, concerned violation of a treaty and a clear, if somewhat prosaic, violation of international law: a falsified passport in the context of a child custody dispute between foreign citizens in 1961.[18]

The other history of ATCA's use was not favourable to CCR and Weiss. In numerous other cases, the Second Circuit had refused the invocation of the 'law of nations' for claims involving the forced sale of property, an air disaster arguably caused by wilful negligence, and a denial of free access to foreign ports.[19] Further, the law of nations had been given a narrow interpretation, thought to be 'those standards, rules or customs... affect[ing] the relationship between states or between an individual and a foreign state'.[20] 'Domestic' human rights violations would rarely seem to rise to such a level of mutual concern as to overcome judicial reticence to take on such disputes. Even universal disapproval of theft was insufficient to persuade one federal appeals panel from giving jurisdiction to a claim by Luxembourgian investors against a US venture capital fund. Claiming that 'thou shalt not steal' does not rise to the 'law of nations', and that ATCA was 'a legal Lohengrin . . . no one seem[ing] to know whence it came', the court in that case could find no treaty or international accord that made that asserted tort grounds for jurisdiction in US courts.[21]

Weiss had contemplated employing ATCA as a tool to gain jurisdiction on two occasions in the decade leading up to *Filártiga*, once following the 1968 Mai Lai massacre in Vietnam and once after the 1973 assassination of Chilean President Salvador Allende. But the others on the legal team

---

[17] *Bolchos* v. *Darrel*, 1 Bee 74, 3 Fed. Cas. 810 (DSC 1795).

[18] *Abdul-Rahman Omar Adra* v. *Clift*, 195 F Supp. 857 (D.Md. 1961) at 863–65.

[19] See *Filártiga* v. *Peña* (1980) at 888.

[20] *Lopes* v. *Reederei Richard Schroder*, 225 F Supp. 292 (E. D.Pa. 1963), cited in *Filártiga* v. *Peña* (1980) 888.

[21] *IIT* v. *Vencap*, 519 2 Fd 1001 (2d Cir. 1975) at 1015.

had to buy into the idea, too. The team at CCR had much respect for their senior Weiss – described as a 'meticulous legal theorist of guru stature' – but it took the force of necessity to overcome their prior scepticism about ATCA and take up any argument that seemed within the bounds of plausibility.[22]

Though the statute was old, the principle of accepting an alien's tort claim had some resonance. From the briefs before the trial judge, the cause of justice was pleaded vigorously, noting that to relinquish jurisdiction to a seemingly more appropriate forum would be short-sighted. While the idea of trying this Paraguayan incident in the United States might strike a judge as curious, 'the consequences of the Filartiga's prior attempt to initiate proceedings against the defendant in Paraguay – the arrest of plaintiff Dolly Filártiga and her mother; the arrest, beating and disbarment of their attorney; and the continuing death threats against the plaintiffs – make it evident that relinquishment of jurisdiction by this court would be an egregious act of injustice'.[23] But given this background, it was no surprise that the district court initially hearing *Filártiga* v. *Peña* rejected the suit for want of jurisdiction, though at least CCR was not 'laughed out of court' as some of the lawyers had feared.[24] The judge had to take seriously the severity of torture as a violation of international norms, but the prevailing understanding of the law of nations excluded how a state treated its citizens.

As the case went to appeal, the political context of the case rose in importance. Though CCR lost the battle to have Peña deposed, and he was deported to Paraguay, CCR pressed for an interpretation of ATCA that at a minimum would link torture to the established precedent of 'affecting the relationship between states' – that is, the court would need to overthrow a conception of international law that divided tort into distinctly domestic and distinctly international spheres, and replace it with one in which domestic violations of human rights are seen as part of the wider law of nations, and thus actionable elsewhere. Given the foreign policy implications of this shift, the court asked for a brief from the US Departments of State and Justice, then under the Democratic administration of Jimmy Carter.

---

[22] White, *Breaking Silence*, p. 215.
[23] Plaintiffs' Memorandum of Law in Opposition to Defendant's Motion to Dismiss, *Filártiga* v. *Peña* (1980), available at Project Diana Online Human Rights Archive, www.yale.edu/lawweb/avalon/diana/filartiga/16june.html (last accessed 27 April 2007).
[24] White, *Breaking Silence*, p. 213.

The government's memorandum in support of Filártiga was decisive in reassuring the court that it would not be overstepping its bounds, as well as rearticulating the legal innovation advanced by CCR. The connection that CCR had drawn between the old law and the new facts meant that there was both a very historical overtone to the court's discussion and a very contemporary inquiry about human rights expectations of the modern world. The court accepted that torture rose to the highest level of status as an offence. It was plain to see the 'universal condemnation' of torture, from UN declarations and US treaties, giving the judges the freedom to recognise torture as a part of the law of nations that rises to the level of global concern even if it occurs domestically. Though one might look more broadly to national practices or judicial opinions for what constitutes the 'general assent of civilized nations' (drawing on eighteenth-century precedent for those terms), the modern evidence in support of Filártiga's claim left no doubt that torture offends customary international law.

But in order to make the link, the judges had to accept the relevance to US law. The court's opinion, written by well-known jurist Irving Kaufman, moved further by recognising that 'the constitutional basis for the Alien Tort Statute is the law of nations, which has always been part of federal common law'.[25] This provided a window that allowed unbridled adaptation of ATCA's eighteenth-century decree. The Framers of the Constitution anticipated, the court argued, that international law would be binding, with evidence for this claim found in Blackstone and early US court dicta. Vitally, international law is not static, Kaufman argued, making the jurisdiction of federal courts organic and evolving. He wrote:

> we believe it is sufficient here to construe the Alien Tort Statute, not as granting new rights to aliens, but simply as opening the federal courts for adjudication of the rights already recognized by international law ... [W]e recognize that questions of jurisdiction "must be considered part of an organic growth, part of an evolutionary process" ... The Framers' overarching concern that control over international affairs be vested in the new national government to safeguard the standing of the United States among the nations of the world therefore reinforces the result we reach today.[26]

In sum, as the world evolves, the country must follow, and the courts must help it do so. If a treaty or other binding decision is unavailable, then, citing a precedent from 1900, 'resort must be had to the customs and usages of civilized nations; and, as evidence of these, to the works of jurists and commentators, who by years of labour, research and experience, have

[25] *Filártiga* v. *Peña* (1980) at 885.   [26] *Filártiga* v. *Peña* (1980) at 887.

made themselves peculiarly well acquainted with the subjects of which they treat'.[27]

In effect, then, although the condemnations of torture are easily gathered from multinational declarations without resort to legal treatises and legal opinions, in the future new torts might be alleged that turn on more creative advocacy to a court, interpreting what is 'universal' in international law. If a tort in violation of international law is found, ATCA provides both a cause of action and jurisdiction in a federal district court. The memorandum from the State Department and Justice Department gave the green light to the judges in matters linked to foreign affairs, recognising that 'the protection of fundamental human rights is not committed exclusively to the political branches of government'.[28]

The Filártiga decision was a stunning synthesis and acceptance of a position once treated by Peter Weiss' friends as a curious pet theory. Its concluding paragraph left no doubt about the shared sympathy for the cause of human rights, finishing in grand terms: 'our holding today, giving effect to a jurisdictional provision enacted by our First Congress, is a small but important step in the fulfillment of the ageless dream to free all people from brutal violence'.[29]

The Second Circuit's findings propelled Filártiga to a positive legal resolution, with a subsequent trial resulting in a $10.4 million judgment against Peña. The inability to collect that award was largely irrelevant to Joelito Filártiga's father and sister, because the process had brought significant attention and diplomatic pressure against Paraguay's dictatorial regime, while also creating a process that future human rights victims could use against their adversaries. For human rights activists and lawyers, too, the landmark case took a conception that had barely a nugget of recognition in the field – merely two supporting cases in two centuries – and had set the foundation for decades of activity in US courts.

B. Challenges

Filártiga was just a beginning. ATCA claims soon returned to the courts throughout the 1980s with new factual situations. There remained real

---

[27] The Paquete Habana, 175 US 677 (1900) at 700, quoted in Filártiga v. Peña (1980) at 880–1.
[28] Memorandum for the United States Submitted to the Court of Appeals for the Second Circuit, Filártiga v. Peña (1980), reprinted as Appendix 1 in David Cole, Jules Lobel and Harold Hongju Koh, 'Interpreting the Alien Tort Statute: Amicus Curiae Memorandum of International Law Scholars and Practitioners in Trajano v. Marcos', Hastings International and Comparative Law Review 12 (1988), 1–47, at 45.
[29] Filártiga v. Peña (1980) at 890.

issues, some of which had arisen in *Filártiga* itself, others in cases that followed, along with a number of potential routes for challenging the new use of ATCA. Indeed, the opinions in some of the subsequent cases, such as *Tel-Oren*, in which a claim for jurisdiction against the Palestine Liberation Movement failed,[30] left many human rights lawyers concerned that *Filártiga*'s principles were 'too fragile a flower' to withstand appeal to the US Supreme Court, and they were relieved when the high court declined to hear it.

There was uncertainty as to whether ATCA did more than deal with jurisdiction, whether it merely allowed US courts to try 'alien torts' if there were other grounds for the suit in US law, or whether that language provided a 'cause of action' – grounds for bringing a case – in itself. However, one of the judicial opinions in the hearing, from Judge Edwards, did clearly assert that ATCA itself provided cause of action, and in the cases that followed courts proved increasingly willing to accept ATCA as sufficient grounds for a suit seeking damages, at least in limited circumstances,[31] collectively adding credibility to ATCA as a valid tool in contemporary human rights litigation.

Significant questions of policy were in play. Was ATCA an appropriate method for implementing international law? International law is rarely self-executing. It usually requires a legislative act to enforce it domestically. Under *Filártiga*, it was argued,[32] all international accords and treaties would become self-executing, by giving any individual a right to sue under the federal common law. There were also questions raised about whether such a small statutory clause justified judges' incorporating a wide swathe of rights into US law without further licence from the legislature, raising constitutional concerns about separation of powers issues. And since ATCA was tapping into foreign affairs, was this an appropriate area for judges in domestic courts to decide, or would it complicate the development of foreign policy by the legislature? These questions were to crop up again and again.

There were other concerns, too. Defences were raised using the doctrine of *forum non conveniens*, arguing that the United States was not a

---

[30] See, *Tel-Oren* v. *Libyan Arab Republic*, 726 F 2d 774 (D.C. Circuit 1984).

[31] *Von Dardel* v. *Union of Soviet Socialist Republics*, 623 F Supp. 246 (D.C.D.C. 1985) at 258, restating Judge Bork's quotation of William Blackstone's *Commentaries* in *Tel-Oren*, 726 F 2d 774 (1984) at 813; *Amerada Hess Shipping Corp.* v. *Argentine Republic*, 830 F 2d 421 (2d Cir. 1987); *Forti* v. *Suarez-Mason*, 672 F Supp 1531 (N.D. Cal. 1987).

[32] Robert H. Bork, *Coercing Virtue: The Worldwide Rule of Judges* (Washington, DC: AEI Press, 2003).

'convenient' forum – not a difficult argument to raise since ATCA cases, by their very nature, involved witnesses from other countries, making it expensive to secure testimony for a US hearing. But, of course, it could in many cases be retorted that the alternative forum, the place where the violation had taken place, was – often, by definition – worse, with records of scant regard of human or civil rights and no meaningful judicial independence or rule of law. In other words, if the central claims of a suit are persuasive, it is likely that the gross nature of the human rights violations will in itself cast doubt on the adequacy of the foreign jurisdiction.

This issue has become a stronger defence in later cases, as ATCA-based litigation has expanded to include non-state actors. Since, in cases against corporate actors, the foreign country is not the primary violator of rights, it may be more charitably characterised as an acceptable forum, and it has been somewhat easier for judges to grant dismissals on these grounds – though even there the challenge is not always successful, as in the *Saro-Wiwa* case brought against Shell over allegations of human rights abuses in Nigeria.[33] Dismissed in 1998 by a district court judge on grounds of *forum non conveniens* (with the United Kingdom as the alternative venue), two years later the Second Circuit gave deference to the resident plaintiff's desire to try the case in the United States and recognised the desire of Congress to give a forum to such difficult human rights suits. The tone of the court's opinion was striking: it embraced the concept that the United States would be a home for international law claims. That, however, was later. In the meantime, post-*Filártiga*, still other defences were being raised.

One defence, where the claim concerned governmental violations (as most of the first claims did) was the 'Act of State' doctrine. This cautioned judges against adjudicating on the legality of acts committed by foreign states within their own borders. Closely related to this was the 'sovereign immunity' defence, giving other states (sovereign powers) immunity from foreign courts, and included in the Foreign Sovereignty Immunities Act of 1976 (FSIA). The courts rejected a number of creative approaches to square ATCA with the FSIA.[34]

However, claims against individuals were much more likely to survive. For individuals like Peña to claim sovereign immunity, they would have to demonstrate that their actions were authorised by their government, but

[33] *Wiwa* v. *Royal Dutch Shell Petroleum*, 226 F 3d 88 (2d Cir. 2000).
[34] *Amerada Hess Shipping Corp.* v. *Argentine Republic*, 830 F 2d 421 (2d Cir. 1987); *Sanchez-Espinoza* v. *Reagan*, 770 F 2d 202 (D.C. Circuit 1985) at 206–7.

because under international law no government can officially sanction international law violations, they are per se acting beyond the sovereign immunity.[35] When officials act beyond the scope of their authority, they are liable to suits. By the end of the 1980s, this point was becoming increasingly settled, especially through suits brought against Ferdinand Marcos and his associates, sued by the family of one of their regime's victims after they had fled to Hawaii in disgrace.[36]

Legal resistance to ATCA's development was, then, failing to undermine the basic principle established in *Filártiga*. What's more – a point noted in the later Supreme Court case *Sosa* – Congress had not stepped in to counter this usage of ATCA. On the contrary, in 1991 it passed the Torture Victim Protection Act, which followed the spirit of ATCA in establishing jurisdiction in cases involving torture and extra-judicial killing. ATCA, however, still had a long way to go.

C. From public to private actors

By the early 1990s, the 'fragile flower' of human rights litigation was blossoming in the minds of creative lawyers. Human rights litigation had begun to attract a range of organisations which sensed its potential as a model of human rights activism. They came to litigation, and ATCA litigation in particular, with an array of backgrounds and objectives. The Center for Constitutional Law, the catalysing counsel for *Filártiga*, began with an organisational focus on US legal issues, but its agenda now included comparative and international dimensions. Amnesty International, founded in 1961 with a focus on prisoners, had reformulated its agenda in the 1980s to include human rights writ large. Numerous other groups, such as EarthRights International, the International League for Human Rights and Human Rights Watch, formed the wider human rights umbrella, including organisations interested in the specific concerns of indigenous peoples, the environment or women. Other 'cause lawyers' had also been litigating human rights issues for years, and some of the successes (e.g., the claims of Holocaust victims) had given them the financial resources to reach out in new ways. The mobilisation of interests and abilities, amidst a hotbed of legal possibilities, made the 1990s a conspicuous time for a human rights litigation agenda.

[35] Tom Lininger, 'Overcoming Immunity Defenses to Human Rights Suits in U.S. Courts', *Harvard Human Rights Journal* 7 (1994), 177–97, at 188.
[36] *Trajano* v. *Marcos*, 878 F 2d 1438 (9th Cir. 1989) and 978 F 2d 493 (9th Cir. 1992).

ATCA litigation at the end of the 1980s was a difficult business. The most serious limitation was the requirement that a defendant be a state actor – the law of *nations* being the operative concept – while not being immune from suit under the Foreign Sovereign Immunities Act. Individuals might be sued, but governments themselves would be immune without revision of the FSIA. The floodgates were opened to new human rights litigation by breaking this logjam in a different way, namely by dispensing with the requirement that a human rights abuser be a state actor, and human rights activists would return to the Second Circuit Court of Appeals, where *Filártiga* had been heard, to find a court willing to step with them outside the box of state action. The case that followed was to become, as a leading participant put it, the 'lynchpin on which the corporate cases have been brought'.

In the early 1990s, a small group of activists was looking to develop human rights law, including but not exclusively via ATCA. Corporate liability was on the minds of many, because experience in the field convinced them of the centrality of corporate behaviour to human rights issues. A wrongful death and negligence claim, based in Pennsylvania state law, against the makers of Israel's tear gas had brought about a settlement and had provided one inspiring model based on a particular theory of corporate liability. Case selection for future suits was haphazard, often emerging from personal connections between lawyers and people working in various hot spots. Lawyers, such as those at CCR, also received a steady stream of inquiries about potential litigation, but mostly these would-be cases had fatal deficiencies, such as a record of abuses that didn't rise to the level necessary to mount an ATCA claim, or a victim unwilling to go public. A number of suits were ultimately filed, but the best vehicle emerged serendipitously out of the tragic conflict in Bosnia-Herzegovina. After voters in the region chose independence from Yugoslavia, Bosnian Serbs attempted to break away from the Croat- and Muslim-dominated regions in the new country, declaring a Bosnian Serb republic and launching a campaign of torture, summary execution, forced prostitution and rape as part of a general strategy of genocide against non-Serbs. As President of the unrecognised republic, Radovan Karadzic possessed ultimate control over military forces operating in the region, and he worked closely with neighbouring Serbia in orchestrating the ethnic cleansing of Serb-dominated areas.

Collaboration among US rights groups developed in order to support the work of women's groups in Bosnia. One part of this multi-faceted effort was a committee exploring the legal options led by Beth Stephens of CCR, who was the lead counsel in the Second Circuit appeal. The information that Karadzic would be visiting the United Nations in New York in February 1993 gave them the legal hook necessary for an ATCA claim, and drove them to quickly make contact with a doctor helping survivors in Croatian refugee camps in order to find some interested and willing litigants. Seeking compensation and punitive damages, these two dozen victims of Serb violence sued Karadzic in federal court in the *Kadic* v. *Karadzic* case, overcoming Karadzic's efforts to avoid being served. At the initial phase, the federal district court judge, who decided on issues not briefed by the parties, found the matter well settled by prior cases – settled against the suit. In *Tel-Oren*, he noted, even Judge Edwards, who had been supportive of ATCA, had concluded it could not reach the Palestine Liberation Organisation (PLO) because it was not 'a recognized member of the community of nations'.[37] By that standard, then, the self-proclaimed Bosnian Serb republic was more difficult to bring under ATCA's ambit, being even less institutionalised and well-recognised than the PLO. Dryly noting this, the judge showed no desire to be the first federal judge to extend customary international law to non-state behaviour.

Nevertheless, in October 1995 the appeals court reversed the decision.[38] As the written opinion signalled at the start, the status of Karadzic in fact – state or non-state – remained in dispute, so much so that both sides contradicted themselves, simultaneously noting in the record that Karadzic was both President and a private individual. Importantly, in retrospect that uncertainty may have made this case a more comfortable vehicle with which to extend ATCA, because it encouraged a freer interpretation of international law, one that could reach someone who had the character of a state official even if by the most formal reading of a recognised state he was not. That ambiguity had to be articulated legally, and one approach taken by human rights lawyers was to allege that Karadzic acted 'under color of law' through his close relationship with the state of Yugoslavia. The appellate court was warm to that suggestion and, in a brief statement, invited future litigation to examine the merits of that charge.

At its heart, however, the appellate court's opinion did not depend on a close fit between law and practice, but rather embraced the victims' central claim that the law of nations, as least as far as ATCA was concerned, did not need the involvement of state actors. The origins of the Act in an era

---

[37] *Tel-Oren* (1984) at 792 (J. Edwards, concurring), cited in *Doe* v. *Karadzic*, 866 F Supp. 734 (SDNY 1994) at 740.

[38] *Kadic* v. *Karadzic*, 70 F 3d 232 (2nd Cir. 1995).

of pirates, described by the Supreme Court in the nineteenth century as 'hostis humani generis' (an enemy of all mankind), made plain that some activities, like piracy and the slave trade, were universally offensive and subject to liability without being state action.[39] Indeed, after World War II, international law conventions prohibiting genocide and war crimes were crafted to apply to all persons, public and private, though some activities such as torture and summary execution are necessarily acts by state officials unless occurring as part of a scheme of genocide and war crimes. The Clinton administration added its weight to the proposition, echoed in other US government positions, that some actions are of such universal concern that private individuals may be liable and states may establish civil remedies. For logical measure, the panel added that nothing in Judge Edwards' Tel-Oren opinion excluded such a position.

In the subsequent trial, Karadzic was found liable and in 2000 a jury issued an award for $4.5 billion. That will never be collected, but the importance of the Second Circuit's decision was understood, as one critic warned of 'the growing forces of international human rights activists pushing for an expanded reading [of ATCA] in order to catch international violators in United States courts'.[40] Perhaps the strongest argument against the step taken in Kadic (and its companion case, Doe v. Karadzic) was the sheer conservatism of prior practice: ATCA since Filártiga had never been applied to private action and thus no case law – the currency of legitimacy in legal reasoning – could be mustered in support of the step. On the other side of the scales, early history and the contemporary political consensus seemed to invite the extension, and so the plaintiffs deployed it persuasively in service of a sympathy-generating set of facts.

More fundamentally, debates about Judge Edwards' opinion notwithstanding, advocates for the extension to private individuals had on their side an evolving legal world in which their claims reverberated. Kadic was recognition of the rising status of the conception of human rights that in international usage had transcended the confines of 'state versus non-state' distinctions in black-letter international law. In this zeitgeist, human rights possessed by people are broader in theory than constitutional rights held against a state; they are inherent to the person and undeniable by state and non-state actors alike. The recognition floated by CCR in their arguments in Kadic, and accepted by the court, suggested that the sources

---

[39] ibid., at 239.
[40] Justin Lu, 'Jurisdiction over Non-State Activity under the Alien Tort Claims Act,' Columbia Journal of Transnational Law 35 (1997) 531–49, at 546.

of human rights might one day be found in wider, less limiting realms of usage and philosophy than the 'law of nations' had previously provided.

Yet, at the same time, the constraint unleashed by those who were now able to see where the ATCA litigation strategy might lead was that the authority for US courts remained lodged in the four walls of ATCA. Could the law of nations, as Congress had written over two hundred years prior, be licence for judges to explore the philosophical boundaries of human rights? Would this, to judges' minds, make them unmoored from their foundations in the US system of government? In the words of one judge in 1996, when denying a claim for a right to the environment, 'in short, plaintiffs' imaginative view of this Court's power must face the reality that United States district courts are courts of limited jurisdiction. While their power within those limits is substantial, it does not include a general writ to right the world's wrongs'.[41] The arguments by litigants pushing forward, then, had to be worked on carefully and creatively in order to bring the force of universal human rights into US jurisprudence.

D. Alien Tort Claims Act and business: Unocal

Litigators tied to the human rights movement began, in the early 1990s, to conceive of ATCA and the law of nations as reaching corporate behaviour. For some, the step was obvious and persuasive, even if untested: if it could reach pirates, it could reach corporations. The first case to be filed with such a theory accused Texaco of perpetrating massive environmental damage in Ecuador. It was brought by Cristóbal Bonifaz, an Ecuadorean native and Massachusetts attorney, aligned with the Philadelphia firm of Kohn, Swift & Graf, which had employed ATCA against Marcos in the 1980s. This first use of ATCA in a corporate case was a specific response to the facts at hand, particularly with what was to the plaintiffs such an extraordinary level of environmental degradation that the case met the legal standards imposed by ATCA. It does not seem to have been part of a conscious strategic bid for a test case that would extend ATCA to corporations more generally. In any event, although the initial motions contained some favourable developments, the litigation stalled for numerous reasons, including the uphill battle to persuade judges of the legal theory.

Other human rights campaigners had taken their first steps against corporations with other legal theories besides ATCA, and by the early 1990s a number of groups were mobilising on areas related to corporate

[41] Aquinda v. Texaco, 945 F Supp 625 (SDNY 1996) at 628.

behaviour. They would need to reach their own acceptance and appreciation of ATCA's potential, in what one activist refers to as the '"Wow!" moment' – the flash of recognition that brought these various interests and strategies together into a new, forward-looking case. After the Texaco suit, some in the movement give credit for developing a strategy with longer-term potential to Jenny Green, a lawyer with CCR, and Paul Hoffman, a Los Angeles attorney. It took a couple of years to reach what another attorney involved in the litigation described as a '"Why not?" moment', when the collaborating attorneys had all the elements of a strong case, factually and legally. Yet another concurred with this latter view, repeating his line that 'there was nothing new, it had just never been done before'. CCR had an ongoing campaign against corporate complicity in human rights abuses, which had begun to gain recognition; the need was only for a theory by which legal strategies could be brought more fully to bear on the problem. To them, the *Kadic* v. *Karadzic* decision seemed to provide one.

Some working on the case were brimming with confidence, and the large team of associated human rights lawyers worked carefully. But following this road presented risks, too, because creative extensions create tensions. The critics of ATCA-based human rights decisions of the 1980s were notable only by their absence: beyond the legal debates, criticism had not coalesced politically. On the brink of this new extension, there were concerns within the human rights movement, first over whether the chances of success were enough to justify optimism, and second over whether the litigation (successful or not) would result in a legislative backlash that could result in a total loss of ATCA. 'Are we ready for this?' was the tenor of conversations (reflected one attorney) even within some of the organisations participating in the suit. To be sure, MNCs can mobilise political power in ways that dictators and torturers cannot. Other lawyers in the movement were less concerned, tending to view the targeting of corporations (in the words of one prominent activist) thus: '[It is a] validation of twenty years-plus of work to be able to use it as a tool against defendants who generally operate with impunity.'[42]

Like earlier cases, human rights lawyers would try to develop ATCA in the context of the most sympathetic facts possible, while self-consciously viewing it as an opportunity to illustrate for others the potential of the human rights movement to target corporations. The facts in *Doe* v. *Unocal*, brought in 1996, provided such an opportunity, with Unocal thought by

---

[42] Confidential interview with authors.

one lawyer involved in the case to be 'as recalcitrant as any corporation can be'. One of the world's leading petroleum companies, Unocal had in 1992 entered into a joint venture with the French company Total, the State Law and Order Restoration Council (SLORC) in Myanmar and the Myanmar Ministry for Oil and Gas Enterprise (MOGE), a unit of the military government. Unocal acquired and placed into wholly owned subsidiaries 28 per cent interests in two complementary projects to extract natural gas from the Yadana natural gas field and build a pipeline to Thailand. From the start, Unocal management was aware of the Myanmar government's reputation as a human rights violator. Since coming to power in 1988, the government had earned a reputation as one of the most repressive regimes in the world.

Under the agreement, the military undertook security for the project, mobilising over two thousand troops, building helipads and clearing roads along the forty-mile pipeline route. The military lived up to – and perhaps exceeded – its reputation, forcing villagers into service in the infrastructure's construction, shooting at those who attempted escape, and in at least one case, throwing an escapee's wife and child into a fire. By the testimony of many, summary execution and rape were common in the course of the forced work. There were other human rights abuses as well. Whole villages were forcibly relocated from along the pipeline route without compensation, and any local opposition was met with execution or indefinite imprisonment without trial. When non-legal alternatives, including a consumer boycott, failed to catch hold, this case emerged as a possible model for an ATCA-based legal strategy against corporations.

A class action lawsuit against California-based Unocal's top executives, as well as Total, MOGE and SLORC, sought an injunction and legal judgment against the company, and damages for eighteen claims of wrongdoing, including forced labour, torture, violence against women, wrongful death and crimes against humanity. CCR and lead lawyer Paul Hoffman were joined by EarthRights International, an NGO with experience in Myanmar. In resolving the first round of pre-trial motions in March 1997, the established principles of sovereign immunity were judged to make the Myanmar government entities SLORC and MOGE immune from suit.[43] One attorney involved in the suit now views this as a blessing in disguise, in terms of the development of corporate accountability, by keeping the Myanmar government out of the case, and allowing it to focus on the corporate issue.

---

[43] *John Doe I* v. *Unocal Corp*, 963 F Supp 880 (C.D. Cal. 1997).

In other respects the district court's ruling was favourable to the plaintiffs, agreeing that it had the authority to hear the substance of the case and denying a dismissal on the basis of the Act of State doctrine. Continuing indeterminacy in ATCA law gives scope for judicial discretion, however. After extensive discovery, including dozens of depositions from company personnel that significantly strengthened the case against Unocal, a replacement federal district court judge (the first having been elevated to the appellate bench) three years later granted a motion for summary judgment, dismissing the case as insufficient. The big issue was whether corporations could be held liable even when they had not themselves carried out the violations but had known what their joint venture partners were doing. The judge conceded that evidence gathered in litigation pointed to Unocal's knowledge of forced labour conducted by their Myanmar collaborators, but he concluded that without evidence revealing Unocal's active desire to use forced labour the company could not be held liable.[44] The plaintiffs were short of the heightened standard that would require showing that Unocal controlled the military, were engaged in state action or 'actively participated' in the forced labour. Nonetheless, even with this limiting decision, one could read the Unocal litigation to that point as a success – and it is cited today in new suits – since it warned that particularly close connections between corporations and foreign states might be sufficient for liability, and – a key accomplishment – it established that corporations were not barred from ATCA suits per se.[45]

In the short term, a more momentous step for ATCA was the appeal and the September 2002 decision to overturn the judge's dismissal.[46] In reviewing the dismissal, the three-judge panel gave a more favourable reading to the evidence supporting the plaintiff's case, while lowering the standard of liability. Restating the principles of earlier decisions, the judges declared a private party can be found liable for violations of international law even without being engaged in state action. Equating forced labour to the historic crimes of slavery and slave-trading, Judge Harry Pregerson added that acts like rape, torture and summary execution can be reached by ATCA when committed by a private party in pursuit of greater crimes like genocide. The key question was the standard for establishing liability. The standard offered by the court was of 'knowing practical assistance or encouragement that has a substantial effect on the perpetration of

---

[44] *John Doe I* v. *Unocal*, 110 F Supp. 2d 1294 (C.D. Cal. 2000) at 1310.
[45] Sarah M. Hall, 'Multinational Corporations' Post-Unocal Liabilities for Violations of International Law', *George Washington International Law Review* (2002), 401–33, at 422.
[46] *Doe* v. *Unocal*, 395 F 3d 932 (9th Cir. 2002).

the crime', under which the evidence was reasonable enough to warrant trial.[47]

Critical of the district judge's 'active participation' standard, which they claimed was used only to overcome the 'necessity defense' of German industrialists at Nuremberg, Pregerson turned instead to the international criminal law applied by the tribunals in Yugoslavia and Rwanda, tribunals that looked as far as the 'moral support' offered by a party. Given the evidence in this case, the court left open whether 'moral support which has . . . a substantial effect' might one day be sufficient to establish liability. Even so, the plaintiffs had been given a firm legal footing to make the case before a jury that Unocal's entry and activities into Myanmar, given its knowledge of how its military partners conduct their work, was a violation of human rights for which it must answer in US courts.[48]

In a number of respects, but particularly regarding the standard for liability, Judge Pregerson's opinion was controversial, thought by some legal commentators to be 'unprecedented' and 'activist'.[49] For the human rights advocates driving this litigation, this new standard would provide a legal instrument that reached much of their wider human rights agenda. It would allow suits against corporations in many parts of the world where firms worked closely with governments that they knew were committing serious human rights abuses. In effect, they would be able to reach out at the globalisation that outsourced violence in order to achieve economic development. Striking so close to the heart of the global economy, the response to the Ninth Circuit decision reflected the new-found intense awareness that ATCA's domestic forum could bring global standards to the transnational operations of US corporations.[50]

Unocal appealed the decision to the full Ninth Circuit, which attested to the significance of the case by agreeing to a hearing by the full bench of judges. In July 2003, a sceptical court focused its questions on whether an

---

[47] *ibid.*, at 947. Judge Stephen Reinhardt concurred with respect to the standard of liability, arguing that the court should instead apply a standard derived from federal common law tort principles, such as agency, joint venture or reckless disregard.

[48] While reinstating the suit for claims of murder and rape, the court did uphold the dismissal of claims of torture, finding these insufficient in the record.

[49] Tawny Aine Bridgeford, 'Imputing Human Rights Obligations on Multinational Corporations: The Ninth Circuit Strikes Again in Judicial Activism', *US University Law Review* 18 (2003), 1009–57; Shanaira Udwadia, 'Corporate Responsibility for International Human Rights Violations,' *Southern California Interdisciplinary Law Journal* 13 (2004), 359–400.

[50] See, e.g., Gary Clyde Hufbauer and Nicholas K. Mitrokostas, *Awakening Monster: The Alien Tort Statute of 1789* (Washington, DC: Institute for International Economics, 2003).

aiding and abetting standard was appropriate for international civil cases. One judge at the hearing was 'a little uncomfortable with the aiding and abetting standard as [the plaintiffs' lawyers were] arguing it as perhaps a little far beyond where the established international law consensus has gotten us'.[51] Although Hoffman, lead lawyer for the plaintiffs, argued that this suit could survive under a higher standard, his final remarks to the court stressed that, 'not having aiding and abetting in Alien Tort Claims Act cases, even beyond this case, would be a disaster. . . . Having the ability to go after a third party for these kinds of egregious crimes in a situation where they provided assistance and encouragement that has that substantial effect is very important'.[52]

The debate here would not be fully resolved. Before the judges completed their work, another ATCA case, Sosa v. Alvarez-Machain,[53] was scheduled to come before the Supreme Court, the first time the creative enforcement of ATCA would be tested at the top of the judicial system. The Unocal case was withdrawn pending the Supreme Court's outcome, in the wake of which other factors were, as we shall see, to intervene.

E. Endorsing the Alien Tort Claims Act: enter the Supreme Court

The Sosa case reached the Supreme Court as a result of events originating in 1985 and a 1992 decision that the facts might give rise to a claim under ATCA. It did not concern corporate behaviour, but rather allegations of the kidnap and arbitrary arrest of a Mexican, Alvarez-Machain, by Sosa, a Mexican ex-policeman employed by the US Drug Enforcement Agency (DEA), who were seeking Alvarez-Machain in connection with the murder of one of their agents. Alvarez-Machain was seized in Mexico, tried in the United States and acquitted. The issue then arose of whether his arrest violated international law and Sosa and the DEA could be pursued under ATCA. Alvarez won against Sosa but the decisions against the US government were less clear.

The importance of Sosa for ATCA and business lay not in the facts of the case but in the fact it was the vehicle that brought the core legal – and, indeed, political – questions before the Supreme Court. The political context had changed significantly from the time of Filártiga and there were concerns on the part of human rights activists about the future of

---

[51] Unofficial transcript of oral arguments in Doe v. Unocal before the Ninth Circuit, en banc, 17 June 2003, available at www.earthrights.org/files/Legal%20Docs/Unocal/enbanctranscript.pdf (last accessed 27 April 2007).
[52] ibid.   [53] 542 US 692 (2004).

ATCA. Business had been lobbying hard for Congress to act against the uses to which ATCA was being put. The *Sosa* case brought the potential implications of ATCA closer to home for the government too, concerning not Paraguayan policemen but a Mexican citizen acting in the employ of a US government agency. What is more, in the wake of 9/11 – the very day the Ninth Circuit judges handed down their decision in favour of the plaintiff – the opponents of ATCA had a new gambit which the *Sosa* case played into, the spectre of judges inhibiting national counter-terrorism efforts. At the next appeal Alvarez won with only a 6–5 majority, with dissenting judges bringing the new context clearly into play in their opening salvo, saying 'we are now in the midst of a global war on terrorism'.[54]

The tenor of the times and the facts at hand made Sosa's appeal to the Supreme Court a vehicle for a full-fledged reconsideration of ATCA, one that had so far been avoided. One concern was that the Supreme Court might conclude that the entire twenty-year foray into ATCA 'has all been a terrible mistake . . . you got it wrong in 1980'. The push for reconsideration came from both Sosa and the Bush administration's Department of Justice, their cases being in effect a sum of all the arguments against the creative interpretation propounded by *Filártiga*, and they asked the Court to return the law to its prior state, in which ATCA would not be a cause of action (only a grant of jurisdiction) and the courts would show greater deference to the political branches overseeing foreign policy.[55]

As it unfolded, human rights activists were able to breathe a sigh of relief. The Supreme Court's 29 June 2004 decision was cast in four parts, with unanimity on two parts and split line-ups on the others. The key point was that there was unanimous agreement from the nine justices that ATCA did apply to contemporary human rights issues. They argued that the first Congress must have intended ATCA to have practical effect from the outset, which meant that it had given licence to courts to hear claims for 'a modest number of international law violations'.[56]

The decision was not unambiguously helpful to the human rights cause, however. A 6–3 majority went on to set a standard for assessing what contemporary claims could be made. The Congress of 215 years previously had apparently only considered piracy, protection of ambassadorial rights and violations of safe conducts, issues no longer at the centre of international law debates. While moving beyond those specific issues, the

[54] *Alvarez-Machain* v. *US*, 331 F 3d 604 (9th Cir. 2003), at 608.
[55] *Sosa* v. *Alvarez-Machain*, No. 03–339, Brief for the United States in Support of the Petition, and Reply Brief for the United States as Respondent Supporting Petitioner, 2003.
[56] *ibid.* at 724.

judges nevertheless decided that the standard for what could be considered grounds for ATCA jurisdiction was to be constrained by the spirit of the original: 'courts should require any claim based on the present-day law of nations to rest on a norm of international character accepted by the civilized world and defined with a specificity comparable to the features of the 18th-century paradigms we have recognized'.[57] This definition was taken to limit the scope for claims. Indeed, it meant that despite the case's affirmation of the use of ATCA for human rights cases, Alvarez's particular claim failed, detention for less than twenty-four hours and transfer to legal custody not being seen as a violation of equal weight to those of 1789.

In *Sosa*, the interpretation of ATCA brought to the courts in *Filártiga*, and expanded since then, had gained the imprimatur of the highest US court. It was bounded – the sense now is that cases brought forward should be limited to egregious human rights violations. There was also material in the case for arguing further constraints, with significant dissenting opinions. What is more, in a substantial footnote, the Court contemplated that in future cases – including the then-ongoing litigation against corporations that participated or aided the former apartheid regime of South Africa – 'there is a strong argument that federal courts should give serious weight to the Executive Branch's view of the case's impact on foreign policy'.[58] This was an argument RioTinto, for example, had already raised.[59] Though *Sosa* left existing case law intact, new litigants might face the reinvigorated limits and the reappearance of old challenges.

The case was, nonetheless, received by human rights activists with relief, including those with a particular interest in corporate accountability. EarthRights International, one of the key organisations behind the *Unocal* case, described *Sosa* as the 'triumph of human rights',[60] noting a report in the *New York Times* in which a lawyer for the US Chamber of Commerce lamented the fact that businesses hadn't succeeded in 'cutting these cases off at the pass'.[61] Nonetheless, it remained to be seen how the case would impact on future judgments.

---

[57] *ibid.* at 725.   [58] *ibid.*, at 733, n. 21.
[59] *Sarei* v. *Rio Tinto* plc, 221 F Supp. 2d 1116 (C.D. Cal. 2002) reinstated Ninth Circuit, 9 August 2006.
[60] EarthRights International, 'In Our Court: ATCA, *Sosa* and the Triumph of Human Rights' (2002), available at www.earthrights.org/index2.php?option = com_content&do_pdf = 1&id = 144 (last accessed 27 April 2007).
[61] Linda Greenhouse, 'Human Rights Abuses are Held to Fall Under U.S. Courts', *New York Times*, 30 June 2004.

F. The complicity issue: Unocal and beyond

While attention had been focused on *Sosa*, the more specific issue of the application of ATCA to business had continued to develop. A number of cases were now in process, such as the *Saro-Wiwa*[62] complaint against Shell over allegations of human rights violations in Nigeria, *Talisman*[63] in relation to genocide in the Sudan, and *Rio Tinto* in relation to environmental and other issues in Papua New Guinea,[64] though other suits had failed to achieve jurisdiction. But the *Unocal* litigation itself also awaited a final resolution.

Complicity, as we have seen, had become a key issue in the business context: could business corporations be held liable where they had aided and abetted, or knowingly assisted, violations, even if they had not directly committed them? Judge Pregerson, in *Unocal*, had said yes, but the corporation had appealed and the full bench deliberations were on hold pending the outcome of *Sosa*. Not all of the plaintiffs' eggs had, however, been in that one legal basket. A case had also been brought against Unocal in the California state court using the same facts but different law, namely the California Constitution's prohibition of slavery and California's Business and Professions Code. Judge Victoria Chaney held in June 2002 that the case should go to trial on questions of whether Unocal's relationship with the Myanmar military triggered vicarious liability for the military's human rights abuses. A jury trial was eventually set, after various objections, for June 2005.

The jury's verdict was, however, never to be heard. Unocal announced in December 2004 that it would settle out of court. This pre-empted both the jury hearing of the California case and the post-*Sosa* assessment by a full bench of judges of Pregerson's approval of complicity as a basis for liability.

While the easy response for human rights activists was to treat Unocal's decision to settle as a welcome capitulation, the situation was in fact more ambiguous. Pre-empting a decision on complicity meant that the issue, an important one for extending ATCA's reach in business, was still left unclear. On the other hand, the decision might not have gone the way the human rights activists wanted, resulting in setback rather than triumph for corporate accountability.[65] At least this way the original decision that

---

[62] *Wiwa* v. *Royal Dutch Shell Petroleum*, 226 F 3d 88 (2d Cir. 2000).

[63] *Presbyterian Church of Sudan et al.* v. *Talisman Energy, Inc.*, No. 01 CV 9882 (SDNY).

[64] *Sarei* v. *Rio Tinto plc*, 221 F Supp 2d 1116 (C.D. Cal. 2002).

[65] A fuller discussion of this theory was offered by Anthony J. Sebok, 'Unocal Announces it Will Settle a Human Rights Suit: What is the Real Story Behind its Decision?', 10 January 2005, at writ.findlaw.com/sebok/20050110.html (last accessed 27 April 2007).

business corporations could be pursued under ATCA suits still stood, along with the potential for establishing liability through close association. As it was, consistent with the Supreme Court's sceptical footnote in *Sosa*, the litigation over corporate complicity in apartheid had been dismissed by a federal judge in November 2004.[66] *Sosa* had been applied narrowly to rule out aiding and abetting as an acceptable standard of proof for corporate liability.

Legal history is, however, a continuing story. Commentators, including human rights activists, have also argued that the apartheid cases were not as strong as *Unocal* for establishing complicity as a basis for liability, the causal connection being more tenuous,[67] whereas the Unocal case required 'a higher standard of corporate involvement', as one lawyer on the case put it in interview, and the evidence against Unocal suggested a strong link. There will be other cases. The complicity issue is still unsettled, but it will not be dropped. Nor is it clear that all of the judiciary will apply *Sosa* as narrowly as in the apartheid cases; there will be liberal and conservative applications. The 'interference with foreign policy' argument pressed in the footnote to *Sosa* has already been rejected, in August 2006, by the Ninth Circuit Judges on the facts of the *Rio Tinto* case.[68] What is more, *Sosa* itself, ironically, at the same time as narrowing the grounds for ATCA, positively *invited* creative legal development. The majority opinion noted the need for caution in creativity but argued that 'the door to further independent judicial recognition of actionable norms . . . is still ajar'. 'Vigilant doorkeeping' was recommended, but creative evolution was still expressly an option, and creative enforcement is certainly set to continue.

There is also ultimately the question of how far human rights abuse, once it has been publicised in all its horrific detail, can be seen to be officially stomached. In that sense the human rights movement stands to benefit from *Sosa*'s message that only clear human rights violations should be pursued. 'If we stick to egregious violations,' said one interviewee

---

66 In *Re South African Apartheid Litigation*, 346 F Supp. 2d 538. (SDNY 2004) – although the judge did so on other grounds extending beyond the narrow confines of Justice Souter's footnote.

67 Rachel Chambers, 'The Unocal Settlement: Implications for the Developing Law on Corporate Complicity in Human Rights Abuses', *Human Rights Brief* 13/1 (2005), 14, available at www.globalpolicy.org/intljustice/atca/atcaindx.htm.

68 *Sarei v. Rio Tinto plc*, 221 F Supp. 2d 1116 (C.D. Cal. 2002) reinstated Ninth Circuit, 9 August 2006. The case had been dismissed in 2002 on grounds including the implications for foreign relations with Papua New Guinea, but these (and other) grounds were rejected and the case reinstated; see www.hagens-berman.com/frontend?command–PressRelease& task=viewPressReleaseDetail&iPressReleaseId=1240iD=1240.

confidently, 'we will win. The courts won't let them be complicit with genocide. No judge, liberal or conservative, can turn their back on that.'

II. Implications

On that front, time will tell. In the meantime, the story so far, at least for the United States and MNCs with subsidiaries in the United States, is one whereby corporate responsibility in the area of international human rights has ceased to be a matter of voluntary policy and has become a matter of legal accountability. That accountability has been established through creative private enforcement of a 1789 statute intended to deal with piracy on the high seas.

The pursuit of business under ATCA has in a practical sense improved the prospects of some human rights victims. Whereas cases against individuals were pursued in the knowledge that any damages awarded would never be collected, cases against US corporations were always likely to have a very different outcome, since they are vulnerable to state enforcement mechanisms and have deeper pockets to draw on. The victims in the *Unocal* case have received sums that can transform their living conditions. However, the payment of damages was not the essential motivation for bringing the case. Justice, publicity and the potential knock-on effects were the primary drivers. As one interviewee put it:

> You can't solve all human rights questions with a lawsuit. We can try to be a pinprick on the conscience of the world, doing this, getting lots of publicity, hoping others come in. You can't make a responsible government from a bunch of thugs, but you can expose them as thugs, and you can shame businesses. That's all we can do, try to do what we can with the rules.

Certainly, the ATCA cases have had a much wider effect, both in the United States and beyond, than their purely legal outcomes. They have brought significant publicity to bear, raising awareness both of human rights violations in general and of business association with them. The esoteric nature of the legal grounds arguably has helped publicity rather than hindered it, with the use of a 'piracy law' against business always making for a good headline.

Business corporations themselves certainly have been made aware of the potentially negative implications for them when they participate in any way – or even share in the knowledge of – unacceptable activities by their business partners, and activists hope for a deterrent effect. Legal risk has extended into market risk, with vulnerability to human rights issues, and specifically ATCA suits, now significant factors in analysts' assessments of companies for the market. Nor has the lobbying by business corporations against ATCA been seen as their finest hour. Arguing on legal technicalities against the *principle* of accountability for forced labour, rape, murder and genocide is not the sort of publicity guaranteed to win business public support.

There may be a message here, too, for the relationship between voluntary CSR and the law. If companies, many of whom have signed up to human rights codes, feel so vulnerable under ATCA, then perhaps they need to look more closely at the real meaning of their voluntary commitments? To ATCA supporters business needs to 'close the gap between corporate citizenship puff and reality'.[69]

For human rights activists there is also the hope that the ATCA cases will help in the growing drive for clear international law on business responsibility in the area of human rights. As Paul Hoffman has put it, 'I don't think you change the world by litigating but I do think that litigation can inspire legislation that can change the world ... International legislation will, at the end of the day, be a better means of curbing corporate behaviour than law suits.'[70] Significantly, the unresolved complicity issue is now under scrutiny by a panel of experts set up by John Ruggie, the UN Special Representative on Human Rights and Business,[71] in order to look into formulating an international law standard on corporate aiding and abetting liability.[72]

These are knock-on effects. ATCA itself is a limited mechanism for dealing with human rights violations. It is civil, not criminal. It currently applies only to very specific circumstances, to businesses with a US base and to egregious violations. Attempts to widen its reach to a broader definition of human rights, such as environmental rights, have so far failed.

Of course, where things go in the future remains to be seen. But that openness in law is, in a sense, the ultimate message of ATCA for business. There has been a powerful business lobby against ATCA, not least because of the creative use to which the statute has been put – its 'misapplication',

---

[69] Quoted in 'Under the Shadow of ATCA', *Foreign Direct Investment*, 5 June 2006. See also R. Shamir, 'Between Self-Regulation and the Alien Tort Claims Act: On the Contested Concept of Corporate Social Responsibility', *Law and Society Review* 38 (2004), 635–63.

[70] Quoted in 'Under the shadow of ATCA' (n. 71).

[71] His full title is the UN Special Representative on Human Rights and Transnational Corporations and Other Business Enterprises.

[72] See, for example, www.Earthrights.org, news, July 2006.

as the US Chamber of Commerce put it.[73] Yet creative use of law is routine corporate practice. Business has been very successful in using legal creativity for its own ends, to fill legal gaps in the law of developing countries in order to facilitate global transactions,[74] or more generally to avoid taxation or escape regulatory controls.[75] No doubt legal creativity will be brought to bear to resist ATCA, too. But legal creativity can also be used in reverse, as the ATCA story has demonstrated, to fill a legal vacuum in a way which enhances control over business. Business may have to come to terms with the fact that legal impunity today cannot be relied on to remain legal impunity tomorrow.

[73] John Howard, Vice President of International Policy and Programs, US Chamber of Commerce, 'The Alien Tort Claims Act' (article in press, October 2002).

[74] D. McBarnet, 'Transnational Transactions: Legal Work, Cross-border Commerce and Global Regulation', in M. Likosky (ed.), *Transnational Legal Processes* (London: Butterworths/North Western, 2002).

[75] D. McBarnet, *Crime, Compliance and Control*, 'Collected Essays in Law' series (Dartmouth: Ashgate, 2004).

6

Bringing corporate social responsibility to the World Trade Organisation

NICOLA JÄGERS

I. Introduction

The call for corporate social responsibility (CSR) has so far focused mainly on business entities. Non-governmental organisations (NGOs)[1] have generally directed their campaigns at corporations, and a rising number has responded to this call by adopting codes of conduct. The emergence of corporate codes of conduct is an important development as it points towards an increasing recognition and support within the business community for CSR. However, ultimately the significance of these voluntary instruments is limited. Corporations tend to be rather selective regarding which issues are addressed in their code. Some corporations that are less susceptible to public pressure might be less inclined to adopt such a code altogether. Moreover, effective implementation and supervision of corporate codes of conduct is frequently lacking.[2] Hence, voluntary commitments are no substitute for action by national governments and international

---

[1] A lot has been written of what exactly constitutes an NGO. Frequently, these entities are defined by what they are not. For the purpose of this chapter the term 'NGO' refers to international and national private organisations that operate independently from a government, are public-interest oriented and of a non-violent character. For more on the issue of definition see, *inter alia*, K. Martens, 'Mission Impossible? Defining NGOs', *Voluntas: International Journal of Voluntary and Nonprofit Organizations* 13, 3 (2002), 271–85; Menno T. Kamminga, 'The Evolving Status of NGOs under International Law: a Threat to the Inter-state System?', in Gerard Kreijen (ed.), *State, Sovereignty and International Governance* (Oxford: Oxford University Press, 2002), pp. 387–406; Peter R. Baehr, 'Mobilization of the Conscience of Mankind: Conditions of Effectiveness of Human Rights NGOs', in E. Denters and N. Schrijver (eds.), *Reflections on International Law from the Low Countries* (The Hague: Kluwer Law International, 1988), pp. 135–55; Steve Charnovitz, 'Two Centuries of Participation: NGOs and International Governance', *Michigan Journal of International Law* 18 (1997), 186–286.

[2] Nicola Jägers, *Corporate Human Rights Obligations: in Search of Accountability* (Antwerp: Intersentia, 2002), pp. 132–6.

agencies. There is a need for strong government commitment to legislate and enforce that legislation. To a certain extent a development towards more legally binding regulation at the national level can be detected. Several national jurisdictions have witnessed a significant increase in CSR litigation against corporations.[3] Nevertheless, a national approach to the issue of CSR ultimately is not enough. To reach goals set by the CSR movement requires that we look beyond the conduct of corporations and states at the bigger picture. Where corporations can avoid national regulation, this is much more difficult if international law takes CSR into account. An international approach to the issue of CSR is important in light of the transboundary nature of international trade.

This chapter will address the relationship between the World Trade Organisation (WTO) and CSR. CSR encompasses many different aspects. A universal definition is lacking but in general CSR usually refers to the concept of integrating economic, social and environmental interests into the activities and structures of corporations. In addition to this common understanding of CSR, the concept can also be understood more broadly to encompass the integration of such concerns into the international structures within which companies operate. The role of the WTO in shaping the international business landscape is imperative.

It is important to keep in mind that the issue of CSR and the WTO can be approached from two different perspectives. First, there is the question whether the WTO is sensitive for CSR in its operations *as an international organisation*. The second approach concerns the tension between CSR issues and trade obligations in the context of the WTO. The focus of this chapter will be on the latter as the WTO, compared to other international organisations, barely develops any policy or (in other words) operates independently from states. Its activities as an international organisation are therefore less controversial than the activities of the member states which emanate from the obligations under the WTO-covered agreements. It is especially those activities that have given rise to the critique discussed in this chapter.

The focus will mainly be on one facet of CSR: the effective protection and enjoyment of human rights. The conclusions drawn can, however, also be applied to other CSR issues, such as the protection of the environment. The question is whether the WTO could, in terms of its legally defined

---

[3] For a thorough overview of this litigation, see Sarah Joseph, *Corporations and Transnational Human Rights Litigation* (Oxford: Hart Publishing, 2004). See also *Commerce, Crime and Conflict: A Survey Response of Sixteen Jurisdictions*, Fafo AIS, www.fafo.no/ liabilities/index.htm (2006).

role, help further the goals of CSR rather than, as is often seen to be the case, obstruct them, and, in particular, whether a greater voice for CSR advocacy could be imported into the WTO via enhanced legal standing for NGOs.

II. The World Trade Organisation and corporate social responsibility

Why is it important to look at the WTO? As stated earlier, serious commitment to CSR requires not only that states hold corporations to account but also that those international rules and mechanisms aimed at facilitating the operations of corporations take CSR into consideration. International trade has greatly benefited from the thrust towards trade liberalisation and the elimination of trade barriers. The catalyst behind this effort is the WTO. This organisation has received strong criticism for an allegedly too narrow focus on trade liberalisation excluding other legitimate public issues such as CSR.

WTO principles such as, *inter alia*, 'most favoured nation treatment'[4] and 'national treatment'[5] can undermine the ability of states to take measures in the field of CSR. For example, prohibiting the import of certain goods produced under slavelike conditions can in fact amount to an illegal trade barrier under WTO law, as it is prohibited to discriminate between products or trading partners.[6] The WTO is fairly exceptional in international law, given its effective binding dispute settlement mechanism. Decisions taken by the WTO Dispute Settlement Body penetrate deeply into states as all WTO members respond mostly by modifying the contested measures or occasionally by accepting resulting sanctions. As will be illustrated below in the context of human rights,[7] governments that

---

[4] The principle of most favoured nation requires that each member of the WTO treats all the other members equally as 'most-favoured' trading partners. If a country improves the benefits that it gives to one trading partner, it has to give the same 'best' treatment to all the other WTO members so that they all remain 'most-favoured'. The principle can be found, *inter alia*, in Article 1 of the General Agreement on Tariffs and Trade (GATT), 3 October 1947, 55 UNTS 194.

[5] Imported and locally-produced goods should be treated equally – at least after the foreign goods have entered the market. The same should apply to foreign and domestic services, and to foreign and local trademarks, copyrights and patents. This principle can be found, *inter alia*, in GATT, Article 3.

[6] It should be noted that, under strict conditions, some exceptions to this principle of non-discrimination are allowed (GATT, Article XX).

[7] See pp. 183–4, n. 25.

attempt to exercise some CSR-control at the national level can run into trouble in the WTO dispute settlement mechanism.

Moreover, not only can WTO rules undermine the ability of states to regulate corporate behaviour, the process of trade liberalisation can also lead to the acceptance of corporate social irresponsibility to secure unlawful competitive trade advantages in global markets, resulting in a race to the bottom. For example, states may be inclined, in violation of their obligations under international human rights law, to turn a blind eye when corporations make use of forced labour or child labour in the production process. States are obligated to protect their citizens by regulating the behaviour of corporations.[8] It is clear that many states fail to do so. This is confirmed, for example, by a recent report by the International Labour Organisation (ILO), entitled *A Global Alliance against Forced Labour*, which reveals that of the 12.3 million people trapped in forced labour, nearly 10 million are exploited in the private economy.[9]

Finally, the WTO deserves more attention from the CSR movement given the fact that currently corporate interests – in contrast to other issues of public concern – are strongly defended in the WTO. States at times turn to the WTO dispute settlement mechanism in order to protect the commercial interests of corporations, providing corporations with considerable indirect access to the WTO.[10] Indeed, several WTO member states have formally adopted internal legislation under which private parties can petition their governments to bring a WTO dispute.[11] It has been argued that, while WTO law formally belongs to the realm of *public* international law, the partnerships between member states and corporations are such that WTO law in fact profits and prejudices private parties.[12] In several cases the influence of entities with a business interest has come to the fore. For example, in the 'reformulated gasoline' case,[13] corporations with major interests in the outcome of the dispute were involved

---

[8] Jägers, *Corporate Human Rights Obligations*, pp. 75–9.

[9] *A Global Alliance against Forced Labour*, Global Report under the Follow-up to the ILO Declaration on Fundamental Principles and Rights at Work (Geneva: International Labour Office, 2005).

[10] For more on the indirect access of corporations to the WTO, see Gregory C. Shaffer, *Defending Interests. Public–Private Partnerships in WTO Litigation* (Washington, DC: Brookings Institution Press, 2003).

[11] See ss. 301–10 of the US Trade Act of 1974 or the Trade Barriers Regulation of the European Communities (Council Regulation 3286/94/EC OJ No. L41/3 23 February 1995.

[12] Shaffer, *Defending Interests*, p. 3.

[13] WTO Doc. WT/DS2/AB/R/, *United States – Standards for Reformulated Gasoline and Conventional Gasoline*, 20 March 1996. This case concerned the prescription by the US government to use so-called reformulated gasoline (gasoline that meets certain requirements

in various stages of the proceedings, including the drafting of written submissions and the preparation of oral arguments.[14] In the cases concerning the importation, sale and distribution of bananas,[15] the United States brought a case against the European Community on behalf of the multinational corporation Chiquita. Another example is where the Kodak Corporation accused Fuji of blocking access to the Japanese market.[16] After considerable pressure from Kodak, the US government decided to bring the case before the WTO dispute settlement system. Both Kodak and Fuji provided substantial support to the United States and Japan respectively.[17] In light of this indirect access of corporations to the WTO dispute settlement system, the question arises whether a CSR-oriented counterbalance is legally feasible.

III. The World Trade Organisation and human rights

This chapter will explore possible avenues to achieve this, focusing specifically on the example of human rights.

In general, it can be argued that the objectives of the WTO go beyond mere trade liberalisation and in fact have much in common with human rights concerns. Both aim to ensure human well-being by promoting peace and stability, non-discrimination and equal opportunities.[18] As can be deduced from the preamble of the WTO, free trade is not an end in itself. The preamble states that the member states of the WTO recognise:

> that their relations in the field of trade and economic endeavour should be conducted with a view to *raising standards of living, ensuring full employment* and a large and steadily growing volume of real income and effective

with regard to its composition and performance) in order to reduce harmful emissions. The requirements for foreign refiners differed from those for domestic refiners. The United States referred to GATT, Article XX. The WTO panel and Appellate Body found no justification for this differential treatment and therefore the US measures were in violation of GATT rules.

[14] August Reinisch and Christina Irgel, 'The Participation on Non-Governmental Organisations in the WTO Dispute Settlement System', *Non-State Actors and International Law* 1 (2001), 127–51, at 137–8. For more examples, see the appendix tables in Shaffer, *Defending Interests*.

[15] WTO Doc. WT/DS27, *European Communities – Regime for the Importation, Sale and Distribution of Bananas*. Appellate Body report adopted on 25 September 1997.

[16] WTO Doc. WT/DS44/R, *Report of the panel*, Parts A–I, *Japan – Measures Affecting Consumer Photographic Film and Paper*, 22 April 1998.

[17] Reinisch and Irgel, 'The Participation on Non-Governmental Organisations', pp. 138–9.

[18] Hoe Lim, 'Trade and Human Rights. What's the issue?, *Journal of World Trade* 35, 2 (2001), 275–300, at 276–8.

demand, and expanding the production of and trade in goods and services, while allowing for the optimal use of the world's resources in accordance with the objective of *sustainable development*, seeking both to protect and preserve the environment and to enhance the means for doing so in a manner consistent with their respective needs and concerns at different levels of economic development (emphasis added).[19]

These goals strongly resemble human rights provisions such as the right to work[20] and the right to an adequate standard of living.[21] The relationship between human rights and WTO law also comes to the fore in Article XX of GATT. That article deals with a number of exceptional circumstances that can justify trade-restrictive measures taken by a state. GATT, Article XX refers, *inter alia*, to measures that are 'necessary to protect human . . . health' (Article XXb) and measures 'relating to products of prison labour' (Article XXe). Article XX (b) and (e) provide states with the possibility to impose trade restrictions against a state that violates international standards. The existence of this article further shows that the object and purpose of the WTO goes beyond trade liberalisation to include respect for fundamental human rights norms. In addition, it can be argued that free trade and the quest for better protection and promotion of human rights can mutually reinforce each other. Respect for human rights may be conducive for trade and easier access to markets can help raise the standard of living, improving the overall human rights situation.

Nevertheless, despite common and complementary goals, the GATT/WTO and the human rights mechanisms have developed on practically separate tracks, with little or no dialogue between the two systems. Unbridled trade liberalisation can, however, have severe consequences for the effective protection of human rights. Under international human rights law, states are obligated to respect, protect and fulfil human rights.[22] Steps taken by states in order to live up to their human rights obligations can pose trade barriers that are illegal under WTO agreements.[23]

---

[19] Marrakesh Agreement establishing the World Trade Organization, 1867 UNTS 154, 33 ILM 1125 (1994), entered into force 1 January 1995.

[20] International Covenant on Economic, Social and Cultural Rights ((ICESR), (16 December 1966 (entered into force 3 January 1976) 993 UNTS 3), Article 6.

[21] ICESCR, Article 11.   [22] Jägers, *Corporate Human Rights Obligations*, pp. 75–9.

[23] These consequences were pointed out in a report on globalisation and human rights written in 2000 by two special rapporteurs of the UN Sub-Commission. They described the WTO as being 'a veritable nightmare for developing countries'. The report points out the impact of trade liberalisation, especially on developing countries and the

It may be argued that the likelihood of human rights issues arising before the dispute settlement mechanism of the WTO is of a largely theoretical nature, as most cases so far have dealt with trade matters of a highly technical nature. However, cases with a human rights dimension have already arisen before the WTO. To name a well-known example, the case brought against the European Union by Canada concerning measures taken by France outlawing the use of asbestos.[24] This case touches upon internationally recognised human rights such as the right to health and the right to life. Another poignant example is the case that the European Union and Japan brought against the United States in 1997 concerning the so-called 'Massachusetts Burma Procurement Law'. Following the call made by Aung San Suu Kyi, leader of the pro-democracy movement in Burma, to disinvest in the country in order to starve the military regime responsible for systematic human rights violations financially,

scant reference to human rights in the WTO. Moreover, the report is critical of the lack of transparency at the WTO. Other reports provide more nuanced contributions to the debate on the social impact of trade liberalisation. See, *inter alia*, the report on the human rights impact of agricultural trade liberalisation, 15 January 2002, at www.unhchr.ch/Huridocda/Huridoca.nsf/(Symbol)/E.CN.4.2002.54. En?Opendocument and the report on the liberalisation on the trade in services and human rights, 25 June 2002, at www.unhchr.ch/Huridocda/Huridoca.nsf/(Symbol)/E.CN.4.Sub.2. 2002.9.En?Opendocument.

[24] This case concerned a dispute between Canada and the European Communities. Canada challenged a French decision taken in 1996 to ban all forms of asbestos fibres and products containing asbestos fibres. The prohibition was issued in the light of mounting awareness of the negative health effects of asbestos. Canada challenged the French ban, stating it severely damaged its export in asbestos and was protectionist in intent. In the proceedings before the panel, the question was addressed whether the measures taken to protect human life and health were in violation of the WTO rules concerning liberalisation of trade. The panel reached the conclusion that the French measures were a justified exception to WTO rules on liberalisation in accordance with Article XX(b) of the GATT. However, as similar domestically produced products were permitted in France, it stated that the French ban on asbestos was of a discriminatory nature and therefore a violation of GATT national treatment obligation (differential national treatment is prohibited by Article III(4) of the GATT). WTO Doc. WT/DS135/R, *Report of the Panel: European Communities – Measures affecting Asbestos and Asbestos-Containing Products [Asbestos Case]*, 18 September 2000, and WTO Doc. WT/DS135/AB/R WTO, *Report of the Appellate Body: European Communities – Measures Affecting Asbestos and Asbestos-containing Products*, 12 March 2001. The Appellate Body confirmed the link between human rights and trade by stating that it seems 'perfectly legitimate for a Member to seek to halt the spread of a highly risky product' in light of the protection of health. Nevertheless, the decision of the Appellate Body has been criticised, as some claim that the line of reasoning was based purely on technical, economic considerations and not on human rights considerations. See Gabrielle Marceau, 'WTO Dispute Settlement and Human Rights', *European Journal of International Law* 13, 4 (2002), 807–8.

several municipal and county governments in the United States terminated contracts with corporations doing business in Burma. Massachusetts was among the states that followed such a policy and adopted a selective purchasing law.[25] Subsequently, the European Union and Japan filed a WTO case claiming the selective purchasing law was a violation of the WTO Agreement on Government Procurement,[26] as it imposed conditions that were not essential to fulfil the contract and were based on political instead of economic considerations.[27] The Massachusetts law was also challenged in the domestic courts of the United States by the National Foreign Trade Council (NFTC), a coalition of corporations, which claimed that the law was unconstitutional, as it infringed the federal government's exclusive authority to regulate foreign affairs.[28] The case went to the Supreme Court, which ruled in favour of the NFTC. The European Union and Japan then decided to suspend their request for proceedings at the WTO. Regrettably, as the case was withdrawn there was no ruling by the panel. It is imaginable, however, that the panel would have agreed with the European Union and Japan that the procurement policies of Massachusetts indeed were illegal under the WTO regime. This case demonstrates how the WTO potentially can restrict the possibilities of States to take measures relating to CSR.

On one occasion the potentially chilling effect of WTO rules on the ability of states to regulate the behaviour of corporations has been acknowledged by the WTO in the context of the trade in so-called 'conflict' diamonds. These diamonds, also known as 'blood' diamonds, are rough diamonds used by rebel groups or their allies to finance armed conflict aimed at undermining legitimate governments. Under the Kimberly Process Certification Scheme for Rough Diamonds, states have taken measures to restrict the import of such diamonds.[29] In 2003, the WTO Council on the Trade in Goods agreed to the request of eleven member states to

---

[25] Act of June 25th, 1996, Chapter 130, 1, 1996, Mass. Acts. 210, codified at Mass. Gen. L. ch. 7. 22G-22M.

[26] Agreement on Government Procurement, 15 April 1994 (entered into force on 1 January 1996), 1915 UNTS 103.

[27] The European Union and Japan considered this to be a violation of Articles VIII(b), X and XIII of the WTO Agreement of Government Procurement. World Trade Organisation, WTO Doc. WT/DS88/1. *United States – Measure Affecting Government Procurement, Request for Consultation by the European Communities*, 26 June 1997.

[28] *National Foreign Trade Council* v. *Baker*, 26 F Supp. 2d 287, 291 (Mass. 1998).

[29] The Kimberly certification process was launched in 2000. For more information see the website, www.kimberlyprocess.com.

recommend that the General Council issue a waiver to these members. According to the council, trade restrictions in this case were acceptable given the 'extraordinary humanitarian nature of this issue and the devastating impact of conflicts fuelled by trade in conflict diamonds on the peace, safety and security of people in affected countries and the systematic and gross human rights violations that have been perpetrated in such conflicts'.[30] It can be argued that this decision was prompted mainly by the major trade interest involved in the trade in diamonds. Also, the use of a waiver shows that the WTO can only deal with human rights issues by recourse to exceptional tools.[31] In any case, so far the decision is exceptional and, in spite of a growing awareness of the linkages between trade and human rights,[32] human rights concerns generally are not taken into consideration in the WTO. However, as pointed out by Pauwelyn,[33] the cases before the WTO adjudicative bodies that concern human rights are likely to increase in the future, given the increasing interaction between WTO law and other branches of international law. Moreover, it is to be expected that member states will turn to human rights law as a possible

[30] See the press release of 26 February 2003 on the website of the WTO at www.wto.org. For more on the WTO waiver for the Kimberly process, see Krista Nadakavukaren Schefer, 'Stopping Trade in Conflict Diamonds: Exploring the Trade and Human Rights Interface with the WTO Waiver for the Kimberly Process', in Thomas Cottier, Joost Pauwelyn and Elisabeth Bügi (eds.), *Human Rights and International Trade* (Oxford: Oxford University Press, 2005), pp. 391–451. She points out, *inter alia*, that a waiver is a short-term, exceptional tool and therefore not adequate to deal with any fundamental incompatibility between WTO obligations and human rights law. In her view a better solution would have been to let the WTO adjudicatory process decide whether such trade barriers are indeed illegal under WTO law.

[31] Kevin R. Gray, 'Conflict Diamonds and the WTO: Not the Best Opportunity to be Missed for the Trade-Human Rights Interface', in Cottier, Pauwelyn and Bügi (eds.), *Human Rights and International Trade*, pp. 451–61. He further argues that the case of conflict diamonds is situational rather than product-related. Such situations can be examined by international human rights institutions.

[32] There is a mounting body of scholarly writing on the issue. For a special focus on the WTO, see for example Cottier, Pauwelyn and Bügi (eds.), *Human Rights and International Trade*; Ernst-Ulrich Petersmann, 'The "Human Rights Approach" advocated by the UN High Commissioner for Human Rights and the International Labour Organization; is it Relevant for WTO Law and Policy?', *Journal of International Economic Law* 7, 3 (2004), 605–27; Marceau, 'WTO Dispute Settlement', 753–815; Lim, 'Trade and Human Rights', 275–300; Robert Howse and Makua Mutua, 'Protecting Human Rights in a Global Economy, Challenges for the World Trade Organization', Policy Paper (Montreal: International Centre for Human Rights and Democratic Development, 2000).

[33] Joost Pauwelyn, 'Cooperation in Dispute Settlement. Human Rights in WTO Dispute Settlement', in Cottier, Pauwelyn and Bürgi (eds.), *Human Rights and International Trade*, pp. 210–11.

defence, given the fact that it is no longer possible to block the formation of a panel or the adoption of a report by the Dispute Settlement
Body.[34]

It has been put forward that the WTO does not have the authority to deal
with issues beyond WTO rules, such as international human rights law.
However, in general it is submitted that, in light of the increasing recognition of the horizontal effect of human rights,[35] the WTO, just as any other
international organisation, cannot disregard fundamental human rights.
The preamble of the Universal Declaration of Human Rights (UDHR)[36]
states that 'every individual and every organ of society . . . shall strive . . .
to promote respect for these rights and freedoms'. Every organ of society
includes the WTO.

What are, more specifically, the implications of this conclusion for the
WTO dispute settlement mechanism? Can it be argued that the WTO
'judiciary'[37] has the authority to include international human rights law
in the proceedings? As described above, the WTO panels and the Appellate
Body are at times confronted with claims of which the underlying issue
involves non-WTO law. Whether the WTO adjudicative bodies can apply
other rules of international law is a matter of controversy. The jurisdiction
of the WTO judiciary is confined to the WTO-covered agreements,[38] and
it is argued that therefore there is no room for other international law, such
as international human rights law.[39] However, it is undisputed that WTO

---

[34] See pp. 196–7 and n. 86.   [35] Jägers, *Corporate Human Rights Obligations*, pp. 36–8.
[36] 10 December 1948, UN Doc. GA Res 217A, United Nations Yearbook (1948–9), 535.
[37] Strictly speaking, the term 'judiciary' is not correct when referring to WTO panels and the
Appellate Body. The panels are established ad hoc and the legal findings of both the panels and the Appellate Body are recommendations that need to be adopted by the Dispute
Settlement Body in order for them to become binding. Nevertheless, the independent functioning of the panels and the Appellate Body in practice gives them a judicial character in
the international law sense. Therefore, the term 'judiciary' will be used in this chapter. This
line of reasoning is followed by several scholars. See, *inter alia*, M. Matsushita, T. J. Schoen-
baum and P. C. Mavroidis, *The World Trade Organization* (Oxford: Oxford University
Press, 2003), p. 18; Joseph H. H. Weiler, 'The Rule of Lawyers and the Ethics of Diplomats:
Reflections on the Internal and External Legitimacy of WTO Dispute Settlement', *Harvard
Jean Monnet Working Paper* 9/00; www.jeanmonnetprogram.org/papers/00/000901.html,
Joost Pauwelyn, 'The Role of Public International Law in the WTO: How Far Can we Go?',
American Journal of International Law 95 (2001), 535–78.
[38] Article 1.1 of the Understanding on Rules and Procedures Governing the Settlement of
Disputes, 15 April 1994, Marrakesh Agreement establishing the World Trade Organization,
Annex 2, 1869 UNTS 401.
[39] Marceau, 'WTO Dispute Settlement', 7; Pauwelyn, 'The Role of Public International Law
in the WTO', 554.

law is part of the wider corpus of international law[40] and, as convincingly argued by Pauwelyn, the fact that a claim before the WTO is limited to the covered agreements does not imply that the applicable law available to the panel or Appellate Body is necessarily limited to these documents.[41] This follows from the simple fact that the dispute settlement mechanism was created and continues to exist in the wider context of international law and the WTO has not 'contracted out' of rules of international law.[42] Furthermore, several articles in the Dispute Settlement Understanding (DSU) are interpreted as requiring that a panel refers to other rules of international law, and from WTO jurisprudence it is clear that panels frequently do so.[43] It can be concluded that WTO panels have the authority to refer to other rules of international law, including international human rights law, as long as this is done in the context of the examination of a WTO claim and both parties to the dispute are bound to the non-WTO rule in question. The latter is undisputable in the case of international human rights norms of a *jus cogens* character, meaning those peremptory norms from which no derogation is allowed.[44] Such norms prevail at all times over all other international norms including WTO rules. *Jus cogens* norms therefore have direct effect within the WTO.[45] The prohibition of slavery is an example of a *jus cogens* norm that is particularly relevant in the context of the WTO as certain labour practices in fact may constitute a modern form of slavery.

In sum, the agreements concluded in the framework of the WTO and especially the binding enforcement mechanism can have a grave impact on the effective enjoyment of human rights. In principle, the WTO cannot ignore international human rights law. So far as substantive law is concerned, where trade rules and human rights concerns intersect, ample consideration must be given to human rights obligations. A legal case can also be made for enhancing the role of agents who would press for such an

---

[40] This was confirmed by the Appellate Body in its first case, *United States – Standards for Reformulated and Conventional Gasoline*, WTO Doc. WT/DS2/AB/R, 20 March 1996, at para. 17; Pauwelyn, 'The Role of Public International Law in the WTO'.

[41] Pauwelyn, 'The Role of Public International Law in the WTO', 560, and Pauwelyn, 'Cooperation in Dispute Settlement', pp. 205–31.

[42] Pauwelyn, 'The Role of Public International Law in the WTO', 562, and Pauwelyn, 'Cooperation in Dispute Settlement', p. 218.

[43] See DSU Articles 3(2), 7, 11. Pauwelyn, 'The Role of Public International Law in the WTO', 562–3.

[44] Vienna Convention on the Law of Treaties (23 May 1963 (entry into force 27 January 1980) 1155 UNTS 331), Article 53.

[45] Marceau, 'WTO Dispute Settlement', 39.

approach, notably NGOs. This is certainly a development that has already begun to occur in other areas of international law.

IV. Evolution of non-governmental organisation participation under international law

The traditional perspective on international law is state-centred. The state is the bearer of international rights and duties. Other entities such as NGOs, however, are gradually moving in on this formerly exclusive domain of the state. The importance of NGO participation has been acknowledged in various authoritative international documents. A general principle of public participation can be deduced from Article 71 of the UN Charter.[46] NGO participation has found its most detailed expression in international human rights law. But also in the field of international environmental law, several major documents have laid down principles regarding public participation.[47] In international human rights law, NGO participation has manifested itself in several different forms. NGOs have developed operational activities in areas such as relief and assistance. They also play an important role as advocates of human rights by exerting pressure on and making available their expertise for negotiating parties in the process of standard-setting, at times as official members of national delegations or by obtaining official observer status.[48] Moreover, the advisory

---

[46] Charter of the United Nations, 26 June 1945, 53 Stat. 1031, Article 71 reads 'The Economic and Social Council may make suitable arrangements for consultation with nongovernmental organizations which are concerned with matters within its competence. Such arrangements may be made with international organizations and, where appropriate, with national organizations after consultation with the Member of the United Nations concerned'.

[47] See, for example, the Rio Declaration on Environment and Development, UN Doc. A/C.151/26 (vol. I), 31 ILM 874 (1994) and Agenda 21, adopted in 1992. Principle 10 of the Rio Declaration acknowledges the importance of NGO participation by acknowledging that '[e]nvironmental issues are best handled with participation of all concerned citizens'. In Agenda 21, chapter 27 is wholly devoted to the role NGOs play as 'partners in sustainable development'. Agenda 21 establishes an action plan for UN institutions, including financial and development agencies, and for all other international organisations and fora to establish formal participatory procedures for the involvement of NGOs at all levels of decision-making and implementation (see paras. 27.9 and 27.13). In a regional, European context, the following document is of interest: the 'Convention on Access to Information, Public Participation in Decision-making and Access to Justice in Environmental Matters' (25 June 1998, 38 ILM (1999)), the so-called Aarhus Convention. The latter is the first international convention exclusively devoted to public participation.

[48] In general, the influence of NGOs on standard-setting conferences has experienced considerable growth in the last few decades. Frequently cited examples are the NGO campaigns

and technical assistance provided by NGOs in the processes of monitoring international human rights standards has proven essential. Due to the proliferation of issues that international organisations have to deal with, there is an increasing need for external input. For example, the Convention on the Rights of the Child[49] recognises a formal role for NGOs in providing for expert advice on the implementation of the Convention.[50] An important aspect of supervision is the availability of information on how national authorities implement international standards. NGOs are often an important source of information for the supervisory bodies in this respect. Finally, NGOs play a valuable role in the dissemination of information regarding international standards, both towards the authorities that need to implement these provisions and towards the public at large.

Besides the NGO participation described above, international human rights law also provides for a more judicial role for NGOs. Legal possibilities have been created for NGOs to participate in proceedings and bring complaints. This concept of civil society acquiring juridical force is particularly challenging to the traditional focus on the state under international law. Legal participation by NGOs can be divided into two categories. First, NGOs may act as parties or as interveners in a dispute. Second, NGOs can participate in the legal process as *amici curiae* (friends of the court). The first type of NGO participation requires *locus standi* (legal standing). This requires that an NGO is sufficiently affected; in other words, has an interest in the matter at hand. In various national jurisdictions, the threshold for establishing such an interest is low and litigation initiated by NGOs for public interest issues is quite common. At the international

regarding the Earth Summit in 1992, the Habitat Conference in 1996, the Banning of Landmines in 1997, the sinking of the Multilateral Agreement on Investment (MAI) in 1998 and the Rome Statute establishing the International Criminal Court in 1998 (entered into force 1 July 2002, 2187 UNTS 90).

[49] Convention on the Rights of the Child, 20 November 1989 (entered into force 2 September 1999), 1577 UNTS 3.

[50] Article 45 reads: 'In order to foster effective implementation of the Convention and to encourage international co-operation in the field covered by the Convention:

(a) . . . The Committee may invite the specialized agencies, the United Nations Children's Fund and other competent bodies as it may consider appropriate to provide expert advice on the implementation of the Convention in areas falling within the scope of their respective mandates.'

The Committee for the Rights of the Child has established a close working relationship with the so-called NGO group for the Convention on the Rights of the Child, a coalition of forty-one NGOs.

level, the requirement of sufficient interest is usually more strictly interpreted, resulting in limited possibilities for NGOs to participate as parties in legal proceedings. Under international human rights law, it has been accepted that NGOs take part in international judicial procedures. The most liberal approach to legal standing is the case where a general public concern can be enough to grant NGOs access to court. This approach amounts to an *actio popularis*, that is an action to obtain a remedy for a group in the name of the general public without being a victim or being explicitly authorised to represent a victim. Such a procedure is provided for in the 1995 optional protocol to the European Social Charter (ESC).[51] This collective complaints procedure allows NGOs to submit complaints with the European Committee of Social Rights concerning an unsatisfactory application of one of the provisions in the ESC. The complaint must be of a general nature and not refer to an individual situation. Under the African Charter on Human and Peoples' Rights (ACHPR),[52] NGOs may submit complaints against alleged violations before the (quasi-)judicial commission without referring to a specific victim.[53] In 2004, the protocol on the establishment of an African Court on Human and Peoples' Rights entered into force, according to which relevant NGOs with observer status before the African Commission may institute cases directly before the African Court.[54] The legal standing of NGOs before the African Court is

---

[51] European Social Charter, 18 October 1961 (revised in 1996, entered into force 1999), 529 UNTS 89; Additional Protocol to the European Social Charter Providing for a System of Collective Complaints, 9 November 1995 (entered into force 1 July 1998), CETS 158. And see www.coe.int/T/E/Human_Rights/Esc/.

[52] African Charter on Human and Peoples' Rights, 27 June 1981, 1520 UNTS 217, 245.

[53] The ACHPR does not contain a specific provision granting NGOs access to the Commission. However, Article 55 speaks of communications other than those of the state parties which is interpreted to include communications from NGOs. Any NGO, in or outside of Africa, may submit such a communication. Article 56 provides a number of procedural requirements: *inter alia* a communication must not be anonymous or contain insulting language, nor should the communication be based solely on news disseminated through the mass media. See Information sheet no. 3, communication procedure, Organisation of African Unity, at www.achpr.org.

[54] Article 5 (3) of the Protocol to the ACHPR. To acquire observer status, an NGO must work in the field of human rights, declare its financial resources and have objectives and activities in consonance with the principles and objectives of the Charter of the Organisation of African Unity, 21 ILM (1982) 59 (replaced by the Constitutive Act of the African Union on 11 July 2000 (entry into force 26 May 2001) OAU Doc. CAB/LEG 23.15 (2001)) Charter and the ACHPR: see Chapter I of the resolution on the criteria for granting and enjoying observer status to NGOs working in the field of human rights with the African Commission on Human and Peoples' Rights, adopted at the 25th meeting of the Commission, 1999. When ratifying the protocol, state parties have to make a separate declaration recognising the jurisdiction of the Court to hear individual or NGO complaints. At the time of writing only Burkina Faso has submitted such a declaration.

potentially – the Court has yet to come into action – far-reaching, as the reach of such a procedure will not be limited to the ACHPR, given that the jurisdiction of the African Court includes other international human rights documents. Moreover, NGOs will also have the right to request an advisory opinion regarding the ACHR and other international human rights treaties.[55] A somewhat more restricted *actio popularis* is provided for under the American Convention on Human Rights (ACHR),[56] where NGOs may lodge a petition with the Inter-American Commission complaining of a violation of the provisions of the American Convention by a member state.[57] The claimant need not be a victim of the alleged violation but should refer to specific victims within the jurisdiction of the Commission.[58] The NGO does not, however, require explicit authorisation by the victim to obtain legal standing.

The second approach to legal standing in international human rights law distinguished here is more restrictive than the *actio popularis* procedures described above. A number of procedures provide access to a court only when an individual right of the complainant is affected, not a general interest. This is the case before the European Court of Human Rights.[59] Moreover, states can declare their intent to recognise procedures allowing for complaints from individuals and groups of individuals claiming to have fallen victim to violations under the international covenants against racial discrimination,[60] discrimination of women[61] and the torture

---

55 What the exact future role of the African Court on Human and Peoples' Rights will be remains, however, to be seen, as it was decided in 2004 that in the future the court will merge with the African Union Court of Justice.

56 American Convention on Human Rights, 22 November 1969 (entered into force 18 July 1978), 1144 UNTS 143.

57 American Convention on Human Rights, Article 44. The requirements that NGOs have to meet to be eligible for participation in the inter-American system are laid down in the 'Guidelines for the Participation of Civil Society Organizations in OAS Activities Adopted in December 1999 by the Permanent Council', CP/RES 759 (1217/99), The NGO needs *inter alia*, to be legally recognised in one or more member states. The main responsibilities are: to answer inquiries from the OAS; to disseminate information on OAS activities; and to present an annual report on its participation in OAS activities, financial situation, sources of funding and coming activities.

58 Report No. 48/96, Case No. 11.553, *Annual Report of the Inter-American Commission of Human Rights 1996* (OEA/Ser.L/V/I/II.95 doc.7 rev.) paras. 27–28.

59 European Convention on Human Rights (ECHR) (Convention for the Protection of Human Rights and Fundamental Freedoms, 4 November 1950 (entry into force 3 September 1953) 213 UNTS 222), Article 34.

60 International Covenant on the Elimination of All Forms of Racial Discrimination (CERD), Article 14. At the time of writing, 45 of the 169 state parties submitted such a declaration and 33 complaints have been registered.

61 Article 2 Optional Protocol to the Convention on the Elimination of all Forms of Discrimination Against Women (CEDAW) (signed 6 October 1999 (entry into force 22 December

convention.[62] Finally, NGOs can play a role without being a victim by representing an individual victim after being explicitly authorised to do so. This is the case, *inter alia*, in proceedings before the Inter-American Court[63] and the Human Rights Committee.[64]

Besides being an actual party to a dispute, an NGO can also play a role as *amicus curiae*. The practice of *amicus curiae* briefs, originally a national concept, is now well-established before international tribunals.[65] In international human rights law, NGOs may participate in proceedings as *amici curiae* under the European Convention on Human Rights (ECHR)[66] and in both advisory and contentious cases before the IACHR.[67] By submitting an *amicus curiae* brief, an NGO does not become a party to the dispute but draws attention to certain arguments. Not being a party to the dispute has the advantage that the interest required to take part in the proceedings will generally be lower than is the case for the parties to the dispute. A general interest is usually sufficient.

From the above it is clear that NGOs have acquired a significant legal role in international proceedings, most notably in the field of international human rights law. It is difficult to quantify the actual influence of NGOs.[68] Nevertheless, especially in the regional human rights systems, many

2000) 2131 UNTS 83), Article 2. At the time of writing, 71 states of the 179 state parties have ratified the optional protocol. So far two decisions/views have been delivered by the Committee.

[62] Article 22 Convention Against Torture and other Cruel, Inhuman or Degrading Treatment (CAT) (10 December 1984 (entry into force 26 June 1987), 1465 UNTS 85), Article 22. At the time of writing, 56 of the 139 parties to the CAT have made declarations to acknowledge the competence of the supervisory committee. In total, 242 complaints have been registered.

[63] Rules of Procedure of the Inter-American Court of Human Rights, Articles 21–23.

[64] See Rules of Procedure of the Human Rights Committee, rule 90.

[65] Ruth Mackenzie, 'The *Amicus Curiae* in International Courts: Towards Common Procedural Approaches', in Tullio Treves, Marco Frigessi di Rattalma, Attila Tanzi, Alessandro Fodella, Cesare Pitea, Chiara (eds.), *Civil Society, International Courts and Compliance Bodies* (The Hague: T.M.C. Asser Press, 2005), pp. 295–311; Jona Razzaque, 'Changing Role of Friends of the Court in International Courts and Tribunals, *Non-state Actors and International Law* 1 (2002), 169–200; Dinah Shelton, 'The Participation of Nongovernmental Organizations in International Judicial Proceedings', *American Journal of International Law* 88, 4 (1993), 611–42.

[66] According to Article 36(2) of the ECHR, permission may be granted to submit written comments within a time-limit in the interest of the proper administration of justice.

[67] The Court receives *amicus curiae* briefs regularly. The only provision regulating their submission is the broadly formulated Article 63.2 of the Rules of the Inter-American Court, stating 'The President may invite or authorize any interested party to submit a written opinion on the issues covered by the request.'

[68] Research shows, however, that the impact of NGOs acting as *amici* has been considerable, notably in the European Court of Human Rights and the Inter-American Court of Human Rights: see Shelton, 'The Participation of Nongovernmental Organizations'.

cases – in the Inter-American system even most – are instigated by NGOs. In any case, it is clear that NGOs are recognised as legitimate partners that fully participate in procedures; it can even be argued that they are expected to fulfil this function.

The different roles described above can be summarised as the development of the role of NGOs from motor to supervisor and even party in a judicial dispute.[69] The practice of international human rights bodies is relevant for other international organisations, as decisions of these courts and tribunals constitute a source of law.

The evolution that has taken place regarding NGO participation in international human rights law is in stark contrast with the role NGOs are granted in international economic organisations. This may be partly due to the rather antagonistic role NGOs have played in the field of trade and investment in the past. An example is the NGO campaign against the Multilateral Agreement on Investment (MAI) in 1998 which effectively blocked its adoption. Contrary to the situation in the human rights field, NGOs are, in general, not considered legitimate participants in international economic organisations. Over the years NGO participation has slightly increased in some organisations. In general, the informal dialogue with NGOs has improved. However, the development towards a more formal, judicial role for NGOs, as has developed in international human rights law, has not taken place. Nevertheless, the concept of individual standing in the field of international trade law is not unprecedented. Several multilateral trade and investment treaties grant legal standing to non-state entities. For example, legal standing is provided to investors at the World Bank's International Centre for the Settlement of Investment Disputes and under the North American Free Trade Agreement (NAFTA).[70] In the European Community NGOs are granted legal standing in several ways before the dispute settlement system.[71] NGOs may directly challenge the legality of legislative and administrative acts[72] or omissions[73] by EC

---

[69] W. J. M. van Genugten, R. A. J. van Gestel, J. E. J. Prins and A. H. Vedder, *NGO's als 'nieuwe toezichthouders' op de naleving van mensenrechten door multinationale ondernemingen. Een beschouwing vanuit internationaalrechtelijk, bestuursrechtelijk en ethisch perspectief* (NGOs as 'new providers of supervision' of the respect for human rights by multinational corporations. Viewed from the perspective of international law, administrative law and ethics) (The Hague: Boom Juridische Uitgevers, 2004), p. 9.

[70] North American Free Trade Agreement, 17 December 1992 (entered into force 1 January 1994) 32 ILM 289, 605.

[71] Marco M. Slotboom, 'Participation of NGOs before the WTO and EC Tribunals: which Court is the Better Friend?', *World Trade Review* 1, 5 (2006), 69–101, at 71–80. As pointed out by Slotboom, it can be difficult in practice for NGOs to meet the requirements. Nevertheless, the *concept* of legal standing for NGOs is not considered problematic.

[72] EC Treaty, Article 230(4).   [73] EC Treaty, Article 232(3).

institutions, appear as interveners in proceedings between other parties[74] and make compensation claims for illegal acts adopted by the EC institutions.[75]

The World Bank group has undergone a radical transformation in the field of transparency and has significantly enhanced civil society participation. It has established the quasi-judicial inspection panel that allows NGOs to challenge any act of the two organs that deal with public-sector projects (the International Bank for Reconstruction and Development (IBRD) and the International Development Association (IDA)) that contravene the policies of the World Bank.[76] The increased attention for CSR in recent years is reflected in the second quasi-judicial avenue established within the World Bank in 1999: the function of Compliance Advisor/Ombudsman. Here, people affected by projects sponsored by the two branches of the World Bank that deal with private-sector financing (the International Finance Corporation (IFC)[77] and the Multilateral International Guarantee Agency) can voice their complaints. From a human rights perspective, work remains to be done towards making the mechanisms in the World Bank group true accountability mechanisms.[78] Nevertheless, the developments in the World Bank so far signal an increased acknowledgement of the principle of public participation in the accountability mechanisms of international economic institutions.[79]

---

[74] Statute of the European Court of Justice (25 March 1957, 298 UNTS 11), Article 40. This right to intervene is interpreted rather widely, allowing NGOs to intervene in cases where the outcome of the proceedings is such as to affect a collective interest. This participation as 'intervener' is broader than *amicus curiae* participation as an intervener is granted legal standing.

[75] Articles 235 and 288 of the EC Treaty. Damages can only be claimed if the NGO has suffered damages itself or has been assigned to claim damages suffered by its members.

[76] IBRD resolution 93-10 (and the identical IDA resolution 93-6) and the Inspection Panel Operating Procedures.

[77] Moreover, in February 2006 the IFC adopted a new set of environmental and social standards, together with a new policy on disclosure. The standards require client companies to have in place effective management systems that allow them to handle social and environmental risks as an integral part of their basic operations. For more information, see www.ifc.org.

[78] Koen de Feyter, 'Self-regulation' in W. J. M. van Genugten, P. Hunt and S. M. Mathews (eds.), *World Bank, IMF and Human Rights* (Nijmegen: Wolf Legal Publishers, 2003), pp. 79–137.

[79] Several regional economic institutions have also adopted compliance mechanisms, such as the Compliance Review Panel of the Asian Development Bank, the Independent Recourse Mechanism of the European Bank for Reconstruction and Development, and the Independent Investigation Mechanism of the Inter-American Development Bank. In each of these compliance mechanisms, NGOs play an important role, as a complaint can only be filed by a group of people affected – or a group representing those affected – by the policies of these institutions.

V. Non-governmental organisation participation in the World Trade Organisation

As can be deduced from the previous section, the tide of increased NGO participation, even in a more judicial role, has not completely bypassed international economic institutions. The situation is quite different in the WTO. Formally, the WTO system is a 'closed' system where non-state actors such as multinational corporations and NGOs are barred from participation. In recent years, the WTO has nevertheless taken steps to improve its relationship with civil society.[80] The legal provision governing this relationship is Article V(2) of the Final Act Uruguay Round (Marrakech agreement),[81] which reads: 'The General Council may make appropriate arrangements for consultation and co-operation with non-governmental organizations concerned with matters related to those of the WTO'.

This provision goes beyond the provision for NGO participation in the United Nations as provided for in Article 71 of the UN Charter, as it also speaks of cooperation and not merely consultation. In 1996, the General Council drew up 'Guidelines for Arrangements on Relations with Non-Governmental Organizations'.[82] According to these guidelines, the Secretariat was given the task of playing 'a more active role in its direct contacts with NGOs who, as a valuable resource, can contribute to the accuracy and richness of the public debate'.[83] A practice has developed of providing NGOs that are 'concerned with matters related to those of the WTO' accreditation to attend the WTO Ministerial Conference. NGOs are not permitted to take part in any of the committees. The WTO has responded to demands for greater release of information concerning WTO policy-making, most notably by constructing an elaborate web-site. In 2002, a long-debated decision was taken on earlier derestriction of documents.[84] Furthermore, the WTO has reached out to NGOs by organising symposia and day-to-day contact between the WTO Secretariat and NGOs. Notwithstanding the importance of these steps, the basic assumption within the WTO seems to be that it is under no obligation to involve further NGOs in its work. The 1996 Guidelines contain the following firm statement:

---

[80] For a survey of this history, see Steve Charnovitz, 'Opening the WTO to Nongovernmental Interests', *Fordham International Law Journal* 24 (November–December 2000).

[81] Marrakesh Agreement Establishing the World Trade Organisation.

[82] Decision adopted by the General Council on 18 July 1996, WT/L/162, 23 July 1996.

[83] Part IV of the Guidelines.

[84] WT/L/452, *Procedures for the derestriction and circulation of WTO documents*, 16 May 2002.

there is currently a broadly held view that it would not be possible for
NGOs to be directly involved in the work of the WTO or its meetings.
Closer consultation and cooperation with NGOs can also be met construc-
tively through appropriate processes at the national level where lies primary
responsibility for taking into account the different elements of public interest which are brought to bear on trade policy-making.[85]

VI. The role of non-governmental organisations in the World Trade Organisation dispute settlement mechanism

This chapter deals with possible NGO participation in a more legal sense
in the WTO. This implies that NGOs could be granted an enhanced role
in the dispute settlement system of the organisation. There are several
reasons for looking into how *judicial* participation can be improved.
The character of the dispute settlement mechanism profoundly changed
after the Uruguay Round of negotiations, from a conciliatory process
to an adjudicative process.[86] The WTO can now be considered the
most 'legalised' international organisation.[87] Consequently, due process
considerations which include public participation are to be taken into
account. Moreover, the exclusive jurisdiction over WTO issues provided
for in Article 23 of the DSU implies that WTO cases that also touch upon
human rights will have to be brought before the WTO dispute settlement
institutions. Moreover, as was pointed out earlier, changes in the dispute
settlement procedure have increased the likelihood that human rights
arguments will be raised in defence by states brought before the WTO
dispute settlement mechanism.[88] In the light of the proper administration of justice, it is essential that the human rights expertise that NGOs
have to offer is utilised. As discussed earlier, corporate interests have made
significant inroads into the WTO dispute settlement mechanism and this

---

[85] Guidelines, Article 6. This point of view was repeated in the report *The Future of The WTO*
(better know as 'The Sutherland Report'); see, *inter alia*, para. 212. This report was written
by eight eminent persons at the request of the Director General of the WTO, Supachai
Panitchpakdi, on the occasion of the tenth anniversary of the WTO. The importance of
the relationship with civil society for the future of the organisation is reflected in the fact
that one of the nine chapters deals with the issue of 'transparency and dialogue with civil
society'. The report is available on the website of the WTO at www.wto.org.

[86] For example, the Uruguay Round of negotiations eliminated the right of individual parties,
typically the one whose measure is being challenged, to block the establishment of panels
or the adoption of a report. Panels are now automatically established and reports adopted
by the Dispute Settlement Body unless there is consensus not to do so.

[87] Shaffer, *Defending Interests*, p. 8.   [88] See p. 185 and n. 34.

needs to be counterbalanced. Allowing more room for NGOs in the system is an option worth considering.

Strictly speaking, the WTO dispute settlement system is an interstate system; only member states can bring a case before the Dispute Settlement Body.[89] Other WTO members with a substantial interest in the dispute may intervene as third parties.[90] Formally, there is no room for NGOs to participate in the legal proceedings of the WTO adjudicative bodies.

However, according to Article 13(1) of the DSU, WTO panels have the authority 'to seek information and technical advice from any individual or body which it deems appropriate'. Based on this provision and the fact that panels are required to make an objective assessment (DSU, Article 11), the Appellate Body has slightly opened the doors for NGO participation in the form of *amicus curiae* submissions. In several cases, panels and the Appellate Body have been confronted with unrequested submissions, mostly from NGOs with an environmental interest and from business associations. In the *US-Shrimp* case the Appellate Body, overturning a panel decision to the contrary, observed that WTO panels have the discretionary authority either to accept or reject non-requested information from NGO sources.[91] The Appellate Body also has this discretionary authority.[92]

NGOs participating in the WTO dispute settlement process as friends of the court have caused considerable controversy among the states parties. Many member states are of the opinion that the Appellate Body trespassed its mandate and allowing for *amicus* participation threatens the interstate character of the organisation.[93] Admitting and considering *amicus curiae*

[89] This was explicitly stated by the Appellate Body in the *US–Shrimp* case: 'it may be well to stress at the outset that access to the dispute settlement process of the WTO is limited to the members of the WTO': WTO Doc. WT/DS/58/AB/R, *Report of the Appellate Body, United States – Import Prohibition of Certain Shrimp and Shrimp Products*, 12 October 1998, para. 101.

[90] WTO Agreement, Annex 2, Article 10, para. 2, 17(4).

[91] WTO Doc. WT/DS58/AB/R, *Report of the Appellate Body, United States – Import Prohibition of Certain Shrimp and Shrimp Products*, 15 May 1998, paras. 108–9.

[92] WTO Doc. WT/DS138/AB/R, *Report of the Appellate Body, United States – Imposition of Countervailing Duties on Certain Hot-Rolled Lead and Bismuth Carbon Steel Products Originating in the United Kingdom*, 10 May 2000. This decision was based on a broad reading of DSU, Article 17(9) which provides the Appellate Body with the authority to draw up working procedures.

[93] The *amicus curiae* controversy in the WTO has been extensively discussed by several scholars. See, *inter alia*, Robert Howse, 'Membership and its Privileges: the WTO, Civil Society, and the Amicus Brief Controversy', *European Law Journal* 9, 4 (2003); Mary Footer and Saman Zia-Zarifi, 'European Communities – Measures affecting

submissions is in line with the practice of other international tribunals. In the field of human rights[94] such NGO participation is common but also in other trade tribunals such as those under NAFTA.[95] However, the relevant issue is not so much what the practice is of other tribunals,[96] but whether WTO law allows for the submission and consideration of such briefs. The Appellate Body has confirmed that the authority of WTO panels to admit and consider briefs from third parties is soundly grounded on Article 13 of the DSU, which gives panels control over the process of informing itself.[97] The Appellate Body has based its own authority on a more procedural article – the right to draw up working procedures (Article 17(9)). More generally, it can be argued that the authority for both the panels and the

Asbestos and Asbestos-containing Products. The World Trade Organization on Trial for its Handling of Occupational Health and Safety Issues', *Melbourne Journal of International Law* 3, 1 (2002), 120–42; Petros C. Mavroidis, '*Amicus Curiae* Briefs before the WTO: Much ado about nothing', Jean Monnet Working Paper, No. 2/01, at www.jeanmonnetprogram.org/papers/01/010201.html; Gabrielle Marceau and Mathew Stilwell, 'Practical Suggestions for Amicus Curiae Briefs before the WTO Adjudicating Bodies', *European Journal of International Law* 1, 1 (2001), 155–87; Georg C. Umbricht, 'An Amicus Curiae Brief on Amicus Curiae Briefs at the WTO', *Journal of International Economic Law* 4, 4 (2001), 773–94; Geert A. Zonnekeyn, 'The Appellate Body's Communication on *Amicus Curiae* Briefs in the *Asbestos* Case. An Echternach Procession?', *Journal of World Trade* 35, 3 (2001), 553–63.

[94] For example, the admission of *amicus curiae* briefs is possible before the International Criminal Court under rule 103 of the Rules of Procedure and Evidence. In general, see Mackenzie, 'The *Amicus Curiae* in International Courts'.

[95] In the Methanex case, a NAFTA tribunal received an unsolicited submission from an NGO. This case concerned a ban in the State of California of a gasoline additive called MTBE manufactured by Canadian-based Methanex Corporation. In response to the ban, Methanex took the US government to the NAFTA tribunal, claiming that under NAFTA, Chapter 11, the ban constituted an unlawful 'expropriation of its business interests'. In 2001, the tribunal ruled it had authority to accept and consider (or reject) *amicus curiae* submissions in this particular case (*Methanex Corp. v. United States of America*, Decision of the Tribunal on Petitions from Third Persons to intervene as 'Amicus Curiae', 15 January 2001). The Tribunal grounded its authority on Article 15(1) of the UNICITRAL Arbitration Rules, according to which the Tribunal has the power to 'conduct the arbitration in such manner as it considers appropriate . . . provided that the parties are treated equally and that at any stage in the proceedings each party is given a full opportunity of presenting its case'.

[96] It has been argued that the NAFTA arbitral tribunals cannot be compared to the WTO in this respect as these already involved private actors as parties to the dispute: see Slotboom, 'Participation of NGOs before the WTO and EC Tribunals', 90. However, in my opinion, this is not relevant for the question whether private parties can participate as *amicus curiae*, which constitutes a different role in the proceedings.

[97] For an opposite view, see Slotboom, 'Participation of NGOs before the WTO and EC Tribunals'.

Appellate Body to receive and accept *amicus curiae* submissions can be derived from the inherent powers of such an international tribunal.[98] In other words, it should be assumed that a dispute settlement mechanism established with the consent of states has those powers it needs in order to safeguard its basic judicial functions. In order for the WTO judiciary to perform its judicial function, the ability to assess all relevant information is a necessary component in the exercise of its judicial function. The WTO agreement is silent on procedural issues and for this relies on principles derived from general international law.[99] It can be argued that, also in respect of *amicus curiae* submissions, the WTO can follow the approach taken in other tribunals to fill this gap.

Amicus participation hardly constitutes a major role for NGOs as such, but can it be argued that this is a first step towards more formal and direct participation by NGOs?[100] Presently this does not seem to be the case, as in practice the WTO judicial organs have dealt with *amicus curiae* briefs in an ad hoc and not very coherent manner. Most submissions are rejected with little or no explanation.[101] This has not, however, stopped NGOs, notably those with an environmental interest, from handing in *amicus* briefs. Environmental NGOs have a considerable head start on human rights advocates as *amicus curiae* in the WTO as environmental issues have been on the WTO agenda for a considerable time.[102] An increasing interest from the side of human rights interest in the activities of the WTO can, however, be detected and this most probably will lead to an increase in the number of *amicus* briefs handed in by these organisations in the future.

---

[98] The doctrine of inherent powers has been formulated by the International Court of Justice (ICJ) in the *Nuclear Tests* case. In this case, the ICJ stated that it 'possesses an inherent jurisdiction enabling it to take such action as may be required, on the one hand to ensure that the exercise of its jurisdiction over the merits, if and when established, shall not be frustrated, and on the other, to provide for the orderly settlement of all matters in dispute . . . Such inherent jurisdiction, on the basis of which the Court is fully empowered to make whatever findings may be necessary for the purposes just indicated, derives from the mere existence of the Court as a judicial organ established by the consent of States, and is conferred upon it in order that its basic judicial functions may be safeguarded' (*Nuclear Tests* case, ICJ Reports 1974, pp. 259–60, para. 23).

[99] Pauwelyn, 'Cooperation in Dispute Settlement', 209–10.

[100] Howse, 'Membership and its Privileges', 497.

[101] Marceau and Stillwell, 'Practical Suggestions for Amicus Curiae Briefs', 163.

[102] See for an overview of this history, the document entitled 'Trade and the Environment at the WTO: background document' on the website of the WTO, www.wto.org.

VII. Suggestions for a future role for non-governmental organisations in the World Trade Organisation

To achieve a better balance of interests in the WTO, an enhanced role for NGOs is worth considering. As has been described above, NGOs in their function as watchdogs have proven invaluable to the development of international human rights law. Can a comparable role be provided for in the WTO?

As pointed out in the introduction, the issue of human rights and the WTO can be approached from two different perspectives. First, there is the impact of the WTO *as an organisation* on the effective enjoyment of human rights. In order to ensure that the operations of the WTO do not impact negatively on human rights, one could think of an accountability mechanism, comparable to the World Bank's Inspection Panel, where NGOs could file a complaint when the WTO violates human rights.[103] Second, a fundamental tension exists between human rights obligations and trade obligations in the context of the WTO. What role can NGOs play in this respect?

One suggestion to improve non-judicial NGO participation would be to actively involve NGOs in the so-called Trade Policy Review Mechanism[104] in a manner comparable to NGO participation in international human rights law. In order to achieve the goals of the multilateral trade agreements, each member state is required to report regularly on its national trade policies. The final report is drawn up by the Trade Policy Review Body, based on the report of the member state and a report drawn up by the WTO Secretariat. NGOs are not involved in the process. Various human rights treaties also require state parties to submit periodic reports. It is a well-established practice for NGOs to submit parallel reports that are accepted and taken into consideration by the human rights monitoring bodies. A similar role can be taken up by NGOs in order to monitor the human rights issues that may arise in the context of the Trade Policy Review process.

Besides enhancing the non-judicial role of NGOs, the role for NGOs in the legal process of the WTO needs to be reconsidered.

---

[103] Pauwelyn, 'Cooperation in Dispute Settlement', 205–31, at 208. For more on the World Bank's Inspection Panel, see Laurence Boisson de Chazournes, 'The World Bank Inspection Panel: About Public Participation and Dispute Settlement', in Treves, *et al.* (eds.), *Civil Society, International Courts and Compliance Bodies*, pp. 187–203, and De Feyter, 'Self-regulation'.

[104] See Annex 3 to the WTO Agreement.

First, the rules regarding the submission of *amicus* briefs must be codified. In the interest of due process and judicial independence, the authority of the WTO adjudicative bodies to deal with unsolicited *amicus* participation needs to be confirmed explicitly, and standard uniform rules regarding such participation need to be established. In light of the fact that WTO panels and the Appellate Body are increasingly confronted with issues beyond the technical aspects of trade liberalisation, expert input from NGOs on public interest issues should be welcomed A standard procedure for *amicus* participation will facilitate the objective assessment of the matters before the WTO adjudicative bodies, as is required by Article 11 of the DSU. Nevertheless, to date the case-to-case approach remains in place, despite calls from member states (notably two heavyweight members, the United States and the European Community) and scholars[105] to formulate a standard procedure for the acceptance of such submissions.

The WTO panels and Appellate Body could also be encouraged to seek more NGO input in the form of an expert opinion. Article 13 of the DSU authorises WTO panels to consult with experts to obtain their opinion on certain aspects of the matter. This article gives considerable flexibility to WTO panels to involve NGOs that have shown interest in providing information as experts. The authority to seek and accept expert advice is discretionary.[106]

It has been argued that NGOs cannot act as resource enhancers as they will not provide objective information.[107] However, it is up to the panel to weigh the information and make an objective assessment pursuant to Article 11 of the DSU. Increasing the role of NGOs in the dispute settlement process will help address the fear expressed by some observers that the adjudicative bodies of the WTO will misinterpret or water down existing human rights obligations.[108]

In light of the inflated controversy of the *amicus curiae* submissions and, more generally, the reluctance felt by many WTO members towards opening up the WTO to non-state participants, it is perfectly clear that, from a political perspective, the WTO is not ready for a further development of an even more judicial type of NGO participation in the proceedings.

---

[105] See, *inter alia*, the suggestions submitted by Marceau and Stilwell, 'Practical Suggestions for Amicus Curiae Briefs'.
[106] WTO Doc. WT/DS26/AB/R, *Appellate Body report EC Measures Concerning Meat and Meat products (Hormones Case)* adopted 13 February 1998, para. 136.
[107] Slotboom, 'Participation of NGOs before the WTO and EC Tribunals', 98.
[108] P. Alston, 'Resisting the Merger and Acquisition of Human Rights by Trade Law: A Reply to Petersmann', *European Journal of International Law* 13 (2002), 815–44.

Nevertheless, it is clear that NGOs can play an important role in those situations where the WTO regime comes into conflict with international human rights law. This in combination with the progress made under international law in the field of NGO participation justifies an exploration of a more legal role for NGOs in the WTO dispute settlement mechanism.

Can we look to the procedures established under the human rights treaties for inspiration? As discussed above, the approach to legal standing for NGOs under the human rights supervisory mechanisms ranges from very liberal (the *actio popularis* procedure created under, *inter alia*, the ESC) to the situation in which an NGO claiming to be a victim of a human rights violation can lodge a complaint. The latter type of complaint clearly belongs in the system of international human rights protection. Where an individual human right is affected, such a claim should be brought before the (quasi-)adjudicative bodies supervising international human rights treaties. Nevertheless, it is necessary that within the WTO trade disputes involving human rights aspects are dealt with in a way that is more receptive to principles and practices of human rights law. WTO policies can impact on human rights, especially economic, social and cultural rights. The collective dimension of these rights can suitably be defended by NGOs. Can a procedure be envisaged where certain selected NGOs may start an *actio popularis*, a claim in the general interest which in fact has underlying human rights issues? As stated, the WTO does not have jurisdiction to enforce international human rights law. However, the situation can occur where human rights violations also amount to a violation of the aims of the WTO. An example is the situation where a state accepts the use of forced labour in the production process. This state is therefore able to produce and export a certain product at very low costs which amounts to an unfair trade advantage in violation of one of the main WTO principles, which is the promotion of fair competition. In response, some states might decide to adopt measures aimed at restricting the import of these products. If these measures are challenged before a WTO panel, justification could possibly be found in the general exception under GATT Article XX. NGOs could fulfil an important role by supporting such a claim acting as *amicus curiae*. However, states may decide, for various – maybe politically motivated – reasons, not to impose any trade restrictions and consequently, in line with the current text of the DSU, it will not be possible to bring a case before the WTO judiciary. Nonetheless, such human rights abuses do in fact constitute a barrier to the important goal of the WTO to promote fair competition. It is clear that in these cases the strict interstate character of the dispute settlement mechanism falls short. A comparison can be made to the international human rights mechanism, where the seldom used interstate complaints mechanisms have brought the necessity to the fore to provide *locus standi* to other actors.[109] An NGO could bring a claim stating a violation of WTO rules as a result of human rights violations. One can also think of a non-violation case where there is no violation of WTO rules as such, but the objectives of a trade agreement or legitimate expectations are not met.[110] For example, the use of child labour in the production process can nullify legitimate expectations regarding the trade value of an international trade concession.[111] It is clear that NGOs cannot be considered the direct beneficiaries of trade concessions. The direct beneficiary is the state. However, in the final analysis, the expected trade value of the concession ultimately belongs to the people of the state concerned. As is the case in *actio popularis* cases, NGOs could act as representatives of the general interest where certain trade behaviour frustrates WTO objectives such as fair competition.

States have limited space to manoeuvre given the political considerations they have to take into account. The possibility of widening the range of actors that can bring a case before the dispute settlement system is worth considering. NGOs could fulfil a valuable role by bringing a case before a WTO panel. WTO panels have the authority to consider other rules of international law. It is submitted here that, if such a claim involves a human rights violation of a *jus cogens* character, the possibility of bringing a claim should also be open to NGOs. Given the fundamental nature of such a claim, such a role for NGOs would seem appropriate.

Notwithstanding the experience with NGO participation in other fields of international law, the concept of *locus standi* for NGOs in the testing context of the WTO gives rise to many practical questions. What would be the implications if a panel decided that human rights violations taking place in a member country indeed amounted to a violation of one of the fundamental aims of the WTO? Could such a judgment provide other WTO members with a ground to impose justified trade restrictions against the country in question? Increasing official NGO participation in the

---

[109] The state complaint mechanisms of the major UN human rights treaties have never been utilised. The ECHR also provides for this possibility but it has been relied on only three times so far.

[110] GATT, Article XXIII 1(a), (b), (c).

[111] See the example provided by Pauwelyn, 'The Role of Public International Law in the WTO', 559.

WTO, especially in the dispute settlement mechanism, will raise concerns. Attention will have to be given to the legitimate concern of southern NGOs regarding the dominance of northern NGOs with large resources. Careful consideration would have to be given to selecting which NGOs are eligible to take on a more legal role in the WTO. Procedural safeguards and substantive criteria would be needed to avoid misconceived and frivolous submissions. The demands placed on NGOs will differ according to the role they (wish to) play. Where NGOs act as friends of the court they bring in new ideas, and selection criteria are less pertinent than is the case where actual legal standing for NGOs is envisaged. Procedural requirements will assist in identifying legitimate NGO contributions.[112] Unfounded claims could also be avoided by establishing an independent body to assist the WTO panel. It has been suggested that such an independent counsel, based on the concept of the Advocate General in the European Community and in several municipal jurisdictions, could inform the panel of relevant issues and additionally could act as a focus and a filter for the concerns of NGOs.[113]

Providing NGOs with legal standing implies a complete overhaul of the system of dispute settlement within the WTO, and therefore, given the political reality, the concept at present is probably not yet feasible. A less far-reaching proposition is the idea of giving NGOs a formal advisory legal role in the WTO judicial system. This could be done by introducing an obligatory consultation process that includes certain selected NGOs. In 2000, the International Law Association recommended that WTO members should strengthen the rule of law in international trade by enhancing the legitimacy and acceptance of WTO rules by in particular '[a]llowing individual parties, both natural and corporate, an advisory locus standi in those dispute settlement procedures where their own rights

---

[112] For more on the issue of the legitimacy of NGOs, see, inter alia: Michael Edwards and Simon Zadek, 'Governing the Provision of Global Public Goods: the Role and Legitimacy of Nonstate Actors', in Inge Kaul, Pedro Conceicao, Katell le Goulven, Ronals U. Mendoza (eds.), Providing Global Public Goods. Managing Globalization (Oxford: Oxford University Press, 2003), pp. 200–24; Hugo Slim, 'By What Authority? The Legitimacy and Accountability of Non-governmental Organisations', International Council on Human Rights Policy (Oxford: Oxford Brookes University, 2002); Steve Charnovitz, 'The Relevance of Non-State Actors to International Law: Comment', in Rudiger Wolfrum and Volker Roben (eds.), Developments of International Law in Treaty Making (Berlin: Springer, 2005), pp. 543–56.

[113] Beatrice Chaytor, Reforming Dispute Settlement for Sustainable Development, SUSTRA International Workshop. Architecture of the Global System of Governance on Trade and Sustainable Development, 2002.

and interests are affected'.[114] NGOs could play a part in advising whether certain national measures fall within the exceptions of GATT, Article XX that allow for trade sanctions. A necessary precondition would be that the panel proceedings would be opened up to some extent.[115] NGOs could be given observer status during formal presentations to dispute panels.

Besides involving NGOs in the dispute settlement mechanism, other avenues to ensure that the WTO takes human rights into account can also be explored. For example, the cooperation with international human rights organisations, such as the Office of the High Commissioner for Human Rights, can be further improved. Moreover, the members of the Appellate Body can include persons with knowledge in the field of human rights.[116]

VIII. Conclusion

CSR is moving beyond voluntary initiatives towards binding regulation. States have an important role to play in this respect. In the field of human rights, states are under the obligation to regulate the behaviour of corporations. However, as has been pointed out in this chapter, agreements concluded in the context of the WTO can undermine the ability of states to regulate CSR issues such as the effective protection of human rights. The question arises how greater attention for CSR can be infused into the WTO, especially in light of the fact that significant indirect access for corporate interests already exists within this organisation. It is submitted that a more judicial type of NGO participation in the WTO as has occurred in the field of international human rights law may assist in securing more attention for CSR issues.

The call for integrating human rights concerns into the work of the WTO does not imply that the WTO is or should act as a human rights tribunal. The protection and promotion of human rights is primarily a task for the human rights machinery. It should be emphasised that, first and foremost, the existing international human rights mechanisms should be better utilised to enforce human rights obligations. All WTO

---

[114] International Law Association, Report of the sixty-ninth conference held in London, 25–29 July 2000, Resolution No. 2/2000, Annex 3.

[115] In August 2005, the WTO, for the first time in its history, decided, upon the request of the parties involved, to open the proceedings in the *Hormones* case (see n. 106 above) to the public through a closed-circuit TV broadcast. This case involved the United States and the European Community, both declared supporters of increasing the transparency of the WTO dispute settlement process.

[116] Pauwelyn, 'Cooperation in Dispute Settlement', 231.

member states are party to at least one of the six principal human rights treaties. Of the 148 WTO member states, 118 have ratified the ICESR and 121 the International Covenant on Civil and Political Rights.[117] The obligations these states have under those treaties should be enforced when decisions they take in the field of trade policy result in a violation of these obligations. Enforcing human rights obligations is not the task of the WTO. Nevertheless, the WTO is not an island in international law. Human rights as an element of general international law are part of the context in which the WTO must function. The WTO should therefore pay more than just lip-service to NGOs and there are precedents to suggest a real participatory role for NGOs could be developed.

[117] International Covenant on Civil and Political Rights, 16 December 1966 (entry into force 23 March 1976), 993 UNTS 171.

7

Meta-regulation: legal accountability for corporate social responsibility

CHRISTINE PARKER

I. Introduction: legal accountability and corporate social responsibility

The very idea that law might make business responsible for corporate social responsibility (CSR) is paradoxical. We might argue that ideally CSR includes compliance with business' legal responsibilities but goes 'beyond compliance'[1] to encompass the *economic* ('to produce goods and services that society wants and to sell them at a profit'), *ethical* ('additional behaviours and activities that are not necessarily codified into law but nevertheless are expected of business by society's members') and even *discretionary* ('those about which society has no clear-cut message for business', but society does expect business to assume some discretionary role, for example making philanthropic contributions) expectations of society.[2] If so, how is it possible for the *law* to make companies accountable for going *beyond the law*?

Research for this chapter was funded by the Australian Research Council Discovery Grant DP0344638 'Meta-regulation and the regulation of law'. I am grateful to my colleagues on that project – John Braithwaite, Colin Scott and Nicola Lacey – for discussions and ideas that have contributed to this paper. I am also grateful to Pamela 'Responsibilisation' Hanrahan, Doreen McBarnet, Greg Restall, Rob Rosen, Ronen Shamir and Aurora Voiculescu for helpful comments and discussions.

[1] See N. Gunningham, R. Kagan and D. Thornton, 'Social Licence and Environmental Protection: Why Businesses go Beyond Compliance?', *Law and Social Inquiry* 29 (2004), 307.

[2] A. B. Carroll, 'A Three-dimensional Conceptual Model of Corporate Performance', *Academy of Management Review* 4 (1979), 497, 500 (italics added). Carroll's definition recognises that all four overlap, some obligations may simultaneously fall into more than one category and obligations may move from being purely ethical to legal over time. They are all aspects of *society's* expectations of what corporations are obligated to do, and hence are *social* responsibilities.

On the other hand, we might argue that CSR is a set of vague, discretionary and non-enforceable corporate responses to social expectations.[3] If so, then might not companies use CSR to stave off more demanding legal regulation? Does not the idea of corporations' taking responsibility themselves for meeting society's expectations undermine the very idea of legal accountability for meeting substantive standards?

This chapter is concerned with the way in which law could (and sometimes does) seek to hold businesses *accountable* for taking their *responsibilities* seriously by using various mechanisms to encourage or enforce businesses to put in place internal governance structures, management practices and corporate cultures aimed at achieving responsible outcomes. Law attempts to constitute corporate 'consciences'[4] – getting companies 'to want to do what they should do'[5] – not just legally compliant outputs or actions. I have previously labelled regulatory initiatives that seek to do this 'meta-regulation' because they represent the (attempted) regulation of internal self-regulation.[6] Meta-regulation – the proliferation of different forms of regulation (whether tools of state law or non-law mechanisms) each regulating one another – is a key feature of contemporary governance.[7] The focus of this chapter, however, is on the meta-regulatory potential only of law.

---

[3] R. Shamir, 'Mind the Gap: The Commodification of Corporate Social Responsibility', *Symbolic Interaction* 28 (2005), 229; and R. Shamir, 'Between Self-regulation and the Alien Tort Claims Act: On the Contested Concept of Corporate Social Responsibility', *Law and Society Review* 38 (2004), 635. For a discussion of the ambiguity of 'corporate social responsibility', see D. Vogel, *The Market for Virtue: The Potential and Limits of Corporate Social Responsibility* (Washington, DC: Brookings Institution Press, 2005), pp. 4–6.

[4] Selznick uses the term 'corporate conscience': P. Selznick, *The Communitarian Persuasion* (Washington, DC: Woodrow Wilson Center Press, 2002), p. 101. See also n. 25 below.

[5] *ibid.*, p. 102

[6] C. Parker, *The Open Corporation* (Cambridge: Cambridge University Press, 2002). For similar uses of 'meta-regulation' or cognate terms, see J. Braithwaite, 'Meta-risk Management and Responsive Regulation for Tax System Integrity', *Law and Policy* 25 (2003), 1; C. Coglianese and D. Lazer, 'Management-based Regulation: Prescribing Private Management to Achieve Public Goals', *Law and Society Review* 37 (2003), 691 (government as 'meta-manager'); P. Grabosky, 'Using Non-governmental Resources to Foster Regulatory Compliance', *Governance* 8 (1995), 527, 543 ('meta-monitoring'). For commentary, see R. Baldwin, 'The New Punitive Regulation', *Modern Law Review* 67 (2004), 351, 374–82; J. Black, 'The Emergence of Risk-based Regulation and the New Public Risk Management in the United Kingdom', *Public Law* Autumn (2005), 512, 543–5; M. Power, *The Risk Management of Everything: Re-thinking the Politics of Uncertainty* (London: Demos, 2004), p. 21.

[7] C. Parker, J. Braithwaite, C. Scott and N. Lacey (eds.), *Regulating Law* (Oxford: Oxford University Press, 2004).

To the extent that law focuses on companies' *internal responsibility processes* rather than *external accountability outcomes*, law runs the risk of becoming a substanceless sham, to the delight of corporate power-mongers who can bend it to their interests. Law might be hollowed out into a focus on process that fails to recognise and protect substantive and procedural rights.[8] If the law itself fails to recognise and protect substantive and procedural rights, then business will doubly fail to do so.

Putting the critique so starkly anticipates the response. This chapter argues that it is possible, in principle at least, to imagine (and even to see partial examples of) legal meta-regulation that holds business organisations accountable for putting in place corporate conscience processes that are aimed at substantive social values. However, this requires that procedural and substantive rights of customers, employees, local communities and other relevant stakeholders, as against businesses,[9] are adequately recognised and protected. 'Meta-regulatory' accountability for corporate responsibility is possible – but it may have little to do with most current business and government 'corporate social responsibility' initiatives.

This chapter:

(1) Sets out what meta-regulating law must do and be in order to hold companies accountable for their responsibility, and briefly explains how this notion of meta-regulating law relates to the plurality of legal, non-legal and quasi-legal 'governance' mechanisms at work in a globalising, 'post-regulatory' world.

(2) Sets out the critique that law which attempts to meta-regulate corporate responsibility will focus on internal governance processes in a way that allows business to avoid the conflict between self-interest and social values, and therefore to avoid accountability.

(3) Argues that law or regulation that falls into this critique does not fall within the criteria I have defined for meta-regulation of corporate responsibility. My conception of legal meta-regulation is a useful tool for evaluating proposals to use law to encourage or enforce CSR precisely because it addresses the main critiques of attempts to regulate CSR.

---

[8] W. Heydebrand, 'Process Rationality as Legal Governance: a Comparative Perspective', *International Sociology* 18 (2003), 325.

[9] Including their senior managers and shareholders: see, for example, Gideon Haigh, *Bad Company: The Strange Cult of The CEO* (London: Aurum Books, 2004) (how remuneration of CEOs affects corporate behaviour); Christopher Kutz, *Complicity: Law and Ethics for a Collective Age* (Cambridge: Cambridge University Press, 2000) (an argument for shareholder liability for corporate irresponsibility).

II. Meta-regulation: legal regulation of corporate conscience

A. Meta-regulation

The concept of meta-regulation can be fitted into a broader literature in which governance is seen as increasingly about 'collaborations', 'partnerships', 'webs' or 'networks' in which the state, state-promulgated law, and especially hierarchical command-and-control regulation, is not necessarily the dominant, and certainly not the only important, mechanism of regulation.[10] States, businesses, non-governmental organisations (NGOs) and people operating even outside these three sectors may all be active in constituting various governance networks that steer (or attempt to steer) different aspects of social and economic life.[11] States and law may be important to a greater or lesser extent in each of these networks, with overlapping forms of governance coming together in different ways to frustrate or accomplish various regulatory goals.[12]

The term 'meta-regulation' itself has been used as a descriptive or explanatory term within the literature on the 'new governance' to consider the way in which the state's role in governance and regulation is changing and splitting. The state is regulating its own regulation as a consequence of policies to apply transparency, efficiency and market competition principles to itself for example: government units that assess the social and economic impact of regulation proposed by other departments before allowing new legislation to be proposed;[13] regulating or auditing the quality assurance mechanisms of semi-independent government agencies (such as schools or universities), newly privatised or corporatised entities (such as prisons, rail operators or telecommunications companies), and

---

[10] See, e.g., J. Braithwaite, 'The New Regulatory State and the Transformation of Criminology', *British Journal of Criminology* 40 (2000), 222; J. Braithwaite and P. Drahos, *Global Business Regulation* (Cambridge: Cambridge University Press, 2000); M. Dorf and C. Sabel, 'A Constitution of Democratic Experimentalism', *Columbia Law Review* 98 (1998), 267; J. Freeman, 'The Private Role in Public Governance', *New York University Law Review* 75 (2000), 543, and 'Collaborative Governance in the Administrative State', *UCLA Law Review* 45 (1997), 1; R. Lipschutz, *Globalization, Governmentality and Global Politics: Regulation for the Rest of Us?* (Abingdon: Routledge, 2005); O. Lobel, 'The Renew Deal: the Fall of Regulation and the Rise of Governance in Contemporary Legal Thought', *Minnesota Law Review* 89 (2004), 342; H. Schepel, *The Constitution of Private Governance: Product Standards in the Regulation of Integrating Markets* (Oxford: Hart Publishing, 2005).

[11] C. Shearing and J. Wood, 'Nodal Governance, Democracy, and the New "Denizens"', *Journal of Law and Society* 30 (2003), 400, 405.

[12] See C. Scott, 'Analysing Regulatory Space: Fragmented Resources and Institutional Design', *Public Law* Summer (2001), 283.

[13] B. Morgan, 'The Economisation of Politics: Meta-regulation as a Form of Nonjudicial Legality', *Social and Legal Studies* 12 (2003), 489.

government departments.[14] 'Meta-regulation' can also entail any form of
regulation (whether by tools of state law or other mechanisms) that regulates any other form of regulation. Thus it might include legal regulation
of self-regulation (for example, putting an oversight board above a self-
regulatory professional association), non-legal methods of 'regulating'
internal corporate self-regulation or management (for example, voluntary accreditation to codes of good conduct and so on), the regulation
of national law-making by transnational bodies (such as the European
Union), and so on.

Some of this governance literature is mainly analytical or descriptive.
Some writers are critical of the 'hollowing out of the state' by plural governance mechanisms. Some actively encourage it. Others are cautiously
optimistic about the possibilities for increased participation in decision-
making entailed by changes in governance. Some seek to suggest ways in
which governance networks might be made more democratic, just, and/or
fair, starting from the assumption that plural governance mechanisms are
(and always have been) a reality for good or for ill. There is no consensus
(among either scholars or practitioners) about what substantive values,
if any, the techniques of meta-regulation and the new governance represent.[15] Nor is there any consensus about what role, if any, law at the
national, and especially international, level can and should play in facilitating, enforcing, regulating or supplanting governance networks.[16]

Why, then, might we be interested in thinking about law 'meta-
regulating' corporate responsibility?

First, and most practically, we would expect that law (or indeed other
forms of regulation/governance) that can focus itself on the inside of

---

[14] M. Power, 'Evaluating the Audit Explosion', *Law and Policy* 25 (2003), 185; C. Scott,
   'Speaking Softly without Big Sticks: Meta-regulation and Public Sector Audit', *Law and
   Policy* 25 (2003), 203. Also see C. Hood, O. James, C. Scott, G. Jones and T. Travers,
   Regulation Inside Government (Oxford: Oxford University Press, 1999); J. Jordana and
   D. Levi-Faur, 'The Politics of Regulation in the Age of Governance', in J. Jordana and
   D. Levi-Faur (eds.), *The Politics of Regulation: Institutions and Regulatory Reforms for the
   Age of Governance* (Cheltenham: Edward Elgar, 2004), p. 1.

[15] See Jordana and Levi-Faur, *The Politics of Regulation*, p. 11 ('the true colours of the regulatory state are still to be determined').

[16] Contrast, for example, Vogel, *The Market for Virtue* (cautious support for the possibility
   of achieving CSR at an international level through market mechanisms and civil society action); Lipschutz, *Globalization* (a substantial argument that current transnational
   governance mechanisms and CSR reform proposals are both based on market regulation
   that exclude political participation and regulation aimed at the common good); Schepel,
   The Constitution of Private Governance (detailed analysis of law and practice to show that
   'private' governance already represents the 'centre' of product safety-setting in a way that
   is ineluctably intertwined with 'public' law on the periphery).

corporations to constitute corporate consciences that go beyond compliance might be able to achieve more sustainable compliance with traditional regulatory goals more effectively and efficiently because it latches onto companies' inherent capacity to manage themselves.[17] Recognition of the plurality of governance provides an opportunity. Meta-regulating law could connect with communities, networks and organisations that are rich with the possibility of regulating themselves and one another responsibly, and work with that possibility to invigorate and enliven their inner commitment to responsibility.

Second, even if meta-regulation cannot be shown to have practical effectiveness and efficiency benefits, we might still think it is good to develop a meta-regulatory aspect to law because it makes the law track more accurately the way we think about organisational responsibility for identifying, preventing and correcting legal and ethical wrongdoing – meta-regulatory law recognises the complex ways in which organisational processes and structures can sometimes lead to wrong actions or outputs, and gives us techniques for holding organisations and their management responsible for the wrongness of those processes, as well as for the wrongness of their outputs.[18]

Finally, in the context of the new governance, meta-regulation might be one of the ways in which the practice and theory of law must be transformed and reconceptualised in order for us to work out how law interacts with other strands of governance.[19] Meta-regulatory law might recognise, incorporate or empower initiatives developed by non-state actors or

[17] See references at n. 6 above, and at n. 30 below. See also B. Fisse and J. Braithwaite, *Corporations, Crime and Accountability* (Cambridge: Cambridge University Press, 1993). Note this argument assumes a certain level of management competence and coherence, assumptions that are not always justified in practice (see critique of meta-regulating corporate responsibility in section III below).

[18] I have set out previously the ways in which more traditional command-and-control regulation of business frequently fails to achieve these first two objectives, and how meta-regulation does: see Parker, *The Open Corporation*.

[19] See C. Sabel and W. Simon, 'Epilogue: Accountability Without Sovereignty', in G. de Búrca and J. Scott (eds.), *New Governance and Constitutionalism in Europe and the US* (Oxford: Hart Publishing, 2006) (on the 'transformation' or 'hybridisation' of law in the context of the 'new governance'). The concept of meta-regulation would be aimed towards similar ideals as those represented by Teubner's idea of 'reflexive' law: G. Teubner, 'Corporate Fiduciary Duties and their Beneficiaries: A Functional Approach to the Legal Institutionalization of Corporate Responsibility', in K. Hopt and G. Teubner, *Corporate Governance and Directors' Liabilities: Legal, Economic and Sociological Analyses of Corporate Social Responsibility* (Berlin: Walter de Gruyter, 1985); Nonet and Selznick's 'responsive' law: P. Nonet and P. Selznick, *Law and Society in Transition: Toward Responsive Law* (2nd edn New Brunswick, NJ: Transaction Publishers, 2001) and, earlier, Durkheim's notion of law as coordinating between different social roles and functions, especially as represented

partnerships of actors that can regulate corporate governance processes (for example by enforcing management system standards developed by international NGOs). Taking a meta-regulatory approach to law might also allow us to recognise that some governance mechanisms that we might not have traditionally thought of as law could in fact be thought of as 'law' in an extended sense, and evaluated according to criteria of legality.[20] And, vice versa, we might understand better the ways in which law's regulatory goals are achieved or frustrated via regulatory forces outside the law (for example pollution limits are only observed by companies to the extent that relevant technology is available and management implements that technology appropriately in corporate production processes), and we might better understand the limits of law's regulatory reach. Meta-regulatory law is a response to the recognition that law itself is regulated by non-legal regulation, and should therefore seek to adapt itself to plural forms of regulation.

B. What would law need to do in order to meta-regulate corporate social responsibility?

Legal regulation characteristically works by holding people *accountable* for meeting 'threshold criteria of good conduct or performance' after the fact.[21] Legal regulation of business has typically involved imposing liability for conduct that has an impact or manifestation external to the business that fails to meet the legal standard, for example pollution, the death or injury of a worker, price-fixing, harmful products and so on.[22] CSR requires *responsibility*. As Philip Selznick puts it, *responsibility* goes beyond accountability to ask 'whether and how much you care about your duties. An ethic of responsibility calls for reflection and understanding, not mechanical or bare conformity. It looks to ideals as well as obligations, values as well as rules ... Responsibility internalizes standards by building them into the self-conceptions, motivations, and habits of individuals and into the organization's premises and routines.'[23]

---

in associational governance regimes: see R. Cotterrell, *Emile Durkheim: Law in a Moral Domain* (Edinburgh: Edinburgh University Press, 1999), pp. 111, 176–80.

[20] See, for example, Schepel's study of product standards developed outside formal legal mechanisms yet incorporated into law and much more important than law in many ways: Schepel, *The Constitution of Private Governance*.

[21] Selznick, *The Communitarian Persuasion*, p. 29

[22] Of course, law does not always regulate by setting standards, monitoring compliance and prosecuting and punishing non-compliance: see Parker, *et al.* (eds.), *Regulating Law*.

[23] Selznick, *The Communitarian Persuasion*, pp. 29, 102.

Responsible institutions, like responsible individuals, must have an inner commitment to doing the right thing[24] – they must have a corporate 'conscience'. For a corporation we need to look at its governance, management and culture in order to see whether, or what kind of, corporate conscience, it has. Selznick puts this well:

> A corporate conscience is created when values that transcend narrow self-interest are built into the practice and structure of the enterprise. This can be done in several ways: by clarifying policies and making them public; by practicing sensitive recruitment of staff; by inculcating appropriate attitudes and habits; by establishing special units to implement policies affecting the well-being of employees, or environmental and consumer protection; and by cooperating with relevant outside groups, such as trade unions and public agencies. All this becomes an 'organisational culture,' a framework within which the main goals of the enterprise are pursued. Although self-interest is by no means rejected, the realities of interdependence are accepted, the benefits of belonging acknowledged. Self-interest is moderated and redirected, not forgotten or extinguished.[25]

Selznick's morally 'thick' conception of what meta-regulation should aim to do set out here can be contrasted with the morally 'thin' reasons for which the critics argue meta-regulation has been adopted. For example, Kim Krawiec argues that meta-regulatory techniques aimed at internal compliance systems have grown in popularity in the United States because policy-proposers and makers see corporate compliance breaches too narrowly as a principal–agent problem – that is, that 'misconduct within organizations results from the acts of single, independent agents who disregard the preferences of shareholder principals and their representatives – the board of directors and senior management'.[26] According to her, meta-regulation is therefore aimed narrowly at giving organisational principals incentives to police their agents more carefully, rather than addressing substantively the ways in which organisational management, systems and culture shape and/or implicitly encourage misconduct. She also argues that 'heightened organizational liability in exchange for a "safe harbor" in the form of mitigation based on internal compliance structures' is 'far

---

[24] P. Selznick, *The Moral Commonwealth* (Berkeley, CA: The University of California Press, 1992), p. 345. See also K. Goodpaster, 'The Concept of Corporate Responsibility', *Journal of Business Ethics* 2 (1983), 1 (corporations should be expected to take ethical responsibility through internal decision-making processes analogous to individual ethical reasoning).

[25] Selznick, *The Communitarian Persuasion*, p. 101.

[26] K. Krawiec, 'Organizational Misconduct: Beyond the Principal–agent Model', *Florida State Law Review* 32 (2005), 1, 28.

less onerous' to business than actually 'altering current business practices or paying damages for agent misconduct', and in that sense it is a public choice response to organisational liability (that is, business preferences have shaped the nature of organisational liability).[27] She may be right or wrong about the factual reasons why US law has incorporated so many apparently meta-regulatory initiatives. But, even if she is right, this does not mean that meta-regulation cannot be justified, and evaluated, on the ethically thicker grounds proposed by Selznick and adopted in this chapter.

In order to instigate, catalyse and hold accountable corporate social *responsibility*, law would have to be aimed at 'regulating' the internal self-regulation of businesses. Following Selznick's formulation of what 'corporate conscience' requires in the quotation above, I suggest that legal 'meta-regulation' of internal corporate self-regulation (or conscience) requires the following three things. Achieving these three things in combination is what would distinguish legal regulation that 'meta-regulates' CSR from other types of legal regulation.[28] If it means anything to hold companies legally accountable for CSR, this is what it must mean:

(1) *Law that meta-regulates CSR must be aimed at making sure that companies meet 'values that transcend narrow self-interest'*
Law that meta-regulates CSR must be aimed clearly at values or policy goals for which companies can take responsibility, not merely compliance with output rules.[29] Social and economic regulation is usually promulgated for specific, articulated policy purposes (albeit vague and/or contested to a greater or lesser extent) – a healthy environment, a fair and competitive market, a high degree of security of financial investment for individuals. Relevant values or policy goals might also come from other sources such as human rights or labour rights instruments at a global level, whether they are seen as law or 'soft law', or neither.

(2) *Law that meta-regulates CSR must be aimed at making sure these values are 'built into the practice and structure of the enterprise'*
An organisation, not being an individual, can only be responsible by building responsibility into its practice and structure. Selznick mentions a

---

[27] *Ibid.*, 41. See also the references at n. 3 above.
[28] Note this chapter is concerned only with considering the *legal* regulation of CSR, not (meta-)regulation by other means.
[29] See J. Braithwaite and V. Braithwaite, 'The Politics of Legalism: Rules versus Standards in Nursing Home Regulation', *Social and Legal Studies* 4 (1995), 307.

number of ways in which responsibility might be 'institutionalised' within a business enterprise. This echoes an extensive literature on what it takes for organisations to be internally committed to legal compliance,[30] and indeed to go 'beyond compliance'.[31] The aim is that each company would have an organisational culture that supports and sustains responsibility, and that management would be carried out in practice in a way that demonstrates responsibility. Generally, in order to achieve these objectives, meta-regulating law would require companies to put in place formal governance structures and management systems that help to produce a responsible culture and management in practice. These might include high-level statements and demonstrations of commitment to compliance with legal and/or ethical obligations; institutionalised in management and worker accountability and performance measurement systems and standard operating procedures; communication and training programmes for disseminating information about these policies and systems; internal reporting and monitoring systems for gathering information about compliance with those obligations and procedures; processes for gathering and resolving relevant complaints, grievances, suggestions and whistleblowing reports from those both internal and external to the organisation; and internal and external reviews or audits of the functioning and performance of the whole system that feeds back to the highest level and into the design and operation of the systems.[32] I have previously argued that these are all ways of making corporate management 'open' or 'permeable' to external values.[33]

---

[30] J. Braithwaite, *Corporate Crime in the Pharmaceutical Industry* (London: Routledge and Kegan Paul, 1984); J. Braithwaite, *To Punish or Persuade: Enforcement of Coal Mine Safety* (Albany, NY: State University of New York Press, 1985); F. Haines, *Corporate Regulation: Beyond 'Punish or Persuade'* (Oxford: Oxford University Press, 1997); B. Hutter, *Regulation and Risk: Occupational Health and Safety on the Railways* (Oxford: Oxford University Press, 2001), pp. 301–12; D. McCaffrey and D. Hart, *Wall Street Polices Itself: How Securities Firms Manage the Legal Hazards of Competitive Pressures* (New York: Oxford University Press, 1998); Parker, *The Open Corporation*, pp. 43–61, 197–244; J. Rees, *Reforming the Workplace: A Study of Self-regulation in Occupational Safety* (Philadelphia, PA: University of Pennsylvania Press, 1988).

[31] N. Gunningham, R. Kagan and D. Thornton, *Shades of Green: Business, Regulation and Environment* (Stanford, CA: Stanford University Press, 2003); A. Prakash, *Greening the Firm: The Politics of Corporate Environmentalism* (Port Chester, NY: Cambridge University Press, 2000).

[32] Parker, *The Open Corporation*, pp. 197–244, includes a more sophisticated analysis of what such systems are likely to require in order to be effective. See also the other references in nn. 30 and 31 above.

[33] See Parker, *The Open Corporation*.

(3) *Law that meta-regulates CSR must recognise that 'the main goals of the organisation' are still to be pursued within the responsibility framework*
The stance of meta-regulating law is to recognise that the main goals of a company are not merely to make sure that it acts socially responsibly, but also to meet its main goals of producing particular goods and/or services, providing a return to its investors, and/or providing paid employment to its workers and managers. Meta-regulating law should allow space for the company itself to take responsibility for working out how to meet its main goals within the framework of values set down by regulation, provided its main goals can be carried on consistently with social responsibility values. Meta-regulating law should be careful to leave space, to the greatest extent possible, to allow the companies it regulates to decide for themselves how to institutionalise responsibility. This means meta-regulating law does not assume command-and-control is the only appropriate technique for regulating social responsibility. It is willing to experiment with more indirect or facilitative techniques for engendering responsibility, including through requiring or capacitating non-state agencies (such as auditors, NGOs or the public at large) to help regulate corporate behaviour (for example, through audit requirements, provision of information about corporate performance to the public and so on). It is also willing to treat firms that show different levels of inner commitment to responsibility in different ways.[34] Note the rider, as much room 'as possible' consistent with ensuring companies do operate within a responsibility framework – meta-regulating law is law, not merely self-regulation.

In summary

Meta-regulation should be about requiring organisations to implement processes (point 2 above) that are aimed at making sure they reach the right results in terms of actions that impact on the world (point 1 above). It recognises, however, that law-makers and regulators may not know exactly what the 'right' processes, and even the right results, will look like in each situation. The people who are involved in the situation are best placed to work out the details in their own circumstances, *if* they can be motivated to do so responsibly (point 3 above). Whenever we see these criteria being met, we see law seeking to make companies responsible – that

---

[34] See N. Gunningham and P. Grabosky, *Smart Regulation: Designing Environmental Policy* (Oxford: Clarendon Press, 1998) and N. Gunningham and R. Johnstone, *Regulating Workplace Safety: Systems and Sanctions* (Oxford: Oxford University Press, 1999) for comprehensive examinations of the various techniques available in two regulatory arenas.

is, meta-regulating companies' internal consciences.[35] Meta-regulating
law can also recognise that motivation, standards, and even monitoring
and enforcement systems, for responsibility come from places other than
law – from consumer activism, voluntary industry codes, the desire to
protect organisational reputation and so on – and that regulators and
regulation can usefully facilitate, coordinate, extend and simply recognise
these other forms of governance.[36] The details of corporate responsibility
processes and their goals will often be 'negotiated' to one extent or another
with industry – by explicitly negotiating standards and goals with individual companies or industry, leaving it for individual companies to decide
exactly how to design a compliance management system for their own
situation, by incorporating into legal requirements voluntary standards
developed by industry, or simply because the relevant law or policy instrument provides only for management systems in the most general terms.

C. Examples of techniques of legal meta-regulation

At a *national level* we will generally find clear examples of legal meta-
regulation of CSR within specific domains of social and economic regulation of business.

The most common method is through determinations of corporate
liability, damages or penalties in civil or criminal law by reference to
whether the corporation has implemented an appropriate compliance
system. Meta-regulating law makes it a good legal risk management practice to implement processes to ensure internal corporate responsibility
for meeting regulatory goals. One of the oldest examples is probably the
duty to provide a safe system of work in relation to occupational health
and safety liability in tort and statutory regulation. The most famous is
the US Federal Sentencing Guidelines for organisations, which state that
the existence of an effective compliance system (as defined in the Guidelines) will provide companies or individuals with a reduction of penalty
if they are found to have breached the law.[37] A variety of other regulatory liability regimes in the United States are now predicated on similar
considerations.[38] In other jurisdictions implementation of a compliance
system is an important aspect in determining liability or penalties in relation to competition and consumer protection law, and vicarious liability

---

[35] For a similar conception, see Coglianese and Lazer, 'Management-based Regulation'.
[36] See Braithwaite and Drahos, *Global Business Regulation*; Vogel, *The Market for Virtue*.
[37] See D. Murphy, 'The Federal Sentencing Guidelines for Organizations: A Decade of
Promoting Compliance and Ethics', *Iowa Law Review* 87 (2002), 697.
[38] For a comprehensive overview, see Krawiec, 'Organizational Misconduct', 14–21.

for sexual harassment and discrimination or unequal employment opportunity.[39] Recent UK and Australian proposals to introduce an offence of corporate manslaughter could also be seen as examples of meta-regulation through the use of liability. For example, the 2005 UK Home Office's Draft Corporate Manslaughter Bill provides that an organisation will be guilty of corporate manslaughter 'if the way in which any of the organisation's activities are managed or organised by its senior managers (a) causes a person's death, and (b) amounts to a gross breach of a relevant duty of care owed by the organisation to the deceased'.[40]

A second technique of legal meta-regulation of corporate responsibility is when regulators 'settle' potential regulatory enforcement actions with businesses only on condition that they implement internal changes to identify, correct and prevent future wrongdoing. Or, where courts make corporate 'probation' orders that require the company to do so as part of the organisation's sentence. The US Sentencing Guidelines state that organisations that do not have an effective compliance programme should be placed on probation to implement one.[41] Regulators in the United Kingdom and other Commonwealth jurisdictions have used discretionary powers to make informal settlements requiring compliance system implementation for years. Similarly, US prosecutors under a number of regulatory regimes consider whether a business has implemented an effective compliance programme or not in deciding whether to prosecute or not.[42] Australian regulatory law seems to be specialising in formalising these types of settlements as 'enforceable undertakings' in legislation.[43]

Another common method of meta-regulation is to make the implementation of internal corporate conscience mechanisms a condition of licences or permissions required before a company can engage in a certain business,

[39] See Parker, *The Open Corporation*, pp. 249–51.
[40] But for a thorough evaluation of the limits of the UK Bill, see Centre for Corporate Accountability, *Response to the Government's Draft Bill on Corporate Manslaughter* (June 2005), available at www.corporateaccountability.org/dl/manslaughter/reform/crownlegal2005.doc (accessed 30 April 2007); see generally A. Hall, R. Johnstone and A. Ridgway, 'Reflection on Reforms: Developing Criminal Accountability for Industrial Deaths' (April 2004), *National Research Centre for Occupational Health and Safety Working Paper* 33, available at www.ohs.anu.edu.au/publications/pdf/WorkingPaper26pdf.pdf (accessed 30 April 2007).
[41] In Australia, see Trade Practices Act 1974 (Cth), s. 86C for provision for corporate probation orders in relation to competition and consumer protection offences.
[42] See C. Parker, *The Open Corporation*, p. 260.
[43] The first was Trade Practices Act 1974 (Cth), s. 87B. See C. Parker, 'Restorative Justice in Business Regulation? The Australian Competition and Consumer Commission's use of enforceable undertakings', *Modern Law Review* 67 (2004), 209.

or build facilities in a certain location. The most common examples are the environmental management systems and local community consultations often required as part of the licence obligations for permissions required from environmental regulators for manufacturing facilities. The licence requirements for financial services firms usually include broad-ranging internal systems for ensuring integrity of funds (preventing fraud, ensuring proper investment decisions, avoiding conflicts of interest and so on) and investor disclosure (including consumer protection measures such as 'know your client' principles) regulation.[44] In New South Wales, the regulator of the corporatised/privatised gas and electricity providers regularly audits their internal compliance systems to make sure they comply with licence obligations, with the frequency of audits partially dependent on the results of the previous audit.[45]

Then there are a number of more voluntary meta-regulatory initiatives that seek to encourage or reward 'beyond compliance' internal management systems by granting extra regulatory flexibility to firms that voluntarily adopt superior internal systems that go 'beyond compliance' – for example, by fast-tracking the granting of permissions or licences to such firms, scheduling inspections less frequently for them, or providing public recognition for them through allowing them to use a seal or logo that is publicised as a mark of superior performance. US environmental and occupational health and safety regulators have been particularly active in experimenting with such schemes.[46]

The law might also seek more indirect or partial methods of meta-regulation. Often more indirect, less coercive, methods of meta-regulation are used (or proposed) for schemes aimed more at the ethical and discretionary aspects of CSR, or for schemes aimed at improving CSR as a whole (rather than focused on the goals of a specific regulatory regime). For example, laws, such as the US *Sarbanes-Oxley Act* (2002), that require certain corporate employees to report suspected corporate fraud to senior management and that require or encourage companies to put in place

---

[44] See, for example, Black, 'The Emergence of Risk-based Regulation'; P. Hanrahan, '(Ir)responsible Entities: Reforming Manager Accountability in Public Unit Trusts', *Company and Securities Law Journal* 16 (1998), 76; H. Lauritsen, 'Enforced Self-regulation under the Financial Services Reform Act: Ensuring the Competency of Financial Intermediaries', *Company and Securities Law Journal* 21 (2003), 468.

[45] See 'Licence Compliance' page in section on Electricity Licensing at www.ipart.nsw.gov.au (accessed 30 April 2007).

[46] See N. Gunningham and D. Sinclair, *Leaders and Laggards: Next-Generation Environmental Regulation* (Sheffield: Greenleaf Publishing, 2002), pp. 111–15; O. Lobel, 'Interlocking Regulatory and Industrial Relations: The Governance of Workplace Safety', *Administrative Law Review* 57 (2005), 1071.

whistleblower policies are a form of partial encouragement to internal corporate conscience, since a corporate policy encouraging and protecting whistleblowers (generally in relation to any breach of legal or ethical obligations, not just financial fraud) would be one element of the sort of processes that companies would need to have in place to ensure their own responsibility.[47] But much more would also be necessary. Laws that simply protect whistleblowers (for example, by providing that they should not be sacked or sued for their actions, and giving them the right to sue for compensation if they are sacked), rather than mandating implementation of policies, provide indirect encouragement to internal corporate conscience.[48] The availability of damages indirectly holds businesses accountable for allowing a culture or management system that ignores and punishes whistleblowers to go unchecked, and encourages whistleblowers to make their concerns known. Other examples might include government 'approved' or sponsored voluntary CSR management accreditation and auditing schemes,[49] voluntary undertakings to implement CSR management systems given to government and enforceable by contract, tax incentives, and government procurement decisions predicated on implementation of CSR systems.[50]

In the final section, we will evaluate some of these more ambiguous examples.

Much discussion about CSR is about corporate observation of human rights at the *transnational level*. It is hard to find good examples of transnational *legal* meta-regulation of CSR because, as is well-known, there are few avenues for holding corporations accountable under international law at all, and none in relation to human rights, the main focus of CSR at the transnational level.[51] (There are many attempts at *non-legal* regulation

---

[47] On the US Sarbanes-Oxley reforms, see R. Rosen, 'Resistances to Reforming Corporate Governance: The Diffusion of QLCC's', *Fordham Law Review* 74 (2005), 1251.

[48] Corporations Act (Cth), Part 9.4AAA (commenced 1 July 2004).

[49] For example EMAS, the Eco-Management and Audit Scheme, a voluntary initiative established by the European Commission (Council Regulation 761/01/EC, OJ No. L114/1. 24 April 2001): see ec.europa.eu/environment/emas/index_en.htm (accessed 30 April 2007).

[50] These had both been proposed by the European Community, but not even that level of legal 'enforceability' is being given to CSR by the European Community at this stage: see Commission of the European Communities, *Communication from the Commission concerning Corporate Social Responsibility: A Business Contribution to Sustainable Development*, Brussels, 2 July 2002 COM (2002) 347 final.

[51] See D. Kinley and J. Tadaki, 'From Talk to Walk: the Emergence of Human Rights Responsibilities for Corporations at International Law', *Virginia Journal of International Law* 44 (2004), 931 (concluding that there is no binding transnational law on human rights obligations for corporations; but there is 'an expanding body of extraterritorial domestic jurisprudence that focuses on the human rights implications of actions taken by

of transnational CSR, with varying degrees of success.)[52] In order to find
examples of *legal* regulation of transnational CSR, we will generally need to
look for situations where nations legally regulate the conduct of transnational corporations (TNCs) in accord with international obligations, or
adopt or enforce voluntary global corporate responsibility standards,[53]
or where national law has an extra-jurisdictional impact on TNCs.[54] In
the future multilateral institutions might also seek to enforce obligations
on TNCs directly, rather than relying on member states to do so.[55] We
might also find international 'networks' of regulation in which state law,
transnational voluntary codes, global civil society organisations and so
on reinforce one another to regulate corporate conscience.[56]

corporations overseas' (at 935); and a number of multilateral institutions have created
'soft-law' human rights standards for the conduct of TNCs, although these have generally
not been implemented, monitored or enforced in any way: at 949–52).

[52] See n. 36 above.

[53] Things like SA8000 (an accreditable and auditable social accountability standard), and
possibly ISO14000, have a focus on internal corporate management systems, but barely
count as law of any kind, even 'soft law'. In the future they might be adopted or encouraged by national laws by being used for reporting standards, liability or incorporated by
contract (by government or by private companies): see Kinley and Tadaki, 'From Talk
to Walk', 957; A. Wawryk, 'Regulating Transnational Corporations through Corporate
Codes of Conduct', in J. Frynas and S. Pegg (eds.), *Transnational Corporations and Human
Rights* (Basingstoke: Palgrave Macmillan, 2003), p. 53; K. Webb and A. Morrison, 'The
Law and Voluntary Codes: Examining the "Tangled Web"', in K. Webb (ed.), *Voluntary
Codes: Private Governance, the Public Interest and Innovation* (Ottawa: Carleton University
Research Unit for Innovation, Science and the Environment, 2002), p. 93. For a compre-
hensive overview of the ways in which environmental management system certification
programmes can be incorporated into, enforced or facilitated by the law, see E. Meidinger,
'Environmental Certification Programs and U.S. Environmental Law: Closer than you may
Think', *Environmental Law Reporter* 31 (2001), 10162.

[54] See, e.g., Alien Torts Claims Act liability in the United States and equivalents in other
jurisdictions and the proposed (but failed) attempts to legislate by the Australian, UK
and US government for companies based in those respective countries to be required to
observe certain human rights standards in overseas operations: Kinley and Tadaki, 'From
Talk to Walk', 939–42. So far these initiatives do not have a meta-regulatory aspect.

[55] See R. Mayne, 'Regulating TNCs; the Role of Voluntary and Governmental Approaches', in
S. Picciotto and R. Mayne (eds.), *Regulating International Business* (Basingstoke: Macmillan Press, 1999), p. 235; cf. T. McInerney, 'Putting Regulation before Responsibility:
the Limits of Voluntary Corporate Social Responsibility' (2005), *The George Washington University Law School Public Law and Legal Theory Working Paper No.* 123, available at
ssrn.com/abstract = 658081 (accessed 30 April 2007) (voluntary CSR is not enough and
global business regulation should develop national capacity to regulate).

[56] See Braithwaite and Drahos, *Global Business Regulation*. The same types of networks
regulate at a national level too, of course (see references at n. 10 above). See also
R. O'Brien, 'NGOs, Global Civil Society and Global Economic Regulation', in S. Picciotto
and R. Mayne (eds.), *Regulating International Business* (Basingstoke: Macmillan Press,
1999), p. 257.

Our concern in this chapter is the extent to which any of these forms of transnational legal regulation of business might be meta-regulatory – that is, aimed at the corporate conscience, not just corporate outputs.[57] One partial example of meta-regulation at the transnational level is the Basel Accord on Banking Regulation, a voluntary multilateral agreement by which G10 nations agree to harmonised standards for national banking regulation. Under this accord, the robustness of banks' internal systems for managing operational risk (a concept that includes breach of legal compliance requirements and reputational loss through breach of ethical obligations to stakeholders and other CSR failures) should be an element in deciding their capital adequacy ratios (the proportion of the investments they hold for customers that they must have available in cash in order to be able to operate).[58]

The World Health Organisation's *International Code of Marketing of Breast Milk Substitutes*[59] is probably the most successful example of international regulation that applies to business organisations. It includes a primitive meta-regulatory aspect: 'manufacturers and distributors of products within the scope of this Code should regard themselves as responsible for monitoring their marketing practices according to the principles and aims of this Code, and for taking steps to ensure that their conduct at every level conforms to them'.[60]

National governments have implemented it to differing degrees but usually only partially as labelling regulation. They have not legally enforced the internal corporate responsibility aspect. An NGO, however, the International Baby Food Action Network has been extremely active in monitoring compliance with the code (including the meta-regulatory provision quoted above) by Nestlé and other baby food companies (as well as governments), and enforcing it through social and political action.[61]

---

[57] For one proposal for a meta-regulatory initiative to be enforced by the World Bank or International Labour Organisation, see A. Fung, D. O'Rourke and C. Sabel, 'Realizing Labour Standards', *Boston Review* 26 (2001), 1, available at www.bostonreview.net/BR26.1/fung.html (accessed 30 April 2007).

[58] Basel Committee on Banking Supervision, *Basel II: International Convergence of Capital Measurement and Capital Standards: A Revised Framework* (June 2004), available at www.bis.org/publ/bcbs107.htm (accessed 30 April 2007). See also D. Ho, 'Compliance and International Soft Law: Why do Countries Implement the Basle Accord?', *Journal of International Economic Law* 5 (2002), 647.

[59] World Health Organisation, 1981.   [60] ibid., para. 11.3.

[61] See the critiques of implementation of the code in internal systems and documents by Nestlé (but also other manufacturers) at the International Baby Food Action Network (IBFAN) webpage: www.ibfan.org (accessed 30 April 2007). Despite its relative success, see the critique of this regime in J. Richter, *Holding Corporations Accountable: Corporate Conduct, International Codes and Citizen Action* (London: Zed Books, 2001).

III. Critique: process at the expense of substance?

The main critique of meta-regulatory-style developments in the law is that they will focus on corporate responsibility processes in a way that allows companies to avoid accountability for substance.[62] Meta-regulatory law runs the danger of hollowing itself out into a focus merely on corporate governance processes that avoid necessary conflict over the substantive values that should apply to corporations. In her work on risk regulation by financial services regulators that utilises firms' internal risk management systems, Julia Black (rather gently) criticises the idea of meta-regulation:

> the firm's internal controls will be directed at ensuring the firm achieves the objectives it sets for itself: namely profits and market share. Whilst proponents of meta-regulation are correct to argue that its strength lies in the ability to leverage off a firm's own systems of internal control, and indeed that regulators should fashion their own regulatory processes on those controls, this *difference in objectives* means that regulators can never rely on a firm's own systems without some modifications. The problem then arises, however, of *locating those differences*, and ensuring both regulator and regulated understand them.[63]

The ability of regulators and stakeholders to locate and hold businesses accountable for those 'differences' – that is, potential conflict between social values and corporate self-interest – is likely to be frustrated in several overlapping ways by companies:

(1) *Companies will avoid conflict over substantive change to their internal management, structure and practices by implementing 'corporate conscience' requirements in a half-hearted, partial and surface-level way.*

---

[62] The critique from the other side (those who are less sympathetic to CSR obligations, and also those who are wary of rule of law values being undermined) is that meta-regulation will appear to focus on allowing companies to set processes that meet their own needs, but so much unaccountable power and discretion will be given to regulators and other stakeholders (who might be given the right to participate in or influence corporate decision-making) that inappropriate and illegitimate substantive values will in fact be imposed on corporations in ways that would not be possible under more traditional legal regulation. See, for example, K. Yeung, *Securing Compliance – A Principled Approach* (Oxford: Hart Publishing, 2004), pp. 204–14. See Lobel, 'Interlocking Regulatory and Industrial Relations', for an examination of the way in which US meta-regulatory initiatives in occupational health and safety have been stymied by administrative laws that impose unsuitable regulatory accountability requirements on them. I have previously addressed Yeung's critique in Parker, 'Restorative Justice in Business Regulation?' (2004).

[63] Black, 'The Emergence of Risk-based Regulation'. For a more robust articulation of a similar critique, see F. Pearce and S. Tombs, *Toxic Capitalism: Corporate Crime and the Chemical Industry* (Aldershot: Ashgate, 1998). (Emphases added by author.)

Companies will implement management systems to the extent necessary to ensure legitimacy, but will make no substantive change to their
ordinary modus operandi, if not necessary.[64] As Lauren Edelman and
her co-authors argue, 'organizations create symbolic structures as visible
efforts to comply with law, but their normative value does not depend
on effectiveness so they do not guarantee substantive change'.[65] They will
be able to satisfy regulators and prosecutors by 'ticking the boxes' that
show they have gone through prescribed processes, but regulators and
prosecutors will not assess whether management systems are producing
outputs that meet the policy goals of the relevant regulatory regime –
indeed, policy goals may not even be defined.[66] It has been suggested that
the whole push for meta-regulation, rather than strict output liability, is
an attempt by corporate interests to avoid substantive internal change by
focusing liability instead on meaningless processes.[67]

(2) *The implementation of corporate conscience requirements may be subsumed into the risk management of legal liability in ways that have little
to do with commitment to social values and which obscure possibilities for
corporate accountability.*[68]

---

[64] Parker, *The Open Corporation*, p. 145; S. Simpson, *Corporate Crime, Law and Social Control*
(Cambridge: Cambridge University Press, 2002), pp. 103–6.

[65] L. Edelman, S. Petterson, E. Chambliss and H. Erlanger, 'Legal Ambiguity and the Politics
of Compliance: Affirmative Action Officers' Dilemma', *Law and Policy* 13 (1991), 73, 75. See
also S. Beder, *Global Spin: The Corporate Assault on Environmentalism* (Melbourne: Scribe
Books, 1997), pp. 128–30; L. Cunningham, 'The Appeal and Limits of Internal Controls
to Fight Fraud, Terrorism, other Ills', *The Journal of Corporate Law* 29 (2004), 267; K.
Krawiec, 'Cosmetic Compliance and the Failure of Negotiated Governance', *Washington
University Law Quarterly* 81 (2003), 487, 514, 542; D. McBarnet, 'Legal Creativity: Law,
Capital and Legal Avoidance', in M. Cain and C. Harrington (eds.), *Lawyers in a Postmodern
World: Translation and Transgression* (New York: New York University Press, 1994), p. 73;
S. Tombs, 'Understanding Regulation', *Social and Legal Studies* 11 (2002), 113; G. Weaver,
L. Trevino and P. Cochran, 'Corporate Ethics Practices in the mid-1990's: An Empirical
Study of the Fortune 1000', *Journal of Business Ethics* 18 (1999), 283 (finding that the vast
majority of US Fortune 1000 firms have committed to the low-cost, possibly symbolic,
side of ethics management).

[66] W. Laufer, 'Social Accountability and Corporate Greenwashing', *Journal of Business Ethics*
43 (2003), 253, 254. See, for example, the critiques of regulators' inadequate use of audit
of required internal management systems in M. Power, *The Audit Society: Rituals of Verification* (Oxford: Oxford University Press, 1997); C. Parker, 'Regulator-required Corporate
Compliance Program Audits', *Law and Policy* 25 (2003), 221.

[67] Krawiec, 'Organizational Misconduct'.

[68] R. Rosen, 'Risk Management and Corporate Governance: The Case of Enron', *Connecticut
Law Review* 35 (2003), 1157, 1180.

As Baldwin says of the 'challenges' of meta-regulation, 'Managers may see regulatory liabilities as risks to be managed, not as ethically reinforced prescriptions'.[69] For example, the internal management systems required by meta-regulating law may be used to obscure senior management/entity responsibility for breaches, and/or to shift blame for breaches onto individual employees (workers, line managers or compliance staff). Thus Laufer suggests that corporations may 'game' regulators to fully insulate the company as an entity and top management from liability by 'reverse whistle-blowing' – offering up culpable subordinate employees, or at least putting all the responsibility for compliance onto employees and line managers.[70] Similarly, regulatory responsibilities might be identified by internal 'corporate conscience' processes but then managed by 'outsourcing' the risk of not acting responsibly – performing ethically or legally questionable activities through separate legal entities that bear the risk of any failure of responsibility. For example, Enron used its joint venture partners to bear responsibility for questionable financial transactions. Brand name retailers have done the same by leaving it to manufacturers in other countries to work out how to comply with labour standards *and* meet production demands at the same time. Insurance, electricity and gas, and telecommunications companies frequently outsource compliance obligations to independent sales agents who must also meet tight sales targets in order to be paid. In Australia, James Hardie famously completely separated off its asbestos compensation responsibilities into a separate legal company set adrift from the rest of the corporate group without adequate financial provision. Socio-legal scholars' critiques of risk management imply that the management of potential legal/regulatory liability is a motivating factor for companies in their adoption of a risk management approach to business.[71] But potential legal accountability may barely rate a passing thought – risk management can be a whole approach to business decision-making, in which it is assumed that legal and compliance risks, like all other risks, can be transformed, hedged or insured against,

---

[69] Baldwin, 'The New Punitive Regulation', 378. See also Power, *Risk Management.*

[70] W. Laufer, 'Corporate Liability, Risk Shifting and the Paradox of Compliance', *Vanderbilt Law Review* 52 (1999), 1341, and 'Corporate Prosecution, Cooperation and the Trading of Favours', *Iowa Law Review* 87 (2002), 643. See also J. Braithwaite, *Corporate Crime,* p. 308 (on the 'vice-president responsible for going to jail'); Hutter, *Regulation and Risk,* pp. 145–7 (British Rail employees believe the purpose of health and safety systems was to shift responsibility away from the Board and pass the buck to staff); Parker, *The Open Corporation,* pp. 149–56.

[71] We are all tempted to think that our own special area of interest is just as important to others as it is to ourselves!

rather than eliminated (by substantive compliance).[72] Meta-regulatory law therefore falls into the trap of giving company lawyers a set of process rules perfectly designed to be manipulated into meaninglessness in the context of a risk management culture.

(3) *Management systems that ostensibly put in place a corporate conscience may be used to contain, mollify and transform dissent about whether the company has followed appropriate values in particular instances without addressing the conflict and allowing it to be authoritatively and accountably resolved.*[73]

Internal corporate governance processes may simply not be capable of resolving such conflict appropriately because of management incompetence or failures of strategic imagination to overcome deadlocks and stultification over dissent.[74] The mollification of dissent and conflict within internal processes may also be more strategic. For example, internal sexual harassment and equal employment opportunity complaints systems have been shown to be a way of containing contestations of equality and reframing appeals to rights as human resources management issues that avoid court action.[75] Similarly stakeholder engagement programmes may simply be a way of 'cooling out' protesters.[76] We normally like to think that legal accountability (ideally anyway) can be a way in which conflicts about corporate behaviour can be brought into open court and determined. Law that mandates corporate responsibility processes gives management the perfect 'legal' cover for keeping conflict out of the public eye and the accountability processes of the courts. Meta-regulatory law requires and rewards them for 'managing' conflict internally.

According to this critique, the development of meta-regulating law in practice and in scholarly writing shows that businesses might be succeeding in shaping the notion of CSR to suit themselves. Meta-regulating law is seen as the spearhead of a corporate campaign to pull back the reach of regulatory accountability through existing command and control regulation of business. Thus, Shamir argues that multinational corporations are responding to the heat of protests against them by seeking to shape the

---

[72] See Rosen, 'Risk Management'.
[73] See Parker, *The Open Corporation*, pp. 156–64.   [74] Baldwin, 'Punitive Regulation', 379.
[75] Edelman, *et al.*, 'Legal Ambiguity'; L. Edelman, H. Erlanger, and J. Lande, 'Internal Dispute Resolution: The Transformation of Civil Rights in the Workplace', *Law and Society Review* 27 (1993), 497; J. Kihnley, 'Unraveling the Ivory Fabric: Institutional Obstacles to the Handling of Sexual Harassment Complaints', *Law and Social Inquiry* 25 (2000), 69.
[76] See J. Conley and C. Williams, 'Engage, Embed, Embellish: Theory versus Practice in the Corporate Social Responsibility Movement', *Journal of Corporate Law* 31 (2005) 1.

notion and practice of CSR in terms of 'a voluntary and altruistic spirit and with notions implying honesty toward investors, with charity-oriented "good citizenship" campaigns, and with more or less elaborate schemes of voluntary self-regulation'.[77] To the extent that scholars and policy-makers focus on achieving CSR through corporate governance processes (i.e., meta-regulation), it 'signifies a decisive move in the direction of abandoning traditional "command and control" state regulatory schemes in favor of "responsive regulation," which is supposed to facilitate – yet not enforce and dictate – self-regulation programs and "compliance-oriented" regulation, which is to be carried out through corporate consent and voluntary organizational processes of reflexive learning'.[78]

The application of substantive standards[79] to corporations is not facil-itated, but conflict forestalled by this 'responsibilisation of subjects who are empowered to discipline themselves'.[80]

Kim Krawiec makes the same point from a different angle. She argues that internal compliance-based liability regimes (meta-regulation) are 'negotiated' – the gaps are filled by firms and their legal compliance pro-fessionals, and they are likely to do so in ways that are favourable to them.[81]

> In short, the incompleteness of law creates room for interpretation and manipulation by a variety of public and private actors. As such, it presents a political opportunity for those with a stake in regulation to push their agenda through renegotiation during the implementation and enforcement phases of governance by constructing a gap-filling interpretation that serves the group's self-interest.[82]

Corporations (their managers, lawyers and compliance professionals) will be able to take advantage of the fact the law is focusing on process to avoid conflict over substantive change.

These critiques of meta-regulating law would apply regardless of whether the meta-regulating law includes enforcement mechanisms or not (and what kind they are – direct or indirect, rewards or sanctions). The

---

[77] Shamir, 'The Alien Tort Claims Act', 644. See also Conley and Williams, 'Theory Versus Practice in the CSR Movement'.
[78] Shamir, 'The Alien Tort Claims Act', 660.
[79] Shamir's concern is with human rights standards.
[80] Shamir, 'The Alien Tort Claims Act', 660. He concludes that 'the idea that human rights standards will be imposed by the courts (whether national or international) and the idea that corporations may be coerced into compliance in this area through formally binding regulations (whether national or transnational) are still far on the horizon' (at 660–1).
[81] Krawiec, 'Cosmetic Compliance', 494.   [82] *ibid.*, 542.

point of the criticisms is that there is nothing worthwhile to be enforced anyway. The problem is that the process orientation of the meta-regulating law leaves too many gaps and too much room for interpretation, in a context where some interests are more equal than others, and relevant social values heavily contested.[83] These are a principled set of objections to meta-regulation.[84]

IV. Response: meta-regulation as a process aimed at a substance

The key feature of each of the three critiques of the idea of meta-regulating CSR above is that meta-regulation runs the risk of creating legal accountability for a vague process without substantive goals because it leaves it up to business itself to define the details of responsibility processes, and then leaves it to the process to define the appropriate outcomes or goals: 'the substance of CSR seems to be process'.[85] Neither the process nor the goals are adequately set from outside business, and therefore we cannot

---

[83] See Scheuerman, 'Reflexive Law and the Challenges of Globalization' *Journal of Political Philosophy* 9 (2001), 101. See also Shearing and Wood, 'Nodal Governance' (for a similar argument that inequality of access to purchasing power is the basis for a governance disparity that means some people are unable to participate in governance processes); Lipschutz, *Globalization* (the new governance is based too much on people participating through markets rather than politics aimed at the public good); cf. Braithwaite and Drahos, *Global Business Regulation* (arguing that seeming powerless interests can sometimes find the right strand to pull in regulatory webs to have a big influence).

[84] Note there is also another set of (related) arguments about whether it is possible to specify standards for internal management systems and how to identify the features of management systems, governance structures or corporate cultures that reliably 'work' to achieve more responsible outcomes in different contexts; how to monitor whether these internal processes have been implemented effectively; what enforcement mechanisms (rewards and sanctions, direct and indirect, persuasive and coercive, formal and informal, etc.), if any, to use; or whether it is better to rely on other diffusion mechanisms that do not rely on legal enforcement. These issues will not be dealt with in detail in this chapter. See R. Kagan, N. Gunningham and D. Thornton, 'Explaining Corporate Environmental Performance: how does Regulation Matter', *Law and Society Review* 37 (2003), 51; V. Nielsen and C. Parker, 'Chapter 4: Degree of Compliance', in *The ACCC Enforcement and Compliance Survey: Report of Preliminary Results* (Canberra: RegNet, ANU, 2005), available at cccp.anu.edu.au/projects/project1.html (accessed 30 April 2007); M. Potoski and A. Prakash, 'Covenants with Weak Swords: ISO14001 and Facilities' Environmental Performance', *Journal of Policy Analysis and Management* 24 (2005), 745. cf. Krawiec, 'Organizational Misconduct'; Krawiec, 'Cosmetic Compliance', 542; M. McKendall, B. De Marr and C. Jones-Rikkers, 'Ethical Compliance Programs and Corporate Illegality: Testing the Assumptions of the Corporate Sentencing Guidelines', *Journal of Business Ethics* 37 (2002), 367.

[85] Conley and Williams, 'Engage, Embed, Embellish'.

expect meta-regulation to make business accountable for anything – there is nothing to be accountable for, no one to be accountable to.

Meta-regulation could be seen as an aspect of a broader shift in the way law regulates in the context of the new governance – 'the creation of a new type of rationality or mode of governance based on a logic of informal, negotiated processes within social and socio-legal networks'.[86] However, as Heydebrand points out, this 'process rationality' can come 'at a heavy cost, namely the emergent deconstruction of procedural and substantive rights, the dissolution of the normative legality that is historically embedded in formal justice, and the deformation of constitutional protections and safeguards';[87] And again, 'Process rationality shares neither the rule-governed, proceduralist schemata of formal legal rationality nor the consensual goal-directedness of substantive rationality. Process drives substance, not the other way around . . . Whatever goals are associated with process rationality tend to emerge dialectically from within the process itself rather than directing it from outside'.[88]

Yet there is nothing inherent in the idea of meta-regulation as a technique that means this must be true, that business must drive the process and the process must drive the substance. We can discriminate between a substance-oriented process (consistent with the distinctives of meta-regulation as defined above) and process driving substance.[89]

Certainly, meta-regulation is about setting a process. *But* it must be a process that is 'going somewhere'.[90] That means it must be set in a context in which it is clearly aimed at social policy goals (or responsibility values) that are defined by the law or by some other mechanism that can garner widespread legitimacy. Conflicts over the meaning of those values must be

---

[86] Heydebrand, 'Process Rationality', 326. See also Scheuerman's assessment of Teubner's notion of reflexive law applied to global business regulation: W. Scheuerman, 'Reflexive Law', 81.

[87] Heydebrand, 'Process Rationality', 334 although Heydebrand does see substantive rationality continuing to operate in areas of administrative regulation where 'social policy and substantive rights protection remain relatively intact' (at 337). Contrast Selznick's idea of 'responsive law' as built upon the foundations of formal justice rather than dissolving it: Nonet and Selznick, *Law and Society in Transition*; Selznick, *The Moral Commonwealth*, pp. 463–5.

[88] Heydebrand, 'Process Rationality', 328.

[89] Compare also Heydebrand, 'Process Rationality', 341 (describing Habermasian communicative rationality as a 'kind of substantively oriented process rationality' and commenting '[i]t is not yet clear, however, to what extent these normative conceptions will remain utopian visions, or else, can be realized and implemented in a concrete, empirical context').

[90] Borrowing Thomas Shaffer's phrase for describing what the 'ethics of care' requires of deliberation between a lawyer and client: T. Shaffer and R. Cochran, *Lawyers, Clients and Moral Responsibility* (Eagan, MN: West Publishing Co., 1994).

capable of external authoritative resolution where corporate management fails to do so appropriately. People who are affected by corporate failure to observe the relevant values or reach the policy goals must be able to contest them within the organisation. If management cannot work out how to resolve cooperatively conflicts over value identified by contestation in this way within the organisation, then the conflict needs to be made obvious and dealt with authoritatively by law or some other mechanism external to the organisation.

In other words, the *substantive goals* at which internal processes are aimed must be adequately specified and enforced external to the company. Moreover, the standards for the companies' internal processes must be specified sufficiently to make sure that those values are represented within internal decision-making processes. This will often involve making sure that stakeholders who might otherwise be excluded from contesting corporate decisions are given specific rights to do so. Meta-regulating law must meet 'traditional formalistic ideals' at least 'by insisting that procedural and organizational norms are relatively clear and cogent'.[91] The aim of meta-regulation in this conception is precisely that substantive conflict between social values and corporate ways of doing things is forced to be dealt with and resolved inside the organisation, or the organisation forced to respond to external resolution.

By stating it that way, we should be able to evaluate some of the proposals for law to be involved in holding companies accountable for CSR and come to a conclusion on whether they are likely to be worthwhile or not.

A. Using 'meta-regulation' to evaluate corporate social responsibility initiatives

The ideal form of meta-regulating law I have set out here is a normative standard that we can use to evaluate various existing approaches and proposals. Whether particular legal mechanisms meet the requirements of meta-regulation that is more than mere process is likely to be highly context-dependent. We will need to examine the surrounding law and governance for each initiative in order to determine whether substantive and procedural rights are adequately specified, or able to be adequately debated and determined in democratically legitimate ways (whether by traditional formal law or by other mechanisms), before we can come to a conclusion on the meta-regulatory value of particular attempts to build CSR.

---

[91] Scheuerman, 'Reflexive law', 99 (rephrasing and referring to I. Maus, 'Sinn und Bedeutung der Volkssouveranitet in der modernen Gesellschaft', *Kritische Justiz* 24 (1991), 137).

Most examples of what governments are doing to promote CSR, beyond traditional business regulation, can barely be stretched to count as law or regulation at all. And where they can, they are not meta-regulatory – that is, they are not focused on constituting corporate consciences internally. One area where government proposals to reform the law might be perceived as meta-regulatory is corporate governance proposals to require companies/directors to report on CSR issues, or even to expand directors' duties to allow them to take into account stakeholder interests.[92] One example was the (now repealed) requirement introduced in the United Kingdom in 2005 that directors of quoted companies should prepare an operating and financial review (OFR) each year in addition to their normal reporting requirements.[93] The OFR included a 'balanced and comprehensive analysis' of:

- the business's development and performance during the financial year;
- the company's (or group's) position at the end of the year;
- the main trends and factors underlying the development, performance and position of the company (or group) and which are likely to affect it in the future.

> This will include a company's (or group's) objectives, strategies and the key drivers of the business, focusing on more qualitative and forward-looking information than has traditionally been included in annual reports in the past. It must include a description of the resources available to the company (or group), and of the capital structure, treasury policies and objectives and liquidity of the company (or group).
>
> In fulfilling these general requirements, directors will need to consider whether it is necessary to provide information on a range of factors that may be relevant to the understanding of the business, including, for example, environment, employee and social and community issues.[94]

[92] For an overview of Anglo-American developments in this area, see C. Williams and J. Conley, 'An Emerging Third Way? The Erosion of the Anglo-American Shareholder Value Construct', *Cornell Journal of International Law* 38 (2005), 493. See, for example, the Australian parliament's Joint Committee on Corporations and Financial Services inquiry into corporate responsibility: www.aph.gov.au/senate/committee/corporations_ctte/corporate_responsibility/tor.htm (accessed 30 April 2007).

[93] The Companies Act 1985 (Operating and Financial Review and Directors' Report, etc.) Regulations 2005 (SI 2005 No. 1011); See also *Guidance on the OFR and Changes to the Directors' Report* (Department of Trade and Industry, April 2005). The OFR requirement has now been repealed by the Companies Act 1985 (Operating And Financial Review) (Repeal) Regulations (SI 2005 No. 3442) on the basis that the OFR requirement essentially duplicated the requirement that the Directors' Report include a Business Review that had been introduced at the same time by s. 234ZZB of the Companies Act 1985.

[94] *Guidance on the OFR*, p. 6.

We might see provisions requiring reports such as the OFR as meta-regulatory because they implicitly require management or directors to collect information about the possibility of breach of CSR obligations (as a risk to reputation and performance).[95] The meta-regulatory hope is that, having collected the information for the report, management will be encouraged to use it in decision-making and to implement systems to manage the risks they have identified, or at least they might be forced to do so by their shareholders.

However, the law requiring OFRs, as with other laws requiring CSR reporting, was purely process-oriented – it was not aimed at any values, it did not require the company to identify and commit to any values, and it gave no external representative of any values any right to participate in defining what values or targets are to be met.[96] Laws requiring CSR reporting may well be a useful, facilitative adjunct to more substantive regimes that do have clear policy values and do give 'stakeholders' rights, but on their own they can achieve no meta-regulation of the corporate conscience.

It is rather like the way the term 'compliance culture' is used in Division 12.3 of Australia's *Commonwealth Criminal Code Act* (1995). 'Corporate culture' is defined in that legislation to mean 'an attitude, policy, rule, course of conduct or practice existing within the body corporate generally or in the part of the body corporate in which the relevant activities take place'. The existence or not of a 'corporate culture' defined in this way can be relevant to the determination of the criminal liability of companies and directors under certain Australian Commonwealth laws. But this is only useful if there are other laws that the definition will apply to. Similarly, proposals to amend directors' duties to allow them to take into account obligations to stakeholders would be purely facilitative – allowing directors to use such information in decision-making and to spend money on ensuring compliance, assuming that they are motivated to do so by some other means. Companies will go through the form and will do as much or as little internally of any substance as they would have done anyway.

---

[95] The OFR might also include information about the company's corporate governance processes, but it is not required: see ibid., p. 7.

[96] See D. Owen, 'Corporate Social Reporting and Stakeholder Accountability: The Missing Link', *International Centre for Corporate Social Responsibility Research Paper Series* No. 32–2005 (Nottingham: Nottingham University Business School, 2005) ('[reporting] reform is viewed in isolation from any necessary institutional reform which may provide the means for stakeholders to hold company directors accountable for actions affecting their vital interests'). One might also object that these reforms generally suggest 'social and environmental issues are only of relevance when there are financial implications for the company' (at 23).

These proposals are too generic in the absence of sufficient meta-regulation aimed at specific values. Contrast Australia's affirmative action regime – a regulatory regime with little teeth which was based purely on requiring companies to report on their process for setting targets and implementing equal employment opportunity measures. Although the affirmative action regime required only reporting of progress and the only sanctions available were being named in Parliament, and possibly losing government contracts, the regime did have a clear set of substantive values (equal employment opportunity) and required companies to go through a clear process and set substantive targets, and was relatively successful in improving the proportion of women employed in companies that came under the regime.[97]

B. A good example: the Environment Protection Authority Victoria's environmental improvement plans[98]

The environmental improvement plan (EIP) requires site representatives to develop an internal compliance management system aimed at improving environmental performance, and monitoring and reporting on those improvements on a regular basis. It is likely to cover issues such as regulatory compliance, waste minimisation, environmental audit, elimination, reduction or control of environmental impacts and risks (for example, greenhouse emissions, offensive odours, reduction of water consumption, introduction of new technology and so on), and arrangements for dealing with accidents and spills. The Victorian Environment Protection Authority (EPA) allows industrial sites to volunteer for the EIP programme, often requires an EIP as a licence condition, as a condition of works approval for new developments and also has legislative power to direct a site to enter into an EIP.[99]

The EIP programme was first developed in response to ongoing conflict between the manufacturers at a large chemical complex in Altona and local residents over odours, air emissions and noise. Not only were the

---

[97] See V. Braithwaite, 'The Australian Government's Affirmative Action Legislation: Achieving Social Change through Human Resource Management', *Law and Policy* 15 (1993), 327.

[98] More details on this case study are available in Gunningham and Sinclair, *Leaders and Laggards*, pp. 157–88; Parker, *The Open Corporation*, pp. 226–7.

[99] Environment Protection Act 1970 (Vic), s. 31C; EPA Victoria, *Guidelines for the Preparation of Environment Improvement Plans* (June 2002, Publication 739). Note that the 2002 *Guidelines* state that community involvement is not necessary for all types of EIPs. The discussion in the text, however, concerns only those EIPs where community participation was required.

site's neighbours unhappy, but the conflict meant it was difficult for the manufacturers to get approval to make any changes to their plants, as community members used the planning approval process to object to all proposed changes. In the late 1980s, the EPA hired a 'community liaison officer' (a social worker) to help set up a community consultation process in which site representatives, local community members (including those who had complained regularly) and local council representatives could meet together and agree an action plan for resolving problems. The success of this process led to the EPA's development of the EIP programme in the early 1990s.

The EIP process required representatives of site management to meet intensively with a Community Liaison Council (CLC) – local community members and local government representatives – which had to be consulted on every aspect of the development of an EIP from target-setting to implementation. Clear targets for performance had to be set as part of this consultative process, and the whole EIP (including the targets) generally became part of the site's licence to carry on its activities from the EPA. This process could take up to twelve months with regular meetings of the CLC and site management over that period. After agreeing the EIP, site representatives had to continue to meet regularly with the CLC and report on the site's implementation of systems and performance on the targets it set for itself. The site's activities also remained subject to local government planning approval and other legal controls (including the possibility of enforcement action for breach of the law or the site's licence) in the normal way. EIPs were not seen as a replacement for the normal application and enforcement of the law.

Gunningham and Sinclair published an in-depth evaluation of the programme in 2002 which concluded that 'as a form of process-based regulation, EIPs frequently generated greater environmental commitment within the enterprise' but 'over and above such process-based changes (and in contrast to initiatives such as ISO 14001 and Responsible Care), the EIP also requires ... [that] enterprises committing to an EIP must meet specified performance targets within a specified time-period (for example, they may commit to upgrade equipment to meet objectives under the plan, or to meet specified emission or waste reduction targets)'.[100] They cite interviews suggesting that entering into an EIP meant that companies incorporated community concerns at an early stage of the planning process for new developments, rather than fighting about them with local residents later on.[101] The EPA itself saw the EIPs as a way to improve how

---

[100] Gunningham and Sinclair, *Leaders and Laggards*, p. 170.   [101] *ibid.*, p. 169.

the companies conducted their businesses generally and communicated with their local communities.[102]

The EIP programme was therefore meta-regulatory and process-oriented. Companies that entered into an EIP had to go through a process of consultation and reporting with the CLC which was mainly focused on internal management issues. But the EIP was not a process-based sham. The companies' legal obligations were reasonably well-known and enforceable. The process itself required them to set clear 'beyond compliance' targets for environmental improvement outcomes for themselves, and made it clear that they would be held accountable for them – by having to face the CLC to report on their performance, and by making the EIP a licence condition.

This type of meta-regulation worked because community representatives were given a right to participate in the EIP process, and their right to participate in that process was backed up by the fact that they had clear rights at general law to object to developments or actions that impacted on the local environment, and the fact that the EPA was acting as broker for the whole consultation and negotiation process. Conflict was not swept under the carpet. Where the programme worked, conflict was brought into the open and dealt with in the CLC meetings – the EPA's community liaison officer reported that the first few meetings of the CLC were often quite heated as conflicting views and values were expressed. Indeed, according to Gunningham and Sinclair's evaluation, the process seemed to work best where conflict was greater and therefore community members' motivation to participate higher. The commitment of the EPA to providing officers to make sure that local community members who vociferously complained about companies' environmental impacts were included in community consultation processes and to guide the CLC through the early stages of negotiating an EIP was clearly key to making this meta-regulatory initiative successful.

V. Conclusion

'Meta-regulation' is a useful way of conceptualising what legal accountability for CSR ought to, and could, look like. As we have seen, it is relatively easy to find examples of partial, or attempted, meta-regulation. It is not so easy to find examples of regulation of CSR that fully meet the normative

---

[102] Environment Protection Authority, *25 Years of Making a Difference* (Melbourne, Victoria: Environment Protection Authority, 1996), p. 13.

criteria for meta-regulation that I have set out here. The argument of this chapter is that legal accountability for CSR must be aimed at making business enterprises put themselves through a CSR process aimed at CSR outcomes. The outcomes must themselves be accountable applications of substantive values to specific situations; and the process must be one that opens up management to external values, stakeholders and regulatory influences, not closes it down. In other words, legal accountability for CSR must amount to meta-regulation – an approach to legal regulation in which the *internal* 'corporate conscience' is *externally* regulated.

If by 'corporate social responsibility' is meant something voluntary and discretionary that businesses on their own can 'take responsibility' for, then the idea of legal accountability for CSR does not make any sense. Indeed, on its own, the whole notion of CSR makes sense only within the context of more substantive discussions of regulatory and social policy which tell us for *what* corporations must take responsibility. Mechanisms for nudging companies towards CSR indirectly (for example, tax incentives or government procurement policies aimed at encouraging CSR) or in a way that is aimed at CSR generically without setting specific substantive standards or goals (such as the United Kingom's repealed OFR requirement) are likely to fail badly unless they are adequately buttressed by specific regulatory regimes which specify social policy goals, and identify and give rights to stakeholders to participate in or contest corporate decisions. These regulatory regimes need not take the form of traditional, hierarchical legal regulation promulgated by nation states. 'Meta-regulating' law might include international networks of governance, more traditional state-based regulatory enforcement activity, and traditional law that authorises, empowers, co-opts or recognises the regulatory influence of industry, professional or civil society bodies to set and enforce standards for CSR processes and outcomes.[103] That type of regime generally only comes about through considerable struggle and conflict.

[103] Compare Gunningham and Grabosky, *Smart Regulation*, pp. 93–134.

PART THREE

Expanding Legal Accountabilities:
Company Law and Beyond

8

Disclosure law and the market for corporate social responsibility

KEVIN CAMPBELL AND DOUGLAS VICK

I. Introduction

While the social role of public companies is an issue that has bubbled near the surface of broader debates about corporate governance for some time now,[1] only fairly recently has corporate social responsibility become an issue of such prominence that it has earned its own acronym: 'CSR' has been the subject of numerous non-binding declarations by governmental bodies, non-governmental organisations (NGOs) and business groups, particularly in the last decade.[2] While there is no clear consensus about

We would like to thank David Stopforth and Claire Lavers for their comments on previous drafts of this chapter, and Lesley Taylor for valuable secretarial assistance. We would also like to acknowledge the valuable feedback we obtained from those who attended our presentations at the Centre for Socio-Legal Studies' Second Seminar Series on Corporate Social Responsibility and the Law in Oxford in 2003, and at the 2004 Socio-Legal Studies Association Annual Conference in Glasgow.

[1] In the United States, arguments about the purposes and public obligations of corporations date from at least the 1930s. See, e.g., A. A. Berle, Jr, 'Corporate Powers as Powers in Trust', *Harvard Law Review* 44 (1931), 1049; E. Merrick Dodd, Jr, 'For Whom are Corporate Managers Trustees?', *Harvard Law Review* 45 (1932), 1145; A. A. Berle, Jr, 'For Whom Corporate Managers *Are* Trustees: A Note', *Harvard Law Review* 45 (1932), 1365.

[2] Early examples are the *OECD Guidelines for Multinational Enterprises*, a series of recommendations first issued in 1976 as part of the Organisation for Economic Co-operation and Development's (OECD) *Declaration on International Investment and Multinational Enterprises*, and the *Global Sullivan Principles*, launched in 1977 by Reverend Leon Sullivan of Philadelphia and initially directed at US companies with investments in South Africa. Both statements subsequently have been expanded in their scope. Other examples of influential declarations include the United Nations' *Global Compact*, a statement of nine principles proclaimed in 1999 and meant to serve as the foundation for a UN-sponsored platform for promoting good corporate practices; the Coalition for Environmentally Responsible Economies' *Statement of Principles*, made in 1989, and the Global Reporting Initiative's *Sustainability Guidelines*, issued in 1999, which focused on the environmental consequences of corporate activities; the Caux Round Table's *Principles for Business*, first published by a coalition of business leaders in 1994; the *ETI Base Code*, issued in 1998 by the Ethical

what exactly CSR means, at a minimum the term implies an obligation on the part of large companies to pursue objectives advancing the interests of all groups (or 'stakeholders', in today's parlance) affected by their activities – not just shareholders but also employees, consumers, suppliers, creditors and local communities. These interests are not just economic but also include environmental, human rights and 'quality of life' concerns. The obligation to be socially responsible is usually conceived of as being over and above the minimum requirements imposed on companies by formal legal rules,[3] although this is not invariably the case.[4]

As a concept, CSR directly challenges the dominant Anglo-American paradigm of corporate governance,[5] which emphasises profit-maximisation for investors as the most efficient means of promoting wealth creation for society as a whole. Consistent with this paradigm, the corporate governance debate in the United Kingdom has focused primarily on making those who run companies accountable to those who effectively own them, the company's members (shareholders), and the preoccupation of company law has been with assuring that company

Business Initiative, a coalition of trade unions, NGOs and business groups based on various conventions adopted by the International Labour Organisation; and *Social Accountability 8000 (SA 8000)*, a set of standards for the protection of workers' rights promulgated by the Council on Economic Priorities Accreditation Agency in 1997.

[3] See, e.g., Commission of the European Communities, *Communication from the Commission Concerning Corporate Social Responsibility: A Business Contribution to Sustainable Development* (Brussels, 2.7.2002) Com (2002) 347 final, p. 5; Department of Trade and Industry, *Business and Society: Corporate Social Responsibility Report 2002*, p. 7.

[4] Mandatory legislation sometimes contains what are classified as CSR initiatives. Recent examples include the Anti-terrorism, Crime and Security Act 2001, which provided that UK companies and company directors could be prosecuted for bribery and corruption offences wherever they are committed in the world (ss. 108–10); amendments to the Income and Corporation Taxes Act 1998 which disallowed tax deductions for payments made outside the United Kingdom which would be criminal offences if made within the United Kingdom; and the Employment Act 2002 and Maternity and Parental Leave etc. and the Paternity and Adoption Leave (Amendment) Regulations 2006, SI 2006 No. 2014, concerning entitlement to maternity, paternity, and adoption leave and pay. Mandatory environmental, health and safety, and anti-discrimination laws are also sometimes seen as part of the CSR agenda.

[5] For purposes of the issues addressed in this chapter, it is useful to refer to an Anglo-American model of corporate governance that is distinguishable from models prevalent in continental Europe. Notwithstanding differences between capitalism as experienced in the United States and the United Kingdom, particularly in connection with welfare provision, there are strong parallels between the two countries in connection with the historical evolution of the corporate form, the law governing it, corporate governance structures and preferred methods of raising finance capital.

directors act in the best interests of the company for the benefit of its members.[6] Policy-makers have been reluctant to interfere with this system – for example, by requiring direct participation of other stakeholder groups in the management of economically significant companies, or by imposing legally enforceable duties on directors that would benefit groups other than shareholders – and have instead preferred to encourage companies to adopt CSR policies voluntarily. Thus, instead of compelling companies to adopt CSR-related policies or undertake CSR-related activities, the present government's strategy for encouraging corporate social responsibility has been to require companies to disclose publicly such policies and activities. In recent years, partly as a consequence of government pressures from within the United Kingdom and elsewhere, there has been a significant growth in CSR self-reporting, with 'social responsibility' statements becoming a common feature in company annual reports.

A basic assumption underlies the government's disclosure strategy: that a company's interests – and the interests of its shareholders – are best served by maintaining a 'positive' CSR profile (the 'enlightened shareholder value' theory). CSR activities, it is assumed, are value-creating because they strengthen a company's relationships with its key stakeholders and because they make the company more attractive to potential customers. This would positively affect a publicly-traded company's share price: if investors believe that disclosure of information demonstrating that a company has a 'good' CSR record will enhance the value of a company, this will be reflected in the price investors are willing to pay for the company's shares. Financial economists postulate that for a publicly-traded company, the most relevant measure of investor perceptions of the value of a company is the market price of the company's shares. In a

---

[6] In this regard, it has been said that the UK corporate system revolves around three groups – directors, shareholders and auditors – with shareholders and auditors monitoring the activities of directors to ensure that they do not act in a way that is contrary to the best interests of the company. See Saleem Sheikh, 'Introduction to the Corporate Governance Themed Issue', *International Company and Commercial Law Review* 9 (1998), 267. The important role of institutional shareholders in the United Kingdom was addressed in 2001 by the Myners Report, which called for pension fund managers to take a more proactive role in the companies in which they invested. The report argued that they should take 'an active interest in the appointment and performance of non-executive directors, exhibiting vigilance in determining an appropriate degree of independence and a proper level of engagement'. *Institutional Investment in the United Kingdom: A Review* (2001), p. 93.

properly functioning market, a company's share price will reflect the collective assessment made by investors of all available relevant information about that company and expectations about the company's future cash flows. If this is true, it is possible to test the validity of the voluntarism principle at the heart of the government's CSR policy by comparing the market performance of companies perceived to have a good CSR record with that of publicly-traded companies that are not.

This chapter will consider how CSR affects the value of companies to shareholders by examining the market performance of companies included in the recently introduced FTSE4Good ethical indices. Developed by the FTSE Group, an independent company that creates and manages indices and related data services used by investment analysts, the FTSE4Good indices provide the 'ethical investment' sector with tools to measure the performance of companies meeting certain CSR criteria. While the FTSE has been criticised for failing to apply their criteria as stringently as they might, nonetheless inclusion in the FTSE4Good indices is, in itself, a signal to the investment community that a company has a desirable CSR reputation. By comparing the companies included in these indices with excluded companies and the market as a whole, it is possible to obtain some empirical evidence concerning investor perceptions of the value-creating potential of CSR activities.

The next section will examine in greater detail the legal approach to corporate social responsibility under the Anglo-American model of corporate governance. The government's CSR strategy is predicated on the notion that companies will produce 'public goods' at levels beyond what is strictly required by law, a notion that challenges the neo-classical conception of the company as a strictly profit-maximising entity. In order to reconcile CSR with established assumptions about the purposes of companies and company law, it is necessary to justify the pursuit of CSR objectives as ultimately being in the company's economic interests. We then discuss the emergence of ethical investment indices in general and the FTSE4Good indices in particular, examining the measurement method employed by FTSE to select companies for these indices. Finally, we describe the results of the empirical tests used to measure the relative performance of companies included in the FTSE4Good indices. By studying the apparent growth of CSR activity from these various perspectives, we can better evaluate whether New Labour's approach in encouraging corporate social responsibility will have a meaningful effect on corporate conduct.

II. Contextualising corporate social responsibility

A. The Anglo-American model of corporate governance

The notion that companies – or at least 'companies of economic significance'[7] – should act in a 'socially responsible' manner begs more fundamental questions about the nature and purposes of companies. Under the Anglo-American model of corporate governance, a company is considered to be the product of individual initiative, possessing powers conferred by its members, and the purpose of companies is to maximise the profits of those members.[8] This has not always been the case: before the mid-nineteenth century, the corporate entity was widely conceived as an artificial creation of the state and entirely dependant on the state for its powers, and incorporation was thought not only to confer privileges on incorporators but to impose responsibilities to further the general public welfare.[9] The relationship between corporate activity and the public welfare was explicit, and company law could almost be seen as an aspect of public law.[10] After the emergence of general incorporation statutes, however,[11] the company was gradually reconceptualised as fundamentally private in nature. So conceived, many questioned the legitimacy of asking corporate executives to spend money 'belonging' to the company's owners to further social interests commonly thought to be the responsibility of the state.[12]

In the United Kingdom, the modern foundations of company law were laid by the Joint Stock Companies Act 1856. As Walter Horrwitz observed, this Act was adopted when 'liberalism was at its peak', and 'the guiding

---

[7] Whether a company is a 'company of economic significance', of course, is often a subject of debate. Tests that have been used have taken into account factors such as whether the company is private or publicly-traded; the size of the company's annual turnover or balance sheet; and the number of persons employed by the company.

[8] See, e.g., Brian R. Cheffins, *Company Law: Theory, Structure and Operation* (Oxford: Oxford University Press, 1997), p. 15.

[9] David Millon, 'Theories of the Corporation', *Duke Law Journal* (1990) 201.

[10] *ibid.*, 211.

[11] See, e.g., Joint Stock Companies Act 1844.

[12] Milton Friedman, for example, dismissed CSR as a dangerous 'socialist' concept in a 1970 article published in the *New York Times Magazine*: see Milton Friedman, 'The Social Responsibility of Business is to Increase Its Profits', reprinted in W. Michael Hoffman and Jennifer Mills Moore, *Business Ethics: Readings and Cases in Corporate Morality* (2nd edn New York: McGraw-Hill, 1990), pp. 153–7. Apparently Friedman later moderated his views. See Saleem Sheikh, *Corporate Social Responsibilities: Law and Practice* (London: Cavendish, 1996), pp. 24–7.

principle then fixed was fullest freedom for shareholders in the formation and management of companies on the condition that fullest information was given to the public'.[13] Company law has evolved since then into a fragmented system of minimal common law and statutory duties and relatively more expansive self-regulation through, for example, the City Code issued by the Panel on Takeovers and Mergers[14] and the codes of best practice and corporate governance applicable to companies listed on the London Stock Exchange.[15] This system is predicated upon a philosophy of minimal state interference with the freedom and flexibility of companies to interpret and respond to market forces. Moreover, it is centred upon a model of agency which sees the company's owners (the shareholders) as principals and company directors as their agents. The owners appoint their agents to run the company, and the agents are required to report back to their principals periodically. While a company's directors may delegate their management function to others, they are ultimately responsible to the shareholders for how a company is operated.

Economically, this model has been justified as the most effective and efficient way to promote wealth maximisation for society as a whole: giving the owners of companies the freedom to pursue their self-interest will lead to productive and allocative efficiency.[16] Companies are the most desirable form of business organisation, and favouring shareholders will induce

---

[13] Walter Horrwitz, 'Historical Development of Company Law', *Law Quarterly Review* 62 (1946), 375.

[14] See *City Code on Takeovers and Mergers* ('Takeover Code') and the *Rules Governing Substantial Acquisitions of Shares* ('SARs'), collectively referred to as 'the Code'.

[15] See, e.g., *The Combined Code: Principles of Good Governance and Code of Best Practice* (May 2000), at www.fsa.gov.uk/pubs/ukla/lr_comcode.pdf, which was based on the *Final Report of the Hampel Committee on Corporate Governance* (London: Gee, 1998), the *Report of the Committee on the Financial Aspects of Corporate Governance* (London: Gee, 1992) ('The Cadbury Report'), and *Directors' Remuneration: Report of a Study Group Chaired by Sir Richard Greenbury* (London: Gee, 1995) ('the Greenbury Report'). The Hampel Committee's Combined Code has been replaced by *The Combined Code on Corporate Governance* (July 2003), available at www.frc.org.uk, in response to Derek Higgs' *Review of the Role and Effectiveness of Non-Executive Directors* (January 2003), at www.dti.gov.uk/files/file23012.pdf, and the report by Sir Robert Smith's Group, *Audit Committees Combined Code Guidance* (January 2003), at www.frc.org.uk/images/uploaded/documents/ACReport.pdf. Applicable to all companies listed on the London Stock Exchange from 1 November 2003, the new Code, like its predecessor, requires listed companies to describe how they apply the Code's main and supporting principles and state whether they comply with the Code's provisions.

[16] Productive efficiency is maximised when production takes place at the lowest possible cost, minimising the waste of resources; allocative efficiency is maximised when goods and services are produced in the quantity and quality demanded by consumers.

market investment and thus facilitate the capitalisation of companies.[17] Legally, this model is effectuated through a rights-oriented approach that recognises and gives priority to property interests in shares. Strictly speaking, the duties imposed on those who manage a company are owed to the 'company', but the company's interests are usually equated with the interests of the company's present and future shareholders.[18] There are limited exceptions to this general rule: directors have a duty to consider the interests of employees in performing their functions (although this duty is virtually unenforceable);[19] and directors are required to consider the interests of creditors when the company is insolvent or on the verge of insolvency.[20] In most situations, however, the notion that directors' duties are owed to a corporate 'entity' is simply a vehicle for protecting the interests of one group of stakeholders, the company's shareholders, at the expense of other groups affected by the company's activities. While courts will not necessarily interfere if a company's directors decide to award other stakeholders, such as employees or local communities, with benefits or gratuities that go beyond the strict limits of the company's legal obligations,[21] they do require that the ultimate objective in awarding these benefits must be 'getting the greatest profit from the business

---

[17] In addition, favouring the position of shareholders potentially provides motivation for shareholders to exercise a supervisory role in relation to the conduct of corporate managers.

[18] See, e.g., J. E. Parkinson, *Corporate Power and Responsibility: Issues in the Theory of Company Law* (Oxford: Clarendon Press, 1993), pp. 76–92. Parkinson notes that a requirement to benefit an artificial entity like 'the company' is, in and of itself, meaningless; an inanimate legal fiction does not really have 'interests' to protect. See *ibid.*, p. 76. As Megarry J. observed in *Gaiman* v. *Association for Mental Health* [1971] Ch 317, at 330, 'I would accept the interests of both present and future members of the company as a whole, as being a helpful expression of a human equivalent' to the legal notion of 'the interests of the company.'

[19] See Companies Act 1985, s. 309 (originally enacted as s. 46 of the Companies Act 1980). Section 309 has been described as 'cosmetic' because employees lack the *locus standi* to bring enforcement actions on behalf of the company unless they are also company shareholders. Sheikh, 'Introduction to the Corporate Governance Themed Issue', 268. See also Ben Pettet, 'Duties in Respect of Employees under the Companies Act 1980' *Current Legal Problems* 34 (1981), 199. Section 719 of the Companies Act 1985 (originally s. 74 of the Companies Act 1980) allows a company to 'make provision' for current or former employees upon cessation or transfer of the company's business, provided this is sanctioned by the company's memorandum or articles, an ordinary resolution, or a resolution of the directors.

[20] See *Lonrho Ltd* v. *Shell Petroleum Co. Ltd* [1980] 1 WLR 627; Insolvency Act 1986, s. 214. See also Andrew Keay, 'The Duty of Directors to Take Account of Creditors' Interests: Has It Any Role to Play?', *Journal of Business Law* (2002), 379.

[21] See, e.g., *Hampson* v. *Price's Patent Candle Co.* (1876) 24 WR 754.

of the company' that is possible[22] – for example by allowing the company to recruit and retain the best employees or improve employee productivity. Finally, to the extent that unconstrained profit-maximisation harms the interests of other groups affected by corporate activities or causes social problems, the Anglo-American system has preferred to deal with these problems from the 'outside' – through legal requirements and prohibitions imposed by primary or secondary legislation – rather than the 'inside' – by incorporating non-shareholder interests into corporate decision-making itself.

The shareholder primacy at the heart of the Anglo-American corporate governance model has not gone unchallenged. E. Merrick Dodd, Jr, in a US law review article published in 1932, argued that a concept of citizenship applicable to individuals – a concept that envisages that sometimes social circumstances require pursuit of other-regarding goals that do not necessarily benefit the individual financially – should also apply to 'corporate persons', and that it should be within the legitimate powers of a company's managers to disregard the company's purely economic self-interest to further other compelling social obligations.[23] This argument recognises that the activities of large, publicly-traded companies affect a wider range of interests than simply those of investors, and asserts in effect that the 'company' to which directors owe duties encompasses those interests as well as the economic interests of shareholders. For example, it is often the case that creditors, employees and local communities bear a far greater risk of loss in the event of a company's failure than the company's 'owners', who individually may possess only a small fraction of the company's shares and are in any event protected by the doctrine of limited liability.[24] A good corporate 'citizen' sometimes must act in a way that shareholders might oppose, even if not expressly required to do so by the strictures of the law (or even by considerations of 'enlightened self-interest'), and such actions should not be regarded as legally or ethically suspect.[25]

Ultimately, Dodd's pluralist vision of corporate governance was not realised. Adolph Berle, for example, argued that if the managers of economically significant companies were allowed to pursue social objectives

---

[22] *Hutton* v. *West Cork Railway Co.* (1993) 23 Ch D 654, at pp. 665–6 (Cotton L.J.).

[23] See Dodd, 'For Whom are Corporate Managers Trustees?', 1161–2.

[24] Moreover, many interests affected by corporate activity – job security and job satisfaction, the environment, the stability of communities in which a company's operations are centred – cannot be translated into economic formulae allowing easy comparison with the financial interests of shareholders.

[25] See Dodd, 'For Whom are Corporate Managers Trustees?', 1161.

on behalf of vaguely defined interest groups, they would be able to exercise tremendous economic, social and political power without really being accountable to anyone.[26] Berle felt that the only effective way to place limits on the power of corporate executives was to make them legally answerable to the one identifiable group unambiguously affected by the company's activities – its shareholders – who through self-interest will monitor management's activities. In fact, the problem of accountability caused by the separation of ownership and management in large, publicly-traded companies soon came to dominate corporate governance discourse in the United States,[27] and concerns about corporate social responsibility faded to the background.[28] This does not mean that US executives did not want to cultivate an image of their companies as caring, socially responsive institutions. But their primary motives seemed to have been to discourage adoption and stricter application of mandatory legislation and anti-monopoly laws and to obtain public relations benefits that could be used for marketing purposes.[29]

In the United Kingdom, CSR remained in 'the realm of "otherness"'[30] until the 1970s, when mainstream participants in public policy debates,

---

[26] See Berle, 'For Whom Corporate Managers Are Trustees', 1367–9. See also Adolph A. Berle and Gardiner C. Means, *The Modern Corporation and Private Property* (New York: Macmillan, 1932), p. 310: 'As an economic organism grows in strength and its power is concentrated in a few hands . . . the demand for responsible power becomes increasingly direct.'

[27] See especially Berle and Means, *The Modern Corporation*. The mainstream view came to be that without a reaction to the actions of managers by investors in the stock market, those managers would be largely unaccountable. The theory is that managers are made accountable by competition in the managerial labour market (investors will force the replacement of under-performing managers) and by the corporate takeover market (a company performing at sub-optimal levels will have stock prices below its true value, making it an attractive takeover target). See Jonathan P. Charkham, *Keeping Good Company: A Study of Corporate Governance in Five Countries* (Oxford: Clarendon Press, 1994), pp. 308–19; Henry Manne, 'Mergers and the Market for Corporate Control', *Journal of Political Economy* 73 (1965), 110.

[28] They did not disappear, however. See, e.g., Howard R. Bowen, *Social Responsibilities of the Businessman* (New York: Harper, 1953); J. W. McGuire, *Business and Society* (New York: McGraw Hill, 1963).

[29] See Sally Wheeler, *Corporations and the Third Way* (Oxford: Hart Publishing, 2002), p. 34. See also Roland Marchand, *Creating the Corporate Soul: The Rise of Public Relations and Corporate Imagery in American Big Business* (Berkeley, CA: University of California Press, 1998); Andrea Tone, *The Business of Benevolence* (Ithaca, NY: Cornell University Press, 1997).

[30] Wheeler, *Corporations and the Third Way*, p. 34. Wheeler notes that for many years, CSR was marginalised from mainstream corporate governance debate, seen as 'being the province of non-conformists such as Congregationalists and Quakers': *ibid.*, pp. 34–5.

like the Confederation of British Industry (CBI), began suggesting that companies must 'have functions, duties and moral obligations that go beyond the immediate pursuit of profit and the requirements of the law'.[31] Shortly thereafter, shareholder primacy was directly challenged when the Bullock Committee contemplated employee representation on company boards.[32] This period also saw a dramatic rise in academic interest in corporate governance issues in general and CSR in particular, an interest that has rarely subsided since then.[33] Often those expressing dissatisfaction with the dominant Anglo-American paradigm looked to the alternative models of corporate governance used in countries like Germany and Japan, whose economies were once considered more successful than those of the United States or Britain. Particularly popular – at least before the economic stresses of reunification damaged the reputation of the German system – was the so-called Rhine Model of corporate governance, which was far less rights-oriented than its Anglo-American counterpart.[34] The Rhine Model conceived the primary function of companies not as profit-maximisation but as assuring that goods and services that a community needs are delivered on a continuing basis.[35] Profits were important, but only as a means to serve this ultimate purpose. This greater emphasis on protecting stakeholders other than shareholders is in part

---

[31] *ibid.*, p. 35, quoting Confederation of British Industry, *A New Look at the Responsibilities of the British Public Company* (London: Confederation of British Industry, 23 January 1973). Around the same time, the accounting profession began devising methods for measuring and publicising a company's community activities: *ibid.*, p. 36.

[32] Committee of Inquiry on Industrial Democracy, *Report* (1977) Cmnd 6706.

[33] Leading works include Charkham, *Keeping Good Company*; Janice Dean, *Directing Public Companies: Company Law and the Stakeholder Society* (London: Cavendish, 2001); Will Hutton, *The State We're In* (London: Cape, 1995); Parkinson, *Corporate Power and Responsibility*; John Plender, *A Stake in the Future: The Stakeholding Solution* (London: Nicholas Brealey, 1997); Sheikh, *Corporate Social Responsibilities*; Wheeler *Corporations and the Third Way*; G. Kelly and J. E. Parkinson, 'The Conceptual Foundations of the Company: A Pluralist Approach', *Company, Financial and Insolvency Law Review* (1998), 174; Paddy Ireland, 'Corporate Governance, Stakeholding, and the Company: Towards a Less Degenerate Capitalism', *Journal of Law and Society* 23 (1996), 287; Ben Pettet, 'The Stirring of Corporate Social Conscience: From "Cakes and Ale" to Community Programmes', *Current Legal Problems* 50 (1997), 279. See also Max B. E. Clarkson (ed.), *The Corporation and Its Stakeholders: Classic and Contemporary Readings* (Toronto: University of Toronto Press, 1998); Klaus J. Hopt and Gunther Teubner (eds.), *Corporate Governance and Directors' Liability: Legal, Economic and Sociological Analyses of Corporate Social Responsibility* (Berlin: W. de Gruyter, 1984).

[34] The foundation of the German system could be found in Article 14(2) of the Basic Law, at www.iuscomp.org/gla/statutes/GG.htm#14, which proclaimed that 'property imposes duties [and its] use shall also serve the public good'.

[35] Charkham, *Keeping Good Company*, p. 10.

reflected in, and in part a consequence of, the legal rules governing the dual-board management structure of German companies. For example, German law gave Work Councils rights to co-determination with the Management Board in connection with dismissal, employee vocational training and grievances; employees were legally entitled to representation on the Supervisory Board of larger companies; and rules requiring banks to act as proxies for shareholders at general meetings assured that a company's major creditors often had a strong influence over corporate behaviour.[36]

While CSR debates continued to be waged by academics in the 1980s and 1990s, it dropped from the policy agenda with the ascendancy of the New Right and its attendant social and economic priorities. In the Thatcher era, Milton Friedman's argument that 'the social responsibility of business is to increase its profits' won out. The pursuit of goals other than profit by company managers was deemed economically inefficient (and thus damaging to the long-term well-being of society as a whole); an unfair infringement of the property rights of shareholders; and an undemocratic concession of power to unelected and publicly unaccountable company directors making decisions about wealth redistribution more properly reserved to a community's elected representatives.[37] In this period, the United Kingdom led the opposition to proposals such as the early version of the EC Draft Fifth Directive on Company Law[38] which would have required larger companies to adopt a German-style two-tier board structure and some form of employee participation in corporate decision-making.[39] Indeed, UK policy-makers resisted any interference with decision-making structures that might have undermined the

---

[36] See generally *ibid.*, pp. 6–58. Perhaps the most striking example of a pluralist approach to corporate governance is that of the regional public broadcasting companies in Germany, which are governed by 'Broadcasting Councils' consisting of representatives of the 'socially significant groups', including ethnic, political, cultural, religious and economic groups. See generally Peter J. Humphreys, *Media and Media Policy in Germany: The Press and Broadcasting Since 1945* (2nd edn, Oxford: Berg, 1994).

[37] See Friedman, 'The Social Responsibility of Business'.

[38] Proposal for a Fifth Directive (company structure and the power and responsibilities of company boards) OJ No. C131, 13 December 1972; amended proposal OJ No. C240, 9 September 1983; further amended OJ Nos. C7, 11 January 1991 and C321, 12 December 1991; finally withdrawn OJ No. C5/20, 12 December 1991.

[39] See Pettet, 'The Stirring of Corporate Social Conscience', 307. See also J. J. Du Plessis and J. Dine, 'The Fate of the Draft Fifth Directive on Company Law: Accommodation Instead of Harmonisation', *Journal of Business Law* (1997), 23. In 2001, after years of negotiation, a Council Regulation was adopted allowing a *Societas Europaea* (European company) registered in one member state to operate throughout the European Union under a single set of rules. See Council Regulation 2157/2001/EC of 8 October 2001 on the Statute for

principle of shareholder primacy, instead identifying the areas of corporate governance in need of greatest reform to be directors' competence,
directors' remuneration, directors' conflicts of interest and shareholders'
remedies.[40]

The approach to CSR taken by the Hampel Committee is indicative of
the consensus that had formed by the 1990s.[41] The Committee insisted
that good corporate governance should take into account the various
stakeholders affected by the company's operations, but was unwilling to
mandate particular management structures giving those stakeholders representation in decision-making processes or to impose legally enforceable
duties benefiting those stakeholders. The Hampel Committee enthusiasti-
cally embraced the proposition that the ultimate objective of the company
was profit maximisation. It concluded that it would be difficult to devise
a system where corporate managers would be legally responsible to stakeholders other than shareholders, as it would require specific identification of the groups to whom duties would be owed and careful definition
of the nature and extent of the duties owed to each group. The Committee maintained, as had Berle decades before, that company directors
effectively could end up being accountable to no one, since the criteria
for judging their performance would inevitably be conflicting and unenforceable. Instead, the Committee proposed that public companies should
be required by the London Stock Exchange's Listing Rules to disclose in
their annual report how they have applied principles of good governance
(including CSR principles), whether they have complied with the provisions of the Combined Code of Best Practice, and when they have not,
explain their failure to do so. This combination of voluntary participation
and mandatory disclosure would form the bedrock of New Labour's CSR
policy after they rose to power in 1997.

a European Company (SE) OJ 2001 No. L294/1. The Regulation allows incorporators to
adopt either a one-tier or two-tier governance structure. The European Union has refused
to adopt a single model of employee participation for the European company in light of the
wide divergence of existing laws in member states, however, though certain disclosure and
consultation requirements have been imposed. See Council Directive 2001/86/EC OJ 2001
No. L294/22; Directive 2002/14/EC of the European Parliament and the Council OJ 2002
No. L80/29. See also Paul L. Davies, 'Workers on the Board of the European Company?',
Industrial Law Journal 32 (2003), 75.

40 See, e.g., *Report of the Committee on the Financial Aspects of Corporate Governance* (The
Cadbury Report); *Directors' Remuneration: Report of a Study Group Chaired by Sir Richard
Greenbury* (The Greenbury Report); Committee on Corporate Governance, *Final Report*
(London: Gee, 1998); Law Commission, *Shareholder Remedies* (1997) Cm 3769; Law Com-
mission, *Company Directors: Regulating Conflicts of Interest and Formulating a Statement
of Duties* (1999) Cm 4436.

41 Committee on Corporate Governance, *Final Report*.

B. *Corporate social responsibility and New Labour*

Before considering New Labour's CSR policies in greater detail, it is worth restating that more direct – and intrusive – options are available to the government than the strategy it prefers, ranging from giving stakeholder groups the right to participate in corporate decision-making to providing mandatory consultation to bestowing a legally enforceable right (akin to that enjoyed by shareholders) to have one's interests considered by directors in decision-making processes. An example of a more robust approach to CSR is found in a Private Members' Bill introduced by Labour backbenchers in 2002 but subsequently dropped.[42] The Corporate Responsibility Bill would have required all companies based or operating in the United Kingdom with an annual turnover of £5 million or more to publish an annual report addressing the broader environmental, social and economic effects of their operations; their employment policies and practices; their financial relationships with governments (including those suspected of human rights abuses) and political parties; and the manner in which they discharged various environmental and social obligations identified in the Bill. In addition, the Bill would have required these companies to consult with, and respond to, all groups affected by any of their proposed major projects, and would have required companies to file impact statements with regulators concerning the environmental, social and economic implications of those projects, with these statements and associated background papers being made available to public inspection. In annual company reports, directors would have been required to disclose whether they had any training, qualifications or experience in connection with environmental or social matters. The Bill's provisions were to be supported by criminal penalties. In addition, stakeholders other than shareholders would have been able to bring private actions against companies or their directors for any breach of the statutory duties imposed by the Act, and if any significant adverse environmental or social effects arising out of a company's operations were associated with the negligence or wilful misconduct of company directors in connection with their duties or disclosure obligations under the Bill, those directors would have been held personally liable.

This robust approach to CSR does not reflect the policy of the current Labour Government. Instead, New Labour's Third Way agenda for the corporate sector emphasises 'non-intervention in a regulatory sense' except

---

[42] This discussion of the Bill is adapted from the analysis in Stephen Copp, 'Corporate Governance: Change, Consistency and Evolution: Part I', *International Company and Commercial Law Review* 14 (2003), 65, at 70.

where necessary to promote competitiveness, with a strong inclination towards 'allow[ing] markets a free reign'.[43] The government is primarily concerned that the United Kingdom's company law remains 'internationally competitive' and assuring 'that we retain our existing companies and attract new ones'.[44] The government has been reluctant to interfere with the management structures of business or the exercise of business judgment by corporate managers. At the same time, the government recognises that market forces alone will not 'create or sustain ethical frameworks'.[45] In March 2000 a Minister within the Department of Trade and Industry (DTI) was given specific responsibility for CSR, and a DTI website dedicated to CSR emphasises the government's support of a voluntary approach to CSR.[46] However, this emphasis on voluntarism is combined with various rules compelling disclosure of the nature and extent of those CSR activities actually undertaken.

One example of this approach is found in secondary legislation adopted in 1999 requiring trustees of occupational pension schemes to include in their published investment policy statements an indication as to the 'the extent (if at all) to which social, environmental or ethical considerations are taken into account in the selection, retention and realisation of investments'.[47] A parallel requirement was imposed on local government pension schemes.[48] The rationale behind these rules is that institutional investors (particularly pension funds) hold a high proportion of publicly traded shares, and given the public scrutiny such disclosure requirements invite, these investors may be encouraged to exercise their power as shareholders in a socially responsible way. This focus on investors is part of the government's efforts to encourage voluntary engagement in 'socially responsible investing' (which has its own acronym,

---

[43] See Wheeler, *Corporations and the Third Way*, p. 36.
[44] Department of Trade and Industry, *Modern Law for a Competitive Economy: Final Report:* vol. I (2001), para. 1.13, quoted by Robert Goddard, "Modernising Company Law': The Government's White Paper', *Modern Law Review* 66 (2003), 402.   -
[45] See Wheeler, *Corporations and the Third Way*, p. 53.
[46] See www.societyandbusiness.gov.uk/.
[47] Occupational Pension Schemes (Investment, and Assignment, Forfeiture, Bankruptcy etc.) (Amendment) Regulations 1999, SI 1999 No. 1849, reg. 11A(a) (amending Occupational Pension Schemes (Investment) Regulations 1996, SI 1996 No. 3127). The amendments were introduced pursuant to s. 35 of the Pensions Act 1995.
[48] Local Government Pension Scheme (Management and Investment of Funds) (Amendment) Regulations 1999, SI 1999 No. 3259 (amending Local Government Pension Scheme (Management and Investment of Funds) Regulations 1998, SI 1198 No. 1831). These regulations were issued pursuant to s. 7 of the Superannuation Act 1972.

SRI).[49] The government identified 'the enhancement of shareholder engagement and a long-term investment culture' as one of the four key objectives of its Company Law Reform Bill, introduced to the Houses of Parliament in November 2005[50] and passed into law in November 2006 as the Companies Act 2006. The Act includes a section which gives the government authority to require institutional investors to disclose how they have exercised their voting rights on resolutions tabled at company meetings.[51]

The Companies Act 2006 is the end product of a lengthy and comprehensive Company Law Review (CLR) launched by the government in March 1998.[52] Although carried out under the auspices of the DTI, much of the work was undertaken by an independent Steering Group consisting of lawyers, academics, business representatives and civil servants. The Steering Group was guided by a larger consultative committee which included representatives from the Trades Union Congress (TUC), and utilised several Working Groups in investigating specific issues of company law and governance. Upon completion of the CLR the government issued an initial, partial response in the form of a White Paper in

---

[49] SRI investing has strong religious roots. In the mid-1700s, John Wesley, the founder of Methodism, noted that the use of money was the second most important subject of New Testament teachings. As Quakers settled in North America, they refused to invest in weapons and slavery, a tradition that is echoed in more modern SRI strategies that avoid so-called 'sin' stocks – typically companies in the alcohol, tobacco and gaming industries. See Social Investment Forum, *2001 Report on Socially Responsible Investing Trends in the United States* (Washington, DC, 2001).

[50] The other key objectives of the Company Law Reform Bill are: ensuring better regulation and a 'Think Small First' approach; making it easier to set up and run a company; and providing flexibility for the future. The Bill was introduced to the House of Lords in November 2005 and brought forward to the House of Commons in May 2006. It received Royal Assent in November 2006 as the Companies Act 2006. It is the longest Act ever to have been passed by Parliament as it repeals, and restates in plain English, almost all of the current Companies Acts, which it largely replaces.

[51] The government's preference is for disclosure to be made on a voluntary basis, but s. 1277 of the Companies Act 2006 provides a reserve power to compel disclosure should a voluntary disclosure regime fail to deliver. See Joanna Gray, 'New Company Law Reform Bill: Power to Order Greater Disclosure of Exercise of Voting Rights by Institutional Investors', *Journal of Financial Regulation and Compliance* 14 (2006), 122.

[52] For an overview, see John De Lacy (ed.), *The Reform of United Kingdom Company Law* (London: Cavendish, 2002); Goddard, 'Modernising Company Law'. Among the consultation documents resulting from the Review are *Modern Law for a Competitive Economy* (1998); *Modern Law for a Competitive Economy: The Strategic Framework* (1999); *Modern Law for a Competitive Economy: Developing the Framework* (2000); *Modern Law for a Competitive Economy: Completing the Structure* (2000); *Modern Law for a Competitive Economy: Final Report:* Vols. I and II (2001).

July 2002 and, following further consultations, a final White Paper, published in March 2005.[53] This latter document contained draft clauses that formed the bulk of the first printing of the Company Law Reform Bill.[54]

From the outset of the review process, the CLR Steering Group indicated that it would not consider fundamental changes to the Anglo-American model of corporate governance:

> We interpret our terms of reference as requiring us to propose reforms which promote a competitive economy by facilitating the operations of companies so as to maximise wealth and welfare as a whole. We have not regarded it as our function to make proposals as to how such benefits should be shared or allocated between different participants in the economy on the grounds of fairness, social justice or any similar criteria.[55]

Moreover, the CLR Steering Group's Final Report and the government's subsequent White Papers all unambiguously endorse the principle of shareholder primacy, reflected in a key section in the Companies Act 2006, which states that 'a director of a company must act in the way he considers, in good faith, would be most likely to promote the success of the company for the benefit of its members [shareholders] as a whole'.[56] However, the section goes on to state that, to achieve this goal, directors should:

> have regard (amongst other matters) to:
>
> (a) the likely consequences of any decision in the long term
> (b) the interests of the company's employees
> (c) the need to foster the company's business relationships with suppliers, customers and others
> (d) the impact of the company's operations on the community and the environment.[57]

---

[53] Department of Trade and Industry, *Modernising Company Law* (July 2002) Cm 5553 – I, II; and, Department of Trade and Industry, *Company Law Reform* (March 2005) Cm 6456.

[54] For an overview of the main issues involved in the consultations on the government's White Papers, culminating in the publication of the Company Law Reform Bill, see House of Commons Library Research Paper 06/30, *The Company Law Reform Bill [HL]* [Bill 190 2005–2006] (2 June 2006).

[55] CLR Steering Group, *Modern Law for a Competitive Economy: The Strategic Framework* (1999), para. 2.5.

[56] Companies Act 2006, s. 172; Directors' general duties have hitherto been found only in case law. By introducing a statutory statement on directors' duties the government's intention is to make the law in this area more consistent and understandable.

[57] *ibid.*, s. 172: two further considerations to which directors should have regard are listed: '(e) the desirability of the company maintaining a reputation for high standards of business conduct, and (f) the need to act fairly as between members of the company.'

These additional considerations reflect the government's acceptance of the 'enlightened shareholder value' approach to company law reform, which assumes that a company's relationship with its stakeholders affects the returns to shareholders, and that it is therefore in shareholders' interests that directors take account of broader stakeholder concerns.[58]

Another CLR Steering Group proposal accepted by the government and incorporated in early drafts of the Company Law Reform Bill (but later discarded) was that all companies of significant economic size be required to produce an Operating and Financial Review (OFR) statement as part of their annual reports.[59] The OFR was envisaged as a forward-looking, qualitative statement concerning a company's performance and future prospects, that was intended to supplement the essentially quantitative and historic information that has long been disclosed. For the most part, the specific content of a company's OFR was to be left to the judgement of company directors,[60] but it was anticipated that any material information relevant to the company's various stakeholders would be included in the statement.[61] The government hoped that the OFR would further the interests of transparency and openness, and that over time the quality of the information disclosed to stakeholders and investors would improve without unduly burdening businesses.

Following extensive consultation, the statute requiring companies to produce an OFR was passed in March 2005[62] and clauses relating to the OFR were included in the Company Law Reform Bill published in early

---

[58] The government also considered, and rejected, an alternative approach identified by the CLR Steering Group – referred to as the 'pluralist' approach – in which the interests of a range of stakeholders are accommodated without the interests of a single group (shareholders) being overriding. See House of Commons Library Research Paper 06/30, p. 11.

[59] The 2002 White Paper indicates that companies of significant economic size are public companies where at least two of three criteria are met: the company's annual turnover is greater than £50 million; the company's balance sheet exceeds £25 million; or the company employs over five hundred people. Private companies can also be considered economically significant, but the criteria are more demanding: a turnover of over £500 million; a balance sheet total of over £250 million; or a work force of over five thousand employees. See DTI, *Modernising Company Law*, para. 4.36.

[60] The Steering Group did identify a few mandatory items that should be included in the OFR. See Saleem Sheikh, 'Company Law for the 21st Century: Part 2: Corporate Governance', *International Company and Commercial Law Review* 13 (2002), 88, at 92.

[61] See DTI, *Modernising Company Law*, para. 4.32.

[62] The Companies Act 1985 (Operating and Financial Review and Directors' Report etc.) Regulations 2005 (SI 2005 No. 1011). The OFR was due to come into force for the financial year ending on or after 31 March 2006.

November 2005.[63] However, the government suddenly decided to abandon the OFR in late November 2005. The surprise announcement was made by the Chancellor of the Exchequer, who cited as the reason for the U-turn the impending introduction, as part of the EU Accounts Modernisation Directive, of a new narrative reporting requirement called the Business Review, as part of the directors' report.[64] It was argued that the Business Review included the key improvements from the OFR but in a more flexible form, and that substituting the Business Review for the OFR would avoid 'gold plating' an EU regulation and help to reduce the regulatory burden on business. However, the Business Review makes no explicit references to the need for companies to report on social and community matters, unlike the OFR, nor does it require companies to declare their policies on social, environmental and employee issues.[65] Regulations repealing the original OFR regulations were introduced in December 2005,[66] and in subsequent parliamentary debates on the Company Law Reform Bill, government ministers found themselves in the uncomfortable position of arguing against legislation that they had promoted on previous occasions. The decision to scrap the OFR in favour of the 'lighter-touch' Business Review may thus signal a weakening of the government's enthusiasm to promote the 'business case' for CSR.

The government's CSR strategy may be viewed as an extension of a long-standing preference for disclosure regimes in company law, designed to facilitate market efficiency by improving information flows. As L. S. Sealy observed a generation ago, given the choice between 'having a fixed rule about something . . . and having no fixed rule as to what a company must do but saying that whatever it does has to be openly disclosed', UK policy-makers usually favour the latter option.[67] Consistent with this

---

[63] *Company Law Reform Bill [HL]* clauses 393–395.

[64] Directive 2003/51/EC of the European Parliament and of the Council of 18 June 2003 (OJ No. L178, 17 July 2003).

[65] See Julian Oram, 'The end of the OFR – and Corporate Responsibility? An Inadequate Approach', *Accountancy Age*, 12 January 2006. However, as pointed out by Timothy Copnall in 'The End of the OFR – and Corporate Responsibility? An Adequate Replacement', *Accountancy Age*, 12 January 2006, although the Business Review does not compel companies to report on employees, the environment, and on social and community issues, neither was there a blanket requirement for such disclosures in the OFR, as they were only required where necessary to enable shareholders to assess the success of strategies adopted by a company.

[66] The Companies Act 1985 (Operating and Financial Review) (Repeal) Regulations 2005 (SI 2005 No. 3442).

[67] L. S. Sealy, *Company Law and Commercial Reality* (London: Sweet and Maxwell, 1984), p. 21.

predilection, the Business Review does not require companies to act in a socially responsible manner but rather encourages them to disclose their CSR policies and activities.

The 'business case' for CSR, as discussed in Chapter 1, is straightforward: by pursuing policies and activities beneficial to society and the environment that go beyond the minimum standards of conduct required by the law, a company enhances its value, provided other stakeholders are aware of these policies and activities. Once information about a company's CSR policies and activities becomes widely available, 'caring' companies, it is believed, will benefit economically in the long term, and those with a reputation for the single-minded pursuit of shareholder value at the expense of other considerations ultimately will do less well as a result of this 'less enlightened' approach. As Robert Goddard observed, the validity of the government's contentions about the 'business case' for CSR is 'dependent on the effect that increased disclosure brings'.[68] To some extent, it is possible to measure this effect, and thereby test the validity of the voluntarism principle at the heart of the government's policy. The rise of socially responsible investing, and the creation of ethical funds and market indices to cater to socially responsible investors, makes it possible to compare the market performance of publicly traded companies perceived to be 'socially responsible' with that of 'less enlightened' companies. If CSR activities are value-creating, as the government's policy assumes, this should be reflected in the share price for companies with a good CSR record. The remainder of this chapter investigates whether there is empirical evidence that this is the case.

III. Doing well by doing good?

A. The rise of socially responsible investing and ethical funds

Even without formal disclosure requirements of the kind contemplated by the government, it was common by the second half of the 1990s for companies to include 'social responsibility' sections in their annual reports (which often were addressed to their 'stakeholders'). In part this was a response to the growth of 'socially responsible' investment strategies worldwide. This expansion was led by US investors: by 2001, one out of every eight dollars under professional management in the United States ($2.32 trillion out of $19.9 trillion) was invested in a portfolio utilising

[68] Goddard, 'Modernising Company Law', 418.

Table 1 *Growth in UK SRI Investment Assets 1997–2001*

	1997	1999	2001
	£bn	£bn	£bn
Church investors	12.5	14.0	13.0
SRI unit trusts	2.2	3.1	3.5
Charities	8.0	10.0	25.0
Pension funds	0.0	25.0	80.0
Insurance companies[1]	0.0	0.0	103.0
TOTAL	£22.7 bn	£52.2 bn	£224.5 bn

[1] *Note:* unit trust assets have been netted off from insurance totals.
Source: Russell Sparkes, *Socially Responsible Investment: A Global Revolution* (London: John Wiley & Sons, 2002).

an SRI strategy.[69] In the United Kingdom, SRI evolved from an activity carried out largely by church-based investors and a few ethical unit trusts to one that is now a mainstream activity among institutional investors (see Table 1). SRI assets under management in the United Kingdom grew from £22.7 billion in 1997 to £224.5 billion in 2001.[70]

Two major developments spurred the growth in the institutional SRI market in the United Kingdom: the disclosure requirements imposed on trustees of occupational pension schemes discussed above,[71] and the move by a number of insurance companies to apply SRI criteria across all their equity funds by actively engaging with companies through dialogue and voting at annual general meetings.[72] This form of shareholder activism, or 'engagement', seeks to protect shareholder value by integrating consideration of SRI issues into the mainstream corporate governance process. An alternative approach to socially responsible investing is to screen

[69] Social Investment Forum, *2001 Report on Socially Responsible Investing Trends in the United States* (Washington, DC: Social Investment Forum, 2001), p. 4.
[70] Russell Sparkes, *Socially Responsible Investment: A Global Revolution* (Chichester: John Wiley & Sons, 2002).
[71] See nn. 47–48 above.
[72] Further impetus to shareholder activism was provided in October 2002 by the launch of a new set of principles, *The Responsibilities of Institutional Shareholders and Agents – Statement of Principles*, drawn up by the Institutional Shareholders' Committee (ISC). This body comprises the Association of British Insurers (ABI), the Association of Investment Trust Companies (AITC), the Investment Management Association (IMA), and the National Association of Pension Funds (NAPF). It speaks for a membership that controls the vast majority of institutional funds in the United Kingdom.

Table 2 *Performance of UK Ethical Funds/Ecological Unit Trusts/OEICS*[1]

	£1,000 after 5 years[2]	% Return	£1,000 after 3 years[3]	% Return	£1,000 after 1 year[4]	% Return
Average for UK ethical/ ecological UT/OEICs	£745.66	−25.4	£661.98	−33.8	£793.84	−20.6
FTSE All Share (xd adj)	£803.66	−19.6	£711.24	−28.9	£824.16	−17.6
Average for All UK UT/OEICs	£908.50	−9.2	£739.53	−26.1	£830.61	−16.9

[1] Open-ended Investment companies.
[2] Showing how much an investment of £1,000 would be worth after 5 years (from 01.06.98 to 01.06.03) in each fund.
[3] Showing how much an investment of £1,000 would be worth after 3 years (from 01.06.00 to 01.06.03) in each fund.
[4] Showing how much an investment of £1,000 would be worth after 1 year (from 01.06.02 to 01.06.03) in each fund.
Source: Standard & Poor's Micropal, 4 June 2003.

companies included in investment portfolios on CSR grounds.[73] Screening is typically the method used by retail ethical funds.[74] The first ethical fund in the United Kingdom was a unit trust called the Stewardship Fund, launched by Friends Provident in 1984; now there are over seventy such funds.[75] Table 2 reveals that the average performance of these ethical funds between June 1998 and June 2003 was inferior to the performance of the UK stock market as a whole (represented by the FTSE All Share Index) and to non-ethical funds, whether measured as a one-year, three-year or five-year investment.

Advocates of ethical investing argue that, standing alone, these figures can be somewhat misleading. For example, it may be that lower returns to ethical funds simply reflect the fact that they incur higher risk than

[73] Screening is usually divided into 'negative' screening to exclude unacceptable shares from a portfolio and 'positive' screening to select companies with superior CSR performance.
[74] As the term is used here, a 'fund' is a portfolio (or collection) of assets, normally shares, that are typically professionally managed.
[75] Standard & Poor's Micropal, 4 June 2003.

unscreened funds because they are insufficiently diversified – the process of ethical screening limits the universe of investments that can be included within an 'ethical' portfolio. Several empirical studies have attempted to control for possible differences in risk associated with different classes of investments in order to determine whether investors value a company's good CSR reputation. Those studies – most of which have been based on US data, but a few of which have dealt with the performance of UK ethical funds – usually conclude that ethical screening leads to similar or slightly lower performance relative to comparable unrestricted portfolios, with any differences in the performance of ethically screened and unscreened portfolios usually found to be statistically insignificant.[76]

There are other difficulties with trying to draw conclusions about the investor response to CSR from studies involving ethical funds. One early UK study found that the companies whose shares are selected by ethical funds for investment tend to be smaller than those included in the market indices typically used for purposes of comparison.[77] When this size bias is adjusted for, the relative performance of ethical funds improves.[78] A number of US papers have also identified industry sector and investment

[76] See, e.g., J. D. Diltz, 'Does Social Screening Affect Portfolio Performance?', *The Journal of Investing* Spring (1995), 64–9; B. Guerard, 'Is There a Cost to Being Socially Responsible in Investing?', *The Journal of Investing* Summer (1997), 11–18; D. A. Sauer, 'The Impact of Social-Responsibility Screens on Investment Performance: Evidence from the Domini 400 Social Index and Domini Equity Mutual Fund', *Review of Financial Economics* 6 (1997), 137. Two studies comparing the returns of ethical and non-ethical US funds to each other, to the S&P 500, and to the Domini Social Index (DSI) (containing only ethically-screened companies), concluded that, after risk was adjusted by using Jensen's alpha (discussed below), there were no significant differences between the returns for ethical and non-ethical funds. S. Hamilton, H. Jo and M. Statman, 'Doing Well While Doing Good? The Investment Performance of Socially Responsible Mutual Funds', *Financial Analysts Journal* 49 (1993), 62; M. Statman, 'Socially Responsible Mutual Funds', *Financial Analysts Journal* May–June (2000), 30–9. A study using an extended sample of US ethical funds – including equity, bond and balanced funds – found that, after differences in risk were controlled by using Jensen's alpha and the Sharpe and Treynor ratios (see n. 105 below), there was no evidence that social screening affected the investment performance of ethical mutual funds in any systematic way. E. F. Goldreyer and J. D. Diltz, 'The Performance of Socially Responsible Mutual Funds: Incorporating Sociopolitical Information in Portfolio Selection', *Managerial Finance* 25 (1999), 23. One early UK study even found some weak evidence that ethical unit trusts outperformed market indices. See R. G Luther, J. Matatko and D. Corner, 'The Investment Performance of UK Ethical Unit Trusts', *Accounting, Auditing and Accountability Journal* 5 (1992), 57.

[77] Luther, Matatko and Corner, 'The Investment Performance of UK Ethical Unit Trusts'.

[78] One study, which confirmed this size bias, found that comparing ethical funds to a small cap benchmark improved their relative performance. See R. G. Luther and J. Matatko, 'The Performance of Ethical Unit Trusts: Choosing an Appropriate Benchmark', *British Accounting Review* 26 (1994), 77. Another study compared a sample of ethical and

'style' biases that can distort comparisons between ethical and conventional funds.[79] In addition, the performance of ethical funds is affected by management fees and transactions costs which are not uniform, and will reflect the ability of individual fund managers to make appropriate decisions concerning asset allocation, sector selection and security selections within each sector. Together, these confounding factors make it difficult to conclude that differences in the performance of ethical funds reflect the impact of SRI strategies on investment performance.[80]

On the other hand, by focusing on the performance of ethical *indices* rather than the performance of ethical *funds*, some of these difficulties can be minimised.[81] A stock market index, in essence, is a number based on a statistical compilation of the share prices of representative stocks. Indices are used by investors as tools for investment analysis, measuring performance, allocating assets and creating index-tracking investment funds. The rise of SRI encouraged the creation of market indices that take into account a company's social and environmental impact as well as the financial factors typically considered when decisions about inclusion in indices are made. Ethical indices represent well-diversified portfolios of screened stocks that are not subject (at least to the same degree) to the

---

non-ethical funds matched on the basis of fund size and formation date and found evidence that ethical mutual funds out-performed on a risk-adjusted basis. See C. A. Mallin, B. Saadouni and R. J. Briston, 'The Financial Performance of Ethical Investment Funds', *Journal of Business Finance and Accounting* 22 (1995), 483. Another study which adjusted for the small cap bias of ethical funds by using a more sophisticated benchmark model found no significant difference between the financial performance of ethical and non-ethical unit trusts. A. Gregory, J. Matatko and R. Luther, 'Ethical Unit Trust Financial Performance: Small Company Effects and Fund Size Effects', *Journal of Business Finance and Accounting* 24 (1997), 705.

[79] See, e.g., D. Di Bartolomeo, 'Explaining and Controlling The Returns on Socially Screened US Equity Portfolios', Presentation to New York Society of Security Analysts, 10 September 1996; Guerard, 'Is There a Cost to Being Socially Responsible in Investing?'; L. Kurtz, 'No Effect, or No Net Effects? Studies on Socially Responsible Investing', *The Journal of Investing* Winter (1997), 37–49. A paper by Bauer, *et al.* addressed this issue by investigating the investment styles of 103 German, UK and US ethical mutual funds and adjusting their performance for any style tilts. They found little evidence of significant differences in risk-adjusted returns between ethical and conventional funds for the 1990–2001 period after such adjustments. However, when they split their sample by time they found evidence of a 'learning effect' whereby older ethical funds catch up after a period of strong under-performance while younger funds continue to under-perform both the index and conventional peers. See Rob Bauer, Kees Koedijk and Rogér Otten, *International Evidence on Ethical Mutual Fund Performance and Investment Style*, Working Paper (2002).

[80] See, e.g., Sauer, 'The Impact of Social-Responsibility Screens on Investment Performance'.

[81] This argument was outlined by Sauer, 'The Impact of Social-Responsibility Screens on Investment Performance', 140.

confounding effects of small firm bias, differences in transaction costs and management 'style' biases that plague studies of ethical funds. A comparison of the performance of ethical indices with the performance of alternative benchmark portfolios could provide a better indication of the potential costs, or benefits, associated with CSR investment behaviour.

B. The FTSE4Good Indices

The oldest ethical index, dating from May 1990, is the Domini 400 Social Index, which monitors the performance of 400 US corporations that pass multiple, broad-based social screens. Other prominent indices used by US investors are the Dow-Jones Sustainability Group Index and the Calvert Social Index. The first indices of this type used in the United Kingdom were the FTSE4Good Index Series. Introduced by the FTSE Group[82] in February 2001 after several years of development, this series initially consisted of eight indices – four benchmark series used as yardsticks for performance measurements, and four tradable series upon which financial products based on their value can be bought and sold. The series allows investors to track the performance of SRI-screened companies in all major financial markets.[83] The FTSE4Good indices cover up to 90 per cent of the world's financial markets, giving investors an unrivalled level of exposure to companies meeting international CSR standards. The FTSE4Good Advisory Committee, consisting of independent experts, oversees the process of determining which companies should be included in the FTSE4Good indices. Company research is provided by the UK firm Ethical Investment Research Service (EIRIS) and its international partners. All the indices are managed and calculated by FTSE according to a published set of ground rules. Certain companies are excluded from the indices altogether because their core business is particularly controversial. Thus, tobacco companies, weapons manufacturers, owners or operators of nuclear power stations, companies involved in mining or processing uranium and companies involved in the production of nuclear weapons systems are ineligible for inclusion in the indices.[84]

---

[82] The FTSE Group, an outgrowth of a joint venture between the *Financial Times* and the London Stock Exchange formed in the 1930s, creates and manages a wide range of market indices. See ftse.com/About_Us/index.jsp.

[83] The series covers four markets – the United States, the United Kingdom, Europe and Global – and a benchmark and tradable index exists for each market covered.

[84] *FTSE 4Good Index Series Inclusion Criteria*, www.ftse.com/Indices/FTSE4Good_Index_Series/Downloads/FTSE4Good_Inclusion_Criteria_Brochure_Feb_06.pdf, p. 1.

The criteria for selecting companies for inclusion in the indices were devised after FTSE identified several common themes running through various statements concerning CSR issued by governmental bodies, non-governmental organisations and business groups.[85] The inclusion criteria are revised regularly and, as of 2006, were grouped under the following five headings: 'environmental'; 'social and stakeholder'; 'human rights'; 'supply chain and labour standards'; and 'countering bribery'.[86] Under the environmental criteria, companies are given an 'impact weighting' of low, medium or high, depending on the industry sector to which they belong: the higher the sector's potential environmental impact, the more demanding the policy, management and reporting criteria that must be met.[87] Under the social and stakeholder criteria, companies must meet at least two of seven indicators to qualify for inclusion.[88] Under the human rights criteria, companies are assessed on a sliding scale, with the most demanding requirements applied to companies in the 'global resource sector' (oil, gas, mining) because of their unique power to influence human rights practices in developing countries, with slightly less stringent standards applied to companies with significant involvement in 'countries of concern' because of their poor human rights records.[89]

The launch of the initial two FTSE4Good indices in July 2001 provoked immediate controversy. Environmental and human rights campaigners protested the inclusion of companies such as BP and questioned the stringency of FTSE's inclusion criteria. On the other hand, the CBI was critical of the potential damage caused to companies that failed to make the list. The exclusion of several leading companies, including Tesco, Marconi and the Royal Bank of Scotland, from the initial FTSE4Good indices attracted significant media attention. However, these companies

[85] FTSE indicated that it had considered, *inter alia*, the United Nations' Universal Declaration of Human Rights; the OECD *Guidelines for Multinational Enterprises*; the United Nations Global Compact; annual reports from Human Rights Watch and Amnesty International; the Ethical Trading Initiative; Social Accountability International; and the Fair Labour Association. See *ibid.*, pp. 5–7.

[86] *ibid.*, pp. 3–11. The first three categories have been used since the launch of the FTSE4Good index in 2001, while the supply chain and labour standards category was introduced in 2004–5 and the countering bribery category was introduced in 2005–6. See *ibid.*, p. 2.

[87] *ibid.*, p. 3.

[88] These criteria are: adopting an equal opportunities policy; adopting a Code of Ethics or Business Principles; providing evidence of equal opportunities systems; providing evidence of health and safety systems; providing evidence of training and employee development systems; providing evidence of systems designed to maintain good employee relations; and, participating in charitable or community support schemes. See *ibid.*, p. 4.

[89] *ibid.*, pp. 5–6.

and others that were initially excluded managed to get in when the Index was reviewed in September 2001. At the second review in March 2002, it was announced that another twenty-four companies had joined the FTSE4Good UK Index, and that index is now made up over three hundred companies, including scores of household names. The inclusive approach that FTSE has adopted has left the FTSE4Good indices open to criticism for not being ethical enough, despite the detailed criteria for admission FTSE has developed. Some of those who think of themselves as ethical investors probably would not want their money going anywhere near some of the oil, gas and drugs companies and high street banks included in the indices.

Notwithstanding the criticism the FTSE4Good indices have attracted, however, it remains true that some companies have been excluded from them. This allows some basis for comparison of the performance of the companies included in the FTSE4Good indices with the 'non-ethical' companies that have been excluded, which in turn allows some empirical testing of the 'business case' for CSR that is at the heart of the government's CSR policy. The results of the empirical tests we have run concerning the performance of the FTSE4Good indices are described in the sections that follow.

C. Absolute investment performance of the FTSE4Good indices

To assess the attractiveness of CSR-screened stocks to investors, we compared the performance of the two FTSE4Good indices created for the UK market (the FTSE4Good UK Index and the FTSE4Good UK 50 Index) with appropriate unrestricted benchmark indices (the FT All Share Index and the FTSE 100 Index respectively), and a hypothetical 'Sin Index' comprised of stocks excluded from the FTSE4Good indices.[90] The unrestricted benchmark indices are representative of the performance of the United Kingdom's publicly traded shares on average. However, there is considerable overlap between the companies included in the FTSE4Good indices and those comprising the benchmark market indices. For example, the FTSE4Good UK 50 Index contains half of the stocks that comprise the

---

[90] The use of a specially created 'Sin Index' was inspired by the 'Sindex' created by the UK magazine *Money Observer* to track the value of twenty-five FTSE 100 index companies initially excluded from the FTSE4Good UK index at its launch in July 2001, and by the US 'Vice Fund' launched on 30 August 2002 by MUTUALS.com, a Dallas-based money management firm.

FTSE 100 Index, as it was constructed so as to enable investors to gain exposure to the ethical stocks with the highest market values. Moreover, after the second review of the constituents of the FTSE4Good indices in March 2002, companies in the FTSE4Good UK Index represented 83 per cent of the FTSE All-Share Index. Thus, comparison of the FTSE4Good UK Index with the 'Sin Index' – a market value-weighted portfolio comprising the tobacco producers, weapons manufacturers, uranium extractors and nuclear power station operators excluded from FTSE's ethical indices[91] – may give a clearer indication of the relative merits of ethical versus non-ethical investment.

Although the FTSE4Good family of indices were only launched on 31 July 2001, it is possible to analyse the performance of the identical hypothetical indices back to 1 July 1996 (assuming the hypothetical indices include the same companies comprising the indices in July 2001).[92] Three time periods are examined. The first period extends from 1 July 1996 (by which time many companies were including CSR reports in their annual statements) to 1 June 2003. The second and third time periods represent a partitioning of the full data-set into two almost equal components; the later component contains the entire period in which the FTSE4Good indices have been in existence. Figure 1 depicts the value of £100 invested on 1 July 1996 in a portfolio tracking each index, assuming a notional 'buy-and-hold' investment strategy.

It is evident from Figure 1 that the 'Sin Index' was the worst performer in the earlier part of the investment time horizon, when the stock market was rising in what has now come to be recognised as a stock market 'bubble' fuelled by unrealistic optimism about the prospects for technology-based stocks, particularly those related to telecommunications and the internet.[93] When the bubble burst in early 2000 and markets began to slide; however, the Sin Index began to outperform the others and has ended up with the greatest value at the end of the investment period. Interestingly, the Sin Index performed the best – and the FTSE4Good UK Index performed the worst – in the period after the creation of

---

[91] Specifically, the Sin Index is constructed as a market value-weighted average of the return on three FTSE sector indices (Tobacco, Mining, and Aerospace & Defence) and on the nuclear power stock British Energy.

[92] Index values based on the initial index constituents are available on a backdated basis through Datastream, a company that provides 'Asset Performance Management' software and services.

[93] See generally Robert J. Shiller, *Irrational Exuberance* (Princeton, NJ: Princeton University Press, 2000).

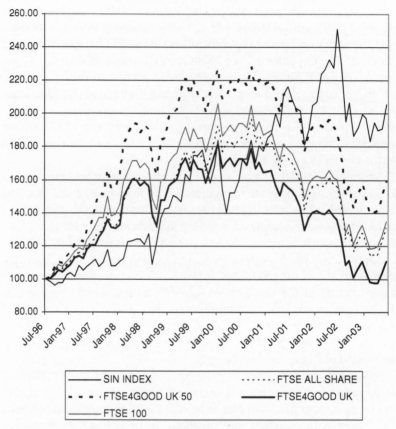

Fig. 1 *Investment value*

FTSE's ethical indices. Table 3 shows that an investment tracking the hypothetical FTSE4Good Index from July 1996 to the beginning of the new millennium would have yielded returns exceeding the value of the other indices, but by the middle of 2003 the Sin Index had appreciated to achieve the greatest value while the FTSE4Good Index had slumped to record the lowest value. This 'reversal of fortune' is not entirely surprising. 'Sin' stocks such as tobacco and defence have been amongst the UK stock market's best performers after the market peaked in early 2000.[94]

[94] For example, in 2002 the UK tobacco sector rose in value by 20 per cent compared to a 25 per cent fall in the FT All Share Index. See R. Miles, 'Fund closes as ethics lose lustre' *The Times*, 15 February 2003.

Table 3 *Value of £100 invested in a tracking fund in July 1996*

Date	SIN INDEX	FTSE4GOOD UK 50	FTSE 100	FTSE ALL SHARE	FTSE4GOOD UK
01.07.1996	£100.00	£100.00	£100.00	£100.00	£100.00
01.01.2000	£184.14	£227.27	£205.87	£192.52	£181.96
01.06.2003	£205.36	£159.42	£135.04	£131.17	£110.81

Tobacco companies are usually considered safe investments in bear markets because they have a reasonably safe and predictable profit flow, and defence companies have benefited from increased arms spending following the terrorist attacks on the United States on 11 September 2001. On the other hand, technology-based companies, which are more likely to be classified as socially responsible as they generally have the least impact on the environment, have been among the worst hit by the new century's stock market slump.[95]

D. Risk-adjusted performance of the FTSE4Good indices

Judging investments on their value alone can be misleading, however, because this does not take account of differences in risk associated with different investments.[96] The interaction between the risk associated with particular investments and the potential financial returns from those investments is a central preoccupation of financial economics. In this context, risk is a measure of the *variability* of an investment's performance, not an indication that the company will perform more poorly than low-risk investment options. To perform a risk-and-return analysis

[95] The lacklustre performance of FTSE4Good stocks is highlighted by the performance of the 'Sindex' created by *Money Observer* magazine (see n. 90 above). Over the twelve-month period to 4 April 2002, the stocks in this 'Sindex' outperformed the seventy-five companies that were included in the FTSE4Good UK Index by 13 per cent. This means that £100 invested in the Sindex would have grown to £108, while the seventy-five FTSE 100 companies included in the FTSE4Good Index fell in value to £95. Over the three-year period to 4 April 2002, £100 invested in the Sindex stocks would have grown to £106, while the 'Saints' would have shrunk to £90. See H. Connon, 'Sinners set to feel the heat', *The Guardian*, 28 May 2002.

[96] This has been a particular problem in assessing the performance of ethical funds, since the process of restricting the 'investment universe' (and the ability to diversify holdings) by using ethical criteria may result in a higher-risk portfolio.

of an investment's relative performance, it is first necessary to calculate the returns on the investment. For an individual company, returns are determined by aggregating the capital gain or loss with dividend income over a given period of time on a percentage basis (so that the performance measure taken can be assessed independent of the size of the investment in the company). For a group of companies, such as those included in a market index, a mean (or average) return ('MR') can be calculated. 'Variance' is a measure of the 'risk' associated with the investment; the greater the variability (or 'volatility'), the greater the risk. Variance is a statistical measure of the deviation of the actual returns ('AR') on the shares from the MR calculated over a time frame immediately before the period studied: one can visualise a graph with a time line in which ARs appear as a dispersion of dots plotted around a line representing the MR. Mathematically, the difference of each AR from the MR is squared,[97] and these squared deviations are added together and averaged. The square root of this average is the standard deviation – and taking the square root of the variance transforms the number into the same units as the returns being analysed.

When the mean monthly returns for the two FTSE4Good indices are compared with appropriate benchmark indices (see Table 4), we see that the average monthly return for the FTSE4Good UK Index is less than that for the FTSE All Share Index between 1 July 1996 and 1 June 2003, but that the average monthly return for the top fifty companies in the FTSE4Good UK Index over that period was greater than that of the top 100 UK companies (represented by the FTSE 100) (see Panel A). These observed differences, however, are not statistically significant – that is, there is insufficient evidence to reject the hypothesis that any observed differences are simply the result of chance.[98] Moreover, no statistically significant differences in monthly returns for the two sub-periods (1 July 1996 to 31 December

[97] They are squared so that the 'positive' and 'negative' deviations do not cancel each other out; all of the deviations are thereby converted into positive numbers.

[98] 'Statistical significance' has a specialised meaning among statisticians. Statistical evidence is usually used to test some hypothesis. For example, the hypothesis might be that the difference in the average monthly returns of the indices being compared is zero (the null hypothesis). Whenever the difference in actual returns differs from zero, this could simply be the product of chance. Statisticians will apply an appropriate statistical test to assess the probability of observing the data actually observed if the null hypothesis is true. The test will yield a 'significance level'; if the significance level is 0.10, for example, one would expect to observe data like that actually observed in one out of every ten times a measurement is taken, if the null hypothesis is indeed true. The smaller the significance level, the less likely it is that the sample came from the population studied assuming the null hypothesis to be true; if the significance level is large, one must conclude that there is insufficient

Table 4 *Mean monthly return and volatility comparison: FTSE4Good UK Index versus FTSE All Share Index and FTSE4Good UK 50 Index versus FTSE 100 Index*

	FTSE4Good UK	FTSE All Share	FTSE4Good UK 50	FTSE 100
Panel A: 1 July 1996 to 1 June 2003				
Mean monthly return	0.23%	0.44%	0.68%	0.48%
Standard deviation	4.71%	4.77%	4.94%	4.88%
Panel B: 1 July 1996 to 31 December 1999				
Mean monthly return	1.47%	1.59%	2.06%	1.77%
Standard deviation	4.29%	4.24%	4.75%	4.48%
Panel C: 1 January 2000 to 1 June 2003				
Mean monthly return	−0.97%	−0.68%	−0.66%	−0.77%
Standard deviation	4.83%	5.04%	4.80%	4.97%

1999 and 1 January 2000 to 1 June 2003) were observed (see Panels B and C). Similarly the observed differences in volatility (as measured by the standard deviation) for the three time periods studied were not statistically significant.[99] Given the large overlap of companies in the indices compared, these results are unsurprising.

Table 5 compares the risk and return of the 'Sin Index' with the two FTSE4Good indices. The mean returns earned by the 'sin' stocks are greater than the mean returns earned by the two FTSE4Good indices over the entire period and in period 2 (Panel C) but not in period 1 (Panel B). Although the significance levels for these results are lower than the findings displayed in Table 4 (indicating there is less of a probability that the observed differences were due to chance), none reach the level that financial economists consider statistically significant. In contrast, the stocks comprising the Sin Index are considerably more volatile than the

evidence against the null hypothesis for it to be rejected. It has been common practice for researchers in the physical and social sciences to refer to a significance level of 0.05 as 'statistically significant' because at this significance level there is a less than 5 per cent chance of erroneously rejecting the hypothesis being tested.

[99] For the statistically minded, a two-tailed t-test assuming unequal variance was used for the difference in mean monthly returns, yielding significance levels ranging from 0.7758 to 0.8973; and a two-tailed F-test assuming unequal variance of each sample was used for the difference in volatility, yielding significance levels ranging from 0.7100 to 0.9393.

Table 5 *Mean monthly return and volatility comparison: UK 'Sin Index' versus FTSE4Good UK indices*

	Sin Index	FTSE4Good UK	FTSE4Good UK 50
Panel A: 1 July 1996 to 1 June 2003			
Mean monthly return	1.06%	0.23%	0.68%
Significance level		0.3325	0.6651
Standard deviation	6.14%	4.71%	4.94%
Significance level		0.0171	0.0510
Panel B: 1 July 1996 to 31 December 1999			
Mean monthly return	1.42%	1.47%	2.06%
Significance level		0.9668	0.5737
Standard deviation	5.44%	4.29%	4.75%
Significance level		0.1384	0.3968
Panel C: 1 January 2000 to 1 June 2003			
Mean monthly return	0.71%	−0.97%	−0.66%
Significancę level		0.1971	0.2920
Standard deviation	6.80%	4.83%	4.80%
Significance level		0.0310	0.0284

stocks which comprise the FTSE4Good indices over the full period and also in period 2 (Panel C), and these findings are statistically significant. Again, these results are unsurprising in view of the shift in the dynamics of the stock market at the turn of the millennium discussed above.

Simple comparisons of raw mean monthly returns and standard deviations between the FTSE4Good indices, the Sin Index and the unrestricted benchmark portfolios ignores possible biases caused by the interaction between the shares included in the indices. The risk of a portfolio of shares depends not only upon the risk associated with individual shares included within the portfolio, but also on how the shares interact with one another. For example, a single set of macroeconomic factors could favour some industries represented in the portfolio and disfavour others. Therefore, it is desirable to examine the performance of the FTSE4Good indices and the Sin Index relative to their unrestricted benchmark portfolios using a commonly applied measure of portfolio performance which adjusts for risk, Jensen's *alpha*.[100] Jensen's *alpha* is ordinarily used to provide

---

[100] See M. Jensen, 'The Performance of Mutual Funds in the Period 1945–1964', *Journal of Finance* 23 (1968), 389.

a risk-adjusted measure of the performance of well-diversified portfolios, and the FTSE4Good indices are intended to provide well-diversified investment options for the 'ethical' investor. Investors in well-diversified portfolios are primarily concerned with their exposure to the investment risk which cannot be diversified away, known as 'market' or 'systematic' risk.[101] Jensen's *alpha* measures the actual return over and above what would be a fair return based upon the widely used capital asset pricing model (CAPM), which incorporates a coefficient (*beta*) to measure the portfolio's exposure to systematic risk.

Jensen's *alpha* is calculated as:

$$\alpha_p = r_{p,t} - [r_{f,t} + \beta_P(r_{m,t} - r_{f,t})]$$

where the term in brackets is the equation for the CAPM; $r_{p,t}$ is the monthly return to the portfolio studied; $r_{f,t}$ is the return earned by a risk-free asset (we use the monthly return to three-month UK Treasury Bills); $r_{m,t}$ is the average return earned by the market as a whole in the relevant time period; and β_p represents the CAPM *beta* coefficient, which is a measure of the portfolio's sensitivity to the stock market as a whole. In our study, the unrestricted FT All Share Index was selected as a proxy for the monthly return to the market portfolio ($r_{m,t}$) in deriving an *alpha* for the FTSE4Good UK Index and the Sin Index, while the FTSE 100 Index was selected as the market proxy for the smaller FTSE4Good UK 50 Index. A positive *alpha* implies superior investment performance relative to the market as a whole for a portfolio with the same market sensitivity (as reflected in the *beta*); a negative *alpha* implies substandard investment performance relative to the market for a portfolio with the same *beta*.

Table 6 summarises the Jensen *alpha* values obtained for the FTSE4Good indices and the Sin Index over the entire period and over the two sub-periods respectively.[102] Over the entire period from July 1996 to June 2003, the *alpha* for the FTSE4Good UK Index was negative and the

---

[101] The evidence suggests that an investment in a random sample of around 15 to 20 stocks eliminates most of the unique (or unsystematic) risk associated with an investment, leaving the investor with exposure to market-wide (or systematic) risk. See, e.g., M. Statman, 'How Many Stocks Make a Diversified Portfolio?', *Journal of Financial and Quantitative Analysis* 22 (1987), 353. The companies included in the FTSE4Good indices are not randomly selected, and thus it cannot be said with confidence that all unsystematic risk has been eliminated. Nonetheless, they consist of large numbers of companies of substantial size, and this significantly reduces unsystematic risk. The Sin Index, on the other hand, is less well-diversified.

[102] These values were obtained from an Ordinary Least Squares (OLS) regression of the sort commonly used to test hypotheses about the relationship between variables. The OLS model used was:

$$r_{p,t} - r_{f,t} = \alpha_p + \beta_P(r_{m,t} - r_{f,t}) + \varepsilon_{p,t}$$

Table 6 *Jensen's Alpha: FTSE4Good UK Index versus the FTSE All Share Index as the Market proxy; FTSE4Good UK 50 Index versus the FTSE 100 Index as the Market proxy; 'Sin Index' versus the FTSE All Share Index as the Market proxy*

	1 July 1996 to 1 June 2003		1 July 1996 to 31 Dec. 1999		1 Jan. 2000 to 1 June 2003	
	α_p	β_p	α_p	β_p	α_p	β_p
FTSE4Good UK						
	−0.0021	0.9575	−0.0007	0.9468	−0.0034**	0.9538
p-value	0.10		0.79		0.00	
FTSE4Good UK50						
	0.0020	0.9918	0.0025	1.0301	0.0006	0.9519
p-value	0.07		0.18		0.64	
'Sin Index'						
	0.0062	0.8604	0.0015	0.7033	0.0141*	1.0231
p-value	0.23		0.84		0.05	

Notes: The *p*-value gives the 'significance level'.
* denotes significant at the 5% level.
** denotes significant at the 1% level.

alpha for the FTSE4Good UK 50 Index was positive, but it cannot be comfortably assumed that these results were not the result of chance.[103] Similarly, the positive *alpha* observed for the Sin Index over the entire study period was not statistically significant. However, when the data are partitioned by time, both the negative *alpha* value obtained for the FTSE4Good

where $r_{f,t}$, $r_{m,t}$ and $r_{p,t}$ are respectively the monthly returns to three-month UK Treasury Bills, the relevant market proxy, and the particular index being studied. The OLS regression was of the excess returns of the index studied against excess returns of the appropriate benchmark index, with excess portfolio returns being defined as those returns obtained over and above the risk-free return (i.e. $r_{p,t} - r_{f,t}$).

[103] The *p*-value represents the significance level. See n. 98 above. The null hypothesis is that Jensen's *alpha* is zero. The significance level for the *alpha* value actually observed for the FTSE4Good UK Index was 0.10, indicating that one would expect to observe data like that actually observed once out of every ten times a measurement is taken, if the null hypothesis is true. Financial economists usually do not deem this significance level low enough to reject the null hypothesis with any confidence; typically, a significance level of 0.05 or lower is required to deem the result 'statistically significant'.

UK Index between 1 January 2000 and 1 June 2003 and the positive *alpha* value obtained for the Sin Index over the same period are statistically significant.[104] It is less clear whether these observed differences are *economically* significant: the results indicate that a well-diversified investor who notionally held a tracker fund tracking the FTSE4Good UK Index over the second period would have had a 0.34 per cent lower risk-adjusted return compared to an investment in an FT All Share Index-tracker, and an investor in a fund tracking the Sin Index would have enjoyed a risk-adjusted return of 1.41 per cent greater than that obtained through a market-tracker. It thus appears that there was a slight penalty suffered by investors who held stocks in the FTSE4Good UK Index in the period from 2000 onward and a somewhat greater reward for investors 'in sin' in the same period, which coincides with the bursting of the stock market bubble in March 2000.[105]

E. Summary of the empirical evidence

To date, most empirical assessments of socially responsible investment strategies have focused on the relative performance of retail ethical funds. In absolute terms, the average performance of such funds has been inferior to that of funds that are not ethically 'screened', and inferior to the stock market as a whole (see, for example, Table 2). The picture is not as discouraging when the measurements of the comparative performance of ethical

---

[104] Jensen's *alpha* for the FTSE4Good UK 50 Index returns are positive in value but insignificantly different from zero, regardless of the time period examined. This suggests that well-diversified investors who restrict their CSR investments to the top 50 CSR stocks did not suffer any adverse impact on their risk-adjusted returns when the FTSE 100 Index is used as the benchmark portfolio.

[105] A second statistical measure of the risk-adjusted performance of an investment is the Sharpe Index, which represents the average risk premium per unit of *total* risk (as opposed to just the systematic risk adjusted for by Jensen's *alpha*). See W. F. Sharpe, 'Mutual Fund Performance', *Journal of Business* 39 (1966), 119, and 'The Sharpe Ratio', *Journal of Portfolio Management* Fall (1994), 49. See also J. D. Jobson and B. Korkie, 'Performance Hypothesis Testing with the Sharpe and Treynor Measures', *Journal of Finance* 36 (1981), 888. Some argue that total risk is a better measure of risk for a socially responsible investor than systematic risk, because the use of CSR screens inadvertently subject investors to otherwise diversifiable risk because the 'investment universe' for them is restricted. The Sharpe Index is calculated as $(r_p - r_f)$ divided by σ_p, where r_p and r_f are the average monthly return to the portfolio and three-month UK Treasury Bills respectively, and σ_p is the standard deviation of monthly portfolio returns over the period in question. The Sharpe index values obtained for the data we have studied pointed in the same direction as the statistical results we have reported here, but none of the values were statistically significant.

funds are controlled for risk: in those studies, the evidence indicates that the performance of ethical funds is similar or slightly worse than that of unscreened portfolios, and that the evidence of weaker performance is not statistically significant.

These studies have limitations, however. Ethical funds typically are not well-diversified and are subject to the confounding effects of 'small firm' bias, differential transaction costs and management 'style' biases. The study described in this chapter largely overcomes these limitations by focusing on the relative performance of ethical indices rather than ethical funds, but the use of indices have limitations of their own. Most problematically, the FTSE4Good indices used in this study have been criticised for being insufficiently selective: as of March 2002 the criteria for inclusion in the FTSE4Good UK Index were satisfied by 83 per cent of the companies in the FTSE All-Share Index, and all of the companies in the FTSE4Good UK 50 Index were in the unscreened FTSE 100 Index. Nonetheless, some companies were excluded from the FTSE4Good indices, and a portfolio containing these companies (a 'Sin Index') provides some basis for comparison.

In absolute terms, a clear pattern is discernible: in the period before the March 2000 stock market crash, the FTSE4Good UK 50 Index (representing the largest companies satisfying the FTSE4Good inclusion criteria) outperformed the market while the FTSE4Good UK Index and Sin Index performed slightly worse than the market as a whole; and after the crash, the Sin Index outperformed the market by a large margin while the ethical indices underperformed the unrestricted market indices (see Figure 1 and Table 3). After adjustments are made for risk, the observed differences in performance of the various indices over the period from 1 July 1996 to 1 June 2003 are not statistically significant, but the better performance of the Sin Index and the weaker performance of the FTSE4Good UK Index after 1 January 2000 is statistically significant (if, perhaps, not particularly great in economic terms) (see Table 6).

In sum, the empirical evidence presented in this chapter concerning the relative performance of the FTSE4Good indices, used as a proxy for socially responsible investments, indicates that over the entire period of our study, the application of CSR screens did not necessarily result in higher volatility or reduced returns. Over the long term, investors would not have been penalised for choosing to invest in the stocks that comprise the FTSE4Good indices. On the other hand, there was no evidence that a good reputation for CSR enhanced a company's value on the stock market, either. There is also clear evidence that as investments 'sin' stocks are substantially more volatile than socially responsible investments and CSR-neutral investments. However, it appears that during bear markets, 'sin' pays: the relative returns of the Sin Index (both in absolute terms, and when adjusted for systematic risk) were much greater, and the relative returns of the ethical investments worse, when times were hard on the stock market. Between 1 January 2000 and 1 June 2003, there was a premium for 'sin' and a discount for 'virtue'.

IV. Conclusion

The central focus of the government's CSR strategy has been to place CSR within a model of the company as a profit-maximising entity. In this view, resources allocated by companies to environmentally benign conduct, enlightened employment policies, charitable giving and other socially worthy activities constitute investments in relationships with key stakeholders. Warm attitudes on the part of customers, suppliers, employees and regulators lead, it is claimed, to enhanced brand value, lower employee turnover, reduced risks of adverse government action and ultimately, to greater returns on investors' capital. In other words, charitable giving and regulatory over-compliance are inputs to the company's overall production process – applied, it can be supposed, at levels calibrated to maximise profits and shareholder returns. The dramatic growth of SRI in recent years indicates that there may be something to the argument that there is a market for corporate social responsibility.

Theories explaining CSR in terms of disguised profit maximisation, however, can generate testable hypotheses. Previous empirical studies of the comparative performance of 'ethical' and 'non-ethical' companies did not provide clear evidence that CSR improved a company's value in the stock market, but they did not clearly indicate that CSR activities hurt performance, either. While the results obtained in our study of the FTSE4Good ethical indices are similarly equivocal, in one respect they are not encouraging: they suggest that while companies recognised by FTSE as having a good CSR record (putting aside questions of whether this reputation was earned) did not fare worse than companies in the 'Sin Index' during bull markets, they were punished by investors when the markets turned bearish.

There are some caveats to keep in mind. FTSE has not been particularly selective in determining whether a company can be included in the FTSE4Good indices, giving rise to the criticism that our study has not compared 'truly' ethical companies with unethical ones, although the

strength of tobacco and defence industries in times of economic uncertainty provides little comfort to socially responsible investors. It is also
possible that the full effects of the government's disclosure strategy have
not been felt, and that once consumers and other stakeholders become
more aware of the CSR records of companies in the marketplace, a good
CSR reputation will have a more positive effect on company value. Our
study also does not take full account of the psychological benefits of the
government's CSR policy: arguably, if company executives are forced to
make CSR disclosure statements, they will internalise CSR considerations,
and this will subtly affect how they carry out their duties.

Nonetheless, the results obtained in our study at least cast doubt on the
vitality of the 'business case' for CSR, which in turn draws into question
the government's reliance on the interplay of voluntary action by company
executives and mandatory disclosure rules. It may be that the most direct
way to assure that companies meet social responsibilities is to impose
legally enforceable obligations through compulsory legislation. Certainly,
the results of our study do not support the abandonment of a strategy
to encourage voluntary CSR, but they do indicate that the benefits of
this approach may only be supplemental to a core strategy based around
mandatory regulation.

9

The board as a path toward corporate social responsibility

LAWRENCE E. MITCHELL

Academic prescriptions to ensure corporate social responsibility (CSR) as such have little hope of achieving significant change. CSR has become a widespread topic of conversation and scholarship over the past decade. But while codes of conduct, principles of investment, corporate codes of ethics and the like fill corporate boardrooms and spill off the presses, often with great fanfare, more often than not they reduce to so much sound and fury. CSR remains ill-defined, if defined at all, and proliferating precatory pronouncements are no better than the paper on which they are written. To the extent that corporations behave in a manner that would achieve consensus description as responsible, they do so for their own reasons and in the course of conducting their quotidian businesses.

At the same time, recent years have witnessed heightened interest in corporate governance from removing anti-takeover protections, featured prominently in the 1990s, to the financial performance of corporations following the collapse of Enron. More recent attacks have been focused on executive compensation and the right of shareholders to veto directors. In contrast to the activists and scholars promoting corporate social responsibility, the actors involved in this aspect of corporate agitation (including institutional investors, hedge funds, corporate governance activists, private equity firms, politicians and pundits) are interested in the financial well-being of shareholders. Unlike the CSR debate per se, the corporate governance debate does repay scholarly attention as a focus of social responsibility, defined as it is by the traditional parameters of corporate law and articulated within a well-developed framework of corporate fiduciary duties. Whereas CSR operates free-form and can seem either superfluous or threatening, corporate governance issues operate within well-defined and accepted structures.

By asserting that the debate over principles of CSR is likely to be fruit-less, I do not mean to suggest that it is an unimportant concern. Quite the contrary. It is precisely because it is so important that it needs to be treated as something central to the corporation's business, not as something the corporation does in addition to its business. Peter Drucker famously dis-tinguished between two kinds of social responsibility. The first deals with issues of social policy external to the corporation, that are decidedly not the business of the corporation (and that we who live in political democ-racies would not want the corporation to solve). The second are social problems created by the corporation itself in the course of its production of goods and services. These latter problems are undoubtedly the cor-poration's responsibility, if for no other reason than that the most basic principles of human behaviour require that we should clean up our own messes.

This latter understanding of CSR, in which management is to take responsibility for the consequences of corporate behaviour, is too impor-tant to be lost in broader arguments over corporate morality. The easier rejection of the latter could make it all too simple for corporate managers to reject the former as well. I have elsewhere argued that corporate direc-tors and managers have the same moral obligations and should exercise the same moral personhood in their corporate roles as in their ordinary lives, and I am not in any way shrinking from this position. My argument here is a more practical one, and is based upon the premise that managers will have a hard time accepting personal moral accountability for their corporate behaviour if they fail to accept the most fundamental notions of corporate responsibility. Facilitating good corporate citizenship is simply too important to insist on perfection.

It is for these reasons that I argue that the most likely way for proponents of CSR to achieve their goals is to recast their issues as issues of corporate governance. This is a position I have taken for years, but as corporate governance reform increasingly, at least in the United States, takes centre stage, issues of corporate responsibility *simpliciter* are easily pushed aside.[1] It is therefore important to talk in terms that will lead corporate decision-makers to listen. And that means talking about corporate responsibility in terms of corporate performance.

[1] Lawrence E. Mitchell, 'Cooperation and Constraint in the Modern Corporation: An Inquiry into the Causes of Corporate Immorality', *Texas Law Review* 73 (1994–1995), 477, 490–1; Lawrence E. Mitchell, 'A Critical Look at Corporate Governance', *Vanderbilt Law Review* 45 (1992), 1263, 1269–73; and Lawrence E. Mitchell, *Corporate Irresponsibility: America's Newest Export* (New Haven, CT: Yale University Press, 2001).

My argument, as developed in this chapter, is intuitive. Corporate management that looks to the best interests of the business over the long term will largely, if not completely, fulfill many of the goals of CSR. Indeed, as one scholar has written, American corporate governance at the height of American industrial dominance, the 1940s and 1950s, was a governance that privileged the interests of workers and customers, two of the principal targets of CSR concern.[2] It may be that expressing CSR concerns in the language of business itself has the potential to marginalise some issues. But these are, more often than not, likely to be the broader societal problems arising from modern corporate capitalism that fall into Drucker's first category. Management that keeps its own house in order, management that understands that running a successful and sustainable business requires it to behave in a manner that does not risk undermining its own legitimacy, is management that will run a corporation that, as a matter of course, will address most of the problems with which CSR is concerned.

How, then, can we guarantee that management keeps its own house in order and in so doing fulfils CSR goals? It is hardly enough to note that a corporation and its managers ought to look to the long term in order to fulfil its social obligations and leave it at that. If nothing else, we also need to understand the incentives and disincentives that affect whether managers are likely to look to the long term in their strategic, tactical and day-to-day operating decisions.[3] The legal structure of the large modern public corporation is particularly sensitive to the stock market and, increasingly over the last twenty-six years, the stock market has become a place to look only for short-term behaviour.[4]

Short-term market pressures can produce two contradictory responses in the boardroom; either the board can bend to the pressure, operating the corporation in the short term to satisfy the market by increasing current earnings and thus stock prices, or it can resist that pressure, weeding out the short-term traders, attracting long-term investors and educating shareholders to understand the benefits of long-term management. The particular approach a board will take will be a function not only of its own philosophy, but of the incentives it creates for its management and itself. Once a board has made its choice clear, we have every right to hold

---

[2] Jeffrey N. Gordon, 'Independent Directors and Stock Market Prices: The New Corporate Governance Paradigm' 59, 6 *Stanford Law Review* (2007, forthcoming).

[3] The constant search for profit guides corporations and their managers to short-term outlook and discourages responsible long-term accountability. Further discussion may be found in Mitchell, *Corporate Irresponsibility*.

[4] Mitchell, *Corporate Irresponsibility*, pp. 4–5, 52.

it accountable for its decisions, the consequences of those decisions and its responses to those consequences.

My argument thus far presumes that the board has a choice. And, of course, in a Kantian sense, if I may misuse Kant by personifying the board, it does. But the practical realities may be different. There is, for example, a huge gulf between Berkshire Hathaway, whose chairman controls the corporation's equity and its shareholders' votes, and Exxon Mobil Corporation – even though a majority of the shares of Exxon Mobil are owned by institutions. And even though institutions are sufficiently concentrated that they might vote in a way that resembles control, those institutions do, and should be expected to, behave very differently from Warren Buffett. Buffett is an individual, a human being, with a human sense of responsibility and clear identification with his corporation such that he is in a very real sense accountable for its actions. Moreover, he makes it publicly known that he stands accountable for his actions.[5] The money managers at Fidelity or the Californian Public Employees Retirement System (CalPERS) are largely unknown to the public and face their own business obligations and imperatives that will affect the way they vote their shares in Exxon Mobil. Buffett therefore has a choice in the free, Kantian sense. The choices facing the managers of Exxon Mobil and CalPERS are far more constrained.

Not only are the choices faced by the boards of large public corporations constrained in non-human ways, but the legal structure of the modern public corporation makes the board a particularly limited and ineffective institution.

The lynchpin concerns the ways in which both the structures of corporate law and the behaviour of the capital markets push corporate boards and officers (to whom I will refer to collectively as 'management') to run the corporation in the short-term interests of the shareholders. In the heyday of efficient capital markets theories, one who identified shareholder short-termism as a problem was a pariah, a voice in the wilderness – or perhaps both.[6] Five years after Enron, the Conference Board, among other business organisations, has finally acknowledged the problem of short-termism as a serious business issue, most recently in its April 2006

---

[5] Warren Buffett, 'Symposium: The Essays of Warren Buffett: Lessons for Corporate America', *Cardozo Law Review* 19 (1997), 5.

[6] Mitchell, 'A Critical Look at Corporate Governance', 1263. I remember a conversation in 1993 with an eminent corporate scholar to whom I voiced my concerns and received, in exchange, an offhand, 'I'm not worried about short-termism' – last I read his work, he is now!

report, *Revisiting Stock Market Short-Termism*.[7] While the multivariate pressures of the stock market, from price punishment for missed earnings estimates to institutional corporate governance proposals, push management to focus on stock price, the structure of corporate law permits the corporation to externalise the costs of short-term performance on the rest of society.[8] When this occurs, corporate irresponsibility follows.

I do not mean to suggest that particular types of irresponsible corporate behaviour – pollution, worker maltreatment, under-investment in research and development, poor quality production, accounting irregularities and the like – are exclusively caused by short-term management. But there can no longer be any question that it is a major factor. The job for those interested in stanching this externalisation, and perhaps reversing it, is to identify the pressure points in the corporate legal and financial structure most likely to be reached effectively and to be responsive to concerns generally articulated by those who advocate CSR.

The most obvious and, I think, perhaps the most effective pressure point is the board of directors. The board has been the corporate institution most roundly criticised by corporate governance activists in the wake of Enron, and is also the target of much of the CSR movement. To the extent that the board is the corporate organ that has most directly been subjected to stock market and institutional short-term pressures, it seems reasonable to believe that focusing CSR efforts on the board is the best method of achieving good results.

But the board is a particularly problematic institution. An examination of the history of the modern American board reveals that, far from ensuring corporate responsibility, the contemporary structure of the board and legal doctrines create disincentives for the board even to protect the shareholders, let alone anybody else. This is because the modern American board was designed to protect directors and managers from liability, not to function effectively. Protection was achieved by combining a minimalist model of board function with a singular focus on shareholders. When this reality is combined with short-term market pressures on the board, it is little wonder that the board fails to perform either for shareholders or other stakeholders. The answer is to insulate the board to some reasonable extent from market and institutional pressures. If we accomplish this result, we will have given the board the choice of how to manage its

---

[7] Matteo Tonello, *Revisiting Stock Market Short-Termism* (New York: The Conference Board, 2006).

[8] Mitchell, *Corporate Irresponsibility*, p. 6.

corporation and, in so doing, made it accountable for its decisions rather than shielding it from that accountability.

I will first discuss the development of the modern board model, the monitoring board, highlighting its implications for CSR. Following that discussion, I will briefly tell the parallel story of how broad economic and social developments grew from 1980 to reinforce the short-term, stockholder-centric nature of board governance. Then I will suggest several different types of reforms that would help break the resulting tight connection between the board and the stock market. Such devices as a revised capital gains tax structure, changes in board terms and the introduction of new accounting principles could go some way toward freeing the board from excessive market pressures, empowering it to function in the best interests of the corporation itself. In short, these reforms would restore meaningful board responsibility.[9]

I. Board reform and the beginning of modern corporate social responsibility

American legal and management scholarship paid very little attention to the role and function of the board of directors before the 1970s. In that earlier period, managerial control with boards comprised largely of insiders of some type was correctly presumed, and there was little apparent reason for concern as long as American corporations were profitable and growing.

The 1970s began a new era. That was a time when legal and social developments threatened the security of managers and directors.[10] Corporate governance, and particularly the role of the board, was on everybody's agenda.[11]

The combination of events that contributed to the atmosphere of crisis was both economic and political. Without the economic problems of that era, political issues would have received little attention. Without the political issues, board reform might not have been as readily embraced by corporate America.

---

[9] A more in-depth analysis of these reforms is discussed in Mitchell, *Corporate Irresponsibility*, pp. 157–61, 162–3, and 203–4.

[10] Roberta S. Karmel, 'The Independent Corporate Board: A Means to What End?', *George Washington Law Review* 52 (1984), 534, 539; Bryan F. Smith, 'Corporate Governance: A Director's View', *University of Miami Law Review* 37 (1983), 273, 276.

[11] Marshall L. Small, 'The Evolving Role of the Director in Corporate Governance', *Hastings Law Journal* 30 (1979), 1353; Melvin A. Eisenberg, 'The Modernization of Corporate Law: An Essay for Bill Cary', *University of Miami Law Review* 37 (1983), 187, 209–10.

The economic problems were dramatic. By the early 1970s, many corporations created during the conglomeration movement of the 1960s were beginning to falter, and the stock market reacted accordingly.[12] The multiplication of businesses in the new conglomerates created significant conflicts of interest for directors, and the overwhelming complexity of disparate and worldwide businesses made meaningful board governance all but impossible.[13] The impregnable Pennsylvania Railroad, once the nation's largest corporation, and itself a giant conglomerate, had gone bankrupt after merging with the New York Central without ever missing a dividend, and with this came a Securities and Exchange Commission (SEC) investigation into its causes, numerous suits against directors and the development of the securities class action.[14] A number of other bankruptcies and severe financial losses, brought on in part by recession, occurred, and with them the resignations or firings of some prominent chief executive officers (CEOs). Chrysler was in need of its eventual federal bailout, and even New York City faced bankruptcy.[15] An activist SEC, aided by the Second Circuit, had a string of successes in its attempt to make the securities laws into a body of federal corporate law with far more teeth than state law had presented.[16]

The economic mess provided an environment in which real and perceived abuses of corporate power received wide attention. The Watergate investigation's revelation of illegal corporate campaign contributions, followed by the SEC's discovery of corporate domestic and foreign bribery,

---

[12] Nader, Green and Seligman describe 1975 as 'a year of reckoning for a dozen major conglomerates'; Ralph Nader, Mark Green and Joel Seligman, *Taming the Giant Corporation* (New York: Norton & Company, 1976), p. 78.

[13] Richard J. Farrell and Robert W. Murphy, 'Comments on the Theme: Why Should Anyone Want to Be A Director?', *Business Law* 27 (1972), 7.

[14] *SEC Staff Study of the Financial Collapse of the Penn Central Co. – Summary* (1972–1973 Transfer Binder), Fed. Sec. L. Rep. (CCH) Par. 78,931 (1972). Numerous lawsuits resulted from the collapse of Penn Central, e.g. *In re Penn Central Transport* Co., 484 F 2d 1300 (3d Cir. 1973); *In re Penn Central Transport* Co., 452 F 2d 1107 (3d Cir. 1971); *SEC* v. *Penn Central Co.*, Fed. Sec. L. Rep. P 94, 527 (E. D. Pa. 2 May 1974). The securities class action first became a practical remedy for shareholders after 1966. J. Vernon Patrick, Jr, 'The Securities Class Action for Damages Comes of Age (1966–1974)', *Business Law* 29 (1974), 159.

[15] Senator William Proxmire, 'Quote, In Quotes', *New York Times*, 25 September 1988.

[16] *Escott* v. *BarChris Construction Corp.*, 283 F Supp. 643 (*SDNY* 1968). See also *Gould* v. *American–Hawaiian SS Co.*, 535 F 2d 761 (3rd Cir. 1976). *Securities and Exchange Commission* v. *Texas Gulf Sulphur*, 446 F 2d 1301 (2d Cir. 1971), *cert. den.* 404 *US* 1005 (1972).

A history of the SEC's attempts to federalise corporate law is told in Roberta S. Karmel, 'Realizing the Dream of William O. Douglas: The Securities and Exchange Commission Takes Charge of Corporate Governance', *Delaware Journal of Corporate Law* 30 (2005), 79.

diminished confidence in the integrity of corporate America and brought forth calls for reform.[17] Corporations' roles in providing material for the Vietnam War, like Dow's manufacture of napalm, opened another avenue of political attack. American corporations were praised for their efforts in ensuring victory in the century's major wars.[18] But those were popular wars and Vietnam was different. Industrial contributions to the military effort in a wildly unpopular war were not publicly separated from the political aspects of the war itself.[19] And the civil rights movement of the preceding decade unleashed criticisms of the large corporations' contributions to economic inequality and workplace injustice.[20] Shareholder proposals by activist groups advocating a variety of social causes were being thrust on corporations and litigated in court.[21]

These events not only created the atmosphere for reform, but they also suggested a particular type of reform. Outside directors had, by the early 1970s, come to constitute the majority of directors on most corporate boards. While outside directors first became a popular way of helping boards to insulate themselves from liability for conflict of interest transactions, they were now beginning to be envisioned as a way of ensuring responsibility to different corporate stakeholders.[22] Moreover, Congress itself was investigating the structure of corporate law with particular attention to the social purpose of the corporation and the role of the shareholder. This necessarily implicated questions of the role and function of the board and its responsibility for economic and social problems.[23] In

---

[17] The story is well-told in Joel Seligman, 'A Sheep in Wolf's Clothing: The American Law Institute Principles of Corporate Governance Project', *George Washington Law Review* 55, 2 (1987), 325, 333–6; Securities and Exchange Commission, *Report on Questionable and Illegal Corporate Payments and Practices* (1976). Karmel gives a less sympathetic account of the era; see Karmel, 'Realizing the Dream of William O. Douglas', 86–90.

[18] See George Wald, 'Corporate Responsibility for War Crimes', *New York Review of Books*, 2 July 1970, 4.

[19] *ibid.*

[20] Suits were brought against corporations under the Civil Rights Act of 1964 alleging racial discrimination in hiring and promotion practices, such as *Claiborne* v. *Ill. C. R.R.*, 583 F 2d 143 and *Marks* v. *Prattco, Inc.*, 607 F 2d 1153 (disapproved of in 1982 by *Knight* v. *Bogalusa*, 673 F 2d 759). These legal challenges to unjust corporate practices spurred feminist activists to launch similar suits opposing corporations' sex discrimination. See *Zambuto* v. *American Telephone and Telegraph Co.*, 544 F 2d 1333.

[21] E.g., *Medical Committee for Human Rights* v. *Securities and Exchange Commission* 432 F 2d 659 (1970).

[22] Victor Brudney, 'Panel Discussion', *University of Miami Law Review* 37 (1983), 319, 321.

[23] Hearings on Corporate Rights and Responsibilities Before the Senate Committee on Commerce, 94th Congress, 2nd Sess. (1976); The Role of the Shareholder in the Corporate World: Hearings Before the Subcommittee On Citizens and Shareholder Rights and Remedies of the Senate Committee On the Judiciary, 95th Congress, 1st Sess. (1977).

1971, Myles Mace published his famous study demonstrating the almost complete passivity of corporate boards.[24] All of these developments put increasing pressure on boards to figure out how to avoid liability. Despite the broad acknowledgement that outside directors could be of some benefit, questions arose as to what the specific function of the outsiders was to be.[25] The first question that had to be asked was, what was the board as a whole expected to do?

Thus, board reform became an important subject of discussion for the first time in American history.[26] But, as Mel Eisenberg pointed out, most reform proposals began with 'the received legal model of the board', that is, the board as manager.[27] And the variety of proposals demonstrates that this idea of board as manager retained a strong hold on the legal imagination, as Eisenberg classifies them into 'those calling for professional directors; those calling for full-time directors; and those calling for fully-staffed boards'.[28]

II. Board reform and the start of modern corporate social responsibility

While originating in an atmosphere of economic crisis, the move to board reform was also an attempt to break managerial control of American corporations in order to ensure their greater political and social accountability. Perhaps the high point of the drive for social reform through board reform is Nader, Green, and Seligman's 1976 book, *Taming the Giant*

---

[24] Myles Mace, *Directors, Myth and Reality* (Boston, MA: Division of Research, Graduate School of Business Administration, Harvard University, 1971).

[25] Cyril Moscow, 'The Independent Director', *Business Law* 28 (1972), 9; Noyes E. Leech and Robert H. Mundheim, 'The Outside Director of the Publicly Held Corporation', *Business Law* 31 (1976), 1799. It was this increase (or recognition of the increase) in the number of outside directors that led the Committee on Corporate Laws to amend section 35 of the Model Business Corporation Act in 1974 to move to a monitoring model of the board. Committee on Corporate Laws of the Section of Corporation, Banking, and Business Law of the American Bar Association, Model Business Corporation Act (with revisions through 1974) 143 (1974). By 1973, according to data published by the Conference Board and the American Society of Corporate Secretaries, 77 per cent of 855 corporations surveyed had a majority of outside directors considering former or retired employees as such, and 62 per cent considering them as management directors. By 1977, the data were 84 per cent and 66 per cent (*Guidebook*, Appendix C).

[26] Indeed Brudney, who observed in 1982 that 'Lawyers, both academic and practicing, have long been concerned with the function of the board' cites literature almost exclusively from the 1970s to support his claim. Brudney, 'Panel Discussion', 603.

[27] Eisenberg, 'The Modernization of Corporate Law', 187, 209–10.   [28] *ibid.*, 149.

Corporation.[29] *Taming the Giant Corporation* captured the deep fear of insulated corporate power that characterised the social moment.[30] The authors shaped their reform suggestions to reflect the extent of corporate power by describing a board composed of representatives from all corporate constituencies and working in the overall public interest.[31] Breaking corporate power over the powerless, or at least redirecting that power to help the powerless, was their goal. Management uncontrolled was management running the country. And management operating in its own interest and that of capital, protected by plutocratic boards, created a particularly worrisome vision of American society.[32]

In the end, the board was reformed. But the shape of reform was not political. It did not result in stakeholder directors or labour representatives or the imposition of environmental and other responsibilities on the board. It did not result in a new vision of the role and purpose of the corporation in modern society. Reform was, instead, highly conservative. While it appeared to respond to concerns about concentrated and unassailable managerial power, reform was structural and internal in a way that could only indirectly be responsive to political concerns.[33] And it was reform embraced by corporate America precisely because it was reform that restructured the board in a way that would protect the board and management from liability.[34] Among the ways it did this was to sharpen the board's focus on the shareholders.[35]

III. The development of the monitoring board

At the height of the 1970s social and economic agitation, Mel Eisenberg published *The Structure of the Corporation,* based on a series of scholarly

---

[29] Christopher Stone, *Where the Law Ends: The Social Control of Corporate Behavior* (New York: Harper & Row, 1975), while not as focused on governance, is another important contribution to the reform literature of the era.

[30] Nader, et al., *Taming the Giant Corporation,* pp. 76–7, quoting Anthony Sampson.

[31] *ibid.,* pp. 120–2. For a more moderate exploration of the social responsibilities of business and a description of a board model to accompany it, see William R. Dill (ed.), *Corporate Governance in America:* Fifty-fourth American Assembly, 13–16 April 1978, Arden House, Harriman, New York.

[32] *ibid.,* p. 76.

[33] John C. Coffee, Jr, 'Beyond the Shut-Eyed Sentry: Toward a Theoretical View of Corporate Misconduct and an Effective Legal Response', *Virginia Law Review* 63 (1977), 1099, 1111–12.

[34] Marcel Kahan, 'The Limited Significance of Norms for Corporate Governance', *University of Pennsylvania Law Review* 149 (2001), 1869, 1880.

[35] Margaret M. Blair, 'Reforming Corporate Governance: What History Can Teach Us', *Berkeley Business Law Journal* 1 (2004), 1, 28–31.

articles he had been writing since the late 1960s. Eisenberg presented the first coherent description and defence of the monitoring board as the appropriate description of the board's function,[36] and *The Structure of the Corporation* became the blueprint for board reform.

Eisenberg studied each of the various possible roles of the board and the structural models that accompanied them – professional directors, full-time directors and fully staffed boards. By a process of elimination, he concluded that the board was, for reasons of time, resources and other practicalities, incapable of performing any of the functions attributed to it by these different models.[37] All that the board could do practically was to hire and fire the chief executive and monitor his performance.[38] These are the functions he targeted for reform by describing a new model of oversight boards with adequate information to perform their tasks. In other words, having eliminated all other possible functions of the board, Eisenberg was left with the monitoring model.[39]

Eisenberg does note that the board is the only corporate organ that can perform the monitoring function (with a similar observation made roughly contemporaneously in financial economics by Jensen and Meckling).[40] Thus, there is a strong normative component to the monitoring model.[41] Monitoring might be all the board could do, but if it was a necessary corporate function and the board was uniquely equipped to perform it, then the board ought to do it.

In order for the monitoring board to work as the reform that Eisenberg planned, the board needed the kind of true independence from management that would provide for serious monitoring. Thus he concludes with a normative recommendation. Legal rules must, 'to the extent possible: (1) make the board independent of the executives whose performance is being monitored; and (2) assure a flow of, or at least a capability for acquiring, adequate and objective information on the executives'

---

[36] M. Eisenberg, *The Structure of the Corporation: A Legal Analysis* (Boston, MA: Little, Brown, 1976). Eisenberg based the book on an earlier set of law review articles including 'Legal Models of Management Structure in the Modern Corporation: Officers, Directors, and Accountants', *California Law Review* 63 (1975), 375. Harvey Goldschmid had also described the monitoring board in a speech given in 1973. Harvey J. Goldschmid, 'The Greening of the Board Room: Reflections on Corporate Responsibility', *Columbia Journal of Law and Social Problems* 10 (1973), 17, 24–5.

[37] Eisenberg, *The Structure of the Corporation*, pp. 156–70.

[38] *ibid.*, pp. 147–8.   [39] *ibid.*, p. 170.

[40] Michael C. Jensen and William H. Meckling, 'Theory of the Firm: Managerial Behavior, Agency Costs, and Ownership Structure', *Journal of Financial Economics* 3 (1976), 305; see also Eugene Fama, 'Agency Problems and the Theory of the Firm', *Journal of Political Economics* 88 (1980), 288.

[41] Eisenberg, *The Structure of the Corporation*, pp. 316–20.

performance'.[42] Had Eisenberg's suggestions been fully adopted, with a substantially independent and adequately informed board, the monitoring board might well have developed with a meaningful function, broad perspective and substantial discretion.[43] Instead, businesses and their lawyers hijacked the model, embracing its structure without its substance. They turned it into a shell of what Eisenberg had imagined – and a very protective shell at that.[44] Eisenberg's reform effort was sandbagged by America's corporate bar during the 1980s when the model received its only real chance for implementation, in the American Law Institute (ALI) *Principles of Corporate Governance*.

IV. The monitoring board as liability shield

Three highly influential groups embraced the monitoring model in different ways and with different emphases in the late 1970s. But despite their differences, the American Bar Association (ABA), the Conference Board and the Business Roundtable all understood how the structure of the monitoring model could be used to protect directors from serious threats of legal liability. And part of that protection was to emphasise the board's focus on shareholders.

V. The American Bar Association's contribution – the Corporate Director's Guidebook: 1978 to 2004

Board reform didn't take the political direction reformers like Nader hoped for. But their agitation, along with the congressional investigation and other events I have described above, did create real concern in corporate boardrooms. The atmosphere created the possibility of new regulation. The fear this engendered in corporate boardrooms led business to organise pre-emptive strikes, launched in particular by three major organisations; the ABA, the Conference Board and the Business Roundtable. Each of these organisations embraced some form of the monitoring board and aimed its focus on the shareholders.

The ABA's publication of the first *Corporate Director's Guidebook* in 1976,[45] with the revised edition published in 1978,[46] was a major salvo

---

[42] *ibid.*
[43] American Law Institute, *Principles of Corporate Governance: Analysis and Recommendations* (Philadelphia, PA: American Law Institute Publishers, 1994).
[44] Kahan, 'The Limited Significance of Norms', 1879–80.
[45] ABA, 'Corporate Director's Guidebook', *Business Law* 32 (1976), 5.
[46] 'Corporate Director's Guidebook', *Business Law* 33 (1978), 1595.

and placed the ABA's imprimatur on the monitoring board aimed at shareholders as the best board model.

It is clear in the 1978 edition that the *Guidebook* was in large part a response to directorial fears of liability. The Introduction notes that: 'As a general observation, it is believed that directors who act within the framework of conduct outlined in this *Guidebook* will not only be performing their directorial functions competently, but will also be reducing the risk of being charged with deficient individual performance as a director.'[47] The *Guidebook* was a guide to avoiding liability. The ABA was attempting to use its powerful influence to create a safe harbour for directorial behaviour.[48] And that safe harbour was the monitoring board and its relatively light directorial responsibilities.

Among its many functions, the *Guidebook* took upon itself the task of presenting a 'proposed model' for corporate governance, taking account of 'current concerns in areas of public policy and emerging trends of corporate governance'.[49] Even a casual reading of the *Guidebook* makes it clear beyond question that the monitoring model is the model it endorses.[50] Directors are to 'review and confirm basic corporate objectives', as well as select and monitor the CEO and senior management.

As I noted earlier, the monitoring model by itself might well have been harmless and perhaps even an improvement in corporate governance. But the monitoring model described by the *Guidebook* had significant implications for the subsequent development of American corporate capitalism and corporate behaviour, implications contained and reflected in its single focus. That focus also made it abundantly clear that the ABA was rejecting the political and social reform that was a large part of public concern:

---

[47] *ibid.*, 1597.   [48] *ibid.*

[49] There never was, nor is there, any model of the board prescribed by statute. To the extent the law prescribes a model of the board it can be inferred from the duty of care. Brudney, in 1982, noted that 'courts have not yet formally addressed the distinction between a duty to manage and a duty to monitor in assessing whether the common law duty of care has been met' (Brudney, 'Panel Discussion', 632). One could argue that the Delaware Supreme Court's opinion in *Graham* v. *Allis-Chalmers*, 188 A 2d 125 (1963), while it long antedated the concept of the monitoring board, did just that. Certainly it has been argued that Chancellor Allen's opinion *In re Caremark International Inc. Derivative Litigation*, 698 A 2d 959 (1996), has the potential to establish a duty to monitor, at least in terms of requiring effective information systems in a corporation operating within a regulated industry. This requirement appears in almost all of the descriptions of the monitoring board.

[50] David Ruder, 'Panel Discussion', *University of Miami Law Review* 37 (1983), 336 ('I was on the committee that drafted the Corporate Director's Guidebook, and I agree with you that the monitoring model was part of the Corporate Director's Guidebook').

> It is important to emphasize that the role of the director is to monitor, in an environment of loyal but independent oversight, the conduct of the business and affairs of the corporation on behalf of those who invest in the corporation. The director should not be perceived as, or perceive himself as, a representative of any other constituency, either private or public. Were the role of any director – whether management or non-management – to be otherwise, profound changes would be required in defining the director's rights and obligations in a variety of contexts.[51]

And there it all is. The monitoring model was the ideal. And the social role of the corporation was clear. Shareholders, and shareholders alone, were to be the objects of directors' concern.[52]

The 1994 edition of the *Guidebook* acknowledges that 'a lot has happened and continues to happen, in the corporate governance world since 1978', justifying a revision of the *Guidebook*.[53] But while the takeover decade had passed, the ALI had adopted its *Principles of Corporate Governance*, institutional investors were beginning to arise from their slumber, and the savings and loan crisis and insider trading scandals of the 1980s were history, the ABA found itself in a position to declare victory in the revised edition. No longer was it modest about its adoption of the monitoring board.

> We deleted the 'proposed model' of the board of a publicly held corporation for two reasons: first, much of this material is now found in the discussion of the structure of the board and its committees; and second, developments in applicable law have removed much of the need for the tentativeness reflected in the concept of a model.[54]

The monitoring board was an accomplished fact. Its shareholder focus was assumed, and the Delaware courts had done their best to reinforce that focus in cases like *Revlon* v. *MacAndrews & Forbes*.[55]

---

[51] Guidebook, 1621.

[52] While the phrase 'those who invest in the corporation' as the sole constituent is ambiguous, it clearly contemplates shareholders. While it is possible that the language could include creditors, that interpretation is improbable given the modern position of creditors in corporate law.

[53] 'Corporate Director's Guidebook, 1994 Edition', *Business Law* 49 (1994), 1247.

[54] *ibid.*, 1248.

[55] *Revlon, Inc.* v. *MacAndrews & Forbes Holdings, Inc.*, 506 A 2d 173 (Delaware Supreme Court, 1986).

Although there was a 2001 revision of the *Guidebook*, the final interesting ABA document is the *Guidebook* revision of 2004.[56] The reason for revision was obvious:

> Since the publication of the third edition, the stunning failures of several prominent US corporations, and the disclosure of abuses of office by some of their senior executives, have led to widespread public concerns about the role and responsibilities of corporate directors . . . The public belief that good corporate governance could have prevented these corporate failures has resulted in a new reality in which corporations perceived not to have good corporate governance will be penalized in the marketplace.[57]

Left unsaid, of course, was that in this new era, penalisation in the marketplace also meant penalisation in the boardroom and the executive suite. The director-protective monitoring board needed some reconsideration.

What was that reconsideration? Not much, except for a strikingly clearer definition of the director's role: 'As a general matter, a business corporation's core objective in conducting its business activities is to create and increase shareholder value.'[58] And monitoring was still the mode of behaviour.[59]

Thus, the monitoring model proposed and refined by the ABA, begun in a climate of political agitation and directorial fear, and most recently revised in a similar climate, specifies relatively minimal duties for directors which, if minimally performed, will allow them to avoid liability.[60] Reform agitation which would recast the board in a way that would make its social responsibilities commensurate with its social power led instead to an increasingly narrow focus on shareholders, at least in part in order to restrict the scope of directorial accountability and liability.[61] In the years between the adoption of the 1978 model up to and including the present, this monitoring board has performed its protective function admirably well and its shareholder-centric nature has continued to dominate.

The history and development of the *Guidebook* is revealing. But there were other significant discussions surrounding the new monitoring model and its focus. The Conference Board and The Business Roundtable endorsed it in the late 1970s, and for the same reason – fear.[62] Again,

---

[56] 'Corporate Director's Guidebook, Fourth Edition', *Business Law* 59 (2004), 1057, 1058.
[57] *ibid.*, 1060.   [58] *ibid.*, 1063.   [59] *ibid.*, 1064.   [60] Guidebook, 27–9.
[61] *ibid.*, 27.   [62] *ibid.*, 27–9.

their reasons for favouring the monitoring board seem clearly aimed at liability protection.[63]

The Conference Board had long paid attention to boards, but its modern contribution began in 1967 with its publication of *Corporate Directorship Practices*.[64] The Conference Board reported that by 1953 a majority of manufacturing companies had a majority of outside directors, growing to 63 per cent by the time of the Report. Nonetheless, the function of these directors – as, indeed, the function of all directors – remained a question. It was clear on one level that the function of outside directors was to sanitise conflict of interest transactions.[65] But, beyond that, they had no particular purpose other than to ratify management's decisions. What else they might do, if anything, was uncertain.[66]

The Report directly confronts the issue, noting that 'it is difficult, if not impossible, to delineate with precision the boundaries between the functions of the board of directors and those of corporate management'.[67] As a general matter, the Report describes the board's appropriate role as a cross between an advisory board and a monitoring board.[68]

By 1975, in a very different atmosphere, the Conference Board had revisited and modified its views. Interestingly, the Report begins not with the question of what the board should do, but to whom it is accountable, and that, unsurprisingly, is the shareholders.[69] This question, it states, is a necessary precondition to determining the board's role, and it is one we

---

[63] Sandra K. Miller, 'What Remedies Should Be Made Available to the Dissatisfied Participant in a Limited Liability Company', *American University Law Review* 44 (1994–95), 465, 495.

[64] National Industrial Conference Board and American Society of Corporate Secretaries, *Corporate Directorship Practices: Studies in Business Policy* No. 125 (1967).

[65] Lucian Ayre Bebchuk and Jesse M. Fried, 'Executive Compensation as an Agency Problem', *The Journal of Economic Perspectives* Summer (2003), 77.

[66] The reality of outsider dominated boards by the 1970s suggests that the outpouring of conversation about outside directors was more about their purpose than their need, although it is fair to say that there was considerable debate about their appropriate identity and the definition of outside directors.

[67] National Industrial Conference Board, *Corporate Directorship Practices*, p. 96.

[68] *ibid.*, p. 93.

[69] *ibid.* The report describes the legal duties of the board as 'to manage the company in the interests of the stockholders' (p. 109), at the same time that it acknowledges that directors 'have a responsibility to the company's employees, its customers, and to the general public, upon whose good will the well-being of the corporation depends. Failure to take cognizance of the responsibility to each of these four groups [including stockholders] can adversely affect the solvency of the corporation' (p. 93). There is little question of the stockholder-centric nature of this position, but it expresses that attitude in a way that, taken seriously, is not far from the position I advocate in this paper. The subsequent history of the development of stockholder valuism seriously has distorted this possibility.   .

have seen the ABA answer in the *Guidebook*, although rather more indi-rectly. The Report describes some sort of a monitoring board, although not quite as pure a one as Eisenberg's model, as its description leaves some significant managerial powers in the board itself.[70] For example, strate-gic planning remains a significant function of the board, a function that still rings of the board's managerial role that was in the process of being phased out.[71] Nonetheless, the Report can be seen as a serious attempt at giving greater specificity to the role of the board at a time when directors felt as if they were coming under increasing legal attack.

The Business Roundtable also provided its own significant endorse-ment of the monitoring board. Like the Conference Board and the ABA, the Business Roundtable began its own statement in fear.[72] 'Some unfor-tunate developments of the last few years have caused the U.S. business community to reexamine intensively board operations and procedures as well as board composition.'[73] The same liability environment that had prompted the ABA and the Conference Board to act also motivated the Business Roundtable.

It was motivated by fear, but adopted a tone of defiance. The *Statement* begins with a defence of the role of American business in our democracy. In a note on 'Corporate Legitimacy and Corporate Power', it states: 'We think it incontestable that the U.S. system has led to greater political free-dom, to better economic performance, and to more personal autonomy, than any other actual – as distinct from idealized – system with which it might be compared.'[74] Defending its members further, it briefly sum-marises the regulatory and competitive environments in which American corporations operated, noting the restraints they imposed on excessive or antisocial behaviour. While the Business Roundtable understood the legitimating effect these restraints created, it was not with unqualified enthusiasm: 'We enumerate all these legal, regulatory and political con-straints on U.S. business organizations with some mixed emotions because a number of them impose excessive and unnecessary costs – costs borne ultimately by the consuming public.'[75] Having asserted its own primacy and exculpation, having tied its own victimisation to that of the American public, it was ready for a substantive discussion of board reform.

That discussion was both more philosophical and considerably more defensive than the statements of the ABA and the Conference Board. Its

---

[70] *ibid.*, pp. 108–9.   [71] *ibid.*, pp. 94–5.
[72] The Business Roundtable, 'Statement on the Role and Composition of the Board of Direc-tors of the Large Publicly Owned Corporation', *Business Law* 33 (1978), 2083.
[73] *ibid.*, 2087.   [74] *ibid.*, 2089.   [75] *ibid.*, 2091.

general thrust was less one of board reform than of corporate legitimacy, defending the corporate enterprise in the atmosphere of legal and social onslaught that characterised the decade. Instead of defining the board's role in terms of what the directors were to do – although it did that as well – it defined the board's role in terms of who it was to serve. And to that question the answer was the same as the ABA's and the Conference Board's – the shareholders. It was this role that legitimated corporate management. The Business Roundtable's approach to protecting directors from increasing liability was to accept the inevitability of the monitoring board but to make sure that the focus of that board was crystal clear, thus also accomplishing the purpose of limiting the scope of director behaviour and thus liability.

Most important for my purposes, the Report also described the board's role in maintaining the corporation's 'social responsibility'. This was the board function perhaps most in keeping with the Business Roundtable's view of the board as legitimating corporate management. But that responsibility was narrow. Long-term profit maximisation that might indirectly benefit other constituents was legitimate, but the interests of the stockholders (and, interestingly, the employees) were first and foremost.[76] While this long-term approach could well be good for business, the Report cautioned, 'other groups affected by corporate activities cannot be placed on a plane with owners', shareholder proposals under Rule 14a-8 should be limited to business, and 'many of the social causes pursued by activist groups represent minority views rather than a prevailing consensus'.[77] More than the two other organisations, the Business Roundtable articulated a vision of corporate social responsibility in keeping with the view I present here, but its emphasis on the stockholders rather than the corporation itself helped to privilege the development of shareholder primacy.

The Business Roundtable bowed to the inevitability of outside directors, noting both the importance of experienced business people on boards and the significant diversification of board membership it had perceived to have already taken place. At the same time, it resoundingly rejected the idea of constituency directors or co-determination, perhaps with the recent publication of *Taming the Giant Corporation* in mind.[78]

Thus, the 1970s ended with substantial convergence by academics, lawyers and business people on a stockholder-centric version of the

---

[76] Mark J. Roe, 'Political Preconditions to Separating Ownership from Corporate Control', *Stanford Law Review* 53 (2000), 539, 542.
[77] *ibid.*, 2100.   [78] *ibid.*, 2105–6.

monitoring model as the dominant vision of board function. That happy state of agreement was about to be blown apart in the 1980s. The political and social atmosphere had rapidly changed and the chance for meaningful corporate reform evaporated. The Supreme Court decision in *Santa Fe* v. *Green*[79] and the election of Ronald Reagan in 1980 significantly diminished the immediate range of political possibilities.[80] It was in this new environment that the American Law Institute was to introduce its version of the monitoring board.

The *American Law Institute Principles of Corporate Governance* (the *Principles* or 'the project') did as much as anything to cement the monitoring board as the dominant model of board governance. But it did not do so until the controversy surrounding the *Principles* almost destroyed the monitoring board and, in the process, did destroy any notion that the monitoring board's visions should extend beyond shareholders. The ABA, the Conference Board and the Business Roundtable collectively did a *volte face* from their position in the 1970s to attack the very model they had unanimously promoted.

There were a number of reasons for the retreat, the most significant of which revolved around the *Principles'* attempt to define and specify the directors' duty of care in a way that neither courts nor legislatures had previously done. Moreover, while corporate groups had been willing to accept reform proposals during the agitation of the 1970s, the atmosphere following Reagan's election in 1980 was different: 'The ALI project was the only significant corporate governance initiative with any reform component remaining.'[81] With real pressure for reform out of the way, all criticism was focused on the one viable reform proposal, no matter how pallid.[82]

Also significant was the fact that the neo-classical, free-market model of the corporation had been developing and was now reaching maturity.[83] A

---

[79] *Sante Fe Industries, Inc.* v. *Green*, 430 US 462 (1977).

[80] By the time of publication of Elliott Weiss's 'Social Regulation of Business Activity: Reforming the Corporate Governance System to Resolve an Institutional Impasse', (*UCLA Law Review* 28 (1981), 343), the chances for political reform had more or less passed. Ronald Reagan had been elected president and the next decade for corporate law was to be centered on the work of lawyers employing the tools of neo-classical economics to make the case for a corporation more strongly grounded in the sanctity of private property. Jensen and Meckling's work had begun to have its influence; the new scripture for this movement was Frank Easterbrook and Daniel Fischel, *The Economic Structure of Corporate Law* (Cambridge, MA: Harvard University Press, 1991), p. 9.

[81] Seligman, 'A Sheep in Wolf's Clothing', 325, 359.   [82] *ibid.*

[83] Easterbrook and Fischel, *The Economic Structure of Corporate Law*, p. 9; Fama, 'Agency Problems', 288; Jensen and Meckling, 'Theory of the Firm'.

vision of the corporation, restrained in its behaviour principally by market mechanisms and able to operate with a freedom that would not be possible when constrained by law, had to be very attractive to business people. Moreover, the model itself led, almost inexorably, to the shareholders as the appropriate focus of the board's attention.[84] The evidence suggests that business groups had a keen awareness of this relatively new scholarship.[85] *Any* specification of director's functions or duties would have restricted this freedom. And now economics seemed to prove that any concern with stakeholders was misplaced.

The *Principles* also famously opened the way to a broader set of board concerns, as set forth in its famous section, 2.01. Although viewed in some quarters as radical, 2.01, with its direction to the board to focus on both the shareholder and the corporation itself, was rather conservative, harking back to the case that is mistakenly taken as the urtext on shareholder primacy, *Dodge* v. *Ford Motor Co.*[86] In light of the shareholder primacy doctrine articulated by the ABA, the Conference Board and the Business Roundtable in the 1970s, not to mention the new, neo-classical arguments for shareholder-centrism, section 2.01 nonetheless sounded like significant reform of the type called for by Nader. But the trouncing administered to the *Principles* by business and the bar led its authors to secure its passage at the expense of meaningful reform. The surrender is reflected in a comment to section 3.02 that first appears in *Tentative Draft 11*, published in 1991 and embodying the first significant changes to section 3.02 (which changes survive in the adopted *Principles*):

> Section 3.02 is intended as a statement of the rules that a court would adopt, giving full weight to all of the considerations (including the judicial precedents) that the courts deem it appropriate to weigh. Section 3.02 is not intended ... to enlarge the scope of a director's legal obligations and liability, the performance expected from directors to comply with the duty of care, or the role and accountability of directors concerning the corporation's compliance with law.[87]

---

[84] Dalia Tsuk Mitchell, 'Shareholders As Proxies: The Contours of Shareholder Democracy', *Washington and Lee Law Review*, 63, 4, (2006) 1503; Dalia Tsuk Mitchell, 'From Pluralism to Individualism: Berle and Means and 20th Century American Legal Thought', *Law and Social Inquiry* 30 (2005), 179.

[85] Seligman, 'A Sheep in Wolf's Clothing', 346–9; The Business Roundtable, 'Statement on the Role and Composition of the Board of Directors', 24, 29.

[86] 170 NW 668 (Mich. 1919).

[87] American Law Institute, Principles of Corporate Governance and Structure: Analysis and Recommendations, Tentative Draft No. 11, 110–11 (Philadelphia, PA: American Law Institute Publishers, 1991).

Section 3.02 was intended to clarify, not expand. It wasn't about reform at all. There was no need for anybody to be upset.

The new economic model of the firm, embraced by legal scholars and remodelled on a set of assumptions that gave rise to a strong statement of shareholder primacy, also made a significant contribution to cementing that model as dominant in American corporate capitalism.[88] The Delaware courts have firmly embraced the monitoring model in this minimalist form.[89]

VI. The broader context

While I have so far broadly described the historical context in which the monitoring model arose and the way in which it developed, the period of its refinement and growth was also an era in which social, economic and financial forces developed together to cement shareholder valuism – and a particularly short-term concept of shareholder valuism at that – as the dominant corporate norm. The 1980 election of Ronald Reagan as President of the United States marked a sharp break with the era of political and social turmoil that began with the Civil Rights movement in the early 1960s, worked its way through the Vietnam War, and ended in America's humiliation in the Iranian revolution.[90] It began an era of looking inward, of looking to new prosperity, of looking to ourselves as the constituency to serve.[91] Reviving a long-dead version of *laissez-faire* social thought, a version that had not been embraced by serious thinkers since the 1880s,[92] the American leadership preached a vision that by looking to maximise your own well-being, your own wealth, you not only would be serving yourself but would be creating more wealth for society as well.[93] The rebirth of an also long-dormant, crabbed form of neo-classical economics in financial and legal scholarship, educated

---

[88] Easterbrook and Fischel, *The Economic Structure of Corporate Law*, pp. 80–1.

[89] Lawrence E. Mitchell, *The Trouble with Boards*, The George Washington University Law School Public Law and Legal Theory Working Paper No. 159 (2005), available at ssrn.com/abstract = 801308.

[90] Philip G. Altbach and Robert Cohen, 'American Student Activism: The Post-Sixties Transformation', *The Journal of Higher Education* January (1990), 33–4.

[91] Leo P. Ribuffo, 'The Burdens of Contemporary History', *American Quarterly* Spring (1983), 11.

[92] Lawrence E. Mitchell, *The Speculation Economy: How Finance Triumphed Over Industry* (San Francisco: Berrett-Koehler, 2007 (forthcoming)).

[93] Graef S. Crystal, *In Search of Excess: The Overcompensation of American Executives* (New York: W. W. Norton, 1991), p. 42.

policy-makers and investors in the new creed.[94] Business leaders were among the last to embrace this notion, which for them meant looking only to the narrow interests of their shareholders – but economic events conspired to pressure them to accede.

The hostile takeover boom of the 1980s is too well known to sustain retelling. The important point to take from that era is that shareholders suddenly found themselves able to maximise the value of their investments in the short term, rather than having to invest and wait for the long term, through the medium of substantial premiums paid by bidders for their stock.[95] While there undoubtedly was some rationalisation of business after the failed conglomerate movement of the 1960s in the form of bust-up takeovers, it is more or less generally recognised that the imperative for the takeover movement was financial, not efficiency-oriented, at least if efficiency is considered to be managing the business for the long term.[96]

The potential of hostile takeovers did exert significant pressure on corporate management.[97] Corporations with share prices that lagged behind market expectations were prime takeover candidates.[98] The logical solution was clear; make sure stock prices rose. Thus the push toward short-term shareholder valuism began.

But that wasn't all. The 1980s were the growth spurt of institutional investors.[99] By the early 1990s, scholars, policy-makers and reformers were all calling for institutional investors to band together and play the active role in corporate governance that the widely dispersed shareholdings of small investors characterised by the Berle-Means corporation denied. Surely, it was argued, institutions largely had the same interests as other

---

[94] Ribuffo, 'The Burdens of Contemporary History', 11.

[95] Martin Lipton and Steven A. Rosenblum, 'A New System of Corporate Governance: The Quinquennial Election of Directors', *University of Chicago Law Review* 58 (1991), 187, 189.

[96] Sanjai Bhagat, Andrei Shleifer, Robert W. Vishny, Gregg Jarrel and Lawrence Summers, 'Hostile Takeovers in the 1980s: The Return to Corporate Specialization, Brookings paper on Economic Activity', *Microeconomics* (1990), 3–4.

[97] Stephen M. Bainbridge, *Corporation Law and Economics* (New York: Foundation Press, 2002), p. 228.

[98] Bengt Holmström and Steven N. Kaplan, 'Corporate Governance and Merger Activity in the United States: Making Sense of the 1980s and 1990s', *The Journal of Economic Perspectives* Spring (2001), 121.

[99] Michael Bradley, Cindy Schipani, Anant Sundaram and James Walsh, 'The Purposes and Accountability of the Corporation in Contemporary Society: Corporate Governance at a Crossroads', *Law and Contemporary Problems* 62, 3 (1999), 18.

shareholders, and any pressure that they could bring to bear on corporate management could only be for the good.[100]

The problem is that institutions had their own short-term pressures. In particular, their compensation systems were structured in a manner that rewarded fund managers for their quarterly performance. If the institutions – or those who managed them – were to use their power for anything, the natural financial incentive would be for them to use their power to increase their own compensation. And so they did.[101] While some reformers saw institutional activism as potentially producing better boards of directors and more responsible corporate governance, and others looked to institutions to pursue social responsibility concerns, the reality, from then until now, has been that institutions use their influence almost always in the service of short-term shareholder profit.[102] Proposals to eliminate classified boards, lift poison pills and otherwise make corporations more takeover-friendly were aimed at precisely this end.[103] And this was as true if the pressure came from the pension funds of the AFL–CIO[104] or TIAA–CREF[105] as if it came from mutual funds. Institutions harnessed their power in the pursuit of short-term profit, and it is in that pursuit they largely continue today.[106]

Compensation further became an issue in executive suites. In 1993, Congress prohibited corporations from deducting more than $1 million in cash compensation for any single employee.[107] The desired response was swift. Boards now began to compensate executives, and often themselves, in stock options, more often than not unrestricted as to exercise.[108] If compensation incentives were powerful for institutional fund managers, they were even more so for the corporate managers who had their hands on the corporate machinery.[109] Management began to bend toward the

---

[100] See Bengt Holmström and Steven N. Kaplan, *The State of US Corporate Governance: What's Right and What's Wrong?*, ECGI – Finance Working Paper No. 23/2003 (September 2003), available at ssrn.com/abstract = 441100.

[101] Bebchuk and Fried, 'Executive Compensation as an Agency Problem', 72.

[102] Kahan, 'The Limited Significance of Norms', 1878.

[103] Mitchell, *Corporate Irresponsibility*, p. 180.

[104] i.e. the American Federation of Labor and Congress of Industrial Organizations.

[105] i.e. the Teachers Insurance and Annuity Association – College Retirement Equities Fund.

[106] *ibid.*, pp. 176–8.

[107] In August 1993, Congress enacted the Omnibus Budget Reconciliation Act (OBRA). Section 162(m) provided that publicly held companies may be limited as to income tax deductions for certain covered executive officers to the extent that their total remuneration exceeds $1 million in any one year. Available at www.businessweek.com/1999/99_16/b3625017.htm.

[108] Bebchuk and Fried, 'Executive Compensation as an Agency Problem', 73.   [109] *ibid.*

short-term imperative, aided by a market that had come to expect short-term gains and now punished those corporations that failed to meet quarterly projections by a swift drop in stock price. Short-termism continued on the rise.[110]

The final straw, perhaps, was the internet bubble of the late 1990s. Initial public offerings (IPOs) that saw stock prices rise multiple times in a day, and investment money rushing to the latest new thing, created expectations in the market that it was a short-term game.[111] The phenomenon of day trading developed to take advantage of this, to the point where by the late 1990s, a full 15 per cent of market volume was represented by day traders (and another 15 per cent was represented by executive stock compensation).[112] Short-termism had become the order of the day, and the market, comprised of the shareholders to whom the monitoring board was responsible, fulfilled the neo-classical dream of controlling the corporation. Until, that is, the market crash in early 2000 and Enron's bankruptcy the next year.[113]

It is not over. Institutional activism continues to create short-term pressures. CEO termination has increased, as boards try to satisfy the market.[114] At the same time, CEO compensation has spiralled to the point of becoming a national issue.[115] Everybody seems to be in it for the short term. And boards have little power, or incentive, to resist.[116]

VII. Some remedies

It is probably unreasonable to expect any major restructuring of the board any time soon. Reform proposals usually centre around the question of inside versus outside director, lead directors, speciality directors (such as the Sarbanes-Oxley mandated audit committee) and the like.[117] The story I have told so far suggests that the board needs space to manage the corporation, space away from the market. While the monitoring board remains a flawed device, certainly as a legal matter, as a practical matter

---

[110] Mitchell, *Corporate Irresponsibility*, pp. 4–5, 52.

[111] Jay R. Ritter and Ivo Welch, 'A Review of IPO Activity, Pricing, and Allocation', *The Journal of Finance* August (2002), 1795.

[112] Brad M. Barber and Terrance Odean, 'The Internet and the Investor', *The Journal of Economic Perspectives* Winter (2001), 49–51.

[113] Mitchell, *Corporate Irresponsibility*, pp. 4–5, 52; Paul M. Healy and Krishna G. Palepu, 'The Fall of Enron', *The Journal of Economic Perspectives* Spring (2003), 3.

[114] Bebchuk and Fried, 'Executive Compensation as an Agency Problem', 75–6.

[115] Mitchell, *Corporate Irresponsibility*, p. 109.   [116] *ibid.*

[117] The remedies discussed here are examined in more detail in Mitchell, *Corporate Irresponsibility*.

I assume, as I always have, that most corporate directors want to do their jobs well. I also assume that most corporate directors, like most of us, have trouble resisting the kinds of pressures that market incentives combined with poorly aligned compensation structures create.[118] The latter is being repaired, albeit slowly. Grants of unrestricted stock options are down. But market pressure continues. So it seems best to address corporate social responsibility from the governance perspective by freeing boards to govern their corporations in their best judgements.

One way of diminishing market pressure on the board is to revisit our concept of capital gains taxation. The on-off switch between what is considered short-term capital gains (and thus tax disadvantaged) and long-term capital gains (tax advantaged) is one year. But one year is not a long term, at least in most businesses. If the point is to relieve the board of short-term pressures, then shareholder tax incentives must properly align with a period that one reasonably could consider to be long term. Thus, capital gains taxes should be tailored toward this goal, giving shareholders an incentive to hold their stock rather than to flip their shares for short-term gains.

In order to accomplish this goal, we might determine a 'long term' on an industry-by-industry basis. The long term for an automobile manufacturer might well be ten years, whereas one year might be legitimate for a new internet company. Short-term trading would be discouraged if we taxed the resulting gains at a punitively high rate, say 90 per cent in the first month (or week or year, depending on the term). We might then tailor the tax rate to diminish over a sliding scale reflecting the long term, ending in tax forgiveness at the end of the holding period. So, for example, we might impose a 90 per cent tax on trading profits for the first six months of our auto maker, diminishing to 50 per cent after five years, and 0 per cent after ten years. Of course I am making up rates and periods purely to illustrate, but the idea should be clear. By creating tax disincentives to sell quickly, and tax incentives to hold, we take pressure off management to perform for the short term while potentially harming the business in the long term. Obviously, we would have to build in reasonable conditions, exceptions perhaps for those who can demonstrate they had to sell out of financial necessity. And we could, I suppose, take the nature of the investor into account. Not only do pension funds typically turn over their portfolios in a year,[119] but they also have begun to invest heavily

---

[118] Crystal, *In Search of Excess*, p. 242.
[119] CalPERS Investments, available at www.calpers.ca.gov/index.jsp?bc = /investments/home.xml.

in hedge funds.[120] While pension funds, whether defined contribution or defined benefit, have to meet certain obligations every year, there is perhaps no investment vehicle so appropriately described as long-term. Pension funds, especially in light of their tax-advantaged status, perhaps should have punitive taxation imposed simply for exceeding a given rate of portfolio turnover in a single year. One can, I think, be reasonably confident that pension fund compensation structures would align accordingly, and long-term management would again become fashionable.

Marty Lipton has suggested another excellent method of removing pressure from boards: hold their elections every five years.[121] While this imposes a 'one size fits all' structure on board elections which might not comport with the long term in every industry, the fundamental idea of providing space for the board to manage is sound. Add to this the fact that average CEO terms run about five years as well,[122] and you provide a reasonably protected space for long-term management. At the end, of course, boards and their managers stand accountable before the shareholders. And if elections were to be held only every five years, this might also provide an opportunity to kick new life into the idea of shareholder democracy, limiting the time a shareholder would have to spend actually learning something about the performance of her company and vote.

The last suggestion I'll make here is one that shifts our ideas of expenses and assets in a way that might help foster long-term corporate well-being. One rather quick way to get stock prices up is to lay off workers. Sometimes too many workers are inefficient, and the only way to correct the inefficiency is to fire them. But that's typically not why stock prices rise; they rise because the diminished payroll promises higher earnings per share.[123] The same is true for workers' salaries, and investments in worker training.[124] These are expenses that hit the bottom line rather hard. Cutting them helps to improve earnings per share.

But workers obviously are the crucial engine that runs the business, at least in most cases. Well-trained, loyal workers, especially in an age of knowledge workers with portable skills, are a real business asset. The same

[120] CalPERS Press Release, 15 November 2004, available at www.calpers.ca.gov/index.jsp?bc=/about/press/pr-2004/nov/calpers–hedge-fund.xml.
[121] Lipton and Rosenblum, 'A New System of Corporate Governance', 190.
[122] Reinier Kraakman and John C. Coates IV, 'Why are Firms Sold? The Role of the Target CEO's Age, Tenure, and Share Ownership' (March 2006), available at repositories.cdlib.org/cgi/viewcontent.cgi?article=1145 &context=berkeley_law_econ.
[123] Roe, 'Political Preconditions to Separating Ownership from Corporate Control', 543.
[124] ibid.

may be true for lower-level workers in an age of substantial outsourcing. In many, if not most, ways, workers are assets, not expenses.

If this is true, then the value of workers to the business has to be reflected on the financial statements. The problem is capitalising workers. But this should not be hard. Taking a note from my capital gains proposal, we might want to determine an industry average salary for workers at each level or job description. Perhaps we would continue to require corporations to deduct that average salary as an expense. But if we were to say to corporations that if they paid their workers above the tabled average they could capitalise that amount and depreciate it over some period, we would remove the current disincentive to pay workers well. We could, of course, do the same for training expenses, thus removing disincentives to substantial corporate investments in training.

This idea presents a few problems. What's to stop the corporation from laying off employees once they've capitalised these expenses? The desire to employ the worker and receive a return on its investment seems obvious enough. But we could also provide that the corporation would have to recapture the depreciation for workers who were terminated prior to the end of the depreciation period. This would provide a strong incentive to make management think twice before engaging in promiscuous layoffs. As with my tax proposal, we would have to allow for exceptions, where demonstrated efficiency or business necessity justify the firings. And corporations could game the system, terminating workers as soon as the depreciation period expired. But the corporation's interest in its own reputation, not to mention its investments (not expenses), should minimise this kind of behaviour.

These suggestions would go a long way towards helping boards govern their corporations the way they see fit, not the way the market sees fit. Price discovery, or valuation, and liquidity, the functions of the market, are not the same things as managing a corporation. But when management is tied to the market, as it has become, the two converge. My suggestions would recreate the space for managers to manage.

In exchange for making the board truly responsible in this way, the board must become more accountable. An institution can never demonstrate the kind of accountability we expect from humans. But institutions are run by humans, and we can expect humans within institutions to step up to the plate. Our current system of disclosure, under the securities laws, attempts to provide accountability by mandating disclosure of a slew of facts about the corporation. But these facts, except for a very limited group (like compensation), are facts in the aggregate. Human accountability is a matter of individual accountability. In order for us to hold corporate managers truly accountable, we need more.

One way of providing this, and perhaps of realising the original Brandeisian goal of disclosure, is to demand that each of the directors of a corporation be given the opportunity to include a thousand-word statement in the corporation's annual report, discussing his or her view of the important events of the year and the important challenges for the future. In this manner, each director would be required to stand exposed, before the corporation's stockholders and all other interested persons, as an individual human being with his or her own ideas, thoughts, positions and values. Those interested in the corporation, including the general public, would start to be in a position to evaluate each director as an individual human being, and to hold each accountable for the fit between his or her decisions, the well-being of the corporation, his or her own attitudes and accepted social norms of business conduct. Such a requirement would force directors to think deeply not only about the immediate effects of his or her decisions on the corporation, but on its broader effects on society and, perhaps most significantly, on his or her personal reputation. While it would be difficult to subject these statements to antifraud provisions, the credibility of their reasoning and the frankness of their statements would likely be enough to compel directors' honesty, and their interests in their own reputations should ensure that their decisions are defensible. As with all decisions, people will disagree. But, like all decisions, board decisions would finally be subjected to a meaningful public test of rationality and defensibility.

There are many more ways of tinkering with both shareholder and managerial incentives within the existing structure of corporate governance. And that, precisely, is the point. History shows us that governance structure is a very difficult thing to change, and change that seems beneficial can be manipulated to produce bad results. History also teaches us that changes in incentives, which are much more easily accomplished as a practical matter (even if they might run into some political haggling), typically have the effect intended, and powerfully so. The problem has not been with the use of incentives but the use of incentives to achieve the wrong ends. Long-term management is socially responsible management. Socially responsible management can occur only when managers are given the space to do the jobs they know how to do.

10

The new corporate law: corporate social responsibility and employees' interests

STEPHEN BOTTOMLEY AND ANTHONY FORSYTH

I. Introduction

Corporate social responsibility (CSR) is back on the corporate law reform agenda. From an Australian perspective, the evidence for this is found in the simultaneous but separate inquiries that have recently been conducted into this topic by the Australian Parliament's Joint Committee on Corporations and Financial Services,[1] and by the Australian Government's Corporations and Markets Advisory Committee (CAMAC).[2] These developments are supported by the many standards, guidelines, principles and codes promulgated by non-government bodies, industry groups and other international organisations.[3]

Cynics might dismiss these developments as part of a regular cycle of corporate law reform. After all, as we will see, this is not the first time that CSR has appeared on the reform agenda. Others might suggest that, finally, this is an idea whose time has come. The purpose of this chapter is to examine the extent to which this renewed, and widespread, attention to CSR is being reflected in the substance of our systems of corporate law.[4] Is it possible, and meaningful, to talk of a 'new corporate law' in which the concerns of people other than shareholders (or, indeed, the non-financial

---

[1] The Parliamentary Committee, established under Part 14 of the *Australian Securities and Investments Commission Act 2001*, commenced its inquiry in June 2005 and reported one year later: *Corporate Responsibility: Managing Risk and Creating Value* (2006).

[2] The Advisory Committee is established under Part 9 of the *Australian Securities and Investments Commission Act 2001*, and operates as a specialised corporate law reform body. It commenced its inquiry with the release of a discussion paper in November 2005: see Corporations and Markets Advisory Committee, *Corporate Social Responsibility: Discussion Paper* (November 2005).

[3] Many of these are referred to elsewhere in this chapter.

[4] When we say 'our systems of corporate law', our reference points will be primarily Australian, with supplementary references to the United Kingdom and the United States of America.

concerns of shareholders) are to be given serious attention? In particular, how far is the new focus on CSR affecting the rights of employees in corporate law?

The plan of the chapter is as follows. We begin with a brief survey of recent developments in different common law jurisdictions, with an emphasis on Australia, that have implications for the idea of CSR. The focus here is not just on statutory developments, but also on the wider array of codes, guidelines and so on that were adverted to earlier. From this base, we then draw and elaborate upon two conclusions. The first is that the shareholder primacy model continues to exert a powerful, although sometimes misunderstood, effect on the capacity of legislators to respond to CSR concerns. In particular, it constrains (though, again, this is not a necessary constraint) the actions of directors in responding to those concerns, it constrains the power of shareholders to put these concerns in front of the board, and it constrains the capacity of non-shareholders to bring these concerns to the attention of company managers. The second conclusion is that much of the action regarding CSR therefore occurs outside the parameters of the statutes, and it is in this sense that we can talk about a 'new corporate law': a system of corporate regulation that depends as much (if not more) on non-statutory mechanisms and methods, which in many cases can have a more immediate impact on corporate operations. The final part of the chapter examines some of these themes in more detail, by way of a 'case study' of the position of corporate employees, particularly in the critical situation of a corporate insolvency. Whatever definition one takes of CSR it is undeniable that the financial and physical well-being of a company's employees must be a central concern. Recent corporate collapses and policy responses to them in Australia provide a stark illustration of the limited extent to which corporate law has been able to respond to the challenges of CSR.

II. Corporate law developments in Australia

There is no express reference to CSR obligations or desiderata in the Corporations Act 2001 (Cth). There are provisions in the Act which deal, in different ways, with matters that fall under the umbrella of CSR, but these have not been inserted as part of any systematic response to the issue. For example, section 299(1)(f) requires the directors' annual report for a company to include details of the company's performance in relation to any 'particular and significant' Commonwealth or state environmental regulation to which the company is subject. Another example is found in Part 5.8A of the Act, which seeks to protect employee entitlements, such as wages, superannuation contributions and leave entitlements, from arrangements intended to defeat the employees' recovery of those entitlements where, for example, there is a restructuring of a corporate group.[5]

As we noted earlier, there are, at the time of writing, two major inquiries being conducted into the extent to which the Australian corporations' legislation should include reference to corporate social responsibility obligations. We will come to these inquiries shortly. First, by way of context, it is useful to look at two earlier events in the history of Australian responses to the problem of legislating for corporate social responsibility.[6]

In May 1988 the Australian Senate asked its Standing Committee on Legal and Constitutional Affairs to inquire into 'the social and fiduciary duties and responsibilities of company directors'.[7] The inquiry was prompted by a request from the Committee itself, arising from perceptions that 'companies are now so dominated by directors that their owners, the shareholders, are denied any effective say in their control' and that 'the corporate sector is now central not only to the economic well-being of society but to most dimensions of community life'.[8] Much of the inquiry was occupied by the duties owed by directors to shareholders and creditors – in other words, the inquiry stayed within the accepted boundaries of corporate law. However the final Report also dealt with the prospect that directors could be given duties to 'outside' interests, with employees, environmental issues and consumers receiving particular attention. Responding to this suggestion, the Committee began with the premise that:

> It is the shareholders' investment that creates the company. Directors' fiduciary duties are premised on this fact and are designed to protect that investment. If company law were to impose new and, at times, contradictory duties (such as looking after interests which may be directly opposed to those of the corporators), directors' fiduciary duties could be weakened, perhaps to the point where they would be essentially meaningless.[9]

The Committee reached the conclusion that '[t]o impose a duty to act fairly between entities as diverse as creditors, employees, consumers, [and]

---

[5] This is discussed further below.

[6] This is not presented as a comprehensive history of developments on the topic.

[7] Australian Senate, Standing Committee on Legal and Constitutional Affairs, *Company Directors' Duties: Report on the Social and Fiduciary Duties and Obligations of Company Directors* (November 1989).

[8] *ibid.*, pp. 8–9.   [9] *ibid.*, p. 98.

the environment, is to impose a broad and potentially complex range of obligations on directors. Such a duty would be vague'.[10] The Committee recommended, therefore, that these 'outside' interests should be dealt with 'not in companies legislation but in legislation aimed specifically at those matters'.[11] The Committee's report had the effect of quieting subsequent debate in Australia about the link between corporate law and corporate social responsibility for a number of years.

The second event occurred in 2000 when an Australian Democrats Senator (the Democrats being a minority party that then held the balance of power in the Senate) introduced the Corporate Code of Conduct Bill into the Senate.[12] The Bill aimed to regulate the overseas activities of Australian companies on matters of human rights, environmental practice, labour relations, and occupational health and safety. The Democrats urged support for the Bill on the grounds that it would promote good corporate citizenship and a broadening of corporate social responsibilities to a wide range of stakeholders. The Democrats argued that the Bill was a necessary response to the failure of voluntary codes, international guidelines and regional initiatives[13] to adequately regulate the activities of multinational corporations. Specifically, the Bill sought to tackle the problem of regulating the conduct of corporate structures which locate the head office functions in one country, separated from the corporate operations in another jurisdiction. The Bill was introduced in the wake of a decision by the House of Lords to permit a group of plaintiffs employed by a South African subsidiary to bring a claim for damages against the UK-based parent company, Cape plc, for injuries suffered in connection with the mining of asbestos.[14] The drafters of the Bill drew on a number of sources for inspiration, including the 1999 EU Resolution on EU Standards for European Enterprises Operating in Developing Countries,[15] a bill introduced in the United States by Congresswoman McKinney,[16] the Universal Declaration of Human Rights, and standards contained in International Labour Organisation conventions.

---

[10] ibid., p. 96.   [11] ibid., p. 99.

[12] The full title of the Bill was 'A Bill for an Act to impose standards on the conduct of Australian corporations which undertake business activities in other countries, and for related purposes'.

[13] Such as the North American Free Trade Agreement: www.dfait-maeci.gc.ca/nafta-alena/menu-en.asp.

[14] Lubbe and Others and Cape plc and Related Appeals [2000] 4 All ER 268, [2000] 1 WLR 1545.

[15] eur-lex.europa.eu/LexUriServ/site/en/oj/1999/c_104/c_10419990414en01800184.pdf.

[16] Bill for a Corporate Code of Conduct Act (H.R. 4596).

The Bill proposed the imposition of obligations on Australian corporations employing more than one hundred persons in another country to take all reasonable measures to prevent any material adverse effect on the environment, and to promote the health and safety of its workers. The Bill required such corporations not to use, or obtain benefit from, forced or compulsory labour or child labour, and to comply with human rights standards concerning equality of opportunity in matters concerning race, colour, sex, sexuality, religion, political opinion, national extraction or social origin. Corporations were required to comply with applicable tax laws, and to ensure that goods and services provided by the corporation complied with relevant consumer health and safety standards and consumer protection and trade practice standards. Corporations would be required to submit detailed annual compliance reports to the Australian corporate regulator, the Australian Securities and Investments Commission (ASIC). A contravention of any of these requirements would make the corporation liable to proceedings for the recovery of a civil penalty.[17] Corporate officers could also incur criminal liability if their involvement in the contravention was done knowingly, recklessly or negligently (and they were in a position to influence the corporation's conduct in relation to the contravention).

The Bill was referred to a Joint Committee of the Australian Parliament for consideration. The Committee received submissions from forty-three individuals and organisations. Some submissions opposed the Bill outright. Others supported the intention of the Bill, but made 'positive criticisms'[18] about its drafting. In its Report,[19] the Committee noted that there was no consensus on whether the Bill should be passed, and came to the conclusion that because there was 'no evidence of systemic failure regarding Australian corporate behaviour',[20] and because the Bill was 'impracticable and unwarranted',[21] it should not be passed. The Bill did not pass the Senate.

As we noted earlier, two inquiries into CSR were established in 2005. The spur for this activity was the Special Commission of Inquiry into matters arising from the restructuring of the James Hardie group of companies in an effort to isolate liability to claimants who had suffered

---

[17] This could include an order to pay a monetary penalty of up to $1 million and/or compensation to a person who suffered loss or damage from the contravention.

[18] A term used in the final report – see para. 4.3.

[19] Parliamentary Joint Statutory Committee on Corporations and Securities, *Report on the Corporate Code of Conduct Bill 2000* (June 2001).

[20] *ibid.*, para. 4.44.   [21] *ibid.*, para. 4.5.

asbestos-related illness associated with James Hardie building products.[22] We can surmise that a further factor was the lingering impact of the collapse of the HIH Insurance group of companies in 2001 (at the time, the largest corporate collapse in Australian history) and the subsequent report of the Royal Commission of Inquiry into the collapse. One matter of concern to the Commission was the potential for abuse by directors of the power to make corporate donations:

> The board of HIH appeared to exert no meaningful control over the amount or direction of the not inconsiderable donations made by the company over the years. There may have been a corporate interest underlying the donations but if so it was not articulated. Credit for the company was not usually sought for having made the donations and there was little if any disclosure of details of the company's magnanimity to the board let alone to shareholders.[23]

Among other detailed recommendations for reforms to Australian corporate regulation, the Report urged companies to develop guidelines for the disclosure of their arrangements for making corporate donations.

In June 2005 the Australian Parliament directed its Joint Committee on Corporations and Financial Services to inquire into corporate responsibility and triple-bottom-line reporting with particular reference, amongst other things, to 'whether revisions to the legal framework, particularly to the Corporations Act, are required to enable or encourage incorporated entities or directors to have regard for the interests of stakeholders other than shareholders, and the broader community'.[24] The Committee received over 145 submissions and conducted hearings, publishing its report in June 2006. Prior to this inquiry, in March 2005 CAMAC was asked by its Minister to inquire into whether the duties of company directors should be revised to include corporate social responsibilities, and whether the Corporations Act 2001 should require certain types of companies to report on the social and environmental impact of their activities. The Committee published a detailed Discussion Paper in November 2005,

---

[22] Report of the Special Commission of Inquiry into the Medical Research and Compensation Foundation (September 2004). See also G. Haigh, *Asbestos House: The Secret History of James Hardie Industries* (Melbourne: Scribe, 2006).

[23] The HIH Royal Commission, *The Failure of HIH Insurance – Volume 1: A Corporate Collapse and its Lessons* (2003), p. 119.

[24] Parliamentary Joint Committee on Corporations and Financial Services, Terms of Reference, 23 June 2005. See the final report, *Corporate Responsibility: Managing Risk and Creating Value* (2006).

seeking submissions.[25] At the time of writing, the CAMAC inquiry has not been completed.

As the Discussion Paper from the CAMAC inquiry observes, alongside the Corporations Act 2001 there are a wide range of codes, guidelines and so on which address corporate social responsibility matters. In Australia these codes fall outside the law in that they are not formally incorporated into, recognised by, or mandated by legislation or other forms of regulation. Some of these have international application and voluntary effect, such as the Organisation for Economic Co-operation and Development (OECD) Principles of Corporate Governance, Principle IV of which states that '[t]he corporate governance framework [of a company] should recognise the rights of stakeholders established by law or through mutual agreements and encourage active co-operation between corporations and stakeholders in creating wealth, jobs, and the sustainability of financially sound enterprises'.[26]

Others have local application. For example, the Australian Stock Exchange (ASX) Corporate Governance Council's Principles of Good Corporate Governance and Best Practice Recommendations encourage companies listed on the ASX to 'recognise legal and other obligations to all legitimate stakeholders'. In support of this the Principles state that '[t]here is growing acceptance of the view that organisations can create value by better managing natural, human, social and other forms of capital. Increasingly, the performance of companies is being scrutinised from a perspective that recognises these other forms of capital'.[27]

The Principles recommend that listed companies should 'establish and disclose a code of conduct to guide compliance with legal and other obligations to legitimate stakeholders'.[28] The suggested contents of such a code include details of a company's responsibilities to the general financial community, to clients, customers and consumers, to employees, to the community and the environment. The ASX Principles are not binding on listed companies. Instead, such companies are required to disclose in their annual reports the extent to which they have followed these best

---

[25] Corporations and Markets Advisory Committee, *Corporate Social Responsibility: Discussion Paper* (November 2005).

[26] Organisation for Economic Co-operation and Development, *Principles of Corporate Governance* (2004), p. 21. See also the OECD *Guidelines for Multinational Enterprises – Revision 2000*, which set out non-binding principles and standards covering human rights, anti-corruption, labour relations, environment and consumer protection.

[27] ASX Corporate Governance Council, *Principles of Good Corporate Governance and Best Practice Recommendations* (March 2003), Principle 10.

[28] *Ibid.*, Recommendation 10.1.

practice principles and, where specific principles have not been followed, these must be identified and reasons given.[29]

Another example of local, non-legislative initiatives is provided by Standards Australia[30] which has published a set of voluntary standards for non-listed private-sector companies as well as not-for-profit organisations and government departments. The standard for corporate social responsibility specifies processes for establishing, implementing and maintaining a programme that deals with employee issues, environmental issues, and matters of health and safety.[31]

In general the Australian situation is replicated in the United Kingdom[32] and the United States.[33] In the United Kingdom, section 309 of the Companies Act 1985, introduced in 1980, states that directors, as part of their duty to the company, are to have regard to the interest of the company's employees in general, in addition to the interests of its members. A generous interpretation of this provision is that it elevates the interests of employees to the same level as those of shareholders. It also leaves it to directors to decide how to balance those interests when they are in competition with each other. A more pessimistic interpretation is that the section 'does not compel the directors to do anything they would not otherwise have been inclined to do'.[34] Instead, it simply requires (and there is debate about its mandatory effect) directors to 'have regard to' employees' interests; that is, 'the duty is merely a procedural one, having no substantive content'. Perhaps this is what lies behind Len Sealy's observation that this section 'is either one of the most incompetent or one of the most cynical pieces of drafting on record'.[35] We make further comment on this statutory provision later in this chapter.

Section 172 of the Companies Act 2006 introduces a 'duty to promote the success of the company'. The section has its origins in the recommendations of the Company Law Review Steering Group which reported

---

[29] ASX Listing Rule 4.10.3.
[30] As described on its website (www.standards.org.au/). Standards Australia, via a Memorandum of Understanding with the Australian Government, operates as the peak non-government standards development body in Australia. It is a company limited by guarantee, with seventy-two members representing groups interested in the development and application of standards and related products and services.
[31] AS 8003–20043.
[32] For a more detailed analysis, see Chapter 9.   [33] See also, Chapters 10 and 17.
[34] J. Parkinson, *Corporate Power and Responsibility: Issues in the Theory of Company Law* (Oxford: Clarendon Press, 1993), p. 84.
[35] L. Sealy, 'Directors' "Wider" Responsibilities – Problems Conceptual, Practical and Procedural', *Monash Law Review* 13 (1987), 164, at 177.

in 2001.[36] The section begins by stating that a director must act in the way that would be most likely to promote the success of the company for the benefit of its members as a whole. The section then goes on to state that in fulfilling this duty, a director must have regard to a range of factors including the interests of the company's employees (thus replacing the present section 309), its suppliers and customers, the impact of the company's operations on the community and the environment, and the desirability of the company maintaining a reputation for high standards of business conduct.[37]

The legislative change in the United Kingdom thus links 'the success of the company' to 'the benefit of the members as a whole'. It attempts to put non-shareholder interests on the directors' managerial agenda, while remaining true to the basic shareholder primacy model that underpins UK (and Australian) corporate law. The difficulty that this presents is emphasised by the indeterminacy of the qualifier used in the proposed section: directors must have regard to these other matters 'so far as reasonably practicable'.

For purposes of comparison we note that, notwithstanding the strong application of the shareholder primacy model in the United States, many states have passed 'corporate constituency' statutes that permit directors to take into account a wider range of constituencies when making corporate decisions in response to a hostile takeover. While the details vary from one state to another, the general pattern of these statutes is to allow directors, when considering the best interests of the corporation, to consider the effects of their proposed action on groups such as employees, customers and suppliers, and communities in which the corporation is located.[38] Unlike the UK proposal, the statutes are permissive, not mandatory, but like the UK proposal they usually do not give any indication about how directors should take the various interests into account.

III. Shareholder primacy

The lesson from the above discussion is that efforts to incorporate the idea of CSR into the general body of corporate law rules and principles

[36] Company Law Review Steering Group, *Modern Company Law For a Competitive Economy – Final Report* (2001, Volume1), Appendix C; see also Department of Trade and Industry, *Company Law Reform White Paper* (March 2005), pp. 20–1.
[37] Again, see further below.
[38] See L. Mitchell, 'A Theoretical and Practical Framework for Enforcing Corporate Constituency Statutes', *Texas Law Review* 70 (1992), 579; B. McDonnell, 'Corporate Constituency Statutes and Employee Governance', *William Mitchell Law Review* 30 (2004), 1227.

inevitably confront two deeply entrenched – and legally enshrined – presumptions. One is the idea that, once elected, directors (and the managers they appoint) should be left to get on with the job. The other is the idea that 'the job' is to maximise shareholder value. Increasingly, this seems to be measured by the daily price of the company's shares. As Paul Redmond explains, '[a] consequence of the shareholder value focus is that the company is seen as a set of income claims and property rights'.[39]

Against the background of this limited shareholder primacy model, efforts by legislators, judges and corporate personnel to tackle the issues of CSR will therefore prove to be difficult. Deciding who counts as a 'stakeholder', how to ensure that their interests count, and how to reconcile competing claims on corporate resources are just three of the many problems to be resolved. On one view, the shareholder primacy model presents a simple solution to these problems: it is the collective interests of the shareholders that matter. We suggest, though, that this argument is often used more as a convenient shield to avoid the problems than as a reasoned attempt to engage with them. Importantly, it also begs some important questions: What *are* the interests of shareholders? Are they always exclusively financial and, even if that is the case, can they only be satisfied by short-term strategies and responses? If shareholders have non-financial interests, such as ethical concerns or a respect for the welfare of the company's workers, how are these to be dealt with? Can shareholders – indeed, *should* shareholders – be a means whereby the interests of non-shareholders may be brought to bear on the decisions of corporate managers?

In posing these questions we accept that, for better or worse, the shareholder primacy model has proven to be resilient, notwithstanding repeated efforts to introduce stakeholder-centred concerns. Despite its limitations, the model continues to exert a powerful grip on the mind-set of legislators, judges, law reformers and corporate managers. As we see it, the first challenge is to see what can be done within the shareholder primacy model.[40] Legally speaking, it is a flexible model; it has the potential to be used in ways that do not necessarily shut out other interests and concerns. The questions posed above suggest there are two key limitations in which the shareholder primacy model has been conceived. One is that

---

[39] P. Redmond, 'Corporate Social Responsibility: An Overview', *Reform* 87 (2005–06), 7, at 9.

[40] Thus, we do not agree with the claim that there is no more work to be done: H. Hansmann and R. Kraakman, 'The End of History for Corporate Law', *Georgetown Law Journal* 89 (2001), 439.

short-term price maximisation has come to be equated with shareholder primacy.[41] The other is that, notwithstanding their 'primacy', shareholders themselves are frequently marginalised in corporate decision-making processes. We suggest, however, that, read carefully, the model does permit attention to be given to shareholders' non-financial concerns (such as concerns for the social or environmental impact of their corporation's activities) and, through the medium of the shareholders, the model can also take account of the interests of non-shareholders.

One way in which this might be achieved is by permitting shareholders to pass advisory resolutions; that is, resolutions on matters of corporate management that fall outside the formal jurisdiction of the general meeting. The long-established common law position is that shareholders may pass resolutions only on those matters that fall within the power of the general meeting, as determined by statute, the company's constitution and (if applicable) the listing rules of the relevant stock exchange. Where, as is most commonly the case, the company's constitution or the legislation[42] gives exclusive managerial power and discretion to the directors, the shareholders have no formal power to dictate or interfere in the directors' exercise of that power.[43]

Nevertheless, advisory resolutions or proposals are permitted in some countries. Legislation in Canada permits a shareholder (with the support of the requisite number of other shareholders) to submit a proposal to the corporation, which the shareholder proposes to raise at a general meeting, of any matter that relates in a significant way to the business and affairs of the corporation.[44] This does not bind the directors to act upon the proposal; it is, in the words of one writer, designed to promote 'shareholder consciousness raising'.[45] In New Zealand, the Companies Act 1993 permits shareholders in a general meeting to pass a resolution that relates to the management of the company; the resolution is not binding on the board

---

[41] D. Millon, 'Why Is Corporate Management Obsessed with Quarterly Earnings and What Should Be Done About It?', *George Washington Law Review* 70 (2002), 890, at 900–2.

[42] In some jurisdictions (e.g. Canada: Canada Business Corporations Act, RSC 1985, s 102; United States: the Revised Model Business Corporations Act § 8.01 (2002); Delaware General Corporation Law, § 141) this division of power is prescribed by statute. In Australia it is the default position that may be varied by a corporation (see the 'replaceable rule' in s. 198A of the Corporations Act 2001).

[43] *Automatic Self-Cleansing Filter Syndicate Co. Ltd* v. *Cunninghame* [1906] 2 Ch 34; *Gramophone & Typewriter Ltd* v. *Stanley* [1908] 2 KB 89; *Shaw & Sons (Salford) Ltd* v. *Shaw* [1935] 2 KB 113.

[44] Canada Business Corporations Act, s. 137

[45] B. Welling, *Corporate Law in Canada: The Governing Principles* (2nd edn, Toronto: Butterworths, 1991), p. 472.

unless the company's constitution provides otherwise.[46] A suggestion that advisory resolutions should be permitted in Australian corporate law was considered in 2000. It was quickly dismissed on the grounds that 'the boundaries . . . between the role of directors and that of the shareholders in general meeting should not become confused'.[47] The concern was that such resolutions might, in practice, be regarded by the board (mindful of the shareholders' power to appoint and dismiss directors) as directive rather than advisory.[48] Notwithstanding this concern, the Corporations Act 2001 was later amended to require that the adoption of the directors' remuneration report at a listed company's annual general meeting be decided by an advisory resolution.[49] This amendment was introduced in the wake of public concern about extravagant rates of pay for directors and senior executives.[50]

We draw attention to the idea of advisory resolutions to emphasise that the shareholder primacy model does not necessarily eliminate the capacity of corporate law to recognise corporate social responsibility concerns. Directors are not necessarily restricted to short-term decisions about shareholder value.[51] Shareholders should not be encouraged to discard wider concerns about the company's operations. However, to achieve this more flexible application of the shareholder model, it is necessary to think of modern corporate regulation in ways that go beyond the usually accepted parameters of corporate law. In the conclusion to this chapter we argue that understanding the new corporate law means understanding the place and role of the many codes, guidelines and other mechanisms that now have a vital role in regulating corporate behaviour.

Having said that, we acknowledge that even an expanded conception of the shareholder primacy model can only push the corporate social responsibility debate so far. More radical proposals, such as the reformulation of directors' formal legal duties to enable and (in some situations) require them to take into account the interests of non-shareholder stakeholders, should be among the options for continued consideration.

---

[46] Companies Act 1993 (NZ), s. 109.

[47] Companies and Securities Advisory Committee, *Shareholder Participation in the Modern Listed Public Company*, Final Report (2000), para. 3.55.

[48] This is notwithstanding the requirement in the Act that the chair of the meeting must allow a reasonable opportunity for shareholders to ask questions about or make comments on the management of the company: s. 250S (see further below).

[49] Corporations Act 2001 (Cth), s. 250R(2) and (3), inserted in 2004.

[50] Parliament of the Commonwealth of Australia, *Corporate Law Economic Reform Program (Audit Reform and Corporate Disclosure) Bill 2003 Explanatory Memorandum* (2003), pp. 165–9.

[51] See Millon, 'Why Is Corporate Management Obsessed with Quarterly Earnings?'.

IV. The position of employees: a case study of the legal limitations on corporate social responsibility

In order to illustrate the limited extent to which recent reforms to the legal framework of corporate governance have involved any real recognition of CSR concerns, we now turn to focus on the position of employees. Along with other non-shareholder stakeholders, employees have traditionally been treated as the 'outsiders' of corporate enterprises under the Anglo-American shareholder primacy model of corporate regulation – with none of the information rights or legal protections of their interests enjoyed by 'insiders', such as shareholders and secured creditors.[52] In Australia, the high-profile collapses of companies like Ansett and One.Tel, and the James Hardie episode, have highlighted the vulnerability of employees within this model. These and many other recent cases of corporate failures and restructures, in which employees' interests have either been overlooked or consciously bypassed, have triggered several regulatory responses. After a brief discussion of the traditional legal position, we examine and evaluate these legislative and policy initiatives. Another significant recent development in Australia – the increasing recourse by unions, lawyers and other representatives of employees to the mechanisms of corporate law to defend and advance workers' interests – will also be explored. Some brief comparisons will then be made of the extent to which employees have received attention in the recent corporate governance debates in Australia, the United Kingdom and the United States.

V. Employees under Australian corporate law

The limited recognition of employees within Australia's traditional arrangements for corporate regulation is best illustrated by the narrow focus of directors' legal duties to act in good faith and in the best interests of the company. At common law and under section 181 of the Corporations Act, company directors must treat shareholders' interests as paramount. The concerns of employees, or other stakeholders, *can* be considered in performing these duties – but only where this would also be in the best interests of the company (that is, the shareholders as a whole). Employee interests cannot generally be placed ahead of those of shareholders, unless this is necessary to ensure that the company meets its obligations to employees under employment, industrial or occupational

---

[52] The 'insider/outsider' terminology is borrowed from B. Bercusson, 'Workers, Corporate Enterprise and the Law', in R. Lewis (ed.), *Labour Law in Britain* (Oxford: Blackwell, 1986), p. 139.

health and safety laws.[53] For example, a company could not make ex gratia redundancy payments to employees in the context of a business closure, where this would run down the funds available for distribution to shareholders. Not even the company's interest in maintaining harmonious industrial relations would warrant directors pursuing such a course of action.[54]

Of course, the greatest threats to the welfare of employees are posed when companies run into financial difficulty and face potential insolvency. At this point, workers' jobs, wages and accrued leave, redundancy and other employment entitlements are placed at considerable risk. Australian case law requires directors to consider creditors' interests when a company is insolvent or near insolvency.[55] However, the cases stop short of establishing a *duty* that is enforceable at the instance of creditors;[56] only the company's liquidator or ASIC can bring an action for compensation or the recovery of company funds to return to creditors. As Symes has indicated, this provides little comfort to employees in insolvency situations: '[f]rom these cases, it is not possible to state that a duty to creditors upon insolvency means that they should take "care" of employees . . .', albeit that employees 'are creditors (statutory priority creditors, in fact) for their unpaid salary and other entitlements'.[57]

This 'priority creditor status'[58] has been one way in which Australian corporate law has attempted to preserve employee rights in situations of company failure and restructuring.[59] Under section 556 of the Corporations Act, employee claims to recover unpaid wages, superannuation,

---

[53] Ensuring compliance with such laws forms part of directors' common law and statutory duties to act with due care and diligence; see, e.g., Justice S. Whelan and L. Zwier, *Employee Entitlements and Corporate Insolvency and Reconstruction*, Research Paper, Centre for Corporate Law and Securities Regulation, University of Melbourne (2005), p. 10.

[54] *Parke* v. *Daily News Ltd* [1962] Ch 927; see also *Hutton* v. *West Cork Railway Company* (1883) 23 Ch D 654.

[55] *Walker* v. *Wimborne* (1976) 137 CLR 1; *Kinsela* v. *Russell Kinsela Pty Ltd* (1986) 4 NSWLR 722. The 'uncommercial transactions' provisions of the Corporations Act (s. 588FB and related provisions in Part 5.7B, Division 2) operate as a form of statutory duty to protect creditors' interests.

[56] See for example *Spies* v. *R* (2000) 18 ACLC 727.

[57] C. Symes, 'A New Statutory Directors' Duty for Australia – a "Duty" to be Concerned about Employee Entitlements in the Insolvent Corporation', *International Insolvency Review* 12 (2003), 133, 137.

[58] Whelan and Zwier, *Employee Entitlements*, p. 4.

[59] For a detailed account of the evolution of the relevant statutory provisions in Australian and English law, see R. W. Harmer, 'Employee Creditors and Corporations', in R. McCallum, G. McCarry and P. Ronfeldt (eds.), *Employment Security* (Sydney: The Federation Press, 1994), p. 227.

injury compensation, leave entitlements and retrenchment payments rank ahead of the claims of other unsecured creditors. However, the claims of secured creditors such as banks and other financiers, and costs incurred in the insolvency process (for example, liquidators' or administrators' fees), take precedence over those of employees. The limitations of the priority treatment for employees become immediately apparent: frequently, there are no assets remaining to meet employee claims once the debts of secured creditors have been fully or partly satisfied.[60]

In a series of high-profile company collapses from the late 1990s – primarily, National Textiles in early 2000, and One.Tel and Ansett in 2001 – thousands of Australian workers lost not only their jobs, but also their accrued leave and redundancy entitlements.[61] In some of these cases, these harsh outcomes were visited upon workers as a result of deliberate corporate strategies to avoid meeting their obligations to employees, or in circumstances where directors had diverted company funds to ensure that payments were made to themselves (for example, in the form of bonuses). The political fallout from these events led the Australian Government to adopt several initiatives aimed at enhancing the level of protection offered to employees under Australian corporate law. However, as the following discussion will reveal, it must be questioned whether that objective has been realised to any appreciable extent.

VI. Moves to enhance the recognition of employee interests – but how far?

The first of these measures was the Corporations Law Amendment (Employee Entitlements) Act 2000 (Cth), which inserted Part 5.8A into the Corporations Act. The new provisions built on the existing duty of directors to prevent companies from trading whilst insolvent,[62] by imposing personal liability on directors where they enter into 'uncommercial transactions' – that is, agreements, transactions or corporate restructures that are *intended* to prevent workers from accessing their accrued

---

[60] R. Campo, 'The Protection of Employee Entitlements in the Event of Employer Insolvency: Australian Initiatives in the Light of International Models', *Australian Journal of Labour Law* 13 (2000), 236.

[61] For an account of some of these corporate collapses and their impact on employees, see Campo, 'The Protection of Employee Entitlements', 243–4, noting that the estimated value of employees' lost entitlements as a result of company insolvencies in Australia is between $140 and $181 million annually; more generally, see CCH, *Collapse Incorporated: Tales, Safeguards and Responsibilities of Corporate Australia* (Sydney: CCH Australia Ltd, 2001).

[62] Corporations Act, ss. 588G–588X.

employment entitlements. Heavy penalties, including fines and imprisonment, are available to deal with breaches of the uncommercial transactions provisions, and employee creditors can themselves initiate legal
proceedings with the liquidator's permission.[63] However, the difficulty of
proving that directors were acting with the requisite intention under these
provisions 'inevitably limit [their] scope and effectiveness as a protective
mechanism for employees'.[64] This assessment is borne out by the fact that
there have been no reported cases to date involving a successful action
by employees under Part 5.8A of the Corporations Act; in fact, only one
case has been initiated under these provisions.[65] In 2004, an influential
Parliamentary Committee recommended that the provisions be reviewed
to determine their effectiveness in deterring companies from adopting
corporate structures (such as 'phoenix' company arrangements) to avoid
meeting employee entitlements, and to consider other possible law reform
options.[66]

Further statutory changes came in the form of the Corporations
Amendment (Repayment of Directors' Bonuses) Act 2003, inserting section 588FDA in the Corporations Act. This provision enables the recovery
by a liquidator of excessive payments made to directors in circumstances
where a company is in no financial position to make such payments – such
as in the One.Tel case, where the once high-flying telecommunications
company's joint managing directors paid themselves $7.5 million each in

---

[63] For detailed discussion of Part 5.8A, see D. Noakes, 'Corporate Groups and the Duties of
Directors: Protecting the Employee or the Insolvent Employer?', *Australian Business Law
Review* 29 (2001), 124.

[64] J. Hill, 'Corporate Governance and the Role of the Employee', in P. Gollan and G. Patmore
(eds.), *Partnership at Work: the Challenge of Employee Democracy* (Sydney: Pluto Press,
2003), p. 119; see further Symes, 'A New Statutory Directors' Duty for Australia', 144–5.

[65] Whelan and Zwier, *Employee Entitlements*, p. 14, referring to *The Creditors of Antal-Air
Pty Ltd (Administrator Appointed)* v. *Australian Securities and Investments Commission*
[2004] FCA 1090, and the appeal decision *Creditors of Antal-Air Pty Ltd* v. *Antal-Air Pty
Ltd* [2004] FCAFC 303; see also C. Symes, 'Will there ever be a Prosecution under Part
5.8A?', *Insolvency Law Bulletin* 3 (2002), 17.

[66] See Parliamentary Joint Committee on Corporations and Financial Services, *Corporate Insolvency Laws: A Stocktake* (Canberra: Commonwealth of Australia, June 2004),
pp. 182–5; the Parliamentary Joint Committee recommended that this review be conducted by CAMAC. While this issue was not referred to CAMAC, in late 2005 the government announced a package of insolvency law reform measures, including proposals
'targeting misconduct by the officers of assetless companies' and 'disqualifying directors .
. . who are involved in repeat phoenix activity': see Australian Government, The Treasury,
'Corporate insolvency reform', 12 October 2005, pp. 5–6, available at www.treasury.gov.au/
contentitem.asp?NavID = 013&ContentID = 1022.

bonuses, in a year when One.Tel had lost $291.1 million.[67] When the company was placed into voluntary administration in May 2001, the union with coverage of its 1,600 employees brought industrial tribunal proceedings to ensure that the workers would be entitled to redundancy payments. These payments were ultimately met in the course of the winding-up process.[68] The new statutory provision aims to prevent companies from providing directors or their associates with payments or other benefits (such as shares), in a situation where no 'reasonable person in the company's circumstances' would enter into such transactions. Again, concerns have been raised about the potential effectiveness of this provision, as it is left to the courts to determine whether payments to directors were 'unreasonable'.[69]

In the wake of the collapse of Ansett Airlines, just prior to the November 2001 Federal election, the government announced several measures to assist the 16,000 unemployed Ansett workers whose employment entitlements were threatened, and to improve the level of protection offered to other employees that might face a similar plight as a result of future corporate insolvencies. First, the government established the Special Employee Entitlements Scheme for Ansett Group Employees (SEESA), to ensure the recovery by former Ansett workers of their employment entitlements.[70] Second, the government replaced the Employee Entitlements and Support Scheme (established in 2000) with the General Employee Entitlements and Redundancy Scheme (GEERS),[71] a more comprehensive scheme enabling employees of insolvent companies to claim recovery of their unpaid entitlements from a government fund. Under GEERS, employees can recover unpaid wages; unpaid annual leave; unpaid long-service leave; payments

---

[67] C. Jay, 'The Day of Reckoning', in CCH, *Collapse Incorporated*, p. 9 at p. 35.

[68] For a detailed account, see L. Floyd, 'Enron and One.Tel: Employee Entitlements after Employer Insolvency in the United States and Australia (Australian Renegades Championing the American Dream?)', *Southern Methodist University Law Review* 56 (2003), 975, 991–5.

[69] See D. Noakes, 'Measuring the Impact of Strategic Insolvency on Employees', *Insolvency Law Journal* 11 (2003), 91, 112; there have been no decided cases as yet on s. 588FDA.

[70] See S. Kinsey, 'A Triumph for Labour over Capital: Employee Entitlements in Insolvency in the Wake of the Ansett Collapse', *Insolvency Law Journal* 10 (2002), 132; see also Whelan and Zwier, *Employee Entitlements*, pp. 32–41, explaining the difficulties encountered by former Ansett workers in recovering their full employment entitlements under SEESA; see further below.

[71] The following description of the operation of GEERS is based primarily on information contained in the most recent version of the GEERS Operational Arrangements (dated 1 November 2005), available at: www.workplace.gov.au/workplace/Category/SchemesInitiatives/EmployeeEntitlements/GEERSV2.

in lieu of notice; and up to sixteen weeks' redundancy pay. Employees must have a legal entitlement to receive such payments under their employment contract, or an applicable industrial award or statutory agreement, or relevant legislation. An overall 'cap' of $98,200 (indexed annually) applies to the level at which entitlements paid out under GEERS are to be calculated.[72] Having advanced payments to employees under GEERS, the Federal Government is able to 'stand in the employees' shoes' as a creditor with the same priority rights in the distribution of the company's assets in liquidation as the employees would have enjoyed.[73]

The establishment of a 'safety net' mechanism such as GEERS represents a welcome improvement in the level of protection offered to Australian employees in the event of employer insolvency – for example, $66.7 million was paid to 8,126 employees in respect of 572 failed businesses in 2004–05. However, the scheme operates subject to a number of important limitations that limit its effectiveness as a protective measure. Most significantly, the establishment of GEERS as a policy instrument, rather than under legislation, means that it is a precarious form of protection compared to the wage protection funds operating in many countries.[74] In *Commonwealth of Australia* v. *Rocklea Spinning Mills Pty Ltd (Receivers and Managers Appointed)*,[75] Justice Finkelstein of the Federal Court of Australia observed that '[GEERS] is not constituted by statute but by an act of the executive government alone'; and, further, that '[t]he scheme is a voluntary scheme. No employee has a right enforceable by action in a court of law to obtain any payment from the money granted by Parliament'.[76] In that case, Justice Finkelstein found that the Federal Government's priority right to recover funds paid to employees under GEERS did not extend to situations where a 'deed of company arrangement' was entered into by creditors.[77] The government's rights of recovery only applied where the insolvency process proceeded to the stage of liquidation of the relevant company.

The decision in *Commonwealth* v. *Rocklea Spinning Mills* was widely considered to threaten the future viability of GEERS. As Justice Finkelstein indicated, the government's priority creditor rights constitute a key feature underpinning the entire scheme: 'if GEERS breaks down because

---

[72] That is, employees who earn more than $98,200 per annum receive payments under GEERS as if that were their level of annual income.

[73] By virtue of s. 560 of the Corporations Act 2001.

[74] See Kinsey, 'A Triumph for Labour over Capital', 141–2.

[75] [2005] FCA 902 ('*Commonwealth* v. *Rocklea Spinning Mills*').

[76] *Commonwealth* v. *Rocklea Spinning Mills* [2005] FCA 902, paras. 3 and 16.

[77] Under Part 5.3 A, Divisions 10 and 11 of the Corporations Act 2001.

parties have found a way to get around the Commonwealth's priority in a winding up there is a real risk that the scheme will be scaled back or itself terminated to the detriment of many employees of insolvent companies'.[78] In response, the government changed the GEERS Operational Arrangements from 1 November 2005, to prevent employees from accessing GEERS payments while the employing entity is under administration or receivership, or is subject to a deed of company arrangement. Claims under GEERS can now only be made once a liquidator has been appointed to 'wind up' the company.[79] The government also extended GEERS to enable employees to recover any wages unpaid in the three months prior to the employer's insolvency; and to make employees who resigned or were dismissed within six months prior to insolvency eligible to recover any unpaid entitlements under GEERS.

A further observation, by way of assessment of GEERS, is that the existence of a government-funded scheme arguably discourages directors from taking greater responsibility for ensuring that companies have sufficient assets to meet their employees' entitlements. While the outcome of GEERS in terms of increased employee protection is commendable, the public policy benefit of effectively transferring directors' potential liability to taxpayers is questionable.[80] Overall, however, the Parliamentary Joint Committee's recent review of GEERS found widespread support for the scheme, arguing that it 'is an important aspect of the overall arrangements for the protection of employee entitlements in Australia and should continue to be a feature of those arrangements'.[81] At the same time, it was recommended that alternative mechanisms for safeguarding employee entitlements should be explored, such as industry trust funds, insurance schemes and employer levies.[82]

---

[78] *Commonwealth* v. *Rocklea Spinning Mills* [2005] FCA 902, paras. 3 and 33.

[79] A complementary measure announced by the government to further improve the security of employee entitlements was a proposed amendment to the Corporations Act, 'to make it mandatory for a deed of company arrangement to preserve the priority available to creditors (as set out in [s.] 556 of the Corporations Act) unless employees agree to waive their priority, or the court upholds the deed on the grounds it offers dissenting creditors a better return than they would receive in liquidation': see Australian Government, 'Corporate Insolvency Reform', p. 2.

[80] Parliamentary Joint Committee, *Corporate Insolvency Laws*, p. 186; for a detailed exploration of the competing arguments and potential alternative arrangements, see Kinsey, 'A Triumph for Labour over Capital', 142–7.

[81] Parliamentary Joint Committee, *Corporate Insolvency Laws*, p. 187.

[82] Parliamentary Joint Committee, *Corporate Insolvency Laws*, pp. 188–90; see further J. Riley, 'Protection for Employee Entitlements: a Legal Perspective', *Australian Bulletin of Labour* 29 (2003), 31, 40–1, 43.

The third measure announced by the Federal Government in response to the Ansett collapse was a promise to place employees' claims to recover unpaid wages and notice and leave entitlements ahead of those of secured creditors in the statutory priority list for distribution of assets upon the insolvency of large companies (the 'maximum priority proposal').[83] After four years of consideration, this proposal was finally abandoned in late 2005, when the government accepted the Parliamentary Joint Committee's recommendations that the maximum priority proposal not be adopted.[84] The Committee had been influenced by many submissions by business interests opposing the proposal. Concerns that were raised included its potential negative impact on lending practices by banks and other finance providers (for example, they would make loans only to companies holding assets without employees, or seek security over the personal assets of proprietors and directors), and the resultant 'stifl[ing of] entrepreneurship' and reduction in investment levels across the economy.[85] Rather than pursuing the maximum priority proposal, the Committee recommended that 'preventative measures' be adopted to modify the behaviour of directors and managers with a view to ensuring that they accept increased responsibility for meeting employee entitlements in future.[86]

It can be seen, then, that the various statutory and policy measures adopted in recent years – especially GEERS – have improved the position of Australian employees in the event of employer insolvency. However, these reforms have done little to bring employees in from 'outside' the corporation. The prevailing corporate governance framework still prioritises the interests of 'insiders', such as directors and shareholders, as well as banks and other secured creditors, at the expense of employees. Employees, unlike these other players, have no access to information about company financial performance (for example, under secured lending instruments) that would enable them to see the warning signs of corporate failure and act to protect their interests.[87] Employees are therefore usually the last to find out about insolvencies or business restructures (such as relocations, closures and mass redundancies) that threaten their

---

[83] D. Macfarlane, 'Put Workers First in Debt Queue, Says PM', *The Weekend Australian*, 15–16 September 2001, p. 7; Parliamentary Joint Committee, *Corporate Insolvency Laws*, pp. 172–3.

[84] Australian Government, 'Corporate Insolvency Reform', p. 3.

[85] See Parliamentary Joint Committee, *Corporate Insolvency Laws*, pp. 175–80.

[86] Parliamentary Joint Committee, *Corporate Insolvency Laws*, p. 181.

[87] See J. Adams and N. Jones, 'Distressed Businesses – Preventing Failure', in CCH, *Collapse Incorporated*, p. 185.

jobs and accrued entitlements.[88] The defeat of the maximum priority proposal illustrates the extent to which business interests continue to hold sway under Australia's shareholder-centred corporate law model,[89] and can be motivated to obstruct the translation of theoretical constructions of CSR into effective legal measures.

VII. Increasing recourse to corporate law mechanisms to advance employee interests

Another significant recent development in Australia has been the increasing resort by unions, lawyers and other representatives of employees to the mechanisms of corporate law to defend and advance workers' interests, through the following types of strategies. First, labour representatives have sought to make more creative use of the limited legal rights of employees in corporate insolvency situations. This approach was pursued with some success to combat the notorious corporate restructuring and forced redundancies of unionised maritime workers by Patrick Stevedores in the 1998 waterfront dispute. In that case, the High Court of Australia ultimately found that the courts could not interfere with the discretion of the Patrick companies' administrators to make decisions in the course of the administration, even if these might be prejudicial to employees' interests.[90] However, the union's pursuit of industrial law claims, in tandem with the assertion of the former employees' rights as creditors, put it in a much stronger position to influence the outcome of settlement negotiations between the disputing parties.[91] Similarly, following the Ansett collapse, unions representing the airline's former employees played a pivotal

---

[88] See further A. Forsyth, 'Corporate Collapses and Employees' Right to Know: an Issue for Corporate Law or Labour Law?', *Australian Business Law Review* 31 (2003), 81.

[89] For example, note the Parliamentary Joint Committee's observation that the proposal 'attacks the rights of legal owners of the property in question': *Corporate Insolvency Laws*, p. 176.

[90] In particular, the administrators could not be required to keep the defunct Patrick companies operating and observe Federal Court orders to reinstate the sacked workers to their positions (these orders had been made on the basis that the Patrick restructure breached applicable industrial laws): *Patrick Stevedores Operations No. 2 Pty Ltd* v. *Maritime Union of Australia* (1998) 195 CLR 1; see M. Gronow, 'Insolvent Corporate Groups and their Employees: the Case for Further Reform', *Company and Securities Law Journal* 21 (2003), 188, 200–1; and P. Spender, 'Scenes from a Wharf: Containing the Morality of Corporate Law', in F. Macmillan (ed.), *International Corporate Law*, vol. I (Oxford: Hart Publishing, 2000), p. 37.

[91] See, e.g., Spender, 'Scenes from a Wharf', p. 43; C. Hughes, 'Towards Pinstriped Unionism: Protecting Employee Entitlements through Securitisation', *Bond Law Review* 12 (2000), 7, 9–10.

role in the voluntary administration process, (unsuccessful) efforts to enable the business to continue operating through another corporate entity, and the subsequent protracted litigation to recover their superannuation benefits and full entitlements under the SEESA scheme.[92] Indeed, in the Ansett case, the Federal Court granted the unions' applications to remove the original administrators (on conflict of interest grounds), and to be recognised as the representatives of the former employees at creditors' meetings without meeting the formal statutory requirements for the appointment of proxies.[93]

In Whelan and Zwier's view, these and other aspects of the Ansett case suggest that 'where the employee claimants are united and organised they have the capacity to have a very significant influence on the course of an insolvency administration'.[94] They point to several other cases indicating both the success of this approach, and the 'growing willingness' of the Australian Council of Trade Unions (ACTU) to engage insolvency practitioners and utilise corporate law devices for the benefit of union members adversely affected by company failures.[95] There are also several recent examples of unions successfully arguing for the 'piercing of the corporate veil' in proceedings under industrial law – for example, to overcome a company's attempts to transfer staff to a subsidiary entity so as to avoid the application of a collective agreement;[96] and to enable the Ansett unions to draw Air New Zealand (the airline's parent company) into negotiations over the employees' redundancy and employment entitlements.[97] Interestingly, these and other cases exhibit an increasing recognition by the judiciary of the need for greater protection of employee interests in corporate restructures and insolvencies. This is perhaps best exemplified by Justice Merkel of the Federal Court's condemnation of the Coogi clothing company's treatment of its 'long serving and loyal employees . . . as if they were serfs, rather than free citizens', by transferring their employment

---

[92] See again Whelan and Zwier, *Employee Entitlements*, pp. 32–41.

[93] See Whelan and Zwier, *Employee Entitlements*, pp. 32–3; and Forsyth, 'Corporate Collapses', 94, discussing *In the matter of Ansett Australia Ltd; Rappas v. Ansett Australia Ltd* [2001] FCA 1348, 39 ACSR 296.

[94] See Whelan and Zwier, *Employee Entitlements*, pp. 42–3.

[95] See Whelan and Zwier, *Employee Entitlements*, pp. 44–6, discussing the Pasminco, Newmont Yandal and James Hardie cases; see also the examination of the Coogi clothing case in Forsyth, 'Corporate Collapses', 81–2.

[96] *Burswood Catering and Entertainment Pty Ltd v. ALHMWU (WA Branch)* [2002] WASCA 354 (Western Australian Industrial Appeal Court); see J. Harris, 'Lifting the corporate veil on the basis of an implied agency: a re-evaluation of Smith, Stone and Knight', *Company and Securities Law Journal* 23 (2005), 7, 21–4.

[97] *ASU and TWU v. Ansett Australia Ltd* (Australian Industrial Relations Commission, Boulton J, PR909513, 24 September 2001).

(without notice) to shell companies with insufficient assets to pay out the workers' entitlements.[98]

The second and third of the corporate law strategies adopted by Australian unions in recent years – 'boardroom activism' and 'shareholder activism' – really amount to attempts to bring employees 'inside' the institutional structures of the corporation, and so take advantage of the shareholder primacy model. Through the concept of *boardroom* activism, the ACTU encourages union representatives on superannuation fund boards to use their positions to ensure 'socially responsible' investment decisions.[99] Boardroom activism has also involved attempts by unions to obtain seats on the boards of major companies, such as the Finance Sector Union's campaign to have a representative elected to the ANZ Bank board. Although (to date) unsuccessful, these efforts have provided a platform for unions to articulate concerns about staff reductions, collective bargaining rights and other employment issues.[100]

The ACTU's *shareholder* activism strategy seeks to utilise the combined voting power of employee and superannuation fund shareholdings to influence decision-making about retrenchments, wage disparities and industrial negotiations at company annual general meetings (AGMs).[101] This approach involves the use of various provisions of the Corporations Act,[102] including those enabling a minimum of a hundred shareholders to submit proposed resolutions at AGMs[103] and to request the holding of extraordinary general meetings;[104] the right of shareholders to ask

---

[98] *McClusky* v. *Karagiozis* [2002] FCA 1137, para. 16. In this decision, Merkel J overturned the company's actions and found that the employees should be regarded as having continued in employment with the original employing entity, making them creditors of that entity and thereby increasing their prospects of recovering their entitlements; see further Forsyth, 'Corporate Collapses', 81–2.

[99] See S. Burrow, 'Whispers Outside the Boardroom Door: Making Working Australia's Money Talk' (Address to the Sydney Institute, Sydney, 29 August 2000); G. Combet, Speech to ACSI Corporate Governance Conference, 9 July 2005.

[100] See K. Anderson and I. Ramsay, *From the Picket Line to the Boardroom: Union Shareholder Activism in Australia* (Research Report, Centre for Corporate Law and Securities Regulation and Centre for Employment and Labour Relations Law, University of Melbourne, December 2005), pp. 22–6.

[101] See Australian Council of Trade Unions, *Corporate Governance Background Paper* (ACTU Congress, 2003); G. Combet, 'Superannuation, Unions and Good Labour Relations' (Address to the Conference of Major Superannuation Funds, Ashmore, 14 March 2002).

[102] See Anderson and Ramsay, *From the Picket Line to the Boardroom*, pp. 1, 50–7.

[103] Corporations Act 2001, s. 249N.

[104] Corporations Act 2001, s. 249D; the Australian Government has proposed to amend this provision so that only holders of 5 per cent of voting shares may requisition a general meeting: see Parliament of Australia, *Inquiry into the Exposure Draft of the Corporations Amendment Bill (No. 2) 2005* (2005), p. 6.

questions of directors at the AGM;[105] and the 'proxy voting' provision.[106] Although unions have not yet obtained shareholder support for their resolutions at any Australian company AGM, shareholder activism has proved successful in enabling unions to focus board and public attention on industrial issues at major companies like Rio Tinto, Boral, Commonwealth Bank, Blue Scope Steel and NRMA.[107] The strategy has been a particularly effective mechanism for unions in obtaining satisfactory outcomes to protracted enterprise bargaining negotiations – that is, after raising concerns about industrial disputes at company general meetings, resolution of the outstanding issues has often quickly followed.[108] As part of their shareholder activism campaigns, unions have also focused on 'mainstream' corporate governance issues, such as the need for independent non-executive directors and limits on executive pay, in order to attract support on industrial issues from other shareholders (especially large institutional investors like superannuation funds).[109]

The increasing recourse by labour representatives to the mechanisms and processes of corporate law represents a considerable shift in the perception of employees and unions as corporate 'outsiders' under the traditional shareholder primacy model.[110] In part, this phenomenon is a response to the removal of many of the long-standing rights and protections for workers and unions under the Australian labour law system since the election of the (conservative) Coalition Government in 1996. This process began with the passage of the Workplace Relations Act 1996 (Cth), and has been taken considerably further by the Workplace Relations Amendment (Work Choices) Act 2005 (Cth), which virtually abolishes the right to strike and significantly constrains employees' rights to access collective bargaining and union representation.[111] Unions have therefore

---

[105] Corporations Act 2001, s. 250S.   [106] Corporations Act 2001, s. 249X.

[107] See the detailed case studies reported in Anderson and Ramsay, *From the Picket Line to the Boardroom*, pp. 10–42.

[108] See Anderson and Ramsay, *From the Picket Line to the Boardroom*, pp. 10–42, 71–6, 83–5.

[109] Anderson and Ramsay, *From the Picket Line to the Boardroom*, pp. 76–8, 85.

[110] See further R. Mitchell, A. O'Donnell and I. Ramsay, *Shareholder Value and Employee Interests: Intersections Between Corporate Governance, Corporate Law and Labour Law*, Research Paper, Centre for Corporate Law and Securities Regulation, Centre for Employment and Labour Relations Law, University of Melbourne (2005).

[111] See A. Forsyth and C. Sutherland, 'Collective Labour Relations under Siege: the Work Choices legislation and collective bargaining', *Australian Journal of Labour Law* 19, 2 (2006) 183. The 2005 legislation also reduces the (already limited) labour law protections for employees in situations of corporate restructure and insolvency, by removing the scope for employees to obtain severance payments through an award variation (as occurred in the case of One.Tel, discussed above) or under statute; and limiting the statutory rights of unions to obtain information and consult with management about mass redundancies.

looked to corporate law as an alternative avenue for influencing management decision-making, and it is expected that this trend will continue
in light of the further diminution of labour law protections under the
2005 legislation.[112] This also challenges the concept of shareholder primacy, as workers' interests increasingly fall into alignment with those of
the broader shareholder base.[113] Not unexpectedly, therefore, a 'backlash'
against union reliance on corporate law has already commenced,[114] once
again illustrating the power of company 'insiders' to fend off incursions
by non-shareholder interests into the corporate realm.

VIII. Employees 'missing' in the debate over corporate governance reform? Australia, the United Kingdom and the United States compared

Employees have received very little attention in the extensive debate
over corporate governance reform in Australia. That debate has been
overwhelmingly shareholder-centred, with legislative responses aimed at
improving board relationships with shareholders and auditor independence.[115] These reform measures make little or no mention of employees,
partly because political actors representing workers' interests (such as the
ACTU and the Australian Labor Party) have not sought to take the corporate governance debate in this direction. Rather, they have supported
moves to strengthen the requirements for independent company auditors, and increased shareholder scrutiny of executive remuneration.[116]
The ACTU has also pressed for legislative reform to enable 'piercing of the
corporate veil' in cases of tortious liability (in response to the James Hardie
episode), and for 'appropriate' regulatory support for voluntary initiatives

---

[112] Anderson and Ramsay, *From the Picket Line to the Boardroom*, pp. 74–6, 86.

[113] See further Anderson and Ramsay, *From the Picket Line to the Boardroom*, pp. 88–92;
Mitchell, O'Donnell and Ramsay, *Shareholder Value and Employee Interests*.

[114] For example, proposed legislative amendments will require unions to obtain the support of at least 5 per cent of a company's shareholders to call an extraordinary general
meeting (rather than only 100 shareholders, as at present); and the Commonwealth
Bank brought (unsuccessful) legal proceedings alleging that the Finance Sector Union's
shareholder activism campaign breached industrial law prohibitions on 'coercion' in
enterprise bargaining: see *Commonwealth Bank of Australia* v. *Finance Sector Union of
Australia* [2006] FCA 1048.

[115] See A. Clarke, 'The Relative Position of Employees in the Corporate Governance Context:
an International Comparison', *Australian Business Law Review* 32 (2004), 111; P. von
Nessen, 'Corporate Governance in Australia: Converging with International Developments', *Australian Journal of Corporate Law* 15 (2003), 1.

[116] See, for example, Senator S. Conroy, *Directions Statement: Improving Corporate Governance* (2002); ACTU, *Corporate Governance Policy* (ACTU Congress, 2003).

to promote corporate responsibility.[117] Several academics have lamented the narrow focus of the corporate governance debate in Australia, arguing that it should be broadened to consider options such as European-style systems for employee representation on company boards.[118] That the ACTU has not embraced the idea of legally-mandated employee representation at board-level demonstrates that, despite the recent developments examined in this chapter, the concept of shareholder primacy remains strongly entrenched in Australia.

In the United Kingdom, recent corporate law developments suggest mixed fortunes for employees. On the one hand, employees have figured far more prominently in the debate over corporate governance reform in the United Kingdom. This has included consideration of a 'major redesign of [company] decision-making structures to permit participation by the relevant stakeholder groups', such as employees.[119] The United Kingdom has also implemented EU laws requiring at least partial adaptation of the shareholder primacy model, to reflect aspects of the European 'stakeholder' approach to corporate regulation – specifically, employee board representation.[120]

On the other hand, as indicated earlier in this chapter, amendments to UK company legislation have seen the provision requiring directors to have regard to the interests of employees as well as shareholders[121] replaced by a more general directors' duty provision.[122] In addition to the criticisms of the former statutory provision discussed above, its effectiveness in protecting employee interests has been questioned on the basis that it does not require those interests to be given priority, and

---

[117] See Australian Council of Trade Unions, *Submission to the Parliamentary Joint Committee on Corporations and Financial Services Inquiry into Corporate Responsibility* (September 2005).

[118] See, for example, R. Markey, 'A Stakeholder Approach to Corporate Governance: Employee Representatives on Boards of Management', in Gollan and Patmore (eds.), *Partnerships at work*, pp. 122, 132–3; Clarke, 'The Relative Position of Employees', 114, 119, 130–1.

[119] J. Parkinson, 'Models of the Company and the Employment Relationship', *British Journal of Industrial Relations* 41 (2003), 481, 499–504; see also P. Davies, 'Employee Representation and Corporate Law Reform: a Comment from the United Kingdom', *Comparative Labor Law and Policy Journal* 22 (2000), 135; J. Williamson, 'A Trade Union Congress perspective on the Company Law Review and Corporate Governance Reform since 1997', *British Journal of Industrial Relations* 41 (2003), 511.

[120] See P. Davies, 'Workers on the Board of the European Company?', *Industrial Law Journal* 32 (2003), 75; C. Barnard and S. Deakin, 'Reinventing the European Corporation: Corporate Governance, Social Policy and the Single Market', *Industrial Relations Journal* 33 (2002), 484.

[121] Companies Act 1985 (UK), s. 309(1).   [122] Companies Act 2006 (UK), s. 172.

because the duty is owed to the company and therefore is enforceable only at the instance of shareholders.[123] However, the enshrinement of the concept of 'enlightened shareholder value' through the new statutory provision[124] means that employees will have to *compete* with a range of other stakeholders for legal recognition.[125]

Finally, in the United States, although employees were significantly adversely affected by massive corporate collapses like Enron and World-Com, the major corporate governance response to these events – the Sarbanes-Oxley Act – did not contain any reforms to improve the protection of employee interests.[126]

IX. Conclusion: the new corporate law

The discussion in this chapter has highlighted the restricted, though still important, role of formal corporate law rules and processes in responding to demands for improved CSR. We have emphasised that the shareholder primacy model, which underpins the Australian and Anglo-American corporate law systems, imposes limits on what can be achieved by corporate legal doctrine and legislative rules. For that reason, rather than focusing solely on attempts to adapt or formalise exceptions to established concepts such as directors' fiduciary duties, we suggest that it may be more fruitful to acknowledge the constraints of formal statutory and judicial rules, and to recognise the growing significance of codes, guidelines and standards, and so on, and their impact on corporate managerial behaviour. Indeed, we argue that the 'new' corporate law in these jurisdictions should be understood not as an attempt to expand or adapt the content of corporate law, but instead as an expanded conception of what counts as corporate law.

Most often the analysis of CSR and how to encourage it begins by assuming a separation between 'the law' and other 'non-legal' phenomena,

---

[123] C. Villiers, 'Section 309 of the Companies Act 1985: is it Time for a Reappraisal?', in H. Collins, P. Davies and R. Rideout (eds.), *Legal Regulation of the Employment Relation* (Dordrecht: Kluwer, 2000), pp. 595–7; Lord Wedderburn, 'Employees, Partnership and Company Law', *Industrial Law Journal* 31 (2002), 99, 106–8.

[124] See P. Davies, 'Enlightened Shareholder Value and the New Responsibilities of Directors: What Does the Best Director Do for the Creditor?' (Inaugural W. E. Hearn Lecture, Law School, The University of Melbourne, 4 October 2005).

[125] B. Wedderburn, *The Future of Company Law: Fat Cats, Corporate Governance and Workers* (London: The Institute of Employment Rights, 2004), p. 43.

[126] Whelan and Zwier, *Employee Entitlements*, p. 16; Clarke, 'The Relative Position of Employees', 121–5.

such as codes and guidelines (for ease of reference, we will use the term 'codes' to refer to this diverse array of material). But, as we have seen in this chapter, corporate law increasingly depends on codes; the law leaves it to codes to fill in the gaps that the law cannot or will not deal with. Where corporate law prescribes general standards, such as 'best interests', 'good faith' or 'care and diligence', codes can supply the further detail. Furthermore, corporate law relies on 'other areas of law which support and create corporations, and the transactions which those corporations enter into'.[127] Rather than viewing corporate law as a discrete, self-referential category of law, we should be concerned with the way in which corporate law interacts with other categories of law, and with other mechanisms for influencing behaviour (such as codes), or non-legislative instruments, to achieve specific outcomes (such as the GEERS policy described above).

Understanding how CSR can be encouraged and enforced means recognising the interdependent nature of corporate law. This does not mean elevating codes to the status of law. Amongst other things, that would carry risks of unaccountable rule-making. And it does not mean assuming that codes are always effective or that they cannot be used in a tokenistic way – as part of CSR 'window-dressing'. Nor does it mean that the law is unimportant, irrelevant or marginal in how we respond to concerns about CSR. The previous discussion about the shareholder activism strategies of Australian unions demonstrates this. It does mean, however, that focusing only on accepted legal categories (and legal limitations) is to miss a big part of the picture. The recent Australian experience of efforts to change formal rules of corporate regulation to accommodate employee interests demonstrates the difficulties that can be encountered in efforts to transpose CSR concepts into meaningful legal rules. For employees, more significant inroads into the shareholder primacy model might be made through reforms to labour law. This could include the adoption of mandatory works councils and other mechanisms for employee 'voice' that can challenge the power of company institutions (such as the board) from which workers are largely excluded.[128]

---

[127] A. Corbett and S. Bottomley, 'Regulating Corporate Governance', in C. Parker, C. Scott, N. Lacey, and J. Braithwaite (eds.), *Regulating Law* (Oxford: Oxford University Press, 2004), p. 63.

[128] For an account of how this has occurred in the United Kingdom under the influence of EU labour law directives, see J. Armour, S. Deakin and S. Konzelmann, 'Shareholder Primacy and the Trajectory of UK Corporate Governance', *British Journal of Industrial Relations* 41 (2003).

In summary, the new corporate law owes more to expanded ideas of regulation than to formal conceptions of what counts as law.[129] The new literature on regulation supplies a means for bringing these parts together. It recognises that, in everyday corporate practice, the boundaries between the law and codes are not always felt so clearly. This idea builds on an argument, developed elsewhere, that the category of law known as 'corporate law' is being transformed into a broader category of rules, which can be called 'corporate governance':

> Corporate law may in the past have been described as a one-dimensional body of law concerned with the regulating the interests of investors, managers and directors. The impact of regulation has been to transform this body of law into an emerging law of corporate governance, which seeks to integrate the policies and concerns of broad areas of regulation into corporate law.[130]

The terrain of CSR, ill-defined though it is, is a prime example of this transformation.

---

[129] The essays in Parker *et al.*, *Regulating Law* explore the impact of 'regulation' on different aspects of the law.

[130] Corbett and Bottomley, 'Regulating Corporate Governance', p. 81.

11

Shareholder activism for corporate social responsibility: law and practice in the United States, Japan, France and Spain

B. AMANN, J. CABY, J. JAUSSAUD AND J. PIÑEIRO

Lewis Gilbert is generally considered the first individual activist shareholder. In 1932, as a holder of ten shares of New York's Consolidated Gas Company, he attended the general meeting of shareholders. He was dismayed at the fact that he could not ask questions. Afterwards, Gilbert and his brother worked towards the implementation of a reform and, in 1934, the Securities and Exchange Commission (SEC) finally enacted a rule allowing shareholders to submit resolutions that might be subject to a vote.[1]

The title of an editorial in the French newspaper *Les Échos* in 2003, 'Shareholders' revolt rises in the City',[2] shows that shareholders are progressively relinquishing their passive attitude and adopting active behaviour patterns. Through resolutions put forward at general meetings, they are trying to influence the company's choices, with or without the agreement of the managers. This activism has seen a rapid rise in the United States and in the United Kingdom and, to a lesser extent, in continental Europe and Japan.

---

[1] Proposing resolutions at general meetings of shareholders has been authorised in the United States by the SEC since 1934. Used for the first time in 1942, these proposals consisted of a brief text submitted by the shareholders requiring a specific action by the management. They are included in companies' annual reports with the response from the management and its recommendations for voting. Even if the proposal obtains a majority, the management is not compelled to implement it. Though the SEC may want it, these proposals are just meant to inform the management of the various shareholders' opinions. Until the end of the 1980s, most of these resolutions came from individual investors or activist social groups and rarely got more than 10 per cent of the votes. Today, these resolutions are more often formulated by institutional investors and obtain much higher percentages of the vote, even the majority.

[2] *Les Échos*, 27 October 2003.

Verstegen Ryan and Schneider[3] define investor activism as 'the use of power by an investor either to influence the process and outcomes of a given portofolio firm or to evoke large-scale change in process or outcomes across multiple firms through the symbolic targeting of one or more portofolio firms'. Le Maux's definition[4] allows us to pinpoint the nature of the ultimate objectives: 'activism includes all actions and procedures undertaken by one (or several) external shareholder(s) with the aim of changing one or several characteristic(s) of the firm in order to better respond to his (or their) financial, social or ethical expectations'.

Thus, activism is the expression of a governance mechanism used by companies which allows all shareholders to express their voices (in the sense of Hirschman)[5] in numerous domains, regardless of their participation in the capital.

Today, activism is primarily pursued by institutional investors.[6] Nowadays, collective management allows households to place their assets in the hands of professional managers. This phenomenon of collectivisation of savings management (that is, the fact that households entrust their saving to huge funds which practise collective management) was hastened by structural evolution. On the one hand, the continuing ageing of the population leads to worries about how to continue financing the contributory pension scheme prevailing in, for example, France. On the other hand, the formidable development of the financial markets in the wake of the deregulations of the 1980s and 1990s provides great investment opportunities with an unparalled liquidity, notably in real estate. This diagnosis is common to all industrialised countries and is even conclusive in those where savings-based retirement has been adopted. The economic weight of institutional investors has become considerable, to the point that their assets overweigh the gross domestic product (GDP) of the (formerly fifteen-member) European Community, Japan and the United States combined. While in the 1960s they held less than 20 per cent of American shares, they now concentrate more than 60 per cent of these shares in their portfolios, and the movement is gathering ground (see Table 1).

[3] L. Verstegen Ryan and M. Schneider, 'The Antecedents of Institutional Investor Activism', *Academy of Management Review* 27, 4 (2002), 554–73.

[4] J. Le Maux, 'L'Activisme: une Protection Active des Actionnaires Minoritaires', in Centre de Recherche en Finance et en Banque, *Recherches récentes en finance* (Paris: Publications de la Sorbonne, 2004).

[5] A. Hirschman, *Exit, Voice and Loyalty* (Cambridge, MA: Harvard University Press, 1973).

[6] The term 'institutional investors' refers to all non-individual investors, such as insurance companies, pension funds, banks and investment funds.

Table 1 *US holding of equities outstanding by investor type*

Types of investors	1990 in US billion dollars (%)	1995 in US billion dollars (%)	2000 in US billion dollars (%)	2001 in US billion dollars (%)
Households Total	1,781 (50.3%)	4,161 (49.1%)	7,317 (41.7%)	5,888 (38.7%)
Institutional Investors Total	1,761 (49.7%)	4,314 (50.9%)	10,249 (58.3%)	9,312 (61.3%)
Public pension funds	285 (8.0%)	679 (8.0%)	1,335 (7.6%)	1,216 (8.0%)
Private pension funds	606 (17.1%)	1,289 (15.2%)	2,195 (12.5%)	1,905 (12.5%)
Pension funds total	*891 (25.1%)*	*1,968 (23.2%)*	*3,530 (20.1%)*	*3,121 (20.5%)*
Mutual funds	233 (6.6%)	1,025 (12.1%)	3,227 (18.4%)	2,836 (18.7%) .
Insurance companies	162 (4.6%)	449 (5.3%)	1,135 (6.5%)	1,076 (7.1%)
Bank personal trust	190 (5.4%)	225 (2.7%)	280 (1.6%)	226 (1.5%)
Foreign	244 (6.9%)	528 (6.2%)	1,748 (10.0%)	1,698 (11.2%)
Others	42 (1.2%)	118 (1.4%)	329 (1.9%)	355 (2.3%)
Total outstanding	**3,543 (100%)**	**8,475 (100%)**	**17,566 (100%)**	**15,201 (100%)**

Source: Securities Industry Association Fact Book 2002.

Taking into account the financial weight they represent, these institutional investors now have the means to wield the power attached to
their rights. They first used their power on traditional issues of corporate
governance, like the compensation of managers.[7] In this context, shareholder activism seems to be mainly a matter of shareholders defending
their financial interests. This can be seen either in the content of resolutions (compensation of managers, for example) or in the authors of the
resolutions (public or private pension funds).

The more recent attention paid to the notion of sustainable development is another outward sign of these attempts to acknowledge the power
of shareholders. Applied to the corporate world, impacting the notion of
sustainable development has led shareholders to be more attentive to
the concerns of all of the stakeholders – personnel, clients and suppliers,
investors and non-governmental organisations (NGOs) – that convey the
expectations of society as well as the environment of the company. For

---

[7] To illustrate, the compensation of the general manager of the British company Glaxo, one
of the worldwide leaders in the pharmaceutical sector, was rejected by the shareholders
during the 2003 general meeting. This was made possible by a July 2002 law adopted by
the London Stock Exchange (LSE) that stipulates that all companies listed in the United
Kingdom must submit their compensation report for the approval of the shareholders
during the annual general meeting starting with fiscal years ending 31 December 2002.

companies, it is thus a matter of undertaking a route of social responsibility with an influence on the practices and processes implemented in domains such as human resources, commercial practices and waste collection. However, such attention to corporate social responsibility (CSR) on the side of shareholders may be regarded as an attempt to protect a company from any potential financial damage resulting from the complaints of any stakeholder.

A study of the relationship between shareholder activism and CSR successively led to:

(1) the characterisation of shareholder activism and its influence on CSR;
(2) a comparison of the situations in Spain, the United States, France and Japan, both in terms of legal contexts and practices observed.

The growing weight of institutional investors will clearly appear as a driving force in the development of shareholder activism, including questions related to CSR in all four countries. However, important differences remain according to the different legal frameworks. These differences go beyond the traditional distinction between common law countries and civil law countries. Shareholder activism will face various restrictions in the different countries, sometimes complicating their access to one mechanism or another.

I. The characterisation of shareholder activism and its influence on corporate social responsibility

A. General characteristics of activism

Verstegen Ryan and Schneider[8] propose a comprehensive model of activism by institutional investors. According to them, their propensity for activism depends on twelve characteristics of funds (see Table 2).

Using this model, these authors can make predictions on the intensity of activism with respect to the type of fund. Public pension funds supposedly show significant activism, private pension funds and investment funds show moderate activism, and banks and insurance companies show low activism. They also indicate that their methodology should remedy the disappointing findings of empirical studies that have tried to highlight the positive influence of activism on companies. Therefore, this model leads to a form of typology of institutional investors.

[8] L. Verstegen Ryan and M. Schneider, 'The Antecedents of Institutional Investor Activism', 554–73.

Table 2 *The influence of the characteristics of funds on the intensity of activism*

Characteristics	Intensity of activism
Fund size	+
Investment time horizon	+
Performance expectation	
– *Purely financial*	–
– *Financial and non-financial*	+
Ability to resist pressure	+
Percentage of the firm stock	+
Percentage represented by the company in the portfolio	+
Proportion invested in equity	+
Legal restraints (law on retirement, law on bankruptcy)	–
Nature of the fund	
– *Defined benefits*	+
– *Defined contributions*	–
Fund's management method	
– *Passive*	+
– *Active*	–
Delegation of management (vs. exercising rights)	+
Exercising voting rights in general meeting (vs. delegation)	+

Source: Verstegen Ryan and Schneider (2002)

Girard[9] used the same type of exercise to draw up a typology of active minority shareholders in France by relying on three criteria: information, influence and control. It distinguishes the small holders, the salaried shareholders, the banks and insurance companies, the private or public American pension funds, and capital risk companies. This author notices that French activism typically implements alternative control mechanisms, like the creation of or recourse to shareholder associations. Furthermore, the strategy of minority shareholders leads to the systematic recourse to legal proceedings. Individual French shareholders thus use the association

[9] C. Girard, 'Une Typologie de l'Activisme des Actionnaires Minoritaires', *Finance Contrôle Stratégie* 4, 3 (2001), 123–46.

mechanism to act collectively within defence associations like ADAM,[10] and prefer giving their claims a public profile rather than referring the case to judicial bodies.[11]

More generally, the relationships between institutional investors and companies can take two main forms: negotiation or conflict. The first happens through informal negotiations meant to bring about an evolution in the governance of the companies concerned. The conflict form, referred to as activism, consists in proposing resolutions at general meetings of shareholders, generally when negotiations have already failed. This latter form is often accompanied by media campaigns meant to bring more pressure to bear on the companies concerned so that they will act in the desired way. Furthermore, the companies compromise fairly frequently, so that the resolutions are withdrawn. Finally, activism is decreasingly individual and increasingly coordinated, notably through organisations such as the Council of Institutional Investors (CII)[12] in the United States.

The US public pension fund California Public Employees Retirement Scheme (CalPERS) is well known for its activism. It is based on the publication and publicising of a 'focus list'[13] made up of listed companies selected for their weak governance and their poor financial performance. Each year, CalPERS draws up a preliminary list and contacts the companies concerned at the end of the summer or in early autumn. During the four to six months that follow, CalPERS meets with the managers and directors to make them aware of their interests and to allow the management to take the necessary steps to get off the list. Sometimes the potential candidates react immediately by initiating share buy-backs and implementing new internal control mechanisms, resulting in the hope of a rapid positive reaction for their stock price and thus avoiding inclusion on the list. In the opposite case, the list is published in February or March: it includes six to twelve names.[14]

Empirical research on the influence of resolutions proposed by institutional investors on companies' performance produces ambiguous

---

[10] Association de Défense des Actionnaires Minoritaires (Association for the Defence of Minority Shareholders), directed by C. Neuville.

[11] Onnée S. *Motivations et Effets Attendus du Retrait de la Côte: le Cas Français* (Grenoble: Université de Grenoble, 1998).

[12] The CII is an organisation that includes more than 130 public and private pension funds. Each October, the CII releases its list of under-performing companies.

[13] This list was created in 1992.

[14] M. Anson, T. White and H. Ho, 'The Shareholder Wealth Effects of CalPERS' Focus List', *Journal of Applied Corporate Finance* 5, 3 (2003), 102–11.

results.[15] Though institutional investors may frequently succeed in bringing about changes in companies' governance structures, this doesn't seem to have an effect on their performance.[16]

In France, Montandrau[17] observed a negative reaction upon the announcement of an alert by the AFG-ASFFI,[18] while Girard[19] measured a negative evolution of the financial market before the public announcement of a contestation process in under-performing companies. Finally, Girard[20] noticed that, generally, French institutional investors withdraw their participation from companies that are subject to shareholder activism.[21]

B. The influence of shareholder activism on corporate social responsibility

This influence is older than it seems and even precedes the mostly financial activism that has been mentioned up to now.[22] In biblical times, the Jewish laws included numerous directives on how to invest ethically. In the middle of the seventeenth century, the founder of the Methodist movement, John Wesley, put the emphasis on the fact that jobs and money were the second most important subject evoked by the teachings of the New Testament. Revisited by the puritanical Americans of the 1920s, ethical investment served various causes. In the beginning, it was a matter of banning gambling, tobacco or pornography, so that for a long time there was a religious dimension. Then, in the 1960s, the boycott of arms manufacturers during the Vietnam War, the first fights for the environment,

---

[15] For a very good review of the empirical literature on this subject, see Le Maux, 'L'Activisme'.

[16] W.-L. Song and S. H. Szewczyk, 'Does Coordinated Institutional Investor Activism Reverse the Fortunes of Underperforming Firms?', *Journal of Financial and Quantitative Analysis* 38, 2 (2003), 317–36.

[17] S. Montandrau, 'Activisme des Investisseurs Institutionnels et Richesse de l'Actionnaire: l'Influence du Conseil d'Administration lors des Alertes AFG-ASFFI', *Cahier de Recherche* (CEROG IAE d'Aix-en-Provence, 2004).

[18] The ASG-ASFFI is the French professional association of funds managers. Since 1999, it has periodically put out alerts on listed companies that do not comply with the rules on corporate governance fixed by their deontological code. Furthermore, Montandrau ('Activisme des Investisseurs Institutionnels') noted that the reaction is all the more negative as the motives are numerous – and all the less as governance is favourable.

[19] C. Girard , 'La Visibilité de la Cause Actionnariale', *Banque et Marchés* 63 (2003).

[20] C. Girard , 'L'Incidence de l'Activisme Actionnarial sur les Mécanismes de Gouvernance: le Cas Français', *Finance Contrôle Stratégie* 7, 3 (2004), 91–116.

[21] Except if the companies concerned have insufficient performance or if they are the object of legal battles.

[22] Le Maux, 'L'Activisme'.

for civil rights, for women's rights, and so on, all secularised the movement. But it was the mobilisation against apartheid in South Africa that brought together all these actors and brought shareholder activism out of its fragmented state.

Sustainable development certainly has ideological content, but it is not merely the expression of a beatifying ideology in search of an ideal society. It is the fruit of a conviction that respecting certain moral values ultimatly results in superior efficiency, for companies in particular and for society in general. Indeed, the social and environmental criteria laid out, notably on ethical grounds,[23] are necessary steps toward a sustainable competitive advantage (of sustainable development) by companies. The ethical question meets the necessity for economic efficiency.

As Derwall, et al. indicated,[24] the creation of a share value that can be attributed to the addition of an ethical dimension to the share selection process is still up for debate. On the one hand, at the corporate level, dedicating financial resources to the improvement of social and environmental performance should lead to a loss of value (increased costs lead to higher prices, a competitive disadvantage and lower profitability). But, on the other hand, improved social and environmental performance could lead to superior efficiency and the creation of new market opportunities. Thus, if the expected profits from social and environmental initiatives are greater (or lower) than their costs, the holders of the socially responsible portfolio should obtain greater (or lower) returns.

Numerous empirical studies have attempted to test the links between social and environmental performance on the one hand, and financial performance on the other, without arriving at truly proven results one way or the other. According to Ullman,[25] and Griffin and Mahon,[26] the conflicting results obtained are mainly due to methodological differences[27]

---

[23] For more insight into ethical funds, see B. Bickart and J. Caby, 'Fonds Éthiques et Développement Durable', in J. Allouche, *Encyclopédie des Ressources Humaines* (Paris: Vuibert, 2003).

[24] J. Derwall, N. Guenster, R. Bauer and K. Koedijk, 'The Eco-Efficiency Premium Puzzle', *Financial Analysts Journal* 61, 2 (2005), 51–63.

[25] A. E. Ullman, 'Data in Search of a Theory: A Critical Examination of the Relationships Among Social Performance, Social Disclosure, and Economic Performance of U.S. Firms', *Academy of Management Review* 10, 3 (1985), 540–57.

[26] J.-J. Griffin and J.-F. Mahon, 'The Corporate Social Performance and Corporate Social Performance Debate. Twenty-Five Years of Incomparable Research', *Business and Society* 36, 1 (1997), 5–31.

[27] When financial performance is measured by stock prices, three types of methodology are used to evaluate the link between the social and environmental performance: event studies, portfolio studies and regression studies.

and to the choice of indicators of financial, social and environmental performance.

Nevertheless, Orlitzky, et al.[28] have carried out a meta-analysis on the numerous empirical studies and observed a significantly positive correlation between social responsibility and several indicators, like return on assets, return on equity and the evolution of share prices. Similarly, Derwal et al.,[29] aided by a methodology that takes into account the insufficiencies normally attributed to studies on the subject, showed that in the United States a portfolio invested in companies that have good records of environmental efficiency had a higher yield than a portfolio of poorly-rated companies for the period from 1995 to 2003.[30] From a strict financial point of view, these superior returns are an anomaly because the profitability–risk arbitrage should take into account the companies' environmental and social performance; these superior returns would thus be due either to the omission of a risk factor or to a bad estimation of the market.[31]

Though shareholder activism in matters of sustainable development is *sui generis* the result of socially responsible investment funds, other actors also come into play – American public pension funds like CalPERS, for example. Johnson and Greening[32] have, furthermore, noted that the shareholders of public pension funds have a positive influence on companies' social and environmental performance, while the presence of traditional investment funds has no effect. According to Woidtke, Bierman and Tuggle,[33] the political aims demonstrated by the managers of public-sector pension funds present a conflict of interest with their fiduciary responsibility vis-à-vis the beneficiaries. The intended social objectives are clearly commendable, but they distract them from their main objective: the profitability of investments. In addition, the administrative costs imposed

---

[28] M. Orlitzky, F. L. Schmidt and S. L. Rynes, 'Corporate Social and Financial Performance: A Meta-Analysis', *Organization Studies* 24 (2003), 403–41.

[29] J. Derwall J. N. Guenster, R. Bauer and K. Koedijk, 'The Eco-Efficiency Premium Puzzle', *Financial Analysts Journal* 61, 2 (2005), 51–63.

[30] To illustrate the methodological problems, these results cannot be explained by the sensitivity of the market, the investment style or specific sectoral characteristics.

[31] This debate goes way beyond the scope of this article. See Campbell and Vick, Chapter 8 in this volume.

[32] R. D. Johnson and D. W. Greening, 'The Effect of Corporate Governance and Institutional Ownership Types on Corporate Social Performance', *Academy of Management Journal* 42, 5 (1999), 564–76.

[33] T. Woidtke, L. Bierman and C. Tuggle, 'Reining in Activist Funds', *Harvard Business Review* (March 2003), 22–3.

upon companies that are the target of these offers are very high (roughly US$100,000).

What is more, shareholder activism in the social domain involves more fundamental risks: disguised protectionism and cultural neo-colonialism.

In the context of globalisation, the international competitiveness of western companies can be weakened by different legislation concerning the environment, workers' rights, social security financing or human rights. The companies in developing countries that are not subject to these constraints may benefit from an undeniable comparative advantage. The inclusion of social and environmental criteria into shareholders' resolutions and into the investment policies of ethical funds can lead to weakening the competitiveness of these companies and a reduction in competition from developing countries. This barrier to the economic development of companies in those countries can materialise itself in two ways. On the one hand, they only benefit from international financing if they accept constraints that lower or eliminate their competitive advantage in terms of costs while local savings are non-existent or insufficient. On the other hand, indirect pressure placed on western multinationals that are donors yields the same effect when these companies operate as subcontractors, as is often the case. Under the guise of good intentions, these measures could thus be considered a means of original and discrete protectionism, albeit efficient and akin to another perverse effect, cultural neo-colonialism.

Even though they were partially abandoned in favour of other influences, the confessional origins of ethical investment are still present because of the ethnocentric character of the main investor countries. The Judeo-Christian roots of most developed countries, with the notable exception of Japan, lend a base of relatively homogenous moral values that is reinforced by the economic weight of the Anglo-Saxon world. On the other hand, numerous developing countries have different cultural values because of their different political and religious history. For example, the concept of human rights does not necessarily possess the universal character that it is given in a country like France. This type of example leads to debates on ethical content which is beyond the scope of this study, but which can seriously flesh out arguments on the existence of a neo-colonialism all the more efficient because it is harmful. The criteria for sustainable development,[34] a reflection of westernised morals, could be the vehicle for this neo-colonialism.

---

[34] Or at least a part of them.

II. Shareholder activism for the benefit of corporate social responsibility: legal mechanisms and implementation

A. A comparative analysis of legal contexts

Any analysis of the legal instruments that allow shareholder intervention or activism vis-à-vis companies (see section 2 below) is inseparable from the evocation of contextual influences (see section 1 below).

1. The influence of contextual variables

Taking into account the general characteristics of national systems of corporate governance is essential. Without developing this issue too much, since it goes beyond the scope of this study, some comments can be made.

Depending on whether one is located in an environment with an Anglo-Saxon type of governance (the United States, for example) or a continental type (France, for example), the instruments available to shareholders are different. The major structural factors of the environment, both microeconomic and macroeconomic, exert a certain influence. Thus, the level of concentration of stock ownership leads to specific methods of protection (for example, in France 48 per cent of SBF 120 companies are controlled by a reference shareholder holding at least one third of the capital). Similarly, the involvement of banks and financial institutions in stock ownership, or the logic of reciprocal shareholding between companies, allows a better understanding of certain French or Japanese regulatory features. The limitation imposed by French law on the number of investments made by boards of trustees is an indirect manifestation. The distinction (perhaps a bit basic) between the Anglo-Saxon model, with the market as the main source of financing and regulation of companies, and the continental model, in which the market is not the main source of financing or influence, can explain the difference between the mechanisms in place to protect shareholders. The importance placed on the role of the market and its efficiency in the United States explains the difficulty faced by the shareholders (especially minority shareholders) in influencing the management. Conversely, it is perhaps the lesser importance of markets in continental Europe (in France and Spain for our purposes), and the relative concentration of the stock ownership, that explains the existence of more powerful mechanisms that allow shareholders to exert an influence over management.

Legal tradition also exerts a strong influence ahead of the perspective of governance. In general, governance systems could be understood with regard to the protective capacity of different legal systems. According to certain authors, the fundamental explanation lies in the origin of the legal tradition seen through the opposition between the Anglo-Saxon tradition of common law and that of civil law.[35] The pertinence of the consideration of these two traditions[36] has given rise to a very lively debate that is far from being settled.[37] The question is that of the overall ability of one or the other legal system to protect (more or less well) the interests of the shareholders and, more broadly, the investors. To this question, La Porta *et al.*[38] have responded in a very decisive (though contested)[39] manner by invoking the superiority of the common law system as regards the protection of investors. One of the main arguments lies in the flexibility of customary laws and their adaptability to evolutions in the environment. Without wanting to get further into this debate, it shows at least the very great influence that legal traditions supposedly have over the mechanisms in place to protect shareholder rights.[40]

It is also appropriate to invoke the weight of history and its influence on legal logic.[41] It is the consequences of the French Revolution which (partially) explain the primacy of the law (as an expression of the people). It is the whole evolution, since World War II, which allows us to understand the change in Japan from *zaibatsu* to *keiretsu* and the whole legal arsenal that ensued (for example, the – legal – organisation of the board of directors in the *kabushiki-kaisha* and the presence of auditors). American influence via the Structural Impediments Initiative in the 1980s

---

[35] Beyond the distinction between different legal systems, the influence of legal rules on the economic development models has long been illustrated by North.

[36] In reality, the distinction is not quite so binary. It is subject to change. On this subject, see T. Beck, A. Demirgüç-Kunt and R. Levine, 'Law, Politics, and Finance', *World Bank Country Economics Department, Working Paper no. 2585* (2001), and G. Charreaux, 'Les Théories de la Gouvernance: de la Gouvernance des Entreprises à la Gouvernance des Systèmes Nationaux', *Cahiers du FARGO* (LEG, Université de Bourgogne, January 2004).

[37] For more details on this matter, see Charreaux, 'Les Théories de la Gouvernance'.

[38] R. La Porta, F. Lopez-De Silanes, A. Shleifer and R. W. Vishny, 'Legal Determinants of External Finance', *Journal of Finance* 52, 3 (1997), 1131–50; R. La Porta, F. Lopez-De Silanes, A. Shleifer and R. W. Vishny, 'Law and Finance', *Journal of Political Economy* 106, 6 (1998), 1113–55; and R. La Porta, F. Lopez-De Silanes, A. Shleifer and R. W. Vishny, 'Investor Protection and Corporate Governance', *Journal of Financial Economics* 58, 1–2 (2000), 3–27; R. La Porta, F. Lopez-De Silanes and A. Shleifer, 'Corporate Ownership Around the World', *Journal of Finance* 54, 2 (1999), 471–517.

[39] See, for example, D. Zetsche, 'Shareholder Interaction Preceding Shareholder Meetings of Public Corporations – A Six Country Comparison', *Arbeitspapiere zum Deutschen und Internationalen Zivil und Wirtschaftsrecht* (Dusseldorf: Henrich-Hein Universität, 2005).

[40] *Ibid.*   [41] Here too, see Beck, Demirgüç-Kunt and Levine, 'Law, Politics, and Finance'.

Table 3 *Main codes and recommendations in France Japan, Spain and United States*

Country	Code	Main objectives	Instruments
France	For better governing of listed companies – Bouton Report (September 2002)	Revision of the Viénot reports following recent events affecting companies.	The *Viénot Reports* serve as a starting point; control of management by the board of directors; competence and diversification of the board, with at least one third being independent of the company; independent external verifiers; audit and compensation committees composed mainly of managers who are not on the board, one third of whom are independent board members; concerns about the instability of the bottom line stemming from the adoption of IAS accounting standards.
Japan	Revised principles of corporate governance – Japan Corporate Governance Forum – (October 2001)	Favour development of healthy corporate governance in Japan.	Optional. Compensation linked to company performance for board members and employees; separation of the management and president; a majority of the managers not part of the board; implementation of committees presided over and mostly made up of outside board members.
Spain	Olivencia Report (February 1998)	Improve company performance, competitiveness and/or access to capital.	Advisory mission to create 'value for the shareholder;' large majority of administrators without management functions, with the number of administrators without a function proportional to the floating ones; same proportion in the boards of directors; opposition force within the council vis-à-vis the general director/president; setting up of other types of committees; compensation based on performance; limitation and control of transactions with linked parties; improvement of participation, information and the shareholder vote.

	Aladama Report (January 2003)	Improve the performance of companies, competition and/or the access to capital and their transparency.	Recommendations similar to the Olivencia report, including recommendations on the transparency of information.
	Commission on Public Trust and Private Enterprise, Conference Board – Rapport Peterson (January 2003)	Treatment of widespread abuses that have led to recent scandals and to a decrease in public confidence in companies, their managers and in American financial markets.	Optional. Principles established for accounting and verification of accounts; readjustment of the functions of the board of directors and the general manager; more independent board members that are more qualified; ethical surveillance; greater participation by shareholders; transparency in compensation linked to company performance.
United States	Corporate governance rules proposals – NYSE (April 2003)	Revision of the standards for admission to listing on the NYSE	Standards for admission to the listings. Evaluation of the cost of call options; reinforcement of the independence of the board of directors, stronger appointment of leaders, committees for the compensation of managers and audits; approval of plans for call options by the shareholders.
	Corporate governance and listing standards – Nasdaq (March 2003)	Revision of the standards for admission to listing on the Nasdaq.	Standards of admission to being listed. Evaluation of the cost of call options; reinforcement of the independence of the board of directors, designation of the strongest personalities, committees for the compensation of managers and for audits.

Source: According to the OECD, *Overview of the evolutions in terms of corporate governance in OECD countries,* 2003.

also plays a role in explaining the evolution of the Japanese commercial code (specifically the parts on companies). To conclude, it is the rarity of legislative intervention in this domain in the United States that explains the weight of the Sarbanes-Oxley Act.

Differences in the institutional and legal framework will deeply impact on shareholder activism and its practices. It may also impact on the importance of CSR as a dimension of shareholders' attention, and even the true nature of their requests in this field: there may be, for instance, more consumer protection orientation in the case of Japan (the Japanese legal framework on consumer protection can be considered weaker than in the other countries of the study); there may be more against sexual discrimination in the case of the United States (see Table 5 below); there may be less workers' protection orientation in the case of France, where legal social protection is strongly developed.

2. The legal instruments of shareholder activism

The countries examined in this analysis belong to different legal traditions. As a hypothesis, the method used here thus includes a relative level of generality,[42] and Table 3 synthesises the main recent sources of recommendations in terms of governance and, by extension, shareholder activism in the countries covered by our analysis.

The issue of compliance with these optional codes and principles changes greatly according to the country. In Spain, for example, the authorities have recorded 80 per cent compliance with the recommendations of the Olivencia Code (Organisation for Economic Co-operation and Development (OECD), 2003).

In terms of the main mechanisms that allow shareholders to be involved in the company's affairs (and allow shareholder activism to influence it), intervening during the general shareholders meeting is the best way. In all the countries included in the study there have been mechanisms allowing the shareholders to be involved more or less easily before and during the meeting – by participating, of course, but also by submitting resolutions which were not initially envisaged by those who called the meeting.

---

[42] It is also necessary to note that, in the United States, internal governance is generally governed by state law, while everything that has to do with financial regulations in a broader sense falls under federal law. This is, for example, the case of the Securities Act of 1933, the Securities Exchange Act of 1934 and more recently of the Sarbanes-Oxley Act of 2002. The complexity of the confusion of two legal standards limits us from going further into this domain here.

Schematically, a meeting proceeds as follows:

- The board drafts the agenda and the resolutions that will be proposed. In most cases, it is the board, which has called the meeting, that determines the agenda. When the board does not do it, various procedures exist to allow the shareholders to do it or to have it done (through legal channels).
- Notices to attend, resolutions from the management and the agenda will be sent out by various means and made generally available.
- There exists the possibility, to a greater or lesser extent, for the shareholders to propose resolutions on their own initiative or to modify resolutions proposed by the author of the convocation. The existence (or not) of this double possibility is far from being neutral for the shareholders' strategies (and may even be a part of them).
- There should be numerous opportunities for the shareholders present to intervene.

Beyond the legal provisions acknowledging this possibility, various restrictions sometimes complicate shareholder access to one mechanism or another (Table 4).

In fact, if the mechanisms for intervening during a general meeting are looked at more carefully, more restrictions are possible. They include the following:

- *The existence of a (quantitative) minimum holding of shares.* Though the justification is generally the avoidance of abusive complications, the threshold (which varies according to the country) can prove to be a significant handicap.
- *The opportunity for managers to disregard the resolution proposed.* In the United States, Rule 14a-8 of the Securities and Exchange Act (SEC)[43] allows for thirteen circumstances under which the company may choose not to take into account a resolution proposed by the shareholders (including a conflict with proposals made by the company, an issue that is under the management's control, something that allows some leeway).
- *The existence of a minimum time period of shareholding.*[44]

---

[43] Code of Federal Regulations (CFR) Ch. II, Sec. 240.14a-8

[44] For example, in the United States, according to Rule 14a-8 (b) subs. 1 of US Regulation 14a, one year before the proposal.

Table 4 *The main limitations on access to general meetings and to the submission of resolutions*

Mechanisms related to the meeting

Country	Minimum prior notice for an annual general meeting	Minimum holding/ Registration	Proposals
France	30 days	Yes/Yes	0.5 to 5% of the capital (based on the size of the company)
Japan	15 days	Yes/Yes	1% of voting rights or 300 votes
Spain	15 days	No/No	5% of the capital (to call a meeting)
United States	30 days	Yes/Yes	1% of the capital and 10% to elect board members

Source: OECD, *Overview of the evolutions in terms of corporate governance in OECD countries*, 2003.

- *A more or less obligatory consideration of the results of the resolution when it was submitted.* In the United States, even if the shareholders' proposal wins the majority, the management is not required to implement it. As the SEC rules, these proposals are only meant to inform the management of the various shareholders' opinions.
- *The time limit for making a request to place a resolution on the agenda for the general meeting.* It varies greatly depending on the country (from 'a reasonable period' for France to 120 calendar days in certain cases in the United States).
- *The content of the resolution.* Depending on the country, it can be a matter of a new resolution or can be meant to modify a resolution proposed by the management (initiative or response). This is the case in France. In other systems (the United States, for example), the limit set for the submission of a resolution prevents any sort of 'response' resolutions and only allows for 'initiatives'. The shareholder strategy is thus less rigid. In some cases, it is also necessary to take into account limits on the number of words that a resolution may contain.
- *Limitations on shareholder representation, in terms of the vote at the general meeting.*

- *The leeway that shareholders are given to ask questions at the general meeting and whether or not the managers are required to answer them.* Here, too, the procedures vary greatly according to country. Generally, it is up to the president to decide who can speak;
- *The cost of the procedure being a potential restriction.*

Beyond this major vehicle for shareholder activism – that is, the shareholder meeting as a means to influence a company's policy – there exist various other mechanisms (whose efficiency, implementation and results are very different for the different countries concerned):

- *Legal challenge, by an individual or on behalf of the company.*
- *Challenging managers for failing to abide by their duties.* American law, notably with the use of the duty of loyalty, part of the fiduciary duties, is the origin of numerous activist demonstrations.
- *Challenging managers to disapprove of management choices (taking control, assignments, etc.).*
- *Demands for information (more or less specific) on managers' assets.* In Japan, any shareholder holding at least 1 per cent of the voting rights, or 300 votes, can propose one or more questions in writing at least eight weeks before the general meeting (Article 232–2 of the Commerical Code, Eibun Horei Sha, 2004).[45] For several years, the general meetings of Toyota and Sony have examined recurring proposals aiming to unveil the compensation of each of the main managers (*Nihon Keizai Shimbun*, 12 and 24 July 2004). So far, these proposals have been rejected. The proposals of resolutions made by shareholders also involve an increase in the amounts of dividends (Tokyo Style in June 2003, Toyota in June 2004, etc.). This type of process has no place in a country like France, where managers' compensation has been published ever since the law on the New Economic Regulations;
- *Exercising the right to information.*

All these considerations must be seen in the light of the concluding remarks in section 1 above. Differences in the institutionnal and legal framework will impact deeply on the importance of CSR as a dimension of shareholders' attention. They will also impact on legal instruments of shareholder activism (and their use) in the area of CSR.

---

[45] Eibun Horei Sha, 'The Commercial Code and the Audit Special Exceptions Law of Japan – 2004', EHS Law Bulletin Series (Tokyo, 2004).

B. A contrasting reality

The American situation serves as a reference for the presentation of the practice of shareholder activism in the countries concerned. In a certain way, the other three countries draw inspiration from the 'American example', which is older and more solidly established. In fact, they are currently in different phases of development, and offer a contrasting reality.

1. The American situation

During the 2003 season of general meetings,[46] more than a thousand resolution proposals concerning corporate governance of social and environmental aspects were filed in the United States (802 in 2002).

Though proposals concerning governance are the most common, those concerning sustainable development are on the increase and deal with a wide variety of topics: the environment, social norms, equality of opportunity, consumer protection, tobacco, military activity and so on. A majority of them are proposed by members of the ICCR (Interfaith Center on Corporate Responsibility), which includes religious institutional investors and socially responsible funds.

Union funds and pension funds have sometimes also been the source of such resolutions in recent years.

In 2003, nearly one third of resolutions (17.91 per cent) obtained more than 20 per cent of favourable votes. Nevertheless, none of the proposals gained a majority without the support of the company's management. Table 5 shows the ten proposals that obtained the most favourable votes in 2003.

It is, however, appropriate to qualify the general impression that resolutions of a social nature always fail despite the increase in percentages obtained. Indeed, when a company accepts the content of a resolution before the general shareholder meeting, the resolution is generally withdrawn by its proponents. Companies that accept this type of agreement are seeking, above all, to improve their image by avoiding bad publicity. This phenomenon occurred numerous times during 2003.

From 1 January to 5 August 2003, 136 proposals had something to do with social and environmental issues. They fall into six main categories:

- *Social norms and international activity* (33). These proposals request that the companies concerned take various measures, such as adopting codes of conduct referring to International Labour Organisation (ILO)

---

[46] All the data on the American situation come from Institutional Shareholder Services and concern the period from 1 January to 5 August 2003.

Table 5 *The ten proposals that obtained the most favourable votes in 2003 in the United States*

Company	Object of the resolution	Percentage obtained
J. C. Penney Co. Inc.	Adopt a policy of no sexual discrimination	98% (with the support of the management)
Dover Corp.	Adopt a policy of no sexual discrimination	42.81%
Gentex Corp.	Increase diversity in the board of directors	39.2%
Yum Brands Inc.	Prepare a report on sustainable development	38.98%
Centerpoint Energy Inc.	Adopt a policy of no sexual discrimination	32.21%
Triquint Semiconductor Inc.	Prepare a report on the environment, health and security	31.52%
Delphi Corp.	Review and modify their international standards	30.07%
Danaher Corp.	Increase diversity in the board of directors	28.68%
American Power Conversion Corp.	Increase diversity in the board of directors	28.61%
Werner Enterprises Inc.	Increase diversity in the board of directors	27.61%

standards in the framework of their international activity. They refer to the respect of human rights. In addition, more and more attention is paid to pandemics in developing countries (AIDS, tuberculosis, malaria) with a view, on the one hand, to increasing the offers of medicines at low prices (pharmaceutical firms) and, on the other hand, understanding the effects of these pandemics on the activity of companies located in these countries and the way in which they face up to them.

- *The Environment* (29). Most environmental resolutions are linked to global warming. In the past, the resolutions mainly related to the improvement of information on greenhouse gas emissions. In 2003, some demanded that companies publish reports on the risks associated with these emissions, while others pressurised companies to develop renewable energy sources.

- *Consumer protection, tobacco, health and safety* (25). Ten proposals had to do with problems surrounding consumer protection, health and safety, such as genetically modified organisms, animal protection and product safety. Fifteen others focused on tobacco; for example, raising consumers' awareness of the danger of light and ultra-light cigarettes.
- *Equal employment opportunity and sexual and racial equality* (19). Numerous resolutions had to do with the Equal Employment Opportunity policy, including sexual equality (nearly 90 per cent of Fortune 100 and 60 per cent of Fortune 500 companies have now adopted such a provision).
- *Involvement* (9). The resolutions demand information from companies concerning their involvement in the development of space weapons, in sales abroad, and so on.
- *Link between manager compensation and social problems* (9). Some resolutions demand that all or part of the compensation for managers be pegged to compliance with social or environmental governance norms.

2. The French scenario

Generally, there have been relatively few resolutions presented in France in five years: Eramet, Azeo, Groupe André, Bull, Vivendi, Pechiney, Rhodia, Euro-Tunnel and Unibail are some examples. They all have to do with classic issues of governance, modifications of protectionist statutes, capital increases, nomination of board members, and so on, and seem largely removed from issues relating to sustainable development. Nevertheless, as the CFIE[47] letter of May 2004 indicates, 'it is not forbidden to think only of the short term, general meetings of large French companies have seen the first indications of resolutions having to do with social and environmental issues'.

Though these resolutions are slow to come in France, numerous questions on social policy are asked during general meetings. The follow-up provided by the CFIE gives an exhaustive description for CAC 40[48] companies from 2002 to 2004 (see Table 6).

The CFIE classification distinguishes between four categories of questions:[49]

---

[47] Centre Français d'Information sur les Entreprises – French Centre for Information on Companies.
[48] The French stock market index that tracks the forty largest French stocks based on market capitalisation on the Paris Bourse (stock exchange).
[49] In reality, the CFIE considers a fifth axis, governance, but it has not been included in the framework of our analysis. CFIE, *Engagement Actionnarial et Développement Durable* (April 2004).

Table 6 *Corporate social responsibility questions asked during the general meetings of the CAC 40 from 2002 to 2004*

	2002	2003	2004
Social policy	79	77	83
Environmental policy	16	16	21
Economic contribution	22	41	38
Community relations	26	45	38
Total	143	179	180

Source: Impact entreprises, the CFIE letter on citizenship and the company (nos. 29, 34 and 40, June–August 2002, May–June 2003, May–June 2004).

- social policy is divided into seven themes: general undertakings, employment and restructuring, labour conditions and safety, equal opportunities (between men and women, for the handicapped), counterbalancing the employment contract (compensation, benefits, training), social relationships, employee profit-sharing (participation in the capital, in the board of directors);
- environmental policy is divided into five areas: general commitments, pressure on the environment, waste, the impact of products and packaging, the impact of facilities;
- the economic contribution has to do with, on one hand, the adequacy of the company's supply and the needs of the population, and on the other hand, the company's business relationships (service providers, suppliers, competitors, clients);
- relationships with the community include three dimensions: supranational (transparency, international institutions), national (states, public institutions) and territorial (population, associations).

It can be noted that they moved toward interrelated categories between 2002 and 2004, with stabilisation between 2003 and 2004. Nevertheless, the relative weakness of environmental issues shows that this area is not yet very important in the eyes of shareholders, while the social dimension remains very important. Though shareholders' social concern increases in France, it remains mainly centred on the traditional idea of an 'employer' company, rather than a 'partnership'.

As regards the questions, it is clearly not possible to measure directly their influence on companies' policies in matters of sustainable development. Even so, in 2003 the CFIE (2004) noted a timid entry onto the

Table 7 *The frequency of questions during general meetings of the IBEX 35 from 1999 to 2003*

	Minimum	Maximum	Average
1999	0	18	5.33
2000	0	17	5.89
2001	0	21	5.31
2002	0	67	7.17
2003	0	41	5.29

scene by institutional investors, notably in the general meetings of Accor and Total. This recent evolution undoubtedly foreshadows more notable changes in the future.

3. The Spanish scenario

In Spain, as in France, sustainable development remains relatively remote from the concerns of the general meetings of shareholders. Specifically, no resolution has ever dealt with this theme. Based on an investigation of IBEX 35 companies,[50] it is clear (Table 7) that there are few questions asked (all concerns taken together), with an average of five, except in 2002 because of exceptional events affecting one of the index's values (Banesto).

As regards the content of these questions, they rarely address social or environmental concerns. Table 8 features a breakdown per year:

Table 8 *Corporate social responsibility questions asked during general meetings of the IBEX 35 from 1999 to 2003*

	1999	2000	2001	2002	2003
Social policy	7	14	13	13	14
Environmental policy	0	3	3	2	4
Community relations	4	7	8	3	12
Total	11	24	24	18	30
Number of companies observed	15	19	26	30	30
Number of questions per company	0.7	1.3	0.9	0.6	1

---

[50] This unreleased investigation was conducted by the authors of the article. The necessary data could only be obtained for thirty of the thirty-five companies that make up the IBEX 35 on 1 December 2004 for the years 1999 to 2003.

Questions about social policy are the most common, but they are concentrated on different companies according to the year: Banesto in 1999 (4 of 7), Indra Sistemas in 2000 (10 of 14), Telefónica mobiles in 2001 (7 of 13) and Inditex in 2002 and 2003 (10 of 13 and 6 of 14, respectively). It is in times of major social difficulty that the questions are used by shareholders as part of a reactive approach rather than a preventive one. Environmental questions are few and far between, even though the index includes seven companies in the oil and energy sector, which is traditionally a target for such questions. Questions related to community relations were, for the most part, aimed at Telefónica.

Shareholder activism, in matters of corporate social responsibility, is practically non-existent on the Spanish stock market. The focus on certain companies in generally difficult circumstances bears out this observation.

4. The Japanese scenario

In Japan, shareholder activism has developed in recent years under pressure from foreign actors, in a context of troubled companies since the crash of the Tokyo stock market in 1990.[51] Until this crash, the regular progression of stock prices recorded by shareholders did not push them to question managers' choices. In addition, shares tended to be held increasingly by companies, banks and other financial intermediaries, in the framework of the development of reciprocal shareholding protection against possible hostile takeovers by western competitors.[52] The profitability of stocks held in this way was not a primary concern for institutional shareholders.

During the 1990s, stock market depreciations were considerable and western investors knew how to profit from them to acquire large portions of the capital of Japanese companies. Non-residents held an average of 20 per cent of the capital of listed companies at the end of March 2003 (*Nihon Keizai Shimbun*, 24 June 2003), while 38.6 per cent of Sony's capital, 49.8 per cent of Canon's capital, 18.2 per cent of Toyota's capital and 32.2 per cent of Honda's capital is now in the hands of foreign investors (Tôyô Keizai Shimpôsha, 2004). Faced with huge losses throughout the decade,

---

[51] B. Amann, J. Jaussaud and A. Kanie, 'Activisme des Actionnaires et Responsabilité Sociale de l'Entreprise au Japon', *Ebisu*, November–December (Tokyo: Maison Franco-Japonaise, 2004).

[52] P. Sheard, 'Intelocking Shareholdings and Corporate Governance', in M. Aoki and R. Dore, *The Japanese Firm, Sources of Competitive Strength* (Oxford: Oxford University Press, 1994); K. Miyashita and D. Russel, *Keiretsu, Inside the Hidden Japanese Conglomerates* (New York: McGraw-Hill, 1996); H. Okumura, *Corporate Capitalism in Japan* (London: Macmillan Press, 2000).

Table 9 *The ISS's orders to reject resolutions in Japan from 2002 to 2004*

	Number of resolutions the ISS ordered rejected during general meetings in June	As a percentage of the total number of resolutions submitted for shareholder vote at general meetings in June
June 2004 (fiscal year 2003)	3519	20%
June 2003 (fiscal year 2002)	3267	28%
June 2002 (fiscal year 2001)	1074	nd

Source: Nihon Keizai Shimbun, July 5, 2002 and July 2, 2004 editions.

numerous Japanese companies and banks had to liquidate their stock portfolios, thus shaking up the system of reciprocal shareholding. Life insurance companies and fund managers who faced difficulties after the collapse of the financial and real estate markets became very sensitive to questions on corporate governance and shareholder value.

Shareholder activism is expressed in Japan, as elsewhere, in various ways.[53] One of the most spectacular ways was the order to reject motions at general meetings given year after year by the Japanese subsidiary of the American company Institutional Shareholders Services, established in Japan since 2001 (Table 9). The Japanese daily newspaper *Nihon Keizai Shimbun* said in its 5 July 2002 edition that these orders were massively followed by the 300 foreign institutional investors present in Japan. Furthermore, this audience extended to Japanese institutional investors, since 20 of them called on the services of Institutional Shareholders Services in 2002, and 35 in 2003 (*Nihon Keizai Shimbun*, June 2, 2003).

It is clear (Table 10) that this form of activism is not directly aimed at issues of CSR. This activism, above all, seeks a higher profitability for companies and the stock, crucial stakes in Japan at the moment, particularly from the point of view of the future of retirement and the solvency of life insurance companies. Questions of social policy are currently totally absent from the concerns of active shareholders. The massive reductions in the workforce of big companies during the 1990s, which posed the

---

[53] Our main source here is *Nihon Keizai Shimbun*, the top business daily in Japan. Numerous articles are available in English in the weekly edition *Nikkei Weekly*, and in a more complete form in the database *Nikkei Net Interactive* at www.nikkei.co.jp, accessible by subscription.

Table 10 *The nature of the resolutions that ISS ordered rejected in June 2003*

Nature of the resolutions that ISS ordered to be rejected in June 2003	Number
Resolutions modifying company by-laws, aiming to delegate to the board of directors the decision for companies to buy back their own shares	1,791
Resolutions concerning the nomination of internal auditors	742
Resolutions concerning proposals of severance pay to auditors or board members	430
Others, notably proposals to pay dividends considered too weak, or the nomination of independent board members judged to be too close to the company	304
Total	3,267

Source: Nihon Keizai Shimbun, 28 June 2003.

problem of corporate social responsibility with regard to employees, were not seen, except in particular cases, as resulting from managerial errors or opportunistic attitudes, but rather as a consequence of the exhaustion of a specific human resource management model, a theme that was widely spread by the Japanese media. The management of large companies strove to lay off as few permanent employees as possible.[54]

The issue of CSR towards employees, which arises in Japan as elsewhere, does not seem, for the time being, to have significantly encouraged shareholder activism.

CSR, however, is not absent from the debate on shareholder activism in Japan: it plays a role of legitimisation.

The success recorded by Japanese companies in the 1980s gave their managers, on the one hand, methods of organisation, decision and control in these companies and, on the other hand, credibility and legitimacy for every challenge. But the difficulties of the 1990s revealed a certain number of serious malfunctions. With the crumbling of profits, the demands of corporate racketeers, such as the *sôkaiya*, became unbearable, and the law of silence fell: many of these affairs were revealed to the general public during the 1990s, affecting even the top companies, like Nomura Securities, Mitsubishi Electric, Mitsubishi Motors, Ito Yokado, Ajinomoto and Kobe

---

[54] J. Jaussaud, 'Le Modèle Japonais de GRH', in J. Allouche, *Encyclopédie des Ressources Humaines* (Paris: Vuibert, 2003).

Steel.[55] When the difficulties continued, all the rules of human resources management were challenged, particularly that of the guaranteed employment of permanent employees.[56] Less protected, employees were no longer in a position systematically to cover up the inappropriate behaviour of their colleagues or superiors. Sexual affairs broke out, to the point that it prompted companies to adopt systems allowing employees to expose irregularities as they happened, namely whistleblowing programmes.

Scandals, other than payments to racketeers, involving big companies with excellent reputations blew up toward the end of the 1990s. Some of these cases truly stunned the general public because they directly threatened the safety of consumers, and the population in general. Mitsubishi Motors, and its subsidiary, Mitsubishi Fuso Truck & Bus, had to acknowledge having hidden from their clients manufacturing flaws that caused serious accidents (*Nihon Keizai Shimbun*, 5 July 2004). Snow Brand Milk was late in informing people that some of its products had gone bad, which caused the food poisoning of about 15,000 people. Tokyo Electric Power had to admit to the falsification of the inspection reports for its nuclear power plants to hide certain malfunctions (*Nihon Keizai Shimbun*, 14 October 2002).

The revelation of these affairs, most often by employees of the companies concerned, seriously affected the confidence that the general public in Japan had in companies and their managers. The idea that these managers had to be monitored and that transparency had to be reinforced quickly spread.

It is in this context that the development of shareholder activism must be assessed in Japan. Until the beginning of the 1990s, any activist shareholder would have been seen as being driven by individual, even selfish, objectives if he questioned the community of interests represented by the company. Today, even though the demands of activist shareholders still reveal pecuniary concerns, they are accepted because shareholder activism seems to be one of the methods of effectively controlling managers whose potential shortcomings no longer need to be proved.

III. Conclusion

As an expression of a mechanism of corporate governance, shareholder activism has ambiguous effects: ambiguity in the relationship between

---

[55] Amann, Jaussaud and Kanie, 'Activisme des Actionnaires'.
[56] Jaussaud, 'Le Modèle Japonais de GRH'.

resolutions filed and company performance, or in the relationship between social responsibility and company performance – social responsibility for which shareholder activism is the vehicle – and, finally, ambiguity in the reality of shareholder activism, which is sharply contrasted in the countries we have studied.

First of all, shareholder activism has changed: Lewis Gilbert's time is long gone and activism is now mainly in the field of institutional investors. The concerns, the issues and the methods are different. No wonder then that it varies from one country to another. The absence (or weakness) of a savings-based retirement plan, for example, can explain a less vigorous activism; the importance of pension funds in the United States as actors in the process is significant. The same reason may explain the small number of resolutions in Spain, France and Japan.

However, whatever the differences from country to country, shareholder activism has been strongly developed in the two last decades, mainly as the result of the growing weight of institutional investors and growing concern on corporate governance issues in all countries in this study.

More generally, there is an increasing shift in societal values and expectations (and, incidentally, a development of the legal framework – see, for example, the French law NRE in 2001). The development of socially responsible investment (SRI) has certainly contributed to this trend. Traditionnaly, SRI is implemented through the investment process and/or the corporate governance process.

There has also been a significant increase in shareholder resolutions, in shareholder groups working in partnership with NGOs challenging companies on key issues of CSR.[57]

Next, because even though legal instruments exist in all the countries examined in the study (and in the logic of improving corporate governance, they have a tendency to increase), there are also numerous obstacles. The existence of these obstacles goes beyond the traditional distinction between common law countries and civil law countries.[58] Even though the United States allows shareholders relatively little leeway to

---

[57] For more about this evolution, see T. R. Guay, J. P. Doh and G. Sinclair, 'Non-Governmental Organizations, Shareholder Activism, and Socially Responsible Investments: Ethical, Strategic, and Governance Implications', *Journal of Business Ethics* 52, 1 (2004), 125–39; J. P. Doh and T. R. Guay, 'Corporate Social Responsibility, Public Policy, and NGO Activism in Europe and the United States: An Institutional-Stakeholder Perspective', *Journal of Management Studies* 43, 1 (2006), 47–73.

[58] A. L. Bebchuk, 'The case for increasing Shareholder Power', *Harvard Law Review* 118, 3 (2005).

question the management, and even though the procedure to make proposals is relatively cumbersome, this is not the case in other common law countries like the United Kingdom. Finally, because it is possible to imagine, more broadly, that the actions of shareholder activism have concerns, in certain cases, that go beyond the company they are trying to influence, but they aim to have a broader influence on society as a whole.

12

The other European framework for corporate social responsibility: from the Green Paper to new uses of human rights instruments

AURORA VOICULESCU

I. Introduction

The European institutions have recently engaged on a path proposing the European Union as a leader in promoting corporate social responsibility (CSR) both at home and abroad. The choice of such a path has a lot to do with three factors: the particular relationship between the member states and the European Union; the fact that the European Union is a major economic and diplomatic player in an increasingly globalised world; and, very importantly, the fact that the Union possesses one of the most established and pervasively applied human rights systems embedded within both EU law and the domestic legal systems of the member states.[1] This chapter looks at the way in which the European Union contributes to the promotion of CSR by attempting to develop a consistent CSR framework, and at whether the European human rights strategy – as identified in European international development cooperation documents – can constitute a platform on which the CSR framework is to be based. After a brief overview of the origin of the CSR debate in Europe, the second part of the chapter offers an account of the variety of domestic regulatory and non-regulatory CSR 'signals' received by the European institutions from the EU member states, highlighting the voluntary versus regulatory dichotomy. The third part focuses on the actual CSR strategy as formulated by various EU documents, and especially by the European Commission. It also looks at the dynamic relationship between the declared voluntary agenda and the potentially regulatory undercurrents arising from these documents. The fourth part addresses the extent to which the European Union can incorporate CSR in its development cooperation agreements, and the

[1] P. Alston (ed.), *The EU and Human Rights* (Oxford: Oxford University Press, 1999), p. 9.

extent to which these international-relations legal tools can become catalysts for socially responsible corporate activities and for CSR-friendly governmental initiatives from all parties in a development agreement.

II. The European journey to corporate social responsibility

The CSR debate has arisen relatively recently on the agenda of European institutions. One of the first steps the EU structures took towards CSR was the 1993 appeal by the European Commission President Jacques Delors to European businesses, urging them to take part in the fight against social exclusion. However, the real catalyst for the beginning of a European CSR strategy appears to have been the shock announcement by the French motor manufacturer Renault, on 28 February 1997, of its decision to close its plant at Vilvoorde in Belgium.[2] Following the Luxembourg Job Summit later the same year, the High-Level Group on Economic and Social Implications of Industrial Change (also known as the Gyllenhammar Group) was established at the invitation of the European Council.[3] In its final report, the Group recommended that businesses with more than a thousand employees should publish voluntarily a 'Managing Change report', an annual report on employment and working conditions in which to give an account of the social impact of their activities.[4] This agenda

---

[2] Renault was criticised both for the tactless manner in which it made public a decision that left 3,000 Renault employees and 1,500 employees in direct-supply companies unemployed, as well as for ignoring legal rules and procedures concerning factory closures. These included a 'cocktail' of International Labour Organisation (ILO) and Organisation for Economic Co-operation and Development (OECD) procedures, national codes of conduct, EU and domestic legislation on collective redundancies and works council rights. For an account of the Renault-Vilvoorde industrial relations incident, classified as part of 'the unacceptable face of capitalism', see European Industrial Relations Observatory On-Line, *The Closure of Renault-Vilvoorde*, available at www.eiro.eurofound.eu.int/1997/03/feature/be9703202f.html (accessed May 2007); also *The Renault Case and the Future of Social Europe*, available at www.eiro.eurofound.eu.int/1997/03/feature/eu9703108f.html (accessed May 2007).

[3] P. Bronchain, *Towards a Sustainable Corporate Social Responsibility* (Luxembourg: The European Foundation for the Improvement of Living and Working Conditions, 2003); study on CSR and working conditions.

[4] European Commission, *Managing Change: Final Report of the High-Level Group on the Economic and Social Implications of Industrial Change* (Luxembourg Office for Official Publications of the European Communities, 1998) (Gyllenhammar Report). The Group indicated that the report should be developed in consultation with employees and their representatives in accordance with national traditions. The Group also suggested a framework, which would deal with policies, practices and performance regarding employment and working conditions, particularly anticipation of structural change, communications, employee involvement and social dialogue, education and training, employee health and safety, and equal opportunities.

was, in its turn, taken over by the Commission's Social Policy Agenda and later included in the Four Year Rolling Programme of the European Foundation for the Improvement of Working and Living Conditions.[5] In March 2000, in line with its objectives for the Lisbon Summit of becoming 'the most competitive and dynamic knowledge-based economy in the world, capable of sustainable economic growth with more and better jobs and greater social cohesion',[6] the European Council also made a special appeal to 'companies' corporate sense of social responsibility' regarding best practices on lifelong learning, work organisation, equal opportunities, social inclusion and sustainable development.[7] From these tentative institutional steps towards CSR, it could be said that the European debate was initially rooted in predominantly domestic concerns.[8]

The European institutional debate on the social responsibility of corporations also appears initially to be more reluctant to acknowledge the concept of CSR itself, as well as its whole baggage of conflicting signals between voluntary and regulatory approaches. Although the concept of 'CSR' was already established in the wider public debate, the initial European documents spoke of 'managing change' and of 'social cohesion', of 'business ethics' and of the 'corporate *sense* of social responsibility'. It was not before July 2001 that the Commission took a proactive approach, acknowledging the term 'CSR' and confronting all the dimensions of the debate, from the definition and the substance of the concept, and from the balance between voluntary and regulatory, to policies and practical mechanisms of implementation both at home and abroad.[9] This new wave is also coupled with a much more proactive general approach taken by the European Union in the area of international development,[10] as

---

[5] European Foundation for the Improvement of Working and Living Conditions, *Four Year Rolling Programme 2001–2004: Analysing and Anticipating Change to Support Socio-Economic Progress*, Working Paper, available at www.eurofound.europa.eu/publications/htmlfiles/ef0082.htm (accessed 2007).

[6] European Council, *Presidency Conclusions: Lisbon European Council*, I(5), available at ue.eu.int/ueDocs/cms_Data/docs/pressData/en/ec/00100-r1.en0.htm (accessed May 2007).

[7] European Council, *Presidency Conclusions: Lisbon European Council*, I(39), available at ue.eu.int/ueDocs/cms_Data/docs/pressData/en/ec/00100-r1.en0.htm (accessed May 2007).

[8] Bronchain, *Towards a Sustainable Corporate Social Responsibility*.

[9] European Commission, Green Paper, 'Promoting a European Framework for Corporate Social Responsibility', COM (2001) 366 final.

[10] Communication from the Commission to the Council, the European Parliament and the Economic and Social Committee of 7 November 2002: 'Participation of non-state actors in EC development policy', COM (2002) 598 final. Available at europa.eu/scadplus/leg/en/lvb/rl2009.htm. For the importance given to the link between trade and development,

well as in promoting human rights and democratisation in developing
countries.[11] This approach is guided by a comprehensive system of rights
and principles contained in provisions of the EU Treaties, in particular Articles 2, 3, 6, 11, 19, 29 and 49 of the Treaty on European Union
(TEU),[12] Articles 11, 13 and 177 of the Treaty Establishing the European Community (EC Treaty),[13] and Articles 6, 7, and 49 of the Treaty
of Amsterdam.[14] These Treaty provisions provide the constitutional basis
for the European Union to extend the promotion of human rights and
fundamental freedoms to trade and development cooperation with third
countries by using a variety of channels, including business and CSR
tools such as codes of conduct, social reporting instruments and public
procurement mechanisms.[15] It also provides for a legal umbrella under
which not only human rights in the 'narrow' sense, but social rights and
environmental protection can be placed as fundamental dimensions of
basic human rights in a wider, human developmental sense.[16] In this
context, in less than a decade, the European debate has made a leap
from business ethics to 'CSR', and from CSR as an item on industry-
based agendas to CSR as a potential dimension of international development cooperation. At the same time, the EU human rights system has
been brought to bear upon the role of corporations in the development
process.

see 'Declaration of the Council and the Commission of 20 November 2000 on the European Community's development policy, based on the Communication from the Commission to the Council at the European Parliament of 26 April 2000 on the same subject'
(not published in the Official Journal), available at europa.eu/scadplus/leg/en/lvb/rl2001.
htm.

[11] See, for instance, 'The Communication on the EU Role in Promoting Human Rights and
Democratisation in Third Countries', COM (2001) 252 final, and 'The Communication
on Promoting Core Labour Standards and Improving Social Governance in the Context
of Globalisation', COM (2001) 416.

[12] Treaty of European Union (TEU), 31 ILM 247; 1992 OJ (C191)

[13] Consolidated Version of the Treaty Establishing the European Community (EC Treaty)
(97/C 340/03).

[14] Treaty of Amsterdam (1997 OJ (C 340)1). This mechanism was further reinforced by the
Treaty of Nice. European Union, *Consolidated Version of the Treaty on European Union
and The Treaty Establishing the European Community* (2002), OJ 2002 C325/1. European
Communities, *The Treaties Establishing the European Communities and Certain Related
Acts* (1997). European Union, The Treaty of Nice, OJ 2001 C80/1.

[15] European Commission, 'Communication Concerning Corporate Social Responsibility: A
Business Contribution to Sustainable Development', COM (2002) 347 final.

[16] For arguments on the way in which environmental protection pertains to human rights,
see A. Sachs, *Eco-Justice: Linking Human Rights and the Environment*, Worldwatch Paper
127 (Washington, DC: Worldwatch Institute, December 1995).

III. European domestic corporate social responsibility policies

Supported by the platform of the EU human rights policies, the European Commission has convened, since 2000, the High-Level Group of National Representatives on CSR as a platform for the exchange of information and dissemination of good practices on national and EU CSR policy developments.[17] This initiative reflects the importance of the domestic CSR signals sent from the member states toward the European institutions, importance derived from the relationship between the member states and the Union. The dynamic relationship between CSR and the law within the European context is inevitably influenced by the nature and the practice of the European institutional arrangements, by the relationship between the Union and its member states, and by the position the European Union takes within the global economy. The close economic and social integration of the member states, coupled with a certain level of retained autonomy,[18] allow for CSR domestic initiatives to emerge on the domestic scene and for some of these initiatives to be absorbed at the higher, European level. The variety of initiatives stemming from the domestic level are without doubt of significance. These initiatives come together in the European public arena to be balanced and taken forward as eventual European CSR dimensions, or, as the case may be, discarded.

CSR has acquired a certain prominence on the public policy agenda not only at the European institutional level but also at the national domestic level of the European member states. While CSR instruments are developed within companies on a complex but largely voluntary basis, in a majority of the member states domestic public authorities also play a key role in setting a reference framework and conditions, which aim not only to induce voluntary CSR initiatives but also to guarantee a level playing field and fair practices for all. In this context, in many member states CSR has grown from a niche issue into a mainstream approach to business management, development cooperation and general global governance. The member states have their own specific policy priorities, reflecting the different economic, political and – not least – cultural contexts. However, their objectives are similar: promoting stakeholder dialogue and

---

[17] 'High-Level Group of National Representatives on CSR: Mandate', available at ec.europa.eu/employment_social/soc-dial/csr/country/CSRHLG_ mandate.htm; European Commission, *Corporate Social Responsibility: National Public Policies in the European Union* (2004).

[18] T. C. Hartley, *The Foundations of European Community Law* (Oxford: Oxford University Press, 2003), pp. 114–17.

public-private partnerships; enhancing transparency and credibility of CSR practices and instruments; raising awareness, increasing knowledge, disseminating and rewarding best practices; and ensuring a more solid and consistent link between sustainable development objectives and public policies.[19] For the purpose of this chapter, the next part offers a brief overview of the domestic CSR landscape, a perspective that can assist in forming an impression of the complexity of the domestic CSR signals received at the European institutional level from the EU member states.

A. Raising corporate social responsibility awareness

The promotion of CSR at the domestic European level takes place through a combination of awareness-raising activities, research, initiation of public–private partnerships, business awards and various other incentives. For instance, many member governments have organised or sponsored – often under the EU umbrella – conferences and symposia focusing on CSR. Belgium, for instance, organised an important European Conference on CSR during its EU Presidency in July–December 2001, with the support of the European Commission's Directorate-General for Employment and Social Affairs.[20] The Austrian Industry Federation, in cooperation with the Federal Ministry of Economic Affairs and Labour and the Austrian Chamber of Commerce, set up in 2002 'CSR Austria', another initiative which aims – through the organisation of events, workshops and surveys – to raise awareness, develop a common understanding on CSR and formulate guidelines on CSR that would offer a framework for 'economic success with social responsibility'.[21] Denmark, another EU member at the forefront of the CSR movement, also used (like Belgium a year earlier) its EU Presidency mandate (July–December 2002) to promote CSR from the European tribune. In November 2002, it organised a European Conference on CSR with the support of, again, the European Commission's Directorate-General for Employment and Social Affairs.[22]

---

[19] European Commission, *Corporate Social Responsibility: National Public Policies in the European Union*. European Commission, Directorate-General for Employment and Social Affairs Unit D.1. (Luxembourg: Office for Publications of the European Communities, 2004), p 3.

[20] See www.socialresponsibility.be.   [21] See www.csr-austria.at.

[22] See www.copenhagencentre.org/sw3362.asp.

Governments of member states have also sponsored CSR reports and have undertaken government-led campaigns for the promotion of CSR. In Denmark, for instance, the Danish Ministry of Economic Affairs, together with the National Business Development Council, published a Report on Ethics in Business.[23] The Report gives an introduction to the main international CSR tendencies, and highlights challenges and opportunities, while analysing the CSR work of the Danish companies both home and abroad. Of similarly wide scope, a Technical Advisors Committee of Experts on CSR was set up in Spain in summer 2003, in association with the Ministry of Employment and Social Affairs. This Committee stemmed from a non-binding resolution of the Spanish Congress of Representatives urging the government to create a national body that would elaborate a wide and flexible CSR framework, and would consider the possibility of creating a certification body for social quality and the implementation of a future social label. The recommendations contained in the Committee's report are expected to have a decisive influence on the CSR national policies in Spain.[24]

There is also a proliferation of CSR research and knowledge centres across Europe. Some of these centres have had a wider impact, beyond the domestic system of origin. The Danish Centre for Human Rights,[25] for instance, has developed the Human Rights Impact Assessment (HRIA), based on over eighty international human rights agreements and treaties.[26] This instrument, which is now regularly referred to as an authoritative CSR instrument both in other member states as well as at the EU institutional level, allows companies operating abroad to voluntarily evaluate their business practices and identify operations that might violate – directly or indirectly – human rights.[27]

The institutional and/or financial governmental sponsorship of international CSR instruments is another way in which the different member states influence the development of the CSR debate. During the French Presidency of the G8 in 2003, for instance, France actively promoted the International Labour Organisation (ILO) Declaration on Fundamental Principles and Rights at Work, the Organisation for Economic Cooperation and Development (OECD) Guidelines and the UN Global

---

[23] See www.ebst.dk/publikationer/rapporter/etikerhvervslivet/index.htm.
[24] See www.mtas.es.
[25] See Human Rights and Business Centre, at www.humanrights.dk/departments/hrb/.
[26] See www.humanrightsbusiness.org.
[27] For details, see www.humanrights.dk, and also www.copenhagencentre.org.

Compact (GC).[28] Similar support was received by these CSR international instruments from other EU countries, such as Germany[29] and Sweden. Sweden, in particular, set up the Swedish Partnership for Global Responsibility (Global Ansvar) in 2002 with the explicit purpose of gathering corporate active support and adherence to the OECD Guidelines and the principles incorporated in the Global Compact.[30]

The awareness-raising instruments are not the only way in which CSR is promoted at the European domestic level. Another important dimension of the European CSR landscape is ensuring transparency – via codes of conduct, social reporting, labels, socially responsible investment initiatives and advertising – and developing CSR-supportive policies – via sustainable development, social and environmental policies, public procurement, fiscal, trade and export policies, and development programmes supported by wider development cooperation agreements. The following pages briefly present some of the CSR codes of conduct and social reporting mechanisms generated at the domestic level and supported through the European institutional approach.

B. Codes of conduct

Once considered the epitome of CSR voluntarism, the codes of conduct are well represented among the domestic CSR instruments, and both the European Parliament and the Commission have become promoters of European code-based strategies and supporters of various codes of

[28] The G8 meeting in Evian in the summer of 2003 adopted a declaration entitled 'Fostering growth and promoting a responsible market economy'. The Declaration encouraged companies 'to work with other parties to complement and foster the implementation of existing instruments' such as the OECD Revised Guidelines and the ILO 1998 Declaration. The impact of the French campaign and support for the Global Compact (France supported the GC financially with €100,000) was noted at least within the French industries. The number of French companies adhering to the Global Compact rose from around thirty in January 2003 to over two hundred in September 2003. The French government set up a national contact point to encourage companies, in particular small and medium enterprises (SMEs), to join the Compact and to exchange information and good practice. See ec.europa.eu/enterprise/csr/ereb/ereb_en_page1.htm.

[29] The German federal government supported the Global Compact financially and co-financed the second Global Compact Learning Forum, held in Berlin in December 2002. See ec.europa.eu/enterprise/csr/ereb/ereb_en_page2.htm.

[30] Companies can join the Global Ansvar based on a statement of support for these two international CSR documents, and they have to provide examples of their CSR work, examples which are posted on the government's website. For the complex work on CSR of the Global Ansvar Secretariat, see www.ud.se/ga.

conduct originating in different domestic settings.[31] The examples given below highlight the competing tendencies between regulatory approaches and voluntarism and the nuances the concept of voluntary action can take in the context of the domestic codifying initiatives. These nuances are sometimes absorbed within the EU institutional debate on CSR and proposed as a possible path for a EU CSR strategy.

Very often the voluntarism once expected to fully underscore such documents is nuanced and qualified via semi-regulatory interventions. A similar movement is emphasised in Chapter [3] in this volume with respect to public procurement policies. The result of such semi-regulatory interventions is what one could call 'interactive voluntarism', where incentives, initiatives and frameworks for such codes originate from within government structures. An example of such a code is the Code of Conduct for the Protection of Children from Sexual Exploitation in Travel and Tourism, signed in 2001 by the Austrian social partners in the tourism industry. The code was the result of a project initiated not by industry under consumer pressure, but by the government mainly under political pressure.[32] The signing of the code generated renewed calls for similar instruments to be adopted in other member states, and finally it generated calls for a European Code of conduct for business, supported by and sanctioned at the European institutional level.[33]

The Ethical Trading Initiative (ETI) is another code-based CSR initiative launched under governmental sponsorship. Initiated in 1998 by the UK Department for International Development (DFID), the ETI – a tri-sector alliance of companies, trade unions and non-governmental organisations (NGOs) – focuses on improving labour conditions in the supply chain of its corporate members. The ETI has developed a model code which participating companies must sign up to. This initiative has crossed the domestic boundaries, first through the national origin of the companies that have signed up to it, and second through the fact that its outlook and methodology is a potential source of inspiration that is being

---

[31] D. Leipziger, *The Corporate Responsibility Code Book* (Sheffield: Greenleaf Publishing, 2003), pp. 35–7.

[32] The actual partners in this project where the Austrian Federal Ministry of Social Security, Generations and Consumer Protection, the Institute for Integrative Tourism and Development (Respect) and Jumbo Touristik, an Asian tour operator. The project includes training of personnel in the country of origin and at travel destinations; a clause in contracts with suppliers repudiating commercial sexual exploitation of children; information to travellers provided in catalogues, ticket shops and home-pages; and reporting.

[33] European Commission, 'Mapping Instruments for Corporate Social Responsibility' (Directorate-General for Employment and Social Affairs, April 2003).

referred to in CSR documents stemming from the EU institutions.[34] This is particularly true of the multi-stakeholder methodologies developed by the ETI in order to monitor and verify compliance with the code.[35]

Of a similarly hybrid origin and outward-looking perspective are the Voluntary Principles on Security and Human Rights in the Extractive Sector. These were launched jointly, by the UK and US governments, in December 2000 following a series of human rights scandals. The document aims to provide practical guidance to companies in the extractive sector who are developing their activities in countries where respect for human rights can be of great concern. The principles were initiated by the two governments and developed in close consultation with oil and mining companies, human rights NGOs, social partners and CSR organisations.[36] Similarly, taking CSR codification a step further towards interactive regulation is also Law 34 on information society services and e-trade, passed by the Spanish Parliament in July 2002. The law creates the framework for the public administration to promote and incentivise the elaboration and implementation of voluntary codes of conduct by companies, associations or commercial and consumer organisations in information services and the e-trade field.[37]

The German domestic debate on CSR is the source of another outward-looking initiative focusing on codes of conduct, initiative that has often been reflected in the European debate.[38] The German federal government set up a multi-stakeholder Round Table on Codes of Conduct.[39] The aim of the Round Table is to improve the implementation of labour and social standards in developing countries through corporate codes of conduct.[40] In order to do this, the Round Table seeks to develop a common understanding of how voluntary codes of conduct can be introduced and applied effectively, transparently and with respect towards all stakeholders, especially the ones in developing countries. Displaying a feature familiar also

---

[34] European Commission, Directorate-General for Employment and Social Affairs, Unit D.1, *Mapping Instruments for Corporate Social Responsibility* (Luxembourg: Office for Publications of the European Communities, 2003).

[35] The ETI members visit their suppliers, identify conditions that do not meet the ETI base code, and then plan improvements in collaboration with their suppliers. See www.ethicaltrade.org.

[36] www.state.gov/g/drl/rls/2931.htm.

[37] There have also been calls that similar laws cover all companies. See ec.europa.eu/employment_social/soc-dial/csr/national_csr_policies_en.pdf.

[38] See www.coc-runder-tisch.de/coc-runder-tisch/rt/f_intro_E.htm.

[39] The Round Table gathers representatives of various ministries, social partners, companies and NGOs.

[40] For details, see www.coc-runder-tisch.de/coc-runder-tisch/rt/f_intro_E.htm.

to the EU CSR debate, the German Round Table – rather than promoting its own code of conduct – focuses on the Universal Declaration of Human Rights and other international human rights conventions, the ILO Declaration on Fundamental Principles and Rights at Work 1998, and the UN Global Compact Initiative.

These are only some of the codes of conduct marking the European domestic CSR spectrum. It can be said that there is no shortage of codes from which the European debate can draw inspiration. Many of these are industry-based and, as such, travel relatively easily across the European borders due to the economic and legal incentives aimed at harmonisation. These codes have, generally, a well-defined, outward-looking perspective on CSR that goes beyond internal labour relations issues. Often they are also initiated by an outside-industry authority, usually the government or governmental agency, with the participation of various stakeholders. While the pool of actors has become more hybrid, with governments and social stakeholders becoming more closely involved in the generation of such instruments, the codes remain generally lodged in the domain of identifying good practice, verifying brands and suppliers, and offering practical guidance and incentives, without taking the final leap and providing a system of sanctions.[41] Another important common feature is that most of these codes refer to international human rights documents, and some of the codification initiatives in fact endeavour to promote these international instruments rather than initiating new ones. As will appear later, all these trends are to be found within the latest CSR debate engendered at the European institutional level.[42]

C. Social reporting

Apart from a wide spectrum of awareness-raising activities and codes of conduct reporting on social issues, another important domestic approach has emerged as reflected in the EU CSR debate and initiatives. The past decade has seen an increase in the number of government imposed or managed reporting schemes, reflecting various regulatory approaches. One of the oldest initiatives dates back to the 1980s, when the Portuguese

---

[41] Leipziger, *The Corporate Responsibility Code Book*, p. 508; ILO, *Codes of Conduct for Multinationals*, available at www.itcilo.it/english/actrav/telearn/global/ilo/guide/main.htm #Implementation.

[42] S. S. Thorsen and A. Meisling, 'A European Perspective', in R. Mullerat (ed.), *Corporate Social Responsibility: The Corporate Governance of the 21st Century* (The Hague: Kluwer Law International, International Bar Association, 2005), pp. 279–81.

government passed Law no. 141/85,[43] that requires companies with more than one hundred employees to submit each year to the Labour Ministry a 'Report on the Social Balance'. Although sometimes controversial in practice, the European Commission and the European Parliament have emphasised the value of the Portuguese Social Balance Report and of other similar domestic initiatives.[44] The Social Balance Report, for instance, is acknowledged as providing essential information on the management of human resources and the effectiveness of social investments undertaken by a company. Both the European Commission and the European Parliament have linked the support for such reporting schemes to a renewed institutional approach to development cooperation and global governance.[45]

France was, however, the first country to make internal social and labour issues, as well as global issues, a matter of reporting for publicly listed companies. According to a law on new economic regulations adopted in May 2001, the annual report of a listed company shall contain information on how the company takes into account the 'social consequences of its activities'.[46] The law[47] applies to French quoted companies at group level and internationally. In their report, companies are required to make use of a set of qualitative and quantitative social indicators specified by a decree.[48] Revealing a strong international outlook, the law requires the companies with international subsidiaries to include in their annual report information on the way in which their subsidiaries respect the ILO

---

[43] Later supplemented by the Decree-law no. 9/92.

[44] G. R. Pinto, *Corporate Social Responsibility: State of the Art in Portugal 2004* (Lisbon: CECOA – Centro de Formação Profissional para o Comércio e Afins (Vocational Trade Centre for Trade), 2004), p. 25, available at www.cecoa.pt/destaques/STATE%20ART%20CSR%20PORTUGAL%202004.pdf (30/01/2006).

[45] European Commission, Communication from the Commission to the Council, the European Parliament and the Economic and Social Committee: 'Promoting Core Labour Standards and Improving Social Governance in the Context of Globalisation', COM (2001) 416 final (18.7.2001); European Commission, Communication from the Commission to the Council and the European Parliament: 'The European Union's Role in Promoting Human Rights and Democratisation in Third Countries', COM (2001) 252 final (8.5.2001).

[46] By 'social', in fact, meaning the reporting on the 'triple bottom line' in its international dimension.

[47] Law No 2001–240, Article 116.

[48] The company, for instance, has to report on its total workforce, on its recruitment policies and the distinction between fixed-term and permanent contracts, redundancies and their motives, overtime and subcontracted labour. Other issues of internal social justice on which French listed companies have to report, and which have been for many years on the EU labour agenda, are the organisation of working hours, their duration for full-time and part-time employees, wages and their evolution, professional equality between men and women, and the importance of subcontracting.

core labour conventions, and on the way in which they promote the ILO conventions with regard to their international subcontractors. Moreover, the law requires reporting on community issues, especially with respect to the way companies take into account the impact of their activities on local development and local populations. The system set up by the law is one of self-reporting. However, the companies must show in their report how they engage with the local stakeholders, including NGOs, consumer groups, educational institutions and local communities. Although it is not a perfect instrument,[49] both the inward- and the outward-looking nature of this reporting system, and its centring on existing authoritative international standards such as the ILO core conventions, is, as shown in the next section, echoed at the EU level.

The breadth of the domestic CSR initiatives is, therefore, wide, covering a variety of tools and methods in various voluntary and regulatory nuances, and interacting in various ways with the CSR debate engendered lately at the EU institutional level. The porosity existing between the domestic and the EU CSR debates and strategies is facilitated by a variety of economic, social, political and legal factors. The economic and social links generated by the EU institutional structures facilitate, by their very nature, an 'integrationist' environment. Politically also, the EU structures offer a platform from which CSR pro-active member states can promote domestic strategies or can hold the EU institutions to commitments already existing in law at the European level but not 'activated' sufficiently to facilitate the promotion of CSR values in a business environment. In addition, strategically, the European Union seeks to speak with one voice,[50] and in order to do this it has to be open to the domestic signals received from the member states. Moreover, the pervasiveness of the European human rights system determines that development cooperation with third countries – until relatively recently seen as a domestic international relations matter, with business and diplomatic dimensions – is now increasingly on the European agenda, coming under the scrutiny of human rights mechanisms from the perspective of human development, sustainability and global governance.[51]

---

[49] Indeed, some classify it as a 'law without the attributes of a law'. See in J. Allouche, F. de Bry, I. Huault and G. Schmidt, 'The Institutionalization of CSR in France: The State Injunction', in J. Allouche (ed.), *Corporate Social Responsibility, Volume 1: Concepts, Accountability and Reporting* (New York: Palgrave Macmillan, 2006), p. 303.

[50] S. Douglas-Scott, *Constitutional Law of the European Union* (London: Longman, Pearson Education Ltd, 2002), p. 35.

[51] P. Fitzpatrick and J. Bergeron (eds.), *Europe's Other: European Law Between Modernity and Postmodernity* (Aldershot: Ashgate, 1998), p. 6.

IV. The European institutional position on corporate social responsibility

The European Commission and the European Parliament are the two European institutions that play out the dynamic relationship between the voluntary and regulatory approaches to CSR. In the complex interactive environment between domestic and European CSR debate, the European Commission initiated a process of inquiry and analysis later summed up by the 2001 Green Paper under the title 'Promoting a European Framework for Corporate Social Responsibility'. The Green Paper was received positively, although by no means uncritically. More than 250 businesses, social partners and public bodies responded and commented on it.[52] Unsurprisingly, the main cleavage between the various stakeholders was between a voluntary versus regulative approach, with business supporting voluntary initiatives and perceiving the role of the Commission as enabler and facilitator, while the social partners such as trade unions and NGOs advocating for a stronger regulatory framework which would ensure the respect of fundamental rights.[53]

The Green Paper invited public authorities at all levels, including international organisations, enterprises from small and medium enterprises (SMEs) to transnational corporations, social partners, NGOs, other stakeholders and all interested individuals, to contribute to the process of promoting CSR through a new framework 'based on European values', which takes into account the interests of both business and stakeholders. In its paper, the Commission used the word 'framework' in a broad sense, inviting all social partners and stakeholders to contribute with proposals which would build on the voluntary nature of corporate social responsibility and identify ways in which it can contribute to achieving sustainable development and a more effective way of governance.[54]

In order to facilitate the creation of such a framework, the Commission started a debate on the concept itself. The objective of such an approach was to define a common ground from which integrated CSR policies – informed by domestic experiences, some of which were highlighted earlier, as well as by existing international standards – would emerge in an organic manner at European level and contribute to the process of sustainable development and global governance. The core of the definition on which the Commission based its position is the one of CSR as 'a concept whereby

---

[52] These comments were published in full on the EU website at www.europa.org.
[53] See ec.europa.eu/employment_social/soc-dial/csr/csr_responses.htm.
[54] European Commission, Green Paper, p. 21

companies integrate social and environmental concerns in their business operations and in their interactions with their stakeholders on a voluntary basis'.[55]

Elaborating on this definition, and making both the social and the business case for CSR, the Commission went on to say that:

> Being socially responsible means not only fulfilling legal expectations, but also going beyond compliance and investing 'more' into human capital, the environment and the relations with stakeholders . . . [Going] beyond legal compliance can contribute to a company's competitiveness. Going beyond basic legal obligations in the social area, e.g. training, working conditions, management-employee relations, can also have a direct impact on productivity. It opens a way of managing change and of reconciling social development with improved competitiveness.[56]

In other words, according to the Commission, a European framework for CSR would be organised according to three guiding principles:

- CSR activities going beyond common regulatory and conventional requirements will be undertaken on a voluntary basis;
- the CSR activities will necessarily be informed by the interaction with all stakeholders in a community;
- the social and environmental concerns constituting the focus of CSR will have to be an integrated part of the business operations.

At the same time, these principles are meant to be applied consistently along two equally essential dimensions of corporate activities, the internal and the external dimensions. The internal dimension covers the responsibility towards employees, including their health and safety, reasonable working hours, diversity in the recruitment process, and due consultation of employees when considering structural changes in the company such as downsizing, restructuring or relocating, issues which set off the initial EU debate on CSR in the late 1990s. Part of this internal dimension is also the responsible management of environmental impacts and efficient use of natural resources. The external dimension of CSR extends beyond the 'walls of the company' to the local community and other stakeholders such as business suppliers, customers, public authorities and NGOs.[57] These

---

[55] *ibid.*, p. 18.   [56] *ibid.*, p. 19
[57] One factor highlighted in the Green Paper is that companies working closely with business partners in supply chains can both reduce costs and increase quality. Building a good relationship with one's suppliers 'may result in fair prices, terms and expectations along with quality and reliable delivery'. See European Commission, Green Paper, p. 13.

elements have acquired an increasing position on the EU CSR agenda and, at the same time, have become an integral part of the EU development cooperation approach.

Human rights play a central role in both these aspects of EU policy. Indeed, in the words of the Commission, all aspects of CSR have 'a strong human rights dimension'.[58] Of course, in the external dimension the link is more obvious, with transnational corporations facing human rights challenges such as child labour, working conditions and relations with governments, where human rights violations are prevalent. Acknowledging that outsourcing is becoming increasingly a mode of production, the Commission, in the Green Paper, draws the companies' attention to their responsibilities towards their new suppliers as well as their staff. Reflecting domestic signals embodied in instruments such as the Danish Human Rights Impact Assessment, as well as other domestic codifying and reporting tools,[59] the Green Paper invites companies not to take their human rights responsibilities lightly and to consider these when setting up business operations in countries where human rights violations occur. At the same time, while the internal dimension appears to focus predominantly on core labour rights and environmental responsibility, the Commission sees both the internal and the external dimensions of corporate social activities as translatable into basic human rights.[60] The acknowledgement of the implications of a company's activities in society reflects the Commission's attempt to propose CSR as part of an 'integrated human rights policy', stemming, as mentioned earlier, from various provisions of EU Treaties and other related documents.[61]

The relationship between the voluntary approach imbued in the Commission's definition of CSR and the potential *legal* expectations attached to business activities – as derived from the human rights principles – should, of course, be reflected in such a policy.[62] The Commission defined the 'legal expectations' attached to business activities as being derived not only from domestic and European law but also from international law.[63]

---

[58] *ibid.*, p. 14.
[59] European Commission, Green Paper, section 2.2.3, paras. 54 and 55, and also para. 16.
[60] Such as health and safety, working hours and conditions, equal opportunities and non-discrimination, as well as working and living in a clean environment, and a sustainable use of resources.
[61] D. C. Horng, 'The Human Rights Clause in the European Union's External Trade and Development Agreements', *European Law Journal* 9 (2003), 678–9.
[62] A. I. Broadhurst, 'Corporations and the Ethics of Social Responsibility: An Emerging Regime of Expansion and Compliance', *Business Ethics: A European Revew* 9 (2000), 94–5.
[63] European Commission, Green Paper, p. 4.

The Commission, therefore, builds into its definition of voluntary corporate action the premise that companies will observe national and international legislation, including the international human rights covenants. Of course, this premise might be an over optimistic one. Most European companies will comply with national legislation but not necessarily and actively with international law. Therefore, they may still violate international law provisions regarding the freedom of association and collective bargaining, the right to equal opportunities on the labour market, or the right to privacy, especially during their activities abroad. However, one could say that taking compliance with international human rights law for granted – as the Green Paper does – is a good signal to give. Moreover, as will be shown later while looking into the CSR potential of the development cooperation agreements, relatively loose regulatory requirements can acquire compliance momentum if guided by business and economic incentives.[64]

The Commission also set out CSR and the law in a dynamic relationship, where it became likely that the balance between voluntary corporate action and legally required action would change constantly, not least because of the endeavour within the European structures. In this sense, although centring the concept of CSR round the notion of voluntarism, the Commission specified that CSR should not be seen as a substitute to regulation or legislation concerning social rights or environmental standards, *including the development of new appropriate legislation*.[65] The Commission specified that in countries where such regulations do not exist, efforts should focus on putting the proper regulatory or legislative framework in place in order to define '*a level playing field on the basis of which socially responsible practices can be developed*'.[66] As will be shown in the next part, this legislative and regulatory dimension in the Commission's policy on CSR is increasingly linked to the Commission's position towards sustainable development and global governance, and is reflected in a novel way of reading CSR *into* EU development cooperation agreements with third countries.

---

[64] Broadhurst, 'Corporations and the Ethics of Social Responsibility'. The corollary of incentives in this context is the notion of 'risk'. The Commission, in its 2002 Communication on CSR, noted the desire of enterprises to improve their risk management, and that risk management is a powerful factor behind CSR: 'Enterprises generally agree that CSR helps them in managing their risks, their intangible assets, their internal processes, and their relations with internal and external stakeholders'. See also the Commission's Communication on CSR, July 2002 final, p. 9.

[65] European Commission, Green Paper, p. 10.   [66] *ibid.*, p. 11 (my emphasis).

Bringing into the picture of corporate action present and future legislation is not the only way in which the Commission's Green Paper nuances
the pure voluntarism one might read into the definition given to the CSR.
Even when on the seemingly safe ground of 'voluntary' corporate codes of
conduct, the Commission, while endorsing such codes, discourages companies from developing their own individual codes, and channels them
towards embracing already existing international standards, such as the
Universal Declaration of Human Rights and the ILO Declaration of Fundamental Principles and Rights at Work, as well as the OECD Guidelines.[67] This has both the advantage of bringing all corporations under
the same rules and of helping corporations speak to their supply chains
with one voice, both these elements making respect for human rights on
the 'First World' side of the global market more likely.[68] In other words,
by recommending companies to subscribe to the same voluntary or 'soft-
regulatory' mechanism and international human rights framework, the
Commission proposes a system that alludes to the qualities of a proto-
regulatory system, characterised by a degree of universality and generality, although backed not by the sheer force of the state but by the 'gentle'
forces of the global market. This preference for supporting established
CSR instruments such as the OECD Guidelines, the ILO core conventions
and the UN initiatives was emphasised even more in the follow-up communication of the Commission in July 2002, document through which
the Commission set up a Multi-Stakeholder Forum,[69] a forum that has as
aim the exchange of experience and good practice between actors at EU
level, the establishment of a common European approach and guiding
CSR principles, and of a basis for international dialogue on CSR.

The relationship between voluntarism and regulation, as set by the
Commission, has to be understood in the context of other CSR initiatives taking place within the EU institutional structures. The European
Parliament is also actively taking part in the CSR debate, contributing
to a 'European CSR policy'. In July 1998, after repeated attempts to initiate a CSR document, the European Parliament published a Report on
CSR (1998 Report), together with a European Code of Conduct covering the activities of the Transnational Corporations (TNCs) operating

---

[67] *ibid.*, pp. 9 and 16.
[68] This approach was reinforced through subsequent communications from the Commission,
the European Council and the Parliament, COM (2001) 36; COM (2002) 347 final; Council
Resolution on Corporate Social Responsibility, OJ C 39/3 (18.02.2003).
[69] 'Communication from the Commission concerning Corporate Social Responsibility: A
business contribution to Sustainable Development', COM (2002) 347 final (2/7/2002).

in developing countries.[70] Unlike the Commission, whose position on CSR has always been rooted in voluntarism, the European Parliament has consistently been in favour of designing better suited regulatory mechanisms. In this sense, the 1998 Report called for the establishment of a European framework setting 'a legal basis' for the TNCs operations all over the world. In the Code, published at the same time, the Parliament set out minimum applicable standards as encapsulated in the ILO Declaration, the OECD Guidelines, the UN Declarations and the two UN Covenants.[71] The Parliament's suggestions did not reach a legally binding status in Europe. However, they have been met with a certain degree of normative success, having largely been taken up through the UN Norms on TNCs with regard to human rights,[72] norms now endorsed at the European institutional level.

Aiming to take advantage of a 'historic opportunity to drive forward the debate', in April 2002 the European Parliament published a Report on the Commission Green Paper.[73] In the Report, the Parliament called for the Commission to take inspiration from and make use of the best practice taking place at domestic level, in the member states, with respect to codes of conduct and social reporting. From the previous section we have seen that these domestic 'best practices' are not always dressed exclusively in the colours of pure voluntarism. Going even further away from voluntary action, the Parliament also called for the Commission to bring out a European Directive that would address all CSR issues. It also called for European legislation that would make reporting on corporate social impact mandatory.[74] Responding to requests from member states, the Parliament supported the creation of a European Forum for CSR that would facilitate enhanced multi-stakeholder dialogue and also serve as a platform for codes of conduct and reporting procedures accreditation.[75] Last but not least, the Parliament called for a systematic mainstreaming

---

[70] European Parliament, 'Resolution on EU standards for European enterprises operating in developing countries: Towards a European Code of Conduct', INI/1998/2075. See also A4–0508/98-Howitt and A4–0198/98-Fassa.

[71] European Parliament, 'Towards a European Code of Conduct'.

[72] UN Norms on the Responsibilities of Transnational Corporations and Other Business Enterprises with Regard to Human Rights, UN Doc. E/CN.4/Sub.2/2003/12/Rev.2 (2003). Adopted on 13 August 2003, by UN Sub-Commission on the Promotion and Protection of Human Rights resolution 2003/16, UN Doc. E/CN.4/Sub.2/2003/L.11 at 52 (2003).

[73] European Parliament, 'Report on the Commission Green Paper on Promoting a European Framework for Corporate Social Responsibility', COM (2001) 366 – C5–0161/2002 – 2002/2069(COS)), A5–0159/2002 Final.

[74] *ibid.*, p. 18.   [75] *ibid.*

by the Commission of the CSR in all areas of community policies and programmes.[76]

The European Parliament's proposal and general position on CSR add to the complex dynamic between voluntarism and regulatory regime in the European CSR debate. While the Commission's basic position promotes voluntarism – notwithstanding its endorsement of international human rights and its tentative openness towards new legislation – the Parliament's position encourages regulation. According to the Parliament's Report, the Commission's definition of CSR would be 'fundamentally flawed' because it would undermine the very idea of global governance. International law exists to promote and safeguard the protection of human life and, according to the Parliament, it should not be left for the companies to decide whether they wish to 'contribute' to this. Moreover, the Commission's definition of CSR would be incorrect because it would give the impression that the only possible approach to CSR is a voluntary one. The Parliament, therefore, disagrees with assigning CSR the position of an optional extra, a feature that can be added on to normal business activities provided it can be reconciled with improved competitiveness, and argues for its mainstreaming into all business activity.[77]

Part of this mainstreaming relates to the use of a human rights clause that would govern all business activities hosted under the umbrella of a bilateral agreement. Such a clause has been defined and refined at the European institutional level since the early 1990s. Since 1992, the European Union has defined respect for human rights and democracy as an 'essential element' of its external relationships and has included in all its bilateral trade and cooperation agreements with third countries a clause in this sense. In order to ensure consistency in the text used and its application, a European Council decision of May 1995 spelt out the basic modalities of this clause.[78] Making human rights observance an 'essential element', and a condition of trade terms and development aid, gives the European Union the ultimate right to suspend all or part of an agreement if a partner country does not fulfil its human rights obligations.[79] This human rights clause is unique to the European Union's bilateral agreements, and it now

---

[76] ibid., p. 19.   [77] ibid., p. 17.

[78] See 'Human Rights and Democratisation Policy' at europa.eu.int/comm/external_relations/human_rights/intro/#4; D. Napoli, 'The European Union's Foreign Policy and Human Rights', in N. A. Neuwahl and A. Rosas (eds.), The European Union and Human Rights (The Hague: Martinus Nijhoff, 1995), p. 304.

[79] V. Miller, 'The Human Rights Clause in the EU's External Agreements', International Affairs and Defence House of Commons Library, Research Paper 04/33 (2004), pp. 43ff; Horng, 'The Human Rights Clause', 677.

applies to over 120 countries. It represents a new model for EU external relations as well as for international cooperation.[80]

In this context, the European Parliament called for the European Council and the Commission to present a firm proposal for applying the human rights clause – including clear, precise and verifiable mechanisms for monitoring and assessing the human rights situation – in trade and development cooperation agreements with third countries by establishing compliance mechanisms, and by ensuring that all human rights and all actors are covered, including EU companies, and that companies should report publicly on these issues and establish sustainability and social impact assessments as part of the process of developing trade policies.[81] This link between the European human rights clause, the trade and development policies, and the CSR objectives was spelt out by a Multi-Stakeholder Forum set up by the Commission during its Round Table on the 'Development Aspects of CSR'.[82] The Round Table emphasised the role of companies in helping to reduce poverty and to achieve sustainable development, and acknowledged foreign direct investment (FDI) as a major force for change in developing countries.[83] For this force to be efficient, however, structures are required to be in place both for government-to-government dialogue (host governments and TNC-exporting governments) and for the private business players to work together with the governmental structures.[84] It is argued, both outside the EU structures and among the EU institutions, that if a meaningful EU CSR framework is to be put forward, it is probably within these parameters.[85]

Set within this European institutional context – with the Commission endorsing a voluntary approach and the Parliament favouring designer regulation, with soft-regulatory tools such as the human rights clause in

---

[80] Miller, 'The Human Rights Clause', 11–12; J. H. H. Weiler and S. C. Fries, 'A Human Rights Policy for the European Community Union: The Question of Competences', Working Paper, Jean Monnet Centre, NY School of Law (1999); E. Fierro, 'Legal Basis and Scope of the Human Rights Clauses in EC Bilateral Agreements: Any Room for Positive Interpretation?', *European Law Journal* 7, 1 (2001), 43.

[81] European Parliament Report on the Commission Green Paper, (54), p. 14.

[82] The Multi-Stakeholder Forum was organised in four main Round Tables. See ec.europa.eu/enterprise/csr/forum_2002_04_index.htm.

[83] Multi-Stakeholder Forum, Round Table on the 'Development Aspects of CSR', at ec.europa.eu/enterprise/csr/documents/rt_dev_finalreport_120504.pdf.

[84] S. A. Aaronsen and J. Reeves, *The European Response to Public Demands for Global Corporate Responsibility* (Washington, DC: National Policy Association, 2002), pp. 4–5.

[85] Communication from the Commission to the European Parliament, the Council, the Economic and Social Committee and the Committee of the Regions, 'Towards a Global Partnership for Sustainable Development', COM (2002) 82 final (13.2.2002), p. 6.

place ready to be interpreted and applied – the relationship between CSR and the law at the European level appears, therefore, as an open-ended dynamic relationship, sponsored by the principle of voluntarism, yet in the continuous vicinity of a subtle, potentially expanding normative regime. The question is, of course, whether this potential will bring anything new and significant to the debate and practice of CSR. In this sense, the Council, while welcoming the Commission's initiative on CSR for promoting a European framework, also warned against adding yet another layer of CSR initiatives,[86] thus contributing to the proliferation of documents and initiatives already existing in the field.

V. Development cooperation agreements as a European corporate social responsibility platform

A good illustration of this expansion of the legal and regulatory mechanisms through which CSR is promoted at the European level is the relatively recent attempt, by the EU institutions, to put international development cooperation agreements firmly within the framework of sustainability, human development and global governance via the promotion of human rights.

Through a unique set of agreements with developing countries and regional groupings, the European Union has at its disposal important instruments for the promotion of CSR at international level. Such agreements have existed since the initial establishment of the European institutions, however it is only lately that the human rights agenda has been stepped up in such agreements and has been more forcefully incorporated. The Cotonou Agreement, for instance, signed in June 2000 between the European Union and the African, Caribbean and Pacific countries (ACP), sets out the parameters of development cooperation centred on human rights and human development rather than on pure economic parameters. In this context, CSR came to be seen as one of the instruments bridging the gap between economic development and human development. From a legal point of view, this bridge is facilitated by the European human rights clause.

The human rights dimension governing the Cotonou Agreement originates well before the EU institutional preoccupation with CSR, and stems from a series of progressive developments within what is known as the

---

[86] Council Resolution on the Follow-up to the Green Paper on Corporate Social Responsibility. OJ C 86/03 (10.4.2002).

'Lomé Conventions'. The four Lomé Conventions were signed following successive negotiations between the EU/EEC and the ACP countries over the span of three decades. The relationships established through these conventions were initially state-to-state based, and human rights were present in the EU-ACP agreements only in the most oblique way. Lomé I, for instance, established the development cooperation based on a relationship of contractual nature, combining aid, trade and some political and social aspects with a long-term perspective.[87] Lomé II, signed in 1979, and Lomé III, signed in 1984, did not bring major changes from this point of view.[88] In a polarised, Berlin-walled world, this allowed the Lomé system to be praised for the 'political neutrality' it displayed, and for the way it kept at bay claims of human rights universality, values which could have otherwise been pressed down on business and economic actors. Such neutrality, however, became difficult to sustain through development cooperation and direct investment projects supported by the European Union in countries where dictatorial regimes made such projects impossible to administer.[89] The pressure, therefore, for introducing human rights into the Lomé Convention system gathered pace during the late 1970s and early 1980s, and by 1984 human rights took a more explicit position in the preamble of Lomé III, acquiring a full position within the body of the succeeding Lomé IV by 1989.

During the review of Lomé IV in the 1994–1995, global market-friendly issues such as the decentralisation of cooperation, the diversification of the ACP economies, and the enhanced promotion of the private sector and private actors appeared on the agenda. At the same time, the human rights agenda was also stepped up, advancing under this umbrella issues of democracy and the rule of law, good domestic and corporate governance, environmental protection and labour rights. Reflecting the EU move towards a systematic use of the human rights clause in the EU bilateral relations, for the first time in the EU–ACP relations respect for a

---

[87] K. Whiteman, 'Africa, the ACP and Europe: The Lessons of 25 Years', *Development Policy Review* 16 (1998), 30; M. Busse and H. Grossmann, 'Assessing the Impact of ACP/EU Economic Partnership Agreement on West African Countries', *Hamburgisches Welt-Wirtschafts-Archiv*, HWWA Discussion Paper 294 (Hamburg Institute of International Economics, 2004).

[88] A. Koulaïmah-Gabriel, 'Beyond the Lomé IV: Future Challenges to EU-Africa Relations', *Review of European Community and International Environment* 6 (1997), 14.

[89] One of the earliest situations when the arrangements set out through the Lomé Convention became a political embarrassment was related to the atrocities committed under the Amin regime in Uganda in the 1970s. David Owen, the British Foreign Secretary at the time, headed a campaign for suspending aid and British direct investment in Uganda.

comprehensive list of human rights – bearing down on a comprehensive list of stakeholders, including business partners – became essential parts of any project of development cooperation and investment between the EU and the ACPs. The importance of this recognition related to a potential for enforcement; the ACP countries that failed to fulfil their human rights obligations risked having their allocated grants withdrawn and the direct investment projects supported by the European Union under the development cooperation umbrella stopped.

In spite of these changes, the 1990s brought growing discontent with the effectiveness of the Lomé system in supporting the ACP countries development effort and needs. Throughout this period, it was widely recognised that the Lomé mechanism had failed to secure sufficient progress regarding both pure trade parameters and the more complex goals of human development to which trade and business relations now seem to be subordinated. This state of affairs determined the European Commission to put forward a Green Paper entitled 'Partnership 2000'.[90] Partnership 2000 prepared the ground for profound changes in the scope, principles and instruments underlying the ACP–EU development cooperation.[91] These changes made CSR part of the panoply of mechanisms for the realisation of the aims of the partnership.

Rather than renegotiating the Lomé Convention as usual, the Commission's Partnership 2000 initiative gave birth to a new arrangement signed as an agreement in Cotonou (Benin, Africa) in 8 June 2000 and entered fully into force on 1 April 2003. The Agreement brings important innovative elements that put the ACP–EU development cooperation on a complex and constructive basis. As such, it creates a potential springboard for the promotion of human rights, using an enhanced open-ended list of implementation mechanisms, some of which are rooted in CSR processes, as well as a wider list of actors in development cooperation projects, including business actors, civil society and community organisations, and social partners.

In the reading of the European Parliament, CSR is part of the panoply of implementation mechanisms available for pursuing the goals of the

---

[90] The Partnership 2000 Green Paper was published in November 1996. For details, see www.eurostep.org/wcm/index.php?option=com_docman&task=cat_view&gid=121& Itemid=41.

[91] M. De la Rocha, 'The Cotonou Agreement and its Implications for the Regional Trade Agenda in Eastern and Southern Africa', World Bank Policy Research Working Paper 3090 (Washington, DC: World Bank, 2003). Available from www.eldis.org/static/ DOC12940.htm.

ACP–EU development cooperation agreements set under the Cotonou Agreement.[92] This is in line with the European Commission's position stating that the European Union can make more effective the promotion of CSR at international level through its unique set of agreements with third countries and regional groupings, including the Cotonou Agreement with the ACP countries.[93] The Agreement takes the form of a set of objectives, principles and options for policy instruments that allow a greater flexibility of action while being long-term programmatic about achieving the central goals of the cooperation, that is human development in the ACP countries. In this sense, Article 2 outlines four fundamental principles on which the Agreement is based: equality of partners and ownership of the development strategies; participation; the pivotal role of dialogue and the fulfilment of mutual obligations; and differentiation and regionalisation. According to the Agreement, the fundamental principle of equality of the partners and ownership of the development strategies has to be exercised with due regard to the essential element described in Article 9 of the Agreement, which is the respect for all human rights and fundamental freedoms. From the CSR perspective, the fundamental principle of participation is particularly important. This principle opens the partnerships based on the Agreement to different kinds of actors – including the private sector and civil society – and not just to central governments.[94]

The implementation mechanisms accompanying the Agreement have, however, been left flexible and have been incorporated in a set of annexes, protocols and a Compendium.[95] The Compendium, for instance, provides reference texts regarding the objectives, policy orientations and operational guidelines in specific areas or sectors of cooperation.[96] The text allows for updating according to the evolving requirements of cooperation; they can be reviewed, completed and/or amended by the Council of Ministers on the basis of recommendation from the ACP–EC Development Finance Co-operation Committee. The list of cooperation areas specified in the Compendium is also not exhaustive but only indicative. New areas which may prove of interest for cooperation strategies can be added. From a legal perspective, therefore, the ACP–EU cooperation

---

[92] European Parliament Report on the European Commission Green Paper on CSR, p. 14.
[93] European Commission, Communication on CSR, July 2002 final, p. 22.
[94] Cotonou, Article 2.
[95] See ec.europa.eu/development/Geographical/Cotonou/CotonouDoc_en.cfm.
[96] European Commission, 'Compendium on Co-operation Strategies', European Commission, Directorate General – Development, Brussels (November, 2001), p. 7.

rests on a 'hard core' of general principles and objectives, and a 'soft law shell' of fairly flexible implementation mechanisms. CSR can be read into this soft shell, which can be redefined and renegotiated according to the specifics of each country, while the Agreement itself – containing the directing principles and objectives – remains the same.[97] The European human rights clause, incorporated in the Agreement and defining human rights as a fundamental element of it, serves as a basis for dialogue with a third country government on human rights. This includes encouraging respect for human rights in their CSR perspective, and in particular for core labour standards, as a necessary underpinning for successful CSR activity by companies investing in developing countries.[98]

The placing of human rights, and potentially of CSR, at the heart of a development cooperation agreement is not limited to the Cotonou system. The EU approach in this area is set out in the Communication on the EU Role in Promoting Human Rights and Democratisation in Third Countries,[99] and the Communication on Promoting Core Labour Standards and Improving Social Governance in the Context of Globalisation.[100] The EU approach, as set out in these documents, includes the use of bilateral dialogue with governments and development assistance to built capacity, and of additional incentives under the EU's Generalised System of Preferences (GSP) where countries comply and apply minimum social and environmental standards. As acknowledged in the Commission's Communication on CSR, the GSP also provides for the temporary withdrawal of preferences where countries commit serious and systematic violations of any of the core labour standards referred to in the ILO Declaration on Fundamental Principles and Rights at Work.[101]

From the point of view of the contribution business can have to the realisation of ACP–EU development cooperation aims, the novel contribution of the Cotonou Agreement consists of the incontestable link it establishes between trade, development and human rights objectives, and of acknowledging the direct impact this link can have on the protection and promotion of human rights.[102] This acknowledgement, while not unprecedented in an intergovernmental document, has great potential

---

[97] The Agreement was set for an unprecedented period of twenty years.
[98] European Commission, Communication on CSR, July 2002 final, p. 22.
[99] European Commission, 'Communication on the EU Role in Promoting Human Rights and Democratisation in Third Countries'. COM (2001) 252 final.
[100] European Commission, 'Communication on Promoting Core Labour Standards and Improving Social Governance in the Context of Globalisation, COM (2001) 416.
[101] European Commission, Communication on CSR, July 2002 final, p. 22.
[102] Miller, 'The Human Rights Clause', p. 14.

for the promotion of human rights. This potential relates to the fact that, apart from setting out human rights objectives, the Agreement also articulates clearly the possibility of suspending development cooperation aid, programmes and subsidies, in the case when insufficient progress is made at the ACP level for the improvement of the human rights situation. This articulation provides the European Union with a classical international law sanctioning tool. The potential of the Cotonou Agreement of co-interesting governments and businesses in the promotion of human rights and CSR is rooted in this sanctioning tool and in the principle of 'mutual obligations' articulated in the Agreement.[103] The human rights agenda of the Agreement is broad, covering all the major international human rights documents and stating that human rights are universal, indivisible and interrelated, thus avoiding any hierarchy of rights and endorsing an obligation to promote and protect all fundamental freedoms and human rights in equal measure, be they civil and political, or economic, social and cultural.[104] In principle, therefore, any serious violation of,[105] or neglect in addressing, the human rights protected through the international agreements can trigger the application of the mutual obligations principle enshrined in the Cotonou Agreement.[106]

The immediate implication of this principle is that the relatively unconditional aid-flow and non-reciprocal trade preferences for the ACP countries – common under the Lomé regime – is no longer a choice. Under the Cotonou regime, the development cooperation will imply not only aid and trade preferences from the European Union, but also acknowledgement and action from the ACP countries with respect to human rights.

Given that the Agreement entered into force only recently, it is difficult to say to what extent it will impact on the trade and development cooperation between European Union and ACP. However, if sympathetically implemented,[107] the Agreement is likely to make European business partners directly interested both in promoting the Cotonou agenda and in endorsing the CSR parameters promoted by the European structures. The system put in place by the Agreement creates the potential for CSR and other human rights initiatives to permeate the development cooperation

---

[103] Cotonou, Article 2.   [104] Cotonou, Article 9(2).

[105] Cotonou, Article 96 refers to 'cases of special urgency' understood as exceptional cases of particularly serious and flagrant violation of one of the essential elements referred to in para. 2 of Article 9, that require an immediate reaction.

[106] See Human Rights Watch, 'World Report 2002', available at hrw.org/wr2k2/americas5. html.

[107] A. I. Broadhurst, 'Corporations and the Ethics of Social Responsibility', 86–98.

agenda through a set of novel mechanisms and procedures introduced through the Cotonou Agreement.[108] While previously – including under the Lomé regime – all the elements of the development cooperation were the exclusive domain of state actors,[109] the Cotonou Agreement opened the door to a much greater non-state actor involvement in both the design and the implementation of development strategies and pro-grammes. The definition of non-state stakeholder was extended in the Agreement to include the private sector, with both economic and social partners.[110] This creates the possibility for a two-way CSR–Cotonou re-enforcement action. First, EU companies with an interest in becoming or staying CSR champions acquire an official outlet of action under the Cotonou human rights umbrella. Second, social stakeholder promoters of CSR acquire an extra mechanism – the Agreement itself – through which to compel or encourage companies to become or stay Cotonou-compatible, and the intergovernmental structures to stay consistent with the Agreement's human rights agenda and to promote CSR. During the Multi-Stakeholder Forum on CSR, for instance, many of the participants (NGOs, trade unions, etc.)[111] expressed their opinion that European inter-governmental cooperation agreements, such as the Cotonou Agreement, should be used *actively* as vehicles for the promotion of CSR. Moreover, the European Parliament, in its comments on the Commission's Green Paper on CSR, stated that in contexts such as the Cotonou Agreement, where the European Union has established formal relations through trade and cooperation agreements, the Commission must seek to jointly include the subject of corporate social responsibility in the official agenda.[112]

---

[108] An important aspect of convergence, for instance, between the European CSR strategy and the Cotonou Agreement is the recognition of the fight against corruption as a 'fun-damental element' in the promotion of human rights, the rule of law and democratic values, and an explicit reference to corruption as both a major development and human rights problem to be addressed (EC Green Paper on CSR, para. 53). Serious cases of corruption, 'including of bribery leading to such corruption', could constitute grounds for suspension of cooperation. This inclusion of a corruption clause in the Agreement aims not only to give an unequivocal sign to aid recipients, but also to promote more transparent activities by European investors and other actors. (The European Union and the ACP have agreed on a specific procedure to deal with such cases of corruption (Article 9).) (EC Green Paper on CSR, para. 53).

[109] With some participatory elements introduced during the review of Lomé IV.

[110] Cotonou, Article 6(1)(b).

[111] See europa.eu.int/comm/employment_social/soc-dial/csr/csr_ responses.htm.

[112] European Parliament, Report on the Commission's Green Paper, (61), p. 15. Mindful of the difficulties encountered in securing jurisdiction over human rights violations that might fall under the ambit of such agreements, the Parliament also called on the Commission

Through the Cotonou Agreement, the traditional state-to-state relations in development cooperation are, therefore, changed towards 'more decentralised and fluid cooperation structures'. These take the form of participatory partnerships that could include a great variety of actors.[113] According to the European Commission, through the Cotonou Agreement the European Union acquires an important role in promoting dialogue between EU and third countries' social structures, including business, industry structures and corporations, and can use this role to further the spread of CSR.[114] Trade unions, consumer associations, human rights defenders and other 'watchdog' mechanisms play an important role in promoting and ensuring respect for fundamental rights. By promoting exchange of experience and sharing of good practice between counterparts in the European Union and developing countries, the European Union can contribute to building the capacity to monitor the on-the-ground application of CSR principles by foreign and domestic investors.[115] Such debate can also promote a convergence of approaches. EU assistance programmes can potentially be used to provide support for such dialogue and capacity-building concerning CSR.[116]

The broadening of the cooperation agents from state-to-state relations to state-to-stakeholders interactions will make partners on both sides more open to scrutiny on human rights issues and, consequently, on the human rights dimension of CSR. Of course, the onus of improving the human rights record remains primarily with the ACP and EU

---

to compile a study of the application of the extraterritoriality principle by courts in the member states of the Union, and called on the EU member states to incorporate the extraterritoriality principle in legislation. Such a principle would be enabled by the 1968 Brussels Convention, consolidated in Regulation 44/2001/EC (OJ No. L134, 30 April 2004, p. 114), according to which the domestic courts of the EU member states have jurisdiction over subsidiaries operating in other countries when these are responsible for (extreme) cases of negligence, leading to manslaughter or other serious harm.

[113] Stemming from Article 5(1), which states that 'the role and potential of initiatives taken by individuals and groups shall also be recognized and fostered in order to achieve in practice real participation of the population in the development process', this type of participation increased the likelihood for issues related to human rights and human development, community orientation and poverty alleviation to be made part of the economic cooperation agenda.

[114] T. Fox and D. Prescott, *Exploring the Role of Development Cooperation Agencies in Corporate Responsibility* (London: IIED/IBLF, 2004).

[115] CSR Multi-Stakeholder Forum, Round Table on the 'Development Aspects of CSR', pp. 7–9.

[116] European Commission, 'Communication on CSR,' July 2002 final, pp. 22–3; for the potential of the European human rights clause to assist with this endeavour, see Horng, 'The Human Rights Clause'.

governments. However, the existence of an appropriate legal framework, such as the one provided by the Cotonou Agreement, also provides for the stakeholders' capacity to hold their governments and their economic agents accountable when cooperation policies and investment projects they choose to support or take part in are inimical to human rights. It also provides the opportunity for business partners to relate directly to the Cotonou Agreement's underlying human rights rationale and to make it work for business in the context of CSR.

VI. Conclusions

The European Union is the world's biggest trading partner and a major source of direct private investment. With such a place in the global market, it is, of course, important that the European Union takes part in the debate refining the concept of CSR and its mechanisms. The EU attempt to develop a CSR framework is dependent upon its constitutional characteristics and upon the complex relationship between the EU institutional core and the member states.

The domestic signals received by the European Union from the member states appear to indicate a certain common ground. First, there is a certain consistency in the references made to international human rights documents and to intergovernmental CSR instruments already in place, such as the OECD Guidelines, the ILO core conventions, the UN Global Compact and, recently, the UN Human Rights Norms. This shared common ground increases the chances for an EU-endorsed mechanism, generated by the OECD or the UN institutions. Second, voluntarism is consistently referred to as the basic approach to CSR. This endorsement, however, is often softened through a variety of means. At the European domestic level, there is a wide range of government initiatives – codes of conduct and reporting mechanisms being among the most common – displaying various degrees of soft-legislation and soft-regulation.

The European Union appears to have incorporated into its institutional approach to CSR both elements mentioned above. First, it has opted for full support of existing intergovernmental mechanisms. Of course, given the European Union's position in relation to international structures such as the OECD and the ILO, this support does not mean only endorsement, but also efforts towards improving and actively promoting those mechanisms. It has been mentioned, in this sense, that the EU initiatives have also been at the heart of the recently adopted UN Human Rights Norms for TNCs. Second, while officially endorsing CSR voluntarism, the EU approach does not appear totally inimical to legislative and regulatory action. The Commission, for instance, acknowledged the legal expectations derived from European and international human rights law in relation to the business actors. It also acknowledged the possibility, to a certain extent, of enacting new legislation and new regulation covering CSR issues. At the same time, the European Parliament has added to the already dynamic relation between the voluntary and the normative action by speaking in favour of a European legislative approach. It is true that the normative 'talk' appears more emphatic when coming from certain EU institutions than from others. However, it is not unusual for new normative domains to develop in this way, and CSR has developed so far as a social discourse mainly through such small steps.

Apart from the issues related to the support for voluntary corporate action and for international and intergovernmental instruments, the European Union also offers another, different, type of platform for CSR. The elements on which this platform is based relate to the EU position in international relations and global trade, as well as to the extent to which the European Union will centre its development cooperation agreements with third countries on human rights. The hard core of principles set out in agreements such as the Cotonou Agreement, and the soft shell of mechanisms of implementation accompanying those principles, render such agreements particularly suited to long-term investment in human rights in general and in CSR in particular. Undoubtedly, however, it also renders them prone to non-implementation, if the implementation mechanisms remain insufficiently developed. At the moment, given the fairly recent ratification of the Cotonou Agreement, an analysis along this line would be premature. However, in the coming years, once development cooperation programmes are set up based on the Cotonou framework, socio-legal research will be required in order to assess whether the human rights and CSR potential of the Cotonou Agreement is matched by the reality of international relations and global market strategies.

The fact that the Cotonou Agreement is conceived in a way that matches the three CSR principles set out in the European Commission's Green Paper (a voluntary approach to CSR, stakeholder involvement and mainstreaming of CSR in all business activities) is likely to bolster the chances of the Agreement to become an effective conveyor of CSR through its human rights provisions. First, through its balance between a hard core of principles and a soft shell of implementation mechanisms, the Agreement allows room for voluntary action, at least at the 'point of commitment', by the signatory countries or participant private actors to the specific human rights responsibilities. Second, although an international law document, setting up an intergovernmental mechanism, the Agreement creates an arena for stakeholder involvement, allowing in principle for both civil society and business actors to take part in the setting up of the agenda of a development cooperation programme supported by CSR. Last but not least, the Agreement is clearly centred on the European human rights clause, and as such, any CSR actor, including the business actors, which would like to take part in a development cooperation project will need to make the requirements of the human rights clause an integral part of their business operations.

It is too early to say whether the guided voluntarism, the stakeholder participation and the semi-regulatory framework provided through the European human rights clause will converge and result in the practical acknowledgement of CSR as part of the instruments of the EU development cooperation agreements. It is, however, evident that the EU approach to CSR and to development cooperation coincide in endorsing these three elements. The regulatory undercurrents, therefore, coming from the EU institutions may well prepare the ground for future changes in the EU approach to CSR, and are likely to support the use of the international law framework offered by the development cooperation agreements in order to promote the CSR values.

PART FOUR

Expanding Legal Accountabilities: Corporate
Responsibility, Human Rights and the
Environment

13

Changing paradigms of corporate criminal responsibility: lessons for corporate social responsibility

AURORA VOICULESCU

I. Introduction

The corporate social responsibility (CSR) debate often focuses on what it is that needs to be protected and how this is to be done. The CSR concept, however, also brings with it a more fundamental normative question related to the nature of responsibility itself. Usually, a normative system – legal or ethical – carries with it the ideas of action and intention, which are placed at the heart of the concept of responsibility. While these ideas connect relatively easily with the concept of an individual human being, they are less evidently applicable to an abstract legal entity such as a corporation. The conceptual issues underlying this difficulty have been at the heart of an ongoing criminal law debate for some time. This chapter analyses recent criminal law developments in a range of jurisdictions, highlighting changes in the paradigms of corporate criminal responsibility and suggesting lessons for CSR.

Corporate responsibility for crime has appeared on the agenda of many international bodies such as the European Union, the Council of Europe, the Organisation for Economic Co-operation and Development (OECD) and the United Nations,[1] and there are calls for an approach which would capture the complexity of corporate activities in the globalised market

The author would like to thank Claire Mayer and Gratia Necsutu for giving their time so generously to discuss a number of issues in the final draft of this chapter and to Doreen McBarnet, Tom Campbell and Marina Kurkchiyan for their comments and suggestions on various drafts of the chapter. All statements and any errors are, of course, the responsibility of the author.

[1] *Norms on the Responsibilities of Transnational Corporations and Other Business Enterprises with Regard to Human Rights (UN Norms)*, UN Doc. E/CN.4/Sub.2/2003/12/Rev.2(2003) 13 August 2003, available at www.business-humanrights.org. See especially para. 18 of the UN Norms. See also *Commentary on the Norms on the Responsibilities of Transnational*

economy. Such an approach calls for a legally binding convention that is internationally enforceable and applicable not only to states but also to corporations, and in addition covers corporate supply-chains as well as corporate subsidiaries.[2]

At the same time, due to the complexity of applying such a convention internationally, the pursuit of a legally enhanced corporate responsibility is expected to take place especially at the domestic level, via the domestic courts.[3] Not surprisingly, therefore, the International Criminal Defence Attorneys Association (ICDAA) has recently launched a project focusing on the potential criminal responsibility of corporations and business executives under both international and national criminal legislation. The first phase of this project focuses on the link between CSR and the various forms of business criminal liability.[4] Moreover, the International Criminal Court (ICC) – given that it does not have business corporations under

---

Corporations and Other Business Enterprises with Regard to Human Rights (hereafter *Commentary*), UN Doc.E/CN.4/Sub.2/2003/38.Rev.2(2003) available at www.umn.edu/ humanrts/links/commentary-Aug2003.html. See Muchlinski in this volume, Chapter 14; also C. Wells and J. Elias, 'Catching the Conscience of the King: Corporate Players on the International Stage', in Philip Alston (ed.), *Non-State Actors and Human Rights: Collected Courses of the Academy of European Law* (Oxford: Oxford University Press, 2003), pp. 5–7. For a reconceptualisation of human rights that would bring transnational corporations more easily under the international fora, see also Sinden, in this volume, Chapter 17; also, Kinley, Nolan and Zerial, in this volume, Chapter 15; The Convention on Combating Bribery of Foreign Public Officials in International Business Transactions, adopted by the Organisation for Economic Cooperation and Development (OECD, 21 November 1997); The Criminal Law Convention on Corruption, adopted by the Committee of Ministers of the Council of Europe [CETS No. 173] (27 January 1999).

2 Christian Aid, *Need for a Legally Binding Regulation of Transnational Corporations*, at www.wdm.org.uk/resources/briefings/index.htm (accessed April 2007). World Development Movement, *Making Investment Work for People: An International Framework for Regulating Corporations* (1999), at www.wdm.org.uk/resources/briefings/chrono.htm (accessed May 2007).

3 B. Stephens, 'The Amorality of Profit: Transnational Corporations and Human Rights', *Berkeley Journal International Law* 20, 1 (2002), 45 at 76; Elliot Schrage, 'Emerging Threat: Human Rights Claims,' *Harvard Business Review* August (2003), 16–18; Stephen R. Ratner, 'Corporations and Human Rights: A Theory of Legal Responsibility,' *Yale Law Journal* 111 (2001), 443; Jordan J. Paust, 'Human Rights Responsibilities of Private Corporations,' *Vanderbilt Journal of Transnational Law* 35 (2002), 801; For a creative extra-territorial application of domestic law capturing CSR issues, see McBarnet and Schmidt in this volume, Chapter 5. On the 'division of labour' between the international and the domestic jurisdictions with respect to CSR, see also Kinley, Nolan and Zerial, in this volume, Chapter 15.

4 ICDAA, *Defence Watch Special Research Project*, at www.aiad-icdaa.org/what_we_do/ corporate_social_responsabilities.php.

its jurisdiction – is looking at developing a concept of *sharing information* and *working with national legal systems* in order to address those corporations and financial institutions the actions of which facilitate gross violations of human rights.[5]

Whether under an international or domestic umbrella, the issue of criminal responsibility of corporations and its forms is, however, still riddled with controversy inasmuch as its conceptual framework is concerned. It oscillates between the image of an aggregate entity, performing aggregated acts and bearing aggregated responsibilities, and – at the other end of the spectrum – an organic, real entity, which is perceived holistically, as more than the sum of its members. The responsibilities of such an entity are seen to be distinct from the ones pertaining to its discrete members. This controversy at the heart of the corporate criminal responsibility debate can only add to the level of controversy CSR enjoys in its own right.[6] Expressions such as 'corporate citizenship', 'the obligation of business to society', 'role and responsibilities of a corporate entity' and 'legitimate corporation', to mention just a few, suggest a strong holistic perspective of the corporate entity being reflected within the concept of CSR.

Moreover, the collectivist rhetoric of this perspective is reflected by (and a reflector of) the fact that an important part of the more traditional CSR tools[7] – by their very nature – addresses the business corporation as a whole rather than targeting specific individuals or categories of its

---

[5] ICC, Communications Received by the Office of the Prosecutor of the ICC: Press Release 16 July 2003, at www.icc-cpi.int/library/press/mediaalert/16_july_english.pdf:; Roberta Cowan, 'International Criminal Court Widens Its Scope', *The Globe and Mail* (Canada), 17 July 2003; G. Soros, 'Open Up the Books', *Corporate Knights* 1 (2003), 41; see also *The International Criminal Court & Business*, at www.aiad-icdaa.org/rpr/csr.html.

[6] Violations of CSR obligations do not have to be characterised as crimes. However, the normative nature of most of the standards included under the CSR umbrella (especially the ones covered by human rights international treaties) makes crime the closest analogy and criminal law an often invoked normative mechanism. It is in this context of increased intertwining of normative mechanisms that criminal responsibility instruments have also appeared on the CSR menu, side by side with the use of major civil penalties; Wells and Elias, 'Catching the Conscience of the King', 25.

[7] This happens largely for want of other practical – i.e., politically acceptable – means. The corporate codes of conduct, CSR reporting systems and ethical labelling systems were developed arguably as a way of pre-emptive action against centrally (domestically or internationally) initiated legal mechanisms; C. Fauset, *What is Wrong with Corporate Social Responsibility?*, Corporate Watch Report 2006, available at www.corporatewatch.org/?lid = 2670, p. 13.

personnel.[8] The holistic image encapsulated, to a certain extent, in the concept of CSR can only be reinforced when it is acknowledged – while also criticised – by organisations known to promote primarily the interests of business. Donald J. Johnston, for instance, the Secretary General of the OECD, declared in February 2006 that corporate social responsibility is not a well-liked term by the OECD: 'At the OECD we prefer to talk about "responsible business conduct".' According to Johnston, the difference between the two terms is that the latter reflects the reality that 'business is conducted by individuals within corporations, not by the corporations themselves', as the term 'CSR' would mistakenly suggest.[9]

The conceptualisation of CSR, therefore, appears to be just as fraught as the one of corporate criminal responsibility. Starting from the controversies regarding this conceptualisation, the present chapter addresses the extent to which the debate on corporate criminal responsibility and the debate on CSR share in the same problematic of corporate agency and responsibility. It also investigates the extent to which the debate on the paradigms of corporate criminal responsibility can further the debate on CSR.

In the corporate criminal responsibility discourse, unlike that in CSR, distinctions and dichotomies have been systematically selected, honed and sanctioned through the legislative process. This is a formalised social debate to which CSR now relates increasingly in a variety of ways and from which CSR may draw re-enforcement. For the purpose of this chapter, therefore, the focus will be on the domestic legal debate stemming from various jurisdictions and on the paradigms of corporate responsibility that emerge from this debate. The domestic platform appears as the most relevant here due to the fact that, on the international arena, corporate criminal responsibility initiatives emerge generally as incentives in search

---

[8] This image still prevails, in spite of the fact that lately there is an increased awareness of the fact that the organisational responsibility for certain CSR issues should be paralleled with an individual responsibility in order to be effective; R. Spencer, *Corporate Law and Structures: Exposing the Roots of the Problem*, Corporate Watch Report 2004, available at www.corporatewatch.org/?lid=2592; David Silver, 'Collective Responsibility, Corporate Responsibility and Moral Taint', *Midwest Studies in Philosophy* 30, 1, 269–78; also L. May, *Sharing Responsibility* (Chicago: University of Chicago Press, 1992), p. 17.

[9] Interestingly, Johnston went on to emphasise precisely the issue of legal liability, saying that 'it is people who choose the legal framework in which they wish to undertake their business whether it be through partnerships, sole proprietorships or, as is most often the case, through corporations with limited liability'; D. J. Johnston, 'Global Corporate Social Responsibility Forum: China' (Beijing, 22 February 2006), available at www.oecd.org/dataoecd/38/55/36196777.pdf.

of domestic solutions.[10] Also, it is more likely that at the domestic level a potential shift in the paradigm of corporate responsibility can reach formal acknowledgement, through law. Such a shift can, therefore, be traced to and reflected in legal initiatives that have reached some kind of legislative conclusion, and so have moved from the domain of social debate into the sphere of legal concepts.[11]

Section II of the chapter looks at the traditional individualist approach to corporate criminal responsibility, identifying its theoretical underpinnings and its practical implications. This approach is illustrated through domestic examples where individualist doctrines have had an impact on the legal framing of corporate criminal responsibility. Section III of the chapter presents some of the more significant domestic changes in the paradigm of corporate criminal responsibility. This is then followed by the discussion of the theoretical foundations of this paradigm shift and its implications for CSR.

II. Corporate social responsibility and the individualist forms of corporate criminal responsibility

Unlike regulatory offences, which do not rely on the requirement of culpability, criminal law brings with it the ideas of intention, knowledge, malice and subjective recklessness. It also has attached to it the idea of enforcement not through compensation, but through punishment and the threat of punishment. Inevitably, these ideas bring controversy in the debate on corporate responsibility within a criminal law framework. Similarly, the CSR debate faces the challenge of proposing corporations as responsible social agents and designing methods and tools of accountability.[12]

Many of the difficulties in proposing the concepts of both corporate criminal responsibility and corporate social responsibility have to do with the difficulty in answering the question whether a collective entity such as a corporation can be held responsible. In practice, some jurisdictions have made corporations criminally liable through various legal mechanisms, while others have been more reluctant to do so. In looking closer at these mechanisms and at their rationale, one can identify elements which are potentially relevant beyond the boundaries of the criminal law domain

---

[10] J. I. Turner, 'Nationalizing International Criminal Law: The International Criminal Court as a Roving Mixed Court', *Stanford Journal of International Law* 41 (2004), 1–53.

[11] D. Patterson, 'Dworkin on the Semantics of Legal and Political Concepts', *Oxford Journal of Legal Studies* 26 (2006), 545–57.

[12] Silver, 'Collective Responsibility', 270–3.

and are thus potentially useful for the understanding of the evolution of CSR processes as such. In order to understand the traditional paradigm of corporate criminal responsibility based on an individualist approach to the notion of organisation, in the next pages we will look into the main issues related to the concept of vicarious liability and the identification doctrine. The shortcomings of the doctrine of identification and its limits for a CSR-enhanced notion of corporate criminal responsibility are illustrated by examples from the UK panoply of health and safety disasters. This will then facilitate the discussion of the individualist underpinnings of the doctrine of identification.

A. Vicarious liability

In certain jurisdictions, criminal law has accepted the idea of the vicarious liability of the employer for the acts of an employee, or of the liability of the principal for the acts of the agent, mainly through mechanisms of blame attribution via strict liability offences when the liability of the employer or principal intervenes regardless of the employee's or agent's behaviour.[13] Alternatively, the employer or principal can be held liable only when the employee or agent is found negligent. The English courts, US federal law and the South-African legal system recognise, to various degrees and through various common law and statutory mechanisms, a vicarious liability principle.[14] In general terms, in order for the corporation to be found vicariously liable, the conduct of an employee must be found at the heart of the offence and must be found to have been performed within the scope of the individual's employment or authority.

In complex situations, however, with intricate chains of command and structures of responsibility, the 'scope of employment' is a difficult concept to prove, with employees and agents often acting under pressure to perform and deliver results regardless of the risks assumed. In these situations, it is possible for the employer to claim that the employee went on a 'frolic and detour', acting in his or her own right rather than in the scope

---

[13] C. Wells, *Corporations and Criminal Responsibility* (Oxford: Oxford University Press, 2001), pp. 99–101; Gary Slapper and Steve Tombs, *Corporate Crime*, Longman Criminology Series (London: Longman, 1999), pp. 197–200; V. S. Khanna, 'Is the Notion of Corporate Fault a Faulty Notion?: The Case of Corporate *Mens Rea*', *Boston University Law Review* 79 (1999), 356–415.

[14] D. Bergman, 'Reckless in the Boardroom', *New Law Journal* 140 [6477] (1990), 1496–1504; M. Goode, 'Corporate Criminal Liability', *Australian Institute of Criminology: Conference Proceedings* (1996), available at www.aic.gov.au/publications/proceedings; B. Fisse, 'Corporate Criminal Responsibility', *Criminal Law Journal* 15 (1991), 166–74.

of the employment. These types of claims are very easy to make in those situations when the chain of command is very long and removed from the place where the violations occur. Vicarious liability has, therefore, been criticised for having both too narrow and too wide a scope:[15] by demanding that liability be necessarily rooted in an individual, vicarious liability, to a certain extent, 'bails out' the corporation itself. At the same time, it is contended that by making the corporation only *vicariously* liable – even if via an individual – the level of blame which would otherwise be associated with the criminal law discourse becomes obscured.

The vicarious liability has also been criticised for being difficult to apply in complex corporate contexts created by the wider global market economy. The principle of the legal separation of the parent corporations from their subsidiaries, and even more so from their supply chains, makes the mechanisms of vicarious liability, for instance, useful only to a very limited extent.[16] Moreover, the vicarious liability of the corporation does not come into play in those situations where the physical integrity of the employees or the local population was affected through acts such as assault or battery committed by employees, unless the use of force was part of their employment (e.g., policy force, security agencies). Generally, it would not apply, for instance, to situations of collusion of interests between a repressive regime and a transnational corporation in the use of excessive force against the local population by security forces.[17] In this sense, international organisations and non-governmental organisations (NGOs) have pointed out the inadequacy of the domestic legal systems in general, and of the domestic corporate criminal law provisions in particular, for opening up to important CSR obligations such as the corporate duty of care for communities and the environment, as well

---

[15] The English legal system, for instance, utilises it only with respect to certain types of regulatory offences; Slapper and Tombs, *Corporate Crime*, p. 197; A. H. Choi and J. C. Bisso, 'Should Vicarious Liability be Based on Negligence or Strict Liability?', *University of Virginia Legal Working Papers Series* (30 March 2006), pp. 28–30, available at ssrn.com/abstract = 89490.

[16] S. Deva, 'Human Rights Standards and Multinational Corporations: Dilemma Between *Home* and *Rome*', *Mediterranean Journal of Human Rights* 7 (2003), 69–97; see also Glinski, in this volume, Chapter 4; S. L. Anand, *Bhopal Gas Disaster and Dow Chemical: Need for CSR*, p. 10, SSRN-id752784[1], available at papers.ssrn.com/sol3/papers.cfm? abstract_id = 752784.

[17] Amnesty International, 'Nigeria: Ten years on: injustice and violence haunt the oil Delta', AI Index AFR 44/022/2005 (November 2005), especially pp. 5–6 and 22ff, available at www.amnestyusa.org/business/nigeriareport/report.pdf. For a creative way of exporting CSR, see McBarnet and Schmidt in this volume, Chapter 5; also, Kinley, Nolan and Zerial, in this volume, Chapter 15.

as to the idea of legal and criminal responsibility of parent companies for the actions of their overseas subsidiaries.[18] The possibility of seeking redress against transnational corporations (TNCs), in the TNC's country of origin (most often a developed country), is also on the CSR agenda. However, it is pointed out that such a redress is not going to produce the desired results if the domestic corporate criminal responsibility provisions rely predominantly on the mechanisms of vicarious and strict liability. Such mechanisms are not designed to cope with the complexity of the social, economic and ultimately legal issues related to the TNC's activities abroad.

Due mainly to these drawbacks, as well as to the gravity of certain corporate acts and to the seriousness of the consequences of those acts, criminal law becomes a recurrent CSR theme, with its fully-fledged concept of blame and accountability. In its turn, however, the criminal law discourse brings along concepts with which domestic legislators and courts are not always at ease in the corporate context. The common law doctrine of identification is a good example in this sense.

B. Identification doctrine

The doctrine of identification is a common law test developed from a series of fraud cases[19] which marked the recognition of corporations as capable of committing offences that required proof of a mental element (*mens rea*). The doctrine essentially means that a company can be liable for a serious criminal offence if one of its most senior officers had acted with the requisite fault. The leading case where the doctrine of identification was expounded was the case of *Tesco* v. *Nattrass*,[20] which limited the relevant personnel for the attribution of fault to those at the centre of corporate power.

Under English criminal law, a corporation, as a legal person, is theoretically in the same position as a natural person and may be convicted for committing criminal offences. 'Corporate manslaughter', for instance, is a term defining an act of homicide committed by a corporation. In practice, however, this equality of positions is less evident, the number of deaths at work and corporate-related accidents and disasters that are not

[18] Christian Aid, 'Report Behind the mask: The Real Face of CSR', available at www.christian-aid.org.uk/indepth/0401csr/csr_behindthemask.pdf. See also B. Stephens, 'The Amorality of Profit: Transnational Corporations and Human Rights', *Berkeley Journal International Law* 20 (2002), 75.

[19] *R* v. *ICR Haulage Ltd* (1944) 30 Criminal Appeal Reports 31.

[20] *Tesco Supermarkets* v. *Nattrass* [1972] AC 153 (HL).

prosecuted greatly outweighing the number of corporate prosecutions.[21] Apart from the usual political reasons related to the lobbying power of big businesses,[22] a chief explanation for the very limited number of successful prosecutions of corporations is the fact that the concept of corporate criminal responsibility is built around the concept of a 'controlling mind', whose actions and intentions can be imputed to the corporation for the purpose of establishing the corporation's criminal responsibility.

The doctrine poses a very stringent evidential requirement regarding with whom the corporation is identified in each particular case. Practically speaking, this prevents, if not prohibits, a wider use of manslaughter prosecutions against corporations, particularly against those with less clear management structures, where the 'office with authority' and the 'directing mind' are more difficult to identify.[23] Moreover, the difficulty in assigning criminal responsibility to corporations is exacerbated by the fact that the test of whether a corporation is guilty of manslaughter depends on whether or not a director or senior manager of the company – a 'controlling mind and will' of the company – is found personally guilty of manslaughter.[24] Therefore, finding a corporate director or manager in charge of an operation which went (criminally) wrong is not enough. For the corporation to be found guilty of manslaughter, the person identified as the 'controlling mind' has to be found personally guilty of manslaughter. Consequently, under the doctrine of identification, if the director or manager is found innocent, the company is declared innocent as well. The corporate body is, therefore, truly *identified* with its directors and managers.

While in theory this process of identification can be argued for, in practice it is very difficult actually to ascertain who had the 'controlling

---

[21] G. Slapper, *Blood in the Bank* (Aldershot: Ashgate Dartmouth, 1999), pp. 202–4; C. Wells, 'Inquests, Inquiries and Indictments: The Official Reception of Death by Disaster', *Legal Studies* 11 (1991), 71; C. Wells, 'Corporate Killing', *New Law Journal* (10 October 2000), 1467–8.

[22] C. M. V. Clarkson, 'Kicking Corporate Bodies and Damning Their Souls', *Modern Law Review* 59 (1996), 557–72; Slapper and Tombs, *Corporate Crime*, p. 208; Slapper, *Blood in the Bank*; F. T. Cullen, W. J. Maakestad and G. Cavender, 'The Ford Pinto Case and Beyond: Corporate Crime, Moral Boundaries, and the Criminal Sanction', in Ellen Hochstedler (ed.), *Corporations as Criminals* (London: Sage Publications, 1984), pp. 103–7.

[23] P. C. Yeager, 'Industrial Water Pollution', in M. Tonry and A. J. Reiss (eds.), *Beyond the Law: Crime in Complex Organisations* (Chicago: University of Chicago Press, 1993), p. 72.

[24] S. Tombs, 'Injury, Death and the Deregulation Fetish: The Politics of Safety Regulation in UK Manufacturing', *International Journal of Health Services* 26 (1996), 327–47; S. Tombs, 'Stemming the Flow of Blood: The Illusion of Self-regulation', *Journal of Human Justice* III, 2 (1992), 75–92.

mind' in a specific situation regarding a specific operation, especially in circumstances in which the corporation has no interest in making its decision structures more transparent than legally required. In principle, the larger the corporation, the more difficult it is to find the evidence necessary in order to prosecute for corporate manslaughter. In this sense, the OECD is arguing not only for more flexible ways of doing business, but also for less 'red tape' in the domestic legal systems, generalisation of lean production methods, footloose enterprises.[25] These elements inevitably influence the balance between the 'three Ps' of CSR – people, planet and profit. In contrast, agencies such as the International Labour Organisation (ILO) highlight the need for simpler and more transparent decision structures both domestically and transnationally, which would link the top and bottom of a working conditions chain, especially with respect to health and safety issues.[26]

The difficulty in disentangling complicated corporate command chains was also one of the major concerns during the discussions related to the Treaty of Rome, which established the ICC.[27] In the case of transnational corporations, this difficulty is exacerbated by a fairly rigid application of the principle of legal separation between the parent company and its subsidiaries, and by the fact that supply chains are 'folded in' the production processes through contractual chains stripped of anything not directly related to production.[28] Moreover, even on the domestic ground, blaming the junior employees and making them individually criminally responsible – for failings of safety systems for which employers are responsible and take profit, for instance – appears more and more as an

---

[25] Y. Fukasaku, 'Revitalising Mature Industries', at www1.oedc.org/publications/observer/ 213/article5_eng.htm.

[26] J. Takala, 'Introductory Report: Decent Work – Safe Work', 17th World Congress on Safety and Health at Work (Orlando, 18–22 September 2005), at www.ilo.org/public/english/ protection/safework/wdcongrs17/intrep.pdf; ILO-OSH, 'Guidelines on Occupational Safety and Health ManagementSystems' (Geneva: ILO, 2001), at www.ilo.org/public/ english/protection/safework/managmnt/index.htm; International and National Standards on occupational safety and health, ILO Standards and Codes of Practice and national legislation data sources, CD-ROM (Geneva, 2002), and www.ilo.org/safework; ILO programme implementation 2002–03, March 2004, at www.ilo.org/public/english/standards/ relm/gb/docs/gb289/pdf/ pfa-10.pdf.

[27] K. Ambos, 'General Principles of Criminal Law', in O. Triffterer (ed.), *Commentary on the Rome Statute of the International Criminal Court* (Baden-Baden: Nomos Verlagsgesellschaft, 2000), p. 476.

[28] For an attempt to deal with this separation, see the analysis of the Australian Corporate Code of Conduct Bill in Bottomley and Forsyth in this volume, Chapter 10; also, Glinski, in this volume, Chapter 4.

unjust and inadequate approach to the corporate reality. The conceptual confusion in relation to corporate criminal responsibility through the doctrine of identification is underlined once more by the fact that, even when successfully applied, the doctrine is misleading as it often spreads confusion as to the rationale of placing criminal responsibility with a specific person. For instance, some of the very few successful convictions for corporate manslaughter in England were against one-man companies, or against very small companies, which raised the questioned whether the conviction in these cases (and maybe even generally) was against the company or against the individual person who happened to own the company.[29]

C. Corporate manslaughter and the principle of identification

In the past two decades, the doctrine of identification has been put to the test, some would say not very successfully. One such case followed the sinking of the P&O ferry *Herald of Free Enterprise* in1987, which killed 192 passengers and members of the crew. In the legal case following the disaster, the prosecution relied on three 'reasonable practicable precautions' which, if taken, would have reduced or even eliminated the risk of the ship ever sailing with its doors open: the use of a system of positive reporting; the installation of comparatively inexpensive bridge indicator lights; and the establishment of a system of revision of orders which, if made, would have enabled the chief officer to check that the doors were closed. The prosecution argued that the serious risk the company was taking should have been obvious and, moreover, easily avoidable, if the P&O Board had facilitated the putting in place of 'reasonable practicable precautions'.[30]

Boardroom decisions, and failures to take appropriate decisions, can in principle support a corporate manslaughter charge under the identification doctrine. However, the level of recklessness required for proving a serious deficiency in the management of the company regarding health and safety issues prevents prosecutions such as the one against P&O from ending in a conviction. And indeed, in October 1990, after protracted legal procedures, the corporate manslaughter charge was dropped for six of the eight defendants, among them P&O European Ferries (Dover) Ltd, two

---

[29] Moreover, if the individual person – 'the brain of the company' – has to be found guilty of manslaughter, then this begs the question as to what exactly is the corporation guilty of.

[30] For the difficulties encountered by the Crown in prosecuting a big company for corporate manslaughter, see Bergman, 'Reckless in the Boardroom'.

directors and a senior manager. Under these circumstances, the Crown prosecution decided that it was 'not in the public interest' to continue with the prosecution of the assistant bosun and the chief officer.

The P&O prosecution was not the only case of a disaster which ended with the manslaughter and corporate manslaughter charges being dropped. Other similar disasters highlighted a variety of weaknesses in the regulatory framework for corporate responsibility, especially with respect to the identification test. Many of the cases of work accidents, however, failed even to be brought to court due to the stringency of evidentiary requirements. On 19 September 1997, for instance, a high speed train (HST) from Swansea to Paddington, London, collided with a freight train crossing the up and down main lines to Southall Yard. The collision resulted in the death of seven passengers and in many injuries. A public inquiry set up in the aftermath of the disaster declared that the immediate cause of the accident was the driver's failure to respond to the two warning signals. However, many other causes also identified by the inquiry pointed towards long-term and systemic corporate failures, which had created the conditions that allowed an inexperienced driver to fail following basic safety procedures.[31]

The public inquiry into the crash, initiated by the Health and Safety Executive (HSE) – the UK health and safety authority – made over ninety recommendations regarding a wide range of issues which could prevent such a tragedy from happening again. No criminal prosecution was instituted due to the very stringent evidential requirements in relation to finding a 'directing mind', combined with the complexity of the corporate activities and decision structures involved.[32] As it came to light later, these recommendations were not pursued effectively.

In October 1999, only two years later, two trains collided at a combined speed of 130mph after one of the trains went through a red signal at

---

[31] Among these other causes were: the failure of the train operator's maintenance system to identify and repair the AWS (Automatic Warning System) fault; the main operator's failure to react to isolation of the AWS; the failure of Railtrack to put in place rules in order to provide for the normal running of a HST with AWS isolated; and the train operator's failure to manage the ATP (Automatic Train Protection) Pilot Scheme so that the ATP equipment was switched on.

[32] As an illustration of the complexity of the case, the five companies involved in the disaster were: (1) Railtrack, which owns the majority of the infrastructure of Britain's railways, and is responsible for the track and signalling on which the crash occurred; (2) Great Western Trains, franchise holder and operator of trains to the west of England and Wales; (3) Angel Train Contracts, owner of the Intercity 125 unit involved in the accident; (4) Mendip Rail, owner of the freight train; (5) English Welsh & Scottish Railways (EWS), operator of the freight train.

Ladbroke Grove. Both drivers, together with twenty-nine passengers, were killed. Over 400 other persons suffered injuries, some of them of a critical nature. The public inquiry set up concluded that the poor lighting of the signal, allied to the effect of bright sunlight at a low angle behind the driver, probably led him to believe that he had a 'proceed aspect' – i.e., that it was safe to continue the train journey. Again, apart from this immediate factor, the inquiry identified a multitude of other probable contributing factors, pointing to systemic failures.[33]

As in the previous Southall inquiry, the committee made numerous recommendations aimed at preventing such disasters from ever happening again. Again, as in the case of the previous disaster, the Crown Prosecution Service decided there was not enough evidence to bring prosecution for corporate manslaughter against any of the companies involved, not even against Railtrack, the infrastructure company, that was accused in the inquiry report of 'serious and persistent' failures.[34]

Both the Southall and Ladbroke Grove public inquiries into the two railway disasters, as well as the prosecution in the P&O ferry disaster,[35] severely condemned company managements for their negligent and even reckless attitude in relation to safety and risk provisions. The findings of these proceedings confirmed earlier findings of the HSE, according to which between 70 and 85 per cent of workplace deaths are preventable by taking no more than *reasonably practicable precautions*. In spite of these findings, prosecutions continue to fail, or are not even initiated. One important contributing factor to this situation is the fragmentation of the decision structures in the context of modern corporate activities, combined with the complexity of the corporate processes and activities involved.[36] In this context, many legal practitioners and scholars have

---

[33] Among these systemic failures were serious deficiencies in the running of the signalling control centre. Wider deficiencies were found in Railtrack's management of the zone, such as: a lack of adequate consideration of the difficulties faced by drivers; failures to convene signal-sighting committees; a failure to carry out risk assessment; a failure to respond to the recommendations of inquiries (such as the Southall inquiry, mentioned above); and a failure to carry out effectively the previously required improvements (including the ones resulted from the public inquiry into the1997 Southall disaster).

[34] See Health and Safety Commission (HSC), *The Ladbroke Grove Rail Inquiry* (The Cullen Report, Cm 3386), (London: The Stationery Office, 2000).

[35] The Hatfield train crash case ended with all the manslaughter charges being dropped in July 2005. In October 2005, engineering firm Balfour Beatty and Network Rail were fined a total of £13.5 million for health and safety breaches in the run up to the Hatfield crash.

[36] M. Tonry and A. J. Reiss, *Beyond the Law: Crime in Complex Organizations* (London: University of Chicago Press, 1993), p. 37.

pointed out the doctrine of identification as an important stumbling block for a more effective corporate manslaughter offence.[37]

D. The individualist underpinnings of the doctrine of identification

Approaches to corporate criminal responsibility such as the one expressed through the doctrine of identification are underscored by what is called an individualist approach to the concept of a corporation.[38] According to this perspective, a corporation does not display identical forms of autonomy and rationality to those displayed by the individual human being and, therefore, could not be seen as a unitary agent, with an existence of its own, distinct from the one of its individual members. This lack of 'unity' means that criminal law can generally acknowledge only individual liabilities of particular members, that is liabilities that are based on the members' direct and intended actions. This would correspond to the classic triangular formula of responsibility, with *mens rea* (intention) and *actus reus* (harmful act) coinciding in the same individual person.[39]

Consequently, from an individualist perspective, for a collective entity to be considered a moral agent for the purpose of criminal law,[40] there is a need for an *identity of nature* between the discrete individuals and the collective organisation to which they belong. This unity of the two entities is, of course, difficult to argue for, and is practically unattainable in a complex corporate context.[41] Essentially, corporations as formal organisations would lack, in any situation, the necessary *mens rea* and *actus reus*, elements which are considered the core of the philosophical, moral and

---

[37] Slapper, *Blood in the Bank*, p. 46; Wells, 'Corporate Killing', 1467.

[38] L. A. Stout, 'On the Nature of Corporations', *Deakin Law Review* 33 (2004), 775; N. H. D. Foster, 'The Theoretical Background: The Nature of the Actors in Corporate Social Responsibility', in S. Tully (ed.), *A Handbook on Corporate Legal Responsibility* (Cheltenham: Edward Elgar Publishing, 2005), p. 27.

[39] The individual liabilities, according to this perspective, could potentially be aggregated, but this would not change the individual nature of the ascribed responsibility; L. May, *Sharing Responsibility* (Chicago: University of Chicago Press, 1992), p. 58.

[40] M. S. Moore, *Placing Blame: A Theory of Criminal Law* (Oxford: Clarendon Press, 1997), pp. 136–8; G. P. Fletcher, *Rethinking Criminal Law* (Boston: Little, Brown, 1978), pp. 57–60; A. Norrie, *Punishment, Responsibility and Justice* (Oxford: Oxford University Press, 2000), pp. 139–41.

[41] Glinski, for instance, speaks about the practical and legal difficulties stemming from the wide application of the principle of legal separation between the parent company and its subsidiaries, and about different domestic mechanisms of coping with this issue in the area of environmental control; Glinski, in this volume, Chapter 4.

ultimately legal notions of responsibility and justice.[42] For instance, the rationality and autonomy exercised by a corporation through its board of directors could not be identified, it is argued, with the rational and autonomous functions performed by the human brain and body.[43] As to the harmful act, or *actus reus*, of the corporation, the performance would belong to the individuals and not to the collective entity. The latter would not act, except vicariously, through its members.[44]

The individualist approach as expounded above has been criticised for failing to account for the reality of corporations, for its lack of institutional imagination and for failure to deliver justice. In spite of the apparent failure to satisfy the social perception of justice through criminal convictions against corporations, the individualist approach could, to a certain extent, be seen as accurate; the corporation, as a formal organisation, can be seen as a legal construction tailored to match, to a certain degree, the sociological reality of the business corporation. However, from the perspective of the law, the individual person can also be seen as just another type of legal construction – another type of fiction.[45] The case of the individual person's autonomy, as seen by law, appears to some extent to be similar. In this sense, May speaks about pseudo-unities proposed as facts.[46] In reality, he argues, these pseudo-unities 'set up oppositions that *arbitrarily separate* those who are included and those who are excluded from a shared conceptualisation or practice'.[47]

Critics of the individualist approach to corporate (criminal) responsibility have argued that if, within the legal sphere, both the corporation and the discrete individual are fictitious legal entities, one has also to consider

---

[42] Velasquez speaks about the notion of *origination*, according to which the 'mental' element would achieve unity with the 'bodily' element; M. G. Velasquez, 'Why Corporations Are Not Morally Responsible for Anything They Do?', in L. May and S. Hoffmann (eds.), *Collective Responsibility: Five Decades of Debate in Theoretical and Applied Ethics* (Savage, MD: Rowman & Littlefield Publishers, 1991), p. 123.

[43] Velasquez, 'Why Corporations Are Not Morally Responsible', 121.

[44] According to this perception of the collective organisation as a fictitious legal entity, the collective entity is related to its members in the same way 'as a legal "principle" is related to those "agents" who are empowered to act on its behalf and whose acts are *conventionally* attributed to the legal "principle"'; Velasquez, 'Why Corporations Are Not Morally Responsible', 129. This conveys the ideas that it could not be the 'principle' which is acting, but the 'agents'.

[45] A. Norrie, *Crime, Reason and History* (Cambridge: Cambridge University Press, 2001), p. 87.

[46] May, *Sharing Responsibility*, pp. 171–3.

[47] May, *Sharing Responsibility*, p. 173 (emphasis added); also, A. Norrie, 'A Critique of Criminal Causation', *Modern Law Review* 54 (September, 1991), 685–701.

that other elements related to those socially constructed entities, such as their needs and their risks, as well as their responsibilities, are all social constructions, dependent upon the system in which they emerge. From this perspective, there should be no reason to expect the concept of responsibility to take the same form when applied to the corporation, as a collective agent, as when it is applied to the individual.[48] Moreover, there should be no reason to expect the corporation, as a fictitious legal construction, to obey the same rules as (just) another fictitious legal construction, such as the individual legal person. While one might agree that, in order to be responsible, an entity should prove a certain degree of autonomy and rationality, there should be no logical necessity to accept a mechanism for the attribution of responsibility which is designed specifically for the individual legal person.[49] From this perspective, the individualist approach to corporate responsibility is less amenable to the new social parameters brought by the concept of CSR. It is also less conceptually supportive of CSR beyond criminal law, and therefore less supportive of the holistic perspective over the concepts of corporate agency and responsibility. As a result, it would also be less instrumental in validating concepts and ideas more in tune with the social perception of the corporate role in society.

In line with this critique of individualism, some authors, in fact, argue that the main source of the organisational power lies in the corporation's *power to organise*.[50] It is thus important to acknowledge the reality of corporations and to look beyond the characteristics of the discrete individual members, while conceiving appropriate mechanisms for corporate action and corporate responsibility.[51] Moreover, from a practical point of view, to rely only on the individual autonomy in order to overcome the corporate power to organise does not seem an appropriate response

---

[48] L. Rosen, 'Intentionality and the Concept of the Person', in J. R. Pennock and J. W. Chapman (eds.), *Criminal Justice* (New York: New York University Press, 1985), pp. 252–4.

[49] P. A. French, 'The Corporation as a Moral Person', in May and Hoffmann (eds.), *Collective Responsibility*, pp. 134–7.

[50] T. Donaldson, *Corporations and Morality* (Englewood Cliffs, NJ: Prentice Hall, 1982), pp. 27–9. See Virginia Held's attribution of responsibility to random collectivities for 'failing to organise'; V. Held, 'Can a Random Collection of Individuals Be Morally Responsible?', in May and Hoffmann (eds.), *Collective Responsibility*, pp. 89–100.

[51] S. Wolf, 'The Legal and Moral Responsibility of Organizations', in Pennock and Chapman, *Criminal Justice*, p. 281; D. F. Thompson, 'Criminal Responsibility in Government', in J. R. Pennock and J. W. Chapman (eds.), *Criminal Justice*, Nomos 27, (New York and London: New York University Press), pp. 204–6.

to the sociological reality of organisations.[52] From this point of view, the corporate environment is seen as designed to subdue the individual autonomy and suppress any values other than the corporate ones.

More sophisticated versions of the individualist approach try to accommodate this critique by acknowledging the fact that a collective agent does not have to be defined solely through the inevitably disqualifying comparison with the parameters of the individual legal person.[53] At the same time, this approach denies corporations the capacity of being 'morally' responsible. This denial, though, is based not so much on an analysis of the traditional concepts of action and intention – which remain inaccessible for a collective agent such as the corporation – but on a 'constitutional' perspective of the organisational structure.[54]

Building on the 'role' of corporations, this perspective claims that corporations are 'controlled' by their very structure. Because of this dominion, organisations would be incapable of exercising moral freedom. The expectation that they evaluate morally their environment would, therefore, be unreasonable.[55] In an endorsement of Milton Friedman's thesis that the role, and hence the social responsibility, of business is to increase its profits,[56] this perspective allows for the perception of formal organisations as rational agencies, but with only a limited autonomy, an autonomy dependent upon their 'specified' or 'empirical' set of goals, i.e. profit-seeking. Accordingly, formal organisations would not possess those qualities which would enable them to change their own goals; they are conceived as profit-pursuing machines which are not designed to morally evaluate their environment. In other words, they are restrained by their structure. And, it is also argued that the structure of a formal organisation cannot be made responsible for reproducing itself.

[52] Norrie, *Crime, Reason and History*, p. 87; J. Casey, 'Actions and Consequences', in C. John (ed.), *Morality and Moral Reasoning* (London: Macmillan, 1971), p. 180. The debates on CSR, but also on corporate governance generally, sustainability, development and global governance, demonstrate plainly an awareness of these issues.

[53] T. Donaldson and P. Werhane, *Ethical Issues in Business: A Philosophical Approach* (Englewood Cliffs, NJ: Prentice Hall, 1979), p. 33–4.

[54] Donaldson, *Corporations and Morality*, p. 2; J. Ladd, 'Morality and the Ideal of Rationality in Formal Organizations', *The Monist* 54 (1970), 498.

[55] Donaldson, *Corporations and Morality*, p. 23. Corporations would belong – according to this view – to the class of 'formal organisations'. By their very nature, formal organisations would be incapable of accommodating moral concerns.

[56] M. Friedman, 'The Social Responsibility of Business is to Increase its Profits', *The New York Times Magazine* (13 September 1970), available at www.colorado.edu/studentgroups/libertarians/issues/friedman-soc-resp-business.html.

The latter argument may well resonate with many of the opponents to the concepts of corporate criminal as well as corporate social responsibility due to the limitations it implies. At the same time, it has also offered conceptual support to the more pragmatic supporters of the concepts of CSR and corporate criminal responsibility since it does away with the need for a moral agency (individual or corporate), by replacing it with a 'learning agency'. In spite of stopping short of acknowledging a form of holistic corporate responsibility, this structural restraint perspective makes an important step forward from the atomising perspective of the traditional individualist approach. It moves the analysis of the corporation as social agency from the moral and criminal discourse, with its stress on individual *mens rea*, to a domain where the corporation is seen as an essentially constructed entity.[57] This entity may not be altered directly, simply by imposing upon the organisation some different *immediate goals* other than its own. However, it is arguable that a collective entity such as a corporation can be responsive and can internalise *socially proposed goals*. This can happen if the appropriate normative environment is created.[58] Of course, the experience with legal instruments such as the identification doctrine, as seen in this chapter, or with codes of conduct[59]

---

[57] It was this nature of the organisation that Rawls sought to address when including formal organisations, along with the individual persons, on the list of parties qualified for occupying the 'original position'. According to Rawls, from this position a social agent would be able to opt in the best interest of society, not blinded by immediate selfish goals; J. Rawls, *A Theory of Justice* (Oxford: Oxford University Press, 1999), p. 146. See also, J. J. Brummer, *Corporate Responsibility and Legitimacy: An Interdisciplinary Analysis* (New York: Greenwood Press, 1991), pp. 165–7. In other writings, though, reflecting the traditional academic ambiguity about the nature of formal organisations, Rawls backtracks on this position and states a certain 'logical priority' of human individuals; J. Rawls, 'Justice as Reciprocity', in S. Gorovitz (ed.), *Utilitarianism* (Indianapolis, IA: Bobbs-Merrill, 1971), pp. 244–5.

[58] Parker speaks about *externally* regulated '*internal* "corporate conscience"'; Parker, in this volume, Chapter 7; see also J. S. Coleman, 'Responsibility in Corporate Action', in K. J. Hopt and G. Teubner (eds.), *Corporate Governance and Directors' Liabilities: Legal, Economic and Sociological Analyses* (Berlin and New York: Walter de Gruyter, 1985), pp. 77–83; for Steimann's arguments and proposed solutions for providing *voice* in the corporate governance for both internal and external interests, see H. Steimann, 'The Enterprise as a Political System', in Hopt and Teubner (eds.), *Corporate Governance and Directors' Liabilities*, pp. 401–27.

[59] See Glinski, in this volume, Chapter 4; also D. Leipziger, *The Corporate Responsibility Code Book* (Sheffield: Greenleaf Publishing, 2003), pp. 35–8; European Commission, Directorate-General for Employment and Social Affairs, Unit D.1, *Mapping Instruments for Corporate Social Responsibility* (Luxembourg: Office for Publications of the European Communities, 2003), p. 4.

and other regulatory instruments, as seen elsewhere in this volume,[60] prove just how difficult it is to create the 'right' normative environment,[61] one which would stimulate corporations to internalise new social standards.[62]

In conclusion, when following legal mechanisms based on the individualist approach, corporate criminal responsibility appears problematic to apply both domestically and, especially, internationally. This is due to legal and practical difficulties inherent to the individualist paradigm. In order to build upon domestic jurisdictions, international initiatives such as those of the ILO, United Nations, European Union, ICC and even the OECD will therefore need to confront the difficulties and challenges coming from the inherent individualist approach of at least some of the jurisdictions.

Nevertheless, the legal mechanisms enabled by this type of approach ought not to be totally dismissed. If legal phenomena such as the new use of the Alien Tort Claims Act (ATCA) in the United States are anything to judge by,[63] there is a search not only for new legal mechanisms that would cover CSR obligations, but also for new modalities of using creatively the existing legal mechanisms.[64] Moreover, the individualist paradigm reminds us – if one-sidedly – that both corporate social and corporate criminal responsibility have arguably two dimensions of accountability: the corporate and the individual one. In this sense, the individualist approach would potentially support – with all the inherent difficulties highlighted in the first part of this chapter – the awareness of a slightly neglected aspect of the CSR discourse: namely, that there is need and scope for CSR to address the individual dimension as well as the corporation.[65]

---

[60] Bottomley and Forsyth, in this volume, Chapter 10; see also Kinley, Nolan and Zerial, in this volume, Chapter 15, about the difficulties encountered at the international level.

[61] See also Parker, in this volume, Chapter 7.

[62] C. D. Stone, *Where the Law Ends: The Social Control of Corporate Behaviour* (Long Grove, IL: Waveland Press, Inc., 1991), pp. 123–5.

[63] McBarnet and Schmidt in this volume, Chapter 5.

[64] Kinley, Nolan and Zerial point out the way in which concepts developed in international criminal law, such as 'aiding and abetting', have been borrowed by US domestic courts, and they suggest the potential of a similar move for giving substance to the UN Norms (UN Doc.E/CN.4/Sub.2/ 2003/12/ Rev.2(2003)); Kinley, Nolan and Zerial, in this volume, Chapter 15.

[65] This is an aspect that has received less attention in the CSR debate, a notable exception being the link between CSR and directors' duties. In order to provide efficiently for an increased awareness of this dimension, though, the domestic systems need to be more adapted to the global market economy context; see R. V. Aguilera, D. Rupp, C. A. Williams and J. Ganapathi, 'Putting the S Back in Corporate Social Responsibility: A Multi-Level

There is, however, no doubt that the conceptual underpinnings of the individualist approach are less supportive of those corporate social obligations rooted in the holistic image of the corporation as a citizen of the world.[66]

III. Corporate social responsibility and the collectivist perspective on corporate criminal responsibility

The focus on the individual as perpetrator of 'corporate' crimes and as bearer of 'corporate' legal and moral obligations is not, however, the only signal received from the domestic corporate criminal law debate. The awareness that the individualist approach fails to capture the complexity of the modus operandi of business organisations has lately crossed more forcefully from the philosophical, ethical and legal academic discourse into the legal legislative debate. In this sense, in the past decade there have been important changes in a number of domestic systems. Such changes generated a critical mass of novel structural approaches to corporate criminal responsibility, with the capacity to infuse and benefit the CSR debate.

A. Management failure: the Law Commission's proposal in the United Kingdom

The growing public dissatisfaction with the difficulties to prosecute corporate offenders, with a very low rate of prosecutions for corporate manslaughter, and an even lower rate of successful prosecutions, has resulted in the past decade in proposals for changing the UK law in the sense of moving away from the doctrine of identification.[67] A proposal for a new crime of 'corporate killing', published by the Law Commission

---

Theory of Social Change in Organizations', *CLPE Research Paper, Academy of Management Review* (2006), available at SSRN: ssrn.com/abstract=820466; S. Cohen, *A Theory of Moral Reasoning: The Framework and Activities of Ethical Deliberation, Argument and Decision-Making* (Oxford: Oxford University Press, 2004); also S. Trotter, 'Corporate Manslaughter', *New Law Journal* 150 [6929] (2000), 454–8.

[66] B. Fisse and J. Braithwaite, *Corporations, Crime and Accountability* (Cambridge: Cambridge University Press, 1993), pp. 43–5; see also A. Crane and D. Matten, *Business Ethics: A European Perspective: Managing Corporate Citizenship and Sustainability in the Age of Globalization* (Oxford: Oxford University Press, 2004), pp. 17–20.

[67] Bergman, 'Reckless in the Boardroom', p. 1499; R. J. Wickins and C. A. Ong, 'Confusion Worse Confounded: The End of the Directing Mind Theory?', *The Journal of Business Law* November (1997), 524–56; for conceptual distinctions accompanying the debate, see C. Wells, 'Involuntary Manslaughter', *New Law Journal* 146 [6734] (8 March 1996), 342–5.

in 1996,[68] was taken forward by the Labour government and included in the Queen's speech in 2000.[69] The proposal addressed some of the pitfalls inherent in existing legal provisions regarding corporate manslaughter, especially with respect to the requirement of the doctrine of identification. The Law Commission – the body in charge of promoting the systematic development, simplification and modernisation of the law in England and Wales – focused on the concept of 'management failure', a theme common to several public inquiries into major disasters and work-place deaths in the United Kingdom.

In its document, the Law Commission proposed the creation of an offence of 'corporate killing'. According to the proposal, section 4(1), a corporation would be guilty of corporate killing if (1) a management failure by the corporation is the cause or one of the causes of a person's death, and (2) that failure constitutes conduct falling far below what can reasonably be expected of the corporation in the circumstances. The Law Commission's proposal specified that 'there is *management failure* by the corporation if the way in which the corporate activities are managed or organized fails to ensure the health and safety of persons employed in or affected by those activities', and if 'such a failure may be regarded as a cause of a person's death notwithstanding that the immediate cause is the act or omission of an individual'.

From this outline, it appears that the Law Commission considered bringing corporate behaviour in line with the social expectations of corporate responsibility for health and safety at work by creating a special offence of 'corporate killing'[70] and by avoiding the requirements of the doctrine of identification.[71] It should also be noted that the proposed crime is not one of conscious wrongdoing but, rather, one of neglect or omission. However, the neglect or omission has to be placed in the context of objectively serious culpability. In an attempt to explain and justify its position with respect to the implications of the proposed offence of corporate killing for the doctrine of identification, the Law Commission stated that:

---

[68] Law Commission of England and Wales, *Legislating the Criminal Code: Involuntary Manslaughter* (Law Comm. 237 1996) (London: The Stationery Office, 1996).

[69] In fact, the Law Commission's process of rethinking the issues began in 1972, immediately after the *Tesco* landmark case for the doctrine of identification; see D. Burles, 'The Criminal Liability of Corporations', *New Law Journal* (3 May 1991), 609–11; also Slapper and Tombs, 'Corporate Crime', p. 33.

[70] This new offence applied the elements of the offence of 'killing by gross negligence', proposed in the same bill for the individual person.

[71] Trotter, 'Corporate Manslaughter', p. 456.

> It is in our view much easier to say that a 'corporation', as such, has failed to
> do something, or has failed to meet a particular standard of conduct than
> it is to say that a corporation has done a positive act, or *has entertained
> a particular subjective state of mind*. The former statements can be made
> directly, without recourse to the intermediary step of finding a *human
> mind and a decision-making process* on the part of an individual within or
> representing the company; and thus the need for the identification theory,
> in order to bring the corporation within the subjective requirements of the
> law, largely falls away.[72]

The introduction by the Law Commission of the concept of 'management
failure' in the debate on corporate criminal responsibility marks, therefore, a tentative shift away from the traditional individualist paradigm
offered by the doctrine of identification towards a model where the corporate structure and functions fulfil a just as important, if not more
important, role in the assessment of the activities of a corporation.[73]
For the time being, though, this shift within the English legal system
remains an open and unfinished chapter. After initially failing to take
up the Law Commission's proposal, the Labour government introduced
to the House of Commons, in July 2006, a Corporate Manslaughter and
Corporate Homicide Bill in which the notion of 'management failure'
was replaced with references to 'activities managed or organised by the
corporate senior managers' and to 'gross breach of a relevant duty of care
owed by the organisation to the deceased'.[74] The Bill has been criticised for
backtracking on some important issues present in the Law Commission's
proposal. *Liberty*, for instance, one of the United Kingdom's leading civil
liberties and human rights organisations, stated in its comments to the
Bill that in order to create a realistic prospect of conviction, the senior
manager test must be removed, and has criticised – among others – the
use of the limitative way in which the 'duty of care' concept appears to be
used in the Bill.[75] The future of the bill is uncertain for other reasons as
well. At the time when this volume went to press, the Home Office ministers were struggling to find a compromise to save it. In February 2007 the

---

[72] Law Commission of England and Wales, *Legislating the Criminal Code*, para. 7.4 (author's
emphasis).
[73] C. Wells, 'Corporate Killing', p. 1469. The problem with the doctrine of identification became known as 'the P&O problem'. See also Trotter, 'Corporate Manslaughter',
pp. 454–6.
[74] *Corporate Manslaughter and Corporate Homicide Blill* (Cm 6497) (London: The Stationery
Office, 2006).
[75] Liberty, 'Corporate Manslaughter Bill', available at www.liberty-human-rights.org.uk/
pdfs/policy06/corporate-manslaughter-bill-second-reading-commons.pdf.

House of Lords rejected the Home Office plans to exclude prisons, police cells and psychiatric hospitals from the remit of the bill, and sent the bill back to the House of Commons. Given that the bill is a 'hangover bill', a remnant of a former parliamentary session, it cannot be transferred to the next parliamentary session.

B. 'Structural negligence' as corporate criminal responsibility tool: Italy

An even more comprehensive approach to corporate (criminal) responsibility can be found in Italian law, in a statute enacted in 2001.[76] Traditionally, under Italian law a corporation could not be convicted of a criminal offence because of the constitutional principle that 'criminal responsibility is individual'.[77] Only natural persons could, therefore, be convicted of a crime. To get around this obstacle, the Italian legislator labelled corporate liability as 'administrative', thus creating a third form of liability that stands between administrative liability proper and criminal liability.[78] Three elements point to the fact that the new liability created is a pseudo-administrative liability, and that in fact it is criminal liability in all but name: first, companies become responsible for criminal offences and not just administrative misdemeanours; second, the cases are heard by criminal courts rather than by administrative tribunals; third, criminal rather than administrative procedures are followed.

The Italian statute creates two types of corporate liability. The first, presumed in the case of a crime committed by a head of the corporation, is a form of vicarious liability, not dissimilar to the English identification doctrine. The second, more radical type of corporate liability is based on the negligence of a corporate body in not considering the possibility of the offence which has occurred and in not having in place a mechanism to avert its commission. This second form of corporate liability is grounded in the concept of *organisational fault*. Very significantly, under Article 8 of the Italian statute, a company can be held responsible even if it is not possible to identify or convict an individual person as the perpetrator of an offence.

---

[76] Decreto Legislativo, 'Disciplina della Responsabilità Amministrativa delle Persone Giuridiche, delle Società e delle Associazioni Anche Prive di Personalità Giuridica', *Gazzetta Ufficiale* No. 140 (19 June 2001).

[77] Italian Constitution, Article 27, para. 1.

[78] 'Consiglio dei Ministri: Via Libera alla Disciplina della Responsabilità Amministrativa delle Persone Giuridiche' (11 April 2001); Maura Castiglioni, 'Societas Delinquere Potest: la Legge 300/2000 ed i Profili di Responsabilità Penale "Diretta" delle Persone Giuridiche', *Magistra, Banca e Finanza*, (November 2002), available at, www.magistra.it.

The innovative dimension of the Italian statute relates to the concept of *structural negligence*. According to the statute, the 'blame' that warrants attaching criminal liability to a corporation is located within such a structural negligence. The corporation needs to have established guidelines and control systems that take into account the *risk* of offences being committed. If it has not, then it will be found to be 'structurally negligent'.[79] Moreover, the control systems need to be detailed and tailored to specific risks. It is, therefore, not enough for a corporation to set up a generic control system. In a format reminding us of Parker's analysis of meta-regulatory approaches,[80] the details and specifics of the guidelines and control systems are, however, left for companies to work out for themselves.[81] A corollary of this approach is that both forms of liability established through the statute can be rebutted by a showing of due diligence.

C. 'Power', 'acceptance' and responsibility: Holland

In other jurisdictions, such as in Holland, legal developments have gone even further in proposing the organisational corporate responsibility as functionally distinct from the responsibility of discrete managers or directors in a corporation.[82]

The Dutch legal position on corporate responsibility is governed by the Criminal Code, which simply states that 'offences can be committed by human beings and by corporations'.[83] The application of this article was framed very broadly through section 15 of the post-war Economic Offences Act, which stated that corporations could be liable for any acts

[79] L. Lombardo, 'Nuova Disciplina sulla Responsabilità Amministrativa delle Società ed Enti', *Diritto & Diritti – Electronic Law Review*, available at www.diritto.it/materiali/ civile/lombardo.html; M. Castiglioni, 'Societas delinquere potest'.

[80] Parker speaks about the possibility of putting in place 'legal meta-regulation' that would hold business organisations accountable 'for putting in place corporate conscience processes that are aimed at substantive social values'; see Parker, in this volume, Chapter 7; L. Lombardo, 'Nuova Disciplina sulla Responsabilità Amministrativa delle Società ed Enti'.

[81] J. Gobert and E. Mugnai, 'Coping With Corporate Criminality: Some Lessons from Italy', *Criminal Law Review* August (2002), 619–29; see also Parker, in this volume, Chapter 7; for arguments regarding the expansion of this law to cover environmental issues, see M. Arena, 'La Responsabilità delle Persone Giuridiche per Illeciti Ambientali', *I Reati Societari: Revista sul diritto penale d'impresa* (30 April 2007), available at www. reatisocietari.it/new/index.php?option=com_content&task=view&id = 173&Itemid=2.

[82] G. Stressens, 'Corporate Criminal Liability: A Comparative Perspective', *International and Corporative Law Quarterly* 43 (1994), 493–520.

[83] Dutch Penal Code, Article 51.

done by persons in the course of their employment or by others who acted in the '*sphere of the corporation*'.[84] This very broad ambit has been gradually reduced as a reflection of the fact that corporations may now be convicted not only as a result of strict liability, but also for crimes widely associated with moral culpability and stigma.

The application of these legal rules allows for corporate responsibility to be attached to any act by an employee in the course of employment which was intended to benefit the corporation. With the court cases evolving towards a more morally charged notion of responsibility, the Dutch Supreme Court moved towards establishing more stringent criteria for corporate responsibility, deciding that the employee's act could only be regarded as the employer's if (1) it was within the defendant's *power to determine* whether the employee acted in this way, and (2) the employee's act belonged to a category of acts '*accepted*' by the firm as being in the course of normal business operations.[85]

The concepts of 'power' and 'acceptance' are very important in the reshaping of the concept of corporate criminal responsibility in that they lead to criteria more suited to the evaluation of a collective enterprise.[86] In the context defined by the two concepts, the stress falls upon the institutionalised practices of the corporation, allowing for corporations to be made accountable for failing to establish appropriate systems of checks and monitoring which would prevent potentially harmful practices. 'Power' and 'acceptance' appear here as *organisational criteria*: the talk of power in this context emphasises the idea of hierarchy and the ability of this hierarchy to influence the acts of individuals and groups within the organisation (of course, the operations of that hierarchy must then be traced to authoritative, constitutionally determined corporate practices). Moreover, 'power' and 'acceptance' point not to the judgment of isolated positive acts by individuals, but rather to continuing collective processes, focusing on decision-making practices.[87] The framework offered by these concepts avoids the trap of any form of the doctrine of identification, making possible – in the process of establishing corporate criminal responsibility – the bringing together not only of acts of various

---

[84] Economic Offences Act, s. 15 (Staatsblad K. 258, 22 June 1950).
[85] IJzerdraad case, Hoge Raad, 23 February 1954, NJ 1954, 378, cited in LegislationOnline, at www.legislationline.org/lawReviews.php?tid=218&jid=37.
[86] J. A. E. Vervaele, 'La Responsabilidad Penal de y en el Seno de la Persona Jurídica en Holanda: Matrimonio entre Pragmatismo y Dogmática Jurídica', *Revista de Derecho Penal y Criminologia* 2, 1 (1998), 153–84.
[87] S. Field and N. Jorg, 'Corporate Criminal Liability and Manslaughter: Should We Be Going Dutch?', *Criminal Law Review* March (1991), 161.

persons, but also of corporate practices and processes. Very importantly, the Dutch law also permits the scrutiny of all corporate rules and practices, not only of the formal ones. This demonstrates an acknowledgement of the fact that often there are no formal corporate licences to break statutory provisions, but that the corporations may create a culture which discourages compliance with those provisions.[88]

D. Corporate culture and responsibility: Australia

A similar emphasis on the 'corporate culture' transpires from the Commonwealth Criminal Code Act 1995 (CCA) (Part 2.5), which has had general application to all Australian Commonwealth offences since December 2001.[89] In Australian law, a corporation is a legal person for the scope of the criminal law in all Australian jurisdictions. Until the CCA1995, an Australian corporation could therefore be tried for all criminal offences, though not for the ones which could only be punished by imprisonment and where the person who made the error of judgement or who acted in a callous way was not the 'guiding mind' of the corporation, or did not 'embody' the 'corporation'.

In this sense, the Criminal Code, in section 12.2, imposes vicarious liability upon the corporation for the physical element of the offence (not the mental element) when committed by an employee, agent and officer within the actual and apparent scope of employment.[90] The innovation of the Act is brought under section 12.3. Section 12.3(1) of the Criminal Code specifies that the requisite element of fault in an offence characterised, for example, by intention, knowledge or recklessness is established on the part of the body corporate itself, where the body corporate has 'expressly, tacitly or impliedly authorised or permitted the commission of the offence'.

Section 12.3(2) sets out several non-exclusive means by which the corporate 'authorisation or permission' can be established. One method would be to prove that the board of directors or a high managerial agent 'intentionally, knowingly or recklessly carried out the relevant conduct, or expressly, tacitly or impliedly authorised or permitted the commission

---

[88] Vervaele, 'La Responsabilidad Penal de y en el Seno de la Persona Jurídica en Holanda', pp. 179ff; see also Field and Jorg, 'Corporate Criminal Liability and Manslaughter', p. 163.

[89] Criminal Code Act 1995 (Cth).

[90] This departs from the *Tesco* principle – doctrine of identification – where the physical element of the offence must be attributable to a high-level officer.

of the offence'.[91] Section 12.3(2) breaks new ground in corporate criminal law in Australia by establishing that the corporation will be understood to have authorised or permitted the commission of an offence if it is proven that 'a corporate culture' existed which either actively encouraged non-compliance (section 12.3(2)(c)), or failed to promote compliance (section 12.3(2)(d)).

The very important concept of 'corporate culture' is defined by the Code as an 'attitude, policy, rule, course of conduct or practice existing within the body corporate generally or in the part of the body corporate in which the relevant activities take place' (section 12.3(6)). According to this, a corporation with a poor corporate culture may be considered as culpable under the Australian Criminal Code as individual directors or senior managers. Significantly, section 12.1 provides that the Code applies equally, with the necessary modifications, to bodies corporate and to natural persons, and that a body corporate 'may be found guilty of any offence, including one punishable by imprisonment'.

Such changes brought within the Australian jurisdiction were designed to capture elements such as 'managerial techniques' and 'corporate unwritten rules', situations where, despite documentation showing the contrary, the reality was that non-compliance was expected and encouraged.[92] The consideration of the 'corporate culture' is considered to parallel the notion of 'intent' and '*mens rea*' involved in personal criminal liability and to be a fair and practical way in which corporations could be held liable both for their policies and practices.[93] It also represents a shift away from an individualist perspective as well as from a focus on the outcomes of corporate decision-making, towards the decision-making

---

[91] For the high managerial agent, there is available the defence of 'due diligence'. 'High managerial agent' is defined in s. 12.3(6) as 'an employee, agent or officer of the body corporate with duties of such responsibility that his or her conduct may fairly be assumed to represent the body corporate's policy'; see C. M. V. Clarkson, 'Corporate Culpability', *Webjournal of Current Legal Issues* (1998), available at www.webjcli.ncl.ac.uk/1998/issue2/clarkson2.html; J. Hill, 'Corporate Criminal Liability in Australia: An Evolving Corporate Governance Technique?', *Vanderbilt University Law School*, Law and Economics Working Paper No. 03–10 (2003), p. 16.

[92] F. Haines, 'Towards Understanding Globalisation and Control of Corporate Harm: A Preliminary Criminological Analysis', *Current Issues in Criminal Justice* 12 (2002), 166.

[93] Standing Committee of Attorneys-General, Criminal Law Officers Committee, *Model Criminal Code*, Chapter 2, *Final Report: General Principles of Criminal Responsibility* (Canberra: ABPS, 1993), Part 5; also Hill, 'Corporate Criminal Liability in Australia', p. 17.

processes themselves.[94] This opens up the corporate criminal responsibility regime to a model which recognises concepts of corporate due
diligence, corporate blameworthiness, corporate culture, enforced self-
monitoring and self-regulation.[95] In time, the presence of such concepts
will increase the potential for issues relating to corporate criminal responsibility to become more closely integrated into corporate governance at an
operational level, and for issues relating to CSR in general to be accepted
more easily on the corporate agenda.[96]

IV. The shift in the paradigm of corporate responsibility and its implications

In the context of Dutch and Australian criminal law (and to a certain
extent in the Italian legal provisions and the UK Law Commission's proposal), a new type of normative approach is manifest, which proposes a
different 'triangle of responsibility' from the one based on the individualist paradigm. The new paradigm can be instrumental in negotiating the
CSR position both within the corporate criminal discourse and beyond
it.[97]

The type of legal responsibility constructed upon the idea of action
and intention originating in the same individual person – as the 'classic'
triangular formula of responsibility and the basic tenet of the individualist approach to corporate responsibility – is complemented in the Dutch
and Australian legal systems with the concepts of *action* and *reason for
action* originating in the same *structure*. The all important intentionality
required for ascribing responsibility is construed here in terms of 'something *done for a reason*',[98] when the reason is placed in 'the sphere of the

---

[94] F. K. Kubler, 'Dual Loyalty in Labour Representatives', in Hopt and Teubner (eds.), *Corporate Governance and Directors' Liabilities*, pp. 441–2.

[95] R. Sarre, 'Responding to Corporate Collapses: Is There a Role for Corporate Social
Responsibility?', *Deakin Law Review* 7 (2002), 5; also W. S. Laufer, 'Integrity, Diligence
and the Limits of Good Corporate Citizenship', *American Business Law Journal* 34 (1996),
157.

[96] See Parker in this volume, Chapter 7, on how this potential can be realised only if there are
other domestic laws to which the framework of corporate criminal responsibility established by the Australian Criminal Code will apply; also Sarre, 'Responding to Corporate
Collapses', 7.

[97] For the analysis of an emerging 'new corporate law' that covers CSR and occurs outside
the parameters of the statutes, see Bottomley and Forsyth in this volume, Chapter 10.

[98] Peter A. French, *Collective and Corporate Responsibility* (New York: Columbia University
Press, 1984), pp. 39–40.

corporation'. This approach attempts to establish an equilibrium among different forms of responsibility and to facilitate a move away from the causal attribution of responsibility, with its requirement of coincidence of intention and action in the same human body, to a collective type of attribution, which requires a coincidence of action and 'reasons for action' in the same structure. This type of approach suggests that the corporation has the capacity for 'collective intelligence' and for the 'actualisation of the potentiality of purposiveness'.[99] The combination of these two elements is proposed as a credible argument for the participation of the corporation in the distribution of normative social responsibility.

The Dutch, Australian and, to a certain extent, Italian statutes suggest a more pragmatic approach to the concept of corporate criminal responsibility (and, implicitly, to the one of moral responsibility). This perspective engenders the idea that corporations have all the necessary apparatus for being able to evaluate and choose their actions and, therefore, the actions of their members,[100] an aspect which entails a certain socially constructed level of organisational autonomy and rationality. According to this perspective, the fact that the corporation *could have* chosen to act differently than it actually did, causing predictable harm, means that the corporation *ought to have* so chosen. Accordingly, both the causal (individual) actor and the actor 'of a more responsible sort' (the corporation) have in common the 'intellectual' or rather cognitive capacity to be sensitive and responsive[101] to complex reasons for and against various actions. This capacity would be a necessary condition for being either morally, or *practically*, a responsible agent.[102] From this perspective, the corporation – as a formal organisation – does not appear as a moral agent, or at least not in the common sense of the word.[103] Although not irreducible moral agents, organisations are nevertheless presented as 'agents of another sort', as social constructions presenting sufficiently distinctive

---

[99] Ernest Weinrib, 'The Intelligibility of the Rule of Law', in Allan Hutchinson and Patrick Monahan (eds.), *The Rule of Law: Ideal or Ideology* (Toronto: Carswell, 1987), p. 82.

[100] Wolf, 'The Legal and Moral Responsibility of Organizations,' pp. 274–9; J. J. Brummer, *Corporate Responsibility and Legitimacy: An Interdisciplinary Analysis* (New York: Greenwood Press, 1991), pp. 165–84.

[101] P. Selznick, 'Self-Regulation and the Theory of Institutions', in G. Teubner, L. Farmer and D. Murphy (eds.), *Environmental Law and Ecological Responsibility: The Concept and Practice of Self-Organization* (Chichester: John Wiley and Sons, 1994), pp. 396–402.

[102] Wolf, 'The Legal and Moral Responsibility of Organizations', p. 277.

[103] Selznick, 'Self-Regulation and the Theory of Institutions', pp. 398–401; Ladd, 'Morality and the Ideal of Rationality', 489–90.

features to make them appropriate bearers of important kinds of normative responsibility.[104]

The acknowledgement of this perspective on corporate responsibility in legal domestic contexts marks a shift in the normative paradigm of
corporate responsibility from an individualist stand towards a more pragmatic organisational (i.e., systemic) approach. Supporters of this kind of
pragmatic view argue for the existence of a different perspective on the
meaning of responsibility. Besides the causal and the moral senses, a 'practical sense' appears as equally important.[105] This dimension, which is not
unknown in the discourse of legal responsibility, especially outside the
criminal law, is used 'when our claim that an agent is responsible for an
action is intended to announce that the agent assumes the risks associated
with that action . . . [that] the agent is considered the appropriate bearer
of damages, should they result from the action, as well as the appropriate
reaper of the action's possible benefits'.[106]

Constructed in this way, the notion of 'practical responsibility' has
implications beyond the limits of criminal law or morality, with much
of the 'CSR and law' debate gravitating around these ideas. Moreover, by
bringing in the notion of 'risk', this view places the implied (practical)
responsibility on the familiar corporate ground of risk assessment, thus
increasing the chances for the desired social values to be internalised as
mediate corporate goals, in other words, to become part of the mainstream thinking about corporate responsibility in general and about CSR
in particular.[107] Although – according to this perspective – corporations
would lack emotional capacities, the presence of cognitive capacities[108]
would suffice for the corporation to be able to internalise new dimensions
of both legal and social responsibility.[109]

---

[104] Wolf, 'The Legal and Moral Responsibility of Organizations', p. 279; C. Wells, *Corporations as Criminals* (Oxford: Clarendon Press, New York: Oxford University Press, 1993),
pp. 39–44.

[105] Brummer, *Corporate Responsibility and Legitimacy*, p. 173; Ladd, 'Morality and the Ideal of
Rationality', 511; Selznick, 'Self-Regulation and the Theory of Institutions', pp. 398–402.

[106] Wells, *Corporations as Criminals*, pp. 2–4.

[107] Parker speaks in this volume about 'meta-regulating law' that makes it a 'good legal risk
management practice' to implement processes to ensure internal corporate responsibility
for meeting regulatory goals; Chapter 7.

[108] Wolf, 'The Legal and Moral Responsibility of Organizations', p. 281–4.

[109] Re-evaluation mechanisms can be built into the very structure of an organisation, or
organisations can be prompted to do it themselves; see Stone, *Where the Law Ends*,
pp. 122–49; also M. Smiley, *Moral Responsibility and the Boundaries of Community: Power
and Accountability from a Pragmatic Point of View* (Chicago: The University of Chicago
Press, 1992), p 161.

V. Conclusions

The shaping of novel legal concepts defining a new paradigm of corporate legal responsibility becomes particularly relevant for the CSR discourse. The legal acknowledgement of this new paradigm, in a range of domestic jurisdictions, contributes to a significant extent to clarifying the legal basis for corporate responsibility in arenas beyond criminal law. Based on the shift in the paradigm of corporate responsibility analysed in this chapter, one can look at the corporate criminal responsibility debate as a debate from which CSR can draw not only normative but also conceptual support. The normative support can intervene through the formal process of bringing under criminal law jurisdiction specific (traditional) CSR issues.[110] It can also take place through an 'infusion' of CSR arguments and justifications into the (traditional) criminal law reasoning.[111] This type of normative support is gradual, it refers to individually selected CSR issues and it always follows the strict requirements of the formal legal debate.

As to the conceptual support, it consists of issues (partially) resolved within the criminal law debate and which are potentially instrumental in placing corporate responsibility on firmer conceptual ground. By selecting, honing and validating a paradigm of corporate responsibility which takes the concept of the corporation away from the simplifying individualist approach, the corporate criminal responsibility debate offers support to those perspectives on CSR that claim that corporations, as opposed to individuals, can and should be held responsible under the law.

The concepts of agency, intentionality and action have the potential to be differently shaped, despite their proceeding from the idea of autonomy and rationality. The social constructedness of these concepts makes them amenable to credible reformulations that are suitable for a new paradigm

---

[110] See, for instance, the issues regarding the domestic extra-territorial criminalisation of sex tourism and the legal implications for the travel and tourism operators and industry; ECPAT, *Consultation on Child Sex: Situational Analysis Studies on Child Sex Tourism in Tourist Destinations of India, Nepal and Sri Lanka* (Kathmandu, Nepal: 19–20 December 2003), at www.ecpat.net/eng/Ecpat_inter/projects/sex_tourism/Executive%20Summary.Web1.pdf, p4-6. See also the Australian attempt to regulate extraterritorial activities of the corporations in Bottomley and Forsyth's discussion of the Australian Corporate Code of Conduct Bill in this volume, Chapter 10; see also Sinden, in the volume, Chapter 17.

[111] The move towards reading environmental 'crimes' into the Italian pseudo-administrative (criminal) corporate responsibility would be an example in this sense; see M. Arena, 'La Responsabilità delle Persone Giuridiche per Illeciti Ambientali'.

of corporate agency and responsibility. Moreover, normative mechanisms built around the notions of 'management failure', 'organisational fault', 'corporate sphere of influence' or 'corporate culture' can all be useful concepts in the development of the concept of CSR. These leave open the possibility of identifying ways in which corporate actors can participate in the distribution of eventual legal responsibilities covered by CSR.

14

Corporate social responsibility and international law: the case of human rights and multinational enterprises

PETER MUCHLINSKI

The concept of corporate social responsibility (CSR) that informs the foundations of this volume poses significant problems when it is cast into the field of international law. Two issues in particular stand out: what is the meaning of an international concept of CSR and how is international law to accommodate such a concept, given the state of existing legal doctrines? These issues will be examined by focusing on the proposed human rights responsibilities of corporations in international law. As such, this chapter builds on the author's existing work in the field, bringing it up to date and developing more fully certain findings previously determined.[1] The chapter is divided into four sections. The first section analyses the meaning of CSR in international law and the role of human rights obligations within this concept. The second will consider the basis of human rights obligations for corporations. The third section looks at the major substantive principles that found the human rights responsibilities of corporations and outlines the most important recent instrument in the field, the UN Norms on the Responsibilities of Transnational Corporations and Other Business Enterprises with Regard to Human Rights (the 'UN

---

[1] See Peter Muchlinski, 'The Development of Human Rights Responsibilities for Multinational Enterprises', in Rory Sullivan (ed.), *Business and Human Rights: Dilemmas and Solutions* (Sheffield: Greenleaf Publishing, 2003), ch. 3; Peter Muchlinski, 'International Business Regulation: An Ethical Discourse in the Making?', in Tom Campbell and Seumas Miller (eds.), *Human Rights and the Moral Responsibilities of Corporate and Public Sector Organisations* (Dordrecht: Kluwer Academic Publishers, 2004), ch. 5; Peter Muchlinski, 'Human Rights, Social Responsibility and the Regulation of International Business: The Development of International Standards by Intergovernmental Organisations', *Non-State Actors and International Law* 3 (2003), 123; Peter Muchlinski, 'Human Rights and Multinationals – Is There a Problem?', *International Affairs* 77 (2001) 31, at 33–5; Peter Muchlinski, 'The Social Dimension of International Investment Agreements', in Julio Faundez, Mary E. Footer and Joseph H. Norton (eds.), *Governance Development and Globalization* (London: Blackstone Press, 2000), p. 373.

Norms').[2] The fourth section examines the practical issues of monitoring and implementation, including the major practical legal issues that will arise in the context of the possible role of intergovernmental organisations (IGOs) in the supervision of adherence to human rights norms.

I. Corporate social responsibility and international law

The introduction of CSR issues into international law poses some basic technical as well as substantive questions. Corporations are not subjects of

[2] *Norms on the Responsibilities of Transnational Corporations and Other Business Enterprises with Regard to Human Rights* (hereafter *UN Norms*), UN Doc. E/CN.4/Sub.2/2003/12/Rev.2(2003) 13 August 2003, available at www1.umn.edu/humanrts/links/norms-Aug2003.html, or www.business-humanrights.org. See also *Commentary on the Norms on the Responsibilities of Transnational Corporations and Other Business Enterprises with Regard to Human Rights* (hereafter *Commentary on the Norms*), UN Doc.E/CN.4/Sub.2/2003/38.Rev.2(2003) available at www1.umn.edu/humanrts/links/commentary-Aug2003.html or www.business-humanrights.org. Other relevant documents are available at www1.umn.edu/humanrts/links/omig.html. See further David Weissbrodt and Muria Kruger, 'Norms on the Responsibilities of Transnational Corporations and Other Business Enterprises with Regard to Human Rights', *American Journal of International Law* 97 (2003), 901; David Weissbrodt, 'The Beginning of a Sessional Working Group on Transnational Corporations within the UN Sub-Commission on Prevention of Discrimination and Protection of Minorities', in M. T. Kamminga and S. Zia-Zarifi (eds.), *Liability of Multinational Corporations Under International Law* (The Hague: Kluwer Law International, 2000), pp. 119–38; Amnesty International, *The UN Human Rights Norms for Business: Towards Legal Accountability* (London: Amnesty International, 2004). The UN Commission on Human Rights appointed a Special Representative on the issue of human rights, transnational corporations and other business enterprises to study further the implications of the extension of such responsibilities to business enterprises: UN Commission on Human Rights (Sixty First Session Agenda Item 17, UN Doc E/CN.4/2005/L.87), 15 April 2005, adopted 20 April 2005 by forty-nine votes to three with one abstention. Opposed by the United States, Australia and South Africa: Amnesty International, '2005 UN Commission on Human Rights: Amnesty International welcomes new UN mechanism on Business and Human Rights' (AI Public Statement 21 April 2005 IOR 41/044/2005). See too UN Commission on Human Rights Report on the Sixtieth Session Resolution 2004/116 (UN Doc. E/CN.4/2004/L.11/Add.7 22 April 2004, pp. 81–2), requesting the UN Commissioner for Human Rights to prepare a report on the 'responsibilities of transnational corporations and related business enterprises with regard to human rights'. The report is contained in UN Doc. E/CN.4/2005/91 15 February 2005. In June 2006 the Commission was replaced by a new Human Rights Council: UN GA Resolution 60/251 'Human Rights Council' 3 April 2006 at www.ohchr.org/english/bodies/hrcouncil/docs/A.RES.60.251_En.pdf. At its latest session on 7 August 2006, the Sub-Commission on the Promotion and Protection of Human Rights, recalling its resolution 2005–06 of 8 August 2005, decided, without a vote, to establish a Sessional working group on the effects of the working methods and activities of transnational corporations on the enjoyment of human rights: Decision 2006/104: Report of the Sub-Commission on Human Rights UN Doc. A/HRC/Sub.1/58/L.11/Add.1 24 August 2006 at www.ohchr.org/english/bodies/subcom/docs/58/A.HRC.Sub. 1.58.L.11.Add.1.pdf

international law as such. Accordingly, it may be said that they can have no duties imposed upon them by international law, only under national law. Equally, it is states, and not private actors, who have the primary responsibility to regulate corporate conduct, including any obligation placed on non-state actors to observe human rights norms. Thus, to extend human rights obligations to corporations appears to make no sense under traditional international law approaches. Nevertheless, certain developments in the work of IGOs suggest that these technical obstacles are not insuperable.

At the heart of these developments lies the idea of CSR resting on the obligations that corporations owe to the societies in which they operate.[3] Such obligations may be seen as the *quid pro quo* for the protection of investors and investments under international investment protection agreements and international economic rules such as those of the World Trade Organisation (WTO). Such obligations can be drawn rather widely. For instance, the Draft United Nations Code of Conduct on Transnational Corporations[4] lists the obligations of transnational corporations (TNCs) across a wide range of issues dealing with such matters as respect for the sovereignty of the host state and its political system, respect for human rights, abstention from corrupt practices, refraining from using the economic power of the TNC in a manner damaging to the economic well-being of the countries in which a firm operates (including observance of tax and anti-monopoly laws) and ensuring full disclosure concerning the activities of the firm. Similarly, the Organisation for Economic Co-operation and Development (OECD) Guidelines for Multinational Enterprises contain a section on 'General Policies' which is worth reproducing in full as it offers an example of what appears to be an emerging consensus on the social obligations of TNCs:[5]

---

[3] For a discussion of the concept of social responsibility and its implications for transnational corporations, see UNCTAD, *The Social Responsibility of Transnational Corporations* (New York and Geneva: United Nations, 1999); UNCTAD, *World Investment Report 1999* (New York and Geneva: United Nations, 1999), Ch. XII; UNCTAD, *World Investment Report 2003* (New York and Geneva: United Nations, 2003), Ch. VI. See too UNCTAD, *Social Responsibility*, UNCTAD Series on issues in international investment agreements (New York and Geneva: United Nations, 2001). All available online at www.unctad.org/iia.

[4] See UNCTAD, *International Investment Agreements: A Compendium* vol. I (New York and Geneva: United Nations, 1996), p. 161.

[5] The remaining chapters include: 'Disclosure, Employment and Industrial Relations, Environment, Combating Bribery, Consumer Interests, Science and Technology, Competition and Taxation'.

Enterprises should take fully into account established policies in the countries in which they operate, and consider the views of other stakeholders. In this regard, enterprises should:

1. Contribute to economic, social and environmental progress with a view to achieving sustainable development.
2. Respect the human rights of those affected by their activities consistent with the host government's international obligations and commitments.
3. Encourage local capacity building through close co-operation with the local community, including business interests, as well as developing the enterprise's activities in domestic and foreign markets, consistent with the need for sound commercial practice.
4. Encourage human capital formation, in particular by creating employment opportunities and facilitating training opportunities for employees.
5. Refrain from seeking or accepting exemptions not contemplated in the statutory or regulatory framework related to environmental, health, safety, labour, taxation, financial incentives, or other issues.
6. Support and uphold good corporate governance principles and develop and apply good corporate governance practices.
7. Develop and apply effective self-regulatory practices and management systems that foster a relationship of confidence and mutual trust between enterprises and the societies in which they operate.
8. Promote employee awareness of, and compliance with, company policies through appropriate dissemination of these policies, including through training programmes.
9. Refrain from discriminatory or disciplinary action against employees who make bona fide reports to management or, as appropriate, to the competent authorities, on practices that contravene the law, the Guidelines or the enterprise's policies.
10. Encourage, where practicable, business partners, including suppliers and sub-contractors, to apply principles of corporate conduct compatible with the Guidelines.
11. Abstain from any improper involvement in local political activities.[6]

As may be apparent from this wide-ranging list of issues, the precise classification of CSR standards is difficult, as potentially the phrase could cover all aspects of corporate regulation. By contrast, the UN Global Compact contains a more specific set of standards. The Ten Principles

[6] OECD Guidelines for Multinational Enterprises, 27 June 2000, pp. 3–4, at www.oecd.org/dataoecd/56/36/1922428.pdf.

on which the Global Compact is founded concern the areas of human rights, labour, the environment and anti-corruption. These are said to enjoy universal consensus and are derived from a number of significant international instruments.[7]

In relation to the drawing up of social responsibility provisions in international law, the key issues identified by the UN Global Compact are by no means exhaustive.[8] Further issues of relevance, to developing countries in particular, can be gleaned from the above-mentioned Draft United Nations Code of Conduct on TNCs and OECD Guidelines for Multinational Enterprises. These include technology transfer, training of the local workforce, the importance of backward linkages and the promotion of local entrepreneurship. Equally, certain issues of interest to both developing and developed countries regarding the proper regulation of corporate behaviour are also present in the Draft Code and the Guidelines. In particular, requirements as to transparency through corporate disclosure, accountability through corporate governance structures to various stakeholder groups, and ethical responsibility in relation to such matters as illicit payments, advertising and product safety and quality could be included under the broad heading of social responsibility.[9] Thus, social responsibility may take both an economic, social and ethical dimension in that TNCs are expected to conduct their economic affairs in good faith and in accordance with proper standards of economic activity, while also observing fundamental principles of good social and ethical conduct. Against this background the remainder of the chapter will now consider

---

[7] See further www.unglobalcompact.org. These are the Universal Declaration of Human Rights; the International Labour Organisation's Declaration on Fundamental Principles and Rights at Work; the Rio Declaration on Environment and Development and the United Nations Convention Against Corruption. The Global Compact asks companies to embrace, support and enact, within their sphere of influence, a set of core values in the areas of human rights, labour standards, the environment and anti-corruption: Human Rights: Principle 1: Businesses should support and respect the protection of internationally proclaimed human rights; and Principle 2: make sure that they are not complicit in human rights abuses. Labour Standards: Principle 3: Businesses should uphold the freedom of association and the effective recognition of the right to collective bargaining; Principle 4: the elimination of all forms of forced and compulsory labour; Principle 5: the effective abolition of child labour; and Principle 6: the elimination of discrimination in respect of employment and occupation. Environment: Principle 7: Businesses should support a precautionary approach to environmental challenges; Principle 8: undertake initiatives to promote greater environmental responsibility; and Principle 9: encourage the development and diffusion of environmentally friendly technologies. Anti-Corruption: Principle 10: Businesses should work against all forms of corruption, including extortion and bribery.

[8] See UNCTAD, *The Social Responsibility of Transnational Corporations*, pp. 7–8.

[9] For a discussion of these further matters, see UNCTAD, *Social Responsibility*.

what is possibly the most significant potential contribution that international law can make to the development of CSR, namely the extension of human rights obligations to the operations of corporations

II. The basis of human rights obligations for corporations

The observance of fundamental human rights can be said to lie at the heart of ethical business practice.[10] However, in relation to business ethics, the use of human rights standards is replete with conceptual difficulties. Indeed, there are a number of strong arguments against an extension of CSR responsibilities, including human rights obligations, to corporations.[11] Some are of general import while others relate more specifically to human rights issues. Turning to general objections first, it may be said that business enterprises are in business: their only social responsibility is to make profits for their shareholders. It is not for them to act as moral arbiters in relation to the wider issues arising in the communities in which they operate. Indeed, to do so may be seen as unwarranted interference in the internal affairs of those communities, something that multinational enterprises in particular have, in the past, been urged not to do.[12] Secondly, the extension of CSR obligations to corporate actors will create a 'free rider' problem.[13] It is predictable that not all states and not all firms will take the same care to observe CSR standards. Thus the more conscientious corporations that invest time and money in observing such standards, and making themselves accountable for their record in this field, will be at a competitive disadvantage in relation to more unscrupulous corporations that do not undertake such responsibilities. They may also lose business opportunities in countries with poor human rights records, in that the host government may not wish to do business with ethically driven corporations and they may not want to do business with it. Turning to more specific, human rights-oriented objections, it may be argued that private non-state actors do not have any positive duty to observe human rights. Their only duty is to obey the law. Thus it is for the state to

---

[10] See John M. Kline, *Ethics for International Business: Decision Making in a Global Political Economy* (London: Routledge, 2005), p. 25.

[11] This section draws on Muchlinski, 'Human Rights and Multinationals', 35–44.

[12] See, for example, the UN Draft Code of Conduct for Transnational Corporations, paras. 15–16 in UNCTAD, *International Investment Agreements: A Compendium*, p. 165.

[13] See Ray Vernon, in Harvard Law School, *Business and Human Rights* (Cambridge, MA: Harvard Law School Human Rights Program, 1999), p. 49.

regulate on matters of social importance and for such actors to observe the law. It follows also that corporations, as private actors, can only be beneficiaries of human rights protection and not human rights protectors themselves. In addition, which human rights are corporations to observe? They may have some influence over social and economic matters, as, for example, by ensuring the proper treatment of their workers, but they can do nothing to protect civil and political rights. Only states have the power and the ability to do that. Finally, unfairness may be exacerbated by the selective and politically driven activities of non-governmental organisations (NGOs), whose principal concern may be to maintain a high profile for their particular campaigns and not to ensure that all corporations are held equally to account.

Such arguments can be answered. First, as regards the extension of social responsibility standards to corporations, it should be noted that such entities have been expected to observe socially responsible standards of behaviour for a long time.[14] This expectation has been expressed in national and regional laws and in numerous codes of conduct drawn up by IGOs, as will be discussed more fully below. Indeed, corporate actors themselves appear to be rejecting a purely non-social role for themselves through the adoption of corporate and industry-based codes of conduct.[15] Second, observance of CSR standards, including human rights, is increasingly being seen by corporate actors as 'good for business'. It is argued that business cannot flourish in an environment where fundamental human rights are not respected – what firm would be happy with the disappearance or imprisonment without trial of employees for their political opinions, thereby being deprived of their labour? In addition, businesses themselves may justify the adoption of CSR and human rights policies by reference to good reputation.[16] The benefit to be reaped from espousing a pro-CSR stance is seen as outweighing any free rider problem, which may be in any case exaggerated.[17]

---

[14] See UNCTAD, *The Social Responsibility of Transnational Corporations*, and *World Investment Report 1999*, Ch. XII.

[15] See, for example, UNCTAD, *World Investment Report 1994* (New York and Geneva: United Nations, 1994), Ch. VIII, and *The Social Responsibility of Transnational Corporations*, pp. 31–42.

[16] See, for example, Simon Williams, 'How Principles Benefit the Bottom Line: The Experience of the Co-operative Bank', in M. Addo (ed.), *Human Rights Standards and the Responsibility of Transnational Corporations* (The Hague: Kluwer Law International, 1999), pp. 63–8. See too Harvard Law School, *Business and Human Rights*, pp. 19–22.

[17] See further Muchlinski, 'Human Rights and Multinationals', 38–9.

Third, the private legal status of corporate actors may be seen as irrelevant to the extension of human rights responsibilities to such entities. As Andrew Clapham has forcefully argued, changes in the nature and location of power in the contemporary international system, including an increase in the power of private non-state actors such as multinational enterprises (MNEs)(which may allow them to bypass traditional state-centred systems of governance), have forced a reconsideration of the boundaries between the private and the public spheres. This, in turn, has brought into question the traditional notion of the corporation as a private entity with no social or public obligations, with the consequence that such actors, including MNEs, may in principle be subjected to human rights obligations.[18] This position coincides with the fear that these powerful entities may disregard human rights and thereby violate human dignity. It follows that corporations, including, in particular, MNEs, should be subjected to human rights responsibilities, notwithstanding their status as creatures of private law, because human dignity must be protected in every circumstance.[19] Furthermore, in response to the view that corporations cannot be subjected to human rights responsibilities because they are incapable of observing human rights designed to direct state action, it may be said that, to the contrary, corporations can affect the economic welfare of the communities in which they operate and, given the indivisibility of human rights, this means that they have a direct impact on the extent that economic and social rights, especially labour rights in the workplace, can be enjoyed. Although it is true that corporations may not have direct control over matters arising outside the workplace, they may nonetheless exercise important influence in this regard. Thus, corporate actors may seek to defend the human rights of their employees outside the workplace, to set standards for their subcontractors and to refuse to accept the benefits of governmental measures that seek to improve the business climate at the expense of fundamental human rights. Equally, where firms operate in unstable environments, they should ensure that their security arrangements comply with fundamental human rights standards.[20] Moreover, where companies have no direct means of influence, they should avoid, at the very least, making statements or engaging in actions that appear to

---

[18] See A. Clapham, *Human Rights in the Private Sphere* (Oxford: Clarendon Press, 1993), pp. 137–8, and A. Clapham, *Human Rights Obligations of Non-State Actors* (Oxford: Oxford University Press, 2006), pp. 544–8.

[19] Clapham, *Human Rights in the Private Sphere*, p. 147.

[20] See Amnesty International UK Business Group, *Human Rights Guidelines for Companies* (London: Amnesty International, 1998), pp. 8–11.

condone human rights violations. This may include silence in the face of such violations. Furthermore, all firms should develop an internal human rights policy which ensures that such concerns are taken into account in management decision-making, and which may find expression in a corporate code of conduct. Finally, the argument that corporations may be subjected to arbitrary and selective targeting by NGOs should not be overstated. While it is true that such behaviour can arise out of what Upendra Baxi has termed 'the market for human rights',[21] in which NGOs strive for support from a consuming public in a manner not dissimilar to that of a service industry, major business enterprises are big enough to take care of themselves.

Despite this strong theoretical and moral case for extending responsibility for human rights violations to corporate actors, the legal responsibility of such non-state actors for such violations remains uncertain. Thus, much of the literature on this issue suggests ways to reform and develop the law towards full legal responsibility, rather than documenting actual juridical findings of human rights violations by MNEs, or indeed other non-state actors.[22] We are yet to see such an event in the courts of the world, although it should be remembered that findings of human rights violations concerning slave-labour practices were made against individual German industrialists at the end of World War II.[23] Against this background, the content of the main substantive human rights obligations of corporate entities will now be considered.

---

[21] Upendra Baxi, 'Voices of Suffering and the Future of Human Rights', *Transnational Law and Contemporary Problems* 8 (1998), 126, at 161–9.

[22] See, for example, David Kinley and Junko Tadaki, 'From Talk to Walk: The Emergence of Human Rights Responsibilities for Corporations at International Law', *Virginia Journal of International Law* 44 (2004), 931; Nicola Jägers, *Corporate Human Rights Obligations: In Search of Accountability* (Antwerp: Intersentia, 2002); Sarah Joseph, 'An Overview of the Human Rights Accountability of Multinational Enterprises', in Menno Kamminga and Sam Zia-Zarifi (eds.), *Liability of Multinational Corporations under International Law* (The Hague: Kluwer Law International, 2000), p. 75; Sarah Joseph, *Corporations and Transnational Human Rights Litigation* (Oxford: Hart Publishing, 2004); Chris Avery, 'Business and Human Rights in a Time of Change', in Kamminga and Zia-Zarifi (eds.), *Liability of Multinational Corporations*, p. 17; Menno Kamminga, 'Holding Multinational Corporations Accountable for Human Rights Abuses: a Challenge for the EC', in Philip Alston (ed.), *The EU and Human Rights* (Oxford: Oxford University Press, 1999), p. 558; Amnesty International and Pax Christi International Dutch Sections, *Multinational Enterprises and Human Rights* (Utrecht, November 1998).

[23] See A. Clapham, 'The Question of Jurisdiction Under International Criminal Law Over Legal Persons', in Kamminga and Zia-Zarifi (eds.), *Liability of Multinational Corporations*, especially pp. 166–71.

III. The major substantive human rights obligations of corporations

The precise content of the human rights obligations of corporations is open to considerable speculation.[24] However, it is clear that corporate actors will not carry the same responsibilities as states. Some state responsibilities are simply impossible for MNEs and other business enterprises to carry out. Examples include protecting rights of asylum, the right to take part in government, rights to nationality and provision of rights of due process. Equally states, as public actors, do not themselves enjoy human rights protection, while, as noted above, corporations, as private actors, can possess rights that may need to be balanced against those of other non-state actors.[25] Against this background the development of substantive obligations will require some adaptation of existing human rights standards. In addition, it may require a wider conception of what obligations may count as human rights obligations for private corporate actors, given their influence over the development of economic and social welfare in the societies in which they operate. The analysis proceeds as follows. First, the relationship between state and corporate spheres of responsibility will be considered, second, the definition of the types of corporate entities that may be subjected to human rights obligations will be assessed and, third, the actual substantive content of possible standards will be briefly discussed. The discussion will be based, in large part, on the UN Norms, owing to their undoubted significance in the developing debate over the nature and scope of human rights obligations for multinational and other business actors.

Historically, the observance of human rights standards has been an obligation of the state alone. Accordingly, the first step in the evolution of substantive standards for MNEs and other business entities requires the assertion of a direct link between the obligations of states, and of non-state actors, to promote universal respect for, and observance of, human rights and fundamental freedoms. An express reference to such a link can be found in the Universal Declaration of Human Rights (UDHR). This instrument is addressed both to governments and to 'other organs of society'. Following this provision, the third recital of the Preamble to the UN Norms recognises that, 'even though States have the primary responsibility to promote, secure the fulfilment of, respect, ensure respect of

---

[24] See further Kinley and Tadaki, 'From Talk to Walk', 966–93; Jägers, *Corporate Human Rights Obligations*, pp. 51–74.
[25] Kinley and Tadaki, 'From Talk to Walk', 967.

and protect human rights, transnational corporations and other business enterprises, *as organs of society*, are also responsible for promoting and securing the human rights set forth in the Universal Declaration of Human Rights' (emphasis added). This is a clear acceptance of the view that corporate entities do have human rights responsibilities on the basis of their social existence. However, the legal status of the UDHR remains that of a non-binding declaration, and so this reference to the UDHR wording in the UN Norms may be no more than a statement of an ethical duty at best, reinforced by the fact that the UN Commission on Human Rights regards the UN Norms as a draft proposal that has no legal standing.[26]

Although the first concern of the UN Norms is to address the obligations of TNCs and other business enterprises in respect of human rights, this instrument continues to address the obligations of governments as well.[27] Thus, paragraph 1 of the UN Norms asserts:

> States have the primary responsibility to promote, secure the fulfilment of, respect, ensure respect of and protect human rights recognized in international as well as national law, including ensuring that transnational corporations and other business enterprises respect human rights. Within their respective spheres of activity and influence, transnational corporations and other business enterprises have the obligation to promote, secure the fulfilment of, respect, ensure respect of and protect human rights recognized in international as well as national law, including the rights of indigenous peoples and other vulnerable groups.

This provision places states over TNCs and other business enterprises as the principal regulators of human rights observance. In addition, it recognises that states and businesses operate in different fields and so each has a specific set of responsibilities in their particular field of operations, thereby obviating the possibility that business enterprises could supplant the state in its obligations to uphold and observe human rights, or that the state could use the UN Norms as an excuse for not taking action to protect human rights.[28]

---

[26] See the discussion in Kinley and Tadaki, 'From Talk to Walk', 948–9, and see UN Commission on Human Rights Res.2004/116 (see n. 2 above) at point (c).

[27] The United States opposed the resolution of 20 April 2005 (see n. 2 above), *inter alia*, on the ground that 'human rights obligations apply to states, not non-state actors, and it is incumbent on states when they deem necessary to adopt national laws that address the obligations of private actors': United States Statement on Item 17 of the Sixty First Session of the UN Human Rights Commission, 20 April 2005, available at www.business-humanrights.org.

[28] See *Commentary on the Norms* (see n. 2 above), para. 2(b).

Turning to the definitional aspects of extending human rights obligations to TNCs, the discussions over the UN Norms in the UN Sub-Commission on Human Rights reflected a desire to see the application of human rights obligations to all business entities and not merely to TNCs. This avoids an otherwise unjustifiable distinction between TNCs and national firms as regards responsibilities to observe fundamental human rights standards. The focus of the debate on international corporate social responsibility has tended to be towards TNCs, given the transnational character of their operations. However, the underlying issues of principle would apply *mutatis mutandis* to national firms as the applicability of human rights standards to private corporate actors does not depend on the mere fact that their business operations cross borders. Such a geographically based justification for applying human rights standards to one class of corporations rather than another would be unprincipled. The focus on TNCs can perhaps be explained as a pragmatic choice, evolving out of their visibility in certain widely publicised cases of mass violations of human rights, and from the perception that TNCs, unlike purely national firms, can take advantage of more lax legal regimes in foreign host countries, which pay scant regard to social welfare concerns, allowing unscrupulous firms to turn this to their commercial advantage.[29] On the other hand, it should be noted that TNCs are more likely than local firms, in countries where social welfare issues are either un- or de-regulated, to observe good practices in this arena. Thus, the real problem may be a lack of proper regulation in the host country of local businesses and institutions for which TNCs may not be responsible. Therefore, any programme of responsibility must take into account the relationship between local and transnational practices and the influence of TNCs thereon.

Taking this into account, the reference to both TNCs and other business enterprises may be said to avoid the risk that an inadequate definition could allow companies to use financial and other structures to conceal their transnational nature and to appear as a domestic company thereby avoiding responsibility under the UN Norms.[30] However, the definition

---

[29] See further *Draft Universal Human Rights Guidelines for Companies: Introduction*, UN Doc. E/CN.4/Sub.2/2001/WG.2/WP.1 (2001), paras. 22–6. See too Working Group of the UN Sub-Commission on Human Rights Report for 2002 (UN Doc.E/CN.4/Sub.2/2002/13 15 August 2002), p. 6, para. 15.

[30] *Draft Universal Human Rights Guidelines Introduction*, paras. 18–21. For an illustrative example of such a strategy applied for the purposes of avoiding a foreign legal liability, see the facts of *Adams* v. *Cape Industries* [1990] Ch 433 (CA).

given of what constitutes a 'transnational corporation' is rather vague. The UN Norms state that this term, 'refers to an economic entity operating in more than one country or a cluster of economic entities operating in two or more countries – whatever their legal form, whether in their home country or country of activity, and whether taken individually or collectively'.[31] Unlike other commonly used definitions of TNCs (or MNEs), this definition does not refer to control, influence or coordination of activities as a key element in determining whether the entity is indeed a TNC. This element must be inferred from the reference to economic entity. Its absence would render the instrument applicable to any type of business relationship that crosses borders. Perhaps that is the intention, given the continued reference to 'other business enterprise', which is defined as including 'any business entity, regardless of the international or domestic nature of its activities, including a transnational corporation, contractor, subcontractor, supplier, licensee or distributor; the corporate, partnership or other legal form used to establish the business entity; and the nature of the ownership of the entity'.[32] This definition continues by presuming that the instrument will apply, as a matter of practice, if the business enterprise has any relation with a TNC, the impact of its activities is not entirely local, or the activities involve violations of the right to security of persons as defined in the text of the instrument at paragraphs 3 and 4. Taking both the definition of 'TNC' and 'other business entity' together, the UN Norms are capable of covering a wide 'sphere of influence' that the activities of a corporate network, whatever its actual form, help to create.[33]

As regards the nature and scope of substantive obligations, the discussions concerning the UN Norms have given rise to a re-examination of the range of sources from which human rights responsibilities for MNEs and other business enterprises can be drawn. From the existing instruments dealing with corporate social responsibility and human rights, as synthesised into the substantive contents of the UN Norms, at least five different types of provisions can be identified. First, there are those which cover 'traditional' civil and political human rights issues, namely:

---

[31] *UN Norms*, para. 20.
[32] *UN Norms*, para. 21. Note the circuitous drafting which replicates the notion of 'transnational corporation' as a part of 'other business entity'.
[33] See Kinley and Tadaki, 'From Talk to Walk', 962–6, and see the Report of the UN Commissioner for Human Rights (see n. 2 above), paras. 37–9.

- the right to equal treatment;[34]
- the right of security of persons as concerns business engagement in, or benefit from, 'war crimes, crimes against humanity, genocide, torture, forced disappearance, forced or compulsory labour, hostage-taking, extrajudicial, summary or arbitrary executions, other violations of humanitarian law and other international crimes against the human person as defined by international law';[35]
- rights of workers dealing, in particular, with those rights listed in Article 2 of the International Labour Organisation (ILO) Declaration on Fundamental Principles and Rights at Work 1998, namely, the prohibition on forced or compulsory labour,[36] the rights of children to be protected against economic exploitation,[37] and freedom of association.[38]

In addition, the UN Norms require respect for other civil and political rights, such as privacy, education, freedom of thought, conscience and religion, and freedom of opinion and expression.[39]

Second, following the contents, in the main, of the ILO Tripartite Declaration of Principles Concerning Multinational Enterprises and Social Policy,[40] the UN Norms contain provisions reflecting the main economic social and cultural rights, including:

- the provision of a safe and healthy working environment;[41]
- compensation of workers with remuneration that ensures 'an adequate standard of living for them and their families';[42]

---

[34] *UN Norms*, Section B, para. 2. See too OECD, *Guidelines on Multinational Enterprises* (Paris: OECD, 2000), Guideline II 'General Policies' and Guideline IV 'Employment and Industrial Relations'; *ILO Declaration on Fundamental Principles and Rights at Work* (Geneva: ILO, 1998), Article 2(d).

[35] *UN Norms*, Section C, para. 3.   [36] *UN Norms*, Section D, para. 5.

[37] *UN Norms*, Section D, para. 6. This formulation in the text replaces the earlier formulation which stated that, 'Companies shall not use child labour and shall contribute to its abolition'. Thus the prohibition in the earlier draft has been modified so that child labour conducted in a non-exploitative manner can be used. This reflects concern that, in some developing countries, the denial of access to labour for children might actually worsen their economic situation and that of their families. In such cases the issue is to make child labour non-abusive. Business enterprises that use child labour must create and implement a plan to eliminate this: *Commentary on the Norms* (see n. 2 above), Section D, para. 6, comment (d). By comparison, the 1998 *ILO Declaration* requires 'the effective abolition of child labour' without qualification.

[38] *UN Norms*, Section D, para. 9.   [39] *UN Norms*, Section E, para. 12.

[40] ILO Tripartite Declaration on Multinational Enterprises and Social Policy 1977 as amended at the 279th Session of the ILO Geneva, 17 November 2000: 41 ILM 186 (2002). See now revision of March 2006 at www.ilo.org which remains in essence unchanged.

[41] *UN Norms*, Section D, para. 7.   [42] *ibid.*, para. 8.

- protection of collective bargaining;[43]
- respect for the social, economic and cultural policies of the countries in which companies operate;[44]
- respect for the rights to health, adequate food and adequate housing, and other economic social and cultural rights such as rights to 'adequate food and drinking water; the highest attainable standard of physical and mental health, adequate housing . . . and refrain from actions which obstruct the realisation of those rights'.[45]

No distinction is made in the UN Norms as to the relative importance of these so-called 'first' and 'second' generation human rights. Indeed, as the Preamble explains, the UN Norms are based on the 'universality, indivisibility, interdependence and interrelatedness of human rights including the right to development'.[46] This approach also covers the so-called 'third generation' rights of collective solidarity, as expressed through the inclusion, in the UN Norms, of the right of development[47] and the obligation on TNCs and other business enterprises to promote, respect and protect the rights and interests of indigenous peoples and other vulnerable groups.[48]

A fourth group of provisions can be said to deal with the special problems created by the operations of TNCs for the realisation of the types of rights listed above. Thus the UN Norms deal with a specific issue that has

---

[43] ibid., para. 9.
[44] ibid., Section E, para. 10. These include transparency, accountability and prohibition of corruption.
[45] ibid., para. 12. The right to drinking water was first included at the inter-sessional meeting of the Working Group in February 2002: Working Group 2002 (see n. 29 above), p. 6, para. 14.
[46] UN Norms, Preamble, Recital 13.   [47] UN Norms, Section E, para. 12.
[48] UN Norms, Section A, para. 1 and Section E, para. 10, as explained in the Commentary on the Norms at Section E, para. 10, comment (c). The UN Norms have dropped any explicit reference to self-determination, which was present in earlier drafts: see Draft Universal Human Rights Guidelines for Companies (UN Doc. E/CN.4/Sub.2/2001/WG.2/WP.1/Add.I (2001), Section E, para. 11. This reference was dropped in 2002. On the issue of indigenous people's rights and TNC obligations, see further the discussion in Kinley and Tadaki, 'From Talk to Walk', 987–93, and Jägers, Corporate Human Rights Obligations, pp. 157–60. See too Mayanga (Sumo) Awas Tinigi Community v. Nicaragua Case No. 79 Inter-American Court of Human Rights, Judgment 31 August 2001 (available at www1.umn.edu/humanrts/iachr/AwasTingnicase.html) which established the right of indigenous peoples to peaceful enjoyment of their traditional lands, requiring the respondent state to protect such rights in granting concessions to foreign investors. See too UN Human Rights Committee Communication No. 511/1992 I. Lansman et al. v. Finland and Communication No. 671/1995 J. Lansman et al. v. Finland discussed in Jägers, Corporate Human Rights Obligations, pp. 158–9.

arisen in a number of cases, namely, the operation of security arrangements for companies. Such arrangements 'shall observe international
human rights norms as well as the laws and professional standards of
the country or countries in which they operate'.[49] This general principle
is further elaborated in the Commentary to the Norms, which requires
companies to observe the emerging best practices evolving in this field
through various codes of conduct, particularly the UN Principles on the
Use of Force and Firearms by Law Enforcement Officials, the UN Code of
Conduct for Law Enforcement Officers, the UN Convention Against Torture and the Rome Statute of the International Criminal Court. Business
enterprises and TNCs are further urged not to supplant the state military
and law enforcement services but only provide for their own preventive
or defensive services, and not to hire individuals known to have been
responsible for human rights or humanitarian law violations.[50] Other
provisions that can be added to this category are the duty to recognise
and respect applicable norms of international law, national laws and regulations, administrative practices and the rule of law,[51] and the final saving
provision which makes clear that 'nothing in these Norms shall be construed as diminishing, restricting, or adversely affecting the human rights
obligations of States under national and international law, nor shall they
be construed as diminishing, restricting, or adversely affecting more protective human rights norms'.[52] Not only does this provision offer a rule
of interpretation favourable to the effective protection of human rights,
but it also emphasises that the operations of business enterprises can
observe higher standards than the minimum standards required by the
UN Norms.

A fifth, and final, group of substantive provisions go beyond a conventional human rights-based agenda and belong more to a general corporate
social responsibility code. This reflects the fact that many of the sources,
referred to as contributing to the Draft Norms,[53] constitute more general codes of business ethics, which, by their nature, will deal with social
issues not usually described as human rights issues. Thus, for example,

[49] *UN Norms*, Section C, para. 4. See further the Amnesty International *Human Rights
Guidelines for Companies* (see n. 20 above).
[50] *Commentary on the Norms* (see n. 2 above), Section C, para. 3, comments (a)–(d).
[51] *UN Norms*, Section E, para. 10. This principle is echoed in the OECD Guidelines and the
ILO Tripartite Declaration.
[52] *ibid.*, Section H, para. 19.
[53] On which see *Draft Universal Human Rights Guidelines for Companies with Source Materials*, UN Doc. E/CN.4/Sub.2/2001/WG.2/WP.1/Add.2 (2001), available at www1.umn.edu/
humanrts/links/omig.html.

the UN Norms require that TNCs and other business enterprises shall act 'in accordance with fair business, marketing and advertising practices and shall take all necessary steps to ensure the safety and quality of the goods and services they provide, including observance of the precautionary principle. Nor shall they produce, distribute, market or advertise harmful or potentially harmful products for use by consumers'.[54] This introduces general consumer protection standards into the instrument. Other such social responsibility provisions include a prohibition against bribery[55] and obligations with regard to environmental protection.[56] Whether these are truly 'human rights' issues is open to debate. On the other hand, as the Preamble to the UN Norms notes, 'new international human rights issues and concerns are continually emerging and . . . transnational corporations and other business enterprises often are involved in these issues and concerns, such that further standard-setting and implementation are required at this time and in the future'. In this light, it may well be that consumer and environmental protection are emergent human rights issues. It has been argued, for example, that a right to a clean and healthy environment is a human right, though this has been disputed.[57] Whether consumer protection is a human right seems rather more tenuous, as it is hard to see how elevating such issues to the status of quasi-constitutional rights makes such protection more effective. In any case, other established human rights could be sufficient. For example, death or serious injury caused by unsafe products or processes could come within the right to life and the right to personal security under Article 3 of the UDHR and Articles 6 and 9 of the International Civil and Political Rights Covenant. Loss of livelihood due to disability could be covered by Article 25 of the Declaration. As for the prohibition against bribery, a human rights approach seems ill-conceived, as it is not entirely clear whether there is an identifiable human victim. This is an area in which the wider social undesirability of such practices is at issue, rather than any significant adverse effects on any one individual. It would thus be better dealt with as a regulatory matter under national law and specialised international conventions than a human rights-oriented instrument.

---

[54] *UN Norms*, Section F, para. 13.
[55] *UN Norms*, Section E, para. 11.   [56] *UN Norms*, Section G, para. 14.
[57] See generally M. Fitzmaurice, 'The Contribution of Environmental Law to the Development of Modern International Law', in J. Makarczyk (ed.), *The Theory of International Law at the Threshold of the 21st Century* (The Hague: Kluwer Law International, 1996), at pp. 909–14.

IV. Monitoring and enforcement

Key to any initiatives concerning the extension of human rights responsibilities to corporations is how to ensure that any emergent substantive
human rights obligations of such entities are actually upheld. This may
involve a mix of informal self-regulation by firms and formal regulation
by way of national and international legal approaches. Corporate self-
regulation on human rights issues is far from developed, as compared with
environmental self-regulation, for example. Whether firms can, or should,
engage in such activity generates controversy. Some business voices feel
that this is a step too far, requiring firms to become quasi-governmental
organisations that would engage in political decisions far beyond the limits
of their capability. Indeed, human rights activism by MNEs might be said
to undermine their position as providers of beneficial foreign investment
to less developed countries that may object to such interference in their
internal political affairs.[58] Equally, human rights concerns may be of such
a fundamentally different magnitude, as compared to other corporate
social responsibility issues (such as environmental protection or day-to-
day employment and health and safety matters), that they should never
be entrusted to self-regulatory responses. On the other hand, in practice some MNEs have found themselves embroiled in situations where
human rights abuses have arisen and their responses have left much to
be desired in terms of avoiding further harm, using their influence with
host governments to mitigate policies of human rights abuse or inadvertently, perhaps even recklessly, contributing to an escalation of harm.[59]
Accordingly, firms may have little choice but to address human rights concerns as part of their business management strategy, particularly where
they invest in conflict zones, politically corrupt states or less developed
countries. Indeed, as will be seen below, the UN Norms expect TNCs and
other business enterprises to develop a human rights policy and appropriate internal monitoring systems. Thus, the trend toward developing

---

[58] See further Frans-Paul van der Putten, Gemma Crijns and Harry Hummels, 'The Ability of
Corporations to Protect Human Rights in Developing Countries', in Rory Sullivan (ed.),
Business and Human Rights (Sheffield: Greenleaf Publishing, 2003), p. 82.

[59] See, for example, the situation of Unocal in Burma or the experience of Shell with the
Ogoni people's rights. See too Rory Sullivan and Nina Seppala, 'From the Inside Looking
Out: A Management Perspective on Human Rights', in Sullivan (ed.), *Business and Human
Rights*, p. 102; Simon Handelsman, 'Mining in conflict zones', in Sullivan (ed.), *Business and
Human Rights*, p. 125; Christopher McDowell, 'Privatising Infrastructure Development:
"Development" Refugees and the Resettlement Challenge', in Sullivan (ed.), *Business and
Human Rights*, p. 155.

clear internal management responses may be inevitable. However, self-regulation, of the kind seen, for example, in relation to environmental matters, may well be inappropriate in the case of human rights issues, as the state remains the prime protector of such rights and it would be politically illegitimate to hand this responsibility over exclusively to the corporation.

Turning to formal legal regulation, at the national level, both standard-setting, through new laws and regulations, and public interest litigation, taken against firms alleged to have broken their human rights obligations, may be used. At the international level there arises the possibility that IGOs have a monitoring role that can supplement such national initiatives, in particular, by requiring states to comply with certain obligations to ensure that their domestic regulatory structures adequately reflect the emergent norms in this area and by providing adequate and effective remedies for those who allege to have been harmed by the failure of firms to observe fundamental international human rights standards.

At the national level, there has, to date, been relatively little progress on standard-setting through new laws or regulations embodying human rights standards.[60] The most significant examples in this regard may be the US and EU initiatives to link labour rights protection to the extension of trade preferences, or the UK Ethical Trading Initiative.[61] Equally, the provision of political risks insurance on the part of national investment and trade guarantee agencies, such as the UK Export Credit Guarantees Department (ECGD), has become subject to human rights and OECD Guidelines compliance requirements.[62] However, specialised legislation on MNEs and human rights is virtually non-existent. One example of what might be possible arose in Australia, where the draft Corporate Code of Conduct Bill contained a provision that subjected the overseas subsidiaries of Australian companies to a general obligation to observe human rights and the principle of non-discrimination.[63] That Bill was never adopted. Similar proposals in the United States and the

---

[60] In this connection, the *UN Norms* state, 'States should establish and reinforce the necessary legal and administrative framework for ensuring that the Norms and other relevant national and international laws are implemented by transnational corporations and other business enterprises': *UN Norms*, Section H, para. 17.

[61] On the United Kingdom, see further www.ethicaltrade.org. For the US and EU position, see M. Trebilcock and R. Howse, *The Regulation of International Trade* (3rd edn, London: Routledge, 2005), pp. 575–6.

[62] See Clapham, *Human Rights Obligations of Non-State Actors*, pp. 197 and 210.

[63] Corporate Code of Conduct Bill 2000: The Parliament of the Commonwealth of Australia draft of 28 August 2000, clause 10.

United Kingdom have also met with little success.[64] On the other hand, at the level of US national law, a degree of direct responsibility for human rights violations on the part of MNEs is being recognised through litigation brought by private claimants against the parent companies of affiliates operating in the claimants' countries under the US Alien Tort Claims Act (ATCA).[65]

Although a finding of direct responsibility on the part of an MNE for human rights violations is as yet unprecedented, there is some support for establishing the indirect responsibility on the part of the state for the conduct of non-state actors that amounts to a violation of the human rights of a third person. Such a responsibility could be established by international convention.[66] No such responsibility has ever been expressly provided for. Instead there is some evidence from the case law under the ECHR that the state may be under an obligation to 'secure' the rights of third persons against interference by a non-state actor. Failure to do so may result in a violation of the Convention.[67] However, this case law is uncertain in its scope and too much cannot be read into it. At most, it is clear that the state cannot absolve itself of its direct human rights responsibilities by hiving them off to a privatised entity.[68]

---

[64] United States: *Corporate Code of Conduct Act* H.R. 4596, 106th Congress (2000), *Corporate Code of Conduct Act* H.R. 2782, 107th Congress (2001); United Kingdom: Corporate Responsibility Bill 2003, available at www.parliament.the-stationery-office.co.uk/pa/cm200102/cmbills/145/2002145.pdf. It should be noted that the UK Bill, introduced as a private members' Bill and not as a governmental initiative, concerns only civil liability and does not create specific human rights obligations on companies.

[65] 28 USC s. 1350. ATCA states: 'The district courts shall have original jurisdiction of any civil action by an alien for a tort only, committed in violation of the law of nations or a treaty of the United States'. For a full discussion, see Joseph, *Corporations and Transnational Litigation*, ch. 2. See too Jägers, *Corporate Human Rights Obligations*, pp. 179–203.

[66] See Kamminga, 'Holding Multinational Corporations Accountable', 559, 569.

[67] See, for example, *Young James and Webster* v. United Kingdom (1981) ECtHR Series A vol. 44; *X and Y* v. *The Netherlands* (1985) ECtHR Series A vol. 91; *Arzte für das Leben* (1988) ECtHR Series A vol. 139. See further Application No. 36022/97 *Hatton and others* v. *United Kingdom* Judgment ECtHR 8 July 2003 (deregulation of night flights at Heathrow Airport did not violate Article 8, right to private and family life) *Hatton* v. *United Kingdom* (2003) 37 EHRR 611, available at cmiskp.echr.coe.int////tkp197/viewhbkm.asp?action=open& table=F69A27FD8FB86142BF01C1166DEA398649&key=11192&sessionId=9966482& skin=hudoc-en&attachment=true; Charles Bourne, 'I'm noisy – fly me', *New Law Journal* 15 (August 2003), 1262. See generally A. Drzemczewski, *European Human Rights Convention in Domestic Law* (Oxford: Oxford University Press, 1983), ch. 8; Clapham, *Human Rights Obligations of Non-State Actors*, pp. 349–420; Jägers, *Corporate Human Rights Obligations*, pp. 36–44 and ch. VI.

[68] *Costello-Roberts* v. *United Kingdom* ECtHR (1993) Series A vol. 247.

Turning to the role of IGOs in monitoring and enforcement, two sets of issues arise.[69] First, what should the legal status of any standard-setting instruments be and, secondly, what kinds of procedures for monitoring and enforcement could be put in place? The discussions over the UN Norms are instructive, as these very questions have had to be faced by the participants. It is clear that the legal status of the UN Norms is yet to be settled and, for the time being, they should be regarded as non-binding.[70] There are arguments in favour of, and against, a binding code.[71] The main advantage of a voluntary instrument is that it could be used in conjunction with existing voluntary corporate codes of conduct to develop a more comprehensive system of internal values to be observed by the company. This would need to be supplemented by an effective system of accountability within the company.[72] However, the discussions on the UN Norms have tended to favour a binding instrument, bearing in mind the past history of non-binding codes, the fact that many non-binding guidelines already exist and also the need for developing practical methods for enforcing human rights standards against TNCs, especially where states might not do so given their need to focus on attracting inward investment.[73] In response, the Introduction to the second draft of the UN Norms (then known as the Draft Guidelines) offers a middle way. It asserts that 'it would be unrealistic to suggest that human rights standards with regard to companies should immediately become the subject of treaty obligations', given that only some of the standards contained in the UN Norms are binding treaty-based norms, and that the precise legal status, in the international legal order, of companies and other non-state

---

[69] See further Kinley and Tadaki, 'From Talk to Walk', 995–1020, covering the possible roles of UN bodies the World Bank and WTO. The IMF is singled out as having suppressed any ability to act as a monitor of TNC human rights practices and as not having the necessary institutional organs to do so: see 996.

[70] But see Weissbrodt and Kruger, 'Norms on the Responsibilities of Transnational Corporations', 913–15, who argue that the UN Norms are 'non-voluntary' and derive a degree of legal authority from the numerous implementation provisions they contain and from the binding sources from which they are derived.

[71] See further *Draft Universal Human Rights Guidelines Introduction*, paras 34–43, on which this discussion draws.

[72] Indeed, a business representative at the 54th Session stressed the need for a voluntary approach and that businesses themselves should develop the draft: Working Group 2002 (see n. 29 above), p. 12, para. 36.

[73] Working Group 2002 (see n. 29 above), p. 9, para. 27, p. 11, paras 32, 35. On the past history of voluntary codes, see P. T. Muchlinski, 'A Brief History of Regulation', in Sol Picciotto and Ruth Mayne (eds.), *Regulating International Business* (London: Macmillan Press/Oxfam, 1999), p. 47.

actors remains uncertain. Indeed, even 'if the Working Group wishes to pursue a legally binding instrument or even a treaty, it would ordinarily start with some form of "soft law" exercise'.[74] This has been the normal pattern of operation in relation to the adoption of other binding human rights instruments.[75] Hence, in the absence of state opinion to the contrary (perhaps an unlikely eventuality),[76] some transition from 'soft' to 'hard' law is more likely to occur, with the Draft Norms being the first step in this process. On the other hand, as David Weissbrodt pointed out at the 54th Session of the UN Sub-Commission on Human Rights, the UN Norms are binding to the extent that they apply human rights law under ratified conventions to activities of TNCs and other business enterprises. Moreover, the language of the document emphasises binding responsibilities through the use of the term 'shall' rather than 'should' and through the inclusion, in more recent drafts, of more comprehensive implementation measures.[77]

Connected with this issue is the question of how to give the UN Norms 'teeth' through effective implementation and monitoring procedures. In this regard, the UN Norms require TNCs and other business enterprises to adopt, disseminate and implement internal rules of operation in compliance with the Norms. In addition, they must incorporate the principles contained in the UN Norms in their contracts or other arrangements and dealings with contractors, subcontractors, suppliers and licensees in order to ensure their implementation and respect.[78] This represents a significant advance on the earlier drafts, which did not contain express provisions on the use of such legal measures to give force to their contents, though such measures were recommended in commentaries on those earlier drafts.[79] The UN Norms also require that TNCs and other business enterprises shall monitor and verify their compliance in an independent and transparent manner that includes input from relevant stakeholders.[80] This may be done by national, international, governmental and/or non-governmental mechanisms in addition to internal review procedures.[81]

---

[74] *Draft Universal Human Rights Guidelines Introduction*, para. 40.
[75] See *ibid.*, paras. 41–3.
[76] However, the UN Millennium Social Forum has indicated its support for a legally binding set of guidelines: UN GAOR, 54th Sess., Agenda Item 49(b), at 11: UN Doc. A/54/959 (2000).
[77] Working Group 2002, p. 6, para. 14, and Weissbrodt and Kruger, 'Norms on the Responsibilities of Transnational Corporations'.
[78] *Draft Norms*, Section H, para. 15.
[79] See UN Doc E/CN.4/Sub.2/2001/WG.2/WP.1/Add.1 (2001), Section H, para. 17, Commentary at (c).
[80] *UN Norms*, Section H, para. 16.　　　[81] *ibid.*

Earlier drafts of the UN Norms focused on corporate implementation. However, the current UN Norms suggest that other actors could use the Norms to assess business practice and performance in the area of human rights responsibilities. For example, they could form the basis of industry monitoring – unions could use them as a benchmark for their expectations of company conduct, as could NGOs – and the UN's human rights treaty bodies could apply the UN Norms to create additional reporting requirements about corporate compliance with this instrument.[82] Furthermore, TNCs must ensure that outside stakeholders have access to information about human rights remediation efforts by firms and that workers have proper avenues by which to make complaints with regard to the violation of the Norms.[83]

In addition, the draft presented to the 54th Session of the UN Sub-Commission on Human Rights in 2002 introduced, for the first time, a provision requiring TNCs and other business enterprises to provide compensation for violations of the UN Norms.[84] The final version reads, 'Transnational corporations and other business enterprises shall provide prompt, effective and adequate reparation to those persons, entities, and communities that have been adversely affected by failures to comply with these Norms through, inter alia, reparations, restitution, compensation and rehabilitation for any damage done or property taken.'[85]

The UN Norms have also introduced some clarification of where such reparation is to be determined. In the words of paragraph 18 of the UN Norms: 'In connection with determining damages, in regard to criminal sanctions, and in all other respects, these Norms shall be applied by national courts and/or international tribunals, pursuant to national and international law.' By taking this approach, the UN Norms envisage a binding enforcement mechanism, centred on national courts and/or international tribunals, which offers directly effective rights of reparation for the individuals or groups affected as a consequence of a violation of the instrument. This pre-supposes a legally binding document that is effective within the national laws of the UN member states that adopt it. Such an effect could not be presumed from a non-binding declaration or recommendation of the United Nations, neither of which normally have the force of positive international law, nor as sources of directly effective individual rights that can be invoked before national tribunals. Arguably, the UN Norms, as an instrument that contains many binding norms of

---

[82] *Commentary on the Norms* (see n. 2 above), Section H, para. 16, comments (a)–(c).
[83] *ibid.*, comments (d)–(e).
[84] See UN Doc. E/CN.4/Sub.2/2002/WG.2/WP.1 29 May 2002, p. 6, para. 17.
[85] *UN Norms*, Section H, para. 18.

international human rights law, may be enforceable by that fact alone. However, as argued above, not all the norms contained in its provisions are uncontroversial in this respect. Some of the rights that are included may not have such a legal status. Therefore, if the reparation mechanism is to be real and effective, it requires the adoption of an instrument that has the force of law within the legal orders of the signatory states, and which recognises the legal effectiveness of all the norms that it contains. This would need to be something akin to an international convention, which contains an obligation to implement its contents and enforcement mechanisms into the municipal law of the signatory state. This is a far cry from a 'soft law' instrument of the kind, as discussed above, usually adopted in this field. Equally, it is unlikely that a UN framework could enforce binding rules and norms relating to the activities of TNCs.[86] In the light of these matters, there is a significant need of further clarification as to what legal form this enforcement mechanism will take and on how it is expected to work. However, given the uncertainty surrounding the status and future importance of the UN Norms in the work of the UN Human Rights Council, which replaced the UN Commission on Human Rights in June 2006, and of the Special Representative appointed to oversee the issue of human rights and TNCs, a clear answer to this question is unlikely in the near future.

A further issue that requires some comment and clarification concerns identifying the precise forum before which any claim for reparations under paragraph 18 can be brought. As it stands, paragraph 18 is silent on this matter. It could, therefore, be presumed that the question of a forum remains to be determined by the national laws of the jurisdiction or jurisdictions in which a claim is brought, or by reference to an international tribunal. If so, then claims brought under the UN Norms may be embroiled in lengthy and unhelpful disputes over jurisdiction, particularly in common law jurisdictions where the doctrine of *forum non conveniens* continues to apply. In such jurisdictions it may be possible for the respondent corporation (particularly if it is an MNE and the *locus* of the alleged violation of the UN Norms is in another jurisdiction) to challenge the appropriateness of the forum chosen by the claimants and, thereby, to gain a procedural advantage either by vacating the case to another forum more sympathetic to the corporation's defence, or simply

---

[86] See Working Group 2002, p. 7, para. 17 (views of Mr Alfonso Martinez, member of the Working Group).

by causing delay while this issue is litigated.[87] In that process the claimants may suffer significant delay in access to justice, not to mention financial loss that might undermine their ability to continue with their claim. Some legal systems are becoming sensitive to such issues[88] but others are not.[89] Thus, the UN Norms may need to establish certain basic rules of jurisdiction so that such legal techniques are not allowed to undermine legitimate claims. One solution would be to make available the jurisdiction of any state that adheres to the UN Norms on the basis of either the locus of the alleged violation or the domicile of the corporation alleged to be responsible, with the claimant having the choice of forum. Equally, it might be necessary to ensure that the corporate (or contractual) separation between affiliates in an MNE group (or network)[90] is not allowed to act as a barrier to jurisdiction against related (or cooperating) entities located outside the jurisdiction where the harm is alleged to have been suffered, but which are seen as complicit in a violation of the UN Norms on the basis of their relationship with the affiliate (or network partner) located in that jurisdiction. This may prove to be rather controversial as it challenges long-accepted notions of separate corporate personality (and, in the case of transnational networks or alliances, freedom of contract) as the basis for attributing liability to legal persons. However, in the absence of some clarification of this matter, national laws may well come to be used to insulate discrete entities involved in an MNE or in a transnational network enterprise, production or retailing chain that leads to a violation of human rights from full responsibility.

[87] See further Peter Muchlinski, 'Corporations in International Litigation: Problems of Jurisdiction and the United Kingdom Asbestos Case', *International and Comparative Law Quarterly* 50 (2001), 1; Michael Anderson, 'Transnational Corporations and Environmental Damage: Is Tort Law the Answer?', *Washburn Law Journal* 41 (2002), 399; Philip Blumberg, 'Asserting Human Rights Against Multinational Corporations Under United States Law: Conceptual and Procedural Problems', *American Journal of Comparative Law* 50 (2002), 493.

[88] See, for example, the House of Lords decision in *Lubbe et al.* v. *Cape plc* [2000] 2 Lloyds Rep 383 [2000] 4 All ER 268.

[89] For a criticism of the US system in this regard, see Blumberg, 'Asserting Human Rights'.

[90] It is necessary to make a distinction between equity-based linkages between affiliates in a corporate group and contractual linkages between cooperating enterprises in a network enterprise or alliance for the purposes of liability, as in the former case the issue of group liability involves the lifting of the corporate veil between the affiliates, whereas in the latter it involves disregarding any contractual warranties or exclusion clauses that seek to limit the liability of some or all of the participating enterprises: see further P. T. Muchlinski, *Multinational Enterprises and the Law* (2nd edn, Oxford: Oxford University Press, 2007), chs. 4 and 8.

The preceding discussion illustrates well the challenges ahead for any IGO that wishes to develop a new social responsibility agenda for MNEs and other business entities. The first point to note is that the process is a slow one and is probably more likely to create 'soft law' obligations. That does not imply that the UN Norms, or any other international CSR instrument, are doomed to complete legal ineffectiveness if they are not legally binding. At the international level, soft law can 'harden' into positive law, where it is seen as evidence of emergent new standards of international law. For these purposes the origin of the legal principle in a soft law instrument, such as a voluntary code of conduct or a non-binding resolution of an international organisation, is of little consequence if a consensus develops that the principle in question should be viewed as an obligatory standard by reason of subsequent practice.[91] Given that many of the most important international expressions of welfare values tend to be in such form,[92] the 'hardening process' may be of especial importance here. Indeed, as the debate over the social content of the unsuccessful Multilateral Agreement on Investment shows, the demand for 'hard law' in this field might be difficult to resist. On the other hand, it should not be forgotten that, even in hard law agreements, provisions concerning controversial social issues have been put into very general, and probably meaningless, hortatory language simply to show that something has been done, but where there is little intention to see these provisions having any real legal effect.[93]

A second significant issue concerns the effect of international instruments at the level of national law. It is arguable that even if the UN Norms were to be adopted as a non-binding voluntary instrument, without direct effect on individual rights under national law, they could conceivably acquire legal force in private law. Private law suits can be brought against any firm or organisation that holds itself out as adopting a voluntary code such as, for example, the UN Norms, by other firms or organisations,

---

[91] See, for example, O. A. Elias and C. L. Lim, *The Paradox of Consensualism in International Law* (The Hague: Kluwer Law International, 1998), pp. 230–2.

[92] *ibid.*

[93] See, for example, the discussion of Article 19 of the Energy Charter Treaty (environmental aspects) by Thomas Waelde in 'Sustainable Development and the 1994 Energy Charter Treaty: Between Pseudo-Action and the Management of Environmental Investment Risk', in F. Weiss, E. Denters and P. de Waart (eds.), *International Economic Law with a Human Face* (The Hague: Kluwer Law International, 1998), pp. 223–70; and see T. Waelde, 'Non-conventional Views on "Effectiveness": The Holy Grail of Modern International Lawyers: The New Paradigm? A Chimera? Or a Brave New World in the Global Economy?', *Austrian Review of International and European Law* 4 (1999), 164.

consumers or other members of the community. Such claims may allege that a failure to comply with the UN Norms, or other international CSR instruments adopted by a company, is evidence that the firm or organisation in question is not meeting standards of conduct that may represent accepted general principles and is, therefore, not exercising reasonable care or due diligence. Moreover, failure to follow the terms of such instruments could be evidence of a breach of contract, where adherence is an express or implied term of the agreement, or of an actionable misrepresentation, as where a firm alleges that its adherence to the instrument in question entitles it to be regarded as qualifying for a governmental standard-setting mark of approval, but where in fact it fails to meet these standards. In such cases, consumers can bring an action if they claim to have been attracted to purchasing the firm's products or services in the light of such assertions of good conduct. Also, the relevant government agency might bring an action for abuse of its certification scheme.[94]

Therefore, to dismiss voluntary sources of international or national CSR standards as irrelevant seems to fail to appreciate how formal rules and principles of law emerge. The very fact that an increasing number of non-binding codes are being drafted and adopted in this area suggests a growing interest among important groups and organisations – corporations, industry associations, NGOs, governments and IGOs – and is leading to the establishment of a rich set of sources from which new binding standards can emerge. Indeed, it is noteworthy that the UN Norms make use of already existing standards produced by other IGOs. In this a kind of 'collective law of IGOs' seems to be developing, in which various organisations working in the field of CSR cross-fertilise each other's initiatives by reference to one another's instruments.

No doubt this process can be, and is being, criticised as one in which corporate interests are trying to capture the agenda through code-making and lobbying before international fora and organisations. It is fair to say that non-business NGOs are attempting the same with their codes. The real issue is when and how will all this 'codification' turn into detailed legal standards that can act as fully binding benchmarks for the control of unacceptable lapses in corporate conduct at the international and national levels. That is, of course, an issue of ideological contest, but one which seems to be veering slowly towards an acceptance of some kind of

---

[94] See Government of Canada, *Voluntary Codes: A Guide for their Development and Use* (Ottawa: Government of Canada, 1998), p. 27; Kernaghan Webb, 'Voluntary Initiatives and the Law', in R. Gibson (ed.), *Voluntary Initiatives: The New Politics of Corporate Greening* (Peterborough, Ontario: Broadview Press, 1999), pp. 32–50.

articulated set of minimum international standards for CSR, as a trade-off for greater corporate freedom in the market. That said, the Special Representative of the Secretary-General on the Issue of Human Rights and Transnational Corporations, John Ruggie, believes that the debate over the UN Norms has been divisive and misleading. In particular he asserts that the imposition of binding obligations by international law on private non-state actors is not possible, as corporations are not subjects of international law, and that, more generally, 'the divisive debate over the Norms obscures rather than illuminates promising areas of consensus and cooperation among business, civil society, governments, and international institutions with respect to human rights.'[95] In this light, the future adoption of the UN Norms by the United Nations itself remains unlikely. However, they remain as a model for debate and in this capacity they already posess persuasive force.

---

[95] See John Ruggie, *Interim Report of the Special Representative of the Secretary-General on the Issue of Human Rights and Transnational Corporations and Other Business Enterprises*, UN Doc. E/CN.4/2006/97 (2006) at www1.umn.edu/humanrts/business/RuggieReport2006.html at paras. 60–5 and 69.

15

'The Norms are dead! Long live the Norms!' The politics behind the UN Human Rights Norms for corporations

DAVID KINLEY, JUSTINE NOLAN AND NATALIE ZERIAL

The heated debate surrounding the content and very existence of the United Nations Norms on the Responsibilities of Transnational Corporations and Other Business Enterprises with Regard to Human Rights[1] (the 'Norms') epitomises the increasingly pervasive influence of non-state actors in the international arena. Beyond the usual friction between northern and southern states, a diverse group of non-government organisations (NGOs), business groups, academics, lawyers and corporations each contributed to the vehement dialogue about the Norms,[2] which the Secretary General's Special Representative on Business and Human Rights (SRSG) has subsequently described as a 'train wreck'.[3] The unfortunate consequence of this furore is that the SRSG has now declared that the Norms are dead,[4] but not the issues that gave rise to their birth.

The putative demise of the Norms was clearly not the fate that their makers' intended. However, this chapter argues that, far from being a

---

The slightly different clarion call, 'The Norms are dead! Long live their Principles!', was suggested by Geoffery Chandler as the banner under which the quest for corporate accountability for international human rights abuses ought now be pursued; in correspondence, April 2006.

[1] 2003, E.CN.4/Sub.2/2003/12/Rev.2, available at www1.umn.edu/humanrts/links/norms-Aug2003.html ('Norms').

[2] The Business and Human Rights Resource Centre, an independent not-for-profit organisation, has catalogued the contributions to the Norms debate on their excellent website. Both sides of the debate are equally covered. See www.business-humanrights.org/Gettingstarted/UnitedNationsNorms.

[3] John Ruggie, remarks delivered at a forum on corporate social responsibility co-sponsored by the Fair Labor Association and the German Network of Business Ethics, Bamburg, Germany, 14 June 2006, at www.reports-and-materials.org/Ruggie-remarks-to-Fair-Labor-Association-and-German-Network-of-Business-Ethics-14-June- 2006.pdf.

[4] *ibid.*

failure, the Norms have been a beneficial and fruitful initiative, reinvigorating debate on the issue of business and human rights, raising new and important concepts regarding regulation of transnational corporations (TNCs) and enforcement of human rights obligations, and articulating a core set of standards for going forward. Before the emergence of the Norms in 2003, the focus of many stakeholders in the corporate social responsibility (CSR) arena seemed stalled and largely focused on the pros and cons of establishing and monitoring codes of conduct. A 'bottom-up' incremental approach to accountability was being pushed often simply at the level of what can and should be done by individual companies. The introduction of the Norms signalled a 'top-down' approach from the United Nations that gave hope to many human rights activists that UN involvement could quicken the pace of human rights protection, while simultaneously provoking concern from some business representatives and from states who did not welcome UN intrusion into the debate. The Norms provoked diverse reactions from the various stakeholders in the CSR community and this chapter aims to map the complex topography of the surrounding debate, including the political and commercial interests that have shaped the landscape and allegedly 'poisoned the water'.[5] While the SRSG may have declaimed on the expiration of the Norms, the debate about human rights standards for corporations is now well and truly alive. From the point of view of the legal development of CSR, the Norms are likely to have an ongoing influence on the direction of future initiatives and dialogue.

I. The development and status of the Norms

The draft status of the Norms has not mitigated the debate over their content, form and aims. The Norms, avowedly still in draft form, were at a very preliminary stage of their life when the furore over them took off around August 2003. The UN sessional working group on multinational corporations, which was responsible for the Norms' development, was only formed in 1998; the decision to develop a code of conduct for TNCs was made in 1999 and the first draft of the Norms appeared in 2000.[6]

---

[5] Robin Aram quoted in SustainAbility, 'In the Hot Seat: Robin Aram, Vice President of External Relations, Policy and Social Responsibility, Shell', 24 February 2005, available at www.sustainability.com/network/business-leader.asp?id = 219.

[6] Human Rights Principles and Responsibilities for Transnational Corporations and Other Business Enterprises, UN Doc, 2000 E/CN.4/Sub.2/2000/WG.2/WP.1. It should be noted that the Norms are not the United Nations' first attempt to engage with the problem of

The din of debate over the Norms got progressively louder once the Sub-Commission on the Promotion and Protection of Human Rights unanimously adopted the draft Norms in August 2003,[7] and continued apace throughout the period leading up to the first consideration of the Norms by the UN Commission on Human Rights (CHR) at their sixtieth session in April 2004. No doubt due to a combination of public and behind-the-scenes lobbying by pro- and anti-Norms groups, the CHR's approach to the Norms has been characterised by prudence, generally encouraging further consultation and analysis. At its sixtieth session, it requested the Office of the High Commissioner of Human Rights (OHCHR) to consult with all the relevant stakeholders, and to compile a report analysing the Norms in light of the various existing initiatives and standards on business and human rights.[8] When debate continued after this OHCHR report was published in February 2005,[9] the CHR requested at its sixty-first session that the UN Secretary-General appoint a Special Representative on the issue of human rights and business (SRSG).[10]

Professor John Ruggie of the Kennedy School of Government at Harvard University was appointed to this position in 2005,[11] and he has since continued the extensive consultation process begun by the OHCHR.[12] He

---

human rights and TNCs. The Centre on Transnational Corporations was established by the United Nations in 1975, and by 1977 it was coordinating negotiation of a voluntary *Draft Code of Conduct on Transnational Corporations*. However, no final agreement was concluded; see Jem Blendell, *Barricades and Boardrooms: A Contemporary History of the Corporate Accountability Movement*, Paper No. 13, United Nations Research Institute for Social Development Programme on Technology, Business and Society (2004), p. 11.

[7] Sub-Com. Res. 2003/16, 'Responsibilities of Transnational Corporations and Other Business Enterprises With Regard to Human Rights', 13 August 2003, in Report of the Sub-Commission on the Promotion and Protection of Human Rights on its Fifty-Fifth Session, 20 October 2003, E/CN.4/Sub.2/2003/43 at 51–53.

[8] UNCHR Dec. 2004/116, 'Responsibilities of Transnational Corporations and Related Business Enterprises with Regard to Human Rights', 20 April 2004, E/CN.4/Dec/2004/116.

[9] 'Report of the United Nations High Commissioner on Human Rights on the Responsibilities of Transnational Corporations and Related Business Enterprises with Regard to Human Rights', 15 February 2005, E/CN.4/2005/91.

[10] UNCHR Res. 2005/69 'Human Rights and Transnational Corporations and Other Business Enterprises', 20 April 2005, E/CN.4/RES/2005/69.

[11] 'Secretary-General Appoints John Ruggie of United States Special Representative on Issue of Human Rights, Transnational Corporations, Other Business Enterprises', 28 July 2005, UN Doc SGA/A/934 www.un.org/News/Press/docs/2005/sga934.doc.htm.

[12] The SRSG, in collaboration with the Business and Human Rights Resource Centre, is maintaining a website where he posts relevant materials on his mandate and the consultation process; see www.business-humanrights.org/Gettingstarted/UNSpecial Representative.

published an Interim Report in 2006,[13] and, at the time of writing, was preparing for his final report, which is to be delivered in mid-2007.[14] The SRSG's interim report, apart from indicating dissatisfaction with the form and reach of the Norms, reflected Ruggie's desire to accommodate both sides of the debate. Admittedly the report, and his surrounding commentary, has been patently critical of some aspects of the Norms, viewing the initiative as 'engulfed by its own doctrinal excesses' and creating 'confusion and doubt' through 'exaggerated legal claims and conceptual ambiguities'.[15] However, Ruggie has acknowledged the usefulness of some of the substance of the Norms, particularly the summary of rights that may be affected by business.[16] No matter what is said about the unsustainable status of the Norms in their present form, it should and will not relegate their substantive content and the debate that has surrounded them to history; these elements will inevitably continue to mark out the contours of deliberations in the area for some time to come. The SRSG's consultation process, while attempting to reconcile both sides of the debate, has already exposed the persistent conflicting reactions to the process of the Norms' creations, and to its form, content and aims.

II. The reaction to the Norms: stepping into the corporate social responsibility debate

CSR itself, particularly the place of human rights in CSR, is already contentious ground. One of the reasons the Norms have engendered such controversy, therefore, is that they have stepped into the middle of this debate, not only by crystallising the connection between human rights and CSR, but by positing a system whereby international law responds directly and forcefully to corporate action that violates such rights. It is thus not surprising that much of the critical commentary on the Norms corresponds with the many of the concerns frequently voiced in respect of other CSR matters, such as the perceived problems that might flow from

[13] Interim Report of the Secretary-General's Special Representative on the Issue of Human Rights and Transnational Corporations and Other Business Enterprises, 22 February 2006, E/CN.4/2006/97.

[14] The SRSG has already noted the 'existing time and resource constraints' (Interim Report, para. 6) which will inevitably limit the scope of his final report; however, there is a strong probability that his mandate will be extended in line with UN practice.

[15] ibid., para. 59.

[16] ibid., paras 57–8. See further, his reiteration of these points in his Opening Statement to the UN Human Rights Council, 25 September 2006, pp. 2 and 4, available at www.reports-and-materials.org/Ruggie-statement-to-UN-Human-Rights-Council-25-Sep-2006.pdf.

soft laws made hard, and from the alleged inappropriateness of placing human rights obligations on corporations.[17]

CSR in its present state is an exceptionally broad-reaching and varied melange of soft and hard law, encompassing subjects as diverse as the environmental and fiscal responsibilities of corporations, as well as occupational health and safety, labour rights and, most importantly for our discussion, human rights obligations. The legal aspects of CSR generally have been promoted through national initiatives,[18] although legal, quasi-legal and political initiatives[19] have proliferated at the international level. To a certain extent, and much to the consternation of their detractors, the Norms were an attempt to remedy this piecemeal approach to CSR by uniting these obligations in one document.[20] For instance, the Norms took a broad-brush approach to defining 'human rights', including, *inter alia*, environmental obligations, consumer protection and labour rights among their provisions. They also sought to conjoin the national and international levels of CSR: while maintaining that states have the primary responsibility for ensuring that business respects human rights,[21] the Norms placed state responsibility in an international framework, articulating global standards for corporate behaviour and recognising that any effective CSR regime in the current global environment required amalgamating states' responsibilities with direct regulation of corporate action.

The Norms were thus an innovative response to at least some of the established problems with CSR. In this context the intensity of the debate is hardly surprising – companies and business organisations were already conversant in CSR and were furthermore mobilised to engage with and

---

[17] For such arguments and their rebuttal, see Parker, in this volume, Chapter 7.

[18] Corporate Code of Conduct Bill 2000 (Australia); Corporate Responsibility Bill 2003 (UK); and Corporate Code of Conduct Bill 2000 (US). See also nn. 65 and 66 below.

[19] For example, see the UN Global Compact (www.unglobalcompact.org); the Organisation for Economic Co-operation and Development Guidelines for Multinational Enterprises, 27 July 2000; and the International Labour Organisation's Tripartite Declaration on Fundamental Principles and Rights at Work (1998).

[20] International Organisation of Employers and International Chamber of Commerce: 'Joint views of the IOE and ICC on the draft "Norms on the responsibilities of transnational corporations and other business enterprises with regard to human rights"': The Sub-Commission's draft norms, if put into effect, will undermine human rights, the business sector of society, and the right to development: The Commission on Human Rights Needs to End the Confusions Caused by the Draft Norms by Setting the Record Straight', March 2004, available at www.reports-and-materials.org/IOE-ICC-views-UN-norms-March-2004.doc, pp. 24–5.

[21] See Article 1.

lobby on it. The Norms had the disadvantage of being frighteningly new on a playing field that was already dominated by experienced, well-funded and often antagonistic players.

III. Two sides (or more) to every debate

At the outset of this discussion, it is worth noting certain key features of the debate about the Norms. The first point is that the debate, which has involved a large but predictable variety of players – human rights and labour NGOs, trade unions, corporations, national and international business organisations, lawyers, and academics from multiple disciplines – has not split along obvious factional lines. While the players have been unsurprising, the sides they have taken have at times defied expectations. For instance, a number of corporations and businesses, most notably those involved in the Business Leaders Initiative on Human Rights (BLIHR), have actively supported the Norms,[22] while a number of international law academics have expressed concerns about the form and content of the Norms, and some human rights organisations, such as Amnesty International, while stressing the valuable contribution that the Norms have made, have accepted that their current format constitutes merely a basis for going forward rather than a blueprint.[23]

The second point is that the polarisation of the debate into two camps – those for the Norms and those against the Norms – is not only a largely artificial division, but has contributed to the present impasse. The Norms are explicitly in draft form, and were brought before the international community with the intention that they would be the subject of amendment, debate and reform.[24] However, instead of looking to how the Norms could be changed to accommodate different views, the polarised debate has prematurely translated a draft document into a static and immutable one, which must be accepted or rejected as a whole. This has split the

---

[22] See www.blihr.org/. The thirteen participating companies are ABB Ltd, Alcan Inc., AREVA, Barclays plc, Gap Inc, Hewlett Packard Co., MTV Europe Networks, National Grid plc, Novartis Foundation for Sustainable Development, Novo Nordisk A/S, Statoil ASA, Ericsson, General Electric and the Body Shop International plc.

[23] See letter from Irene Khan, Secretary-General, Amnesty International to John Ruggie Special Representative on Human Rights and Transnational, 27 April 2006, available at web.amnesty.org/library/index/engior500022006.

[24] The Commission on Human Rights expressly recognised their status as such: see Commission on Human Rights, Agenda Item 16, UN Doc. E/CN.4/2004/L.73/Rev.1 (2004). For discussion, see J. Nolan, 'With Power comes Responsibility: Human Rights and Corporate Accountability', *University of New South Wales Law Journal* 28, 3 (2005) 581, at 604–5.

proponents of the Norms between those who can envisage substantive changes to the Norms that will still achieve the aims of human rights regulation of business, and those who believe that Norms need to be preserved wholly or largely in their present form. The polarisation has also allowed those companies who dislike the Norms – for the simple self-serving reason that they wish to avoid their human rights obligations – to hide behind the more eloquent and often cogent arguments of those who oppose the Norms for particular formal or practical reasons. Companies can thus conveniently denigrate the Norms without hurting their corporate image.[25]

IV. Critical responses to the Norms

The arguments for and against the Norms have been discussed in greater depth elsewhere.[26] This chapter is concerned less with the merits of these arguments than with asking who is voicing the various objections to the Norms, and why. In particular, the following discussion tries to expose how the two issues discussed above – the players and the artificial polarisation – have impacted on the various criticisms levelled at the Norms.

The challenges to the Norms have been underlined by criticism of the process of their creation. Primarily, states, corporations and business groups have complained about the failure of the Sub-Commission and the Working Group to engage in sufficient consultation.[27] However, the accuracy of this criticism has been disputed.[28] Multi-stakeholder consultations were conducted,[29] and included, among others, the International Business Leaders Forum and the World Business Council for Sustainable Development.[30] According to one commentator, the responsibility for any

---

[25] See claims made about Shell and Robin Aram (Shell's Vice-President of External Relations and Policy Development) in this regard: 'Shell Leads International Business Campaign Against UN Human Rights Norms', Corporate Europe Observatory, *CEO Info Brief*, March 2004, available at www.corporateeurope.org/norms.html.

[26] David Kinley and Rachel Chambers, 'The UN Human Rights Norms for Corporations: The Private Implications of Public International Law', *Human Rights Law Review* 6, 3 (2006), 18–35; and Nolan, 'With Power comes Responsibility', 584–605; and Mushlinki, in this volume, Chapter 14.

[27] IOE–ICC, 'Joint views of the IOE and ICC' pp. 18–19, 29. See Kinley and Chambers, 'The UN Human Rights Norms for Corporations'.

[28] Corporate Europe Observatory (n. 25 above).

[29] David Weissbrodt and Muria Kruger, 'Norms on the Responsibilities of Transnational Corporations and Other Business Enterprises with Regard to Human Rights', *American Journal of International Law* 97 (2003), 901, 904–5.

[30] Corporate Europe Observatory (n. 25 above).

feelings of disenfranchisement lies directly with the business groups themselves who 'instead of communicating their views directly to the working group [chose] back-channel lobbying against the Norms'.[31] Similarly, a number of states indicated their displeasure at their lack of involvement in the Norms' development, which they in part indicated in the 2004 CHR resolution, when they declared that the Norms had not been created at their instigation.[32] This is despite the fact that, as the delegate for Cuba highlighted, 'studies did not always have to have been requested in advance by the Commission'.[33] The SRSG's conspicuous and wide-ranging programme of consultation has been a more or less successful attempt to remove any grounds for such accusations in respect of future initiatives. Given that the CSR community involves a very broad range of stakeholders, to move beyond the impasse of the Norms and achieve real prospects for progress in the protection of human rights in the business arena, all voices must be heard. While trade unions and NGOs often claim the moral ground of speaking for workers, companies too must be involved and empowered in the development of CSR.[34] However, calls for further engagement should not be used as a delaying tactic or simply because some players are unhappy with the shape the debate is taking. Notably, in this respect the International Chamber of Commerce on the one hand had called for a 'more systematic' consultation process,[35] while on the other commenting to the SRSG that it had decided to drop out of negotiations on the basis that 'the topic of discussion became the shape of the table in the tribunal chamber where companies would be tried'.[36] Good faith consultation is necessary and beneficial; but participation cannot be predicated on any particular stakeholder getting their own way.

In relation to the Norms themselves, their most polarising feature is their apparent attempt to impose obligations directly on companies, in addition to parallel obligations on states. This sought to address one of

---

[31] *ibid.*   [32] CHR 2004 Resolution, Agenda Item 16, para. (c).

[33] E/CN.4/2004/SR.56, 26 April 2004, 60th Session, 56th Meeting, 20 April 2004, at 10 a.m., para 155.

[34] See the International Chamber of Commerce's stakeholder submission, p. 6; their definition of 'consultation' is a process 'which is based on open discussion without pressure, among a group of equals, feedback and joint reflection, and some effort to arrive at joint conclusions'.

[35] International Chamber of Commerce stakeholder submission to the OHCHR: letter from Maria Livanos Cattaui, International Chamber of Commerce, to Dzidek Kedzia, OHCHR, dated 7 September 2004, pp. 5–6, at www.ohchr.org/english/issues/globalization/business/docs/intchamber.pdf.

[36] Ruggie address to FLA, Bamburg, Germany, 14 June 2006 (n. 3 above).

the most significant barriers to regulating TNCs: the fact that, due to their transnational nature, they often operate in a legal vacuum, particularly in states that are themselves human rights violators or which are too weak to prevent or remedy violations. Directly binding TNCs through international law could be one way of overcoming this problem, but it is an unorthodox step, and is exaggeratedly portrayed by the Norms' detractors as turning international law on its head.[37] The unfavourable reactions to these perceived legal implications of the Norms range across quizzical academic commentary,[38] through states' scepticism,[39] to outright corporate hostility.[40] On the other hand, for many human rights NGOs, this kind of legal progressivism is essential to achieving change in corporate human rights behaviour. The debate over this particular aspect of the Norms reflects the broad debate in CSR about the appropriate response of international law to corporate misbehaviour. Minimalists argue that international law is not the appropriate method of dealing with corporations – beyond, that is, the limited scope of soft international law initiatives, such as the United Nations' Global Compact, which are voluntary and exhortatory rather than legally binding[41] – while maximalists argue that international law can and should be used to bind corporations, and even lobby for an instrument analogous to the Rome Statute of the International Criminal Court, that might impose international law directly

---

[37] See Kinley and Chambers, 'The UN Human Rights Norms for Corporations', 35–40. Such portrayal is exaggerated, at least in the sense that since the Nuremberg Trials international law has taken note of, and imposed obligations upon, individuals and other non-state entities; on which history, see Andrew Clapham, *Human Rights Obligations of Non-State Actors* (Oxford: Oxford University Press, 2006), pp. 59–83. The direct imposition of obligations on non-state entities by international law is perhaps most clearly illustrated today by the Statute of the International Criminal Court 1998, Article 25, of which sets out the conditions under which individual criminal liability for war crimes and crimes against humanity are to be established. In respect of the less conspicuous (but extant) instances of international law binding corporations, see discussion in Kinley and Tadaki, 'From Talk to Walk: The Emergence of Human Rights Responsibilities for Corporations at International Law', *Virginia Journal of International Law* 44 (2004), 931, at 993–4.

[38] For example, Upendra Baxi, 'Market Fundamentalisms: Business Ethics at the Altar of Human Rights', *Human Rights Law Review* 5 (2005), 1.

[39] See Kinley and Chambers, 'The UN Human Rights Norms for Corporations', at n. 72 and accompanying text.

[40] See nn. 46 and 47 below.

[41] www.unglobalcompact.org/. See also J. Nolan, 'The United Nations' Compact with Business: Hindering or Helping the Protection of Human Rights?' *University of Queensland Law Journal* 24, 2 (2005), 445; and S. Deva, 'The Global Compact For Responsible Corporate Citizenship: Is It Still Too Compact To Be Global?', paper presented at the 3rd ASLI Conference on The Development of Law in Asia: Convergence versus Divergence, Shanghai, 25–26 May 2006.

on corporations through an international adjudicative body.[42] More than any other subject, this controversy has prevented the Norms from going forward, mainly because it is not a problem of drafting, but concerns the fundamental mechanism and design of any standards seeking to regulate corporate action that violates human rights.

Part of the perceived problem with imposing international legal obligations directly on corporations has been that it 'privatises human rights'.[43] Under the extreme version of this argument, the Norms are accused of absolving states of their international human rights law responsibilities by placing obligations on institutions that are neither democratically elected nor qualified to make the sorts of difficult decisions regarding human rights that are required by international law. Human rights obligations can be interpreted as involving qualitative assessments of what might constitute compliance, and is thus arguably distinguishable from the occupational health and safety, financial reporting, environmental and other obligations that domestic laws increasingly impose on corporations. However, it appears more likely that it is the twin costs of compliance, and (the potentially even higher costs of) non-compliance with such obligations which constitute the prime motivating factors spurring on corporate objections to such legal obligations.

A closely related controversy concerns the intended legal status of the Norms. In contrast to the voluntary and generally aspirational format of existing international instruments and codes on TNCs, the Norms seek ultimately to impose binding legal obligations on states and on corporations, and suggest the possible use of international as well as national courts and tribunals to uphold the Norms' principles and impose damages on recalcitrant corporations.[44] The explanations for opposition to the legal character of the Norms have included both specific arguments that it upsets the legal order,[45] as well as more whimsical or rhetorical objections, such as the claim that there are too many 'whereases' in the

---

[42] The ICC currently has jurisdiction over genocide, war crimes and crimes against humanity with respect to individuals only, but that includes individuals acting in their capacities as directors, employees or agents of corporations; see further, n. 63 below; and also Nolan, 'The United Nations' Compact with Business', 450–1.

[43] IOE-ICC, 'Joint views of the IOE and ICC', p. 1.   [44] Norms, Article 18.

[45] Mendelson , 'In the Matter of the Draft "Norms on the Responsibilities of Transnational Corporations and other Business Enterprises with Regard to Human Rights": Opinion of Professor Emeritus Maurice Mendelson QC', 4 April 2004, at para. 29, available as 'Report I' to CBI's stakeholder submission to the Report of the High Commissioner for Human Rights, at www.ohchr.org/english/issues/globalization/ business/contributions.htm.

text of the Norms for businesses to be comfortable.[46] In fact, there is not a single 'whereas' in the Norms. Instead, there are many instances of a more admonitory and a far more discomforting legal word for businesses interesting in escaping concrete responsibilities: 'shall'. The professed disdain for legalese seems to be a façade behind which some businesses are hiding their fear of being exposed to new and relatively unprecedented avenues of legal liability. This concern of the corporate lobby is perhaps well founded. The cases brought under the United States' Alien Torts Claims Act (ATCA) have already demonstrated that human rights can be costly for corporations.[47] Yet the practicality of such an objection, let alone its morality, is questionable. A fear of unmeritorious claims is forgivable, albeit one that should be viewed critically in light of the cost of litigation and other factors. However, to the extent that corporations are seeking to prevent genuine claims of abuse by appealing to a need to maintain the current legal status quo, they are engaging in the type of corporate self-interest and protectionism that has led to the often bad human rights reputation of business worldwide.

A final objection to note is the evident distrust of the language of 'sphere of influence' and 'complicity' as used in the Norms. Related to the anxiety over legalese – especially international legalese – some corporations and their legal advisers have railed against the vagueness of certain terms and provisions in the Norms.[48] One critic has even suggested that a corporation that pays tax to a government 'suspected of past or, possibly, future human rights abuses' might thereby be considered 'complicit' in human rights violations under the Norms.[49] In large measure, this type of reaction to the terminology used in the Norms is the clearest example of the degree of the scare factor behind the corporate campaign to kill off the Norms. It is widely acknowledged, even by the Norms' supporters,

---

[46] As reported of Shell's Robin Aram, see Corporate Europe Observatory (n. 25 above).

[47] See generally, S. Joseph, *Corporations and Transnational Human Rights Litigation* (Oxford: Hart Publishing, 2004). No case has yet gone through to judgment under ATCA but costs are still incurred, both in defending the allegation and in several cases paid through out of court settlements, for example; see Rachel Chambers, 'The Unocal Settlement: Implications for the Developing Law on Corporate Complicity in Human Rights Abuses', *Human Rights Brief* 13 (2005), 14.

[48] IOE–ICC, 'Joint views of the IOE and ICC', which argued that the draft Norms are 'extraordinarily vague' and as such, actions taken to enforce the Norms 'will result in widespread arbitrariness – violating the interests and rights of business' (p. 3); see also Mendelson, 'In the Matter of the Draft Norms', p. 9.

[49] Statement by Timothy E. Deal, Senior Vice President, Washington, United States Council for International Business, to the Fund for Peace, Human Rights and Business Roundtable, Washington, DC, 6 February 2004, at www.uscib.org/index.asp?documentID=2823.

that these terms do indeed need further definition, and that the process of refining their meaning should draw on well-established concepts in tort, criminal law or even contract law, building on tests such as those for causation and duty of care.

In fact, this process has already begun. Defining the scope of a company's 'sphere of influence' and clarifying the limitations on corporate complicity in human rights violations is a specific part of the SRSG's mandate. Further, the companies involved in the BLIHR have also taken up the gauntlet in a very practical manner to delimit what conduct such terms might incorporate.[50] The question of who or what falls within the sphere of activity and influence of a corporation – that is, especially to which stakeholders the obligations to protect, promote, respect and secure the fulfilment of human rights are owed – will likely not turn on legal principles alone. The same can be said of determining the limits of corporate complicity.[51] But these are issues where debate and practical experience is essential in clarifying the terms and setting limits on liability. Calling for the outright rejection of the Norms because of lack of precision in the terms it uses is an extreme reaction – especially in light of their current draft status, which is precisely disposed to ironing out through debate and discussion just such textual difficulties. Concurrently, much of the NGO support for the Norms overlooks the need for further clarification in these areas. For the debate to move forward, the shortcomings of the language used and the need for rearticulating certain principles has to be both acknowledged and addressed.

V. Constructive responses to the Norms

Having painted a rather bleak picture of the Norms' reception, we now turn to the more enthusiastic and constructive responses to the Norms and their aims. As a matter of fact, the strong opposition to the Norms has been matched by an equally robust, and at times equally single-minded, movement in support of them. There can be no doubt that the more fundamentalist Norms' supporters have, like the Norms' fundamentalist detractors, exacerbated conflict over the Norms. While the Norms' creators were modest about the legal status of the initiative, some NGOs incorrectly trumpeted the Norms as a codification of customary international law.[52]

---

[50] See nn. 53–55 below.
[51] In this respect, see the work of the International Commission of Jurists, at n. 56 below.
[52] See Summary Report of CHR meeting 2004 on Agenda Item 16.

They have also vociferously advocated that part of the initiative that suggests the direct imposition of obligations on corporations, despite the practical difficulties of achieving consensus on this issue and the equally important problems of implementation.

Some of the most constructive approaches to the Norms have come from a small but influencial part of the corporate sector itself, which, although not providing uncritical support for the initiative, has tried to build on the substance of the Norms in order to formulate best practice regulation of corporate behaviour in relation to human rights. Specifically, this has been the approach of BLIHR, which consists of a growing number of companies that have sought to demonstrate and develop the Norms' potential by 'road-testing' them in the context of their existing business operations.[53] BLIHR has now produced three reports documenting their approach and the lessons they have learnt throughout this process. Apart from showing the possibility of engagement with, in contrast to opposition to, human rights by business,[54] the group has also shown that some of the most controversial features of the Norms are much less confronting than the bulk of the corporate lobby has suggested. An excellent example of this is the work that the BLIHR companies have done on refining the concepts of 'sphere of influence' and 'complicity' in the practical setting of everyday commercial activity.[55]

Another worthwhile response to the Norms has been from a number of international lawyers and academics who have sought to use this process to develop the international legal aspect of CSR. Here notably, the International Commission of Jurists (ICJ) has begun work on defining the legal aspects of corporate complicity and human rights with direct reference to the Norms and the debate the Norms have engendered.[56] The ICJ initiative has kick-started a lively and constructive legal debate about the way international law should address corporate crime, and the SRSG has expressly indicated he will keep a keen eye on these discussions, from which he will certainly gain.[57] CSR can only benefit from fuller engagement with

---

[53] Originally ten companies, there are now thirteen participating companies (see list in n. 22 above).

[54] Business Leaders Initiative on Human Rights, *Report 3: Towards a Common Framework on Business and Human Rights: Identifying Components* (June 2006), p. 1.

[55] *ibid.*, pp. 9–11.

[56] See www.icj.org/news.php3?id_article=3961&lang=en.

[57] See Mallen Baker, 'Mapping the Way Ahead for Business and Human Rights', *Business Respect* 90 (12 March 2006), at www.mallenbaker.net/csr/CSRfiles/page.php?Story_ID=1554.

the academic and legal community on the difficult issues that arise in attempts at regulation.

VI. Moving past the politics? Ruggie's response

As SRSG, Professor John Ruggie has tried to move past the 'divisive debate over the Norms' and to reconcile the pro- and anti-Norms lobbyists by illuminating what unites rather than what divides the two camps.[58] In order to achieve this aim, he has declared that the manner in which the Norms are framed must be abandoned, but has confirmed that their substance may be resurrected in a new and less controversial format.[59] This could be done in part by choosing to focus on further clarifying the rights relevant to business and by setting limits on their applicability by defining what falls within a corporation's sphere of influence, while leaving actual implementation and enforcement to national law mechanisms. This will not satisfy all parties but would be a beneficial, if incremental, step toward refining the legal aspects of CSR. Of more interest in the present context is how Professor Ruggie has responded to the Norms' reception, and his vision for moving forward.

Professor Ruggie is a political scientist rather than a lawyer, and he has approached his mandate with the goal of engaging with the politics surrounding the initiative, rather than ignoring or trying to escape it. This has its benefits and disadvantages. The political response to the Norms has been characterised by inappropriate and unfortunate division and confrontation, with extreme views being expressed by both sides. While disengagement with any stakeholder is not a viable option, international law, particularly international human rights law, cannot simply be subordinated to political engagement. Ultimately the purpose of any human rights initiative for business is not to placate or stifle business but to ensure that human rights are protected, respected and upheld as part of good business practice. Complaints and concerns from the corporate sector must be acknowledged, but should also be viewed in their proper context. Formal human rights standards will inevitably place some burden on business. However, as BLIHR has shown, the size of that burden need not be excessive and, if business chooses, they can embrace such an initiative and the supplementary benefits of clearer and universal standards as well as the benefits of human rights compliance for their corporate culture and image. However, at the same time the socio/political reality of the context in which greater corporate accountability is being sought

[58] Interim Report of the SRSG, para. 69.   [59] Hence, the choice of title for this chapter.

must be acknowledged. Incremental steps that clarify the circumstances under which corporations can and do have human rights responsibilities are positive but should not be the final step.

The SRSG shares the traditional view that the best way to regulate corporations is via state responsibility, although he has also recognised that states are not always willing or capable of implementing human rights regulations. That said, his primary engagement with this problem has thus far focused on discussion of 'weak governance zones',[60] and his vicarious concern with corporate complicity in states' human rights abuses.[61] He has yet to address the far more controversial issue that all states can fail in terms of corporate human rights regulations, and that developed states can be – and have been – party to corporate human rights abuses.[62] Reconciling the traditional academic view of international law with the real human rights failings of all states is one of the SRSG's most difficult tasks. From a purely theoretical point of view, the maximalists are undeniably correct about the capacity of international law to speak directly to corporations, if and when states consent to do so. A corporate equivalent of the International Criminal Court is not only possible, it has already been mooted, albeit unsuccessfully to date,[63] and, as Ruggie points out, 'there are no inherent conceptual barriers to States deciding to hold corporations directly responsible [for violations of international law] . . . by establishing some form of international jurisdiction'.[64] Indeed, the objections to the legal aspects of the Norms do not dispute the possibility of international law binding corporations, although they are careful to mount the argument that no such international legal apparatus exists at the moment – rather they dispute the practicality of trying, first, to obtain consent from states for such an instrument, and, second, to implement such a system.

The SRSG's conclusions on enforcement mechanisms are also of interest. Thus far, he seems to be keen on formulating universal and consensual human rights standards rather than creating enforcement mechanisms. This is certainly helpful in avoiding going over the same contested ground

---

[60] Interim Report of the SRSG, paras. 27, 30 and 75.

[61] See nn. 56 and 57 above.

[62] Complaint to the Australian National Contact Point, regarding allegations of human rights abuses in immigration detention centres run by a private security firm – namely, Global Solutions Ltd. See further www.bsl.org.au/pdfs/FinalStatement_GSL_Australia.pdf.

[63] A proposal by France that the Rome Statute include a provision that extended criminal liability beyond individuals to include legal persons such as corporations was never adopted. See 'Developments – International Criminal Law', *Harvard Law Review* 114 (2001), 1943, 2031–2.

[64] Interim Report of the SRSG, para. 65.

as before with the Norms, as any initiative involving real legal teeth is going to result in strong resistance from a number of states and corporations. However, NGOs are rightly critical of the value of any initiative that does not have any meaningful enforcement provisions. Voluntarism has its limits. Consensual and universal standards are undoubtedly a laudable aim, but they will be unlikely to satisfy any but the corporate sector who are already happy with the manifold voluntary codes that seek to regulate their behaviour.

VII. Where to from here for corporate social responsibility and international law

After all of the political furore, what has been achieved? A great deal, one might say, particularly from the perspective of CSR. The Norms and the surrounding debate have brought renewed attention to the issue of corporate influence on human rights and have forced states, corporations and international corporate groups such as the International Chamber of Commerce to think seriously about this issue. The Norms have also identified a path to crystallising soft law on CSR into hard law, although, as we have noted, any such path to that end remains one of the most controversial aspects of the Norms.

Despite the intriguing and cogent arguments for an international document that speaks directly to corporations, the way forward will inevitably be through the international legal orthodoxy of state responsibility. International law must be the spine of any serious effort to reform this area, and by utilising the traditional modes of regulation some of the poisoned ground may be bypassed, and states may be more willing to come to the table. However, this does not mean that the process would be irrelevant for corporations outside of domestic regulation. As BLIHR has shown, initiatives in this area can and should be embraced by corporations, not merely out of fear of legal liability, but as best practice requires.

The next big question is how effectively to extend state responsibility in respect of TNCs. There are increasing examples of states trying to regulate corporate behaviour, particularly in areas of environmental protection and even social responsibility,[65] as well as corporate (especially fiscal)

---

[65] See, for example, in the United Kingdom, the Companies Act 2006, s. 172(1)(c), which, within the general duty of directors to act in ways that 'promote the success of the company', obliges directors to have regard to 'the impact of the company's operations on the community and the environment'; see www.publications.parliament.uk/pa/cm200506/cmbills/218/ 2006218a.pdf.

governance,[66] however few of these have an extraterritorial reach.[67] It may be necessary to incorporate some form of extraterritorial jurisdiction in a state's internal regulations in order to properly address the TNC phenomenon. Alternatively, the possibility for some form of international dispute mechanism holds certain benefits.

In our view, any further push to have the Norms adopted in their current form is a lost cause – whatever the merits of such an argument. That said, insofar as there is need and value in formulating international standards for corporate respect for human rights (and we believe there is on both counts), then it is hard to see past the existing core substantive provisions of the Norms. If one were indeed to start all over again, then the list of rights relevant to corporate enterprise one would almost certainly draw up, the emphasis on the direct but not exclusive legal responsibility being borne by states, and the attendant directions given to states as to how and what policies and procedures they should implement domestically to enforce those standards, would look not unlike what the Norms provide today. In which case, perhaps, the lesson to be learnt from the political debate that has surrounded the Norms thus far is that even if we do have to go over some of the same ground again, at least this time we will have all stakeholders present, primed and above all engaged in what will certainly be a lengthy, but hopefully fruitful and measured debate.

---

[66] See, for example, in the United States, the Sarbanes-Oxley Act (2002) Pub. L. No. 107–204.

[67] CSR legislation introduced into the legislatures of the United States, the United Kingdom and Australia in recent years has sought expressly to apply extra-territorially; none of these initiatives, however, was successful. For discussion, see Kinley and Tadaki, 'From Talk to Walk', 942; and Adam McBeth, 'A Look at Corporate Code of Conduct Legislation', *Common Law Review* 33 (2004), 222.

16

Corporate environmental responsibility: law and the limits of voluntarism

NEIL GUNNINGHAM

I. Introduction

The increasing interest in corporate social responsibility (hereafter CSR) has, somewhat belatedly, sparked interest amongst law and society scholars in its relationship with law. Is CSR a purely voluntary enterprise, in which corporations unilaterally raise their standards beyond those required by law? Or does law help shape both definitions and outcomes of CSR initiatives, and if so how? Is the relationship between CSR and law unidirectional (law impacting on CSR) or is that relationship multidirectional and interactive, and if the latter, what influences that interaction? Can one sensibly examine the relationship between CSR and law in isolation from other social forces, or must those forces also be factored into any explanation? And from a normative perspective, can and should law be invoked to shape CSR and, if so, what legal techniques might best be suited to this task?

It is likely that the answers to these and related questions are complex and contextual, and that more insights may be gained by focused, evidence-based research than by abstract analysis. This chapter examines the relationship between CSR and law in one substantive area, that of environment protection. Within this area, it seeks to develop arguments and draw conclusions based on empirical inquiry with regard to three industry sectors that have more reason than most to become engaged in CSR initiatives: mining, chemicals, and pulp and paper. All involve large reputation-sensitive companies, all are industries which potentially cause substantial environmental degradation, and all have at some stage experienced pressure from environmental non-government organisations

I am grateful to Darren Sinclair for his comments on an earlier draft, and to Niamh Lenagh-McGuire for research assistance.

(ENGOs) and/or local communities. Since the remainder of this chapter is confined to CSR initiatives in the area of environment, the term 'corporate environmental responsibility', and the acronym CER, will be used throughout. For present purposes, a conventional definition of CER is adopted, implying voluntary and unenforceable action beyond that which is required by law, as a response to public pressures and social expectations.[1]

In exploring the relationship between CER and law, a useful starting point is to ask *why* corporations might engage in CER initiatives. The existing literature on CER, or 'corporate greening', and on the reasons for moving 'beyond compliance' with environmental regulation, is rather limited.[2] My own previous work with Kagan and Thornton, based on an in-depth study of fourteen pulp and paper companies in four countries, suggests that corporate environmental management might usefully be viewed in terms of five ideal types. The first three of these (environmental laggards, and reluctant and committed compliers) are of little interest for present purposes since they do not aspire to CER. However, the last two may provide some useful insights into corporate motivation for CER, and are summarised in Box 1.

Box 1

Environmental Strategists: Environmental Strategists have a broad, future-oriented conception of their environmental objectives, which they see as closely linked to their business goals. As a matter of long-term 'business sense', they believe it is desirable to fully meet current and anticipated regulatory requirements with a margin of safety. They often seek to 'over-comply' with existing permit requirements in order to maintain a reputation as a good environmental citizen with regulators, environmental activists, neighbours, customers and financial markets. They also act strategically and proactively in their relationship with regulators, seeking to build a positive reputation for honesty and reliability where they believe that will generate long-term economic

---

[1] See, for example, David Vogel, *The Market for Virtue* (Washington, DC: The Brookings Institution, 2005). It should be noted that this definition is contested by ENGOs, who seek to give the term obligatory and enforceable meaning. See, for example, the United Nations' 'Global Compact' initiative (www.unglobalcompact.org).

[2] For an overview, see N. Gunningham, R. Kagan and D. Thornton, *Shades of Green: Business, Regulation and the Environment* (Stanford, CA: Stanford University Press, 2003), ch. 2.

benefits. However, they strive to reshape regulation (at its formulation stage) so as to minimise its economic impact upon them, and to provide greater flexibility.

Environmental Strategists believe that, in a range of circumstances, environmental improvements can lead to improved economic performance. Hence they establish highly professional environmental management departments which actively scan for and seek out 'win-win' opportunities. They place emphasis on the integration of economic and environmental performance, establishing sophisticated internal control and auditing systems. They are willing to make substantial environmental investments that cannot be justified, *ex ante*, as directly profit-enhancing, but that can be viewed qualitatively, and in the long term, as adding to the economic health of the corporation. For similar strategic reasons, Environmental Strategists often accommodate to community demands, taking environmental measures that go well beyond legal compliance. However, Environmental Strategists also take initiatives designed to shape community attitudes, educating local interest groups and governmental officials about the firm's environmental policies and the constraints it faces. Information is also carefully managed, for fear that this might be misinterpreted, misunderstood and/or used against them by environmental groups or their competitors. For this reason they have only very limited transparency, at least as compared to True Believers.

True Believers: True Believers, like other firms, have to make decisions that ensure that they remain economically viable. Nevertheless, they approach those decisions with a distinctive attitude toward their environmental responsibilities, explaining their decisions on environmental issues not purely in pragmatic terms (the 'business case'), but also in terms of principle, as 'the right thing to do'. They see a reputation for environmental excellence as an important key to business success, as do many Environmental Strategists. They therefore adopt many of the same strategies of such Environmental Strategists, but make that goal more central to their corporate identity. They have an extremely broad perception of what constitute win-win opportunities. This makes them more inclined to define investment in 'beyond compliance' environmental measures as 'good business decisions', even if the numerical payoff can't be calculated *ex ante*. True Believers constantly scan for such opportunities, both internally and externally, and are prepared to invest in them both for the short and the long term. Because they believe that establishing trust with local communities is essential, they are more inclined than Environmental Strategists to accept the need to be fully transparent. Accordingly, they disclose whatever information the community requests about their environmental impacts, and they are even more inclined than Strategists to go 'beyond compliance' in remedying environmental impacts that disturb their neighbours.

Source: Neil Gunningham, R. Kagan and D. Thornton, *Shades of Green, Business, Regulation and Environment,* Stanford University Press, 2002, pp. 100–2.

Based the work of my collaborators and myself on the pulp and paper, mining, and chemical industries,[3] it would appear that the large majority of those engaged in CER initiatives do so for motives which approximate those of 'Environmental Strategists' as described above. There are relatively few 'True Believers', and those that exist are likely to experience long-term market pressure to reduce their levels of environmental expenditure.[4]

This finding is consistent with the broader CSR literature,[5] which suggests that the large majority of those committing additional resources to CER do so because they are convinced of the 'business case' for going beyond compliance. For example, the mining sector perceives the business case for CER as being based on cost reduction, competitive advantage and reputational enhancement.[6] Similarly, interviews with large chemical companies suggest that they usually go beyond compliance for reasons related primarily to the perceived need to protect their reputation and maintain the trust of local communities.[7] And in all three industry sectors, the predominant focus of the business case is risk management, the principal driver being the fear that without taking measures to protect

[3] See Neil Gunningham and Darren Sinclair, *Leaders and Laggards: Next Generation Environmental Regulation* (Sheffield: Greenleaf Publishing, 2002), ch. 7; N. Gunningham, D. Thornton and R. Kagan, 'Motivating Management: Corporate Compliance in Environmental Protection', *Law and Policy* 17 (2005), 2.

[4] See Gunningham, *et al.*, *Shades of Green*, ch. 5.

[5] For a useful overview, see Vogel, *The Market for Virtue*. See also F. L. Reinhardt, *Down to Earth: Applying Business Principles to Environmental Management* (Harvard, MA: Harvard Business School Press, 2000).

[6] J. Walker and S. Howard, *Finding the Way Forward: How Could Voluntary Action Move Mining Towards Sustainable Development?* (London: International Institute for Environment and Development and WBCSD, 2002).

[7] Gunningham, *et al.*, 'Motivating Management', 301.

one's reputation, communities, ENGOs, regulators or others may take action which will adversely affect the corporate bottom line.[8]

Where does that leave the role of law? At first blush, it might appear that law is largely irrelevant to those committed to environmental CER. After all, if they are truly to 'walk the talk' (and those who do not are increasingly exposed by sophisticated ENGOs), then they must do considerably more than the law requires. Yet a closer examination will suggest that CER and law are in fact inextricably intertwined, that the relationship between them is interactive, negotiable and complex, and that understanding this relationship has important normative implications.

Section II will examine why corporations engage in CER initiatives at individual and collective levels, suggesting that CER can best be understood in terms of a complex and multi-faceted 'licence to operate'. The central strands of this licence, it will be demonstrated, involve legal, social and economic dimensions, which themselves are interconnected and interactive. And in some circumstances, an important fourth strand may be found in the form of a broader collective pressure imposed on industry by an industry association or equivalent body. What this means for the relationship between CER and law will be examined through an empirical analysis of the three industry sectors identified above. The normative implications of the above analysis, particularly in terms of state intervention to strengthen the terms or enforcement of the social and collective license strands, are the subject of section III . Section IV concludes.

II. Explaining corporate environmental responsibility initiatives

Whereas the scholarly literature has sought to explain corporate environmental performance in terms of various external 'drivers' of corporate behaviour – such as closeness of regulatory or community scrutiny, threats to corporate reputation, and various market-based factors – in the course of field research, my colleagues and I came to regard the concept of drivers as somewhat impoverished.[9] It implies the existence of independent, unidirectional and unambiguous pressures – whether from regulation, civil society or markets – which impact upon corporations with sufficient force that they react to them, often by developing some form of CER initiative. Yet we found that these external factors, rather than operating independently, often gain their force through mutual interaction, and that they do not operate unidirectionally. On the contrary, their thrust and content

---

[8] Reinhardt, *Down to Earth*, ch. 6.
[9] See generally Gunningham, *et al.*, *Shades of Green*, ch. 3.

often are determined by the way regulated enterprises interpret, confront and counter them.

The external pressures that push enterprises towards CER can be divided into three broad categories: economic, legal, and social. These categories are a convenient means of classifying the expectations of various stakeholders. Economic stakeholders include shareholders (including institutional investors), banks and customers (including other businesses and final consumers). Legal stakeholders include regulators, legislators and citizens (including environmental organisations) seeking to enforce regulations. Social stakeholders include neighbours (the local community), environmental activist organisations and the general voting public. We can usefully think of (and indeed industry itself increasingly thinks of) each of these expectations or requirements as terms or conditions of a 'licence to operate'. As one international mining association chairman put it:

> The most obvious fact is that our activities risk being intrusive on the environment and disruptive to the social fabric of the communities we work in. As individual companies, we can continue to operate only as long as local communities and national governments continue to accord us a licence to operate. By consistently demonstrating our progress towards sustainable development we can keep this licence live.[10]

The concept of a licence to operate, we came to feel, captures the complexity of the relationship between the regulated enterprise and key stakeholders in a way that the concept of 'drivers' does not. First, the concept of a licence encapsulates the extent to which various stakeholders can bestow or withdraw privileges from a company. It emphasises that business is dependent upon, and has a direct relationship with, the various economic, regulatory and social stakeholders who define, measure and enforce the terms of the licence. Second, the relationship between companies and stakeholders, as between many regulated firms and licensing authorities, is an interactive one, with many of the terms of the licence open to negotiation. Third, the notion of an overall licence to operate encompasses our empirical observation that there is considerable interaction among its three different components, which we label the regulatory licence, the economic licence and the social licence.

Traditionally, the notion of a business' licence to operate referred only to the company's legal obligations. For example, in order to operate legally,

---

[10] David Kerr, 'We Want to and Can, Conduct our Businesses in a Responsible Way', *ICMM Newletter* 3 (2004), 2.

a pulp mill operator had to obtain a land-use and a construction permit before building a new facility. It had to introduce particular pollution control technology. Once operating the facility, it had to maintain certain process and performance standards (for example, concerning hazardous waste disposal and workplace safety). Together, these regulatory obligations and permits might be referred to as a facility's legal or regulatory licence. Today, however, the concept of licence to operate must include 'economic reality' requirements such as the need to meet debt obligations, show growth in earnings, and maximise shareholder return on investment (or at least to provide a reasonable rate of return). The terms of this *economic licence* – what is an adequate rate of return on investment or level of profitability – are not written down in detail like a regulatory permit, of course; they may vary over time, 'tightening' and 'loosening' with market conditions and each firm's economic performance. The economic licence to operate is particularly relevant to the study of corporate environmental performance insofar as it operates as a brake on (or, in some circumstances, a spur to) 'beyond compliance' investments and expenditures.

In addition, the licence to operate concept has been extended to include the demands of social actors. Neighbours may complain about odour, international environmental groups may demand the use of less hazardous bleaching chemicals, and both groups may threaten a variety of informal sanctions if industry fails to respond. An extremely serious violation of community expectations – such as a death-dealing explosion in a mill, or a chlorine leak that results in severe threats to human health or severe ecological damage – can trigger political demands to close a plant down. Even short of that, while the terms of the social licence are not precisely delineated and may be subject to negotiation and manipulation, a company's failure to meet social expectations concerning environmental performance can impair the firm's reputation, adversely affect recruiting and trigger demands for more stringent and intrusive legal controls. Indeed, in some instances the conditions demanded by 'social licensors' may be tougher than those imposed by the current legal licence, resulting in beyond compliance corporate environmental measures, or what are commonly referred to as CER initiatives.

A. The interaction between corporate environmental responsibility, regulation and economic pressures

What is the relationship between CER and law or (couched in terms of the framework set out above) between the social and regulatory licences to operate? Rather than CER operating in isolation of law, an analysis in terms of the licence model described above suggests that CER is a direct response to multiple licence pressures – social, legal and economic. Moreover, as the following section will illustrate, these licence pressures often gain their force through interaction. Indeed, the interactions among the regulatory, economic and social strands of the licence to operate often result in the intensification of the overall constraints under which companies operate. In other cases, however, there are tensions between the different economic, social and regulatory forces that may pull firms in different directions. The economic licence, for example, often calls for limits on or even reductions in environmental expenditure, while the terms of the social licence usually push for an increase.

We explore the implications of these interactions for CER below, distinguishing for heuristic purposes between legal and social interactions and economic and social interactions, while recognising that in the real world all three may interact. Given the subject matter of this book, the principal focus will be on interactions between the legal and social licence, while recognising that a variety of other interactions, between the economic and the social, the legal and the economic, also take place.

1. Legal expansion of the social licence

In terms of legal and social interactions, the regulatory licence often extends the reach and impact of the social licence, either by directly empowering social licensors, or by giving them access to information which they can then use to pressure target enterprises. Conversely, the scope of the legal licence can also be expanded as a result of its interaction with the social licence, for example as social pressures on legislators and regulators feed through in terms of enactment, monitoring and enforcement of regulation.

The most common influence of the legal on the social licence is that of empowerment. For example, the relative power and influence of the local community may be connected directly to the extent to which it is enabled by legislation to participate in decision-making about a facility's future. In New Zealand, almost all our respondents emphasised the enormous impact of the Resource Management Act 1991, which gave individuals the right to make submissions and challenge any variation of the consent (the basic permit or licence to operate) and whose interventions might hold up a new project for a considerable period. As one pulp mill manager described it: 'It became a very public process. In 1994–95 there were 169 submissions regarding the mill. We had very strong protests. People were finally able to have their say. We had 32 people speaking at the public hearings.' This created an environment in which there was a strong incentive for corporations to listen and respond to community concerns because if they failed to do so they risked delays, possibly for years, in obtaining the consents they needed in order to introduce technological and other changes.

Similarly, in the Australian state of Victoria, the introduction of Environmental Improvement Plans by legislation required polluting companies to engage in dialogue with local communities 'in the shadow of the law'. Process-based requirements under that legislation prompted companies to develop more effective internal management and planning, and to agree to improved environmental targets, against a backdrop of tougher regulation if they did not. But it was the institutionalisation by law of dialogue with the community that empowered communities to act as environmental 'watchdogs' and as surrogate regulators, at least in circumstances where they are ready, willing and able to take on these roles.[11]

Laws requiring disclosure of environmental information at firm level can also act to empower local communities, albeit indirectly. For example, 'community right to know' (CRTK) legislation and pollution inventories can require individual companies to estimate their emissions of specified hazardous substances. This information is then used to compile a publicly available inventory, which can then be interrogated by communities, the media, individuals, environmental groups and other ENGOs who can ascertain, for example, the total emissions of particular companies. This information enables comparison of different firms' emissions and can be used to compile a 'league table' which identifies both leaders and laggards in terms of toxic emissions. The evidence suggests that well-informed communities use this information both to ensure tight enforcement of regulations and to pressure companies to improve their performance even in the absence of regulations.[12]

These examples do not exhaust the list of ways in which the terms of the legal licence expand the social licence. Rights of standing to sue either a company or a regulatory agency, broader issues of access to information, legal duties of companies to consult with local communities, and penetration of the legal decision-making process that can result in delay, if not termination, of facility plans can serve to expand the scope

---

[11] Gunningham and Sinclair, *Leaders and Laggards*, ch. 8.
[12] A. Fung and D. O'Rourke, 'Reinventing Environmental Regulation from the Grass Roots Up', *Enviromental Management* 25, 2 (2000), 115–27.

of the social licence. In addition to criminal sanctions and administrative notices (and in the United States, civil penalties), companies that breach their legal obligations are also vulnerable to either individual or class actions from citizens injured as a result of the facility's illegal activities. In the case of local residents, they can oppose, by both legal and political means, any expansion of the facility, thereby slowing or halting its economic growth. For example, they may challenge or oppose variation in the permit requirements or in local ordinances, or they may lobby local and state governments to limit any expansion of the mill under planning and land-use laws.

The extent to which a company complies with regulation is also used by community and environment groups as a performance indicator by which the community judges compliance with the broader social licence. For this reason, some companies fear enforcement not so much because of any penalty likely to be inflicted by the regulator but rather because of the resulting adverse publicity, and as a consequence the informal sanctions imposed by the public, the media and perhaps also by markets. For example, large chemical corporations reported that conforming to regulation was particularly important in terms of protecting their reputation because of the stigma associated with being sanctioned.[13]

Certainly compliance with regulation will not in itself be sufficient to satisfy broader community concerns, which often extend well beyond the standards embodied in regulation, and commonly include issues such as noise and odour which may not even be directly addressed in the permit itself. However, at the very least, substantive non-compliance with the permit and regulation will send broader signals to the community concerning the company's failure to deliver on its claims to corporate environmental responsibility.

2. Social expansion of the legal licence

While the terms of the legal licence commonly serve to expand the scope of the social, the converse is also true: a social licence can expand the scope of law. For example, a failure to respond appropriately to the social licence involves the risk of expanding the regulatory licence, as politicians and – ultimately – regulators respond to community demands. As one senior corporate official pointed out: 'local communities have the ability through the political process to create the regulations that allow you to do business ... we operate under a licence from the public in every place we do

[13] Gunningham, et al., 'Motivating Management'.

business so we have to be sensitive to public concerns'. Again, so sensitive are some companies to the messages they send to local communities that they are willing to compromise substantially on the terms of their legal licence and permit conditions. Thus as one pulp company recounted:

> We didn't like the permit limit but we didn't want to appeal it because that would send a wrong message to the community. We had some trust to build up, we didn't want to appeal the permit for that reason – we asked, what do *you* want in the permit – and so sent a message out and saved our reputation [with the community]. The public has the ability to appeal the permit – nobody appealed it but was very controversial – every other pulp company in the state appealed their permit.

However, we also found that enterprises sometimes use compliance with the social licence to gain some respite from some of the terms of the regulatory licence. For example, good community relations can sometimes be used to gain additional regulatory leverage. As one environmental manager argued: 'If you can sell something to the local community they will stand in front of the regulators on your side.' This manager gave the example of a dispute between the regulator and the mill concerning a Superfund site. Although the company wanted to proceed with a clean-up plan, the government was reluctant to sign off on anything: '[B]ut the environmental groups mobilized behind us and that got EPA [Environmental Protection Agency] and [the state regulator] in the room and to achieve the first settlement of Superfund site in the country without litigation . . . it saved us millions of dollars.'

More broadly, the way enforcement agencies exercise their discretion may be influenced substantially by community mores and expectations. On occasion, regulatory action could even be viewed almost as a surrogate for community action, with the company regarding their main licence as being social rather than regulatory. For example, in the Australian case cited earlier, the regulator's policy appeared to be not to prosecute simply because there had been a breach of environmental standards, but rather to do so only when the level of community complaints about a particular incident was judged to be sufficiently high.

From the above account it will be apparent that the social licence is monitored and enforced by a variety of social stakeholders, who commonly seek leverage by exploiting a variety of licence terms. Environmental groups not only enforce the terms of the social licence directly (e.g., through shaming and adverse publicity), but also seek to influence the terms of the economic licence (e.g., generating consumer boycotts of environmentally damaging products) and of the regulatory licence (e.g., through citizen suits or political pressure for regulatory initiatives). Thus the effect of the interaction between the different types of licence often exceeds the effect of each acting alone. The terms of some legal licence provisions extend the reach and impact of the social licence by directly empowering social activists or by giving them access to information which they can use to pressure target enterprises. Conversely, a company which fails to respond appropriately to social licence obligations risks a tightening of its regulatory licence, as frustrated community activists turn for help to politicians and regulators. At the same time, the interaction between a firm's economic licence and the demands of social stakeholders help determine how far it will go beyond legal compliance.

Finally, it should be apparent from the above that the role of the corporations whose CER behaviour is influenced by this diversity of interacting licence terms is far from passive. On the contrary, large, reputation-sensitive companies, either directly, or in some cases through their industry associations, do a great deal to shape both the licence terms themselves and their enforcement. For example, a campaign to challenge all prosecutions, and outspend the regulator until such time as the latter admits defeat and pursues smaller fish elsewhere, not only protects a corporation's regulatory licence but also (since they will no longer have to report successful prosecutions in their annual environmental report) benefits the social licence. Companies may also seek to lobby directly for regulatory change, go on the offensive with public relations campaigns designed to influence public opinion and enhance their social licence, and benefit their economic licence through a variety of campaigns intended to exclude or disadvantage rivals, either locally or internationally.

B. The fourth strand: the collective licence to operate

Responding to the sorts of licence pressures identified above, an increasing number of companies have engaged in their own CER initiatives, largely independent of broader industry sector policy. However, there are limits to what can be achieved at individual corporate level and, for this reason, some industry sectors, in some circumstances (usually through their peak bodies), have turned to *collective* CER schemes to achieve a variety of broader objectives. This section summarises the experience of the principal form of collective CER initiative – industry self-regulation – and explains why such initiatives have developed and how they have effectively imposed a fourth licence to operate upon industry members.

It then examines the relationship between such a purportedly voluntary, industry-driven approach and law.

1. Why collective action is necessary

Over the last decade, a proliferation of industry-specific collective and voluntary initiatives have evolved which, from an industry perspective, have a variety of attractions. The main impetus for their introduction (mainly in the form of industry codes of practice) is the need for industry to pre-empt the threat of tougher legislation and to maintain its environmental credibility with a broad range of stakeholders.[14] Put differently: 'Strategic maneuvering of corporations in the CSR field consists of two basic moves: one that resists attempts to subject MNCs [multinational companies] to an enforceable legal framework, and another that engages in actively consolidating a self regulatory regime in CSR that is based on a host of voluntary and non-enforceable instruments.'[15]

The experience of the mining and chemicals industries is representative. Both these sectors have a substantial and high-profile environmental impact, both have had a poor public environmental image, and both need to protect their reputation capital in order to maintain access to development opportunities across a diverse range of countries, to ward off more interventionist government regulation, and to maintain credibility with external stakeholders. For example, in the case of the mining industry, as one commentator has pointed out:

> ... worldwide, mining is faced with a pattern of low credibility and social opposition, which drives from a general perception that mining is a dirty business. Mining is seen as inherently destructive, in that it destroys the environment, and leaves nothing positive behind when it packs up and goes. The image of abandoned mines, tailings dumps, waste-rock piles, and abandoned communities has significant resonance with the general public.[16]

As a result, the mining industry faces an urgent need to gain and maintain legitimacy and social acceptance.[17] It is particularly vulnerable to

---

[14] This chapter recognises that voluntarism is a question of degree, not an absolute, and embraces within it initiatives which in significant part may be a response to external forces.

[15] R. Shamir, 'Between Self-Regulation and the Alien Tort Claims Act: on the Contested Concept of Corporate Social Responsibility', *Law and Society Review* 38 (2004), 348.

[16] Anon, 'Focus and Comment: Earning a Social Licence', *The Mining Journal* (1999).

[17] For a general analysis of CER in the mining sector, see H. M. Jenkins, 'Corporate Social Responsibility and the Mining Industry: Conflicts and Constructs', *Corporate Social Responsibility and Environmental Management*, 11 (2004), 23–34.

criticisms from a combination of local and international ENGOs. The Brent Spar saga, albeit in another resource sector, is a dramatic illustration of the impact which sophisticated NGO media campaigns can have on corporate reputation and profits. The environmental and social damage caused by the Ok Tedi mine in Papua New Guinea at one stage threatened to become a comparable media disaster for its owners, at least at the regional level.

Against this background, how can industry convince society that it is acting responsibly in the way it exploits resources, and that it is doing so in a manner which is compatible with the concept of sustainable development? A crucial distinction here is between action which is required to protect the reputation of an individual company, *and action which is needed to protect the reputation of an entire industry*. In the case of some industries – particularly those that rely on intermediaries to market their products directly to consumers – only collective action will be effective in protecting the social licence of the industry in its entirety. This is because: 'industries that manufacture commodities that require further processing before sale to end-users tend to assume a collective identity in the public's mind. The problems of one company color public perception of the entire industry.'[18] As a result, individual initiatives will not be sufficient to protect the reputation of an industry as a whole, and yet unless the industry as a whole is trusted, then the prospects of individual companies within it may be threatened. This is because a major environmental incident involving an individual company commonly tarnishes the reputation of the entire industry, exposing it to the risk of tougher regulatory requirements, obstacles to development and community backlash. This is precisely what happened to the chemical industry following the Bhopal explosion and the Love Canal site contamination. Although they took place many years ago, these incidents provided the chemical industry with direct intimations of what it means to lose (or almost lose) its social licence. Thus, like nuclear power companies in the wake of the Three Mile Island incident, chemical companies feel themselves, in Joseph Rees's apt phrase, 'hostages of each other'.[19]

The result is that each company in such industries must act as its brother's keeper. Thus a mechanism must be found, nationally and

---

[18] J. Nash, 'Voluntary Codes of Practice: Non-Governmental Institutions for Promoting Environmental Management in Firms', Paper presented to Workshop on Education, Information on Voluntary Measures in Environmental Protection, Washington, DC, November 2000), p. 7.

[19] J. Rees, *Hostages of Each Other: The Transformation of Nuclear Safety since Three Mile Island* (Chicago, IL: University of Chicago Press, 1994).

internationally, which enables the industry to continuously improve the environmental performance of all companies, large and small. Such a mechanism must be capable of improving the industry's poor public image, restoring public faith in the industry's integrity and taking the heat out of demands for stricter government regulation.[20]

In the case of the chemical industry, such a mechanism was developed in the form of the 'Responsible Care' self-regulatory initiative. Responsible Care evolved in the aftermath of the chemical industry disaster at Bhopal, India, in 1984, at a time when the industry internationally faced a serious credibility problem and feared draconian government regulation and serious public opposition to many of its activities. Responsible Care is intended to reduce chemical accidents and pollution, to build industry credibility through improved performance and increased communication, and to involve the community in decision-making. It is built around a series of industry codes of practice and greater levels of public disclosure and participation with administration by chemical industry associations at national level. The relevant associations rely largely on promulgating norms of industrial conduct, peer pressure, technical assistance and transfer, data collection and self-reporting by members to institutionalise responsibility and ensure compliance.

The mining industry, substantially following the chemical industry model, has also explored a variety of mechanisms to achieve similar results. Internationally, these include the International Council of Metals and Mining Sustainable Development Framework[21] and participation in the Global Mining Initiative (developing a mining and metals supplement to the Global Reporting Initiative's Sustainability Reporting Guidelines).[22] At country level, the most advanced example of what a mining industry code might involve is the Australian Minerals Industry Code for Environmental Management (AMICEM), which is concerned to protect the reputation of the Australian mining sector as a whole through the development and implementation of industry codes of practice and other voluntary approaches which establish industry standards of environmental performance.

[20] As former Canadian Chemical Producers Association President Jean Belanger put it: 'if we could figure out a way of becoming proactive, then we could lessen demands for that degree of regulation'; quoted in R. Mullin, 'Canadian Deadline Approaches: Contemplating continuous improvement', Chemical Week 128 (1992).

[21] International Council on Mining and Metals, Sustainable Development Framework, www.icmm.com/sd_framework.php.

[22] See generally www.globalreporting.org/ (accessed 6 January 2006). See also the UN sponsored guidelines on mining and environment, www.natural-resources.org/minerals/index.htm and www.mineralsresourcesforum.org.

In both industries, what has effectively occurred is the development of industry-wide self-regulation *in a form designed to protect the collective social licence of the industry*. This, in effect, imposes a fourth licence term on each of the individual companies who are pressured to sign up for, and comply with, such self-regulatory initiatives. The terms of this collective licence are set out in the contract entered into by each participant and the industry association which administers the self-regulatory initiative, and enforced through such informal sanctions as peer group pressure, shaming and the threat of expulsion from the industry association.

Those self-regulatory initiatives also set out a charter for CER in their respective industries. While some companies might seek to achieve standards beyond those established by the relevant codes of practice, none can credibly claim CER credentials without demonstrably meeting those terms. Whatever criticisms ENGOs may have of industry self-regulation (and there are many), they are not reticent in criticising any corporation that might manifestly fail to achieve them.

2. Corporate environmental responsibility, the collective licence and law

The collective licence does not, of course, operate in isolation from the other licence strands. For example, there is substantial interactivity between the collective licence and the regulatory and legal licences as they play out in the mining and chemical industry self-regulatory initiatives.

First, as indicated earlier, a powerful motivation for developing such industry-sponsored collective licences is to ward off stronger legal intervention in the affairs of the industry. Accordingly, far from being independent of law, such mechanisms are developed directly in the shadow of the law, and strongly influenced by the fear of future legal developments. Although there is a long history of self-regulation being used as a façade to ward off government regulation without attempting to achieve genuine improvement in collective performance, this interpretation cannot be supported in the case of the mining and chemical industries. Certainly there may be recalcitrants, who left to their own devices will only make tokenistic efforts. But there is little doubt that industry leaders, and indeed many of the largest companies, did indeed intend that Responsible Care and more recent mining self-regulatory initiatives should substantially improve the environmental performance of the industry as a whole and provide a credible alternative to state regulation.[23]

---

[23] See generally, N. Gunningham and P. Grabosky, *Smart Regulation: Designing Environmental Policy* (New York: Oxford University Press, 1998), ch. 4.

Second, a 'two track' system of environmental regulation may also spur the development of a collective licence (and vice versa). Under this approach, those who are accredited to and demonstrably meet the performance criteria established by the self-regulatory programme are provided with regulatory flexibility and become a 'low inspectoral priority' in a manner that others do not.[24] In this way, the self-regulatory initiative becomes a form of 'soft law', influencing the behaviour of the formal regulatory system.

Third, collective licences, while privately negotiated and voluntary, are substantially influenced by a variety of forms of civil law. For example, Glinski points out that private self-regulation has private law consequences and that advertising law can be applied to prevent or provide redress for misleading information provided to consumers, that contract law will ensure enforcement as between signatories to the contract, that tort law may impose minimum standards and civil liability for failure to achieve them, and so on.[25] Similarly, what have been called 'market information legal rules' regulate firms' voluntary (and mandatory) disclosures and assign potential liability for false disclosures. These may also have a powerful impact, given the sensitivity of firms to their market reputation.[26] Indeed, according to Johnston: 'the legal rules that are most crucial in improving CSR are not regulations that try to mandate SR corporate behavior, but rather those determining when and if companies are liable for either failing to disclose or falsely communicating about their social and environmental performance'.[27]

Not all the licence terms, however, may pull in the same direction. For example, there is a substantial tension between the collective and the individual social licence for, although it will be important to industry leaders to maintain the reputation of the entire industry (the collective licence), they also actively seek means to distinguish themselves in the eyes of the public from the 'rump' of their industry (individual social licence). In particular, the environmental efforts of the most environmentally responsible corporations have largely gone unrecognised by communities and unrewarded by markets 'because of the absence of a credible mechanism

---

[24] On two track regulation, see N. Gunningham and R. Johnstone, *Regulating Workplace Safety: Systems and Sanctions* (New York: Oxford University Press, 1999), ch. 4.

[25] Glinski, Chapter 4 in this volume.

[26] See generally J. Johnston, *Signaling Social Responsibility: On the Law and Economics of Market Incentives for Corporate Environmental Performance* (Philadelphia, PA: University of Pennsylvania, 2005).

[27] See *ibid.*, p. 8.

that can differentiate companies on the basis of their environmental and social performance'.[28] To overcome this problem, they must find means (in the form of credible 'league tables' and independent performance indicators) to distinguish themselves from the remainder of the industry. For example, according to one analysis:

> while the desire to avoid regulation may have driven the development of the [Minerals Council of Australia] Code... the main motivation for adopting the MCA code was the opportunity it provided for companies seeking to improve their reputation. The Code not only required signatures to disclose instances of poor performance, *it also offered them an opportunity to publish information about their good performance.*[29]

(emphasis added)

III. The interaction of corporate environmental responsibility and law: normative implications

The findings described above have important public policy implications, for they suggest that rather than simply relying on conventional legal/regulatory instruments, policy makers can and should seek to enhance the variety of licences to operate (legal, social, economic, and collective) that have the potential to enhance the adoption of CER. Often, given the web of interactions noted above, public policy interventions will trigger multiple forms of licence to operate simultaneously. Also, there are numerous opportunities for policy intervention, with different strategies targeted at different licence terms. Rather than examine all the possible permutations, the following section will focus on three of the most potentially powerful interactions between CER and law.

A. Procedural empowerment

Procedural empowerment through law (the regulatory licence) is a particularly potent means of expanding the terms of the social licence and

---

[28] World Wildlife Fund – Australia, *Mining Certification Evaluation Project: WWF – Placer Dome Asia Pacific Discussion Paper*. Whether independent certification (as under the model of the Forest Stewardship Council or the Marine Stewardship Council) would provide a mechanism which allows minerals and metals from well-managed mines to access environmentally sensitive markets is uncertain and untested.

[29] P. Schiavi, 'Regulating the Social and Environmental Performance of the Australian Minerals Industry: A Sociological Analysis of Emerging Forms of Governance', Paper presented to Regulatory Institutions Network Conference, Australian National University, Canberra, 7–9 December 2005.

thereby the scope of CER. Community and environmental advocacy groups in particular tend to act as effective watchdogs and de facto regulators, exploiting the fear of reputation damage to shame and otherwise pressurise companies into beyond compliance environmental performance. While they can sometimes play this role in the absence of any form of state intervention, their effectiveness is enhanced by various statutory provisions designed to empower community and environmental groups through citizen suit provisions and compliance certification requirements in major permit programmes, and information disclosure provisions such as the US Toxic Release Inventory (further described below).

Research suggests that government actions that *procedurally* empower social actors to delay changes to facility infrastructure or operations would be particularly important in changing corporate environmental behaviour. Such actions include requiring facilities to consult local communities, requiring that facilities respond formally to community concerns, and having regulatory or judicial review of the response if it is deemed by the community to be arbitrary and capricious. In New Zealand, enterprises reported having become much more responsive to community environmental concerns after communities were given the legal right to challenge the terms of each facility's 'consent' (permit), and thereby gained the power to delay the introduction of new processes or technology. In an Australian jurisdiction, similar effects flowed from a new law that obligated firms to prepare and comply with an environmental improvement plan, including a commitment to consultation with local communities.[30] In Canada and the United States, the permitting process has long been open to the public and allowed for public comment on permitting decisions. Such public access has been extended in the United States through programmes such as Project XL and the Wisconsin Green Tier Program,[31] which made it a condition for providing greater regulatory flexibility that participating companies provide information to, and consult with, local communities.[32]

---

[30] See further Gunningham and Sinclair, *Leaders and Laggards*.

[31] See dnr.wi.gov/org/caer/cea/environmental/ accessed 10 January 2006.

[32] See generally Gunningham and Sinclair, *Leaders and Laggards*, ch. 6. Note that procedural empowerment raises two important concerns. First, a badly designed process could be hijacked by small extremist elements able to delay actions that most in the community or the country support. Procedural empowerment would have to provide a mechanism that allowed more broadly based coalitions to block extremist delaying tactics. This would provide an incentive for companies to invest in community relations so as to obtain sufficient reputation capital to overcome extremist attacks. Second, the process could be hijacked by well-meaning incompetents, more concerned with phantom threats than real ones, or with impossibly expensive demands. But once again, real outreach and investment in the community seems likely to minimise this risk.

B. Comparative information

A second potentially important means of using the regulatory licence to expand the social licence is through legal requirements to disclose comparative information. While current regulation often requires companies to report environmental information, this information is not usually designed to be explicitly comparative and allow the lay public (or indeed, other interested parties) to rank facilities in terms of their environmental performance.[33] Certainly, the Unites States Toxic Release Inventory, which simply obligates firms to publish their total estimated emissions of potentially hazardous chemicals, permits comparisons, but the quality of the data and a host of other problems detract from its usefulness.[34] Explicitly comparative information dramatically increases the social meaning of environmental information because it identifies both the leaders in an environmental arena and the laggards. It therefore provides incentives to the best performers to do better and to the worst performers to improve because leaders can be rewarded for their excellence while laggards can be punished. This has implications for both the social and economic licences, through informing communities and consumers and enabling them to impose social and economic pressure respectively.

In addition, comparative information standards might well work in circumstances where enforcement is weak, political officials unresponsive and regulators overwhelmed because they make it easy to target laggards (and reward leaders) in the market. For example, in Indonesia, under the PROPER PROKASIH programme, regulators rank the performance of individual facilities using surveys, a pollution database of team reports and independent audits. An enterprise's pollution ranking is readily understood by the public, being based on a colour coding (gold and green for the best performers, black, blue and red for those not in compliance). The programme has reportedly been very successful in improving the environmental performance of participating firms.[35]

---

[33] Instead, information is often designed to determine whether or not legal limits or other requirements have been met, not whether they have been met more quickly, more efficiently or more completely than others.

[34] See Mark Cohen, 'Information as a Policy Instrument in Protecting the Environment: What Have We Learned?', *Environmental Law Reporter* 31 (2001). The vast majority of information standards are those that require facilities to monitor their air emissions and water discharges. These requirements are not explicitly comparative.

[35] See Afsah and Vincent, *Putting Pressure on Polluters: Indonesia's PROPER Program* (Cambridge, MA: Harvard Institute for International Development, 1997).

C. Enhancing self-regulation

An important question in terms of public policy concerns the extent to which collective licences (in the form of self-regulatory CER initiatives) can be relied upon as stand-alone instruments to achieve improved environmental performance. Unfortunately, most evidence suggests that such initiatives have at best a very mixed track record.[36]

While no credible evaluations have yet been conducted of the evolving minerals industry self-regulatory programs, it can be said the performance of Responsible Care, some twenty years since its inception, is disappointing. For example, one evaluation found that because Responsible Care has operated without explicit sanctions for malfeasance, 'it has fallen victim to enough opportunism that it includes a disproportionate number of poor performers',[37] while another study concluded that in the majority of firms studied, Responsible Care primarily helped relations with external constituencies without significantly changing internal behaviour.[38] These analyses may be unduly harsh insofar as they do not take account of soft effects (which are difficult to measure), such as the development of an industrial morality – a set of norms which generate a sense of obligation, emphasising particular values and structuring choice.[39]

Nevertheless, at best such programmes have achieved only very limited success, raising the important normative questions as to whether, to what extent and how their effectiveness might be increased by linking them to various forms of state regulation. The argument is that, whatever their shortcomings, collective licences have the considerable advantages of providing greater flexibility to enterprises in their response, greater ownership of solutions which they are directly involved in creating, less resistance, greater legitimacy, greater speed of decision-making, sensitivity to market

---

[36] The evidence suggests that such codes are rarely effective in achieving compliance (i.e., obedience by the target population/s with regulation/s) – at least if used as a stand-alone strategy without sanctions. This is because self-regulatory standards are often weak, enforcement is commonly ineffective and punishment is secret and mild. Moreover, self-regulation commonly lacks many of the virtues of typically conventional state regulation, 'in terms of visibility, credibility, accountability, compulsory application to all, greater likelihood of rigorous standards being developed, cost spreading, and availability of a range of sanctions': K. Webb and A. Morrison, *Legal Aspects of Voluntary codes: In the Shadow of the Law* (Ottawa: Industry Canada, 1996). For a comprehensive survey, see M. Priest, 'The Privatization of Regulation: Five Models of Self-Regulation', *Ottawa Law Review* 29 (1998–99).

[37] Nash, *Voluntary Codes of Practice*, p. 7.

[38] C. Coglianese and J. Nash, *Regulating from the Inside: Can Environmental Management Systems Achieve Policy Goals?* (Washington, DC: Resources for the Future, 2001).

[39] N. Gunningham and J. Rees, 'Self-Regulation', *Law and Policy* 19 (1999), 4.

circumstances and lower costs. If their weaknesses can be compensated for by integrating them with the regulatory licence, then the result in terms of CER might plausibly be better than that achieved by either state regulation or self-regulation operating in isolation.

Those who advocate this approach begin by identifying the major shortcomings of industry-wide self-regulation and suggesting ways in which this might be compensated for by greater, but complementary, state regulation. For example, of the various challenges confronting self-regulation, perhaps the most crucial is free riding – seeking to benefit from self-regulatory initiatives without contributing a share of the costs – which arguably might be overcome by state intervention. For example, where a significant number of players refuse to join the self-regulatory programme, and cannot be induced to do so by threats or incentives provided by other players, then government might plausibly intervene directly to curb the activities of non-participants.[40] A related challenge is that of effective monitoring and enforcement. The range of enforcement mechanisms that might potentially be invoked under a collective self-regulatory initiative is quite broad, ranging, at the lower levels, from education, incentives and peer pressure, through to the ultimate sanction of expulsion from the industry association. However, expulsion may have little direct impact, and associations will be reluctant to invoke it for fear of revealing their ultimate lack of regulatory clout. It is at this point that most collective voluntary initiatives are vulnerable to failure. Lacking the ultimate capacity to invoke sanctions at the tip of an 'enforcement pyramid',[41] the credibility of sanctions at lower levels is also weakened. Again, there is a compelling need to complement self-regulation with some form of government (or third-party) involvement. In broad terms, collective voluntary initiatives are much more likely to achieve CER objectives if they operate in the shadow of rules and sanctions provided by the general law, for it is these which are the most obvious and visible (but not the only) means of giving regulatees the incentive to comply with the self-regulatory programme.[42]

---

[40] Gunningham and Grabosky, *Smart Regulation*, ch. 4.

[41] I. Ayres and J. Braithwaite, *Responsive Regulation* (Oxford: Oxford University Press, 1992).

[42] Note also the evidence suggesting that domestic legislation is by far the most important influence on environmental management practices. See Organisation for Economic Co-operation and Development (OECD) Directorate for Financial, Fiscal and Enterprise Affairs, 'Public Policy and Voluntary Initiatives: What Roles have Governments Played?' (Working Papers on International Investment No. 2001/4: OECD, 2001), 5. This is not to suggest that state law is invariably the best underpinning for self-regulation. Indeed, in the

Finally, the importance of utilising a broader regulatory mix cannot be over-emphasised. Often the best solution is to design complementary combinations using a number of different licence terms. Thus self-regulation, government regulation and third-party oversight through the social licence may be capable of being combined in complementary combinations that work better than any one of these instruments, or even two acting together. For example, in the case of Responsible Care, even though the industry as a whole has a self-interest in improving its environmental performance, collective action problems and the temptation to free-ride mean that self-regulation and its related codes of practice alone will be insufficient to achieve that goal. However, a tripartite approach, involving co-regulation and a range of third-party oversight mechanisms, may arguably be a viable option. This might involve creating greater transparency through a community right-to-know about chemical emissions; greater accountability through the introduction of independent third-party audits; and an underpinning of government regulation which, in the case of companies which are part of the scheme, need only 'kick in' to the extent that the code itself is failing or when individual companies seek to defect from their obligations under it and free-ride.

IV. Conclusion

To return to the questions with which this chapter began, it is clear that CER is not a purely voluntary matter. Corporations participate in CER initiatives for essentially pragmatic reasons, usually justifying that participation in terms of a 'business case', in which particular emphasis is placed upon risk management. Thus 'voluntary' CER initiatives are likely to be a calculated response to external pressures rather than an expression of any internal moral or philanthropic commitment.

The risks that CER initiatives may help to circumvent and the opportunities that CER provides can best be thought of in terms of a socially constructed 'licence to operate'. This licence includes economic and social

context of developing countries, the law is rarely a credible and effective policy tool, and environmental regulators are usually vastly under-resourced and sometimes vulnerable to capture and possibly corruption. Accordingly, we must look elsewhere for means to bolster the effectiveness of voluntary initiatives. See generally J. Cooney, 'Mining in Developing Countries: New Rules for an Old Game', Paper presented to Natural Resources Canada MMS Manager Conference, Gatineau, Quebec, 2 November 2005, and L. Zarsky 'Havens, Halos and Spaghetti: Untangling the Evidence about Foreign Direct Investment and the Environment', Paper presented to OECD Conference on FDI and the Environment, The Hague, 28–29 January 1999, p. 49.

demands as well as the demands of government regulators: what were termed the economic, social and regulatory licences respectively. Sometimes, a fourth licence strand – a *collective* social licence – also comes into play. This occurs when an industry sector (or at least the leading companies within it) perceives a compelling need to protect the reputation of the industry as a whole, and establishes some industry-wide initiative designed to do so. One by-product of such an initiative is to establish what are in effect *minimum* CER credentials for corporations operating in that sector.

What a company decides to do in terms of CER can be explained largely by how it interprets and responds to the various strands of the licence to operate. In particular, it was suggested, the various licence terms are interactive and interconnected. For example, corporations fear that not meeting the requirements of the social licence will ultimately result in increased regulation or greater economic costs to the company. Moreover, the interaction of the different types of licence often exceeds the effect of each type of licence acting alone. Thus the terms of some legal licence provisions extend the reach and impact of the social licence by directly empowering social activists or by giving them access to information which they can use to pressure target enterprises. Conversely, a company which fails to respond appropriately to social licence obligations risks a tightening of its regulatory licence, as frustrated community activists turn for help to politicians and regulators.

However, corporations are not merely reactive to various external licence pressures. On the contrary, they often actively seek to shape the licence terms themselves, variously lobbying to restrict the regulatory licence, engaging in outreach or public relations initiatives to influence their social licence or seeking opportunities in so doing to expand their economic licence.

From this analysis it is clear not only that CER is intimately connected to law (the regulatory licence) but also that this interconnection cannot be understood without taking account of the broader interactions with the social licence and the collective licence (which are likely to increase CER expectations) and the economic licence (which may well decrease them).

This analysis has important normative implications. For understanding the connections between the different strands of the licence to operate also enables policy-makers to understand more clearly how various licence terms, especially the regulatory licence, might be invoked to shape CER. For example, procedural empowerment through law (the regulatory licence) was found to be a particularly potent means of expanding the terms of the social licence and thereby the scope of CER, as was the use of the regulatory licence to expand the social licence through requirements to disclose comparative information. And collective licences (in the form of self-regulatory CER initiatives), while unlikely to make a substantial contribution to improved corporate environmental performance as a stand-alone policy instrument, might nevertheless do so if used in conjunction with an underpinning of state or third-party oversight, or as a form of co-regulation.

The broader conclusion is that CER is part of a complex web involving law, social, economic pressures and, on occasion, collective licence pressures, and without understanding this web one cannot explain why companies seek to engage in improved corporate environmental performance.

17

Power and responsibility: why human rights should address corporate environmental wrongs

AMY SINDEN

I. Introduction

A. The problem

Deep in the Ecuadorian Amazon rain forest is a region known as the Oriente. It is teeming with life, supporting more biodiversity than perhaps any spot on the globe: 5 per cent of all species on earth live here, in an area smaller than the state of Alabama. The Cofan Indians have called this region home for centuries and, until a generation ago, their way of life had changed little from that of their ancestors. They lived in small clan groups in thatched hut villages. They hunted wild monkeys, turkeys and pigs with spears and blow guns. The biodiversity of the forest was stitched through the very fabric of their lives – from the grasses they used to build their huts to the animals they hunted for food, to the plants and herbs they used to heal the sick. Just to make a blow gun, a Cofan hunter would gather sixty different materials from the rich bounty of the rain forest.[1]

But in 1972 life began to change drastically for the Cofan. Through a deal struck with the Ecuadorian government, Texaco came to the Oriente. Bulldozers began cutting roads through the thick forest. Oil rigs began pumping black crude through a pipeline that snaked its way 500 kilometres across the rain forest, up 13,000 feet through the Andes, and finally down to the sea. Then, strange things began to happen. Huge pools of bubbling black liquid appeared in remote areas of the forest. Rivers and streams ran black with oil. Trees withered and died. A Cofan hunter shot a wild pig with a blow gun, just as his ancestors had done for centuries, but found its body so soaked with oil that the meat was inedible. Tribe members began to complain of strange skin rashes and intestinal problems. Children were

[1] Joe Kane, *Savages* (New York: Alfred A. Knopf, 1996), pp. 33–5; Joe Kane, 'Battle for the Rain Forest', *Scholastic Update* 131 (8 February 1999), 6.

born with birth defects that made them so bowlegged they could barely walk. Cancer rates quadrupled.[2]

Complaints began coming from residents of the Oriente, but the weak and corruption-prone government of Ecuador, which derives half of its revenue from oil production, was unresponsive. It took decades before international investigations eventually began to reveal the enormous scope and depth of the harm that Texaco had wrought. By the time the company finished operations and left Ecuador in 1992, the pipeline had spilled 17 million gallons of crude oil into the forests and streams of the Oriente, half again as much as was spilled by the Exxon-Valdez in Alaska. But that was the least of it. For twenty years Texaco had been dumping more than 4 million gallons of waste water each day into hundreds of unlined pits throughout the region – an antiquated practice that has long been illegal in the United States. These pits left a lasting legacy, continuing to leach arsenic, lead and other cancer-causing chemicals into the rivers and creeks of the Oriente long after the company had left, producing levels of contamination in drinking water a thousand times higher than those allowed in the United States.[3]

Meanwhile, in another remote corner of the globe, the New Orleans-based mining company, Freeport-McMoran, has been under contract with the Indonesian government since the 1960s to operate copper, gold and silver mines in the forests of Papua New Guinea. The contract gives Freeport broad powers over the population, including quasi-governmental authority, like the power of eminent domain. It also promises 'flexibility' in the enforcement of Indonesia's environmental laws – a promise that the Indonesian government has assiduously kept. Indeed, environmental enforcement has been so 'flexible' as to be virtually non-existent.

Freeport's mining operations have deposited huge quantities of mine tailings and other toxic wastes directly into the region's rivers and streams, leaving environmental devastation in their wake. The trees that the local people used to build houses and canoes have died off, the animals that people had hunted for food are gone, and in at least five documented incidents, people eating shellfish from rivers polluted by mine tailings have died of copper poisoning. In the 1980s and 1990s, when there were signs that the local people might protest, Freeport hired the Indonesian military to 'protect their investment', paying tens of millions of dollars as

---

[2] Judith Kimerling, *Amazon Crude* (New York: Natural Resources Defense Council, Inc., 1991), pp. 43, 55–84; Eyal Press, 'Texaco on Trial', *The Nation* 268 (1999), 11.

[3] Chris Jochnick, 'Amazon Oil Offensive', *Multinational Monitor* 16 (January/February 1995); Kimmerling, *Amazon Crude*, pp. 31, 48.

well as providing helicopters and other equipment. The result has been brutal repression of any attempts to speak out against Freeport's operations. Torture, rape, murder, arbitrary detention and surveillance of local residents by Indonesian soldiers have all been documented.[4]

B. Toward a solution

These stories and others like them have been important drivers of the Corporate Social Responsibility (CSR) movement. Indeed, it is in response to damaging publicity over atrocities like these committed in the developing world that many transnational corporations (TNCs) have begun in recent years to adopt codes of conduct, promising to conform business practices to ethical standards that combine attention to short-term shareholder profits with a new respect and commitment to social and environmental values.[5]

But, as stories like these continue to emerge, there is increasing scepticism about the capacity of purely voluntary ethical codes to adequately address the problem. Additionally, there is a sense that the magnitude and profundity of such harms demands a stronger response, both functionally and rhetorically. Accordingly, the public debate surrounding environmental atrocities like these increasingly employs the language of human rights. There have been numerous pieces in the academic literature urging the application of human rights norms to TNCs.[6] There have been a series of attempts in US courts to use the Alien Tort Claims Act (ATCA) to

---

[4] Abigail Abrash, *Human Rights Abuses by Freeport in Indonesia: Observations on Human Rights Conditions in the PT Freeport Indonesia Contract of Work Areas with Recommendations* (Robert F. Kennedy Memorial Center for Human Rights, July 2002), available at www.mpi.org.au/campaigns/rights/human_rights_abuse_freeport_indo/.

[5] See Doreen McBarnet, 'Human Rights, Corporate Responsibility and the New Accountability', in Tom Campbell and Seumas Miller (eds.), *Human Rights and the Moral Responsibilities of Corporate and Public Sector Organisations* (Boston: Kluwer Academic Publishers, 2004), pp. 63, 66–7.

[6] See Steven R. Ratner, 'Corporations and Human Rights: A Theory of Legal Responsibility', *Yale Law Journal* 111 (2001), 443; Menno T. Kamminga, 'Holding Multinational Corporations Accountable for Human Rights Abuses: A Challenge for the EU', in Philip Alston (ed.), *The EU and Human Rights* (Oxford: Oxford University Press, 1999), p. 553; Tom Campbell, 'Moral Dimensions of Human Rights', in Campbell and Miller (eds.), *Human Rights*, p. 11; Nicola Jägers, *Corporate Human Rights Obligations: In Search of Accountability* (New York: Intersentia, 2002); Meno T. Kamminga and Saman Zia-Zarifi (eds.), *Liability of Multinational Corporations under International Law* (Boston: Kluwer Law International, 2000); Rebecca M. Bratspies, '"Organs of Society": A Plea for Human Rights Accountability for Transnational Business Enterprises and Other Business Entities', *Michigan State Journal of International Law* 13 (2005), 9.

hold TNCs responsible for human rights violations in connection with environmental harms.[7] And a number of international instruments have actually begun to define (though not in binding terms) a set of specific duties imposed on TNCs by human rights norms.[8]

Certainly, there is an intuitive appeal to the idea of applying human rights norms against TNCs. It seems to provide some legal credibility to the sense of moral outrage that these incidents engender. And given that part of the problem stems from the inadequacy of domestic regulation, it seems desirable to try to shift the locus of enforcement from domestic to international regimes. Calling something an 'international human rights violation' begins to effect that shift.

But there are two big problems with trying to impose human rights norms directly on corporations. First, human rights have traditionally been defined solely against states.[9] Some maintain that to view human rights as imposing duties on private corporations 'changes the very foundations of human rights'.[10] Second, some of the bad things done by TNCs do not quite seem to fit our traditional notions of the kinds of injuries that constitute human rights violations.[11] When, for example, Freeport hires the Indonesian military to beat demonstrators to death, that looks very much like a human rights violation. But what about the people who died from eating poisoned shellfish? When Freeport dumps toxic mine tailings in the rivers with impunity, is that a human rights violation? Those people

---

[7] See James Boeving, 'Half Full . . . or Completely Empty: Environmental Alien Tort Claims Post Sosa v. Alvarez-Machain', *Georgetown International Environmental Law Review* 18 (2005), 109; Hari M. Osofsky, 'Environmental Human Rights under the Alien Tort Statute: Redress for Indigenous Victims of Multinational Corporations', *Suffolk Transnational Law Review* 20 (1997), 335.

[8] Sub-Commission on the Promotion and Protection of Human Rights, *UN Norms on the Responsibilities of Transnational Corporations and Other Business Enterprises with Regard to Human Rights*, UN Doc. E/CN.4/Sub.2/2003/12/Rev.2 (2003), available at www.unhchr.ch/html/menu2/2/55sub/55sub.htm; OECD Guidelines for Multinational Enterprises (2000), available at www.oecd.org/dataoecd/56/36/1922428.pdf. See generally Jägers, *Corporate Human Rights Obligations*, pp. 99–131.

[9] See Campbell and Miller (eds.), *Human Rights*, p. 14; Ratner, 'Corporations and Human Rights', 465–6. There are a few exceptions. Human rights against genocide, war crimes and crimes against humanity have, since the aftermath of World War II, been enforceable against individuals: see Ratner, 'Corporations and Human Rights' at 466–8; Convention on the Prevention and Punishment of the Crime of Genocide, 9 December 1948, Article 4, S. Exec. Doc. O, 81–1 (1949) ('[P]ersons committing genocide . . . shall be punished whether they are constitutionally responsible rulers, public officials, or private individuals').

[10] Peter T. Muchlinski, 'Human Rights and Multinationals: Is there a Problem?', *International Affairs* 77 (2001), 31, 32.

[11] See Campbell and Miller (eds.), *Human Rights*, pp. 14–15, 22.

are just as dead as the people killed by the military, and their death evokes a similar sense of moral outrage. Intuitively, it feels like a human rights violation. But it doesn't fit as clearly into traditional categories of human rights because it is not the kind of thing that states typically tend to do. It is the kind of thing that corporations tend to do.

Most of the academics who have been urging the adoption of human rights norms against TNCs have approached the question primarily from the perspective of positive law.[12] That is, they have sought to answer the question, is this a human rights violation? by asking, is this something that could be treated as a human rights violation under currently existing standards and structures of international law? And for many who have posed that question, the answer has been: perhaps not yet, though international law is arguably moving in that direction.

But human rights are more than just a product of positive law. One of their 'prime roles' is also 'to provide a basis for criticism of positive law'.[13] Accordingly, I would like to take a different approach by stepping back and asking the normative question, are the bad things that TNCs do things that we *should* treat as human rights violations? This requires us to ask, what are human rights, and what are the concerns and values that underlie them? What are the qualities that raise an injurious act to the level of a human rights violation? Do the acts described above committed by TNCs share those qualities? Is there a legitimate theoretical basis for arguing that the rubric of human rights should include claims by individuals against TNCs as well as claims by individuals against states?

In the remainder of this chapter I will argue that many of the environmental wrongs committed by TNCs *are* things that we should treat as human rights violations. Rights are at bottom a response to the problem of power. During the Enlightenment, when the idea of civil and political rights was born, states were by and large the biggest aggregations of power in society. Rights were therefore crafted to protect individuals from abuses of power by states. But today, TNCs often wield as much or even more power than many states, and the conditions of individuals'

---

[12] See, e.g., Kamminga, 'Holding Multinational Corporations Accountable'; Andrew Clapham, *Human Rights in the Private Sphere* (Oxford: Clarendon Press, 1993); Muchlinski, 'Human Rights'; Jägers, *Corporate Human Rights Obligations*; Dinah Shelton, 'Protecting Human Rights in a Globalized World', *Boston College International and Comparative Law Review* 25 (2002), 273. Indeed, some argue that international human rights cannot possibly be described or defined in other than positive law terms because there exists no international consensus on the moral or normative foundations for human rights. See Louis Henkin, *The Age of Rights* (New York: Columbia University Press, 1990), p. 32.

[13] Campbell, 'Moral Dimensions', p. 17.

lives are shaped as much by TNCs as by states. From this perspective, it seems obvious that TNCs are far more like states than like individuals, and thus should be located on the public rather than the private side of the public–private divide in assigning human rights and duties. The problem is that our legal and political discourse has become so permeated with the logic of welfare economics that we have come to reflexively envision social relations in terms of private actors competing in markets and to ignore distributions of wealth and power. But once we view rights through the lens of power rather than through the lens of welfare economics, the idea that human rights obligations should be imposed against TNCs begins to seem natural.

The remainder of this chapter proceeds in three further sections. Section II defines 'human rights', narrowing the argument to civil and political rights, and arguing that these rights have always been rooted in significant part in the perceived need to counteract the power imbalance between the individual and the State. Section III argues that, even though corporations are traditionally categorised on the private side of the public–private divide, the significant power wielded by TNCs makes that an awkward fit. TNCs often wield much the same kind of power as that wielded by states and, in such circumstances, human rights duties should be imposed directly on TNCs. Section IV describes the particular types of human rights claims that ought to apply against TNCs, discusses the extent to which such claims would provide protections not already available through the enforcement of common law rights, and considers the question of compliance.

II. The nature of rights

The term 'rights' can mean many things in many different contexts. Accordingly, it will be helpful to define the sense in which I use the term here. To begin with, it is useful to distinguish between two basic types of rights. On one hand, there are 'human rights'. In this category, I lump together both international human rights and the constitutional rights that exist within domestic jurisdictions. These rights are traditionally understood as rights that individuals enjoy against government.[14] On the other hand, there are 'private rights' that government enables individuals

---

[14] See Rex Martin, 'Human Rights and Civil Rights', in Morton E. Winston (ed.), *The Philosophy of Human Rights* (Belmont, CA: Wadsworth 1989), pp. 75, 79–81.

to enforce against each other.[15] Traditionally, these were the rights of tort and contract, although recently those common law rights have been extensively supplemented by statutory rights.

There is, of course, no question that private rights can be asserted against TNCs (or against any corporation). My focus is rather on human rights. But that category can be further divided into at least two subcategories: civil and political rights arose out of the Enlightenment and form the basis for the US Constitution and the French Declaration of the Rights of Man. They are rooted in a conception of the person as an autonomous individual, and they stress the protection of individual autonomy and dignity from government interference. Economic and social rights, in contrast, trace their lineage to Karl Marx, and are rooted in the notion that government has affirmative obligations to protect individuals from deprivation of the basic material necessities of life. In addition to these two well-established categories, what some are calling a 'third generation' of human rights has also recently begun to emerge, protecting group rights to the preservation of cultural identity and self-determination.[16]

Second generation economic and social rights – or even third generation group rights – might at first blush seem more amenable to the accommodation of a right against environmental harm of the type I seek to promote here. Nonetheless, my argument focuses solely on civil and political rights. These are the rights with the longest historical pedigree and the rights that command the most respect and acceptance in the developed world.[17] Since the developed world wields substantial power and influence in international law and is where most TNCs are rooted, culturally if not also physically, I have chosen to frame my argument around the kinds of rights that the developed world understands. Accordingly, in the following pages I attempt to construct a theoretical basis for the imposition of human rights duties directly on TNCs for environmental

---

[15] See Peter Laslett (ed.), *Locke: Two Treatises of Government* (Cambridge: Cambridge University Press, 1988), pp. 271–2, 357–63 (government's purpose to protect rights of individuals against invasion by each other, but in serving that function, government necessarily accrues power, which it has duty to citizens not to abuse).

[16] See Winston (ed.), *The Philosophy of Human Rights*, pp. 4–5, 18–19; Tom Campbell, *Rights: A Critical Introduction* (New York: Routledge, 2006), pp. 5–10.

[17] Moreover, the International Covenant on Economic, Social, and Cultural Rights (16 December 1966, S. Exec. Doc. D, 95-2 (1978), 993 UNTS 3) is written in less binding terms than the International Covenant on Civil and Political Rights (19 December 1966, S. Exec. Doc. E, 95-2 (1978), 999 UNTS 171). The former only calls on states to 'take steps' to achieve the enumerated rights 'up to the maximum of available resources'. Henkin, *Age of Rights*, p. 20.

harms solely on the basis of the civil and political rights that are rooted in the Enlightenment tradition and exemplified by US constitutional law.

A. Human rights as mediators of power imbalance between the individual and the state

For civil and political human rights at the international or domestic level, the prototypical rights holder is the individual and the prototypical duty holder is the state.[18] These rights come into play when for some reason we cannot trust the political system to protect certain individual interests through the usual forms of private law. Usually that occurs when there is some reason to worry about abuse of power by the state itself. In those instances, we cannot trust the state to police itself. We need some higher source of authority to act as a check on state power. Within domestic legal systems, that higher source of authority is the constitution. In international law, it is international human rights norms.[19]

A great deal has been written about the basis and justifications for civil and political human rights. For our purposes, it is sufficient to observe that two dominant strands of thought consistently emerge in efforts to identify the concerns and values underlying these rights. I will call them (1) the individual autonomy strand and (2) the power imbalance strand.[20] In the words of Richard Pildes, the individual autonomy strand 'reasons out' from the conception of the person.[21] It views the integrity, dignity and autonomy of the individual as paramount, and as requiring the delineation of a sphere of immunity around each person within which the state cannot intrude. The power imbalance strand, on the other hand, 'reasons in' from actual experience with government practice and from the risk that government will abuse power.[22] This strand views rights as providing a counterweight to the imbalance of power between the individual and the state.

---

[18] See Campbell and Miller (eds.), *Human Rights*, p. 17.

[19] See Ratner, 'Corporations and Human Rights', 466; Louis Henkin, 'International Rights as Human Rights', in Winston (ed.), *The Philosophy of Human Rights*, pp. 129, 131.

[20] See Amy Sinden, 'In Defense of Absolutes: Combating the Politics of Power in Environmental Law', *Iowa Law Review* 90 (2005), 1405, 1460–84.

[21] Richard H. Pildes, 'Why Rights are Not Trumps: Social Meanings, Expressive Harms, and Constitutionalism', *Journal of Legal Studies* 27(1998), 725, 729.

[22] *ibid.*; see also Christina Brooks Whitman, 'Emphasizing the Constitutional in Constitutional Torts', *Chicago-Kent Law Review* 72 (1997), 661, 669 (constitutional rights 'are defined with reference to the unique power that government has over those subject to its jurisdiction').

Both strands emerge clearly from, for example, the vast literature on freedom of expression. One prominent view follows the individual autonomy strand, seeing freedom of expression as primarily aimed at protecting values of individual autonomy, self-realisation and self-fulfilment.[23] But another robust line of theory views freedom of expression as essential to countering the power of government – as providing a crucial check on the abuse of state power. Freedom of speech, freedom of assembly and association, and freedom of the press all serve this checking function, ensuring that the power of the state is not used to suppress information and ideas critical of government.[24]

Both strands also animate criminal procedure rights. The power imbalance between the individual and the state is perhaps nowhere more vivid and palpable than when the individual is pitted against the vast power and resources of the state in a criminal proceeding. Accordingly, it is no surprise that four of the ten amendments that make up the US Bill of Rights are devoted to the rights of the criminally accused. Certainly, the individual autonomy strand is very much in evidence here, since a criminal proceeding involves possibly the most severe limitations conceivable on individual freedom and autonomy – imprisonment and even death. But the power imbalance strand is also prominent. Many criminal procedure rights are explicitly justified by courts and commentators in terms of the need to counteract the vast disparity of power between the state and the accused. These include the right to counsel,[25] the right against self-incrimination,[26] the double jeopardy guarantee,[27] and the beyond-a-reasonable-doubt standard,[28] to name a few. Through these various

---

[23] See Thomas Scanlon, 'A Theory of Freedom of Expression', *Philosophy and Public Affairs* 1 (1972), 204, 215–22.

[24] See Vincent Blasi, 'The Checking Value in First Amendment Theory', *American Bar Foundation Research Journal* (1977), 521.

[25] See *United States* v. *Gouveia*, 467 US 180, 189 (1984) (right to counsel aimed at correcting the imbalance of power between the government and the accused).

[26] See *Miranda* v. *Arizona*, 384 US 436, 460 (1966) (right against self-incrimination aimed at ensuring 'the proper scope of governmental power over the citizen . . . and maintaining a fair state-individual balance').

[27] See *Green* v. *United States*, 355 US 184, 187–8 (1957) ('The underlying idea [behind the double jeopardy clause], one that is deeply ingrained in at least the Anglo-American system of jurisprudence, is that the State with all its resources and power should not be allowed to make repeated attempts to convict an individual for an alleged offense, thereby subjecting him to embarrassment, expense and ordeal and compelling him to live in a continuing state of anxiety').

[28] See Andrew Ashworth, *Principles of Criminal Law* (New York: Oxford University Press, 1991), p. 74.

mechanisms, the procedural protections provided to criminal defendants operate to level the playing field between the individual and the state.

In the civil context as well, due process rights implicate both the individual autonomy strand and the power imbalance strand underlying civil and political rights. Certainly, the deprivation of an individual's life, liberty or property by the state implicates his or her individual autonomy. But we could say the same about a deprivation of life, liberty or property committed by any private individual. Why, then, do we raise such deprivations to the status of civil and political rights when they are committed by the state? The answer is that because of the power imbalance between the individual and the state, we are particularly worried that such deprivations will occur at the hands of the state, and that when they do the usual remedies will not be sufficient to redress them.[29] Due process, then, gives individuals something when the state deprives them of life, liberty or property that they do not get when another private individual commits such a deprivation – that is, procedural due process: notice and an opportunity to be heard. Procedural due process operates to shift power from the state to the individual by giving the individual the right to demand information and to participate in decision-making processes that affect her or him.

B. The nature of power

Thus, civil and political human rights are justified in part by the need to counteract the power imbalance between the individual and the state. But what is this thing called power? Perhaps the words of the Due Process Clause best capture what the framers of the US Constitution had in mind when they worried about power as wielded by government: the ability to 'deprive [persons] of life, liberty or property'. This implies the ability to alter the quality of people's lives or the conditions of their existence along all dimensions: physical (life), spiritual (liberty) and material (property). Certainly, one obvious reason that governments have this capacity is because they control the police and the military. They can literally call in the troops, put people in jail or, in some jurisdictions, even put people to death.

---

[29] See *Daniels* v. *Williams*, 474 US 327, 331 (1986) (acknowledging 'the traditional and common-sense notion that the Due Process Clause, like its forebear in the Magna Carta, was "intended to secure the individual from the arbitrary exercise of the powers of government"').

But the direct application of physical force is not the only form that power takes. Perhaps more importantly, the power to alter the conditions of a person's life through direct physical force also implies the power to alter the conditions of his or her life through coercion. Thus, if A can alter the physical, spiritual or material conditions of B's life through the application of direct physical force, then it necessarily follows that A can also get B to do things that B would not otherwise do by *threatening* to alter the conditions of B's life. This is Robert Dahl's well-known formulation of the concept of power.[30] Thus, we pay taxes and stop at red lights at least in part because of the coercive power wielded over us by government (the threat of physical force).

Of course, I do not literally worry that a police officer will put a gun to my head if I run a red light or fail to pay my taxes. I worry instead about having to pay the traffic ticket or the fines or penalties that will likely be imposed if I fail to comply with the law. I suppose we can say that in some ultimate sense, all exercises of government power are backed up by the threat of physical force. Initially, my refusal to pay my traffic ticket would only result in further demands for monetary penalties, but eventually repeated refusals to pay could conceivably land me behind bars for contempt of court. But for most people in the modern world, physical manifestations of government power are far removed from daily life. Instead, for most of us most of the time, government power manifests itself in economic rather than physical terms. Government alters the material conditions of my existence by assessing taxes or imposing fines or penalties. And it exercises coercive power over me – getting me to do things I would not otherwise do – by threatening to impose economic penalties on me if I engage in certain activities (like running a red light).

But this description still fails to capture the full spectrum of government power in modern society. While the Enlightenment-era thinkers

---

[30] Robert A. Dahl, 'The Concept of Power', *Behavioral Science* 2 (1957), 201, 202–3. Subsequent critiques of Dahl's formulation have argued that power can take other subtler forms as well. See Steven Lukes, *Power: A Radical View* (2nd edn, New York: Palgrave, 2005), p. 167; Steven L. Winter, 'The "Power" Thing', *Virginia Law Review* 82 (1996), 721; Michel Foucault, *Power/Knowledge: Selected Interviews and Other Writings, 1972–77* (New York: Pantheon, 1980). While these later and more complex understandings of the concept of power are important to any general investigation of the role of power relationships in society, because they are probably outside the realm of the conception of power that animated the Enlightenment-era architects of civil and political rights, and because Dahl's definition is sufficient to draw the analogy between state power and TNC power necessary for my argument here, I am confining my analysis to the narrower conception of power captured by Dahl's original formulation.

who first formulated civil and political human rights tended to conceptualise government power only in negative terms – as the capacity to *deprive* – the flip side of taking is giving, and government can exercise power as much through giving as taking away.[31] This positive aspect of government power is far more difficult to ignore in the modern welfare state, where government largesse affects the conditions of its citizens' existence through countless programmes, regulatory schemes and initiatives that are intricately woven into the fabric of economic life. Farm subsidies, welfare payments, corporate bail-outs, tax-breaks and below-market mineral leases on public lands all look like government *giving* rather than *depriving*. But, at least in the economic realm, these are simply flip sides of a single coin. Thus, the distinction between depriving of a right and withdrawing a benefit is often difficult to draw – as is the distinction between ceasing to impose a deprivation and conferring a benefit. Does the termination of welfare benefits deprive the recipient of a right or withdraw a benefit?[32] Does the conferral of a tax break confer a benefit or cease the imposition of a deprivation? Accordingly, the capacity to confer benefits that alter the physical, material and spiritual conditions of existence is an important aspect of government power and intimately related to the capacity to deprive.

And, like the capacity to deprive, the capacity to confer benefits also implies the power of coercion. That is, government may get me to do things I would not otherwise do by offering a benefit (as well as by threatening a deprivation). I may, for example, choose to buy rather than rent a house, in part because of the tax benefit conferred on me by the US government in the form of the mortgage interest deduction if I do so. Similarly, the promise of a tax benefit may cause a corporation to locate a plant in one location rather than another. While these examples seem relatively innocuous, the capacity to confer benefits – like the capacity to deprive – creates a significant potential for abuse of this coercive power, as when a

---

[31] See Lukes, *Power*, p. 83 ('[T]here is really no reason for supposing that the powerful always threaten rather than sometimes advance, the interests of others').

[32] See *Goldberg* v. *Kelly*, 397 US 254, 262 (1970) (rejecting right/privilege distinction). Even a more traditional form of property – like a piece of land to which I hold title – can be viewed as a benefit conferred by the state rather than a pre-existing right. My ability to possess, use and exclude others from the property, after all, exists only by virtue of the state's administration of a system of property rights definition and enforcement. See Joseph William Singer, *Entitlement: The Paradoxes of Property* (New Haven, CT: Yale University Press, 2000), p. 7. Under this view, a deprivation of that property by the state constitutes simply the withdrawal of a benefit rather than the deprivation of a right.

state social worker makes a teenage mother's continued receipt of welfare benefits contingent on her 'agreement' to undergo sterilisation.[33]

Finally, government power affects us indirectly as well as directly. By influencing countless private decisions, government power shapes not only our relations with government itself, but our relations to other private actors as well. It affects how private resources are used and distributed in society, which in turn affects the physical, material and spiritual conditions of our existence: whether a polluting facility can locate in my neighbourhood, or whether an employer has to pay me a minimum wage.[34]

States, of course, are not the only entities that exercise power in society. Private individuals exercise power over other private individuals all the time. When a mugger holds me up at gunpoint, he is exercising power over me. He is getting me to do something I would not otherwise do – hand him my purse – by threatening to alter the physical conditions of my life. When a private law firm offers me a pay cheque, it is getting me to do something I wouldn't otherwise do – go to work every day – by altering the material conditions of my life. But the framers of the US Constitution did not give me a constitutional right against the mugger or the law firm. Nor do international human rights norms give me such a claim.[35] Civil and political human rights do not generally address the myriad power imbalances that exist between private individuals.[36]

Why do civil and political rights only apply to exercises of power by the state? What makes the power exercised by the state different from the power exercised by a private individual? The difference is that when the state itself exercises power over me, there is no higher authority – no one to whom I can appeal. When the mugger takes my purse, I can call on the superior power of the state to arrest the mugger and put him in jail. When the law firm fails to pay me, I can file a lawsuit, get a judgment against

---

[33] See Cox v. Stanton, 529 F 2d 47 (4th Cir. 1975).

[34] See Susan Strange, The Retreat of the State: The Diffusion of Power in the World Economy (New York: Cambridge University Press, 1996), pp. 16–43.

[35] The only exception would be if the mugger's acts fell within the definition of genocide war crimes or crimes against humanity. See n. 9 above.

[36] Equal protection rights can be viewed as an exception – that is, they can be viewed as aiming to counteract power imbalances between private groups in society rather than between private individuals and government. See Ruth Colker, 'Anti-Subordination Above All: Sex, Race, and Equal Protection', New York University Law Review 61 (1986), 1003, 1007; Laurence H. Tribe, 'Constitutional Calculus: Equal Justice or Economic Efficiency?', Harvard Law Review 98 (1985), 592, 604. The equal protection clause, however, was not part of the original Enlightenment-era civil and political rights in the US Constitution. Moreover, the equal protection guarantee is subject to the state action requirement and so, as a matter of US constitutional law anyway, is limited to discrimination by the state.

the law firm, and, if necessary, get the sheriff to execute the judgment. But when a government soldier puts a gun to my head, there is no higher authority to whom I can complain.[37] The state is the final decision-maker. Human rights, then – whether they are international human rights or domestic constitutional rights – by standing outside of and above the apparatus of the state, serve to constrain the exercise of ultimate, final, unappealable power by the state.

III. Positioning transnational corporations within the public–private divide

Civil and political human rights, then, are the mechanism by which law mediates the power relationship between the state and the individual, or, more generally, between the private and public realms. Where does the TNC fit in within this structure? In general, the treatment of corporations in both domestic and international law is premised on the notion that they are private, not public, entities – that is, that they are more like individuals than like states. This follows naturally from the economic world view, which dominates current conceptions of law in general and corporations in particular.[38] Under this view, corporations are participants in the free market, accountable only to shareholders. Like individual people, they are rational profit maximisers competing in the market. This now dominant conception of social relations places corporations in general (including TNCs) squarely on the private side of the public–private divide. That is, they are analogised to and categorised with individuals rather than states. Accordingly, with respect to human rights, they are treated as rights holders rather than duty holders.[39]

---

[37] See *Bivens* v. *Six Unknown Federal Agents*, 403 US 388, 394 (1971) ('[W]e may bar the door against an unwelcome private intruder, or call the police if he persists in seeking entrance . . . [but] the mere invocation of [government] power by a . . . law enforcement official will normally render futile any attempt to resist an unlawful entry or arrest by resort to the local police, and a claim of authority to enter is likely to unlock the door as well').

[38] See Cynthia A. Williams, 'Corporate Social Responsibility in an Era of Economic Globalization', *UC Davis Law Review* 35 (2002), 705, 711–14; Kellye Y. Testy, 'Linking Progressive Corporate Law with Progressive Social Movements', *Tulane Law Review* 76 (2002), 1227; Lawrence E. Mitchell, *Corporate Irresponsibility: America's Newest Export* (New Haven, CT: Yale University Press, 2001).

[39] The US Supreme Court has held that corporations are 'persons' entitled to assert constitutional rights. See Daniel J. H. Greenwood, 'Markets and Democracy: The Illegitimacy of Corporate Law', *University of Missouri-Kansas City Law Review* 74 (2005), 41, 59. The European Court of Human Rights has also held that corporations possess rights to property, free speech, a fair trial and privacy. See Michael Addo, 'The Corporation as Victim

But if we think about the values and concerns that underlie civil and political human rights, under either the individual autonomy or the power imbalance strand of rights jurisprudence, the TNC seems an awkward fit on the private, rights-holder side.[40] From the perspective of the individual autonomy strand, a TNC is certainly not a human being with needs for bodily integrity, self-realisation, self-fulfilment and so on, and thus hardly seems an appropriate rights holder. Indeed, Joseph Raz rests his theory of rights in part on the Kantian condition that the individual rights holder's well-being is of 'ultimate value', or 'an end in itself' – a condition that clearly applies to human beings but is problematic as applied to TNCs. In order to make his theory fit with the reality of existing legal doctrine, he tacks on corporations (or 'artificial persons') as an additional category of rights-holders, almost as an afterthought.[41] But the very fact that they need to be added as a separate category only serves to highlight the lack of fit between corporations and the fundamental concept of rights-holder.

The fit seems awkward from the perspective of the power-imbalance strand as well. It has become almost cliché these days to observe that many TNCs wield more economic power than most nations.[42] And even with respect to 'the ability to wield physical force, corporations are as powerful as . . . government[s]: private security forces employ more people than public police departments'.[43] But if TNCs are really as powerful – or more powerful – than many states, does it make sense to put them on the private side of the divide? Given the extraordinary power wielded by TNCs, would it not make more sense to put them on the other side – to treat them as duty-holders vis-à-vis the human rights claims of individuals, just as states are?[44] After all, while the state was viewed as representing the greatest aggregation of power and therefore the greatest threat to individual liberty

of Human Rights Violations, in Michael K. Addo (ed.), *Human Rights Standards and the Responsibility of Transnational Corporations* (Boston: Kluwer Law International, 1999), pp. 187–97.

[40] See Greenwood, 'Markets and Democracy', 55, 87.
[41] Joseph Raz, 'On the Nature of Rights', in Winston (ed.), *The Philosophy of Human Rights*, pp. 44, 45.
[42] See Kamminga, 'Holding Multinational Corporations Accountable', p. 553.
[43] Greenwood, 'Markets and Democracy', 58–9.
[44] See Clapham, *Human Rights*, p. 137 ('[T]he definition of the public sphere has . . . to be adapted to include . . . new centres of power . . . such as . . . multinationals . . . that the individual now perceives [as sources of] authority, repression, and alienation'); Shelton, 'Protecting Human Rights', 315; Campbell and Miller (eds.), *Human Rights*, p. 18; Peter Muchlinski, 'International Business Regulation: An Ethical Discourse in the Making?', in Campbell and Miller (eds.), *Human Rights*, pp. 81, 91.

and autonomy at the time the Bill of Rights was drafted, cannot we now say that TNCs are wielding power on the same scale as states?[45]

Accordingly, under both the individual autonomy and the power imbalance strands of human rights jurisprudence, TNCs may be more appropriately treated as duty holders (like states) than as rights holders (like individuals).[46] This argument has a certain intuitive appeal, but to test its legitimacy, we must carefully consider two questions. First, do states wield power over TNCs in the same way they wield power over individuals? Second, do TNCs wield power over individuals in the same way that states do?

In one sense, a state's control over the military and the police creates power over corporations within its jurisdiction of the same or similar kind that states wield over individuals. The state has the power to fine a corporation and to put its officers in jail. This implies the concomitant power to force a corporation to comply with regulatory restrictions on its activities through the threat of such sanctions. Indeed, since a corporation itself exists only by virtue of a benefit conferred by the state, the state that has incorporated it also has the power to disband it. This, however, assumes that the corporation is incorporated, headquartered and doing business all within one state. As TNCs become more and more international, they become more difficult for individual states to control.[47] Certainly, where a TNC does business in a host state, but is incorporated and headquartered in a separate home state, the host state's ability to exert power over the TNC is substantially diminished.

As the last section explored, a state may exert power through positive as well as negative incentives. Thus, it may exert power over a corporation by offering tax-breaks, subsidies or leases to mineral rights on public lands. The strength of this power, however, depends on the wealth of the state. Developing nations are often cash poor and desperate for foreign investment.[48] TNCs, on the other hand, often wield wealth that dwarfs the GNP of the developing country with which they are negotiating. Thus, in the developing world, power in the form of the capacity to offer money and/or valuable resources may often flow in the opposite direction, from

---

[45] See Ratner, 'Corporations and Human Rights', 461.

[46] While the application of human rights norms to TNCs is frequently described as giving human rights 'horizontal effect,' or '*Drittwirkung*' (see Jägers, *Corporate Human Rights Obligations*, p. 38), my argument in effect reconceptualises the relationship between individuals and TNCs from a horizontal to a vertical orientation.

[47] See Ratner, 'Corporations and Human Rights', 463; Kamminga, 'Holding Multinational Corporations Accountable', p. 553.

[48] See Ratner, 'Corporations and Human Rights', 459–60.

the TNC to the state. That is to say, the TNC may have more of an ability to get the state to do things it would not otherwise do than vice versa.[49]

The relationship between Texaco and the government of Ecuador provides an instructive example. On the one hand, Ecuador exercised positive power over Texaco, offering it concessions to state-owned land on which the oil company could search for oil. Additionally, Ecuador exercised negative power, imposing taxes on Texaco's operations, collecting royalties and requiring the company to invest in infrastructure, including roads and airports, as a *quid pro quo* for access to Ecuadorian oil reserves. On the other hand, substantial power ran in the other direction as well. Texaco had the money, technology and expertise necessary to explore and drill for oil. These were resources that the Ecuadorian government did not have and desperately needed. In order to transform its oil reserves into much-needed cash, Ecuador was dependent on outside investment from a company like Texaco. And Ecuador – with a national debt that had by 1991 grown to a staggering $12.4 billion (more than its GNP) – desperately needed the revenue that oil development could bring.[50]

Thus, Ecuador had sovereignty over its territory and the oil reserves within its borders and therefore had at least the formal power to deny Texaco access or set conditions on its access. But Texaco had the capacity to make vast sums of money for the Ecuadorian government – money that the government desperately needed. For Texaco, this translated into the power to push back against Ecuador's demands for royalty payments, taxes and environmental controls.[51] Thus, the power relationship between Texaco and the government of Ecuador was complicated, with substantial power running in both directions and Texaco arguably wielding even more power than the state of Ecuador.[52] This relationship looked nothing like

---

[49] See Jägers, *Corporate Human Rights Obligations*, pp. 8–9. Cf. Hari Osofsky, 'Litigating Energy's Externalities: A Modern Westphalian Geography of Corporate Responsibility' (2005), available at ssrn.com/abstract=796204 (analysing complex and changing regulatory relationship between TNCs and nation states in context of climate change litigation).

[50] Kimerling, *Amazon Crude*, p. 46.

[51] *ibid.*, p. 43. The Ecuadorian government's dual role with respect to Texaco as both regulator and business partner created an inherent conflict of interest. This is a common feature of oil development in the developing world. See Robert Dufresne, 'The Opacity of Oil: Oil Corporations, Internal Violence, and International Law', *New York University Journal of International Law and Politics* 36 (2004), 331, 355–6.

[52] For a nuanced historical portrait of the complex power relationships between developing nations and the companies to which they have granted concessions for natural resource extraction, see Rebecca Hardin, 'Concessionary Politics in the Western Congo Basin: History and Culture in Forest Use', Working Paper Series: Environmental Governance in Africa (Washington, DC: World Resources Institute, 2002). See also Dufresne, 'The Opacity of Oil'.

the prototypical relationship between the state and the individual that forms the basis for civil and political human rights.

In answer to the first question, then, there seems little doubt that states – particularly cash-poor, developing nations – do not wield power over TNCs in anything like the way states typically wield power over individuals. This indicates that it may be inappropriate simply to equate TNCs with individuals by placing them on the private side of the public–private divide. But is it appropriate to place them on the other side – to treat them the same as states, with human rights duties toward individuals? This brings us to the second question, do TNCs wield power over individuals in the same way that states do?

Applying the definition of power developed in the last section, there can be no question that Texaco exercised power over the Cofan. By poisoning their water and destroying the animals and plants that provided them food, shelter and subsistence, Texaco unquestionably altered the physical, material and spiritual conditions of the Cofan's lives. Indeed, some have called the results of the ecological destruction wrought by Texaco's operations 'cultural genocide'.[53] And the same has been said of Freeport-McMoran's impact on the people of Papua.[54] The company drastically altered the conditions of the Papuans' lives both through the ecological destruction it wrought on the resources they depended on and – to the extent that Freeport is found to be a causal agent in the military repression of the Papuans – through the torture, rape, murder and detention of Papuan citizens.

To say that these TNCs exercised power over the people of Ecuador and Papua is probably relatively uncontroversial. But the crucial question is whether the *kind* of power exercised by the TNCs is the same *kind* of power that is typically exercised by states, and therefore the same kind of power that civil and political human rights were created to counteract. In the last section, I argued that what makes state power different from private power, and what necessitates the mechanism of human rights to curtail and control state power, is the fact that it is ultimate and final – there is no higher authority to whom one can appeal. This appears to have been true of the power exercised by Texaco and Freeport over the people of Ecuador and Papua. When the tribes of the Oriente organised and petitioned the Ecuadorian government to stop Texaco from poisoning the land and water on which they depended for life, the government –

---

[53] *ibid.*, p. 34 (Cofan tribe reduced from 15,000 to 300 during Texaco's tenure).
[54] *Beanal* v. *Freeport-McMoran*, 969 F Supp. 362, 366 (E. D. La. 1997).

itself dependent on investment by foreign oil companies for half its revenue – did not respond.[55] When government troops paid for by Freeport tortured, raped and killed those who attempted to speak out against the corporation's activities in Indonesia, there was no higher authority to which the people of Papua could appeal.

In sum, while states may wield some power over TNCs, it is not anything like the prototypical power dynamic that exists between government and the individual. TNCs often wield considerable power back against states, particularly when those states are developing countries in desperate need of revenue to pay off staggering debt. Accordingly, it is inappropriate simply to put TNCs in the same category as individuals for the purposes of analysing human rights. Moreover, in some circumstances at least, TNCs wield power over individuals that looks very much like the kind of power that states wield over individuals and that civil and political human rights were created to counteract. Specifically, this is true where a TNC has the ability to alter the physical, material or spiritual conditions of existence for individuals and those individuals have no higher authority to which they can appeal.

There are two circumstances in which we find TNCs exercising final, ultimate authority of this kind. The first occurs where the state has become so weak and/or corrupt as to be non-functional. It therefore fails to regulate corporate behaviour, and in some instances the TNC may even become the de facto provider of state services.[56] The second circumstance occurs where the TNC has so much power and influence within the domestic government that it essentially controls state decision-making. These circumstances, or combinations of the two, are widespread in the developing world today. Where these circumstances exist, TNCs are exercising state-like power over individuals, and therefore should be subject to human rights duties in order to prevent abuses of that power.[57] The imposition of such duties is not some radical new departure from existing human rights norms, but is entirely consistent with the values and justifications that underlie our traditional and hallowed conceptions of civil and political rights.

---

[55] Only after Texaco made the decision to leave in 1992 did the government in Ecuador begin to take some steps to oppose Texaco, though these were largely symbolic and ineffective.

[56] See Ratner, 'Corporations and Human Rights', 500.

[57] TNCs may also be centrally involved in human rights violations where they work in concert with a state. Those acts, however, are reachable under the state action doctrine as applied to existing interpretations of human rights. See *Kadic* v. *Karadzic*, 70 F. 3d 232 (2nd Cir. 1995).

IV. Defining and enforcing the human rights duties of transnational corporations

It is one thing to say in general terms that the civil and political human rights held by individuals should be viewed as imposing duties directly on TNCs, but what particular rights are we talking about? And how can such rights be enforced? This section addresses these questions.

A. Definition

Clearly not all the rights enforceable against states are relevant in the context of TNCs. A TNC is unlikely to act in the role of criminal prosecutor, for example. Thus, the whole range of criminal procedure rights that make up so much of the lexicon of traditional civil and political rights are unlikely to be applicable against TNCs.[58] There may be some need, then, for a 'creative adaptation' of human rights norms to the context of TNCs.[59]

My aim here is not to exhaustively catalogue all of the specific rights that could apply against TNCs, but rather to simply sketch a few broad categories of rights that may be appropriate in light of the above analysis. There are three rights that have a long pedigree in the civil and political rights tradition and seem like particularly good candidates for applying against TNCs that engage in environmental wrongs in the circumstances defined above. Free expression is one such category. Where TNCs are making decisions that have widespread and significant impacts on the health and welfare of the surrounding community – like a decision to build a polluting facility or to engage in environmentally destructive extractive activity – the same concerns that underlie free expression rights against states are implicated. In such circumstances, human rights norms should ensure a free flow of ideas – including ideas critical of the corporate decision-makers. TNCs should have a duty, for example, not to suppress free expression among employees and community members aimed at publicising information relating to the environmental impacts of the TNC's facilities. Acts or threats of violence against demonstrators and those who speak out against a TNC's practices would clearly constitute

---

[58] TNCs may, however, sometimes act in concert with government officials in a prosecutorial role, as Shell Oil did in Nigeria (see n. 51 above), in which case such rights might be logically applied against them. See Ratner, 'Corporations and Human Rights', 492–3.

[59] Campbell and Miller (eds.), *Human Rights*, p. 18. See Jägers, *Corporate Human Rights Obligations*, pp. 48–74.

such suppression. But so could less violent tactics, like economic reprisals against outspoken employees.

Similar concerns weigh in favor of recognising procedural due process rights against TNCs. Thus, TNCs should have a duty to provide information to employees and community members before making decisions that may affect the physical, spiritual or material conditions of their lives, and a duty to allow employees and community members to participate in such decision-making by presenting information and arguments to corporate officials. Where, for example, a TNC is considering building a facility that may cause pollution or other environmental degradation, these rights would impose certain procedural due process obligations on the TNC for the benefit of employees and community members. At a minimum, these should include the duty to turn over information about the potential harms the facility may cause. A stronger version of such rights would require the TNC to allow employees and community members to participate in decision-making by, for example, presenting arguments and evidence relevant to the decision. This could occur either through a procedure akin to notice and comment rule-making or through some type of formal hearing. Additionally, due process might require the TNC to prepare and distribute for public comment an environmental impact statement, demonstrating that the decision-makers have adequately considered potential environmental impacts of and alternatives to the proposed facility.

Procedural rights like these are a common feature of environmental law, both domestically and internationally.[60] Such rights play an important role in promoting environmental protection. Existing laws, however, differ from what I am suggesting here in that they impose duties directly on government and only indirectly on corporations. Thus, a government agency is usually charged with gathering information from private corporations and then distributing it to the public. Additionally, the decision-making processes in which individuals are given the right to participate are usually those of the government itself, which may be deciding whether, for example, to grant a permit to a private corporation to build a polluting facility. But where government is dysfunctional or beholden to a more economically and politically powerful TNC, such procedural rights against the state are of little use. For such rights to be meaningful, the

---

[60] See Claudia Saladin, 'Public Participation in the Era of Globalization', in Romina Picolotti and Jorge Daniel Taillant (eds.), *Linking Human Rights and the Environment* (Tucson, AZ: University of Arizona Press, 2003), p. 57.

duties must be imposed directly on the real decision-maker, which in such circumstances is the TNC itself.

Finally, rights to personal security – to life and bodily integrity – should also apply against TNCs.[61] Such rights would certainly apply where a TNC hires a security force to beat demonstrators,[62] just as the assault of an individual by a police officer constitutes a clear violation of traditional civil and political rights. In my view, however, such rights should also apply in certain instances of indirect, unintentional harm – where, for example, a TNC causes environmental harm that results in significant adverse health impacts to members of the surrounding community.

In this second scenario, the TNC certainly exercises power over those harmed by the pollution – it alters the physical, material and spiritual conditions of their lives – and where the state is non-functional and/or the TNC controls state decision-making, this is the kind of power that I argued in the last section should trigger human rights norms. But not all exercises of power by the state constitute human rights violations, nor should all exercises of power by a TNC.[63] The state does not violate my rights every time it assesses a tax against me or issues me a traffic ticket, as long as it follows appropriate procedures. Nor are my human rights violated when a state employee driving negligently causes her car to crash into mine. The question is whether there has been an *abuse* of power.[64] The US Supreme Court has answered this question in the context of constitutional rights by looking at the mental state of the state official causing the injury. Generally, the Supreme Court has found that something more than negligence – deliberate indifference or gross negligence – is necessary in order for an unintentional injury caused by a state official to rise to the level of the kind of abuse of power necessary for a violation of constitutional rights.[65]

---

[61] See Cristina Baez, Michele Dearing, Margaret Delatour and Christine Dixon, 'Multinational Enterprises and Human Rights', *University of Miami International and Comparative Law Review* 8 (1999), 183, 255; *Ingraham* v. *Wright*, 430 US 651, 673–4 (1977) ('Among the historic liberties . . . protected [by the Due Process Clause] was a right to be free from . . . unjustified intrusions on personal security' including 'bodily restraint' and/or the infliction of 'appreciable physical pain').

[62] The practice of TNCs – particularly those engaged in extractive industries in the developing world – hiring private security forces and/or government military units to repress political opposition to their operations and protect their facilities is widespread. See Dufresne, 'The Opacity of Oil', 335–8, 344–5.

[63] See Ratner, 'Corporations and Human Rights', 472.

[64] See *Daniels* v. *Williams*, 474 US 327, 332 (1986).

[65] See *Estelle* v. *Gamble*, 429 US 97, 104 (1976) ('deliberate indifference' to prisoners' medical needs rises to level of constitutional rights violation); *Youngberg* v. *Romeo*, 547 US 307, 322 (1982) (conduct of state mental hospital employee must constitute a 'substantial departure

If we were to apply a similar standard to TNCs, then, a human rights violation might be found where environmental harm caused by a TNC could be traced to gross negligence and/or deliberate indifference by TNC officials.[66]

While US constitutional law provides a useful analogy, it need not, of course, be binding in this context. Certainly, an argument can be made that, at least in some situations, negligence itself may rise to the level of the kind of abuse of power that ought to constitute a human rights violation where certain other factors are present.[67] Thus, where the harm is severe, long-lasting and widespread – as was the environmental destruction wrought by Texaco in the Amazon and Freeport in Papua – mere negligence might rise to the level of an abuse of power. Additionally, where the power exercised was unique to the TNC – the power to create widespread environmental devastation, for example, as distinguished from every citizen's 'power' to cause a car accident – abuse of power might be found even where the responsible officials exhibited a less culpable mental state.

Defining the actual contours of the rights that might be asserted against TNCs obviously raises deep and complex issues that need far more development than I have space for here. I have simply tried to suggest some of the broad outlines that such an analysis might follow.

B. Enforcement

Even if the imposition of human rights duties on TNCs for environmental harms can be justified as a matter of theory, what difference would it make

from professional judgment, practice, or standards' to violate constitutional rights); *Doe* v. *New York City Department of Social Services*, 709 F 2d 782, 790 (2nd Cir. 1983) (calling *Youngberg's* professional judgement standard 'essentially a gross negligence standard' and applying it to mistreatment of child in foster care).

[66] US courts have generally applied standards lower than intent – like deliberate indifference, recklessness or gross negligence – only in custodial situations like prisons and mental hospitals, otherwise requiring a showing of actual intent in order to find constitutional liability. In *County of Sacramento* v. *Lewis*, 523 US 833 (1998), however, the Supreme Court clarified that the basis for this distinction is not the fact of custody per se so much as the fact that prison and hospital officials generally have time to deliberate before taking action, unlike, for example, police officers conducting a high speed chase. *Lewis*, 523 US at 851. Under this logic, the actions of the officials of a TNC that result in environmental degradation – typically actions taken with ample forethought over the course of many years – would clearly fall within the ambit of the deliberate indifference or gross negligence standards even though those harmed are not in the custody of the TNC.

[67] See Christina Brooks Whitman, 'Emphasizing the Constitutional in Constitutional Torts', *Chicago-Kent Law Review* 72 (1997), 661, 689–90.

in practice? Does a human rights approach present advantages over other approaches to CSR in terms of gaining actual compliance by TNCs? One might well ask, why bother? Why not simply leave TNCs on the private side of the public–private divide and rely on private rights and consumer pressures in the marketplace to temper corporate conduct? After all, if a TNC hires security guards who beat up a demonstrator, surely the demonstrator has a tort claim for assault and battery against the TNC, regardless of whether any human rights duties apply? And surely the private market itself provides an incentive for TNCs to avoid involvement in activities that in the age of internet communications are likely to produce negative publicity and hurt their image among consumers?

While negative publicity campaigns aimed at TNCs committing environmental atrocities have certainly had some effect, prompting some TNCs to adopt corporate codes of conduct and to discontinue particularly offensive activities, such effects are necessarily limited. Corporate codes of conduct are entirely voluntary, and when ethical behaviour requires sacrificing profits, ethics is unlikely to win out.[68] Moreover, such publicity campaigns depend largely on cash-strapped and overextended NGOs to monitor and publicise TNC activities and so are unlikely to occur in every instance in which they are warranted. Finally, such campaigns are most effective against high-profile, brand-driven products, but may be far less effective against firms that don't depend on a prominent public image.[69] Thus, to the extent that a human rights approach offers the possibility of supplementing market incentives with formal court enforcement, it offers distinct advantages.

Additionally, even in the absence of formal enforcement mechanisms, the recognition of human rights duties against TNCs may have a positive effect on corporate behaviour. In addition to directly proscribing particular activities, law serves an expressive function, both reflecting and shaping societal values.[70] In today's world, the language of human rights carries a universally recognised moral force.[71] Accordingly, in those instances where NGOs do have the resources to generate publicity regarding atrocities like those of Texaco in Ecuador and Freeport in Indonesia, the ability

---

[68] See Mitchell, *Corporate Irresponsibility.*   [69] See Muchlinski, 'Human Rights', 39.

[70] Jane B. Baron and Jeffrey L. Dunoff, 'Against Market Rationality: Moral Critiques of Economic Analysis in Legal Theory', *Cardozo Law Review* 17 (1996), 431, 487–90; Christopher Stone, 'The Law as a Force in Shaping Cultural Norms Relating to War and the Environment', in Arthur H. Westing (ed.), *Cultural Norms, War and the Environment* (Oxford: Oxford University Press, 1988), pp. 64, 65.

[71] See Campbell, *Rights*, p. 3.

to condemn such actions in the language of human rights lends a weight and moral authority to such accusations that is likely to intensify public pressure against these TNCs.

Finally, while formal enforcement against TNCs faces many hurdles, enforcement of human rights is ultimately far more likely to be effective than enforcement of private rights. The environmental atrocities committed by a TNC may well constitute common law torts, but, in the circumstances in which the human rights duties I have proposed apply (the non-functional state and the TNC-controlled state), the host government is by definition not adequately enforcing private rights against TNCs. Private rights are therefore of little use. There is a need for some outside authority to impose duties on TNCs. And in order for such an outside tribunal to act with credibility, it needs some universally accepted source of substantive law, like human rights.

But what tribunal outside the host state could enforce human rights duties against TNCs? Existing institutions offer two possibilities: (1) courts in the TNC's home state enforcing a domestic statute that incorporates international law principles, like the US ATCA, or (2) an international human rights tribunal. Under current law, obstacles exist to the prosecution of human rights claims against private parties in these fora, but reconceptualising substantive human rights norms in the way I have suggested here could be a first step toward breaking down those barriers. If, as I have argued, environmental atrocities committed by TNCs fit within traditional understandings of civil and political human rights as mechanisms for counteracting power imbalance, then there is perhaps some hope that some such claims might some day fall within the scope of the 'present day law of nations' recognised as actionable under the ATCA, even under the narrow reading of that concept recently provided by the US Supreme Court.[72] Since the state action requirement under the ATCA only applies to the extent that the law of nations defines the human rights standard at issue solely against states,[73] the reconceptualisation of human rights norms that I urge here could also conceivably provide a rationale for loosening or eliminating that requirement. Even if the US ATCA continues to be read narrowly by the courts, domestic courts in other home countries could conceivably provide fora for such claims.[74] Similarly, this new understanding of human rights norms provides an argument for

---

[72] *Sosa* v. *Alvarez-Machain*, 542 US 692, 749 (2004).
[73] See *Kadic* v. *Karadzic*, 70 F 3d 232 (2nd Cir. 1995).
[74] See Jägers, *Corporate Human Rights Obligations*, pp. 203–12.

altering the procedural requirements of the European Court of Human Rights and other human rights tribunals that currently recognise only claims against state parties.[75]

V. Conclusion

This chapter has attempted to construct a normative justification for the imposition of human rights duties on TNCs that commit environmental wrongs in the developing world. Under the now near-hegemonic world-view of welfare economics, TNCs are analogised to individuals competing in the marketplace and thus placed squarely on the private side of the public–private divide. If we step outside of the economic world view, however, and recognise the extent to which the normative justifications for civil and political human rights have traditionally been rooted in a perceived need to counteract the imbalance of power between the individual and the state, it becomes clear that it is frequently far more appropriate to treat TNCs as 'like states' than 'like individuals'. Accordingly, at least where one of two sets of factual circumstances exist, human rights duties should be imposed directly on TNCs for environmental harms: (1) where the state has become so weak and/or corrupt as to be non-functional, or (2) where the TNC has so much power and influence within the domestic government that it essentially controls state decision-making.

[75] See Clapham, *Human Rights*, p. 91.

PART FIVE

Moral and Analytical Issues in Corporate Social Responsibility and the Law

18

The normative grounding of corporate social responsibility: a human rights approach

TOM CAMPBELL

I. Introduction

The theme of this book is the intermingling of social and legal pressures on business organisations to behave in a socially responsible manner. The increasing impact of corporate social responsibility (CSR) thinking on corporate legal liability, and the acceptance that law has an important role to play in encouraging the corporate world to give more attention to the social implications of their activities, can be taken to be established matters of fact in contemporary society, although the extent to which these developments actually impact on business practice remains unclear.[1] What has yet to emerge, however, is an agreed normative grounding that provides a convincing and generally accepted moral basis for the practice of CSR and for the legitimation of the pressures that are deployed to encourage its development. Most of the contributors to this book adopt a morally neutral stance with respect to this normative grounding of CSR, with more or less implicit positive attitudes to CSR, with some explicitly arguing in its favour. This chapter directly addresses the normative grounding of the CSR phenomenon, concentrating mainly on the analysis of CSR from a normative perspective and the significant but limited extent to which the discourse of human rights can be successfully deployed to provide moral justifications for and limitations to CSR, as well as the use of legal devices to promote, enforce and curtail it.

Warm thanks are due to Dr Craig Taylor for his contribution to the preparation of this chapter, and to those who made helpful comments on early drafts at seminars in the Centre for Applied Philosophy and Public Ethics (CAPPE), at the Australian National University, and at the Philosophy Department, Charles Sturt University, Wagga Wagga.
[1] For a mildly sceptical view, see Gunningham, in this volume, Chapter 16, with respect to corporate environmental responsibility.

A great deal of the literature on CSR takes for granted not only what CSR is, but also that CSR is, by and large, a good thing, it being assumed that the prime issue is how best to achieve its implementation, a major common theme throughout most of the chapters in this book.[2] True, there is a flourishing critical literature that is opposed to the whole idea of CSR[3] and there are plenty of succinct and successful demolitions of the more extreme versions of these critiques,[4] but there is a dearth of debate as to the precise way in which various varieties and degrees of CSR may or may not be justified. This is important because the normative grounding of CSR raises complex and difficult issues whose neglect threatens the credibility of CSR programmes and impedes the articulation and implementation of CSR policies within business, government and civil society. Moreover, confusion as to the concept of CSR and its moral basis gives credence to a very limited form of CSR that amounts to little more than intelligent business practice that enhances long-term rather than short-term profitability, to the virtual exclusion of responsibilities that are not justifiable in terms of the economic interests of the corporations in question. There is, therefore, a need for more sustained attention being given to these normative issues and for the articulation of some principles and rationales that can be used to clarify and focus the debate as to what forms and degree of CSR, if any, have moral legitimacy, in that they deserve the support of citizens, businesses, employees and governments.

Such normative debates about the legitimacy of CSR as do occur are frequently focused on the issue of whether social responsibility is good for business.[5] This is an important topic and one that is crucial when calculating the prospect of successfully implementing CSR programmes,

---

[2] Particularly Chapters 2, 3, 4, 7, 8, 10 and 15.

[3] See Muchlinski, this volume, Chapter 14, p. 436. Much of this derives from the work of Milton Friedman: see 'The Social Responsibility of Business is to Increase Profits', *New York Times Magazine*, 13 September 1970, pp. 33, 122–6, and Milton Friedman, *Capitalism and Freedom* (Chicago, IL: Chicago University Press, 1962 and 1982). And more recently, David Henderson, *Misguided Virtue: False Notions of Corporate Social Responsibility* (Wellington: New Zealand Business Round Table, 2001). See also John Hasnas, 'Two Normative Critiques of Business Ethics: A Critique', *Business Ethics Quarterly* 8 (1998).

[4] Thus, Thomas Donaldson, *Corporations and Morality* (Englewood Cliffs, NJ: Prentice Hall, 1982); Elizabeth Vallance, *Business Ethics at Work* (Cambridge: Cambridge University Press, 1995), ch. 2; Damian Grace and Stephen Cohen, *Business Ethics* (Melbourne, Oxford University Press, 2000), ch. 2.

[5] See Campbell and Vick, this volume, Chapter 8, pp. 259–64, and, more generally, Ben Schiller and Lisa Roner, 'What's the real benefit of ethical practice?', *Ethical Corporation*, September 2006, pp. 35–7.

or enabling corporations to respond positively to socially minded share-holders or to head off legislative changes that explicitly permit or require CSR policies, but it is not as central to the normative assessment of CSR as is generally supposed. For a start, one of the core reasons in favour of the 'business case' for CSR is that it pleases customers and investors, thus indirectly generating economically beneficial good will, which is of vital importance, particularly to those corporations whose success depends on their favourable public reputation. This does not, however, address the underlying normative questions as to whether CSR *ought* to have the support of such groups, and whether CSR would or would not be morally justified, or required, in the absence of such support. Moreover, the real crunch questions in CSR concern what to do when the business case does not hold because it is not economically wise for a particular economic unit or business sector to 'do the right thing'. Long-term self-interest may counsel general conformity to some CSR standards, but this is not always the case. Indeed, it may be argued that it is precisely when the often contestable harmony of morality and self-interest does not hold that ethical commitment to CSR is most needed and CSR comes into its own as a distinctive moral factor within business decision-making.

This chapter directly confronts these normative questions, taking up themes that emerge in the earlier parts of the book, with a view to exploring the nature and extent of the moral legitimacy of CSR in its various forms. I use the term 'legitimacy' here to refer to a practical form of normative discourse that is used to develop justifications of (and by implication, limitations on) the use of social, political and economic power, justifications that can reasonably be expected to be acceptable to those involved in and those affected by the institutions and conduct in question. What is sought is not so much an abstract philosophical justification as one that takes for granted both the desirability and necessity of achieving a working consensus on, in this case, the proper roles of business organisations and how these are to be articulated and implemented.[6] In this context,

---

[6] Richard C. Warren, 'Company legitimacy in the new millennium', *Business Ethics: A European Review* 8.4 (1999), 214–24, at 214:

> Legitimization is a term used to analyze the relationship of power that exists between an institution and society. In a society, a legitimation crisis arises when the power of an institution is challenged, or when it comes into conflict with other groups who ask questions about the authority and scope of the institution. For an institution to function, its activities have to be generally accepted and the decisions of its leaders complied with both inside and outside the institution. Consequently, an institution needs a certain amount of authority if it is to pursue its purpose in society.

the assumption is that we are seeking a normative scheme that has the potential to be accepted as common ground by the regulators, civil society, citizens, consumers and business itself, so that there can be willing compliance with such state-enforced regulations as are democratically endorsed, as well as the prospect of trusting corporations to implement effective internal procedures to fulfil their socially agreed non-legal obligations, and also a framework for deciding what are the proper roles and methods that should be adopted in civil society by organisations and individuals seeking to influence corporate conduct. The legitimation that is sought is one which promotes a broadly based democratic endorsement of the objectives and methods to be permitted and fostered within, in this case, progressive liberal capitalism, and establishes some sort of guidelines for the developing debate around CSR.

An essential preliminary to this normative debate is the clarification of what is to count as 'corporate social responsibility'. This is not an easy task. Given the diversity of terms deployed to cover the various ethical issues relating to business, it is impossible to find a meaning that will accommodate even the majority of actual uses of the term 'CSR',[7] let alone its increasingly popular surrogate 'corporate sustainability'.[8] However, the conceptual and terminological confusion in this area requires that any adequate treatment of the topic has to adopt a clear and coherent use of the key terms involved.[9] Contention here derives in part from the competing interests that are at stake and the use and abuse of such terms as 'CSR' and 'sustainability' in the realm of public relations and political rhetoric. In such circumstances, a measure of terminological stipulation is inevitable if the substance of rival normative arguments are to be clearly expressed.

With all this in mind, the first part of the chapter develops two overlapping but reasonably distinct components of 'corporate responsibility' (CR), which I use as the generic term for socially or legally required

---

[7] See Marcel van Marrewijk, 'Concepts and Definitions of Corporate Social Responsibility and Corporate Sustainability: Between Agency and Communion', *Journal of Business Ethics* 44 (2003), 95–105, at 96: 'an "all-embracing" notion of CSR has to be broadly defined and is therefore too vague to be useful in academic debate. A set of different approaches, matching the various ideal type contexts in which companies operate, could be the alternative'.

[8] See Parker, this volume, Chapter 7, p. 208. 'Sustainability' tends to be associated with a heady combination of long-term profitability, environmental protection and reputational risk management.

[9] The astonishing variety of uses is exhibited in efforts to compare what is taught in Business Schools. See Dirk Matten and Jeremy Moon, 'Corporate Social Responsibility in Education in Europe', *Journal of Business Ethics* 45 (2004), 323–37.

corporate conduct. Generic CR is then divided into what I categorise as (1) 'corporate business responsibility' (CBR), which relates to market-oriented conduct where responsibility is to the shareholders of the corporation and to the social and legal norms that govern an open and competitive market, sometimes referred to as 'the rules of the game', (2) 'corporate philanthropy' (CP), which I identify as the utilisation of corporate wealth to further humanitarian goals not directly connected with its business operations, and then, in the core sense of a term that is sometimes confused with CR in general, (3) 'corporate social responsibility' (CSR), which, when broadly conceived, concerns those duties that relate to the actual and potential social consequences of mainstream business decisions. Within CSR, so defined, I go on to distinguish a purely instrumental form of CSR, in which the social consequences in question are pursued for business reasons alone, and an intrinsic form of CSR, in which the social consequences involved are adopted as worthwhile objectives or ends in themselves rather than, for instance, as a means of enhancing the corporation's long-term profitability.

Using these distinctions, the chapter goes on to explore three normative themes: (1) the often overlooked significance of (principally consequentialist) moral arguments for what I term corporate business responsibility (CBR), arguments that have distinct moral significance even if these often conflict with the requirements of both CP and CSR; and (2) the very significant but nevertheless limited potential for human rights discourse to identify the morally justified aims and limits of CSR, particularly intrinsic CSR. This second theme should not be confused with the more commonly debated issue of whether corporations have a responsibility to respect human rights, which in general terms can hardly be given anything other than an affirmative answer. Rather, the issue debated is whether human rights discourse is a useful grounding for determining the limited extent to which corporations may, in both moral and legal terms, be legitimately required to engage in intrinsic CSR – that is, CSR which is not justified by long-term corporate self-interest. The overall conclusion is that social and legal pressure on corporations to engage in quite extensive CSR, beyond that which is in its business interests, can be usefully expressed and debated in human rights terms. My tentative thesis is that intrinsic CSR, and the imposition of social and legal pressures in its support, are morally justified if and only if this is a legitimate human rights requirement. This position is most clearly and cogently formulated if we distinguish CSR in what I take to be its core or specific meaning from corporate business responsibility (CBR) on the one hand and corporate philanthropy (CP) on the other.

II. Defining corporate social responsibility

Assessing the legitimacy of CSR is seriously hampered by the tangle of overlapping and conflicting terminology within the literature and the many different understandings of the concept amongst practitioners. Most of the ambiguities and confusions involved can be traced to the fact that the word 'social' as it features in defining CSR can be taken in at least three different ways, the first relating to the question of whom corporate responsibilities are owed to (namely 'society');[10] the second pointing to the contrast between 'social' and legal; and the third having to do with the content of the obligations in question, namely those obligations that relate to promoting the interests of groups (often referred to as 'stakeholders') other than the shareholders, senior managers and board members of the corporation.

Thus, drawing on the first meaning of 'social', some definitions of CSR are based on an inclusive coverage of all the duties that may be attributed to corporations. It makes sense to use the term 'CSR' in this all-encompassing way if we take it that all duties are ultimately owed to society, for if it is society to which corporations are responsible, then all its responsibilities are in this sense 'social' rather than prudential. They are responsibilities to others, not to themselves. This collective approach to corporate responsibilities is illustrated in the idea that corporations have a 'triple bottom line', with distinct obligations to 'profit, people and the planet', the crucial point being that, for a business, making a profit is a duty as well as a right. This point can be made, however, without categorising all corporate responsibilities as CSR, and I suggest, therefore, that we reject this conceptualisation of CSR as too broad and speak instead of corporate responsibility (CR), leaving it an open question whether the duty to make a profit is a duty the corporation owes to itself or to society in general.

Other definitions of CSR take 'social' in the term 'CSR' to identify those corporate duties that are not legal obligations and depend directly and only on social expectations. This approach, in which the 'social' in CSR is contrasted with 'legal', is favoured by those who hold the view that CSR is, by definition, a voluntary matter.[11] Arguments are given below to the

[10] As Muchlinski, this volume, chapter 14, p. 433: 'the idea of CSR resting on the obligations that societies owe to the societies in which they operate'.

[11] As with the notorious definition in the European Commission Green Paper 'Promoting a European Framework for Corporate Social Responsibility' (2001), according to which CSR 'is a concept whereby companies integrate social and environmental concerns in their business operations and in their interactions with their stakeholders on a voluntary basis'; see Voiculescu, this volume, Chapter 12 (p. 378).

effect that this crucial question is a substantive one that should not and need not be settled conceptually by defining CSR in a way that requires it to be non-legal.

This then takes us to those definitions interpreting the word 'social' in CSR to refer to the content of the duties in question, 'social duties' being those that a corporation has to persons and groups other than themselves and perhaps, at its broadest, to society in general.[12] We therefore have a triple ambiguity as to the meaning of 'social' in CSR: covering either (1) to whom the responsibilities are owed, or (2) non-legal responsibilities, or (3) responsibilities that are, from the point of view of the corporation in question, other-regarding with respect to their content.

Given the dramatic differences between these definitions of CSR, it is clear that coherent debate as to its normative rationales cannot proceed without some basic conceptual clarification and stipulation as to what 'CSR' is taken to mean. Perhaps any one of a number of definitions will do as long as we are clear about our own use of the term and stick to it consistently. Certainly, there is no one definition of CSR that can be declared to be correct on empirical, normative or conceptual grounds. On the other hand, there are more and less useful definitions for the purpose of discussing the legitimacy of CSR.

Helpful definitions of CSR in this context should, I suggest, be to some extent constrained by facts about the actual social movements that have used and contributed to this discourse, and also by the analytical need to identify what is distinctive in the idea, as well as the prospect of arriving at a measure of conceptual consistency within public discourse. My particular analysis of the term is also shaped by the wish to express clearly the different normative rationales that feature in CSR legitimation and business ethics generally. This requires, for instance, resisting the view that CSR is necessarily a voluntary matter, a view that is particularly prevalent in some (but not all) European CSR discourse, but which is unhelpful in that it places a conceptual stop on an open debate about how CSR should be enforced or achieved. It also suggests that we should adopt a definition of CSR that enables us to identify any distinctive moral rationales that underpin the social movement in question, as otherwise it

---

[12] Geoff Lane, 'Corporate Social Responsibility: Trickier than it looks', *European Business Forum* March (2003): 'In essence, CSR is about a company recognising and responding to the needs of its key stakeholders, and demonstrating this publicly. This means focussing on its impact on the environment, its people, the marketplace, and the wider community'. See Kinley, Nolan and Zerial in this volume, Chapter 15, p. 460.

will always tend to be resubmerged in the shareholder paradigm.[13] And again, it seems question-begging and dogmatic to define CSR in general as relating either only to social responsibilities that are undertaken for the (usually long-term) benefit of the corporation in question, or only for those social responsibilities of corporations that are undertaken purely for their social benefits. Even if we think CSR is, in general, good business and this is the basis for its justification, we cannot reasonably make this part of the very meaning of CSR.

Seen through an historical perspective, CSR is generally viewed as a movement to extend the range of corporate legitimating objectives beyond the shareholders to other groups, such as employees, suppliers, creditors and consumers (the so-called stakeholder dimension), and perhaps also to public goods beyond gross domestic products (such as environmental goods and social capital).[14] However, there has been no agreement as to whether 'CSR' should be confined to these 'new' objectives or responsibilities that transcend the core economic goals that have been thought to constitute the very idea of what a business corporation is.[15] If the term 'CSR' is confined to concerns beyond shareholder profitability, then it must be contrasted with 'corporate business responsibility' (CBR), which takes the key or sole stakeholder to be the owner or shareholders of the corporation in question and the responsibilities of business as having to do with the rules of the market game. Within CBR shareholder interests are paramount, albeit within the laws that govern business conduct with respect to such matters as honesty, fair trading, anti-corruption and open competition.

This contrast of CSR and CBR fits with the common assumption that CBR is solely a matter of self-interest under conditions of fair competition, whereas the broader concerns of CSR are socially oriented in that they take into consideration people other than the corporate owners and are therefore in some ways altruistic. This is illustrated by the clear division between types of shareholder activism identified by Amann, Cuby,

---

[13] See Campbell and Vick, this volume, Chapter 8, pp. 241–4.

[14] Thus Arlene I. Broadhurst, 'Corporations and the ethics of social responsibility: an emerging regime of expansion and compliance', *Business Ethics: A European Review* 9, 2 (2000), 86–98, at 89: 'The concept of "stakeholder interest" substantially broadens the scope of corporate ethical concern from its original basis of protection for its own workers to the including of "society", "community" and the environment'.

[15] Archie B.Carroll, 'A Three-Dimensional Conceptual Model of Corporate Performance', *Academy of Management Review* 4 (1979), 497–505, at 500: 'The first and foremost social responsibility of business is economic in nature. Before anything else, the business institution is the basic economic unit in our society'.

Jaussaud and Piñeiro.[16] However, this way of looking at the matter tends to obscure the fact that the pursuit of profitability within market norms may itself be regarded as a socially beneficial activity, certainly in a market economy. Moreover, CBR cannot be confined to the pursuit of profitability exclusively, without reference to its economic and political significance. In a normative analysis, the assumption must be that justifiable profitability is achieved within the framework that serves important social and economic goals.[17] Further, many paradigm examples of what constitutes CSR, such as treating employees well, can and usually do enhance profitability. It would not be helpful to exclude such duties from CSR simply because they may sometimes, or even often, be justified by reference to the interests of shareholders. It is best, therefore, to sustain the analytical distinction between CBR and CSR, but without, at this stage, taking any position as to the moral justifications of these distinct responsibilities. In particular, it is important to resist the idea that CBR is amoral or even immoral, while CSR enshrines all the ethical aspects of business responsibilities. Rather we have to elucidate the distinctive (and perhaps conflicting) normative grounding of these different types of CR.

The moral justification of the pursuit of profit in a market system is frequently overlooked or distorted in CSR debates because the norms of the competitive market that are essential to the justification of profit are largely submerged within the general obligation of business to stay within the law. In fact, the rules of the market economy are not exhaustively contained in laws, and laws that are binding on corporations deal with other matters as well as fair competition. We can, however, identify as a distinctive element within CBR those requirements of a free market that are essential for an economy in which the pursuit of private property works out to the general advantage of society by promoting the efficient production and distribution of desired goods. For this reason, it makes sense to include in CBR those legally and socially based obligations that circumscribe the ways and means that may be legitimately adopted in the pursuit of profit if an economic system is to maximise, in Adam Smith's terms, 'the wealth of nations'.[18] This brings out both

---

[16] This volume, Chapter 11.

[17] See Wesley Cragg, 'Human Rights, Globalisation and the Modern Shareholder Owned Corporation', ch. 6, in Tom Campbell and Seumas Miller (eds.), *Human Rights and the Moral Responsibilities of Corporations and Public Sector Organisations* (Dordrecht: Kluwer, 2004), pp. 105–27.

[18] Interestingly, while Smith's general justification of market systems is founded primarily on utilitarian considerations (the 'invisible hand' analysis), he incorporates in his theory

the moral justification for permitting business organisations to pursue their own profitability, and the framework within which this justification operates, which enables us to say that CBR is a social matter both to the extent that it, like most obligations, is owed to society, and because it is ultimately justified mainly in terms of general social utility.[19] However, CBR includes only those business norms that derive from or are presupposed by the concept of a free and fair market, leaving 'CSR' to cover the further and more controversial corporate objectives and normative frameworks.

I have noted that a common conceptual alternative at this point is to define 'CSR' so as to encompass all three of the triple bottom lines for which corporations are to be held accountable (their own property, the interests of other people and the protection of the planet).[20] This has the advantage of highlighting the full range of corporate responsibilities as being largely dependent on their social benefits and recognises that corporations are responsible for much more than the profitability that some had taken to be exclusively definitive of the purpose of the corporation. However, this line of thought is equally well met by using the generic term of corporate responsibility (CR).[21]

One advantage of the narrower analysis of CSR (excluding CBR) is that it focuses attention on the historically neglected aspects of CR and highlights the 'new' responsibilities to other groups and to society generally. On the other hand, an advantage of the much wider analysis of CSR (including CBR) is that it prompts us to acknowledge that profitability is *prima facie* a positive moral factor in that it is a requisite of the viability of organisations that are (or may) be morally justified by the economic contribution they make to society at large. This avoids the false antithesis

of social behaviour a major role for justice as a socially developed moral sentiment that prohibits actions that cause harm to others in a way and to an extent that evokes the sympathetic resentment of the 'impartial spectator', a moral force that, in his view, would justify the legal imposition of what we would now call CSR, even in its intrinsic form. See T. D. Campbell, *Adam Smith's Science of Morals* (London: Allen & Unwin, 1971); P. H. Werhane, *Adam Smith and His Legacy for Modern Capitalism* (New York: Oxford University Press, 1991).

[19] Although there are also rights-based reasons that underpin certain aspects of CBR, such as those concerned with freedom of association and equality of opportunity.

[20] See Jägers, this volume, Chapter 6, p. 178: 'CSR usually refers to the concept of integrating economic, social and environmental interests into the activities and structures of corporation'. See also Carroll, 'A Three-Dimensional Conceptual Model' (n. 15 above). Also Voiculescu, this volume, Chapter 12, p. 367.

[21] See Doreen McBarnet, this volume, Chapter 1, p. 10.

between business and morality that skews so many of the debates on business ethics.[22] It also makes it clear that the triple bottom lines are, at least to some extent, in direct competition with each other. For instance, an exclusive concern with CBR is incompatible with a commitment to intrinsic CSR. However, by speaking of corporate business responsibility rather than corporate business rights, these morally important aspects of CBR are accommodated within the discourse.

On balance, therefore, it seems less misleading to retain the distinctiveness of CSR by excluding CBR from its scope. Note, however, that excluding CBR from CSR does not involve denying that business responsibility relates not only to the *prima facie* acceptance of private profitability but also to the public goods related to and justifying the economic system in operation. In the present context, this means the prerequisites of free and (market) fair economic competition both with respect to rival corporations and consumers. The major part of corporate law deals with precisely such matters and is designed to prevent fraud, insider trading, misleading information, inadequate financial audits, anti-competitive behaviour and other market-oriented responsibilities. These are obligations of a type that pre-date current preoccupations with CSR, although business ethics clearly requires the integrity and commitment to the rule of market law[23] that their proper fulfilment requires.

Stressing the analytical importance of distinctiveness as a criterion for a useful definition of such terms as CSR, it is tempting to add, as a necessary defining criterion, the notion that CSR is a voluntary matter, not subject to legal control and coercive enforcement.[24] Here the term 'social' in CSR is juxtaposed to 'political' or 'legal', to bring out that the obligations in question are 'societal' in the sense that the rules and norms they articulate are part of social morality and are not legal requirements. Such voluntarist definitions of CSR have some considerable historical basis and current use in that CSR remains a term generally adopted by those who oppose increasing state regulation and encourage corporate

---

[22] Thus business leaders are frequently prompted to protest that they are engaged in promoting human rights through their economic activities. See David Rice, 'Human Rights Strategies for Corporations', *Business Ethics: A European Review* 11, 2 (2002), 134–6.

[23] See Jägers, this volume, Chapter 6, on the traditional role of the World Trade Organisation.

[24] Thus Parker notes that it seems paradoxical to discuss the legal enforcement of CSR: this volume, Chapter 7, p. 207: 'the very idea that law might make business responsible for their corporate social responsibility is paradoxical'. Also discussed by McCrudden, this volume, Chapter 3, pp. 103–4 and Voiculescu, this volume, Chapter 12.

self-regulation, either explicitly or implicitly, often as a way of heading off external controls.[25]

Nevertheless, adding the criterion of voluntariness to our definition of 'CSR' does not provide a workable basis for addressing questions about how well the different modes of regulation promote the goals of CSR for normative purposes. We need a definition of CSR that is open-ended as to how the various social goods advocated under CSR are best achieved. This must include the option of utilising legal means of one sort or another. It is at least an open question whether or not CSR should be externally regulated, therefore CSR cannot, for the purpose of moral analysis, usefully exclude legal control by definition. This means that we must start, at least, in terms of an analysis that identifies the objectives of CSR, and does so in terms of social objectives, although it is clear that a major feature of any effective implementation to CSR is having internal procedures to address the fulfilment of any legal and social obligations that are involved.

It is true that most business persons regard CSR as voluntary (and in so doing, it is worth noting, they are accepting the narrow analysis of CSR as excluding CBR, much of which is uncontroversially enshrined in law), but this is more an ideological or evaluative point than an analytic or descriptive one. Thus Milton Friedman, the famed opponent of CSR, happily endorses the obligation of business to obey the law, but opposes laws that require business to be socially responsible except for instrumental economic reasons.

Finally, it is important not to include within CSR philanthropic off-shoots from corporate activity, including those that utilise the managerial and other skills of business to provide services to deserving causes. Such activity is important, may be admirable, and is often also good for business, but it does not equate with the, perhaps morally justified, social (and perhaps legal) demands that any acceptable corporation must take into account in the actual running of the business in question and may often be contrary to the economic interests of the corporation in question.[26] Corporate philanthropy (CP) is sometimes distinguished from CSR by its greater moral optionality, and this is generally true (although this is

---

[25] Thus, Standards Australia, 'Australia Standard: Corporate Social Responsibility' (Sydney: Standards Australia International Ltd, 2003), at 1.4.1: '**Corporate Social Responsibility (CSR)**: A mechanism for entities to voluntarily integrate social and environmental concerns into their operations and their interactions with their stakeholders, which are over and above the entity's legal obligations'.

[26] See the discussion by Bottomley and Forsyth, this volume, Chapter 10 (p. 312) on the collapse of the Australian company HIH.

not always the case), in that the possession of great wealth can engender very powerful moral obligations to help those in dire need.[27] However, CP is mainly distinguishable from CSR by its more extraneous connection with the mainstream of corporate management.[28] This may sometimes be a hard line to draw, particularly with respect to intrinsic CSR where the social objectives involved are being promoted for their own sake. CP may also be seen as a form of CBR where it is being undertaken to secure the market benefits of a good reputation. It is important, however, to distinguish responsibilities that bear on the processes whereby profit is sought from those that arise in the distribution of the profits so created. CP needs to be distinguished from CSR principally because CP is not directly connected to core business activities even though it involves the redistribution of profits and may indeed enhance the reputation and so promote the business interests of the donor corporation.

To summarise this conceptual analysis, I commend and adopt a broad but not over-inclusive working definition of CSR to the effect that CSR constitutes those obligations (social or legal) which concern the major actual and possible social impact of the activities of the corporation in question, whether or not these activities are intended or do in fact promote the profitability of the particular corporation.[29] This analysis does not confine the use of the generic term 'CSR' to corporate activities that either do promote or are undertaken in order to promote the profitability of the organisation in question (what I call 'instrumental CSR'). Nor does it conceptually require that 'CSR' is only CSR if it is undertaken to achieve certain social benefits for their own sake, irrespective of their impact on profitability (what I call 'intrinsic CSR'). However, once we move on to debate the normative issues it soon becomes clear that it is relatively

---

[27] See Tom Campbell, 'Poverty as a Violation of Human Rights: Inhumanity or Injustice?', in Thomas Pogge (ed.), *Freedom from Poverty as a Human Right: Who Owes What to the Very Poor?* (Oxford: Oxford University Press, 2007).

[28] Paul Tracey, Nelson Phillips and Helen Haugh, 'Beyond Philanthropy: A Community Enterprise as a Basis for Corporate Citizenship', *Journal of Business Ethics* 58 (2005), 327–44, at 328:

> We believe that these difficulties stem partly from corporations' continued reliance on philanthropy as the dominant mode for delivering CSR initiatives which fall outside the boundaries or core operations of the firm, and which in practice consist mainly of uncoordinated and piecemeal donations to 'worthy' local causes. This is symptomatic of the fact that these kinds of CSR activity are regarded as peripheral in many companies, with the relevant departments and teams operating quite separately from other management functions.

[29] This is in line with the introductory analysis of CSR given by Doreen McBarnet, this volume, Chapter 1 (p. 9).

easy to justify instrumental CSR, roughly along the same lines as CBR may be morally justified, while it is relatively difficult to justify intrinsic CSR. It is in relation to the latter that the human rights thesis comes into play to suggest that CSR can be legitimated if and only if human rights are at stake. However, the conceptual scheme outlined here leaves open for normative debate such questions as (1) the circumstances in which we should legally permit the fulfilment of some or all CSR, (2) the circumstances in which we may legally require the fulfilment of some or all CSR, and (3) if and when the fulfilment of CSR may properly override maximising profitability, even within the confines of CBR.[30]

III. Opening the way for corporate social responsibility

CSR (as broadly defined above) includes the possibility that some corporate responsibilities go above and beyond the fiduciary duty of a corporation to making maximal (short/middle/long-term) profits for shareholders. As far as instrumental CSR is concerned, there is no special problem as to its moral grounding. For this purpose, instrumental CSR can be subsumed under the general justification of economic activity, and, as such, comes under the same justifications as apply to CBR.[31] On the most conservative of assumption, there is an open normative door for those who wish to practice instrumental CSR. This means that the first controversial normative issue regarding CSR, which is addressed in this part of the

[30] This side-steps the question of how to classify environmental responsibilities which are routinely both encompassed within 'CSR' and yet also frequently distinguished from social responsibilities. The problem, which is not addressed here, is whether obligations to the environment are to be seen as indirect obligations to people, including future generations, or are to be seen as a matter of protecting the environment for its own sake. See Lawrence Tribe, 'From Environmental Foundations to Constitutional Structures: Learning from Nature's Future', *Yale Law Journal* 84 (1975), 545.

[31] The view that all legitimate CSR is instrumental in maximising profitability is commonly used to justify the conclusion that the legal legitimacy of CSR is not in any doubt. Thus, see Parliamentary Joint Committee on Corporations and Financial Services, *Corporate Responsibility: Managing Risk and Creating Value* (Canberra: Commonwealth of Australia, 2006), at 4.76:

> The committee considers that an interpretation of the current legislation based on enlightened self-interest is the best way forward for Australian corporations. There is nothing in the current legislation which genuinely constrains directors who wish to contribute to the long term development of their corporations by taking account of the interests of their stakeholders other than shareholders. An effective director will realise that the wellbeing of the corporation comes from strategic interaction with outside stakeholders in order to attract the advantages described earlier in the chapter.

chapter, is whether the possibility of engaging in intrinsic CSR – that is, CSR for its own sake – should be morally affirmed and legally permitted.[32]

In order to open the way for intrinsic CSR, it is necessary to establish that shareholder profitability is (1) not the sole justifying objective of business organisations, or (2) is, in any case, subject to moral limitations as to how profits may be obtained. In this part of the chapter, I argue that there are good moral reasons for permitting corporations to engage in intrinsic CSR, before moving on to the even more controversial question as to what extent, if any, CSR ought to be accepted as a duty, and whether, and in what circumstances, it is legitimate to give that duty legal form.

If we start our moral discussion of the corporate right to engage in intrinsic CSR by assuming that corporations are agents of their members,[33] it is not problematic to insist that there are the same sort of limitations on what corporations can do morally as there are on individuals. Equally, it might be argued, corporations, if they are voluntary associations of individuals, are legitimate instruments of these individuals, so that if individuals are entitled to pursue profit individually, they are entitled to do so collectively, with the same moral limitations in both cases. Following this line of thought, it would appear that a core argument that is used to justify the pursuit of profit maximisation – freedom of choice – can also be used to legitimate other corporate objectives, such as intrinsic CSR or CP, through shareholder rights.

This would seem sufficient to establish that, *ceteris paribus*, while corporations are entitled to maximise profits they should also be entitled to do other things as well, if their members so choose. In this case, we would appear to have made the first step in justifying intrinsic CSR by showing that maximising shareholder profits is not necessarily the sole justifiable objective of corporations. Collective shareholder sovereignty includes the right to do what they will with their own, subject to the same limitations as apply to individuals. This does not mean, of course, that managers are entitled so to act without the (perhaps implicit) consent of shareholders.

However, the matter does not rest there. Of course, people may start up and join any association they like for a range of different acceptable purposes, and, within the constitutional provisions of such associations, they may vary these purposes at will, but not all of these associations are

---

[32] The vicissitudes of this debate are outline by Campbell and Vick, this volume, Chapter 8.
[33] Andrei Schleifer and Robert Vishny, 'A Survey of Corporate Governance', *Journal of Finance* 52 (1997), 461–88.

businesses. Such associational rights apply to religious, sporting, political and charitable associations. Yet such associations are not businesses. The defining objective of business is profit-making, it may argued, so that there is a necessity, if you engage in business, to confine the operation to profit-making. The idea here is that there may be good reasons for having distinct sorts of associations for different purposes and that these associations may carry with them different sets of rights and responsibilities.

This rejoinder is sometimes presented as a conceptual point about the nature of business.[34] However, considered as such, exclusive commitment to profitability is a very culture-specific definition of 'business', and one which makes sense only within a purist liberal capitalist system, so even if we accept that this is what 'business' means, or used to mean, in developed western cultures, this presents no conceptual veto to adopting a wider conception of business. Indeed, it is relatively easy to say that even the western concept of business is sufficiently flexible to apply to organisations in which profitability, but not maximising profits, is a necessary condition of being in business, in that other objectives may be incorporated provided they are not incompatible with the level of profitability that is necessary for the survival of the organisation. This would appear to make room for intrinsic CSR defined as those obligations of corporations other than making profits, even if we take the degree of profitability required for corporate survival to be lexically prior to other considerations, in that its requirements have to be met before other legitimate demands may be taken into consideration. Profitability is, of course, affected by shareholder reluctance to invest in corporations that do not maximise the return on their investment, so the line between being profitable and being maximally profitable may be hard to draw in practice, especially for small businesses. However, there is no conceptual veto on shareholders adopting a measure of intrinsic CSR.

But we are not there yet. A further, more economics-based argument can then be made, to the effect that corporations have a duty to maximise profits, irrespective of the wishes of their members. The point here may be that individual business associations are part of a system, a system that depends on each of its participant organisations pursuing profits. Any organisation that fails to do so is undermining the economic system whose overall success requires that profit-seeking is the form of activity that members of society have a right to expect from a business. From this

---

[34] Thus, Elaine Sternberg, *Just Business: Business Ethics in Action* (2nd edn, Oxford: Oxford University Press, 2000), pp. 30–61.

economic perspective, having 'rogue' businesses that put others things before profit undermines the workings, and hence the benefits, of the system as a whole – in which case a full commitment to unit profitability is morally required and may properly be legally required.

Note, however, that, to be morally compelling, this position must assume that there is some justifying benefit to be derived from an economic system that is purely profit-driven.[35] What is that benefit? If profit is a good in itself, it may be no more than that the more profit the better. Yet it is not clear that a system in which every economic unit pursues its own profits as the sole end is one that actually maximises profit over all. Moreover, as profit is measured in monetary terms, its value must presumably be what money can buy, and this depends on the available pool of consumer products and services. Making profits, if justifiable, must surely be justified by reference to what money can buy, and that depends on the availability of desired goods at accessible prices. This points us to the evident fact that profit is not (characteristically) an end in itself but a means to a genuinely or intrinsically desirable outcome, such as the efficient production of wealth – that is, consumer goods and services – and perhaps even also its appropriate distribution.

Let us assume, then, that these social benefits provide a core or foundational justifying aim of business as such. If it is the case that only if every unit in the economic system pursues its own profit does an economic system maximise wealth, then we have an instrumental basis for saying that those engaging in business have a duty to be motivated only by profit-making, and that this duty overrides their rights to associate for any legitimate purpose. If people want to be altruistic, or to pursue other goals, then they should do so as individuals or via organisations other than businesses.

Evidently this economic analysis has some force in a capitalist system of production, but, when fleshed out, it brings with it the recognition that such harmony of self-interests requires certain preconditions, such as fidelity to contracts, absence of monopolies, adherence to the conditions of uncoerced trading, the absence of legal, political and social restrictions on trade, and equality of opportunity in the job market, and other factors that feature in CBR.

Let us call a system with these normative constraints a business or market system and note that, within this view, pursuit of profit is the

---

[35] See Cragg, 'Human Rights, Globalisation and the Modern Shareholder Owned Corporation', 118–21.

only legitimate business goal, while noting that such a thesis lacks all plausibility if it cannot be shown to maximise some further good, such as real wealth. This enables us to say that such a system has its own internal morality deriving from the material benefits of the system and the preconditions of its effective operation, which we may call, for brevity's sake, fair trading. It is this internal market morality that gives rise to what I have called corporate *business* responsibility (CBR). Such a morality may, of course, have justifications other than its instrumental role in maximising wealth production, in that some elements at least may be valued in terms of norms such as justice, autonomy and honour, quite independently of their contribution to wealth maximisation.

Given these assumptions, we have a strong *prima facie* argument for it being the responsibility of business organisations in a capitalist society to maximise their profits within the confines of CBR. But this *prima facie* responsibility cannot rule out there being sound moral reasons for departing from this model, at least as far as departing from the norm of maximum profitability goes. Social justice relating to equalising distribution, including preserving the environment for future generations and providing tolerable conditions of employment, are just some examples of considerations that compete with and may sometimes override maximising profits. From a wider moral perspective, markets do not achieve all priority goals. And, of course, where actual markets, through market failures, do not in practice maximise wealth, this gives further grounds for modifying the total commitment to rules that are based on the assumption of market perfection. Thus, there can be good moral reasons to justify business organisations making adequate but not maximal profitability their goal, and/or adopting other objectives (such as producing goods that are needed for reasons of human well-being), even at the expense of maximising the bottom business line and reducing overall wealth.

Nevertheless, in a well-operating market, profits are reduced to the lowest feasible, as the equilibrium affects of supply and demand kick in, and this does not create much opportunity for letting matters other than profitability and business morality determine business decisions. Indeed, it would seem to be the case that only in imperfect markets with restrictions on fair competition could be there much scope for intrinsic CSR – that is, making business decisions for social not profits-based reasons – although this limitation does not apply to instrumental CSR where social goals are adopted for business reasons, like improving brand image to enhance market appeal.

Of course, in actual markets, some corporations are so profitable that they could engage in extensive intrinsic CSR and generous CP at the expense of maximal profitability, and the arguments outlined above suggest that they be permitted so to do, if their members so wish, as long as they give due weight to the CBR requirement to promote their own profitability as a contribution to maximising economic productivity generally. The next question is, are they morally obliged so to do? Should there be a social, even perhaps a legal, obligation on corporations to follow CSR within the limits of economic viability? And should this obligation be strong enough to override the *prima facie* obligation to follow the internal business morality of fair competitive self-interest, the absence of which may have put them in a position to engage in extensive intrinsic CSR?

This is the point at which it is difficult to identify moral rationales that are good enough but not too good – that is, moral reasons that justify setting up powerful social obligations that are binding on corporations and may even provide a basis for establishing legal obligations where appropriate, but obligations that are not so stringent as to be effectively open-ended, turning businesses into charities and/or governments. We need strong but circumscribed moral reasons for intrinsic CSR that justify measures that impact negatively on the potential bottom line, but nevertheless lie within the prime function of business as wealth production, albeit within the (often very demanding) morality of free markets.

Where do we look for such moral rationales? Do we plunder traditional political philosophy and apply arguments to corporations we used to apply to states? That seems to beg the question as to the legitimacy of CSR by ascribing the responsibilities of states to corporations. Inevitably, we must eventually draw on the core concepts of political philosophy, such as social contract, utilitarianism, social justice and individual rights, but when doing so we should be on the lookout for disanalogies between corporations and states. To this end, it is sensible to see what help may be had from discourses that have been developing from within business ethics itself. There are not many of these, but stakeholder theory is certainly one of them and its terminology is now commonplace.[36]

IV. Stakeholder theory

A principal contribution to business ethics by stakeholder discourse, with its affirmation that corporations have responsibilities to a range of groups in addition to shareholders, has been that, by adopting it, practitioners

---

[36] 'The 'licence to operate', with the idea that there is a practical compromise or agreement struck between the polity or community that permits and enables business to operate and the businesses in question as to the terms on which their economic activity is tolerated or encouraged. See Neil Gunningham, this volume, Chapter 16, p. 482.

are acknowledging the significance of social responsibilities of business beyond those that flow from maximising profits for shareholders.[37] The extent of this advantage can be greatly exaggerated, as the priority stakeholders are the shareholders, and the second and often the only other category of stakeholders given much weight are those groups on whom corporations depend, such as their customers, their employees and their suppliers. Neither of these stakeholders (shareholders and those on whom they depend) take us as far as the objects of intrinsic CSR, and characteristically only point to the familiar instrumental fact that such employees, customers and suppliers make important contributions to the financial bottom line of a corporation.

There is, however, another reading of this rather limited version of stakeholder theory that goes beyond the idea of corporate dependence and suggests that groups such as employees, who have contributed to business success in the past, merit reward for their contribution.[38] This line of thought comes to the fore if we consider stakeholders to be, in a fairly literal sense, those who have a stake in the business enterprise in that they have invested money, time and life opportunities, and developed ways of life, that make them dependent on the business in question: people who have invested much (and not simply money) and who have therefore something at risk in the operation, such as long-serving employees now skilled in the ways that are adapted to the business in question. These would appear to be stakeholders in the most literal sense in that they have put something into the corporation and may be thought to be owed something in return. There is an argument here for such things as the intrinsic value of reciprocal loyalty and the justice of rewarding past contributions.

However, on a yet broader conception of 'stakeholder', there are stakeholders in the sense of those groups that are vulnerable to the activities of a corporation in that they are actually or potentially affected by the business unit's activities.[39] This can also involve current employees and suppliers,

---

[37] The approach stems from R. Edward Freeman, *Strategic Management: A Stakeholder Approach* (Boston, MA: Pitman, 1984). Having been initially presented as 'those groups without whose support the organisation would cease to exist' (pp. 31–2), stakeholders are now seen as 'any group or individual who can affect, or is affected by, the achievement of a corporation's purpose' (p. vi).

[38] Thus, Robert Phillips, 'Stakeholder Legitimacy', *Business Ethics Quarterly* 13, 1 (2003), 25–41, seeks to distinguish normative legitimacy from 'derivative legitimacy'.

[39] Campbell and Vick, this volume, Chapter 8 (p. 241): 'While there is no clear consensus about what exactly CSR means, at a minimum the term implies an obligation on the part of large companies to pursue objectives advancing the interests of all groups (or "stakeholders" in today's parlance) affected by their activities.'

but also those whose traditional way of life is threatened by the intrusion of corporate activities, or customers as people who might be harmed by a product, or even competitors who might be damaged by unfair trading practices. Those who are categorised as stakeholders because of their vulnerability could include a wider catchment of persons, including those whose economic futures are affected by the activities of a corporation, such as poor people whose meagre livelihood is threatened, or those who have become addicted to the products of a tobacco and alcoholic beverage corporation. This might take us as far as including as stakeholders all those in need who could be benefited by corporate activity. This is a very fuzzy and controversial conception of stakeholding but it is not excluded by the basic concept of the theory.

The major line to be drawn or redrawn here is between those who are vulnerable to positive actions by corporations and those who have simply not been well served by corporations. They have not obtained jobs, they have not had cheap basic food supplied, they have not had the medicines they need, the clean water they lack, and so on. Do those in need who could be beneficiaries of corporations count as 'vulnerable' – can we see them as stakeholders of business simply because business could benefit them if it was conducted differently? Here we might make a distinction between those who might benefit from corporate largesse (CP), and those who might benefit by becoming employees, suppliers, or satisfied customers, something that is more at the core of CSR.

In short, we have at least four categories of stakeholder: (1) owners; (2) those on whom a business depends; (3) those who are deserving of special consideration, perhaps due to their past involvement; and (4) those who are affected by or are vulnerable in that they could benefit or suffer as a result of corporate activity or inactivity. Each category is associated with rather different bases for their claims on a corporation, the first depending on ownership rights, the second what they can contribute, the third on what they deserve and the last on their needs. The stakeholder approach thus incorporates the full gamut of distributive claims from bare ownership rights to full welfare considerations. At one extreme, where vulnerability is broadly construed so as to include the very poor, stakeholder theory could end up going beyond capitalism to embrace the public ownership or control of the means of production for the purpose of meeting the basic needs of everyone. The current consensus is that such a system of production and distribution does not work, and so we are sent back to learn the basics of the rationale for liberal capitalism: the opportunity to harnesses human creative potential to maximise the wealth of peoples through division of labour and market competition.

A more moderate form of the vulnerability analysis is that business responsibility to meet the needs of the poor is limited to abiding by the norms of business responsibility, including fair employment opportunities, and morally requiring that some strategic business decisions involve engaging in the efficient production of goods designed to meet the needs of the poor, but within the confines either of de facto profitability, or some theory of externally determined 'just' levels of profit. The problem is that the stakeholder theory lacks the resources to distinguish between stakeholders and determine the force of their respective claims because it lacks a general theory of justice.

As it stands, stakeholder theory is likely to mean rather little beyond the prudential exhortation to remember the prerequisites of long-term profit maximising, such as a loyal workforce. Thus balancing stakeholder interests comes down to a matrix for balancing is taken to be a form of profitability evaluation. It does not, therefore, take us beyond the justification of instrumental CSR. Certainly, stakeholder theory, as currently developed, seems to provide no way of determining what weight, if any, should be given to the needs of, for instance, the poor, if they are included as stakeholders at all, or indeed of stakeholders generally. If what we are talking about is working through a mixed politico-economic system in which free market capitalism is compromised with ingredients of socialist redistribution and political control, then it is from such a hybrid system that we must read off who are stakeholders and which groups have priority. While some have read into the theory certain commitments to consultation based on respect for persons' rights to determine their own futures,[40] in itself stakeholder theory does not have the internal resources to contribute to this larger debate.[41] Thus, while 'local communities' are frequently mentioned as an illustrative category of stakeholder, this tends to be seen as a reference to the communities from which employees are drawn and within which corporate activities may lead to direct environmental

[40] W. M. Evan and R. E. Freedman, 'A Stakeholder Theory of the Modern Corporation: Kantian Capitalism', in T. L. Beauchamp and N. Bowie (eds.), *Ethical Theory and Business* (Englewood Cliffs, NJ: Prentice Hall, 2004), p. 79. See Michelle Greenwood and Helen De Cieri, 'Stakeholder Theory and the Ethicality of Human Resource Management', in Ashly Pinnington, Robert Macklin and Tom Campbell (eds.), *Human Resource Management: Ethics and Employment* (Oxford: Oxford University Press, 2007).

[41] For a more sweeping critique which argues the incompatibility of other stakeholder rights if we take the fiduciary duty to shareholders seriously, see Alexei M.Marcoux, 'A Fiduciary Argument Against Stakeholder Theory', *Business Ethics Quarterly* 13 (2003), 1–24.

and social harm. 'The poor' as the totality of those persons in extreme need do not feature as such. Stakeholder theory, on its own, can provide no reason for this omission. And in the case of more narrowly drawn stakeholder boundaries, it cannot, from within its own resources, provide guidance for the prioritisation of different types of shareholder. There is a lack of substance to the theory that leaves the questions crucial to the normative grounding of intrinsic CSR unanswered.[42]

V. Human rights as a justifying rationale

Stakeholder theory is useful for formulating, but not for determining, the crucial legitimation issues surrounding CSR and CP. Theoretically, it leaves us with a package of normative issues unresolved. Is it justified for corporations to promote stakeholder and public good objectives even when these conflict with the interests of shareholders? If so, it follows that they should be legally permitted so to do. But should CSR be legally required, and if so, to what extent? And, whether or not it is legally permitted, there are further legitimation questions about the sort of participation to which non-shareholder[43] stakeholders are entitled, and what sort of activities are acceptable on the part of other groups in the process of pressuring corporations to adopt and fulfil their legal and social obligations. Should shareholders act on the basis of their non-economic interests? What rights should non-governmental organisations (NGOs) have to put pressure on corporations to change their CR objectives? Should consumers have duties as well as rights with respect to their marketplace decisions?

We do not have a comprehensive theory that enables us to address these questions in any systematic way. We have economic theories about the most productive form of economic system, we have political theories about the just distribution of benefits and burdens in a liberal society, we have various unsuccessful attempts, such as stakeholder theory and

---

[42] A similarly respectful but unenthusiastic comment may be made about the attempt to harness the political concept of a social contract, as developed in the seminal work of John Rawls, to the question of business rights and responsibilities. See, for instance, Donaldson, *Corporations and Morality*; Gillian Brock, 'Are Corporations Morally Defensible?', *Business Ethics Quarterly* 8 (1998), 703–21. As a method of moral reflection, it is able to diminish the impact of the everyday prejudices that often pervert our moral reasoning, but this does not give sufficient input to the substantive questions that the method seeks to deploy.

[43] See Amann, *et al.*, on 'shareholder activism', Chapter 11, this volume, and Campbell and Vick on 'ethical investment', Chapter 8, this volume.

business versions of the 'social contract' approach,[44] and we have neo-Aristotelian theories of private and public virtue.[45] But none of these can claim to have worked out a coherent and plausible set of answers to the CSR legitimation questions identified above.

It is in this context that I have chosen to explore the extent to which the political philosophy underlying human rights discourse can be used to give more substance to stakeholder theory. Certainly, the discourse of human rights, particularly human rights law, features prominently in many discussions of CSR, including in this book.[46] Potentially at least, the human rights tradition has the advantage that it provides a powerful rationale for identifying corporate responsibilities that extends beyond the narrow confines of strictly business goals and norms. Every person and every organisation has obligations to respect human rights, although these obligations vary with the social roles of the individuals and organisations involved. This is surely a powerful enough moral basis for imposing obligations and placing morally justified limits on corporate conduct. At the same time, human rights norms are reasonably circumscribed so that their imposition on business does not necessarily lead to open-ended demands that divert corporations from their primary social functions. Human rights may mark the limits of the legitimate imposition of CSR as well as its positive justification. This is a controversial thesis, but it does enable us to articulate the thesis that corporations can get on with their business role according to market norms, provided they do not violate human rights, or, more positively, as long as their business aims and methods are adopted at least in part in order to actually promote certain human rights. This might work as a CSR legitimation test, at least for intrinsic CSR.

The idea that human rights might provide the justifying rationale for intrinsic CSR enables us to draw on a rich tradition of thought on the exercise of power in society, its dangers and its benefits, its failures and its successes.[47] Moreover, when we set out to list the distinctive socially oriented and uncontroversial obligations of business entities, this does appear to take us straight into human rights issues. Thus, in relation to

---

[44] Donaldson, *Corporations and Morality*; Brock, 'Are Corporations Morally Defensible?'; Ben Wempe, 'A Defense of a Self-disciplined, Domain-specific Social Contract Theory of Business Ethics', *Business Ethics Quarterly* 15, 1 (2005), 113–35. Of course, contract theory may be used as a decision-making mechanism for deriving the content of human rights.

[45] Robert C. Solomon, *Ethics and Excellence: Cooperation and Integrity in Business* (Oxford: Oxford University Press, 1993).

[46] Particularly Chapters 5, 7, 12, 13, 14 and 17.   [47] See Sinden, this volume, Chapter 17.

employees,[48] there are issues of child labour, forced labour, unreasonable disciplinary practices, grossly excessive working hours, minimum wages, freedom of association, freedom of speech, discrimination, and serious risks to health and safety, matters that also arise in considering the operations of suppliers, and, with respect to health and safety at least, clearly apply to consumers as well. In the case of environmental responsibilities, whether these are regarded as a human rights matter depends on whether the environment is to be protected for its own sake or for the health and well-being of this and future generations.

However, while the sphere of CSR is replete with human rights concepts (and vice versa), serious problems arise when we seek to articulate the specific human rights responsibilities of corporations, particularly if we are going to argue that intrinsic CSR is confined to human rights responsibilities. Business leaders generally accept that they do have some such responsibilities,[49] but is their scope and content to be equated only with those that apply to individual citizens, or, at the other extreme, are their human rights responsibilities to be compared to those of states?[50]

It is tempting to view these issues as legal questions for which we should look to human rights law for an answer. Several of the chapters in this book deal with the prospect and reasonableness of implementing human rights law as it is currently and potentially embodied in international law or in domestic constitutions.[51] However, these important questions are cognate with, but not the same as, the issue as to how human rights ideas and values might be used to justify CSR, whether or not these responsibilities are to be legally articulated and enforced irrespective of the current content of human rights law, international and domestic. When using human rights discourse to legitimate CSR (and indeed to legitimate existing and proposed human rights law), we are drawing on the moral and political discourse of human rights on which social as well as legal obligations may be founded. In this mode, human rights are those basic human interests that ought to be recognised and guaranteed by the social, economic and political arrangements in place in all human societies. What we are drawing on here is the idea of basic universal interests of overriding moral

---

[48] See Bottomley and Forsyth, this volume, Chapter 10.

[49] Thus Chandler 1998. Rice, 'Human Rights Strategies for Corporations'.

[50] See the discussion in Muchlinski, this volume, Chapter 14, pp. 436–9, Kinley, et al., this volume, Chapter 15, p. 468, and Sinden, this volume, Chapter 17, pp. 515–19.

[51] Particularly, this volume, Chapter 14, where Muchlinski, referring to John M. Kline, *Ethics for International Business: Decision-Making in a Global Political Economy* (London: Routledge, 2005), goes so far as to say that 'The observance of fundamental human rights can be said to lie at the heart of ethical business practice' (p. 436).

significance, rather than any existing set of international conventions or positive legal systems.[52]

That said, it is useful to illustrate this tradition by reference to the Universal Declaration of Human Rights, as long as we take note of the fact that this foundation document of the United Nations was formulated almost entirely on the assumption that the responsibilities correlative to these rights apply to states. Corporations are not states, and we cannot assume that fundamental rights established to guide and control states are necessarily applicable to corporations. Yet, if we can identify the principal ways in which corporations pose a threat to the sort of interests identified in the Universal Declaration, we can find grounds articulating corporate human rights obligations, many of which will readily be recognised as similar or equivalent to the requirements of CSR. This is more of a philosophical exercise in moral justification than an analysis of possible legal developments on the basis of current human rights law. It is directed primarily at the formulation of opinion within the democratic process, not advice to judges as to how they might creatively use their interpretive powers.

In existing corporate codes of conduct, respect for human rights is in practice given a rather limited connotation, having come to be associated with complicity of multinational companies (MNCs) in governmental civil rights violations in foreign jurisdictions and extreme examples of labour exploitation, particularly child labour and grossly unsafe workplaces.[53] Indeed, in such codes it is often unclear precisely what is meant by human rights, as many of the rights which might seem to the reader to be paradigmatic human rights, such as the right to form associations, are listed alongside human rights, as if they were distinct from human rights.[54] However, the actual range of human rights, even if we just stay within the confines of the Universal Declaration of Human Rights, is much wider than this and incorporates the sort of significant social, cultural and economic rights that feature in the expression of the stakeholder rights of employees, customers and members of the public.[55] Once we adopt

---

[52] I develop this in Tom Campbell, *Rights: A Critical Introduction* (London: Routledge, 2006).

[53] Susan Ariel Aaronson, '"Minding Our Business": What the United States Government has done and can do to Ensure that U.S. Multinationals Act Responsibly in Foreign Markets', *Journal of Business Ethics* 59 (2005), 175–98.

[54] For more on this, see Tom Campbell, 'A Human Rights Approach to Developing Voluntary Codes of Conduct for Multinational Corporations', *Business Ethics Quarterly* 16.2 (2006), 255–69.

[55] Voiculescu (this volume, Chapter 12) makes the interesting points that 'while the US debate on CSR was fuelled largely by observations on the impact of corporate activities abroad, the European debate was initially rooted in predominantly domestic concerns' and that

a more expansive domain for human rights with parameters similar to the Universal Declaration, it becomes feasible to raise the question as to whether human rights can serve as the normative grounding for all CSR, or, more restrictively, all intrinsic CSR – or, more narrowly still, all CSR which it is reasonable to enforce through legal mechanisms.

This approach works best in relation to negative human rights where the responsibilities involved require corporations to refrain from harming others in specified ways.[56] Many of the ills arising from corporate activity are constituted by just such harms – for instance to life, sustenance and health – brought about directly or indirectly by the activities of the corporations in question. Here we can draw on the values underlying the affirmation of state-oriented human rights, and apply them to the rather different role of corporations. The basic human interests that require protection are the same but the threats and protection mechanisms are likely to be rather different in the case of corporations.[57] It may be, for instance, that corporate human rights responsibilities have rather different content and focus and impact in a more negative way than is the case with states. Corporate human rights responsibilities may be viewed primarily in terms of the limits they impose rather than the more positive human rights responsibilities that apply to states – not that the boundaries in relation to the negative aspect of human rights responsibilities are easy to draw. As far as physical protection and basic health are concerned, the concerns for the well-being of employees in these respects as ends in themselves and as exemplified in the principal focus of the International Labour Organisation would be clearly within the parameter of corporate human rights responsibilities, and the same might be said about much of what goes on under the umbrella of consumer protection, particularly with respect to dangerous products. Less clear is where to locate equally significant harms caused to other people through the economic and health care injuries resulting from the 'normal' consequences of economic competition.

---

the Treaty on the European Union 'provides for a legal umbrella under which not only human rights in the "narrow" sense, but social rights and environmental protection can be placed as fundamental dimensions of basic human rights in a wider, human development sense'.

[56] See Glinski, this volume, Chapter 4, pp. 136–7.

[57] In this volume, Chapter 17, Sinden explores some issues in relation to civil human rights and makes a strong case for the propriety of seeing corporations as important players in prompting such rights, based on the analogy between political and economic power. However, given that corporations are business entities and their power is essentially economic power, it seems appropriate to view their human rights potential, for good and ill, primarily in economic terms.

The application of human rights to CSR works less well in relation to protecting public goods, such as clean air and unpolluted water, where individual interests are not so directly involved, and it is therefore more difficult to articulate these harms in terms of rights.[58] We may see these public goods as aspects of CSR that are justified in general utilitarian terms, such as those which are commonly invoked to support CBR, where it is the prosperity of society rather than the interests of identifiable individuals to which appeal is made. Arguably CBR requires a different form of justification that has more to do with the preconditions of the proper functioning of the economic system in question, where the rationale is more focused on the operation of the corporation as an economic entity. While this is certainly about the achievement of the same ends as social and economic rights, namely the attainment of a decent standard of living for all, the connection of corporate responsibilities to economic well-being is not of the direct and individual sort that is characteristic of human rights responsibilities.

Significant problems arise when we utilise positive or affirmative human rights to legitimate CSR, where the correlative obligation is to take action to promote a human rights objective, something that is not normally associated with a special obligation arising from having been responsible for the harm in the first place, or the residual welfare obligations of states. Such obligations are readily attributable to governments, whose assumed role is to promote the well-being of its members. Corporations, it might be thought, have restricted obligations in this sphere that can extend at best to an inner circle of vulnerable stakeholders who have actually been harmed or are at serious risk of harm. Even if we note that neo-liberal capitalist states are withdrawing from their commitment to welfare provision, no one seriously suggests that this vacuum should be filled by comprehensive, corporately funded services for the poor and indigent sick. This may be one reason why it is important to distinguish CSR from CP, for while the State has welfare obligations to its citizens that are clearly based on human rights considerations, it is not clear that the same applies to corporations, wealthy as they may often be. While it is arguable that there should be a human right to relief from poverty, it is difficult to hold that the correlative obligations here apply to corporations as such, although this remains a key human rights issue that is as

---

[58] The idea of 'collective rights' may be invoked here, which works quite well in relation to the interest of specific and clearly identifiable minority groups but less well in relation to societies as a whole, at which point rights-discourse and utilitarian calculation tend to merge.

yet unresolved. As Muchlinski points out, this is likely to be neither an efficient nor a fair way to redistribute wealth.[59]

At this point answers to our legitimation questions in relation to positive economic and social rights depend on the calculation of available resources and appropriate distributive mechanisms. It may be argued, for instance, that while many corporations have the means to make a very substantial contribution to welfare services, they lack the mechanisms, namely taxation and social administration, to carry out such a function fairly (to corporations as well as clients) and effectively. Here we have a moral (equitable distribution of burdens) and a practical consideration (inefficacy in providing the necessary welfare services) that undermine the *prima facie* human rights argument that those with the means to do so should assist those in greatest basic need. Or so the argument might go. Very little can be read off here from the specific state-oriented human rights responsibilities that have evolved in other contexts. The debate has to go back to identifying priority human interests, the affirmation of equality of human worth, and assessing the most effective mechanisms for promoting these values.

It would be extravagant to suggest that a human rights approach could fill this legitimation vacuum, if only because human rights themselves are in large part asserted and posited rather than systematically justified. In this respect, a human rights approach is in much the same boat as stakeholder theory in that the concept of human rights provides only a framework within which to draw moral conclusions. However, a human rights approach to CSR provides us with a rich discourse for the articulation of moral priorities in contemporary societal contexts that has clear relevance to emerging social expectations that corporations make a more proactive contribution to the solution of grave social problems.

One major advantage of human rights discourse here is that it invites us to articulate overriding moral priorities in a way that potentially justifies legal enforcement but does not actually require this. This has the justificatory advantage that there is no reason in principle why CSR obligations should not be legislated and enforced at law if that is likely to be effective. On the other hand, another set of moral and practical arguments that bear on this issue relate to my suggestion that the idea that CSR should have, if not by definition at least in practice, a presumption of voluntarism. The moral argument is that those working for a corporation have a human right to be involved in its decision-making processes, particularly with

---

[59] This volume, Chapter 14, p. 436.

respect to its CSR programmes, an argument that can be extended to the right of other stakeholders to be consulted on such matters. The practical argument for voluntary CSR is that legal regulation can rarely succeed in enforcing anything except minimum standards in matters that can be easily policed. Indeed, it may often be counterproductive. If members of an organisation, especially its leaders, do not have a moral commitment to CSR then it is unlikely that CSR will feature in that organisation beyond its subsidiary role as a tactical way of seeing to CBR or doing the minimum to conform with the letter of CSR laws.[60] It may be that seeing the justification of CSR in terms of human rights may help to generate such moral commitment.

While it may be agreed that both states and corporations should have human rights obligations beyond those of individuals, a problem with the human rights approach is that it does not identify the distinctive obligations of each type of entity. Here the task is to identify the different contributions that different types of organisations should be expected to make to realising what are in effect common goals. It is not enough to argue, at this point, that all individuals and organisations have a responsibility to respect human rights. This division of labour has to be determined in large part by reference to the means that the types of organisation in question have at their disposal. Thus, where it is desirable to have fixed clear rules universally applied and impartially enforced, then the responsibilities in question must fall on state governments, and where what is required is entrepreneurial initiative and effective resource management, the responsibilities would fall more appropriately on corporations. This means that the government responsibilities do in principle include legislating to control corporate activities to foster those very objectives that also feature in the articulation of corporate responsibilities generally. To that extent, a human rights approach to CSR leads to a mandatory framework for encouraging corporations to formulate and achieve their most important CSR objectives.

Nevertheless, there is a case for saying that the idea of CSR must include a rebuttable presumption that there should be internal mechanisms and cultural processes that support a 'moral' or social, rather than a purely legal, approach to the wider (non-shareholder) obligations of corporations. Indeed, it can be argued, on what are in effect human rights grounds, that employees, and maybe a wider range of stakeholders, have a right to

---

[60] G. More, 'Hives and Horseshoes, Mintzberg and MacIntyre: what future for corporate responsibility?', *Business Ethics: A European Review* 12, 1 (2003), 41–53.

participate in the process whereby CSR policies are arrived at and implemented.[61]

On the other hand, it is a mistake to assume that non-legal obligations are morally as well as legally voluntary in the sense that whether or not such obligations are met is not a matter for the most stringent moral assessment and criticism. Because something is legally permitted does not make it morally optional. It therefore makes perfect sense, for instance, to speak of the moral obligation to respect and further human rights.[62] This means that NGOs, for instance, are entitled to put as much pressure on corporations over failure to respect their moral (or societal) human rights obligations as those which are also legal obligations.

VI. Problems with the human rights approach to corporate social responsibility

The position I have outlined so far offers encouragement to the United Nations in its efforts to establish 'Norms of Responsibilities of Transnational Corporations and Other Business Enterprises with Regard to Human Rights' (the 'UN Norms') that are discussed in some detail in Chapters 12 and 13 of this book. While there is a danger that such developments lead to an over-emphasis of existing state-oriented human rights and corporate complicity with the human rights violations of host states, rather than the distinctive potential of corporations for promoting and damaging fundamental human interests, this does seem an appropriate forum for political debate as to the content and enforcement of intrinsic CSR and the modifications this might require to instrumental CSR and CBR. However, there are some further problems with the human rights approach to CSR to which attention should be drawn.

One drawback to a human rights approach to CSR is the potential to use human rights more generally, and particularly the human right to own property, as a basis for asserting shareholder rights taking priority over other stakeholder needs. That is, there is the prospect that the outcome will be to affirm the human rights, not the human rights responsibilities,

---

[61] Thus, P. Maclagan, 'Corporate Social Responsibility as a Participative Process', *Business Ethics: A European Review* 8 (1999), 43–9, at 47: 'Ideally, a participative process aimed at enhanced CSR would require mechanisms to ensure adherence to the Kantian principle of respect for persons.'

[62] See Tom Campbell, 'The Moral Dimensions of Human Rights', in Campbell and Miller, (eds.), *Human Rights*, ch. 1.

of corporations.[63] However, there is no convincing case for combining the right to property and the right to association to produce an aggregate absolute right on shareholders to determine corporate policies irrespective of their social consequences. Corporations are, in large part, social creations that do not automatically take on the rights of those who form them, particularly, as 'the concessions theory' points out, if the associations in question are given certain legally protected privileges, such as limited liability and intellectual property rights. Nevertheless, there is a real possibility that the sphere-specific human rights responsibilities that are ascribed to corporations are given an ultra-liberal interpretation that sees them as directed largely at protecting individuals against policies that promote public goods and redistributive goals.

Another disadvantage of viewing CSR from a human rights perspective is that it raises certain assumptions as to the proper mechanism for articulating and enforcing CSR. Within the community of human rights advocates, it is commonly assumed not only that human rights are essentially legal phenomena that call for comprehensive legal enforcement, but that this is an area of law in which judicial law-making should dominate. The difficulty here is not that a human rights approach will lead to a measure of legal enforcement, for that, in itself, may be a good thing.[64] The difficulty is rather that, through the prevalence of US-style Bills of Rights in domestic constitutions, it has come to be expected that judiciaries should have a leading role in working out the proper content of human rights obligations. This expectation is not inevitable, as democratic governments have a long history of establishing human rights legislation, much of it to override judge-made law, but in current political culture it is likely that identifying CSR with human rights may open the way for judicial creativity with respect to formulating the precise content of the correlative obligations that would be imposed on corporations, as is illustrated many times over in other chapters. Evidently judiciaries are neither in the best nor the most legitimate position to undertake this task and either will not do so at all or will do so ineffectively or erroneously. Here the legal initiaitives associated with the Alien Torts Act in the United States makes interesting reading.[65] On the other hand, it is not clear where the best domestic fora for working through these issues may be. Chapter 13

---

[63] Thus, in some jurisdictions, such as the United States and Canada, there is a legally recognised human right to freedom of speech that is used to protect corporations against certain restrictions on advertising. See Shaw, *Business Ethics* (4th edn, Boston, MA: Wadsworth), pp. 160–2.

[64] See Parker, this volume, Chapter 7, pp. 213–17.   [65] This volume, Chapter 5.

charts recent developments with respect to the UN Norms. It is clear that, important as this arena for debate and decision has become, it will be necessary for these issues to be taken up more dynamically within domestic democratic jurisdictions if they are eventually to achieve international political consensus and political legitimacy. However, the influence that corporations have within the domestic political processes of democratic regimes is such that only major shifts in public opinion are likely to have much impact on representative assemblies and elected governments.

A further concern about adopting a human rights approach to CSR is that it seems too restricted in that there are lots of CSR concerns that have moral significance but do not have a human rights rating.[66] Some of this concern may be met by harking back to the distinctions drawn earlier in the chapter between CSR, CBR and CP. CBR is of the highest moral importance with respect to the efficient outcomes of a liberal capitalist economy, but CBR is not primarily a matter for human rights assessment, although it could be if the autonomy elements in the contractual rights involved in liberal economic systems are given a human rights interpretation, as when antidiscrimination provisions are seen as part of fair trading norms. Similarly, CP is not primarily a matter of protecting or furthering human rights, although, again, there is scope for a human rights element entering into CP in so far as we are deal with gross disparities of wealth and available capacities of wealth corporations that could be deployed for the relief of extreme poverty. However, if we put CBR and CP to one side, it remains plausible to argue that business should not be diverted from its economic role except where human rights violations are at issue, particularly if the correlative obligations are to be legally enforced or encouraged through the use of incentives together with social and political pressures. Yet confining our attention to CSR does not entirely solve the problem since many facets of CSR, especially those that are seen to be 'good for business', do not have the moral importance we attach to human rights. Refining and confining the scope of the relevance of human rights to the legitimation of CSR takes us back to the thesis that it is with respect to intrinsic CSR, where the interests of the corporation are not the justifying

---

[66] Perhaps for this reason the draft UN Norms appear rather too broad in their scope in places. See Kinley, et al. this volume, Chapter 15, p. 463, and Muchlinski, this volume, Chapter 14, p. 446: 'many of the sources, referred to as contributing to the Draft Norms, constitute more general codes of business ethics, which, by their nature, will deal with social issues not usually described as human rights issues'. Note also Muchlinski's comments on the Draft United Nations Code of Conduct on Transnational Corporations and the OECD Guidelines for Multinational Enterprises, in this volume, Chapter 14, pp. 432–6.

rationale, that moral legitimacy depends on there being corporate human rights responsibilities in play, whereas with instrumental CSR, where the interests of the corporation are central and enforceability is not, therefore, such a pressing question, justification may be made, if required, on other, more utilitarian, grounds.

VII. Conclusion

On the evidence of this book, it can be said that CSR has become part of the discourse of the regulatory state and that the governance involved in its implementation draws extensively on norms and mechanisms deriving from the activities of civil society and developed within corporations for a variety of motivations and purposes. This has been something of a back-door process in which there is considerable adherence to the rhetoric of voluntarism and self-regulation, and a postulate that all acceptable CSR can be reduced to a business case resting on the long-term advantages that accrue to the socially responsible corporation or business sector. One message of the book is that there is more going on than this in the interaction between law and CSR. For all the enhanced power that corporations enjoy through the process of globalisation, which has released them from much of their previous dependence on the political authority of the countries in which they operate, corporations are individually vulnerable to world public opinion, and collectively at risk through the delegitimation of the economic system within which they currently flourish.

It is the contention of this concluding chapter that the largely unresolved problem of establishing an acceptable normative grounding for CSR, particularly intrinsic CSR – that is, CSR undertaken purely for the benefit of persons beyond the confines of the business organisation – needs to be openly and persistently addressed. Beyond the analytical proposals made in the course of defining the term CSR, and distinguishing it from other corporate responsibilities (corporate business responsibility and corporate philanthropy),the substantive thesis of the chapter is that (1) the legitimation of CSR has to involve justifying in principle its legal enforcement where appropriate, notwithstanding that there are important moral and practical reasons for holding back on the juridification of CSR and maintaining a substantial degree of voluntarism, and (2) that this justification should be seen as grounded in the particular human rights obligations arising from the distinctive capacities that corporations have for vitally important human harms and benefits. In its strongest form, the thesis is that intrinsic CSR is justified if and only if it is required to fulfil a corporation's human rights responsibilities, not as set by current human rights law, but as justified by the underlying philosophy of human rights as applied to corporations. In a weaker form the thesis is that this is the least controversial rationale for intrinsic CSR.

This is in itself not much more than a framework for approaching currently intractable issues about the propriety of imposing even meta-regulatory CSR legal obligations on corporations, and the moral defensibility of bringing market and political pressure to bear on corporations through mechanisms that operate in civil society. Drawing on the philosophical underpinnings of human rights discourse, including the characteristic rationales for adopting and developing human rights law, does not enable us to side-step deploying the broad range of moral values and institutional considerations associated with the classical disputes within moral and political philosophy on which our determination of the form and content of human rights requirements must ultimately be grounded. There are no incontrovertible moral intuitions that can take the place of such complex practical reasoning. Yet human rights discourse does embody a powerful tradition of social and political thought and experience, albeit largely in a different institutional context, which frames the issues in fruitful ways, pointing us to the identification of the unacceptable social harms that arise from some business activities and suggesting how we might institutionalise arrangements to ensure that these harms are minimised.

This approach to the normative grounding of CSR fits in with much of the current debate on CSR in relation to the UN Norms and the significant role of international NGOs in the movement for developing stronger and more effective forms of CSR, although there is a tendency for that debate to stray beyond the bounds of human rights. At the same time, a human rights approach to CSR provides potential legitimation of those NGO activities designed to pressure corporations to conduct their core business in a more socially responsible direction. Many of the rights of NGOs to bring pressure to bear on corporations can be derived from basic civil and political rights, such as freedom of speech, communication, association and property. More difficult questions arise when politically unaccountable civil society organisations are treated as representative of the community beliefs and values that are at the core of democratic legitimacy, and are given a place in corporate or global governance that may not be merited by the interests they represent. But again, there is a framework here for dealing with these issues in the standard civil and political rights that relate both the democratic governance and market freedoms.

Bringing human rights to the centre of the CSR stage may be thought to vindicate the fears of corporate leaders that they will be forcibly diverted from the 'business of business' to become surrogate states with complex political and welfare obligations and hence become less effective as economic organisations. Yet even if we remain within this business perspective, it important to note the serious economic consequences for corporations, and economic systems generally, that lose the moral respect of the public, and to repeat the point that moral justifications, particularly human rights legitimations, circumscribe as well as affirm the scope of CSR. Viewing the business case for CSR within this wider moral perspective does render the normative grounding of CSR, particularly its implementation through legal mechanisms and legislative change, much more complex and problematic. This, as is illustrated throughout the book, is, however, how the movement to CSR is developing as a phenomenon 'beyond the law' with respect to its social drivers, 'through the law' with respect to its implementation, and 'for the law' as a way of providing moral legitimacy for the social and political forces sustaining the new corporate accountability.

INDEX

accountancy, CSR industry, 20
accounting, 10, 47
Act of State doctrine, 159
actio popularis, 190, 191–2, 202
ADAM, 341
advertising
  freedom of expression, 560
  misleading advertisements, 126–8
  TNC practices, 447
AFG-ASFFI, 342
African Charter on Human and
    Peoples' Rights, 190–1
Air New Zealand, 328
Ajinomoto, 361
Allende, Salvador, 154
Amann, Bruno, 536
Amazon rainforest, 63, 501–2
American Bar Association, 290–4,
    295
American Law Institute, 290, 292,
    297–9
AMICEM, 490
amici curiae, 189, 192, 201, 204
Amin, Idi, 387
Amnesty International, 15, 27, 30, 39,
    60, 148, 160, 464
Amnesty International Business
    Group, 24
Amnesty International USA, 38
Amoco Cadiz, 143
Anglo-American paradigm
  See also shareholder primacy
  challenges, 248–9
  corporate governance model, 245–52
  corporate ownership models, 346
  CSR and, 9, 242–3, 315–18
  efficiency, 246–8

flexible model, 316
  New Labour endorsement, 256
Annan, Kofi, 142
Ansett Airlines, 319, 321, 323, 326,
    327–8
Aon, 17
apartheid, 343
Aram, Robin, 465, 469
arms manufacturers, 10, 264, 268,
    342
Arthur Andersen, 20
asbestos, 183, 310, 312
ASrIA, 62
AstraZeneca, 64, 68
auditing
  business reviews, 35
  chemical emissions, 498
  supplier contract conditions
    effectiveness, 77–8
  external audits, 76–7
  in-house auditing, 75–6
Aung San Suu Kyi, 183
Australia
  affirmative action, 234
  annual reports, 308
  codes of conduct, 313–14
  company collapses, 319, 321
  compliance culture, 233
  Corporate Code of Conduct Bill,
    310–11, 449, 463
  corporate criminal responsibility,
    424–7
  corporate culture, 424–6
  corporate law developments, 308
  corporate manslaughter, 219
  corporate veil, piercing, 328
  CSR agenda, 307–8

5373347R10332

Printed in Great Britain
by Amazon.co.uk, Ltd.,
Marston Gate.